Families First Act and CARES Act, Selected Provisions

Law, Explanation and Analysis

Editorial Staff Publication

Wolters Kluwer

ISBN 978-1-5438-2620-3

Printed in the United States of America

Introduction

Families First Act and CARES Act Deliver Relief to Struggling Workers and Businesses During the COVID-19 Pandemic

Responding to the COVID-19 crisis that hit the United States in early 2020, Congress came together to fast-track much needed relief for both workers and businesses struggling to survive in a climate of quickly spreading infections, social distancing directives, state and local stay-at-home orders, and mounting business closures and layoffs. The necessary relief came in phases.

On March 18, 2020, President Trump signed into law the Families First Coronavirus Response Act (FFCRA) (P.L. 116-127) in an attempt to limit the spread of the COVID-19 pandemic and support relief efforts, mainly for employees and small- and medium-size businesses. This was the phase-two measure that followed a phase-one supplemental appropriations bill to combat the hard-hitting impact of the coronavirus pandemic.

Phase-three bipartisan relief came on March 27, 2020, when President Trump signed into law the Coronavirus Aid, Relief, and Economic Security Act (CARES Act) (P.L. 116-136), largely targeted toward stabilizing the economy. It provided a massive $2 trillion tax and spending COVID-19 emergency relief package.

The Families First Coronavirus Response Act includes: provisions that expand the Family and Medical Leave Act to include public emergency paid family and medical leave; emergency unemployment insurance; emergency paid sick leave; health care relief provisions; and tax credits to employers for paid sick and paid family and medical leave.

The CARES Act contains significant relief for companies and individuals, including rebates for individual taxpayers and the creation of three new unemployment insurance programs, as well as a multitude of tax benefits for companies of all sizes and significant payroll relief. The CARES Act also clarifies the emergency paid family leave and paid sick leave provisions in the FFCRA, among other relief.

Note that the Families First Coronavirus Response Act was effective April 1, 2020, and certain provisions in the CARES Act took effect immediately. Professionals will need to move quickly to understand the impact of both measures.

Explanation and Analysis

Families First Act and CARES Act, Selected Provisions: Law, Explanation and Analysis provides a thorough analysis of important aspects of the Families First Coronavirus Response Act and the CARES Act, affecting a broad range of individuals, workers, and businesses of all sizes. The detailed analysis will assist labor and employment, human resources, employee benefits, and payroll professionals.

About This Work and Wolters Kluwer

Wolters Kluwer is providing practitioners with a single integrated law and explanation of the Families First Coronavirus Response Act and the CARES Act, which continues the Wolters Kluwer tradition of empowering labor and employment, human resources, employee benefits, and payroll professionals with the information and resources necessary to help them understand and work with new laws as they take effect. Other products related to the new legislation, including *Labor & Employ-*

ment Law Daily, HR Compliance Library, Employee Benefits Management, and the *Payroll Management Guide* may be found at www.lrus.wolterskluwer.com

April 2020

Wolters Kluwer
EDITORIAL STAFF

¶1 Features of This Publication

This publication is your complete guide to selected provisions of the *Families First Coronavirus Response Act* (P.L. 116-127) and the *Coronavirus Aid, Relief and Economic Security Act (CARES Act)* (P.L. 116-136) (the "2020 Coronavirus Response Acts").

The core portion of this publication contains the Explanations of these Acts. The explanations outline all of the public health emergency leave provisions under Title I of the Family and Medical Leave Act, and the similarly new emergency paid sick leave available to assist workers during the COVID-19 pandemic. Additionally, explanations cover unemployment insurance stabilization and access, health and privacy, tax credits and other payroll relief, pension plan changes, economic stabilization for distressed sectors of the U.S. economy, and air carrier workers support.

The publication also contains numerous other features designed to help you locate and understand the changes made by these Acts. These features include cross references to related materials, detailed effective dates, finding tables, and a topical index. A more detailed description of these features appears below.

HIGHLIGHTS

Highlights are quick summaries of the major provisions of the 2020 Coronavirus Response Acts. The Highlights are arranged in chapter and paragraph order. At the end of each summary is a paragraph reference to the more detailed Explanation on that topic, giving you an easy way to find the portions of the publication that are of most interest to you. *Highlights begin at ¶5.*

EXPLANATIONS

Explanations are designed to give you a complete, accessible understanding of the new law. Explanations are arranged by subject for ease of use. There are two main finding devices you can use to locate explanations on a given topic. These are:

- A detailed table of contents at the beginning of the publication listing all of the Explanations of the new law; and
- A table of contents preceding each chapter.

Each Explanation contains special features to aid in your complete understanding of the new law. These include:

- A summary at the beginning of each explanation providing a brief overview of the new law;
- A background or prior law discussion that puts the law changes into perspective;
- Editorial aids, including examples, comments, and compliance tips, that highlight the impact of the new law;
- Captions at the end of each explanation identifying existing law sections added, amended or repealed, as well as the Act sections containing the changes;
- Cross references to the law paragraphs related to the explanation; and

- A line highlighting the effective date of each law change, marked by an arrow symbol.

The Explanations begin at ¶100.

2020 Coronavirus Response Acts

While the primary focus of this book is on the employee leave and unemployment insurance-related provisions of the 2020 Coronavirus Response Acts, other provisions of the Acts are also part of the discussion. Thus, the Acts have been reproduced in their entirety, *beginning at ¶1000.*

AMENDED LAW PROVISIONS

Changes to the Family and Medical Leave Act appear at ¶3000, and selected provisions, as amended, of the following laws appear at: ¶5000 Internal Revenue Code; ¶6000 Employee Retirement Income Security Act; ¶7000 Social Security Act; and ¶8000 Fair Credit Reporting Act. Changes to these laws are all *set out in italics.*

REGULATION

This publication also includes the full text of 29 CFR Part 826, Paid Leave under the Families First Coronavirus Response Act; temporary regulations issued by the U.S. Department of Labor's Wage and Hour Division. The preamble to the Temporary Rule promulgating the regulations is included (*see* ¶9000).

SPECIAL TABLES

Other special tables and finding devices in this book include:

- Family Medical Leave Act Section to Explanation Table (*see* ¶10,001);
- Family Medical Leave Act Sections Added, Amended or Repealed (*see* ¶10,005);
- Act Sections Amending Family Medical Leave Act Sections (*see* ¶10,010);
- Internal Revenue Code Section to Explanation Table (*see* ¶10,015);
- Internal Revenue Code Sections Added, Amended or Repealed (*see* ¶10,020);
- Act Sections Amending Internal Revenue Code Sections (*see* ¶10,025);
- ERISA Section to Explanation Table (*see* ¶10,030);
- ERISA Sections Added, Amended or Repealed (*see* ¶10,035);
- Act Sections Amending ERISA Sections (*see* ¶10,040);
- Social Security Act Section to Explanation Table (*see* ¶10,045);
- Social Security Act Sections Added, Amended or Repealed (*see* ¶10,050);
- Act Sections Amending Social Security Act Sections (*see* ¶10,055);
- Fair Credit Reporting Act Section to Explanation Table (*see* ¶10,060);
- Fair Credit Reporting Act Sections Added, Amended or Repealed (*see* ¶10,065); and
- Act Sections Amending Fair Credit Reporting Act Sections (*see* ¶10,070).
- CARES Act Sections Amending Families First Coronavirus Response Act Sections (*see* ¶10,075).

¶2 Table of Contents

TOPICAL INDEX

¶3 Detailed Table of Contents

CHAPTER 3. EMERGENCY PAID SICK LEAVE

CHAPTER 4. HEALTH AND PRIVACY PROVISIONS

CHAPTER 5. TAX CREDITS AND OTHER PAYROLL RELIEF

CHAPTER 6. PENSION PLANS PROVISIONS

CHAPTER 7. ECONOMIC STABILIZATION PROVISIONS

CHAPTER 8. AIR CARRIER WORKERS SUPPORT

¶5 Highlights

EMERGENCY FAMILY AND MEDICAL LEAVE EXPANSION

¶100 **Public Health Emergency Leave.** The Family and Medical Leave Act is expanded to require employers with fewer than 500 employees to offer eligible employees paid FMLA leave if the employee is unable to work (or telework) due to a need to care for the employee's minor child because a COVID-19 public health emergency has forced the closure of the child's school or place of care. Employees must provide employers with notice of the need for such leave, to extent foreseeable and practicable. Entitlement to public health emergency leave begins April 1, 2020 and ends December 31, 2020.

¶110 **Covered Employers/Eligible Employees.** The public health emergency leave requirement (see ¶100) generally applies to employers with fewer than 500 employees. Exemptions for businesses with fewer than 50 employees or for employees deemed to be health care providers and emergency responders may apply. Employees employed by the employer for at least 30 calendar days are eligible for public health emergency leave.

¶120 **Relationship to Paid Leave.** Employers must provide paid leave for public health emergency leave after the initial 10 days of leave, which employers may designate as unpaid leave.

¶130 **Restoration to Position.** The Family and Medical Leave Act's job restoration requirements do not apply to employees of an employer with fewer than 25 employees in situations where public health emergency leave is taken.

¶140 **Employment Under Multi-Employer Bargaining Agreements.** Under multiemployer bargaining agreements, employers may satisfy their obligations regarding the public health emergency leave provisions by making contributions to a multiemployer fund that permits such contributions. Employees who work under a multiemployer collective bargaining agreement and whose employers pay into a multiemployer plan may access emergency paid leave under the Families First Coronavirus Response Act.

¶150 **Special Rule for Certain Employers.** Businesses with fewer than 50 employees are exempt from civil damages in employee-initiated lawsuits for violations involving the extended emergency FMLA leave.

¶160 **Special Rule for Health Care Providers and Emergency Responders.** An employer of a health care provider or emergency responder may choose to exempt these employees from the application of the public health emergency leave provisions.

EMERGENCY UNEMPLOYMENT INSURANCE STABILIZATION AND ACCESS

¶200 **Emergency Transfers for Unemployment Compensation Administration.** The Secretary of Labor is authorized to provide $1 billion in emergency administrative grants to the states for activities related to the processing and payment of unemployment benefits in fiscal year 2020 under certain conditions.

¶210 **Temporary Assistance for States with Advances.** Any interest payment otherwise due from a state for Federal Unemployment Account Trust Fund advances shall be deemed to have been made by the state and no interest shall accrue from March 18, 2020, through December 31, 2020.

¶220 **Technical Assistance and Guidance for Short-Time Compensation Programs.** The Families First Coronavirus Response Act provision pertaining to technical assistance and guidance for short-time compensation programs is repealed.

¶230 **Full Federal Funding of Extended Unemployment Compensation for a Limited Period.** The Families First Coronavirus Response Act amends, for a limited period, the Federal-State Extended Unemployment Compensation Act to provide 100% (formerly 50%) federal funding beginning March 18, 2020, and before December 31, 2020, for extended benefits in states that experience an increase of at least 10% or more of unemployment compensation claims over the same quarter in the previous calendar year and receive emergency grant funding.

¶235 **Pandemic Unemployment Assistance.** The Secretary of Labor must provide unemployment benefit assistance to a covered individual while he or she is unemployed, partially unemployed, or unable to work due to COVID-19. The individual must not be entitled to any other unemployment compensation or waiting period credit. The total number of weeks that an individual may receive assistance may not exceed a maximum of 39 weeks.

¶240 **Emergency Unemployment Relief for Governmental Entities and Nonprofit Organizations.** The Secretary of Labor must provide funds to states to reimburse government agencies, nonprofits, and Indian tribes for half the costs they incur through December 31, 2020, in providing unemployment benefits.

¶245 **Emergency Increase in Unemployment Compensation Benefits.** An additional $600 per week payment will be given to each recipient of unemployment insurance or Pandemic Unemployment Assistance in states that enter into an agreement with the Secretary of Labor for the additional amount through July 31, 2020.

¶250 **Temporary Full Federal Funding of First Week of Compensable Regular Unemployment for States with No Waiting Week.** Federal funding is provided to pay the cost of the first week of unemployment benefits through December 31, 2020, for states that choose to pay recipients as soon as they become unemployed instead of waiting one week before the individual is eligible to receive benefits.

¶255 **Federal and State Agreements for Pandemic Emergency Unemployment Compensation.** Under the Pandemic Emergency Unemployment Compensation program, individuals whose state has entered into an agreement with Secretary of Labor and who have exhausted benefits they otherwise would be entitled to are eligible for an additional 13 weeks of unemployment benefits. The extended benefits are available through December 31, 2020.

¶260 **Temporary Financing of Short-Time Compensation Payments in States with Programs in Law.** Temporary federal financing is provided for states that currently have a short-time compensation program set forth in state law. The Coronavirus Aid, Relief, and Economic Security Act (P.L. 116-136)) provides financing for 100 percent of short-time compensation paid under such a program for weeks of unemployment beginning on or after the date of enactment (March 27, 2020) and ending on or before December 31, 2020.

¶265 **Modification of PBGC Premiums for Cooperative and Small Employer Charity (CSEC) Plans.** Temporary federal financing is provided for federal-state short-time compensation agreements, ending on or before December 31, 2020. Under those agreements, the state agency must make payments of short-time compensation under a plan approved by the state, and employers must pay the state an amount equal to 50 percent of the amount of the short-time compensation paid under the plan (states would be eligible for temporary federal financing of 50 percent of the amount of short-time compensation paid).

¶270 **Grants for Short-Time Compensation Programs.** A maximum of $100 million is earmarked for the Secretary of Labor to award grants to states for the implementation and administration of approved short-time compensation programs and for the promotion and enrollment of employers in such programs.

¶275 **Assistance and Guidance in Implementing Short-Time Compensation Programs.** The Secretary of Labor is directed to develop model legislative language and provide technical assistance and guidance to states in establishing short-time compensation programs.

¶280 **Waiver of Waiting Period Under the Railroad Unemployment Insurance Act.** The seven-day waiting period for unemployment and sickness benefits under the Railroad Unemployment Insurance Act is temporarily eliminated.

¶285 **Enhanced Benefits Under the Railroad Unemployment Insurance Act.** An additional recovery benefit of $1,200 per two-week registration period is provided for each recipient of railroad unemployment benefits beginning on or after April 1, 2020, through July 31, 2020.

¶290 **Extended Benefits Under the Railroad Unemployment Insurance Act.** Railroad workers who received regular unemployment insurance benefits during the period from July 1, 2019, to June 30, 2020, may be eligible to receive extended benefits.

¶295 **Funding for the DOL Office of Inspector General for Oversight of Unemployment Provisions.** Funds are appropriated to the Office of the Inspector General of the Department of Labor to carry out audits, investigations, and other authorized oversight activities of the CARES Act's unemployment insurance provisions.

¶297 **Implementation.** The Secretary of Labor may issue any operating instructions or other guidance necessary to carry out the Act's unemployment insurance provisions.

EMERGENCY PAID SICK LEAVE

¶300 **Paid Sick Time Requirement.** Private employers with fewer than 500 employees (as well as public employers and other non-private entities with at least one employee) must temporarily provide their employees with paid sick time for designated reasons related to COVID-19. This requirement is scheduled to expire on December 31, 2020.

¶305 **OMB Waiver of Paid Sick Leave.** The Office of Management and Budget is authorized to exclude for good cause certain federal government employees from the provisions of the Emergency Paid Sick Leave Act.

¶310 **Definitions.** Terms pertaining to the Emergency Paid Sick Leave Act are defined. Key information about eligible employees, covered employers, and calculating compensation for paid sick time is included in the definitions.

¶320 **Notice.** Employers are required to post notice in a conspicuous location for employees about the Emergency Paid Sick Leave Act and its requirements.

¶330 **Prohibited Acts.** Employers are prohibited from taking any action, including discriminating against, disciplining, or terminating, an employee who takes leave in accordance with the Act; has filed a complaint; instituted a proceeding relating to the enforcement of the Act; or has testified, or is about to testify, in such a proceeding.

¶340 **Enforcement.** Employers who violate the Emergency Paid Sick Leave Act are considered to have violated the FLSA and will be subject to a potential fine, incarceration, and other punitive action.

¶350 **Employment Under Multi-Employer Bargaining Agreements.** Employers participating in a multi-employer collective bargaining agreement (CBA) may meet their paid leave obligations by paying into a multi-employer fund to which their employees are entitled while working under the multi-employer CBA provided the plan allows employees to secure pay based on the hours they have worked under the multiemployer CBA for paid leave taken under the new public health emergency leave and paid sick time provisions.

¶360 **Regulatory Authorities.** The Secretary of Labor has the authority to issue regulations consistent with the enforcement of this Act, including the exclusion of certain health care providers and emergency responders from the definition of employee.

HEALTH AND PRIVACY PROVISIONS

¶400 **Coverage of Testing for COVID-19.** Effective immediately, and for the duration of the national emergency, group health plans and health insurance issuers will be required to provide coverage of COVID-19 diagnostic tests and office visits, urgent care center visits, and emergency room visits that result in an order for or administration of such tests without application of any cost sharing.

¶410 **Insurer Pricing of Diagnostic Testing.** Group health plans and health insurance issuers must reimburse providers of COVID-19 diagnostic tests in accordance with rates negotiated prior to the public health emergency or in an amount equal to the cash price for the service as listed on the provider's website. Providers must make the cash price of COVID-19 diagnostic tests public or face civil money penalties.

¶420 **Rapid Coverage of Preventive Services and Vaccines for Coronavirus.** Group health plans and health insurance issuers offering group or individual health insurance are required to cover—without cost-sharing—qualifying coronavirus preventive services, including COVID-19 immunizations.

¶430 **Health Savings Account (HSA) Eligibility.** For plan years beginning on or before December 31, 2021, a safe harbor for health savings accounts (HSAs) provides that a health plan will not fail to be treated as a high-deductible health plan (HDHP) for failing to impose a deductible for telehealth or other remote care services.

¶440 **Medical Care Expenses for HSAs, Archer MSAs, HRAs, and Health FSAs.** The requirement that individuals obtain a prescription in order to be reimbursed for over-the-counter medicines and drugs has been eliminated for expenses paid or incurred after December 31, 2019, for health savings accounts (HSAs), Archer medical savings accounts (MSAs), health flexible spending accounts (FSAs), and health reimbursement arrangements (HRAs). In addition, expenses paid or incurred for the purchase of menstrual care products after December 31, 2019, are eligible medical care expenses for purposes of HSAs, Archer MSAs, health FSAs, and HRAs.

¶450 **Confidentiality and Disclosure of Records Relating to Substance Abuse Disorder.** After a patient's prior written consent has been obtained, a covered entity, business associate, or program may use or disclose the contents of substance use disorder records for purposes of treatment, payment, and health care operations, and re-disclose the information, as permitted by the Health Insurance Portability and Accountability Act of 1996 (HIPAA) regulations.

¶460 **Guidance on Protected Health Information.** The Secretary of Health and Human Services (HHS) must—within 180 days of the enactment of the Coronavirus Aid, Relief, and Economic Security Act (P.L. 116-136)—issue guidance on the sharing of patients' protected health information during the COVID-19 public health emergency.

TAX CREDITS AND OTHER PAYROLL RELIEF

¶500 **Payroll Credit for Required Paid Sick Leave.** An employer is allowed a credit against the Old-Age, Survivors, and Disability Insurance (OASDI) tax or Railroad Retirement Tax Act (RRTA) tax imposed on the employer for each calendar quarter in an amount equal to 100% of the qualified sick leave wages paid by the employer for the calendar quarter, subject to a few limitations. The credit is refundable and can be obtained in advance.

¶510 **Allowance of Required Paid Sick Leave Credit for Certain Health Plan Expenses.** The qualified sick leave wage credit will be increased by the amount of an employer's qualified health plan expenses that are properly allocable to the qualified sick leave wages for which the credit is allowed.

¶520 **Special Rules for Required Paid Sick Leave Credit.** An employer cannot take both the payroll credit allowed for sick leave against the Old-Age, Survivors, and Disability Insurance (OASDI) tax or Railroad Retirement Tax Act (RRTA) for each calendar quarter under the Families First Act and the current credit allowed under Code Sec. 45S. Employers can elect not to participate. The credit does not apply to governments.

¶530 **Transfers to Federal Old-Age and Survivors Insurance Trust Fund for Sick Leave Credit.** Amounts equal to the reduction in revenues to the Treasury by reason of the payroll credit for paid sick leave will be appropriated to the Federal Old-Age and Survivors Insurance Trust Fund and the Federal Disability Insurance Trust Fund.

¶540 **Payroll Credit for Required Paid Family Leave.** An employer is allowed a credit against the Old-Age, Survivors, and Disability Insurance (OASDI) tax or Railroad Retirement Tax Act (RRTA) tax imposed on the employer for each calendar quarter in an amount equal to 100% of the qualified family leave wages paid by the employer for the calendar quarter, subject to a few limitations. The credit is refundable and can be obtained in advance.

¶550 **Allowance of Required Family Leave Credit for Certain Health Plan Expenses.** The amount of the family leave credit will be increased by the amount that the employer's qualified health plan expenses are properly allocable to the qualified family leave wages for which the credit is allowed.

¶560 **Special Rules for Required Paid Family Leave Credit.** An employer cannot take both the payroll credit allowed for family leave against the Old-Age, Survivors, and Disability Insurance (OASDI) tax or Railroad Retirement Tax Act (RRTA) for each calendar quarter under the Families First Act and the current credit allowed under Code Sec. 45S. Employers can elect not to participate. The credit does not apply to governments.

¶570 **Transfers to Federal Old-Age and Survivors Insurance Trust Fund for Family Leave Credit.** Amounts equal to the reduction in revenues to the Treasury by reason of the payroll credit for required paid family leave will be appropriated to the Federal Old-Age and Survivors Insurance Trust Fund and the Federal Disability Insurance Trust Fund.

¶575 **Special Rule Related to Tax on Employers.** The employer portion of Social Security (FICA) or railroad retirement (RRTA) taxes will not be collected from employers from sick or family leave paid under the Families First Act.

¶580 **Exclusion for Certain Employer Payments of Student Loans.** Certain payments made by an employer on a qualified student loan of an employee before January 1, 2021, are excluded from the employee's gross income. The payments can be made to either the employee or a lender to be applied to the employee's student loans and could cover principal or interest.

¶590 **Employee Retention Credit for Employers Subject to Closure Due to COVID-19.** To encourage employers to keep employees on their payroll during the COVID-19 crisis, the employee retention credit is a refundable tax credit against the Old-Age, Survivors, and Disability Insurance (OASDI) tax or Railroad Retirement Tax Act (RRTA) tax imposed on the employer for each calendar quarter equal to 50% of the qualified wages an eligible employer pays to employees after March 12, 2020, and before January 1, 2021.

¶595 **Delay of Payment of Employer Payroll Taxes.** Employers can defer payment of the employer's share of the Social Security tax that they otherwise are responsible for paying on wages. The deferral applies to taxes normally required to be paid from March 27, 2020, through December 31, 2020. The deferred tax must be paid over two years, with half to be paid by December 31, 2021, and the other half to be paid by December 31, 2022.

¶597 **Temporary Relief for Federal Student Loan Borrowers.** Payroll garnishment of wages for the purpose of paying federal student loans that are in default are halted during the period in which the Secretary of Education suspends payments on a loan.

PENSION PLANS PROVISIONS

¶600 **Coronavirus-Related Distributions from Retirement Plans.** The 10-percent additional tax under Code Sec. 72(t) is waived for any qualified coronavirus-related distributions from a retirement plan. Eligible individuals who take such distributions can include them in gross income over a three-year span and have three years to repay the amount.

¶605 **Coronavirus-Related Plan Loans from Retirement Plans.** The threshold limit on loans from an employer-sponsored retirement plan for a qualified individual affected by the coronavirus is increased to the lesser of $100,000 or 100 percent of the present value (but not less than $10,000) of the plan participant's benefits under the plan.

¶610 **Temporary Waiver of Required Minimum Distributions.** For the 2020 calendar year, the required minimum distribution (RMD) requirements generally applicable to retirement plans are temporarily suspended with respect to defined contribution retirement plans, including individual retirement accounts (IRAs).

¶620 **Minimum Funding Rules for Single-Employer Retirement Plans.** Minimum required contributions to a single-employer retirement plan otherwise due in calendar year 2020 (including any quarterly contributions) are delayed until January 1, 2021. The amount of each such contribution is increased by any interest accruing for the period between the original due date (without regard to the delay) for the contribution and the payment date. A plan sponsor also may elect to treat the plan's adjusted funding target attainment percentage for the last plan year ending before January 1, 2020, as the adjusted funding target attainment percentage for plan years that include calendar year 2020.

¶630 **Cooperative and Small Employer Charity (CSEC) Pension Plans.** The list of Cooperative and Small Employer Charity (CSEC) pension plans has been amended to add a class of plans belonging to any Code Sec. 501(c)(3) organization in existence since at least 1938 that conducts medical research directly or indirectly through grant making and whose primary exempt purpose is to provide services with respect to mothers and children.

¶640 **Expansion of Department of Labor Authority to Postpone Certain Deadlines.** The Department of Labor has the authority to postpone ERISA compliance deadlines for up to one year in the event of a public health emergency declared by the Secretary of Health and Human Services.

ECONOMIC STABILIZATION PROVISIONS

¶700 **Loans, Loan Guarantees, and Other Investments.** The Coronavirus Aid, Relief, and Economic Security Act (CARES Act, P.L. 116-136) authorizes up to $500 billion of funding to provide liquidity to eligible businesses, states, and municipalities experiencing financial distress as a result of the COVID-19 national emergency. The Department of the Treasury may make up to $46 billion in direct loans and loan guarantees to passenger air carriers and related businesses, cargo air carriers, and businesses critical for national security. The Treasury may use the remaining $454 billion for programs established by the Federal Reserve to facilitate direct lending and guarantees and to support lending through banks or other lenders. One of these programs would provide financing to banks and other lenders that make direct low-interest loans to mid-sized businesses.

¶710 **Limitations on Certain Highly Paid Officer and Employee Compensation.** The Secretary of the Treasury may only enter into an agreement to make a loan or loan guarantee to eligible passenger air carriers (and specified related businesses), cargo air carriers, and businesses critical to maintaining national security (as described in Section 4003(b)(1), (2), and (3) of the Coronavirus Aid, Relief, and Economic Security Act (P.L. 116-136)) if the businesses agree to specified limitations on total compensation of certain highly paid officers and employees.

¶720 **Temporary Sunshine Act Relief.** The Board of Governors of the Federal Reserve System may conduct meetings without regard to the Sunshine Act requirements during the covered period for the COVID-19 national emergency if the Chairman of the Board of Governors of the Federal Reserve System determines, in writing, that unusual and exigent circumstances exist.

¶730 **Temporary Hiring Flexibility.** The Department of Housing and Urban Development, the Securities and Exchange Commission, and the Commodity Futures Trading Commission are granted additional hiring flexibility during the COVID-19 national emergency.

¶740 **Credit Protection During COVID-19.** The Fair Credit Reporting Act is amended to require data furnishers to report to the credit bureaus that consumers are current on their credit obligations if they enter into an agreement with a consumer affected by COVID-19 to defer, forbear, modify, make partial payments, or get any other assistance on their loan payments from a financial institution and the consumer fulfills those requirements.

¶750 **Protection of Collective Bargaining Agreement.** A loan to an air carrier or other eligible business cannot be conditioned on whether that air carrier or eligible business is preparing to enter into negotiations for a collective bargaining agreement regarding pay or other terms and conditions of employment.

AIR CARRIER WORKERS SUPPORT

¶800 **Pandemic Relief for Aviation Workers.** The Coronavirus Aid, Relief, and Economic Security (CARES) Act (P.L. 116-136), earmarks $32 billion in financial assistance (*i.e.*, payroll support) to aid the commercial airline industry and its employees affected by travel cutbacks due to the coronavirus pandemic. These funds are in addition to loans and loan guarantees provided to passenger air carriers and businesses critical to maintaining national security provided elsewhere in the statute.

¶810 **Procedures for Providing Payroll Support.** Payroll support funds provided to airlines and airline contractors will be determined based upon the recipients' salaries and benefits incurred during the six-month period between April 1—September 30, 2019, and will be made available under expedited application and payment procedures beginning five days after the enactment of the Coronavirus Aid, Relief, and Economic Security (CARES) Act (P.L. 116-136).

¶820 **Required Assurances.** Airlines and airline contractors receiving payroll support funds must agree to refrain from furloughing employees or reducing their pay and benefits through September 30, 2020, as well as from engaging in stock buy-backs through that date and paying dividends or other capital distributions to shareholders.

¶830 **Protection of Collective Bargaining Agreements.** Payroll support funds to airlines and airline contractors cannot be conditioned upon the recipients' implementation of measures to enter into negotiations with the collective bargaining representatives of their employees regarding wages or other working conditions.

¶840 **Limitations on Certain Employee Compensation.** Airlines and airline contractors receiving payroll support funds must enter into an agreement with the Secretary of the Treasury that limits the total compensation to be received by corporate officers and employees during any 12-month period between March 24, 2020, and March 24, 2022, to 2019 levels.

Chapter 1—Emergency Family and Medical Leave Expansion

1

¶100 Public Health Emergency Leave

SUMMARY OF NEW LAW

The Family and Medical Leave Act is expanded to require employers with fewer than 500 employees to offer eligible employees paid FMLA leave if the employee is unable to work (or telework) due to a need to care for the employee's minor child because a COVID-19 public health emergency has forced the closure of the child's school or place of care. Employees must provide employers with notice of the need for such leave, to extent foreseeable and practicable. Entitlement to public health emergency leave begins April 1, 2020 and ends December 31, 2020.

BACKGROUND

The Family and Medical Leave Act (FMLA) generally provides eligible employees of employers with 50 or more employees with 12 workweeks of unpaid leave during any 12-month period in certain situations (FMLA Secs. 101(4); 102(a)(1)). Leave is available due to the birth of the employee's child; to the placement of a child with the employee for adoption or foster care; the serious health condition of the employee's family member; the serious health condition of the employee; or in certain situations where the employee's family member is on covered active duty in the Armed Forces (FMLA Sec. 102(a)(1)(A-E).

NEW LAW EXPLAINED

Public health emergency leave.—During the period beginning on April 1, 2020 and ending December 31, 2020, entitlement to FMLA leave is expanded to include leave related to a qualifying need related to a public health emergency (FMLA Sec. 102(a)(1)(F), added by Act Sec. 3102(a) of the Families First Coronavirus Response Act (P.L. 116-127).

Qualifying need. A "qualifying need related to a public health emergency" means the employee is unable to work (or telework) due to a need to care for the employee's son or daughter under 18 years old if, due to a public health emergency:

(1) The school or place of care has been closed, or

(2) The child care provider of the employee's child is unavailable (FMLA Sec. 110(a)(2)(A), as added by Act Sec. 3102(b) of the Families First Act).

> **Comment:** "Son or daughter" includes: the employee's biological or adopted child under 18 years of age; a legal ward, or a child for whom the employee stands *in loco parentis*. Also included is an adult child who is incapable of self-care due to a mental or physical disability (29 CFR § 826.10).

Public health emergency. A public health emergency is an emergency related to COVID-19 declared by a Federal or State or local authority (FMLA Sec. 110(a)(2)(B), as added by the Families First Act).

Child care provider. For purposes of the emergency leave, a "child care provider" is one who is compensated for providing child care services on a regular basis, including eligible child care providers offering subsidized child care to low-income working families (FMLA Sec. 110(a)(2)(C), as added by the Families First Act).

School. Public health emergency leave is available to parents of children whose "elementary" and "secondary" schools have closed due to a public health emergency. This provision applies to a nonprofit institutional day or residential school (including a public charter school) that provides elementary or secondary education as determined under state law, except not beyond grade 12 (FMLA Sec. 110(a)(2)(D), as added by the Families First Act).

Employers with fewer than 500 employees are generally required to provide public health emergency leave to employees employed for at least 30 days (FMLA Sec. 110(a)(1)(B), as added by the Families First Act). See ¶110.

Notice to employer. When an employee's need for public health emergency leave is foreseeable, the employee must provide the employer with notice of such leave. Notice is required to the extent such notice is practicable (FMLA Sec. 110(c), as added by the Families First Act).

> **Comment:** Under regulations issued by the Labor Department, notice may not be required in advance, and may only be required after the first workday for which an employee takes expanded family leave. Employers may require oral notice, as well as enough information to determine whether the requested leave is covered by the Act (29 CFR § 826.90(c)). Employees must document their need for leave by supplying the employer (prior to taking leave), with, among other things, an oral or written statement that the employee is unable to work due to

NEW LAW EXPLAINED

the qualified reason for the leave; the name of the school or child care provider that has closed; a representation that no other suitable person will be caring for the child while expanded leave is taken; and any additional information as needed for the employer to support a request for tax credits. The employer is not required to provide leave if materials sufficient to support the applicable tax credit have not been provided (29 CFR § 826.100).

> **Expert Guidance:** Notice to employees. According to the law firm Ogletree Deakins, "The FFCRA requires eligible employers to maintain, in a conspicuous location, where notices to employees are customarily posted, in all work locations, a notice prepared or approved by the Secretary of Labor. In addition, and particularly given the prevalence of employees working remotely due to COVID-19, employers may provide notice through email or direct mail to employees or by posting on an employee-facing intranet or external website. The model notice posting applicable to private employers is now available in English, Spanish, and Korean. The DOL permits emailing the poster to those already teleworking." Michael M. Shetterly, Matthew K. Johnson and Sarah J. Platt, The Families First Coronavirus Response Act FAQs: The FMLA Amendments and paid Sick Leave Requirements of the New Law (https:/ogletree.com/solutions/coronavirus-covid-19-resource-center/). The model notice posting is at dol.gov/sites/dolgov/files/WHD/posters/FFCRA_Poster_WH1422_Non-Federal.pdf.

Paid leave. After the initial 10 days of public health emergency leave (which may be unpaid), employers must provide paid leave (FMLA Sec. 102(c), as amended by Act Sec. 3102(a)(2) of the Families First Act). See ¶ 120.

▶ **Effective date.** The Act takes effect April 1, 2020 (not later than 15 days after the date of enactment (Act Sec. 3106 of the Families First Act).

Law Source: Law at ¶1027, ¶1031, ¶3005, and ¶3013.

— Act Sec. 3102(a)(1) of the Families First Coronavirus Response Act (P.L. 116-127), amending FMLA Sec. 102(a)(1) by adding subsection (F).

— Act Sec. 3102(a)(2) of the Families First Act, amending FMLA Sec. 102(c).

— Act Sec. 3102(b) of the Families First Act, amending Title I of the FMLA by adding Sec. 110.

— Act Sec. 3106 of the Families First Act, providing the effective date.

¶110 Covered Employers/Eligible Employees

SUMMARY OF NEW LAW

The public health emergency leave requirement (see ¶100) generally applies to employers with fewer than 500 employees. Exemptions for businesses with fewer than 50 employees or for employees deemed to be health care providers and emer-

SUMMARY OF NEW LAW

gency responders may apply. Employees employed by the employer for at least 30 calendar days are eligible for public health emergency leave.

BACKGROUND

Generally, to be covered by the FMLA, a private employer must employ 50 or more employees for each working day during each of 20 or more calendar work weeks in the current or preceding calendar year (FMLA Sec. 101(4)). In addition, a company must employ at least 50 employees within 75 miles of a worksite before it is required to provide FMLA leave (FMLA Sec. 101(2)(B)(ii)).

To be eligible to take FMLA leave, an employee must have worked for an employer for at least 12 months total. In addition, the employee must have worked at least 1,250 hours during the 12-month period immediately before the leave is scheduled to begin (FMLA Sec. 101(2)(A)).

NEW LAW EXPLAINED

Covered employers and eligible employees for public health emergency leave.— The public health emergency leave requirement applies to employers with fewer than 500 employees, although exemptions for businesses with fewer than 50 employees or for health care providers and emergency responders may apply. Employees employed by the employer for at least 30 calendar days are eligible for public health emergency leave (FMLA Sec. 110(a)(1), as added by Act Sec. 3102(b) of the Families First Coronavirus Response Act (P.L. 116-127).

Fewer than 500 employees. For purposes of public health emergency leave, the Families First Act replaces the FMLA's "50 or more employees during a 20-week period" threshold with a requirement that all employers with fewer than 500 employees must provide the public health emergency leave (FMLA Sec. 110(a)(1)(B), as added by the Families First Act).

According to the Wage and Hour Division of the Department of Labor, an employer must provide leave if, at the time the employee's leave is taken, the employer employs fewer than 500 full-time and part-time employees within the United States. Typically, a corporation, including its separate establishments or divisions, is considered to be a single employer for purposes of the 500-employer threshold. Employers should include the following employees when making this determination:

- Employees on leave
- Temporary employees who are jointly employed by the employer and another employer (regardless of whether the jointly employed employees are maintained on the employer's payroll); and
- Day laborers supplied by a temporary agency (regardless of whether the employer is the temporary agency or the client firm if there is a continuing employment relationship).

NEW LAW EXPLAINED

Note that independent contractors are not employees for purposes of the 500-employee threshold (*Families First Coronavirus Response Act: Questions and Answers*, Q/A-2, issued by the Department of Labor, dol.gov/agencies/whd/pandemic/ffrca-questions).

Relief for small employers. The Secretary of Labor is authorized to issue regulations that would exempt small businesses with fewer than 50 employees from compliance with the leave requirement if compliance would jeopardize the viability of the business (FMLA Sec. 110(a)(3)(B), added by the Families First Act).

Under Labor Department regulations issued pursuant to the Act, for a small business to claim the exemption, an authorized officer of the business must determine that at least one of the following conditions is satisfied:

- Providing the expanded family leave would cause the employer's expenses to exceed available revenues remedies and cause the small business to cease operating at minimal capacity;
- Absence of employees with specialized knowledge or skills would entail a substantial risk to the financial health of the business; or
- The small business lacks enough workers to perform the work of the employees requesting the expanded family leave.

The employer must retain for its records documentation that such a determination has been made. The documentation should not be sent to the Wage and Hour Division (29 CFR § 826.40(b)).

Eligible employees. Employees who have been employed for at least 30 calendar days by the employer are eligible for public health emergency leave (FMLA Sec. 110(a)(1)(A), as added by the Families First Act). This includes a rehired employee who had been laid off by the employer (not earlier than March 1, 2020), had worked for the employer for not less than 30 of the last 60 calendar days prior to the layoff, and was then rehired by the employer (FMLA Sec. 110(a)(1)(A)(ii), added by Act Sec. 3605 of the Coronavirus Aid, Relief, and Economic Security Act (P.L. 116-136).

> **Expert Guidance:** As to what qualifies as "30 calendar days" under the Act, the law firm Ogletree Deakins comments: "The employee must have been on payroll (again, any time worked as a temporary employee for the employer also counts as being on payroll) for 30 calendar days, no matter how many days he or she worked"(Michael M. Shetterly, Matthew K. Johnson and Sarah J. Platt, The Families First Coronavirus Response Act FAQs: the FMLA Amendments and Paid Sick Leave Requirements of the New Law, https:/ogletree.com/solutions/coronavirus-covid-19-resource-center/).

Health care workers and emergency responders. The Secretary of Labor is authorized to issue regulations excluding health care providers and emergency responders from the definition of eligible employee (FMLA Sec. 110(a)(3)(A), as added by the Families First Act).

> **Comment:** Regulations issued by the Labor Department offer broad definitions of "health care provider" and "emergency responder" for purposes of this

NEW LAW EXPLAINED

exemption. For example, the definition of "health care provider" encompasses all employees of hospitals, doctor's offices, nursing homes, home health providers, etc., as well as workers making medical products, including medical equipment, tests and vaccines. The governor of a State has the authority to designate individuals as health care providers or emergency responders for this purpose (29 CFR § 826.30(c)).

Federal employees. Most federal employees are not entitled to the expanded family and medical leave because while the Act only amended Title I of the FMLA, most federal employees are covered instead by Title II of the FMLA (*Families First Coronavirus Response Act: Questions and Answers*, Q/A-53, issued by the Department of Labor, dol.gov/agencies/whd/pandemic/ffrca-questions). In addition, the Director of the Office of Management and Budget has the authority under the Act to exclude some categories of the U.S. Government Executive Branch with respect to expanded family and medical leave (FMLA Sec. 110(a)(4), as added Act Sec. 3604(a) of the CARES Act). However, Congressional employees otherwise covered by the FMLA who have been employed for at least 30 calendar days are covered (FMLA Sec. 110(a)(1)(A)**(iii)[sic]**, as added by Act Sec. 19008 of the CARES Act).

Impact of regulations. The Families First Act authorizes the Labor Department to issue regulations as necessary to implement the Act, including to ensure consistence between the Act and existing provisions of the FMLA (FMLA Sec. 110(a)(3), as added by the Families First Act). Regulations were issued by the Labor Department's Wage and Hour Division on April 6, 2020 (85 FR 19326).

▶ **Effective date.** The Act takes effect April 1, 2020 (not later than 15 days after the date of enactment) (Act Sec. 3106 of the Families First Act).

Law source: Law at ¶1027, ¶1031, ¶2121, ¶2123, ¶2240, and ¶3013.

— Act Sec. 3102(b) of the Families First Coronavirus Response Act (P.L. 116-127), amending Title I of the FMLA by adding Sec. 110.

— Act Sec. 3106 of the Families First Act, providing the effective date.

— Act Sec. 3605 of the Coronavirus Aid, Relief, and Economic Security Act (P.L. 116-136), adding FMLA Sec. 110(a)(1)(A)(ii).

— Act Sec. 3604(a) of the CARES Act, adding FMLA Sec. 110(a)(4).

— Act Sec. 19008 of the CARES Act, adding FMLA Sec. 110(a)(1)(A)**(iii)[sic].**

¶120 Relationship to Paid Leave

SUMMARY OF NEW LAW

Employers must provide paid leave for public health emergency leave after the initial 10 days of leave, which employers may designate as unpaid leave.

BACKGROUND

Leave under the Family and Medical Leave Act is normally unpaid leave: employers are not required to compensate employees for time spent on FMLA leave. In addition, the FMLA generally gives employers the option of requiring employees to take paid leave that they have already earned at the same time as all or part of the 12-week FMLA leave entitlement (FMLA Sec. 102(c)).

NEW LAW EXPLAINED

Relationship to paid leave.—Employers must provide paid leave for public health emergency leave after the initial 10 days of leave, which employers may designate as unpaid leave. Paid leave is capped at $200 per day and $10,000 in the aggregate (FMLA Sec. 102(c), as amended by Act Sec. 3102(a)(2) of the Families First Coronavirus Response Act (P.L. 116-127) and FMLA Sec. 110(b), as added by Act Sec. 3102(b) of the Families First Act).

While employers may require employees to take the first 10 days of public health emergency leave on an unpaid basis, the employee may elect (or the employer may require the employee) to substitute any accrued vacation leave, personal leave, or medical or sick leave for unpaid leave, as set forth in FMLA Sec. 102(d)(2)(B) (FMLA Sec. 110(b)(1)(B), as added by Sec. 3102(b) of the Families First Act).

Paid leave commences. After the initial 10 days of leave, employers must provide paid leave equal to not less than two-thirds of the employee's regular rate of pay and the number of hours the employee would otherwise be normally scheduled to work, or the number of hours calculated for employees who have varying schedules (FMLA Sec. 110(b)(2)(B)(i), as added by Sec. 3102(b) of the Families First Act).

> **Expert Guidance:** According to the law firm Ogletree Deakins: "After the first two weeks of [public health emergency leave] (Congress said 10 days, but the concept of days does not align with the FMLA), the [Act] offers paid leave for up to another 10 weeks (depending upon need and whether the employee has already exhausted some FMLA leave for other qualifying reasons). During the last 10 weeks of leave, an employer must pay the employee two-thirds of the employee's average rate of pay (i.e., total compensation other than discretionary bonuses) over the past six months, subject to a statutory cap of $200 per day and $10,000 total (the aggregate maximum of all paid FMLA leave under this provision). An employer may choose to pay more, but tax credits will be limited to the amount required. Employers with unions can use multiemployer collective bargaining agreement plans to pay out these amounts so long as the plans are amended to make the payments provided, and the employer funds the plan to pay for the leave." (Michael M. Shetterly, Matthew K. Johnson and Sarah J. Platt, The Families First Coronavirus Response Act FAQs: The FMLA Amendments and paid Sick Leave Requirements of the New Law, (https:/ ogletree.com/solutions/coronavirus-covid-19-resource-center/)).

Calculating paid leave for part-time workers or those with varying hours. Where an employee's schedule varies from week to week and the employer is unable to

NEW LAW EXPLAINED

determine with certainty the number of hours the employee would have worked if the employee had not taken leave, the hours are to be calculated based on: a number equal to the average number of hours that the employee was scheduled per day over the 6-month period ending on the date on which the employee takes such leave, including hours for which the employee took leave of any type and, if the employee did not work over such period, the reasonable expectation of the employee at the time of hiring of the average number of hours per day that the employee would normally be scheduled to work (FMLA Sec. 110(b)(2)(C), as added by Act Sec. 3102(b) of the Families First Act).

Cap on paid leave. An employer is not required to pay more than $200 per day and $10,000 in the aggregate for each employee for paid public health emergency leave (FMLA Sec. 110(b)(2)(B)(ii), as added by Sec. 3102(b) of the Families First Act and amended by Act Sec. 3601 of the Coronavirus Aid, Relief, and Economic Security Act (P.L. 116-136).

▶ **Effective date.** The Act takes effect April 1, 2020 (not later than 15 days after the date of enactment) (Act Sec. 3106 of the Families First Act).

Law source: Law at ¶1027, ¶1031, ¶2118, ¶3005, and ¶3013.

— Act Sec. 3102(a)(2) of the Families First Coronavirus Response Act (P.L. 116-127), amending FMLA Sec. 102(c).

— Act Sec. 3102(b) of the Families First Act, amending Title I of the FMLA by adding Sec. 110(b).

— Act Sec. 3106 of the Families First Act, providing the effective date.

— Act Sec. 3601 of the Coronavirus Aid, Relief, and Economic Security Act (P.L. 116-136), amending FMLA Sec. 110(b)(2)(B), as added by the Families First Act.

¶130 Restoration to Position

SUMMARY OF NEW LAW

The Family and Medical Leave Act's job restoration requirements do not apply to employees of an employer with fewer than 25 employees in situations where public health emergency leave is taken.

BACKGROUND

Employees returning from leave under the FMLA generally have the right to be restored to the same or an equivalent job position with the same or equivalent benefits, pay and other terms and conditions of employment. An equivalent position is one that is virtually identical to the employee's former position in terms of pay, benefits and working conditions, including privileges and status (FMLA Sec. 104(a)(1)).

NEW LAW EXPLAINED

Job restoration provisions suspended for smaller employers.—The FMLA's job restoration requirements do not apply to employees of an employer with fewer than 25 employees as long as the following conditions are met:

A. The employee takes leave under the public health emergency leave provision.

B. The position held by the employee when the leave commenced no longer exists, due to either economic conditions or other changes in the employer's operating conditions that affect employment and are caused by a public health emergency during the period of leave.

C. The employer makes reasonable efforts to restore the employee to a position equivalent to the position that the employee held when the leave commenced, with equivalent employment benefits, pay, and other terms and conditions of employment.

D. If the employer's reasonable efforts under subparagraph (C) fail, the employer makes reasonable efforts for a one-year period to contact the employee if an equivalent position becomes available. The one-year period begins on the earlier of the date on which the qualifying need related to a public health emergency ends; or 12 weeks following the leave's commencement (FMLA Sec. 110(d), added by Act Sec. 3102(b) of the Families First Coronavirus Response Act (P.L. 116-127)).

> **Comment:** Note that federal agencies are required to interpret requirements in the FMLA and the Families First Act in a consistent manner (FMLA Sec. 110(a)(3)(C), as added by Act Sec. 3611(7) of the Coronavirus Aid, Relief, and Economic Security Act (P.L. 116-136). Regulations issued by the Labor Department explain that in most instances, apart from the exemption for employers with fewer than 25 employees, employers are required to provide the same (or a nearly equivalent) job to an employee who returns to work following leave. However, employees are not protected from layoffs and other employment actions that would have affected the employee regardless of whether leave was taken. In addition, job restoration may be denied to key eligible employees, including the highest paid 10 percent of all employees (29 CFR § 826.130).

▶ **Effective date.** The Act takes effect April 1, 2020 (not later than 15 days after the date of enactment) (Act Sec. 3106 of the Families First Act).

Law source: Law at ¶1027, ¶1031, ¶2129, and ¶3013.

— Act Sec. 3102(b) of the Families First Coronavirus Response Act (P.L. 116-127), amending Title I of the FMLA by adding Sec. 110(d).

— Act Sec. 3106 of the Families First Act, providing the effective date.

— Act Sec. 3611(7) of the Coronavirus Aid, Relief, and Economic Security Act (P.L. 116-136), amending FMLA Sec. 110(a)(3), as added by the Families First Act.

¶140 Employment Under Multi-Employer Bargaining Agreements

SUMMARY OF NEW LAW

Under multiemployer bargaining agreements, employers may satisfy their obligations regarding the public health emergency leave provisions by making contributions to a multiemployer fund that permits such contributions. Employees who work under a multiemployer collective bargaining agreement and whose employers pay into a multiemployer plan may access emergency paid leave under the Families First Coronavirus Response Act.

BACKGROUND

The Family and Medical Leave Act requires an employer with 50 or more employees (within a 75-mile radius) to give eligible employees 12 weeks of unpaid leave for births, adoptions, and family illnesses. While this leave can be unpaid, many employers provide paid FMLA leave.

FMLA regulations require an employer to continue contributing to a multiemployer health plan on behalf of an employee on FMLA leave, unless the plan contains an explicit FMLA provision for maintaining coverage such as through pooled contributions by all employers who are party to the plan.

In light of the urgent need created by the COVID-19 pandemic, expanded emergency FMLA provisions, including provisions for emergency paid leave, have been enacted.

NEW LAW EXPLAINED

Special rules for multiemployer bargaining agreements.— An employer who is a signatory to a multiemployer collective bargaining agreement, consistent with its bargaining obligations and its collective bargaining agreement, may fulfill its obligations (see ¶ 120) under FMLA Sec. 110(b)(2), as added by the Families First Coronavirus Response Act (P.L. 116-127), by making contributions to a multiemployer fund, plan, or program based on the paid leave each of its employees is entitled to under such section while working under the multiemployer collective bargaining agreement (FMLA Sec. 110(b)(2), added by Act Sec. 3103(a) of the Families First Act).

This special rule applies if the fund, plan, or program enables employees to secure pay from such fund, plan, or program based on hours they have worked under the multiemployer collective bargaining agreement for paid leave taken (see ¶ 110) under FMLA Sec. 102(a)(1)(F), as added by the Families First Act. If such an arrangement is not in place, individual employers are still obligated to provide expanded emergency FMLA benefits under the Families First Act. (FMLA Sec. 102(a)(1)(F), added by Act Sec. 3103 of the Families First Act).

> **Comment:** An employer may satisfy its obligations regarding the expanded emergency FMLA leave by other means, provided that those means are consis-

NEW LAW EXPLAINED

tent with its bargaining obligations and collective bargaining agreement (*Families First Coronavirus Response Act: Questions and Answers*, issued by the Department of Labor; https://www.dol.gov/agencies/whd/pandemic/ffcra-questions).

Employees. Employees who work under a multiemployer collective bargaining agreement into which their employers make contributions may secure pay from such fund, plan, or program based on hours they have worked under the multiemployer collective bargaining agreement for paid leave taken (see ¶110) (FMLA Sec. 102(a)(1)(F), added by Act Sec. 3103(b) of the Families First Act).

▶ **Effective date.** The Act takes effect April 1, 2020 (not later than 15 days after the date of enactment) (Act Sec. 3106 of the Families First Act).

Law source: Law at ¶1028, ¶1031, ¶3005, and ¶3013.

— Act Sec. 3103(a) of the Families First Coronavirus Response Act (P.L. 116-127), adding FMLA Sec. 110(b)(2).

— Act Sec. 3103(a) of the Families First Act, adding FMLA Sec. 102(a)(1)(F).

— Act Sec. 3106, providing the effective date.

¶150 Special Rule for Certain Employers

SUMMARY OF NEW LAW

Businesses with fewer than 50 employees are exempt from civil damages in employee-initiated lawsuits for violations involving the extended emergency FMLA leave.

BACKGROUND

Family and Medical Leave Act (FMLA) rights are enforceable through civil actions by employees who may sue for damages and equitable relief. Further, the Department of Labor may bring a civil suit to recover damages for rights violated under the FMLA. Any amounts recovered are held in a special deposit account and paid to each affected employee. The DOL also may bring suit against employers to restrain interference violations of the law, including withholding payment of wages, salary, employment benefits, or other compensation, plus interest, that is due to eligible employees. The DOL may seek equitable relief, including employment, reinstatement, and promotion, in U.S. district courts.

NEW LAW EXPLAINED

Small employers exempted from civil lawsuits by employees.— Employers with fewer than 50 employees are exempted from civil FMLA damages in an FMLA lawsuit arising out of the public health emergency leave provisions of the Families First

NEW LAW EXPLAINED

Coronavirus Response Act (P.L. 116-127), thus shielding smaller employers from being liable for back pay or liquidated damages (Act Sec. 3104 of the Families First Coronavirus Response Act (P.L. 116-127), as amended by Act Sec. 3611(4) of the Coronavirus Aid, Relief, and Economic Security Act (P.L. 116-136)).

> **Comment:** Although these small employers are protected from employee-initiated lawsuits for any violations of the expanded emergency FMLA provisions of the Families First Act, these employers would remain subject to civil actions brought by the Labor Department, which could continue to bring enforcement actions for violations.

▶ **Effective date.** The Act takes effect April 1, 2020 (not later than 15 days after the date of enactment) (Act Sec. 3106 of the Families First Act).

Law source: Law at ¶1029, ¶1031, and ¶2129.

— Act Sec. 3104 of the Families First Coronavirus Response Act (P.L. 116-127), as amended by Act Sec. 3611(4) of the Coronavirus Aid, Relief, and Economic Security Act (P.L. 116-136).

— Act Sec. 3106, providing the effective date.

¶160 Special Rule for Health Care Providers and Emergency Responders

SUMMARY OF NEW LAW

An employer of a health care provider or emergency responder may choose to exempt these employees from the application of the public health emergency leave provisions.

BACKGROUND

The Family and Medical Leave Act (FMLA) defines the term "health care provider" as (1) a doctor of medicine or osteopathy who is authorized to practice medicine or surgery (as appropriate) by the state in which the doctor practices; or (2) any other person determined by the Secretary of Labor to be capable of providing health care services. However, the FMLA does not contain a definition of "first responder."

As the COVID-19 pandemic unfolds, health care facilities nationwide are experiencing a shortage of trained health care providers, as well as equipment and supplies.

NEW LAW EXPLAINED

Health care providers and emergency responders may be exempted from expanded FMLA provisions.—Under the Families First Coronavirus Response Act (P.L. 116-127), employers who employ health care providers or emergency responders may

NEW LAW EXPLAINED

choose to exempt those employees from the newly-enacted expanded emergency FMLA provisions (see ¶ 100) (Act Sec. 3105 of the Families First Coronavirus Response Act (P.L. 116-127)).

The Secretary of Labor is authorized by the Families First Act to exclude certain health care providers and emergency responders from the definition of "eligible employees" under the expanded emergency provisions (FMLA Sec. 110(a)(1)(A), as added by the Families First Act).

Health care providers. The FMLA statute itself defines the term "health care provider" as including (1) a doctor of medicine or osteopathy who is authorized to practice medicine or surgery (as appropriate) by the state in which the doctor practices; or (2) any other person determined by the Secretary to be capable of providing health care services (FMLA Sec. 101(6)).

However, the Department of Labor has clarified that, for purposes of the expanded emergency FMLA, a health care provider is anyone employed at any doctor's office, hospital, health care center, clinic, post-secondary educational institution offering health care instruction, medical school, local health department or agency, nursing facility, retirement facility, nursing home, home health care provider, any facility that performs laboratory or medical testing, pharmacy, or any similar institution, employer, or entity. This definition includes any permanent or temporary institution, facility, location, or site where medical services are provided that are similar to such institutions (*Families First Coronavirus Response Act: Questions and Answers*, issued by the Department of Labor; https://www.dol.gov/agencies/whd/pandemic/ffcra-questions).

According to the DOL, this definition of health care provider includes any individual employed by an entity that contracts with any of these institutions described above to provide services or to maintain the operation of the facility where that individual's services support the operation of the facility. This also includes anyone employed by any entity that provides medical services, produces medical products, or is otherwise involved in the making of COVID-19 related medical equipment, tests, drugs, vaccines, diagnostic vehicles, or treatments. This also includes any individual that the highest official of a state or territory, including the District of Columbia, determines is a health care provider necessary for that state's, territory's, or the District of Columbia's response to COVID-19.

First responders. The Department of Labor has clarified the definition of "emergency responders," for purposes of the expanded emergency FMLA, as including anyone necessary for the provision of transport, care, health care, comfort and nutrition of such patients, or others needed for the response to COVID-19. This includes, but is not limited to, military or national guard, law enforcement officers, correctional institution personnel, fire fighters, emergency medical services personnel, physicians, nurses, public health personnel, emergency medical technicians, paramedics, emergency management personnel, 911 operators, child welfare workers and service providers, public works personnel, and persons with skills or training in operating specialized equipment or other skills needed to provide aid in a declared emergency, as well as individuals who work for such facilities employing these individuals and whose work is necessary to

NEW LAW EXPLAINED

maintain the operation of the facility. This "first responders" definition also includes any individual whom the highest official of a state or territory, including the District of Columbia, determines is an emergency responder necessary for that state's, territory's, or the District of Columbia's response to COVID-19.

▶ **Effective date.** The Act takes effect April 1, 2020 (not later than 15 days after the date of enactment) (Act Sec. 3106 of the Families First Act).

Law source: Law at ¶1030 and ¶1031.

— Act Sec. 3105 of the Families First Coronavirus Response Act (P.L. 116-127).

— Act Sec. 3106, providing the effective date.

Chapter 2—Emergency Unemployment Insurance Stabilization and Access

2

¶200 Emergency Transfers for Unemployment Compensation Administration

SUMMARY OF NEW LAW

The Secretary of Labor is authorized to provide $1 billion in emergency administrative grants to the states for activities related to the processing and payment of unemployment benefits in fiscal year 2020 under certain conditions.

BACKGROUND

State and federal unemployment insurance (UI) payroll taxes collected from employers are maintained in the U.S. Treasury Department's Unemployment Trust Fund. The trust fund consists of 53 state accounts (here "state" includes the District of Columbia, Puerto Rico, and the Virgin Islands) and separate federal accounts for specific purposes. Funds flow into these accounts from state and federal payroll taxes, loans from other accounts, and loans and transfers from the federal general fund. Funds flow out of the accounts for benefit payments, administrative costs, and the provision of loans to other accounts.

Federal law authorizes appropriations to assist states in the administration of their unemployment compensation laws. The Secretary of Labor certifies to the Secretary of Treasury for payment to states such amounts as the Secretary of Labor determines to be necessary for the proper and efficient administration of unemployment compensation during the fiscal year for which the payment is made. The Secretary of Labor's determination must be based on the population of the state, an estimate of the number of persons covered by the state's unemployment compensation law and the cost of proper and efficient administration of such law, and such other factors as the Secretary of Labor finds relevant. The Secretary of Labor may not certify for payment a total amount which exceeds the amount appropriated for the fiscal year.

Title IX of the Social Security Act allows a certain portion of federal unemployment taxes to be used for administrative purposes or benefits by the states. Further, the Social Security Act describes the conditions under which excess funds may be transferred to state accounts in the Unemployment Trust Fund (Social Security Act Sec. 903).

NEW LAW EXPLAINED

Emergency transfers in fiscal year 2020.—The Families First Coronavirus Response Act provides $1 billion for emergency relief grants to the states for activities related to the administration of unemployment benefits in fiscal year 2020 under certain conditions. The funding will be distributed based on each state's proportionate share of regular UI administrative funding provided through annual appropriations. States are eligible for two equal and distinct allotments, each with specific application criteria

NEW LAW EXPLAINED

(Social Security Act Sec. 903(h), added by Act Sec. 4102(a) of the Families First Coronavirus Response Act (P.L. 116-127)).

> **Comment:** The Department of Labor (DOL) advises that funds provided through the emergency grants may only be used for the administration of unemployment compensation programs and not for the payment of unemployment compensation itself (*DOL Unemployment Insurance Program Letter No. 13-20,* March 22, 2020).

Allotment I: Immediate additional funding. Five hundred million dollars of the total grant is earmarked to provide immediate funding to all states for unemployment program staffing, technology, systems, and other administrative costs. The amounts must be transferred with respect to each state not later than 60 days after the March 18, 2020 date of enactment of the Families First Act upon a certification by the Secretary of Labor to the Secretary of the Treasury that the state has satisfied certain basic requirements for ensuring access to earned benefits for eligible workers (SSA Sec. 903(h)(1)(C)(i), as added by the Families First Act).

Under the Act, states must:

- Require employers to provide notification of potential UI eligibility to laid-off workers;
- Ensure that workers have, to the extent practicable, at least two ways (for example, online and phone) to apply for benefits; and
- Notify applicants when an application is received and is being processed and if the application cannot be processed, provide information to the applicant about how to ensure successful processing (SSA Sec. 903(h)(2), added by Act Sec. 4102(a) of the Families First Act, as amended by Act Sec. 3603 of the Coronavirus Aid, Relief, and Economic Security Act (P.L. 116-136)).

States to report on outcomes. States receiving emergency administration grant funding under Allotment I are required to report on the number of eligible individuals who received UI benefits and the state's efforts to ensure access within one year of the date of enactment of the legislation (SSA Sec. 903(h)(5), as added by the Families First Act).

Allotment II: Emergency grants tied to 10% increase in unemployment. Another $500 million is reserved for emergency grants to states that experience at least a 10 percent increase in unemployment over the same quarter in the previous calendar year. Those states are eligible to receive an *additional* grant, in the same amount as the initial grant, to assist with costs related to the unemployment spike (SSA Sec. 903(h)(1)(C)(ii), as added by the Families First Act).

In order to receive such an emergency grant, states must:

- Commit to maintain and strengthen access to the UI system, including through initial and continued claims; and
- Take steps to temporarily ease eligibility requirements that are limiting access to UI benefits during the COVID-19 outbreak, including work search requirements, required waiting periods, and non-charging employers directly impacted by COVID-19 due to an illness in the workplace or direction from a public health

NEW LAW EXPLAINED

official to isolate or quarantine workers (SSA Sec. 903(h)(3), as added by the Families First Act).

> **Comment:** For purposes of determining if and when a state's initial unemployment claims have increased by 10 percent over the same quarter in the previous calendar year, the DOL will aggregate initial claims reported on the ETA 5159 report which contains monthly information on claims activities and the number and amount of payments under state and federal unemployment programs. In addition, the DOL notes that states have the option of applying for each of the two allotments separately, which may be beneficial if a state has not met the 10 percent increase in initial claims activity to meet the requirement of the second allotment. States that meet the requirements for both allotments may submit a single application (*DOL Unemployment Insurance Program Letter No. 13-20*, March 22, 2020).

Emergency state flexibility. The Act provides flexibility regarding any actions taken that require changes to state law or policy to ease unemployment eligibility requirements on an emergency, temporary basis as needed to respond to the COVID-19 outbreak (Act Sec. 4102(b) of the Families First Act, as amended by Act Sec. 2106 of the CARES Act).

Provisions of state law listed in the Act as appropriate for temporary flexibility include:

- Work search;
- Waiting week;
- Good cause;
- Employer experience rating; or
- Personnel standards on a merit basis.

Staffing flexibility. The emergency flexibility for personnel standards on a merit basis shall only apply through December 31, 2020, and is limited to engaging of temporary staff, rehiring of retirees or former employees on a non-competitive basis, and other temporary actions needed to quickly process applications and claims (Act Sec. 4102(b) of the Families First Act, as amended by Act Sec. 2106 of the CARES Act).

> **Comment:** The DOL encourages states to adopt these permissible flexibilities. The DOL cautions, however, that any changes to state laws and policies to implement the flexibilities must be limited to the timeframe in which the COVID-19 pandemic is being addressed. Further, the DOL recommends states to consider tracking COVID-19-claims activity separately from regular UI program administration (*DOL Unemployment Insurance Program Letter No. 13-20*, March 22, 2020; *DOL Unemployment Insurance Program Letter No. 14-20*, April 2, 2020).

Guidance authorized. The Secretary of Labor may prescribe any regulations, operating instructions, or other guidance as necessary to carry out the emergency UI relief provisions (Act Sec. 4102(c) of the Families First Act).

State deadlines for submission. States must submit a completed SF-424, Application for Federal Assistance, to the DOL by May 8, 2020, for the first allotment and by

NEW LAW EXPLAINED

September 15, 2020, for the second allotment (*DOL Unemployment Insurance Program Letter No. 13-20,* March 22, 2020).

▶ **Effective date.** The Act does not specify an effective date for the amendments. Accordingly, the amendments are effective on the March 18, 2020, date of enactment of the Families First Coronavirus Response Act (Act Sec. 4102 of the Families First Coronavirus Response Act (P.L. 116-127)).

Law source: Law at ¶1034, ¶2027, ¶2120, and ¶7001.

— Act Sec. 4102(a) of the Families First Coronavirus Response Act (P.L. 116-127), adding Social Security Act Sec. 903(h).

— Act Sec. 4102(b) of the Families First Act.

— Act Sec. 4102(c) of the Families First Act.

— Act Sec. 2106 of the Coronavirus Aid, Relief, and Economic Security Act (P.L. 116-136), amending Act Sec. 4102(b) of the Families First Act.

— Act Sec. 3603 of the CARES Act, amending Social Security Act Sec. 903(h)(2)(B).

¶210 Temporary Assistance for States with Advances

SUMMARY OF NEW LAW

Any interest payment otherwise due from a state for Federal Unemployment Account Trust Fund advances shall be deemed to have been made by the state and no interest shall accrue from March 18, 2020, through December 31, 2020.

BACKGROUND

States with insufficient reserves in their unemployment funds to meet regular state benefit obligations may borrow funds from the Federal Unemployment Account in the Unemployment Trust Fund, pursuant to Title XII of the Social Security Act.

States are liable for interest on advances they receive from the federal unemployment account unless certain conditions are fulfilled.

The purpose of Title XII is to allow a state to continue paying benefits when, because of poor economic conditions, its fund falls below solvency levels or becomes totally depleted.

NEW LAW EXPLAINED

Interest payments temporarily waived.—The Social Security Act is amended to provide that interest payments for Title XII advances will be waived and no interest will accrue during the period of March 18, 2020, through December 31, 2020 (Social Security Act Sec. 1202(b)(10)(A), amended by Act Sec. 4103 of the Families First Coronavirus Response Act (P.L. 116-127)).

NEW LAW EXPLAINED

Accordingly, any interest payment otherwise due from a state during the period of March 18, 2020, and ending December 31, 2020, will be deemed to have been made by the state and no interest will accrue during the same period on an advance or advances made to a state.

▶ **Effective date.** The Act does not specify an effective date for the amendments. Accordingly, the amendment is effective on the March 18, 2020, date of enactment of the Families First Coronavirus Response Act (Act Sec. 4103 of the Families First Coronavirus Response Act (P.L. 116-127)).

Law source: Law at ¶1035 and ¶7003.

— Act Sec. 4103 of the Families First Coronavirus Response Act (P.L. 116-127), amending Social Security Act Sec. 1202(b)(10)(A).

¶220 Technical Assistance and Guidance for Short-Time Compensation Programs

SUMMARY OF NEW LAW

The Families First Coronavirus Response Act provision pertaining to technical assistance and guidance for short-time compensation programs is repealed.

BACKGROUND

Short-time compensation is a variation of the unemployment insurance program that is designed to help avert layoffs. States may pay *pro rata* benefits to individuals who are working less than full time because their employer has a plan approved by the state agency that provides for a reduction in work hours for employees rather than temporary layoffs. Also known as work sharing or the shared-work program, short-time compensation is overseen by the Department of Labor and administered by the states.

The Act directed the Secretary of Labor to assist the states in establishing, implementing, and improving employer awareness of short-time compensation programs to help avert layoffs. Specifically, the Secretary was charged with promoting awareness of the programs through technical assistance and guidance (Act Sec. 4104 of the Families First Coronavirus Response Act (P.L. 116-127).

NEW LAW EXPLAINED

Repeal of short-time compensation assistance.—Section 4104 of the Families First Act has been repealed (Sec. 2111(d) of the Coronavirus Aid, Relief, and Economic Security Act (P.L. 116-136)).

NEW LAW EXPLAINED

> **Comment:** The unemployment insurance provisions of the CARES Act include support for short-time compensation programs (see ¶¶260—275).

▶ **Effective date.** The CARES Act does not specify an effective date for the repeal. Accordingly, the repeal is treated as effective on the March 27, 2020, date of enactment (Act Sec. 2111(d) of the Coronavirus Aid, Relief, and Economic Security Act (P.L. 116-136)).

Law source: Law at ¶1036 and ¶2032.

— Act Sec. 4104 of the Families First Coronavirus Response Act (P.L. 116-127).

— Act Sec. 2111(d) of the Coronavirus Aid, Relief, and Economic Security Act (P.L. 116-136), repealing Act Sec. 4104 of the Families First Act.

¶230 Full Federal Funding of Extended Unemployment Compensation for a Limited Period

SUMMARY OF NEW LAW

The Families First Coronavirus Response Act amends, for a limited period, the Federal-State Extended Unemployment Compensation Act to provide 100% (formerly 50%) federal funding beginning March 18, 2020, and before December 31, 2020, for extended benefits in states that experience an increase of at least 10% or more of unemployment compensation claims over the same quarter in the previous calendar year and receive emergency grant funding.

BACKGROUND

All state unemployment insurance laws contain provisions limiting the period over which benefits can be paid to a single claimant. Although the manner in which this is done varies from state to state, the most common maximum duration of benefits, exclusive of extended-duration benefits, is 26 weeks.

As part of the Employment Security Amendments of 1970, Congress enacted the Federal-State Extended Benefits Program, which provides benefits to unemployed workers who have exhausted their entitlement to regular state benefits during periods of high unemployment. Generally, when the rate of insured unemployment is at specified levels, the extended benefits program is triggered and offers benefits at the same rate as the weekly benefit computed under state law for up to an additional 26 weeks of benefits after the regular benefit weeks of entitlement have expired.

The program is financed equally from federal and state funds and becomes operative on a state level.

NEW LAW EXPLAINED

NEW LAW EXPLAINED

Extended benefits financing.—The Federal-State Extended Unemployment Compensation Act of 1970 is amended, for a limited period, to provide 100% (as opposed to one-half of) federal funding beginning on March 18, 2020, and before December 31, 2020, for extended benefits in states that experience an increase of at least 10% or more of unemployment compensation claims over the same quarter in the previous calendar year. States also must receive emergency grant funding under Section 903(h)(1)(C) of the Social Security Act (Federal-State Extended Unemployment Compensation Act of 1970 Sec. 204(a)(1), as amended by Act Sec. 4105(a) of the Families First Coronavirus Response Act (P.L. 116-127)).

Waiting week penalty temporarily waived. The Act suspends the financial penalty within the extended benefits program for states that do not provide the usual one-week waiting period for benefits beginning on March 18, 2020 and ending on or before December 31, 2020. The provision allows for the temporary federal matching of the first week of extended benefits for states with no waiting week provision (Federal-State Extended Unemployment Compensation Act of 1970 Sec. 204(a)(2), as amended by Act Sec. 4105(b) of the Families First Act).

Regulations may be issued. The Act notes that the Secretary of Labor may prescribe any operating instructions or regulations necessary to implement the changes to the extended benefits program (Act Sec. 4105(d) of the Families First Act).

▶ **Effective date.** The Act does not specify an effective date for the amendments. Accordingly, the amendments are effective on the March 18, 2020, date of enactment of the Families First Coronavirus Response Act (Act Sec. 4105 of the Families First Act).

Law source: Law at ¶1037.

— Act Sec. 4105(a) of the Families First Coronavirus Response Act (P.L. 116-127), amending Federal-State Extended Unemployment Compensation Act of 1970 Sec. 204(a)(1).

— Act Sec. 4105(b) of the Families First Act, amending Federal-State Extended Unemployment Compensation Act of 1970 Sec. 204(a)(2).

— Act Sec. 4105(d) of the Families First Act.

¶235 Pandemic Unemployment Assistance

SUMMARY OF NEW LAW

The Secretary of Labor must provide unemployment benefit assistance to a covered individual while he or she is unemployed, partially unemployed, or unable to work due to COVID-19. The individual must not be entitled to any other unemployment compensation or waiting period credit. The total number of weeks that an individual may receive assistance may not exceed a maximum of 39 weeks.

BACKGROUND

The self-employed, independent contractors, and those with limited work history are not normally entitled to unemployment benefits. Act Sec. 2102 of the Coronavirus Aid, Relief, and Economic Security Act (CARES Act) (P.L. 116-136) provides assistance for such individuals who are unable to work due to the COVID-19 emergency.

NEW LAW EXPLAINED

Unemployment benefit assistance.—From January 27, 2020 through December 31, 2020, the Secretary of Labor must provide a covered individual with unemployment benefit assistance while he or she is unemployed, partially unemployed, or unable to work due to COVID-19 and not entitled to any other unemployment compensation or waiting period credit (Act Sec. 2102(a), (b), and (c) of the Coronavirus Aid, Relief, and Economic Security Act (P.L. 116-136)).

Covered individual defined. The term "covered individual" means an individual who is not eligible for regular compensation or extended benefits under state or federal law or pandemic emergency unemployment compensation under Act Sec. 2107 of the CARES Act (see ¶ 255) and who self-certifies that he or she is otherwise able to work and available for work but is unemployed, partially unemployed, or unable or unavailable to work because:

1. the individual has been diagnosed with COVID-19 or is experiencing symptoms of COVID-19 and seeking a medical diagnosis;
2. a member of the individual's household has been diagnosed with COVID-19;
3. the individual is providing care for a family member or a member of the individual's household who has been diagnosed with COVID-19;
4. a child or other person in the household for which the individual has primary caregiving responsibility is unable to attend school or another facility that is closed as a direct result of the COVID-19 public health emergency and the school or facility care is required for the individual to work;
5. the individual is unable to reach the place of employment because of a quarantine imposed as a direct result of the COVID-19 public health emergency;
6. the individual is unable to reach the place of employment because a health care provider has advised the individual to self-quarantine due to concerns related to COVID-19;
7. the individual was scheduled to start employment and does not have a job or is unable to reach the job as a direct result of the COVID-19 public health emergency;
8. the individual has become the breadwinner or major support for a household because the head of the household has died as a direct result of COVID-19;
9. the individual has to quit his or her job as a direct result of COVID-19;
10. the individual's place of employment is closed as a direct result of the COVID-19 public health emergency; or

NEW LAW EXPLAINED

11. the individual meets any additional criteria established by the Secretary for unemployment assistance (Act Sec. 2102(a)(3)(A)(ii)(I) of the CARES Act).

A "covered individual" also includes an individual who is self-employed, is seeking part-time employment, does not have sufficient work history, or otherwise would not qualify for regular unemployment or extended benefits under state or federal law or pandemic emergency unemployment compensation under Act Sec. 2107 of the CARES Act and meets the above requirements (Act Sec. 2102(a)(3)(A)(ii)(II) of the CARES Act).

Excluded from the definition of "covered individual" are individuals who: (1) have the ability to telework with pay; or (2) are receiving paid sick leave or other paid leave benefits, regardless of whether the individual meets a qualification described in Act Sec. 2102(a)(3)(A)(ii)(I)(aa) through (kk) (Act Sec. 2102(a)(3)(B) of the CARES Act).

Duration of assistance. A covered individual is limited to 39 weeks' assistance, including any week for which he or she received regular compensation or extended benefits under any federal or state law. However, if, after March 27, 2020, the duration of extended benefits is extended, this 39-week limitation will be extended by the number of weeks by which the extended benefits were extended (Act Sec. 2102(c)(2) of the CARES Act).

Amount of assistance. The amount of assistance for a week of unemployment, partial unemployment, or inability to work will be the weekly benefit amount authorized under the unemployment compensation law of the state where the covered individual was employed, except that the amount may not be less than the minimum weekly benefit amount described in 20 C.F.R. §625.6, and the amount of Federal Pandemic Unemployment Compensation under Act Sec. 2104 of the CARES Act. If the weekly benefit amount increases after March 27, 2020, the assistance authorized under Act Sec. 2102 will be increased by the same amount (Act Sec. 2102(d)(1) of the CARES Act).

If, however, a covered individual is self-employed, would not otherwise qualify for unemployment compensation under state law, or lives in Guam, the Northern Mariana Islands, American Samoa, Micronesia, the Marshall Islands, or the Trust Territory of the Pacific Islands (see 20 C.F.R. §625.6(c) and (d)), the amount of assistance will be calculated in accordance with 20 C.F.R. §625.6 and will be increased by the amount of Federal Pandemic Unemployment Compensation under Act Sec. 2104 of the CARES Act (Act Sec. 2102(d)(2) of the CARES Act).

Waiting period. Notwithstanding state law, no waiting period will apply for purposes of assistance authorized under Act Sec. 2102 (Act Sec. 2102(e) of the CARES Act).

Agreements with states. The Secretary of Labor must provide pandemic unemployment assistance through agreements with states (including the District of Columbia, the Commonwealth of Puerto Rico, the Virgin Islands, Guam, American Samoa, the Northern Mariana Islands, Micronesia, the Marshall Islands, and the Republic of Palau) that have an adequate system for administering such assistance through existing state agencies. The Secretary will pay each state an amount equal to 100% of the total amount of assistance provided by the state pursuant to the agreement and any additional administrative expenses incurred by the state due to the agreement, including expenses

NEW LAW EXPLAINED

necessary to process applications online or by telephone rather than in-person (Act Sec. 2102(a)(5), (f)(1) and (2) of the CARES Act).

Amounts payable to a state under such an agreement are payable, either in advance or by way of reimbursement, in amounts that the Secretary estimates the state will be entitled to receive for each calendar month. The payment will be reduced or increased by the amount by which the Secretary finds that his estimates for any prior calendar month were greater or less than the amounts that should have been paid to the state. These estimates may be made on the basis of statistical, sampling, or other method that the Secretary and state agree upon (Act Sec. 2102(f)(3) of the CARES Act).

Funding for pandemic unemployment assistance. The Secretary of Labor must use funds in the extended unemployment compensation account of the Unemployment Trust Fund, as transferred from the general fund of the Treasury, to make payments to states. In addition, the Secretary must use funds in the employment security administration account of the Unemployment Trust Fund, as transferred the general fund of the Treasury, to reimburse states for administrative expenses (Act Sec. 2102(g) of the CARES Act).

Disaster unemployment assistance. If Act Sec. 2102 of the CARES Act conflicts with the disaster unemployment assistance provisions of 20 C.F.R. part 625, part 625 applies as if: (1) the term "COVID-19 public health emergency" were substituted for the term "major disaster" each place it appears in part 625; and (2) the term "pandemic" were substituted for the term "disaster" each place it appears in part 625 (Act Sec. 2102(h) of the CARES Act).

Guidance. On April 5, 2020, the Department of Labor released Program Letter 16-20, which provides information on Act Sec. 2102 of the CARES Act. Letter 14-20 explains the unemployment-related provisions of the CARES Act.

▶ **Effective date.** The Act does not specify an effective date. Accordingly, the provision is effective on the March 27, 2020, date of enactment of the CARES Act.

Law source: Law at ¶2023.

— Act Sec. 2102 of the Coronavirus Aid, Relief, and Economic Security Act (P.L. 116-136).

¶240 Emergency Unemployment Relief for Governmental Entities and Nonprofit Organizations

SUMMARY OF NEW LAW

The Secretary of Labor must provide funds to states to reimburse government agencies, nonprofits, and Indian tribes for half the costs they incur through December 31, 2020, in providing unemployment benefits.

BACKGROUND

Prior to the 1970 Employment Security Amendments, a state could not allow nonprofit organizations to finance benefit payments by means of the reimbursement method, due to the requirement in the federal law that an employer's unemployment insurance taxes must be based on the employer's experience with unemployment (or other factors bearing a direct relation to unemployment risk) as reflected in an experience rate, after being subject to the state law for a certain period of time. However, the 1970 Amendments made it mandatory for a state to allow any of the nonprofit organizations it was required to cover the option of reimbursing the state directly for benefits paid to its employees. Also, the states were permitted to cover (and to allow reimbursement financing to) nonprofit organizations generally.

The 1976 Amendments made it mandatory that the states cover most services performed by state and local government employees, and specifically provided that governmental agencies may elect to reimburse the state fund in lieu of paying contributions.

Amendments to the Federal Unemployment Tax Act (FUTA) in 2000 required coverage of certain services performed by federally recognized Indian tribes. These amendments also required that the states permit these entities to elect to make payments in lieu of contributions, or reimbursements, to a state's unemployment fund. Prior to these amendments, states were not permitted to allow Indian tribes to finance their employees' benefits on a reimbursable basis because of the experience-rating provisions of the law.

NEW LAW EXPLAINED

Unemployment assistance.—From March 13, 2020 through December 31, 2020, the Secretary of Labor must transfer to states' unemployment trust funds half of the amounts of compensation (as defined in Internal Revenue Code Section 3306(h)) attributable under their state laws to service to which Internal Revenue Code Section 3309(a)(1) applies that the states paid for weeks of unemployment. States must use these funds exclusively to reimburse governmental entities, nonprofits, and Indian tribes for amounts paid into the state unemployment funds. These funds do not need to be repaid by the entities (Soc. Sec. Act Sec. 903(i), as added by Act Sec. 2103(b) of the Coronavirus Aid, Relief, and Economic Security Act (P.L. 116-136)).

Guidance to states. The Secretary of Labor may issue guidance to allow states to interpret their unemployment compensation laws in a way that would provide maximum flexibility to reimbursing employers as it relates to timely payment and assessment of penalties and interest pursuant to state law.

▶ **Effective date.** The Act does not specify an effective date. Accordingly, the provision is effective on the March 27, 2020, date of enactment of the CARES Act.

Law source: Law at ¶2024.

— Act Sec. 2103(b) of the Coronavirus Aid, Relief, and Economic Security Act (P.L. 116-136), adding Social Security Act Sec. 903(i).

¶245 Emergency Increase in Unemployment Compensation Benefits

SUMMARY OF NEW LAW

An additional $600 per week payment will be given to each recipient of unemployment insurance or Pandemic Unemployment Assistance in states that enter into an agreement with the Secretary of Labor for the additional amount through July 31, 2020.

BACKGROUND

The unemployment insurance program is run by the states, with some oversight from the Department of Labor. Most states provide up to 26 weeks of benefits to unemployed workers, replacing about half of their previous wages, on average. The Coronavirus Aid, Relief, and Economic Security Act (P.L. 116-136) enacted a number of provisions related to the emergency unemployment insurance relief for covered individuals.

NEW LAW EXPLAINED

Emergency increase in unemployment compensation benefits.—The Coronavirus Aid, Relief, and Economic Security Act (P.L. 116-136) provides individuals who are collecting unemployment insurance or Pandemic Unemployment Assistance with an additional $600 in federal benefits per week for weeks of unemployment ending on or before July 31, 2020, in states that enter into an agreement with the Secretary of Labor for the additional amount (Act Sec. 2104(a) and (b) of the Coronavirus Aid, Relief, and Economic Security Act (P.L. 116-136)). The CARES Act refers to this increase in compensation as the Federal Pandemic Unemployment Compensation (FPUC) (Act Sec. 2104(b)(1)(B) of the CARES Act).

The additional amount may be paid together with the regular amount of benefits owed or paid separately by the state, but it must be paid on the same weekly basis as the regular benefit amount (Act Sec. 2104(b)(2)(A) and (B) of the CARES Act). In addition, the states are prohibited from changing the computation method covering regular unemployment compensation in a way that results in the reduction of the average weekly benefit amounts or the number of weeks of benefits payable (*i.e.*, the maximum benefit entitlement) (Act Sec. 2104(c)(1) and (2) of the CARES Act). The maximum benefit entitlement must not be less than what would otherwise have been payable during such period under state law as of January 1, 2020 (Act Sec. 2104(c)(1) of the CARES Act).

The additional amount is available in the U.S., the District of Columbia, Puerto Rico, and the U.S. Virgin Islands, provided the state/territory signs an agreement with the Department of Labor (Act Sec. 2104(i) of the CARES Act). The provisions of the agreement apply to weeks of unemployment beginning after the state enters into the

NEW LAW EXPLAINED

agreement with the Secretary of Labor and ending on or before July 31, 2020 (Act Sec. 2104(e)(1) and (2) of the CARES Act). The state may, upon providing 30 days' written notice to the Secretary of Labor, terminate the agreement (Act Sec. 2104(a) of the CARES Act).

Full reimbursement of benefits payable under the FPUC will be made available to state agencies (Act Sec. 2104(d)(1)(A)(i) of the CARES Act). In addition, the federal government will reimburse any additional administrative expenses incurred by the state for the FPUC (as determined by the Secretary) (Act Sec. 2104(d)(1)(A)(ii) of the CARES Act). The Secretary of Labor will determine the amount payable to a state, either in advance or by reimbursement, through estimates based on statistical, sampling, or other methods agreed upon by the Labor Department and the state (Act Sec. 2104(d)(1)(B) of the CARES Act). The Secretary of Labor will notify the Treasury Department of the amount payable to each state. Note that the funds for the FPUC are appropriated from the general fund of the Treasury, without fiscal year limitation (Act Sec. 2104(d)(2) and (3) of the CARES Act).

Finally, if an individual knowingly makes a false statement or representation of material fact or causes another to do the same, or knowingly has failed, or caused another to fail, to disclose a material fact, and has received FPUC amounts to which he or she was not entitled, that individual will be ineligible for further funds from the FPUC and will be subject to prosecution (Act Sec. 2104(f)(1)(A) and (B) of the CARES Act). If an individual receives FPUC benefits to which he or she was not entitled, the payments must be repaid to the state agency with certain exceptions (Act Sec. 2104(f)(2)(A) and (B) of the CARES Act). Specifically, the state agency may waive the repayment if it determines that the payment of the FPUC was not the fault of the individual and the repayment would be contrary to equity and good conscience.

▶ **Effective date.** No specific effective date is provided by the Act. The amendments made by this section are, therefore, considered effective on March 27, 2020, the date of enactment of the CARES Act.

Law source: Law at ¶2025.

— Act Sec. 2104 of the Coronavirus Aid, Relief, and Economic Security Act (P.L. 116-136).

¶250 Temporary Full Federal Funding of First Week of Compensable Regular Unemployment for States with No Waiting Week

SUMMARY OF NEW LAW

Federal funding is provided to pay the cost of the first week of unemployment benefits through December 31, 2020, for states that choose to pay recipients as soon as they become unemployed instead of waiting one week before the individual is eligible to receive benefits.

BACKGROUND

The unemployment insurance program is run by the states, with some oversight from the Department of Labor. Most states provide up to 26 weeks of benefits to unemployed workers, replacing about half of their previous wages, on average. When an unemployment claim is approved, individuals typically begin receiving benefits after a one-week waiting period. The Coronavirus Aid, Relief, and Economic Security Act (P.L. 116-136) enacted a number of provisions related to the emergency unemployment insurance relief for covered individuals.

NEW LAW EXPLAINED

Temporary full federal funding of the first week of compensable regular unemployment.—Federal funding is provided to pay the cost of the first week of unemployment benefits through December 31, 2020, for states that choose to pay recipients as soon as they become unemployed, instead of waiting one week before the individual is eligible to receive benefits, and that enter into an agreement with the Secretary of Labor for the temporary full funding (Act Sec. 2105(a) and (b) of the Coronavirus Aid, Relief, and Economic Security Act (P.L. 116-136)).

The federal government will reimburse 100 percent of the benefits paid to a state under the agreement during the first week of an individual's unemployment if a state waives its waiting period (Act Sec. 2105(c)(1)(A) of the CARES Act). The federal government also will cover the costs of any additional administrative expenses incurred by the state, as determined by the Secretary (Act Sec. 2105(c)(1)(B) of the CARES Act).

This funding is available for weeks of unemployment beginning after the date on which the state enters into an agreement with the Department of Labor and ends on or before December 31, 2020 (Act Sec. 2105(e)(1) and (2) of the CARES Act). Any state that is a party to the agreement may, upon providing 30 days' written notice to the Secretary, terminate such agreement (Act Sec. 2105(a) of the CARES Act). The Secretary of Labor will determine the amount payable to a state, either in advance or by reimbursement, through estimates based on statistical, sampling, or other methods agreed upon by the Labor Department and the state (Act Sec. 2105(c)(2) of the CARES Act). The Secretary of Labor will notify the Treasury Department of the amount payable to each state. Note that the funds for this section are appropriated from the general fund of the Treasury, without fiscal year limitation (Act Sec. 2105(d) of the CARES Act).

Finally, if an individual knowingly makes a false statement or representation of material fact or causes another to do the same, or knowingly has failed, or caused another to fail, to disclose a material fact, and has received funds to which he or she was not entitled, that individual will be ineligible for further funds from the program and will be subject to prosecution. If an individual receives unemployment benefits to which he or she was not entitled, the payments must be repaid with certain exceptions (Act Sec. 2105(f) of the CARES Act, cross-referencing Act Sec. 2107(e) (see ¶ 255)). Specifically, the state agency may waive the repayment if it determines that the payment of the compensation was not the fault of the individual and the repayment would be contrary to equity and good conscience.

NEW LAW EXPLAINED

▶ **Effective date.** No specific effective date is provided by the Act. The amendments made by this section are, therefore, considered effective on March 27, 2020, the date of enactment of the CARES Act.

Law source: Law at ¶2026 and ¶2028.

— Act Sec. 2105 of the Coronavirus Aid, Relief, and Economic Security Act (P.L. 116-136).

— Act Sec. 2107(e) of the CARES Act.

¶255 Federal and State Agreements for Pandemic Emergency Unemployment Compensation

SUMMARY OF NEW LAW

Under the Pandemic Emergency Unemployment Compensation program, individuals whose state has entered into an agreement with Secretary of Labor and who have exhausted benefits they otherwise would be entitled to are eligible for an additional 13 weeks of unemployment benefits. The extended benefits are available through December 31, 2020.

BACKGROUND

The unemployment insurance program is run by the states, with some oversight from the Department of Labor. Most states provide up to 26 weeks of benefits to unemployed workers, replacing about half of their previous wages, on average. The Coronavirus Aid, Relief, and Economic Security Act (P.L. 116-136) enacted a number of provisions related to the emergency unemployment insurance relief for covered individuals.

NEW LAW EXPLAINED

Federal and state agreements for pandemic emergency unemployment compensation.—Under the Pandemic Emergency Unemployment Compensation (PEUC) program, individuals who have exhausted benefits they otherwise would be entitled to are eligible for an additional 13 weeks of unemployment benefits (Act Sec. 2107(a) and (b) of the Coronavirus Aid, Relief, and Economic Security Act (P.L. 116-136)). Therefore, eligible individuals may receive unemployment benefits up to a maximum of 39 weeks (previously, most states capped regular benefits at 26 weeks).

The extended benefits are available for weeks of unemployment beginning after the state enters into an agreement with the Department of Labor and ending on or before December 31, 2020 (Act Sec. 2107(g)(1) and (2) of the CARES Act). Any state that is a party to an agreement may, upon providing 30 days written notice to the Secretary of Labor, terminate the agreement (Act Sec. 2107(a) of the CARES Act).

NEW LAW EXPLAINED

This program covers individuals who:

A. have exhausted all rights to regular compensation under state or federal law for a benefit year beginning on or after July 1, 2019;

B. have no rights to regular compensation for a week under that state's or any other state's unemployment compensation law or to compensation under any other federal law;

C. are not receiving compensation with respect to a week under the unemployment compensation law of Canada; and

D. are able to work, available to work, and actively seeking work (Act Sec. 2107(a)(2)(A)-(D) of the CARES Act).

However, states should offer flexibility in meeting the "actively seeking work" requirement if individuals are unable to search for work because of COVID-19, including because of illness, quarantine, or movement restriction (Act Sec. 2107(a)(7)(B) of the CARES Act).

Individuals are considered eligible for the additional 13 weeks of unemployment benefits when they have exhausted their rights to unemployment benefits. Under the CARES Act, this means that an individual cannot receive benefits because they have received all the benefits available to them during the base period, or the base year has expired (Act Sec. 2107(a)(3) of the CARES Act).

The amount of PEUC payable to an individual each week is equal to the amount of his or her regular compensation (including dependents' allowances) (Act Sec. 2107(a)(4)(A) of the CARES Act). This amount also must include the extra $600 Federal Pandemic Unemployment Compensation for weeks prior to July 31, 2020 (Act Sec. 2107(a)(4)(A)(ii), cross referencing Act Sec. 2104(b)(1)(B) and (e)(2) of the CARES Act (see ¶ 245)). Payment of extended benefits that an individual is eligible to receive must be deferred until after the payment of Pandemic Emergency Unemployment benefits (Act Sec. 2107(a)(5) of the CARES Act).

After entering into an agreement, the states are prohibited from changing the computation method covering regular unemployment compensation in a way that results in the reduction of the average weekly benefit amounts or the number of weeks of benefits payable (*i.e.*, the maximum benefit entitlement) (Act Sec. 2107(a)(6)(A) and (B) of the CARES Act). The maximum benefit entitlement must not be less than what would otherwise have been payable during such period under state law as of January 1, 2020 (Act Sec. 2107(a)(6)(A) of the CARES Act).

The federal government will reimburse 100 percent of the benefits paid through the PEUC program (Act Sec. 2107(c)(1) of the CARES Act). Under the agreement with the state, the federal government will establish an account for each eligible individual who files for benefits under the PEUC (Act Sec. 2107(b)(1) of the CARES Act). The amount in the account will be equal to 13 times the individual's average weekly benefit amount, which also will include the extra $600 Federal Pandemic Unemployment Compensation for weeks prior to July 31, 2020 (Act Sec. 2107(b)(2), cross referencing Act Sec. 2104(b)(1)(B) and (e)(2) of the CARES Act (see ¶ 245)). The Secretary of Labor will

NEW LAW EXPLAINED

determine the amount payable to a state, either in advance or by reimbursement, through estimates based on statistical, sampling, or other methods agreed upon by the Labor Department and the state (Act Sec. 2107(c)(3) of the CARES Act). The Secretary of Labor will notify the Treasury Department of the amount payable to each state. Note that the funds for this section are appropriated from the general fund of the Treasury, without fiscal year limitation (Act Sec. 2107(d) of the CARES Act).

Finally, if an individual knowingly makes a false statement or representation of material fact or causes another to do the same, or knowingly has failed, or caused another to fail, to disclose a material fact, and has received PEUC benefits to which he or she was not entitled, that individual will be ineligible for further funds from the PEUC and will be subject to prosecution (Act Sec. 2107(e)(1) and (2) of the CARES Act). If an individual receives PEUC benefits to which he or she was not entitled, the funds must be repaid with certain exceptions (Act Sec. 2107(e)(2)(A) and (B) of the CARES Act). Specifically, the state agency may waive the repayment if it determines that the payment of the PEUC was not the fault of the individual and the repayment would be contrary to equity and good conscience.

▶ **Effective date.** No specific effective date is provided by the Act. The amendments made by this section are, therefore, considered effective on March 27, 2020, the date of enactment of the CARES Act.

Law source: Law at ¶2025 and ¶2028.

— Act Sec. 2107 of the Coronavirus Aid, Relief, and Economic Security Act (P.L. 116-136).

— Act Sec. 2104 of the CARES Act.

¶260 Temporary Financing of Short-Time Compensation Payments in States with Programs in Law

SUMMARY OF NEW LAW

Temporary federal financing is provided for states that currently have a short-time compensation program set forth in state law. The Coronavirus Aid, Relief, and Economic Security Act (P.L. 116-136)) provides financing for 100 percent of short-time compensation paid under such a program for weeks of unemployment beginning on or after the date of enactment (March 27, 2020) and ending on or before December 31, 2020.

BACKGROUND

Short-time compensation is a variation of the unemployment insurance program that is designed to help avert layoffs. States may pay *pro rata* benefits to individuals who are working less than full-time because their employer has a plan approved by the

BACKGROUND

state agency that provides for a reduction in work hours for employees instead of temporary layoffs.

Also known as work sharing or the shared-work program, short-time compensation is overseen by the Department of Labor and administered by the states.

The unemployment insurance provisions of Title II of the CARES Act also include support for these short-time compensation programs.

NEW LAW EXPLAINED

Temporary financing of current state programs.—Temporary federal financing is provided for states that currently have a short-time compensation program, as defined under Code Sec. 3306(v), set forth in state law (Act Sec. 2108(a)(1) of the Coronavirus Aid, Relief, and Economic Security Act (P.L. 116-136)). The Coronavirus Aid, Relief, and Economic Security Act provides financing for 100 percent of short-time compensation paid under such a program for weeks of unemployment beginning on or after the date of enactment (March 27, 2020), and ending on or before December 31, 2020 (Act Sec. 2108(b)(1) and (2) of the CARES Act).

Terms of payments. Payments that are made to a state under the temporary financing of current state programs are payable by way of reimbursement in such amounts as the Secretary of Labor estimates the state will be entitled to receive under the financing program for each calendar month. This amount may be reduced or increased, as needed, by any amount by which the Secretary of Labor finds that its estimates for any prior calendar month were greater or lesser than the amounts which should have been paid to the state. These estimates may be based on such statistical, sampling, or other method as may be agreed upon by the Secretary of Labor and the state agency of the state involved (Act Sec. 2108(a)(2) of the CARES Act).

Limitations on payments. The CARES Act sets forth the following limitations on payments:

1. No payments can be made to a state for short-time compensation paid to an individual by the state during a benefit year in excess of 26 times the amount of regular compensation (including dependents' allowances) payable under the state law for a week of total unemployment; and
2. No payments can be made to a state for short-time compensation paid to an individual if the individual is employed by the participating employer on a seasonal, temporary, or intermittent basis (Act Sec. 2108(a)(3)(A) and (B) of the CARES Act).

Applicability. Payments to states under the temporary financing of current state programs are available for weeks of unemployment beginning on or after the March 27, 2020 date of enactment of the CARES Act and ending on or before December 31, 2020 (Act Sec. 2108(b)(1) and (2) of the CARES Act).

New programs. If, after March 27, 2020, a state passes a law providing for the payment of short-time compensation under an approved program, then the state will be eligible

NEW LAW EXPLAINED

for this temporary financing (Act Sec. 2108(c) of the CARES Act). This provision is subject to the applicability end date above.

Funding and certifications. The CARES Act appropriates funding, as may be necessary, to carrying out the temporary financing of current state programs. The Secretary of Labor shall, from time to time, certify to the Secretary of the Treasury payment to each state the amounts payable to that state (Act Sec. 2108(d)(1) and (2) of the CARES Act).

Definitions. The CARES Act clarifies that it is the Secretary of Labor who is to implement the program under this provision. Further, the Act makes it clear that terms "state," "state agency," and "state law" have the meanings as those terms have in Act Sec. 205 of the Federal-State Extended Unemployment Compensation Act of 1970 (P.L. 91-373) (Act Sec. 2108(e)(1) and (2) of the CARES Act).

Further, the Act makes a technical correction to Code Sec. 3306(v)(6), defining short-time compensation program, to make it clear that the definition refers to the Workforce Innovation and Opportunity Act (P.L. 113-128) (Act Sec. 2108(f) of the CARES Act).

▶ **Effective date.** The CARES Act does not specify an effective date for the amendments. Accordingly, the amendments are treated as effective on the March 27, 2020, the date of enactment of the CARES Act.

Law source: Law at ¶2029 and ¶5009.

— Act Sec. 2108 of the Coronavirus Aid, Relief, and Economic Security Act (P.L. 116-136).

— Act Sec. 2108(f) of the CARES Act, amending Code Sec. 3306(v)(6).

¶265 Temporary Financing of Short-Time Compensation Agreements

SUMMARY OF NEW LAW

Temporary federal financing is provided for federal-state short-time compensation agreements, ending on or before December 31, 2020. Under those agreements, the state agency must make payments of short-time compensation under a plan approved by the state, and employers must pay the state an amount equal to 50 percent of the amount of the short-time compensation paid under the plan (states would be eligible for temporary federal financing of 50 percent of the amount of short-time compensation paid).

BACKGROUND

Short-time compensation is a variation of the unemployment insurance program that is designed to avert layoffs. States may pay *pro rata* benefits to individuals who are working less than full-time because their employer has a plan approved by the state

BACKGROUND

agency that provides for a reduction in work hours for employees instead of temporary layoffs.

Also known as work sharing or the shared-work program, short-time compensation is overseen by the U.S. Department of Labor and is administered by the states.

NEW LAW EXPLAINED

Federal-state agreements.—Temporary federal financing is provided for any state that enters into, and participates in, a federal-state short-time compensation agreement, provided that such state's law does not currently provide for payment of short-time compensation under a short-time compensation program (as defined in Section 3306(v) of the Internal Revenue Code of 1986). Any state that is a party to such an agreement can terminate the agreement upon providing 30 days' written notice to the Secretary of Labor. Under the agreements, the state agency must make payments of short-time compensation under a plan approved by the state. The plan must provide that payments are made in accordance with the requirements under Section 3306(v) of the Internal Revenue Code of 1986 (Act Sec. 2109(a) of the Coronavirus Aid, Relief, and Economic Security Act (P.L. 116-136)).

Definitions. The term "Secretary" means the Secretary of Labor, while the terms "state," "state agency," and "state law" have the meanings given those terms in section 205 of the Federal-State Extended Unemployment Compensation Act of 1970 (26 U.S.C. 3304 note) (Act Sec. 2109(f) of the CARES Act).

Limitations on plans. A short-time compensation plan approved by a state must not permit the payment of short-time compensation to an individual by the state during a benefit year in excess of 26 times the amount of regular compensation (including dependents' allowances) under the state law payable to such individual for a week of total unemployment, nor can the plan provide payments to an individual if such individual is employed by the participating employer on a seasonal, temporary, or intermittent basis (Act Sec. 2109(b)(2) of the CARES Act).

Employers' payment of costs. Any short-time compensation plan entered into by an employer must provide that the employer will pay the state an amount equal to one-half of the amount of the short-time compensation paid under the plan. The amount must be deposited in the state's unemployment fund and must not be used for purposes of calculating an employer's contribution rate under Section 3303(a)(1) of the Internal Revenue Code of 1986 (Act Sec. 2109(b)(3) of the CARES Act).

Payments to states. States would be eligible for temporary federal financing of one-half of the amount of short-time compensation paid as well as any additional administrative expenses incurred by the state by reason of the federal-state agreement (as determined by the Secretary of Labor). Payments made to a state must be payable by way of reimbursement in such amounts as the Secretary estimates the state will be entitled to receive under this section for each calendar month, reduced or increased by any amount by which the Secretary finds that the Secretary's estimates for any prior calendar month were greater or less than the amounts which should have been paid to

NEW LAW EXPLAINED

the state. Such estimates can be made on the basis of such statistical, sampling, or other method as may be agreed upon by the Secretary and the state agency of the state involved (Act Sec. 2109(c) of the CARES Act).

Funding. The sums necessary for purposes of carrying out the temporary financing of short-time compensation agreements are appropriated out of moneys in the Treasury (Act Sec. 2109(c)(3) of the CARES Act).

Certifications. The Secretary of Labor must, from time to time, certify to the Secretary of the Treasury for payment to each state the sums payable to such state under the short-time compensation program (Act Sec. 2109(c)(4) of the CARES Act).

Applicability. Federal-state agreements apply to weeks of unemployment beginning on or after the date on which such agreement is entered into and ending on or before December 31, 2020 (Act Sec. 2109(d) of the CARES Act).

Special rule. If a state has entered into such a federal-state agreement and subsequently enacts a state law providing for the payment of short-time compensation under a short-time compensation program, then the state will not be eligible for payments under the federal-state agreement for weeks of unemployment beginning after the effective date of such state law (Act Sec. 2109(e)(1) of the CARES Act).

Note: A state that enacts its own short-term compensation program would then be eligible for payments under Section 2108 of the CARES Act (see ¶ 260) after the effective date of the state law (Act Sec. 2109(e)(2) of the CARES Act).

▶ **Effective date.** The Act does not specify an effective date. Accordingly, this provision is considered effective on March 27, 2020, the date of enactment of the CARES Act.

Law source: Law at ¶2030.

— Act Sec. 2109 of the Coronavirus Aid, Relief, and Economic Security Act (P.L. 116-136).

¶270 Grants for Short-Time Compensation Programs

SUMMARY OF NEW LAW

A maximum of $100 million is earmarked for the Secretary of Labor to award grants to states for the implementation and administration of approved short-time compensation programs and for the promotion and enrollment of employers in such programs.

BACKGROUND

Short-time compensation is a variation of the unemployment insurance program that is designed to avert layoffs. States may pay *pro rata* benefits to individuals who are working less than full-time because their employer has a plan approved by the state

BACKGROUND

agency that provides for a reduction in work hours for employees instead of temporary layoffs.

The Secretary of Labor may award grants for short-time compensation programs.

NEW LAW EXPLAINED

Grants.—The Secretary of Labor is directed to award grants to states for: (1) the implementation or improved administration of short-time compensation programs (as defined in Section 3306(v) of the Internal Revenue Code of 1986); and (2) the promotion and enrollment of employers in such programs (Act Sec. 2110(a) of the Coronavirus Aid, Relief, and Economic Security Act (P.L. 116-136)).

Eligibility. The Secretary is directed to determine eligibility criteria for such grants. States administering a short-time compensation program that does not meet the definition of a short-time compensation program under Section 3306(v) of the Internal Revenue Code of 1986, as well as states with a federal-state short-time compensation agreement under Act Sec. 2109 of the CARES Act (see ¶ 265), will not be eligible to receive a grant under this section until such time as the state law of the state provides for payments under a short-time compensation program that meets such definition and such law (Act Sec. 2110(a)(3) of the CARES Act).

Definitions. The term "Secretary" means the Secretary of Labor, while the terms "state," "state agency," and "state law" have the meanings given those terms in section 205 of the Federal-State Extended Unemployment Compensation Act of 1970 (26 U.S.C. 3304 note) (Act Sec. 2110(i) of the CARES Act).

Amount of grants. The maximum amount available for making grants to a state must be equal to the amount obtained by multiplying $100,000,000 (less the amount used by the Secretary for administration) by the same ratio as would apply under Section 903(a)(2)(B) of the Social Security Act (42 U.S.C. 1103) for purposes of determining such state's share of any excess amount (as described in subsection (a)(1) of such section) that would have been subject to transfer to state accounts, as of October 1, 2019, under the provisions of subsection (a) of such section. Of the maximum incentive payment determined with respect to a state, one-third must be available for a grant for the implementation or improved administration of a short-time compensation program, and two-thirds must be available for a grant for the promotion and enrollment of employers in a short-time compensation program (Act Sec. 2110(b) of the CARES Act).

Grant application and response. States seeking a grant must submit an application to the Secretary, complete with such information as the Secretary may require. The Secretary will not award a grant for an application submitted after December 31, 2023. Within 30 days after receiving a complete application, the Secretary will notify the state agency of the Secretary's findings regarding the requirements for a grant (Act Sec. 2110(c) of the CARES Act).

Certification and dispersal. If the Secretary finds that the state-law provisions meet the requirements for a grant, the Secretary must make a certification to that effect to the Secretary of the Treasury, together with a certification as to the amount of the grant

NEW LAW EXPLAINED

payment to be transferred to the state account in the Unemployment Trust Fund (as established in Section 904(a) of the Social Security Act (42 U.S.C. 1104(a))) pursuant to that finding. The Secretary of the Treasury must make the appropriate transfer to the state account within seven days after receiving the certification. No certification will be made with respect to any state whose: (1) state law is not otherwise eligible for certification under Section 303 of the Social Security Act (42 U.S.C. 503) or approvable under Section 3304 of the Internal Revenue Code of 1986; or (2) short-time compensation program is subject to discontinuation or is not scheduled to take effect within 12 months of the certification (Act Sec. 2110(c) of the CARES Act).

Use of funds. A grant must be used for the implementation and overall administration of short-time compensation programs, as well as for the promotion and enrollment efforts associated with those programs, such as through: (1) the creation or support of rapid response teams to advise employers about alternatives to layoffs; (2) the provision of education or assistance to employers to enable them to assess the feasibility of participating in short-time compensation programs; and (3) the development or enhancement of systems to automate the approval of plans and the filing of new and ongoing short-time compensation claims (Act Sec. 2110(d) of the CARES Act).

Administration. The Secretary is authorized to use 0.25 percent of the funds appropriated in this section to provide for outreach and to share best practices with respect to short-time compensation programs (Act Sec. 2110(e) of the CARES Act).

Recoupment. The Secretary is directed to establish a process to recoup the amount of any grant if the Secretary determines that, during the five-year period beginning on the first date that any such grant is awarded to the state, the state either terminated its short-time compensation program or failed to meet appropriate requirements with respect to that program (as established by the Secretary) (Act Sec. 2110(f) of the CARES Act).

Funding. One hundred million dollars is appropriated from the Treasury to the Secretary to carry out this section. This amount will remain available without fiscal year limitation (Act Sec. 2110(g)) of the CARES Act).

Reporting. The Secretary is permitted to establish reporting requirements for states receiving a grant in order to provide oversight of grant funds (Act Sec. 2110(h) of the CARES Act).

▶ **Effective date.** The Act does not specify an effective date. Accordingly, this provision is considered effective on March 27, 2020, the date of enactment of the CARES Act.

Law source: Law at ¶2031.

— Act Sec. 2110 of the Coronavirus Aid, Relief, and Economic Security Act (P.L. 116-136).

¶275 Assistance and Guidance in Implementing Short-Time Compensation Programs

SUMMARY OF NEW LAW

The Secretary of Labor is directed to develop model legislative language and provide technical assistance and guidance to states in establishing short-time compensation programs.

BACKGROUND

Short-time compensation is a variation of the unemployment insurance program that is designed to avert layoffs. States may pay *pro rata* benefits to individuals who are working less than full-time because their employer has a plan approved by the state agency that provides for a reduction in work hours for employees instead of temporary layoffs.

Section 4104 of the Emergency Unemployment Stabilization and Access Act of 2020, which is contained in Division D of the Families First Coronavirus Response Act (P.L. 116-127), directed the Secretary of Labor to assist states in establishing, implementing, and improving employer awareness of short-time compensation programs, such as by providing technical assistance and guidance.

NEW LAW EXPLAINED

Assistance and guidance in implementing short-time compensation programs.— To assist states in establishing, qualifying, and implementing short-time compensation programs (as defined in Section 3306(v) of the Internal Revenue Code of 1986), the Secretary of Labor is directed to: (1) develop and periodically revise model legislative language for use by states in developing and enacting such programs; (2) provide technical assistance and guidance in developing, enacting, and implementing such programs; and (3) establish reporting requirements for states, including reporting on the number of estimated averted layoffs and the number of participating employers and workers. The model language and guidance must allow sufficient flexibility by states and participating employers while ensuring accountability and program integrity (Act Sec. 2111(a) and (b) of the Coronavirus Aid, Relief, and Economic Security Act (P.L. 116-136)).

Consultation. The Secretary of Labor is directed to consult with employers, labor organizations, state workforce agencies, and other program experts in developing the model legislative language and guidance. Existing model legislative language that has been developed through such a consultative process is deemed to meet the consultation requirement of this provision (">Act Sec. 2111(c) of the CARES Act).

Repeal. Section 4104 of the Emergency Unemployment Stabilization and Access Act of 2020 (contained in division D of the Families First Coronavirus Response Act (P.L.

NEW LAW EXPLAINED

116-127)) is repealed (Act Sec. 4104 of the Families First Act, repealed by Act Sec. 2111(d) of the CARES Act).

▶ **Effective date.** The Act does not specify an effective date. Accordingly, this provision is considered effective on March 27, 2020, the date of enactment of the CARES Act.

Law source: Law at ¶1036 and ¶2032.

— Act Sec. 2111 of the Coronavirus Aid, Relief, and Economic Security Act (P.L. 116-136).

— Act Sec. 4104 of the Families First Coronavirus Response Act (P.L. 116-127), repealed by Act Sec. 2111 of the CARES Act.

¶280 Waiver of Waiting Period Under the Railroad Unemployment Insurance Act

SUMMARY OF NEW LAW

The seven-day waiting period for unemployment and sickness benefits under the Railroad Unemployment Insurance Act is temporarily eliminated.

BACKGROUND

The Railroad Unemployment Insurance Act (RUIA) provides qualified railroad employees with the payment of unemployment insurance (UI) benefits to restore part of their lost wages during periods of unemployment. Also, the RUIA provides for the payment of sickness insurance (SI) benefits for days of sickness. Benefits are based on biweekly claims filed with the Railroad Retirement Board, the federal agency responsible for administering the RUIA.

The unemployment insurance provisions of the Coronavirus Aid, Relief, and Economic Security Act (P.L. 116-136) include amendments to the RUIA.

NEW LAW EXPLAINED

Waiting period temporarily eliminated.—The Coronavirus Aid, Relief, and Economic Security Act (P.L. 116-136) temporarily waives the seven-day waiting period for unemployment and sickness benefits under the Railroad Unemployment Insurance Act (RUIA). With respect to any registration period beginning on or after the date of enactment, March 27, 2020, and ending on or before December 31, 2020, the waiting period shall not apply (Act Sec. 2112(a) of the Coronavirus Aid, Relief, and Economic Security Act (P.L. 116-136)).

> **Comment:** The Railroad Retirement Board (RRB) cautions that the temporary waiver of the waiting period is the only RUIA provision of the CARES Act that applies to both UI and SI benefits (*Unemployment and Sickness Benefit Flexibilities*

NEW LAW EXPLAINED

Under the Railroad Unemployment Insurance Act (RUIA) during the COVID-19 Virus Outbreak FAQs, issued by the RRB, April 2, 2020).

Operating instructions. The RRB may prescribe any operating instructions or regulations necessary to carry out the temporary waiver of the waiting period (Act Sec. 2112(b) of the CARES Act).

Funding. The CARES Act appropriates $50 million to cover the costs associated with the temporary elimination of the waiting period. Once the funds appropriated are exhausted, the waiting-week waiver shall no longer apply (Act Sec. 2112(c) of the CARES Act).

Registration period. The CARES Act provides that for the purposes of the temporary waiver of the waiting period, the term "registration period" has the meaning given in Sec. 1 of the RUIA. Under the RUIA, a "registration period" is normally a period of 14 days, beginning with the first day on which the employee claims benefits by properly registering (Act Sec. 2112(d) of the CARES Act).

▶ **Effective date.** The Act does not specify an effective date. Accordingly, the provisions are treated as effective on the March 27, 2020, date of enactment of the CARES Act.

Law source: Law at ¶2033.

— Act Sec. 2112(a) of the Coronavirus Aid, Relief, and Economic Security Act (P.L. 116-136).

— Act Sec. 2112(b) of the CARES Act.

— Act Sec. 2112(c) of the CARES Act.

— Act Sec. 2112(d) of the CARES Act.

¶285 Enhanced Benefits Under the Railroad Unemployment Insurance Act

SUMMARY OF NEW LAW

An additional recovery benefit of $1,200 per two-week registration period is provided for each recipient of railroad unemployment benefits beginning on or after April 1, 2020, through July 31, 2020.

BACKGROUND

The Railroad Unemployment Insurance Act (RUIA) provides qualified railroad employees with unemployment insurance benefits to restore part of their lost wages during periods of unemployment. Benefits are based on biweekly claims filed with the Railroad Retirement Board, the federal agency responsible for administering the RUIA.

BACKGROUND

The funds to pay unemployment insurance benefits are provided by payroll taxes on railroad employers only. Employees do not pay railroad unemployment insurance taxes.

The unemployment insurance provisions of the Coronavirus Aid, Relief, and Economic Security Act (P.L. 116-136) include amendments to the RUIA.

NEW LAW EXPLAINED

Enhanced recovery benefits.—Additional recovery benefits of $1,200 per two-week registration period are provided for each recipient of railroad unemployment insurance benefits. This benefit is in addition to the current biweekly unemployment benefit maximum received by most claimants. The enhanced unemployment benefits apply to registration periods beginning on or after April 1, 2020, through July 31, 2020 (Railroad Unemployment Insurance Act Sec. 2(a), amended by Act Sec. 2113 of the Coronavirus Aid, Relief, and Economic Security Act (P.L. 116-136)).

> **Comment:** Under the RUIA, a "registration period" is normally a period of 14 days, beginning with the first day on which the employee claims benefits by properly registering (Railroad Unemployment Insurance Act Sec. 1(h)).

> **Comment:** The Railroad Retirement Board advises that a railroad employee is eligible for the CARES Act recovery payment for registration periods for which the employee (1) is receiving unemployment insurance benefits or (2) would be receiving unemployment insurance benefits if he or she had not already exhausted unemployment insurance benefits for benefit year 2019. The 2019 benefit year began on July 1, 2019, and ends on June 30, 2020 (*Unemployment and Sickness Benefit Flexibilities Under the Railroad Unemployment Insurance Act (RUIA) during the COVID-19 Virus Outbreak FAQs*, issued by the Railroad Retirement Board, April 2, 2020).

Funding. The CARES Act appropriates $425 million to pay for the additional recovery benefits. Once the funds appropriated are exhausted, the enhanced benefits shall no longer be payable (Act Sec. 2113 of the CARES Act).

▶ **Effective date.** The Act does not specify an effective date. Accordingly, the provisions are treated as effective on the March 27, 2020, date of enactment of the CARES Act.

Law source: Law at ¶2034.

— Act Sec. 2113 of the Coronavirus Aid, Relief, and Economic Security Act (P.L. 116-136), amending Railroad Unemployment Insurance Act Sec. 2(a).

¶290 Extended Benefits Under the Railroad Unemployment Insurance Act

SUMMARY OF NEW LAW

Railroad workers who received regular unemployment insurance benefits during the period from July 1, 2019, to June 30, 2020, may be eligible to receive extended benefits.

BACKGROUND

The Railroad Unemployment Insurance Act (RUIA) provides qualified railroad employees with unemployment insurance benefits to restore part of their lost wages during periods of unemployment. Benefits are based on biweekly claims filed with the Railroad Retirement Board, the federal agency responsible for administering the RUIA.

The funds to pay unemployment insurance benefits are provided by payroll taxes on railroad employers only. Employees do not pay railroad unemployment insurance taxes.

The unemployment insurance provisions of the Coronavirus Aid, Relief, and Economic Security Act (P.L. 116-136) include amendments to the RUIA.

NEW LAW EXPLAINED

Extended benefits.—Railroad workers who received regular unemployment insurance benefits during the period from July 1, 2019, to June 30, 2020, may be eligible for extended benefits. No extended benefit period will begin after December 31, 2020 (Railroad Unemployment Insurance Act Sec. 2(c)(2)(D)(iii), amended by Act Sec. 2114(a) of the Coronavirus Aid, Relief, and Economic Security Act (P.L. 116-136)).

Pursuant to the CARES Act:

- Workers with 10 years or more of service, who were previously eligible for up to 65 days of extended benefits, will be eligible for up to a total of 130 days of extended benefits within 13 consecutive two-week registration periods.
- Workers with less than 10 years of service will be eligible for up to 65 days of extended benefits within seven consecutive two-week registration periods.

Comment: Under the RUIA, a "registration period" is normally a period of 14 days, beginning with the first day on which the employee claims benefits by properly registering (Railroad Unemployment Insurance Act Sec. 1(h)).

▶ **Effective date.** The Act does not specify an effective date. Accordingly, the provisions are treated as effective on the March 27, 2020, date of enactment of the CARES Act.

NEW LAW EXPLAINED

Law source: Law at ¶2035.

— Act Sec. 2114(a) of the Coronavirus Aid, Relief, and Economic Security Act (P.L. 116-136), amending Railroad Unemployment Insurance Act Sec. 2(c)(2)(D)(iii).

— Act Sec. 2114(b) of the CARES Act, providing clarification on authority to use funds.

¶295 Funding for the DOL Office of Inspector General for Oversight of Unemployment Provisions

SUMMARY OF NEW LAW

Funds are appropriated to the Office of the Inspector General of the Department of Labor to carry out audits, investigations, and other authorized oversight activities of the CARES Act's unemployment insurance provisions.

BACKGROUND

The Office of Inspector General (OIG) at the U.S. Department of Labor (DOL) conducts audits to review the effectiveness, efficiency, economy, and integrity of all DOL programs and operations, including those performed by its contractors and grantees. This work is conducted in order to determine whether: the programs and operations are in compliance with the applicable laws and regulations; DOL resources are efficiently and economically being utilized; and DOL programs achieve their intended results.

NEW LAW EXPLAINED

Oversight activities.—An appropriation of $25,000,000 has been made from the Treasury to the Office of the Inspector General of the Department of Labor to carry out audits, investigations, and other oversight activities authorized under the Inspector General Act of 1978 that are related to the provisions of, and amendments made by, the Coronavirus Aid, Relief, and Economic Security Act (P.L. 116-136). The funds will remain available without fiscal year limitation (Act Sec. 2115 of the Coronavirus Aid, Relief, and Economic Security Act (P.L. 116-136)).

► **Effective date.** The Act does not specify an effective date for the amendments. Accordingly, the amendments are treated as effective on the March 27, 2020, the date of enactment of the CARES Act.

Law source: Law at ¶2036.

— Act Sec. 2115 of the Coronavirus Aid, Relief, and Economic Security Act (P.L. 116-136).

¶297 Implementation

SUMMARY OF NEW LAW

The Secretary of Labor may issue any operating instructions or other guidance necessary to carry out the Act's unemployment insurance provisions.

BACKGROUND

The Coronavirus Aid, Relief, and Economic Security Act or CARES Act (P.L. 116-136) enacted a number of provisions related to emergency unemployment insurance relief for covered individuals. Pursuant to the legislation, certain implementation requirements are set forth.

Responsibilities assigned to the Secretary of Labor that relate to employment services, job training, and unemployment insurance are fulfilled via the Employment and Training Administration through a variety of programs.

NEW LAW EXPLAINED

Operating instructions.—The Secretary of Labor may issue any operating instructions or other guidance necessary to carry out the provisions of, or the amendments made by the Relief for Workers Affected by Coronavirus Act of the Coronavirus Aid, Relief, and Economic Security Act. In addition, the Paperwork Reduction Act does not apply (Act Sec. 2116(a) of the CARES Act (P.L. 116-136)).

▶ **Effective date.** The Act does not specify an effective date for the amendments. Accordingly, the amendments are effective on the March 27, 2020, date of enactment of the CARES Act.

Law source: Law at ¶2037.

— Act Sec. 2116(a) of the Coronavirus Aid, Relief, and Economic Security Act (P.L. 116-136).

— Act Sec. 2116(b) of the CARES Act (P.L. 116-136).

Chapter 3—Emergency Paid Sick Leave

3

¶300 Paid Sick Time Requirement

SUMMARY OF NEW LAW

Private employers with fewer than 500 employees (as well as public employers and other non-private entities with at least one employee) must temporarily provide their employees with paid sick time for designated reasons related to COVID-19. This requirement is scheduled to expire on December 31, 2020.

BACKGROUND

Paid sick leave provides employees with a source of income during the period of time they are unable to work due to illness. For the most part, employers voluntarily provide paid sick time to their employees as part of their employee benefits packages. According to the U.S. Bureau of Labor Statistics, 76 percent of workers in private industry and state/local government have access to paid sick leave. This includes 86 percent of full-time employees and 43 percent of part-time employees. Only 66 percent of employees working for small establishments (with fewer than 100 workers) have access to such benefits. For workers covered by plans with a fixed amount of sick days, the median number of days provided is seven per year (*National Compensation Survey: Employee Benefits in the United States*, March 2019).

States have led the way in enacting paid sick leave mandates—over a quarter of the states have such laws with Connecticut, California and Massachusetts among the earliest adopters. Measures requiring paid sick leave also have passed at a more local

BACKGROUND

level, including in the District of Columbia. Some laws allow employees to use paid sick leave to care for ill family members as well as themselves. In response to the COVID-19 crisis, a number of states and localities have enacted emergency legislation to mandate paid sick leave for employees affected by the virus.

On a federal level, Executive Order 13706, signed by the president on September 7, 2015, requires federal contractors and subcontractors to provide full- and part-time employees performing work under federal contracts with up to seven days of paid sick leave annually, including paid leave allowing for family care. The order has a limited reach, however. Up until now, there has been no federal law requiring employers to provide workers with paid sick leave due to a national public health emergency.

On March 18, 2020, President Trump signed the Families First Coronavirus Response Act (P.L. 116-127), which provides relief for both employers and employees in connection with the COVID-19 crisis. The Act's Division E is called the Emergency Paid Sick Leave Act. The Coronavirus Aid, Relief, and Economic Security Act (P.L. 116-136), enacted on March 27, 2020, added dollar limitations to the paid sick time provision; the limitations were previously set forth only in the law's definitions.

NEW LAW EXPLAINED

Paid sick time required.—The Emergency Paid Sick Leave Act requires private employers with fewer than 500 employees to provide each employee with paid sick time of 80 hours for full-time employees (or the average number of hours worked over a two-week period for part-time employees) when the employee is unable to work or telework due to a need for leave because the employee (Act Sec. 5102 of the Families First Coronavirus Response Act (P.L. 116-127), as amended by Act Sec. 3602 of the Coronavirus Aid, Relief, and Economic Security Act (P.L. 116-136); Act Sec. 5110(2) of the Families First Act, as amended by Act Sec. 3611(6) of the CARES Act):

1. is subject to a federal, state, or local quarantine or isolation order related to COVID-19;
2. has been advised by a health care provider to self-quarantine due to concerns related to COVID-19;
3. is experiencing symptoms of COVID-19 and seeking a medical diagnosis;
4. is caring for an individual who is subject to a federal, state, or local quarantine or isolation order related to COVID-19, or has been advised by a health care provider to self-quarantine due to COVID-19 concerns;
5. is caring for the employee's son or daughter when the school or place of care has been closed, or the child care provider is unavailable, due to COVID-19 precautions; or
6. is experiencing any other substantially similar condition specified by the Secretary of Health and Human Services in consultation with the Secretary of the Treasury and the Secretary of Labor.

NEW LAW EXPLAINED

The sick time requirements also apply to public agencies or other non-private entities with one or more employees, persons acting directly or indirectly in the interest of an employer in relation to an employee, and successors in interest of an employer (Act Sec. 5110(2) of the Families First Act, as amended by Act Sec. 3611(6) of the CARES Act). See ¶ 310 for more about the definition of "employer."

Expert Guidance: According to the law firm of Ogletree Deakins, an employer with 500 or more employees can offer emergency paid sick leave, and often must do so given state and local requirements. However, employers with 500 or more employees are not *required* to provide such leave under the Act and are not eligible for tax credits provided by the Act (Michael M. Shetterly, Matthew K. Johnson and Sarah J. Platt, *The Families First Coronavirus Response Act FAQs: The FMLA Amendments and Paid Sick Leave Requirements of the New Law*, https:/ogletree.com/insights/the-families-first-coronavirus-response-act-faqs-the-fmla-amendments-and-paid-sick-leave-requirements-of-the-new-law).

Employers of health care providers or emergency responders may elect to exclude such employees from the paid sick time provisions (Act Sec. 5102(a) of the Families First Act).

Comment: To minimize the spread of COVID-19, the Department of Labor (DOL) encourages employers to be judicious when exempting health care providers and emergency responders from paid sick leave. Employers that elect not to exclude otherwise-eligible health care providers or emergency responders are eligible for the tax credit for paid sick leave. Also, note that exercising the exclusion does not prevent an employee who is a health care provider or emergency responder from taking earned or accrued leave in accordance with established employer policies.

Qualifying reasons. In temporary regulations, the DOL provided clarifying guidance on the six qualifying reasons for taking paid sick time:

- *Reason 1.* Quarantine or isolation orders include a broad range of governmental orders (including those that advise citizens to shelter in place, stay at home, quarantine, or otherwise restrict their mobility). However, an employee may take paid sick leave for the first reason only if "but for" being subject to the order, he or she would be able to perform work (or telework) that is otherwise allowed by the employer. In other words, the employee may not take paid sick leave where the employer does not have work for the employee as a result of the order or other circumstances. This is because the employee would be unable to work even if he or she were not required to comply with the order (29 CFR § 826.10(a) and 29 CFR § 826.20(a)(2)).
- *Reason 2.* An employee may take paid sick leave for the second reason if a health care provider advises the employee to self-quarantine based on a belief that he or she has, may have, or is particularly vulnerable to COVID-19 and following the health care provider's advice to self-quarantine prevents the employee from being able to work or telework (29 CFR § 826.20(a)(3)).

NEW LAW EXPLAINED

- *Reason 3.* An employee may take paid sick leave for the third reason if he or she has a fever, dry cough, shortness of breath, or other COVID-19 symptoms identified by the Centers for Disease Control and Prevention (CDC). However, the paid sick leave is limited to the time the employee is unable to work because he or she is taking *affirmative steps* to obtain a medical diagnosis, such as making, waiting for, or attending an appointment for a test for COVID-19 (29 CFR § 826.20(a)(4)).
- *Reason 4.* An employee may not take paid sick leave for the fourth reason unless "but for" a need to care for an individual, the employee would be able to perform work (or telework) for his or her employer. An employee caring for an individual may not take paid sick leave where the employer does not have work for the employee. Sick leave may be taken if the employee is unable to perform work for his or her employer and if the individual depends on the employee to take care of him or her and is either subject to a quarantine or isolation order or has been advised to self-quarantine by a health care provider because of a belief that the individual has, may have, or is particularly vulnerable to COVID-19. Also, the "individual" cared for must be the employee's immediate family member, a person who regularly resides in the employee's home, or someone with whom the employee has a relationship that creates an expectation that the employee would care for him or her. It does not include people with whom the employee has no personal relationship (29 CFR § 826.20(a)(5)).
- *Reason 5.* An employee may not take paid sick leave to care for his or her son or daughter unless "but for" a need to care for an individual, the employee would be able to work (or telework) for his or her employer. Again, the employee may not take paid sick leave where the employer does not have work for the employee. Also, during the period of leave, no other suitable person may be available to care for the son or daughter (29 CFR § 826.20(a)(8)).
- *Reason 6.* Clarification about the sixth qualifying reason for taking paid sick time was not included; however, the temporary regulations note that a "substantially similar condition" may be defined at any point during the effective period (April 1, 2020, to December 31, 2020) (29 CFR § 826.20(a)(1)).

Expert Guidance: The DOL regulations clearly state that an employee is not entitled to receive paid sick leave when the employer does not have work for him or her as a result of a government order or other circumstances, Ogletree Deakins pointed out (Katrina Grider and Sarah J. Platt, *No April Fools: FFCRA Went Into Effect and the DOL Issued Regulations,* https:/ogletree.com/insights/no-april-fools-ffcra-went-into-effect-and-the-dol-issued-regulations).

Also, if the employer reduces an employee's scheduled hours (or furloughs the employee temporarily) due to a lack of work, the employee may not be paid for hours the employee is not scheduled to work (Michael M. Shetterly, Matthew K. Johnson and Sarah J. Platt, *The Families First Coronavirus Response Act FAQs: The FMLA Amendments and Paid Sick Leave Requirements of the New Law,* https:/ogletree.com/insights/the-families-first-coronavirus-response-act-faqs-the-fmla-amendments-and-paid-sick-leave-requirements-of-the-new-law).

NEW LAW EXPLAINED

Use of paid sick time. Paid sick time is available for immediate use for the specified purposes regardless of an employee's length of service (Act Sec. 5102(e) of the Families First Act). Employers may end it beginning with the employee's next scheduled work shift immediately following termination of the need for paid sick time (Act Sec. 5102(c) of the Families First Act). Note that paid sick time does not carry over from one year to the next (Act Sec. 5102(b) of the Families First Act).

> **Comment:** Intermittent use of paid sick leave is allowed if there is a mutual agreement between the employer and employee; however, there are some restrictions. For employees reporting to the worksite, intermittent leave may be taken in any agreed-upon increment *only* if the leave is for the fifth qualifying reason: to care for the employee's son or daughter whose school or place of care is closed (or whose child care provider is unavailable) because of reasons related to COVID-19. More flexibility is allowed for employees who telework due to a lower risk of spreading the virus. For those employees, paid sick leave may be taken intermittently in any agreed-upon increment for any of the qualifying reasons when the employee is unable to telework due to a COVID-19-related reason. Note that only the amount of paid sick leave actually taken will count toward an employee's leave entitlement (29 CFR § 826.50).

> **Comment:** A full-time employee who has taken all 80 hours of paid sick leave and then changes employers is not entitled to additional paid sick leave from the new employer. If fewer than 80 hours were taken, the employee is entitled only to the remaining portion from the new employer (29 CFR § 826.160(f)).

Prohibitions. Employers may not require employees to use other paid leave before using paid sick time (Act Sec. 5102(e) of the Families First Act). Requiring employees to find replacement workers to cover their paid sick time hours is also prohibited (Act Sec. 5102(d) of the Families First Act).

> **Expert Guidance:** Ogletree Deakins notes that paid sick time under the Act is in addition to any paid sick leave already offered by an employer (including subject to state or local requirements). Even if an employer has a generous paid sick leave policy offering more than the 80 hours required by the Act, the Act requires additional paid sick leave for COVID-19 purposes (Michael M. Shetterly, Matthew K. Johnson and Sarah J. Platt, *The Families First Coronavirus Response Act FAQs: The FMLA Amendments and Paid Sick Leave Requirements of the New Law*, https:/ogletree.com/insights/the-families-first-coronavirus-response-act-faqs-the-fmla-amendments-and-paid-sick-leave-requirements-of-the-new-law).

Calculating paid sick time. Information about calculating compensation for paid sick time, a reduced rate for the care of individuals, and handling varied scheduled hours for part-time employees is included in the Act's definition of "paid sick time." For details, see ¶ 310.

Limitations. There are caps on the amount of paid sick time required based on the aforementioned reasons why the employee is taking leave. An employer is not required

NEW LAW EXPLAINED

to pay more than (Act Sec. 5102(f) of the Families First Act, as added by Act Sec. 3602 of the CARES Act):

- $511 per day and $5,110 in the aggregate for each employee when the leave is for reason (1), (2), or (3); or
- $200 per day and $2,000 in the aggregate for each employee when the leave is for reason (4), (5), or (6).

Rules of construction. Nothing in the Emergency Paid Sick Leave Act should be construed to diminish rights or benefits that an employee is entitled to under any other federal, state, or local law; collective bargaining agreement; or existing employer policy. It also should not be construed to require employers to provide financial or other reimbursement for unused paid sick time upon an employee's termination, resignation, retirement, or other separation from employment (Act Sec. 5107 of the Families First Act).

Temporary regulations issued. The DOL has issued temporary regulations on paid leave under the Families First Coronavirus Response Act (29 CFR Part § 826; 85 FR 19326, April 6, 2020). The regulations contain further details about paid sick leave, including leave entitlements (29 CFR § 826.20), pay (29 CFR § 826.22), employer coverage (29 CFR § 826.40), intermittent leave (29 CFR § 826.50), the intersection between the Emergency Paid Sick Leave Act and the Emergency Family and Medical Leave Expansion Act for childcare (29 CFR § 826.60), employee notice (29 CFR § 826.90), and documentation (29 CFR § 826.100), among other topics.

▶ **Effective date.** The provision is effective not later than 15 days after the date of enactment, which was March 18, 2020 (Act Sec. 5108 of the Families First Coronavirus Response Act (P.L. 116-127)). The DOL clarified that the effective date is April 1, 2020 (29 CFR § 826.10(b) and *Families First Coronavirus Response Act: Questions and Answers*, issued by the Department of Labor; https:/www.dol.gov/agencies/whd/pandemic/ffcra-questions). The provision is scheduled to sunset on December 31, 2020 (Act Sec. 5109 of the Families First Act).

Law source: Law at ¶1040, ¶1045, ¶1046, ¶1047, ¶1048, ¶2119, and ¶2129.

— Act Sec. 5102 of the Families First Coronavirus Response Act (P.L. 116-127).

— Act Sec. 5107 of the Families First Act.

— Act Sec. 5110 of the Families First Act.

— Act Sec. 5108 of the Families First Act, providing the effective date.

— Act Sec. 5109 of the Families First Act, providing the sunset date.

— Act Sec. 3602 of the Coronavirus Aid, Relief, and Economic Security Act (P.L. 116-136), amending Act Sec. 5102 of the Families First Act.

— Act Sec. 3611 of the CARES Act, amending Act Sec. 5110 of the Families First Act.

¶305 OMB Waiver of Paid Sick Leave

SUMMARY OF NEW LAW

The Office of Management and Budget is authorized to exclude for good cause certain federal government employees from the provisions of the Emergency Paid Sick Leave Act.

BACKGROUND

The Families First Coronavirus Response Act (P.L. 116-127) provides relief for both employers and employees in connection with the coronavirus (COVID-19) crisis. The Act's Division E, the Emergency Paid Sick Leave Act, requires certain employers, including the federal government, to temporarily provide their employees with paid sick and family leave time for designated reasons related to COVID-19. This requirement is scheduled to expire on December 31, 2020.

NEW LAW EXPLAINED

Authority to exclude certain federal employees.—The Coronavirus Aid, Relief, and Economic Security Act (P.L. 116-136) amended the Emergency Paid Sick Leave Act (EPSLA) to authorize the Director of the Office of Management and Budget (OMB) to exclude, for "good cause," certain federal executive branch employees from the EPSLA's requirements. Employees that may be excluded from EPSLA coverage include (Act Sec. 5110(1)(E), (F) of the Families First Coronavirus Response Act (P.L. 116-127); Act Sec. 5112 of the Families First Act, as added by Act Sec. 3604(b) of the Coronavirus Aid, Relief, and Economic Security Act (P.L. 116-136)):

- a federal officer or employee covered under 5 U.S.C. chapter 63, subchapter V (Family and Medical Leave); and
- any other individual in a position in the civil service (as defined in 5 U.S.C. 2101(1)).

The CARES Act also authorizes OMB to make "good cause" exemptions from EPSLA requirements for certain federal government employers: executive agencies (as defined in 5 U.S.C. 105), the U.S. Postal Service, and the Postal Regulatory Commission (Act Sec. 5110(2)(A)(i)(V) of the Families First Act; Act Sec. 5112 of the Families First Act, as added by Act Sec. 3604(b) of the CARES Act).

▶ **Effective date.** The Emergency Paid Sick Leave Act is effective not later than 15 days after the date of enactment, which was March 18, 2020 (Act Sec. 5108 of the Families First Coronavirus Response Act (P.L. 116-127)). The EPSLA is scheduled to sunset on December 31, 2020 (Act Sec. 5109 of the Families First Act).

The CARES Act does not specify an effective date for Section 3604(b). Accordingly, the section is treated as effective on March 27, 2020, the date of enactment of the CARES Act.

NEW LAW EXPLAINED

Law source: Law at ¶1046, ¶1047, ¶1048, ¶1050, and ¶2121.

— Act Sec. 5108 of the Families First Coronavirus Response Act (P.L. 116-127), providing the effective date.

— Act Sec. 5109 of the Families First Act, providing the sunset date.

— Act Sec. 5110 of the Families First Act.

— Act Sec. 5112 of the Families First Act.

— Act Sec. 3604(b) of the Coronavirus Aid, Relief, and Economic Security Act (P.L. 116-136), adding Act Sec. 5112 of the Families First Act.

¶310 Definitions

SUMMARY OF NEW LAW

Terms pertaining to the Emergency Paid Sick Leave Act are defined. Key information about eligible employees, covered employers, and calculating compensation for paid sick time is included in the definitions.

BACKGROUND

On March 18, 2020, President Trump signed the Families First Coronavirus Response Act (P.L. 116-127), which provides relief for both employers and employees in connection with the coronavirus (COVID-19) crisis. The Act's Division E, the Emergency Paid Sick Leave Act, requires certain employers to temporarily provide their employees with paid sick time for designated reasons related to COVID-19. This requirement is scheduled to expire on December 31, 2020.

The Emergency Paid Sick Leave Act contains its own set of definitions, and many of them draw off definitions in other laws. The Coronavirus Aid, Relief, and Economic Security Act (P.L. 116-136), enacted on March 27, 2020, made several technical changes to these definitions.

NEW LAW EXPLAINED

Terms defined.—For purposes of the Emergency Paid Sick Leave Act, as amended, the following terms are defined:

Employee. The term "employee" encompasses a wide range of individuals employed by both private- and public-sector employers. An individual who meets the definition of "employee" under the Fair Labor Standards Act of 1938 (FLSA) (29 U.S.C. 203(e)) is specifically included, as is an employee of the Government Accountability Office, a state employee under 42 U.S.C. 2000e-16c(a), a covered employee under 2 U.S.C. 1301 (other than an applicant), a covered employee under 3 U.S.C. 411(c), a federal officer or employee under 5 U.S.C. Ch. 63 (Subchapter V), or any other individual in a position in

NEW LAW EXPLAINED

the civil service (as defined in 5 U.S.C. 2101(1)) (Act Sec. 5110(1) of the Families First Coronavirus Response Act (P.L. 116-127), as amended by Act Sec. 3611(5) of the Coronavirus Aid, Relief, and Economic Security Act (P.L. 116-136)).

Employer. In general, the term "employer" includes a person who is a "covered employer" (discussed below), an entity employing a state employee (under Sec. 304(a) of the Government Employee Rights Act of 1991), an employing office (as defined in Sec. 101 of the Congressional Accountability Act of 1995 or 3 U.S.C. 411(c)), or an executive agency (as defined in 5 U.S.C. 105) including the U.S. Postal Service and the Postal Regulatory Commission. An employer must be engaged in commerce (including government), or an industry or activity affecting commerce (including government) (Act Sec. 5110(2)(A) of the Families First Act).

Importantly, a "covered employer" is any person engaged in commerce (or in an industry or activity affecting commerce) that employs fewer than 500 employees if it is a private entity or individual, or employs one or more employees if it is a public agency or other non-private entity. This term includes a person acting directly or indirectly in the interest of an employer in relation to an employee, and a successor in interest of an employer. A "covered employer" also includes a public agency (as defined in 29 U.S.C. 203(x)), the Government Accountability Office, and the Library of Congress (Act Sec. 5110(2)(B) of the Families First Act, as amended by Act Sec. 3611(6) of the CARES Act).

> **Comment:** To determine whether private employers have fewer than 500 employees, the count is taken at the time each employee would take leave—sometimes referred to as a "snapshot" approach. For purposes of this count, every part-time employee is counted as if he or she were a full-time employee. Consider those employed within the United States, the District of Columbia, or any U.S. territory or possession. Include currently employed employees, employees on leave, employees of temporary placement agencies who are jointly employed, and day laborers supplied by a temporary placement agency. All common employees of joint employers and all employees of integrated employers must be counted together. Independent contractors, as well as laid-off or furloughed workers, are excluded (29 CFR § 826.40(a)).

Employ, state, health care provider, and son or daughter. The terms "employ" and "state" have the same meanings as in FLSA Sec. 3 (29 U.S.C. 203), while "health care provider" and "son or daughter" have the meanings set forth in Sec. 101 of the Family and Medical Leave Act of 1993 (29 U.S.C. 2611) (Act Secs. 5110(3) and 5110(4) of the Families First Act).

Paid sick time. The term "paid sick time" means an increment of compensated leave that is provided when the employee is unable to work or telework due to a need for leave because the employee (Act Secs. 5102(a) and 5110(5) of the Families First Act):

1. is subject to a federal, state, or local quarantine or isolation order related to COVID-19;
2. has been advised by a health care provider to self-quarantine due to concerns related to COVID-19;

NEW LAW EXPLAINED

3. is experiencing symptoms of COVID-19 and seeking a medical diagnosis;
4. is caring for an individual who is subject to a federal, state, or local quarantine or isolation order related to COVID-19, or has been advised by a health care provider to self-quarantine due to COVID-19 concerns;
5. is caring for the employee's son or daughter when the school or place of care has been closed, or the child care provider is unavailable, due to COVID-19 precautions; or
6. is experiencing any other substantially similar condition specified by the Secretary of Health and Human Services in consultation with the Secretary of the Treasury and the Secretary of Labor.

The definition also provides information for calculating the amount of paid sick time. In addition, the Secretary of Labor was charged with issuing guidelines to help employers with the calculation; the guidelines were due no later than 15 days after the date of enactment, which was March 18, 2020 (Act Sec. 5110(5)(D) of the Families First Act). On April 6, 2020, the U.S. Department of Labor (DOL) issued temporary regulations that cover the number of hours and amount of pay for paid sick leave (29 CFR § 826.21 and 29 CFR § 826.22).

Paid sick time is based on an employee's "required compensation" and the number of hours the employee would otherwise be normally scheduled to work. Required compensation is the greater of the employee's regular rate of pay under the FLSA (29 U.S.C. 207(e)), the federal minimum wage rate, or the applicable state or local minimum wage rate. Importantly, for paid sick time taken for reasons (4), (5) or (6) above, the employee's required compensation is reduced to two-thirds of this amount (Act Secs. 5110(5)(A) and (B) of the Families First Act).

Comment: Because the law does not specify which workweek to use to compute the regular rate, employers should use a weighted average. Compute the regular rate for each full workweek in which the employee has been employed over the lesser of the six-month period ending on the date the employee takes paid sick leave, or the entire period of employment. Then figure the average of the weekly regular rates, weighted by the number of hours worked for each workweek. In other words, add all compensation that is part of the regular rate over the relevant period and then divide that sum by all hours actually worked over the same period. An employee's commissions, tips, and piece rates are incorporated into the regular rate to the same extent that they are included in the calculation of the regular rate under the FLSA (29 CFR § 826.25).

The law's definition of paid sick leave also sets forth caps on the amount of paid sick time required based on the aforementioned reasons why the employee is taking leave (Act Sec. 5110(5)(A) of the Families First Act):

- for reasons (1), (2), or (3), the cap is $511 per day and $5,110 in the aggregate; and
- for reasons (4), (5), or (6), the cap is $200 per day and $2,000 in the aggregate.

Also, where a part-time employee's schedule varies from week to week such that an employer is unable to determine with certainty the number of hours the employee

NEW LAW EXPLAINED

would have worked if he or she had not taken paid sick time, the employer should use the following (Act Sec. 5110(5)(C) of the Families First Act):

- the average number of hours that the employee was scheduled per day over the six-month period ending on the date on which the employee takes the paid sick time (including hours for which the employee took leave of any type); or
- when the employee did not work over the six-month period above, the employee's reasonable expectation at the time of hiring of the average number of hours per day that the employee would normally be scheduled to work.

> **Comment:** A part-time employee is entitled to paid sick leave of up to 14 times the calendar-day amounts. If the part-time employee has not been employed for six months, the number is based on the average number of hours per calendar day that the employee and the employer agreed to at the time of hiring (29 CFR §826.21).

The definition makes clear that after the first workday (or portion thereof) for which an employee receives paid sick time, the employer may require him or her to follow reasonable notice procedures in order to continue receiving it (Act Sec. 5110(5)(E) of the Families First Act).

> **Expert Guidance:** The law firm of Ogletree Deakins cautions that an employer may not require an employee to provide notice in advance of taking leave, and notice may only be required after the first workday (or portion thereof) for which the employee takes paid leave under the Families First Coronavirus Response Act.
>
> The firm also notes that an employer may not require an employee's notice of a leave request to include documentation beyond what is allowed in the DOL regulations. This includes the employee's name, the dates for which the employee is requesting leave, the qualifying reason for the leave, and oral or written statements that the employee is unable to work because of the qualified reason for leave (however, note that IRS guidance indicates that employers must receive a written request to substantiate a tax credit to recover paid leave). Depending on the qualifying reason for the leave, additional documentation is required, including the name of the government entity that issued the quarantine or isolation order; the name of the health care provider who advised the employee (or individual being cared for) to self-quarantine; and the name of the son or daughter being cared for, the name of the school/place of care/child care provider that has closed or become unavailable, and a representation that no other suitable person will be caring for the son or daughter during the period for which the employee takes paid sick leave. Employers may request additional material as needed for the employer to support a request for tax credits.
>
> These records must be maintained by employers for four years, according to Ogletree Deakins, regardless of whether employees' requests for leave are granted or denied (Katrina Grider and Sarah J. Platt, *No April Fools: FFCRA Went Into Effect and the DOL Issued Regulations*, https:/ogletree.com/insights/no-april-fools-ffcra-went-into-effect-and-the-dol-issued-regulations).

NEW LAW EXPLAINED

Temporary regulations issued. The DOL has issued temporary regulations on paid leave under the Families First Coronavirus Response Act (29 CFR Part 826; 85 FR 19326, April 6, 2020). The regulations include additional definitions, including those for child care provider, COVID-19, place of care, school, and telework (29 CFR § 826.10(a)). Also defined are a health care provider and emergency responder for purposes of the exemption from paid sick time (29 CFR § 826.30(c)).

▶ **Effective date.** The provision is effective not later than 15 days after the date of enactment, which was March 18, 2020 (Act Sec. 5108 of the Families First Coronavirus Response Act (P.L. 116-127)). The DOL clarified that the effective date is April 1, 2020 (29 CFR § 826.10(b) and *Families First Coronavirus Response Act: Questions and Answers*, issued by the Department of Labor; https:/www.dol.gov/agencies/whd/pandemic/ffcra-questions). The provision is scheduled to sunset on December 31, 2020 (Act Sec. 5109 of the Families First Act).

Law source: Law at ¶1040, ¶1046, ¶1047, ¶1048, ¶2119, and ¶2129.

— Act Sec. 5102 of the Families First Coronavirus Response Act (P.L. 116-127).

— Act Sec. 5110 of the Families First Act.

— Act Sec. 5108 of the Families First Act, providing the effective date.

— Act Sec. 5109 of the Families First Act, providing the sunset date.

— Act Sec. 3602 of the Coronavirus Aid, Relief, and Economic Security Act (P.L. 116-136), amending Act Sec. 5102 of the Families First Act.

— Act Sec. 3611 of the CARES Act, amending Act Sec. 5110 of the Families First Act.

¶320 Notice

SUMMARY OF NEW LAW

Employers are required to post notice in a conspicuous location for employees about the Emergency Paid Sick Leave Act and its requirements.

BACKGROUND

Generally, under current law, employers are not required to provide employees with paid sick leave. However, many employers have sick pay provisions which offer access to a finite number of hours or days to employees who are unable to work due to illness, while other employers have merged paid sick leave with vacation and personal time off into paid time off (PTO) policies. Under specific circumstances, the Family and Medical Leave Act (FMLA) provides job-protected, unpaid leave to eligible employees for multiple reasons, including a serious health condition.

NEW LAW EXPLAINED

NEW LAW EXPLAINED

Conspicuous posting of notice.—Starting in April 2020, employers are required to post, and keep posted, onsite in a conspicuous place with other required notices, a notice prepared or approved by the Secretary of Labor describing the Emergency Paid Sick Leave Act and its requirements (Act Sec. 5103 of the Families First Coronavirus Response Act (P.L. 116-127)).

▶ **Effective date.** The provision is effective not later than 15 days after the date of enactment, which was March 18, 2020 (Act Sec. 5108 of the Families First Coronavirus Response Act (P.L. 116-127)). The DOL clarified that the effective date is April 1, 2020 (29 CFR §826.10(b) and *Families First Coronavirus Response Act: Questions and Answers*, issued by the Department of Labor; https:/www.dol.gov/agencies/whd/pandemic/ffcra-questions). The provision is scheduled to sunset on December 31, 2020 (Act Sec. 5109 of the Families First Act).

Law source: Law at ¶1041, ¶1046, and ¶1047.

— Act Sec. 5103 of the Families First Coronavirus Response Act (P.L. 116-127)

— Act Sec. 5108 of the Families First Act, providing the effective date.

— Act Sec. 5109 of the Families First Act, providing the sunset date.

¶330 Prohibited Acts

SUMMARY OF NEW LAW

Employers are prohibited from taking any action, including discriminating against, disciplining, or terminating, an employee who takes leave in accordance with the Act; has filed a complaint; instituted a proceeding relating to the enforcement of the Act; or has testified, or is about to testify, in such a proceeding.

BACKGROUND

Generally, under current law, employers are not required to provide employees with paid sick leave. However, many employers have sick pay provisions which offer access to a finite number of hours or days to employees who are unable to work due to illness, while other employers have merged paid sick leave with vacation and personal time off into paid time off (PTO) policies. Under specific circumstances, the Family and Medical Leave Act (FMLA) provides job-protected, unpaid leave to eligible employees for multiple reasons, including a serious health condition. Employers are prohibited from interfering with or discriminating against employees who take leave under the FMLA.

NEW LAW EXPLAINED

Prohibition on discrimination, discipline, or discharge.— The Emergency Paid Sick Leave Act division of the Families First Coronavirus Response Act (P.L. 116-127),

NEW LAW EXPLAINED

states that it is unlawful for any employer to discharge, discipline or in any way discriminate against any employee who: (1) takes leave in accordance with the Act, or (2) has filed any complaint, instituted or caused to be instituted a proceeding that seeks enforcement of the Act, or has testified in or about to testify in such a proceeding (Act Sec. 5104 of the Families First Act, as amended by Act Sec. 3611(8) of the Coronavirus Aid, Relief, and Economic Security Act (P.L. 116-136)).

▶ **Effective date.** The provision is effective not later than 15 days after the date of enactment, which was March 18, 2020 (Act Sec. 5108 of the Families First Coronavirus Response Act (P.L. 116-127)). The DOL clarified that the effective date is April 1, 2020 (29 CFR §826.10(b) and *Families First Coronavirus Response Act: Questions and Answers*, issued by the Department of Labor; https:/www.dol.gov/agencies/whd/pandemic/ffcra-questions). The provision is scheduled to sunset on December 31, 2020 (Act Sec. 5109 of the Families First Act).

Law source: Law at ¶1042, ¶1046, ¶1047, and ¶2129.

— Act Sec. 5104 of the Families First Coronavirus Response Act (P.L. 116-127).

— Act Sec. 3611(8) of the Coronavirus Aid, Relief, and Economic Security Act (P.L. 116-136), amending Act Sec. 5104(1) of the Families First Act.

— Act Sec. 5108 of the Families First Act, providing the effective date.

— Act Sec. 5109 of the Families First Act, providing the sunset date.

¶340 Enforcement

SUMMARY OF NEW LAW

Employers who violate the Emergency Paid Sick Leave Act are considered to have violated the FLSA and will be subject to a potential fine, incarceration, and other punitive action.

BACKGROUND

Generally, under current law, employers are not required to provide employees with paid sick leave. However, many employers have sick pay provisions which offer access to a finite number of hours or days to employees who are unable to work due to illness, while other employers have merged paid sick leave with vacation and personal time off into paid time off (PTO) policies. Under specific circumstances, the Family and Medical Leave Act (FMLA) provides job-protected, unpaid leave to eligible employees for multiple reasons, including a serious health condition.

NEW LAW EXPLAINED

Possible punishment for employer violators.— Any employer who violates the paid sick time requirement (Act Sec. 5102 of the Families First Coronavirus Act (P.L.

NEW LAW EXPLAINED

116-127)) (see ¶ 300) shall be considered to have failed to pay minimum wages in violation of section 6 of the FLSA (29 U.S.C. 206) and will be subjected to penalties including a fine in an amount up to $10,000 and/or up to six months imprisonment. Employers may also be subject to payment of damages and attorney's fees and costs (29 U.S.C. 216; 217) (Act Sec. 5105 of the Families First Act).

An employer who willfully violates Act Sec. 5104 of the Families First Act (see ¶ 300) by unlawfully terminating an employee shall be considered to have violated section 15(a)(3) of the FLSA (29 U.S.C. 215(a)(3)) and will be subject to penalties including a fine in an amount up to $10,000; up to six months imprisonment; payment of damages; and attorney's fees and costs (29 U.S.C. 216; 217) (Act Sec. 5105 of the Families First Act).

The Secretary of Labor may investigate and collect data to ensure compliance as authorized by sections 9 and 11 of the FLSA (29 U.S.C. 209-211) (Act Sec. 5105 of the Families First Act, as added by Act Sec. 3611(9) of the Coronavirus Aid, Relief, and Economic Security Act (P.L. 116-136).

▶ **Effective date.** The provision is effective not later than 15 days after the date of enactment, which was March 18, 2020 (Act Sec. 5108 of the Families First Coronavirus Response Act (P.L. 116-127)). The DOL clarified that the effective date is April 1, 2020 (29 CFR §826.10(b) and *Families First Coronavirus Response Act: Questions and Answers*, issued by the Department of Labor; https:/www.dol.gov/agencies/whd/pandemic/ffcra-questions). The provision is scheduled to sunset on December 31, 2020 (Act Sec. 5109 of the Families First Act).

Law source: Law at ¶1043, ¶1046, ¶1047, and ¶2129.

— Act Sec. 5105 of the Families First Coronavirus Response Act (P.L. 116-127).

— Act Sec. 3611(9) of the Coronavirus Aid, Relief, and Economic Security Act (P.L. 116-136), adding Families First Act Sec. 5105(c).

— Act Sec. 5108 of the Families First Act, providing the effective date.

— Act Sec. 5109 of the Families First Act, providing the sunset date.

¶350 Employment Under Multi-Employer Bargaining Agreements

SUMMARY OF NEW LAW

Employers participating in a multi-employer collective bargaining agreement (CBA) may meet their paid leave obligations by paying into a multi-employer fund to which their employees are entitled while working under the multi-employer CBA provided the plan allows employees to secure pay based on the hours they have worked under the multiemployer CBA for paid leave taken under the new public health emergency leave and paid sick time provisions.

BACKGROUND

Generally, under current law employers are not required to provide employees with paid sick leave. However, many employers have sick pay provisions which offer access to a finite number of hours or days to employees who are unable to work due to illness, while other employers have merged paid sick leave with vacation and personal time off into paid time off (PTO) policies. Under specific circumstances, the Family and Medical Leave Act (FMLA) provides job-protected, unpaid leave to eligible employees for multiple reasons including a serious health condition.

NEW LAW EXPLAINED

Employers participating in multi-employer CBAs.— Employers that are signatory to a multi-employer collective bargaining agreement (CBA) may, consistent with their bargaining obligations and its CBAs, meet their paid leave obligations by contributing to a multi-employer fund, plan, or program based on the paid leave to which each of their employees is entitled while working under the multiemployer CBA, provided that the fund, plan, or program permits employees to secure pay based on the hours they have worked under the multi-employer CBA for paid leave taken under the new public health emergency leave and paid sick time provisions (Act Sec. 5106(a) of the Families First Coronavirus Response Act (P.L. 116-127)).

Conversely, employees who work under a multi-employer CBA into which their employers make contributions as provided above, may secure pay from the fund, plan, or program based on hours they have worked under the multi-employer CBA for paid leave and paid sick time taken undertaken under the public health emergency leave and paid sick time provisions (Act Sec. 5106(b) of the Families First Act).

▶ **Effective date.** The Act takes effect April 1, 2020 (not later than 15 days after the March 18, 2020, date of enactment of the Families First Act) (Act Sec. 5108 of the Families First Coronavirus Response Act (P.L. 116-127)). The Act and its requirements will expire on December 31, 2020 (Act Sec. 5109 of the Families First Act).

Law source: Law at ¶1044, ¶1046, and ¶1047.

— Act Sec. 5106 of the Families First Act Coronavirus Response Act (P.L. 116-127).

— Act Sec. 5108 of the Families First Act, providing the effective date.

— Act Sec. 5109 of the Families First Act, providing the sunset date.

¶360 Regulatory Authorities

SUMMARY OF NEW LAW

The Secretary of Labor has the authority to issue regulations consistent with the enforcement of this Act, including the exclusion of certain health care providers and emergency responders from the definition of employee.

BACKGROUND

Generally, under current law employers are not required to provide employees with paid sick leave. However, many employers have sick pay provisions which offer access to a finite number of hours or days to employees who are unable to work due to illness, while other employers have merged paid sick leave with vacation and personal time off into paid time off (PTO) policies. Under specific circumstances, the Family and Medical Leave Act (FMLA) provides job-protected, unpaid leave to eligible employees for multiple reasons including a serious health condition.

NEW LAW EXPLAINED

Regulation authority.—The Secretary of Labor has the authority (sections 553(b)(B) and 553(d)(3) of title 5, United States Code) to issue regulations (Act Sec. 5111 of the Families First Coronavirus Response Act (P.L. 116-127), as amended by Act Sec. 3611(2) of the Coronavirus Aid, Relief, and Economic Security Act (P.L. 116-136)):

(1) To exclude certain health care providers and emergency responders from the definition of employee by allowing the employer of such health care providers and emergency responders to opt out;

(2) To exempt small businesses with fewer than 50 employees from the requirements of section 5102(a)(5) when the imposition of such requirements would jeopardize the viability of the business as a going concern; and

(3) As necessary, to carry out the purposes of this Act to ensure consistency between this Act and Division C and Division G of the Families First Coronavirus Response Act.

Temporary regulations issued. The DOL has issued temporary regulations on paid leave under the Families First Coronavirus Response Act (29 CFR Part § 826; 85 FR 19326, April 6, 2020). The regulations contain further details about paid sick leave, including leave entitlements (29 CFR § 826.20), pay (29 CFR § 826.22), employer coverage (29 CFR § 826.40), intermittent leave (29 CFR § 826.50), the intersection between the Emergency Paid Sick Leave Act and the Emergency Family and Medical Leave Expansion Act for childcare (29 CFR § 826.60), employee notice (29 CFR § 826.90), and documentation (29 CFR § 826.100), among other topics.

▶ **Effective date.** The Act takes effect April 1, 2020 (not later than 15 days after the March 18, 2020, date of enactment of the Families First Act) (Act Sec. 5108 of the Families First Coronavirus Response Act (P.L. 116-127)). The Act and its requirements will expire on December 31, 2020 (Act Sec. 5109 of the Families First Act).

Law source: Law at ¶1046, ¶1047, ¶1049, and ¶2129.

— Act Sec. 5111 of the Families First Coronavirus Response Act (P.L. 116-127), as amended by Act Sec. 3611 of the Coronavirus Aid, Relief, and Economic Security Act (P.L. 116-136).

— Act Sec. 5108 of the Families First Act, providing the effective date.

— Act Sec. 5109 of the Families First Act, providing the sunset date.

Chapter 4—Health and Privacy Provisions

4

¶400 Coverage of Testing for COVID-19

SUMMARY OF NEW LAW

Effective immediately, and for the duration of the national emergency, group health plans and health insurance issuers will be required to provide coverage of COVID-19 diagnostic tests and office visits, urgent care center visits, and emergency room visits that result in an order for or administration of such tests without application of any cost sharing.

BACKGROUND

Generally, companies have broad latitude in designing group health plans. Employer-provided health plans do not have to cover all expenses that are considered medical care expenses for federal income tax purposes (although companies may choose to cover all such expenses). However, an ever-increasing number of federal laws require employers to provide coverage for specified benefits or to provide the coverage they do offer on a nondiscriminatory basis.

For example, the Patient Protection and Affordable Care Act (P.L. 111-148) imposes significant mandates on group health plans and health insurance issuers offering group coverage. Plans in the small group market are required to cover minimum essential benefits, and large employers face penalties if they do not offer employees

BACKGROUND

minimum essential coverage. Group health plans are required to provide coverage, without cost-sharing, for certain preventive services. And, insured group health plans are subject to an increasing number of coverage requirements under state law.

NEW LAW EXPLAINED

Coverage of testing for COVID-19.—For the duration of the national emergency, group health plans and health insurance issuers will be required to provide coverage of COVID-19 diagnostic tests and office visits, urgent care center visits, and emergency room visits that result in an order for or administration of such tests without application of any cost sharing (Act Sec. 6001(a) of the Families First Coronavirus Response Act (P.L. 116-127)). Cost-sharing includes copayments, coinsurance, and deductibles.

The Families First Act specified that the covered COVID-19 testing and treatment should be approved by the FDA (Act Sec. 6001(a)(1) of the Families First Act). However, the CARES Act expands this provision to apply to additional forms of approved testing during the public health emergency (such as certain state-approved tests or other HHS-approved tests) (Act Sec. 3201 of the Coronavirus Aid, Relief, and Economic Security Act (P.L. 116-136)). The expansion covers testing that has not yet made it through the FDA approval process but is being utilized, so that an individual who is given such a test does not have his or her health plan deny coverage for the diagnostic test as an experimental treatment or care.

This provision applies to both self-insured, insured, and grandfathered health plans (Act Sec. 6001(a) of the Families First Act).

The Department of Health and Human Services, Labor, and Treasury are directed to implement this provision of the Act through sub-regulatory guidance, program instruction, or otherwise (Act Sec. 6001(c) of the Families First Act). In addition, the Departments will enforce this provision of the Act, as applicable (Act Sec. 6001(b) of the Families First Act).

▶ **Effective date.** No specific effective date is provided by the Acts. The provisions are, therefore, considered effective on March 18, 2020, the date of enactment of the Families First Act, and March 27, 2020, the date of enactment of the CARES Act.

Law source: Law at ¶1052 and ¶2071.

— Act Sec. 6001 of the Families First Coronavirus Response Act (P.L. 116-27).

— Act Sec. 3201 of the Coronavirus Aid, Relief, and Economic Security Act (P.L. 116-136), amending Act Sec. 6001(a)(1) of the Families First Act.

¶410 Insurer Pricing of Diagnostic Testing

SUMMARY OF NEW LAW

Group health plans and health insurance issuers must reimburse providers of COVID-19 diagnostic tests in accordance with rates negotiated prior to the public health emergency or in an amount equal to the cash price for the service as listed on the provider's website. Providers must make the cash price of COVID-19 diagnostic tests public or face civil money penalties.

BACKGROUND

Act Sec. 6001(a) of the Families First Coronavirus Response Act (P.L. 116-127), as amended by Act Sec. 3201 of the Coronavirus Aid, Relief, and Economic Security Act (P.L. 116-136), requires group health plans and health insurance issuers to provide coverage, without cost-sharing, for in vitro diagnostic testing for COVID-19 and items and services that lead to or are related to the administration of in vitro diagnostic testing for COVID-19.

The coverage requirement applies to health care provider office visits (including in-person visits as well as telehealth visits), urgent care center visits, and emergency room visits. Items and services under the provision must lead to the order of a COVID-19 test and relate either to the furnishing or administration of a test itself or to the evaluation of such individual for purposes of determining the need for that test.

NEW LAW EXPLAINED

Reimbursement rates. — Group health plans and health insurance issuers must reimburse the provider of diagnostic testing under Act Sec. 6001(a) of the Families First Act either: (1) a negotiated rate between the insurer and provider that was in effect prior to the declaration of a public health emergency; or (2) if no such negotiated rate exists, an amount that equals the cash price for such service as listed by the provider on a public internet website. Group health plans and health insurance issuers may also negotiate a rate with a provider that is lower than the publicly listed cash price (Act Sec. 3202(a) of the Coronavirus Aid, Relief, and Economic Security Act (P.L. 116-136)).

Price publication. — During the emergency period, providers of COVID-19 diagnostic tests must make public the cash price for such a test on its public internet website. A provider that fails to publish the cash price of its COVID-19 diagnostic test and does not complete a corrective action plan to comply with the publication requirement will be subject to a $300 per day civil money penalty as long as the noncompliance is ongoing (Act Sec. 3202(b) of the CARES Act).

▶ **Effective date.** The Act does not specify an effective date. Accordingly, the provision is effective on the March 27, 2020, date of enactment of the CARES Act.

NEW LAW EXPLAINED

Law source: Law at ¶2072.

— Act Sec. 3202 of the Coronavirus Aid, Relief, and Economic Security Act (P.L. 116-136).

¶420 Rapid Coverage of Preventive Services and Vaccines for Coronavirus

SUMMARY OF NEW LAW

Group health plans and health insurance issuers offering group or individual health insurance are required to cover—without cost-sharing—qualifying coronavirus preventive services, including COVID-19 immunizations.

BACKGROUND

Section 2713(a) of the Public Health Service Act (PHSA) and the accompanying regulations at 26 C.F.R. § 54.9815-2713, 29 C.F.R. § 2590.715-2713, and 45 C.F.R. § 147.130 require a group health plan and a health insurance issuer offering group or individual health insurance coverage to provide, without cost-sharing, coverage for, among other preventive services:

- evidence-based items or services that have in effect a rating of "A" or "B" in the current recommendations of the United States Preventive Services Task Force; and
- immunizations that have in effect a recommendation from the Advisory Committee on Immunization Practices of the Centers for Disease Control and Prevention with respect to the individual involved.

NEW LAW EXPLAINED

Coverage requirement.—Pursuant to section 2713(a) of the PHSA, group health plans and health insurance issuers offering group or individual health insurance are required to cover, without cost-sharing, qualifying coronavirus preventive services. This coverage requirement is notwithstanding section 2713(b) of the PHSA, which imposes a minimum one-year time period between a recommendation or guidance and the plan year to which it is effective (Act Sec. 3203(a) of the Coronavirus Aid, Relief, and Economic Security Act (P.L. 116-136)).

Qualifying coronavirus preventive service.—The term "qualifying coronavirus preventive service" means an item, service, or immunization that is intended to prevent or mitigate COVID-19 and that is also an evidence-based item or service that has:

- in effect a rating of "A" or "B" in the current recommendations of the United States Preventive Services Task Force; or

NEW LAW EXPLAINED

- an immunization that has in effect a recommendation from the Advisory Committee on Immunization Practices of the Centers for Disease Control and Prevention with respect to the individual involved.

(Act Sec. 3203(b)(1) of the CARES Act).

▶ **Effective date.** The coverage requirement described in Act Sec. 3203 of the CARES Act will take effect with respect to a particular qualifying coronavirus preventive service 15 business days after the date on which a recommendation is made relating to the qualifying coronavirus preventive service (Act Sec. 3203(b)(2) of the CARES Act).

Law source: Law at ¶2073.

— Act Sec. 3203 of the Coronavirus Aid, Relief, and Economic Security Act (P.L. 116-136).

— Act Sec. 3203(b)(2) of the CARES Act, providing the effective date.

¶430 Health Savings Account (HSA) Eligibility

SUMMARY OF NEW LAW

For plan years beginning on or before December 31, 2021, a safe harbor for health savings accounts (HSAs) provides that a health plan will not fail to be treated as a high-deductible health plan (HDHP) for failing to impose a deductible for telehealth or other remote care services.

BACKGROUND

A health savings account (HSA) is a trust established for the exclusive purpose of paying for qualified medical expenses of the account beneficiary. To be eligible for an HSA, an individual must be covered under a high deductible health plan (HDHP). Furthermore, the individual cannot be covered under any health plan which is not an HDHP and which provides coverage for any benefit which is covered under the HDHP (Code Sec. 223(c)(1)(A)).

Certain coverage is disregarded for purposes of determining whether an individual is covered only by an HDHP. Disregarded coverage includes coverage for accidents, disability, dental care, vision care, or long-term care. It also includes certain permitted insurance and coverage under a health FSA (Code Sec. 223(c)(1)(B)). Such coverage can be provided without having to satisfy a deductible requirement.

HSAs can make distributions to pay or reimburse qualified medical expenses (Code Sec. 223(d)(2)). These include a medicine or a drug only if prescribed (determined without regard to whether such drug is available without a prescription) or is insulin (Code Sec. 223(d)(2)(A)).

NEW LAW EXPLAINED

NEW LAW EXPLAINED

HSA safe harbor for absence of deductible for telehealth.—For plan years beginning on or before December 31, 2021, a plan is treated as a high deductible health plan (HDHP) even if it does not impose a deductible for telehealth or other remote care services (Code Sec. 223(c)(2)(E), added by the Coronavirus Aid, Relief, and Economic Security (CARES) Act (P.L. 116-136)). Telehealth and remote care (for plan years beginning on or before December 31, 2021), are added to the list of coverage items that are disregarded for purposes of determining HDHP deductibles (Code Sec. 223(c)(1)(B)(ii), as amended by the CARES Act).

> **Expert Guidance:** William D. Elliott, Of Counsel, Elliott, Thomason & Gibson, LLP, in Dallas, notes that the effect of Section 3701 of the Act is to create a safe harbor from the high deductible health plan rules for failing to have a deductible for telehealth and other remote care services.

Comment: Telehealth services and other remote care services permit patients and practitioners to interact electronically rather than the more traditional face-to-face method of providing medical care. They are generally less costly for providers and help to keep overall medical costs down. Telehealth services are already considered an eligible expense for use with an HSA. The CARES Act provides temporary relief during the COVID-19 crisis from any requirement that a plan participant must meet a minimum deductible before such expenses are covered by an HSA.

The IRS has also provided emergency relief for HSAs for expenses related to COVID-19. Health plans that otherwise qualify as HDHPs will not lose that status merely because they cover the cost of testing for or treatment of COVID-19 before plan deductibles have been met. In addition, any vaccination costs will count as preventive care and can be paid for by an HDHP (Notice 2020-15).

▶ **Effective date.** The amendments made by this section take effect on March 27, 2020, date of the enactment (Act Sec. 3701(c) of the Coronavirus Aid, Relief, and Economic Security (CARES) Act (P.L. 116-136)).

Law source: Law at ¶2131 and ¶5005.

— Act Sec. 3701(a) of the Coronavirus Aid, Relief, and Economic Security (CARES) Act (P.L. 116-136), adding Code Sec. 223(c)(2)(E);

— Act Sec. 3701(b), amending Code Sec. 223(c)(1)(B);

— Act Sec. 3701(c), providing the effective date.

¶440 Medical Care Expenses for HSAs, Archer MSAs, HRAs, and Health FSAs

SUMMARY OF NEW LAW

The requirement that individuals obtain a prescription in order to be reimbursed for over-the-counter medicines and drugs has been eliminated for expenses paid or incurred after December 31, 2019, for health savings accounts (HSAs), Archer medical savings accounts (MSAs), health flexible spending accounts (FSAs), and health reimbursement arrangements (HRAs). In addition, expenses paid or incurred for the purchase of menstrual care products after December 31, 2019, are eligible medical care expenses for purposes of HSAs, Archer MSAs, health FSAs, and HRAs.

BACKGROUND

Amounts received as reimbursements for medical care are excludable from gross income (Code Sec. 105(b)). For this purpose, medical expenses includes the cost of medicine but reimbursements for medicine or drugs will only meet the definition of medical expenses if the medicine or drug is a prescribed drug or insulin (Code Sec. 106(f)). This means that reimbursements by health flexible spending arrangements (FSAs), health reimbursement arrangements (HRAs), and other employer health plans for the cost of nonprescription drugs are not excludable from tax.

Health FSAs and HRAs. A flexible spending arrangement (FSA) is an employer-established benefit program under which amounts credited to an employee's account may be used to reimburse the employee for health care, dependent care, or adoption expenses that would otherwise be excludable from the employee's gross income if paid by the employer (Prop. Reg. § 1.125-5). A health reimbursement arrangement (HRA) is an employer-funded plan that reimburses employees for qualified medical care expenses (Notice 2002-45, amplified by Rev. Rul. 2006-36). An HRA is funded solely by employer contributions and may not be funded through employee salary deferrals under a cafeteria plan.

Health Savings Accounts. A health savings account (HSA) is a trust established for the exclusive purpose of paying for qualified medical expenses of the account beneficiary. To be eligible for an HSA, an individual must be covered under a high deductible health plan (HDHP) (Code Sec. 223). Furthermore, the individual cannot be covered under any health plan which is not an HDHP, and which provides coverage for any benefit which is covered under the HDHP. HSAs can make distributions to pay or reimburse qualified medical expenses. These include a medicine or a drug only if prescribed (determined without regard to whether such drug is available without a prescription) or is insulin.

Archer MSAs. Archer MSAs were an earlier version of HSAs that a small employer could set up for itself between 1997 and 2007. Existing MSAs were grandfathered after that, and still operate (Code Sec. 220). MSAs also require HDHPs. MSAs can make distributions to pay or reimburse qualified medical expenses. These include a

BACKGROUND

medicine or a drug only if prescribed (determined without regard to whether such drug is available without a prescription) or is insulin.

NEW LAW EXPLAINED

Over-the-counter medicines, drugs, and menstrual care products treated as medical expenses. The requirement that individuals obtain a prescription in order to be reimbursed for over-the-counter medicines and drugs has been eliminated for health savings accounts (HSAs), Archer medical savings accounts (MSAs), health flexible spending accounts (FSAs), and health reimbursement arrangements (HRAs) for amounts paid or incurred after December 31, 2019 (Code Secs. 106(f), 220(d)(2)(A), and 223(d)(2)(A), as amended by the Coronavirus Aid, Relief, and Economic Security Act (P.L. 116-136)).

> **Comment:** Amounts paid or incurred for medicine or a drug before January 2, 2020, are qualified medical expenses only if the medicine or drug is a prescribed drug (determined without regard to whether such drug is available without a prescription) or is insulin.

Expenses paid or incurred for menstrual care products purchased after December 31, 2019, are also treated as qualified medical expenses for use with HSAs, Archer MSAs, health FSAs, and HRAs. Menstrual care products as defined for this purpose include a tampon, pad, liner, cup, sponge, or similar product used by individuals with respect to menstruation or other genital-tract secretions (Code Sec. 223(d)(2)(D), as added by the CARES Act).

> **Comment:** The elimination of the rule against treating over-the-counter medications as qualified medical expenses, as well as the inclusion of menstrual care products as qualified medical expenses, is part of the CARES Act. However, the changes are permanent and not specifically related to providing temporary relief for the COVID-19 crisis.

▶ **Effective date.** The amendments made by this section for health savings accounts (HSAs) and Archer medical savings accounts (MSAs) apply to amounts paid after December 31, 2019. The amendment made by this section for reimbursements applies to expenses incurred after December 31, 2019 (Act Sec. 3702(d) of the Coronavirus Aid, Relief, and Economic Security (CARES) Act (P.L. 116-136)).

Law source: Law at ¶2132, ¶5001, ¶5003, and ¶5005.

— Act Sec. 3702(a) of the Coronavirus Aid, Relief, and Economic Security (CARES) Act (P.L. 116-136), amending Code Sec. 223(d)(2)(A) and adding (d)(2)(D);

— Act Sec. 3702(b), amending Code Sec. 220(d)(2)(A);

— Act Sec. 3702(c), amending Code Sec. 106(f); and

— Act Sec. 3702(d), providing the effective dates.

¶450 Confidentiality and Disclosure of Records Relating to Substance Abuse Disorder

SUMMARY OF NEW LAW

After a patient's prior written consent has been obtained, a covered entity, business associate, or program may use or disclose the contents of substance use disorder records for purposes of treatment, payment, and health care operations, and re-disclose the information, as permitted by the Health Insurance Portability and Accountability Act of 1996 (HIPAA) regulations.

BACKGROUND

Public Health Service Act (PHSA) Sec. 543 and 42 C.F.R. Part 2 govern the use and disclosure of substance use disorder records. Before amendment, PHSA Sec. 543 provided simply that substance use disorder records could be disclosed with the patient's prior written consent, for specific purposes only, and it only prohibited the use of such records to initiate or substantiate criminal charges against, or investigate, a patient, except as authorized by a court order.

HIPAA regulations in 45 C.F.R. and the Health Information Technology and Clinical Health (HITECH) Act govern the use and disclosure of protected health information, and Soc. Sec. Act Secs. 1176 and 1177 establish penalties for violations of HIPAA rules. Act Sec. 3221 of the Coronavirus Aid, Relief, and Economic Security Act (P.L. 116-136) attempts to align requirements concerning substance use disorder records with HIPAA regulations.

NEW LAW EXPLAINED

Patient's written consent.—Substance use disorder records may be used or disclosed in accordance with the patient's prior written consent. Once the patient's prior written consent has been obtained, a covered entity, business associate, or program may use or disclose the contents for purposes of treatment, payment, and health care operations, and re-disclose the information, as permitted by the HIPAA regulations. It is permissible for a patient's prior written consent to be given once for all such future uses or disclosures for purposes of treatment, payment, and health care operations, until he or she revokes the consent in writing. Section 13405(a) and (c) of the Health Information Technology and Clinical Health (HITECH) Act applies to all such disclosures (PHSA Sec. 543(b)(1), as amended by Act Sec. 3221(b) of the Coronavirus Aid, Relief, and Economic Security Act (P.L. 116-136)).

Regardless of whether the patient gives written consent, the content of a substance abuse disorder record may be disclosed to a public health authority, as long as such content meets the standards established in 45 C.F.R. § 164.514(b) for creating de-identified information (PHSA Sec. 543(b)(2), as amended by Act Sec. 3221(c) of the CARES Act).

NEW LAW EXPLAINED

Use of records in civil, criminal, administrative, or legislative proceedings.—Except as authorized by a court order or by the consent of the patient, a substance abuse disorder record, or testimony relaying the information contained in such a record, may not be disclosed or used in any civil, criminal, administrative, or legislative proceedings conducted by a federal, state, or local authority against a patient. For example, the record or testimony must not: (1) be entered into evidence in any criminal prosecution or civil action before a federal or state court; (2) form part of the record for decision or otherwise be taken into account in any proceeding before a federal, state, or local agency; (3) be used by any federal, state, or local agency for a law enforcement purpose or to conduct any law enforcement investigation; or (4) be used in an application for a warrant (PHSA Sec. 543(c), as amended by Act Sec. 3221(e) of the CARES Act).

Penalties.—Soc. Sec. Act Secs. 1176 and 1177 apply to violations of PHSA Sec. 543. The reference to "this subsection" in Sec. 1176(a)(2) will be treated as a reference to "this subsection (including as applied pursuant to section 543(f) of the Public Health Service Act)". In Sec. 1176(b), each reference to "a penalty imposed under subsection (a)" will be treated as a reference to "a penalty imposed under subsection (a) (including as applied pursuant to section 543(f) of the Public Health Service Act)" and each reference to "no damages obtained under subsection (d)" will be treated as a reference to "no damages obtained under subsection (d) (including as applied pursuant to section 543(f) of the Public Health Service Act)" (PHSA Sec. 543(f), as amended by Act Sec. 3221(f) of the CARES Act).

Discrimination prohibited.—Entities are prohibited from discriminating against an individual on the basis of information received pursuant to an inadvertent or intentional disclosure of substance use disorder records or information contained in records in (1) admission, access to, or treatment for health care; (2) hiring, firing, or terms of employment, or receipt of worker's compensation; (3) the sale, rental, or continued rental of housing; (4) access to federal, state, or local courts; or (4) access to, approval of, or maintenance of social services and benefits provided or funded by federal, state, or local governments. In addition, recipients of federal funds, in affording access to the services provided with those funds, are prohibited from discriminating against an individual on the basis of information received pursuant to an intentional or inadvertent disclosure of records or information contained in substance abuse records (PHSA Sec. 543(g), as added by Act Sec. 3221(g) of the CARES Act).

Notification of breach.—If a breach of substance use disorder records occurs, Sec. 13402 of the HITECH Act applies to a program or activity relating to substance use disorder education, prevention, training, treatment, rehabilitation, or research to the same extent as the provisions apply to a covered entity in the case of a breach of unsecured protected health information (PHSA Sec. 543(j), as added by Act Sec. 3221(h) of the CARES Act).

Regulations.—The Secretary of Health and Human Services (HHS) is required to revise regulations as necessary for implementing and enforcing the amendments made by Act Sec. 3221 of the CARES Act, with amendments applicable to uses and disclosures

NEW LAW EXPLAINED

of information occurring on or after March 27, 2021 (Act Sec. 3221(i)(1) of the CARES Act).

By March 27, 2021, the HHS Secretary must update 45 C.F.R. § 164.520 so that covered entities and entities creating or maintaining substance abuse disorder records provide notice, written in plain language, of privacy practices regarding such records, including: (1) a statement of the patient's rights, including self-pay patients, with respect to protected health information and a brief description of how the individual may exercise these rights; and (2) a description of each purpose for which the covered entity is permitted or required to use or disclose protected health information without the patient's written authorization (Act Sec. 3221(i)(2) of the CARES Act).

▶ **Effective date.** The Act does not specify an effective date. Accordingly, the provision is effective on the March 27, 2020, date of enactment of the CARES Act.

Law source: Law at ¶2082.

— Act Sec. 3221(a) of the Coronavirus Aid, Relief, and Economic Security Act (P.L. 116-136), amending PHSA Sec. 543(a) and (h).

— Act Sec. 3221(b) of the CARES Act, amending PHSA Sec. 543(b)(1).

— Act Sec. 3221(c) of the CARES Act, amending PHSA Sec. 543(b)(2).

— Act Sec. 3221(d) of the CARES Act, adding PHSA Sec. 543(k).

— Act Sec. 3221(e) of the CARES Act, amending PHSA Sec. 543(c).

— Act Sec. 3221(f) of the CARES Act, amending PHSA Sec. 543(f).

— Act Sec. 3221(g) of the CARES Act, adding PHSA Sec. 543(i).

— Act Sec. 3221(h) of the CARES Act, adding PHSA Sec. 543(j).

¶460 Guidance on Protected Health Information

SUMMARY OF NEW LAW

The Secretary of Health and Human Services (HHS) must—within 180 days of the enactment of the Coronavirus Aid, Relief, and Economic Security Act (P.L. 116-136)—issue guidance on the sharing of patients' protected health information during the COVID-19 public health emergency.

BACKGROUND

Section 264(c) of the Health Insurance Portability and Accountability Act of 1996 (HIPAA) provided the HHS Secretary with authority to promulgate privacy standards that govern:

(1) the rights that an individual who is a subject of individually identifiable health information should have;

(2) the procedures that should be established for the exercise of such rights; and

BACKGROUND

(3) the uses and disclosures of such information that should be authorized or required.

The authority under section 264(c) gave rise to the HIPAA Privacy and Security rules, which established national standards to protect individuals' medical records and other personal health information by requiring covered entities to undertake certain safeguards to secure such information.

NEW LAW EXPLAINED

Requirement to promulgate guidance.—Within 180 days of the enactment of the Coronavirus Aid, Relief, and Economic Security Act (P.L. 116-136), the HHS Secretary must promulgate regulations on the sharing of patients' protected health information under 45 C.F.R. § 160.103 and the regulations enacted under section 264(c) of HIPAA. The guidance must pertain to the sharing of patients' protected health information during the COVID-19 public health emergency and policies that may come into effect during the emergency (Act Sec. 3224 of the CARES Act).

Guidance. The HHS Office for Civil Rights (OCR) has published guidance designed to explain civil rights laws and the HIPAA Privacy Rule in the context of the COVID-19 emergency (HIPAA, Civil Rights, and COVID-19, https://www.hhs.gov/hipaa/for-professionals/special-topics/hipaa-covid19/index.html).

▶ **Effective date.** No specific effective date is provided by the Act. The amendments made by this section are, therefore, considered effective on March 27, 2020, the date of enactment of the CARES Act.

Law source: Law at ¶2085.

— Act Sec. 3224 of the Coronavirus Aid, Relief, and Economic Security Act (P.L. 116-136).

Chapter 5—Tax Credits and Other Payroll Relief

5

¶500 Payroll Credit for Required Paid Sick Leave

SUMMARY OF NEW LAW

An employer is allowed a credit against the Old-Age, Survivors, and Disability Insurance (OASDI) tax or Railroad Retirement Tax Act (RRTA) tax imposed on the employer for each calendar quarter in an amount equal to 100% of the qualified sick leave wages paid by the employer for the calendar quarter, subject to a few limitations. The credit is refundable and can be obtained in advance.

BACKGROUND

Federal employment taxes are imposed on wages paid to employees and include taxes imposed under the Federal Insurance Contributions Act (FICA), the Federal Unemployment Tax Act (FUTA), and the Internal Revenue Code (IRC). In addition, Tier 1 of the Railroad Retirement Tax Act (RRTA) imposes a tax on compensation paid to railroad employees and representatives.

FICA taxes are comprised of two components: OASDI (Social Security) and HI (hospital insurance or Medicare). The Social Security tax rate is 12.4% with half (6.2%) imposed on the employee (Code Sec. 3101(a)) and the other half (6.2%) imposed on the employer (Code Sec. 3111(a)). The tax is assessed on covered wages up to the Social Security wage base ($137,700 in 2020). The Medicare tax rate for employees (Code Sec. 3101(b) and employers (Code Sec. 3111(b)) is 1.45% on all of employees' earnings. An additional 0.9% of Medicare taxes are withheld from employees on earnings above $200,000 ($250,000 for joint filers). Individual income tax rates vary under the IRC (Code Sec. 1).

Employers must withhold the employee portion of FICA taxes (Code Sec. 3101) and personal income tax in accordance with IRS withholding tables or computational procedures (Code Sec. 3402) from paychecks and deposit with the federal government as required by the applicable deposit rules. The employer is liable for the employee portion of FICA taxes, in addition to its own share, whether or not the employer withholds the amount from the employee's wages.

Generally, the term "wages" for tax purposes means all remuneration for "employment," including the cash value of all remuneration (including benefits) paid in any medium other than cash, with certain exceptions. Wages includes salaries, vacation allowances, bonuses, deferred compensation, commissions, and fringe benefits. Sick leave is generally taxed as income and subject to payroll tax withholding. The term "employment" is generally defined as any service, of whatever nature, performed by an employee for the person employing him or her, with certain specific exceptions.

> **Note:** Railroad workers do not participate in the OASDI system. Compensation subject to RRTA tax is exempt from FICA taxes. The RRTA imposes a tax on compensation paid by covered employers to employees in recognition for the performance of services. Employees whose compensation is subject to RRTA are ultimately eligible for railroad retirement benefits that fall under a two-tier structure. Rail employees and employers pay Tier 1 taxes at the same rates as other employment taxes.

NEW LAW EXPLAINED

Payroll credit for required paid sick leave.—An employer is allowed a credit against the employer portion of OASDI (Social Security) tax (Code Sec. 3111(a)) or RRTA (Code Sec. 3221(a)) tax imposed for each calendar quarter in an amount equal to 100% of the qualified sick leave wages paid by the employer with respect to that calendar quarter, subject to the limits described below (Act Sec. 7001(a) of the Families First Coronavirus Response Act (P.L. 116-127)). Qualified sick leave wages are wages as defined in Code Sec. 3121(a)) and compensation as defined in Code Sec. 3231(e) paid

NEW LAW EXPLAINED

by an employer which are required to be paid by reason of the Emergency Paid Sick Leave Act (EPSLA) (Act Sec. 7001(c) of the Families First Act).

Payroll credit limitations. The amount of qualified sick leave wages that an employer may take into account for an employee has some limitations based on different circumstances under which qualified sick leave wages are paid (Act Sec. 7001(b) of the Families First Act).

The amount of qualified sick leave wages taken into account for purposes of the credit may not exceed $511 for any day (or any portion thereof), or $5,110 in the aggregate for each employee, for which the individual is paid sick time because: (1) the employee is subject to a federal, state, or local quarantine or isolation order related to COVID-19; (2) the employee has been advised by a health care provider to self-quarantine due to concerns related to COVID-19; or (3) the employee is experiencing symptoms of COVID-19 and seeking a medical diagnosis (Act Sec. 7001(b)(1) of the Families First Act).

The amount of qualified sick leave wages taken into account may not exceed $200 for any day (or portion thereof), or $2,000 in the aggregate for each employee, for which the individual is paid sick time because: (1) the employee is caring for an individual who is subject to a federal, state, or local quarantine or isolation order; (2) the employee has been advised by a health care provider to self-quarantine; the employee is caring for the employee's son or daughter if the school or place of care of the son or daughter has been closed, or the child care provider is unavailable due to COVID-19 precautions; or (3) the employee is experiencing any other substantially similar condition specified by the Secretary of Health and Human Services in consultation with the Secretary of the Treasury and the Secretary of Labor; (Act Sec. 7001(b)(1) of the Families First Act).

In addition, the aggregate number of qualified sick leave days to be taken into account for the calendar quarter for an employee may not exceed the excess (if any) of 10 over the aggregate number of days so taken into account for all preceding calendar quarters (Act Sec. 7001(b)(2) of the Families First Act).

Medical expense credit increase. The credit is increased by the amount of the employer's qualified health plan expenses as are properly allocable to the qualified sick leave wages for which the credit is allowed (Act Sec. 7001(d) of the Families First Act) (see ¶ 510).

Medicare tax credit increase. In addition, the credit is increased by the amount of the employer's share of Medicare tax (but not for the RRTA Medicare tax) (Act Sec. 7005(b) of the Coronavirus Aid, Relief, and Economic Security Act (P.L. 116-136)) (see ¶ 575).

OASDI and RRTA cap. The credit allowed may not exceed the OASDI tax or RRTA tax imposed on the employer, reduced by any credits allowed for the employment of qualified veterans and the research expenditures of qualified small businesses for that calendar quarter on the wages paid for all the employer's employees (Act Sec. 7001(b)(3) of the Families First Act).

NEW LAW EXPLAINED

Credit is refundable and payable in advance. However, if for any calendar quarter the amount of the credit exceeds the OASDI tax or RRTA tax imposed on the employer, as reduced by any credits taken for the employment of qualified veterans and research expenditures of qualified small businesses, the excess is treated as a refundable overpayment (Act Sec. 7001(b)(4)(A) of the Families First Act, as amended by Act Sec. 3606(a)(1)(A) of the CARES Act).

Employers can get the payroll tax credit in advance. The Secretary of the Treasury (or the Secretary's delegate) is required to issue forms and instructions as are necessary to allow the advance payment of the credit to be calculated through the end of the most recent payroll period in the quarter (Act Sec. 3606(a)(1)(B) of the CARES Act, adding Act Sec. 7001(b)(4)(A)(ii) to the Families First Act). The IRS has issued Form 7200, Advance Payment of Employer Credits Due to Covid-19, together with instructions.

Credit mechanics. The IRS has issued several examples of the mechanics for using the credit (IRS News Release IR-2020-57, March 20, 2020; IRS COVID-19-Related Tax Credits for Required Paid Leave Provided by Small and Midsize Businesses FAQs (https://www.irs.gov/newsroom/covid-19-related-tax-credits-for-required-paid-leave-provided-by-small-and-midsize-businesses-faqs)).

> **Comment:** Before an advance payment can be received, the employer must retain (use up) all available employment taxes including withheld federal income taxes and the employee and employer share of Social Security and Medicare taxes, rather than depositing them with the IRS.

> **Comment:** If the federal employment taxes yet to be deposited are not sufficient to cover the employer's cost of qualified leave wages, plus the allocable qualified health plan expenses and the amount of the employer's share of Medicare tax imposed on those wages, then the employer can file a request for an advance payment from the IRS.

Example 1: An eligible employer pays $10,000 in qualified sick leave wages and qualified family leave wages in Q2 2020. It does not owe the employer's share of Social Security tax on the $10,000, but it will owe $145 for the employer's share of Medicare tax. Its credits equal $10,145, which include the $10,000 in qualified leave wages plus $145 for the eligible employer's share of Medicare tax (this example does not include any qualified health plan expenses allocable to the qualified leave wages). This amount may be applied against any federal employment taxes that the eligible employer is liable for on any wages paid in Q2 2020. Any excess over the federal employment tax liabilities is refunded in accord with normal procedures. The eligible employer must still withhold the employee's share of Social Security and Medicare taxes on the qualified leave wages paid.

Example 2: An eligible employer paid $5,000 in qualified sick leave wages and qualified family leave wages (and allocable health plan expenses and the

NEW LAW EXPLAINED

eligible employer's share of Medicare tax on the qualified leave wages) and is otherwise required to deposit $8,000 in federal employment taxes, including taxes withheld from all of its employees, for wage payments made during the same quarter as the $5,000 in qualified leave wages. The eligible employer may keep up to $5,000 of the $8,000 of taxes the eligible employer was going to deposit, and it will not owe a penalty for keeping the $5,000. The eligible employer is then only required to deposit the remaining $3,000 on its required deposit date. The eligible employer will later account for the $5,000 it retained when it files Form 941, Employer's Quarterly Federal Tax Return, for the quarter.

Example 3: An eligible employer paid $10,000 in qualified leave wages (and allocable qualified health plan expenses and the eligible employer's share of Medicare tax on the qualified leave wages) and is otherwise required to deposit $8,000 in federal employment taxes, including taxes withheld from all of its employees, on wage payments made during the same quarter. The eligible employer can keep the entire $8,000 of taxes that the eligible employer was otherwise required to deposit without penalties as a portion of the credits it is otherwise entitled to claim on Form 941. The eligible employer may file a request for an advance credit for the remaining $2,000 by completing Form 7200.

Deposit penalty waivers. The Secretary of the Treasury (or the Secretary's delegate) will waive any penalty under Code Sec. 6656 for failure to make a deposit of the OASDI or RRTA taxes if the Secretary determines that such failure was due to the anticipation of the new credit allowed (Act Sec. 3606(a)(3) of the CARES Act amending Sec. 7001 of the Families First Act).

Application of law. The law provisions apply for the period that begins on a date within 15 days of the date of enactment (March 18, 2020), prescribed by the Secretary of the Treasury (or the Secretary's delegate), and that ends on December 31, 2020. (Act Sec. 7001(g) of the Families First Act). The IRS has determined that the tax credits for qualified sick leave wages and qualified family leave wages required to be paid will apply to wages paid for the period beginning on April 1, 2020, and ending on December 31, 2020 (IRS Notice 2020-21, IRB 2020-16, April 13, 2020).

Upcoming regulations. The Secretary of the Treasury (or the Secretary's delegate) will be issuing regulations or other guidance to carry out the law including: (1) to prevent the avoidance of the purposes of the limitations; (2) to minimize compliance and record-keeping burdens; (3) providing for waiver of penalties for failure to deposit amounts in anticipation of the allowance of the credit; (4) for recapturing the benefit of credits determined under this provision in cases where there is a subsequent adjustment to the credit; (5) to ensure that the wages taken into account conform with the paid sick time required to be provided under the Emergency Paid Sick Leave Act, and (6) regulations or other guidance to permit the advancement of the credit (Act Sec.

NEW LAW EXPLAINED

7001(f) of the Families First Act, as amended by Act Sec. 3606(a)(2)(C) of the CARES Act).

▶ **Effective date.** No specific effective date is provided. The provisions are, therefore, considered effective on March 18, 2020, the date of enactment of the Families First Coronavirus Response Act (P.L. 116-127). However, the provisions related to overpayments and advance payments of refunds are effective on March 27, 2020, the date of enactment of the Coronavirus Aid, Relief, and Economic Security Act (P.L. 116-136).

Law source: Law at ¶1063 and ¶2124.

— Act Sec. 7001 of the Families First Coronavirus Response Act (P.L. 116-127).

— Act Sec. 7001(g) of the Families First Act.

— Act Sec. 3606(a)(1)(A) of the Coronavirus Aid, Relief, and Economic Security Act (P.L. 116-136), adding Act Sec. 7001(b)(4)(A)(i) of the Families First Act.

— Act Sec. 3606(a)(1)(B) of the CARES Act, adding Act Sec. 7001(b)(4)(A)(ii) of the Families First Act.

— Act Sec. 3606(a)(2)(C) of the CARES Act, adding Act Sec. 7001(f)(6) of the Families First Act.

¶510 Allowance of Required Paid Sick Leave Credit for Certain Health Plan Expenses

SUMMARY OF NEW LAW

The qualified sick leave wage credit will be increased by the amount of an employer's qualified health plan expenses that are properly allocable to the qualified sick leave wages for which the credit is allowed.

BACKGROUND

Currently, employer-paid premiums for health insurance are exempt from federal income and payroll taxes. Employee-paid premiums are excluded from taxable income.

Generally, the term "group health plan" means an employer plan (including a self-insured plan) or a plan contributed to by an employer to provide health care to the employees. In addition, employer-paid expenses related to health insurance (for employees or for dependents) are 100% tax-deductible as ordinary business expenses.

NEW LAW EXPLAINED

Allowance of credit for certain health plan expenses.—The amount of the qualified sick leave wage credit allowed under this law will be increased by the amount of the employer's qualified health plan expenses that are properly allocable to the qualified

NEW LAW EXPLAINED

sick leave wages for which the credit is allowed. The amount of qualified sick leave wages taken into account for purposes of the credit may not exceed $511 for any day (or any portion thereof) for which the individual is paid such sick time. (Act Sec. 7001(d)(1) of the Families First Coronavirus Response Act, P.L. 116-127; Joint Committee on Taxation Report JCX-10-20, Technical Explanation of Division G, Tax Credits For Paid Sick and Paid Family And Medical Leave, of H.R. 6201, March 17, 2020).

Qualified health plan expenses. The term "qualified health plan expenses" means amounts paid or incurred by the employer to provide and maintain a group health plan (as defined in Code Sec. 5000(b)(1)), but only to the extent that such amounts are excluded from the gross income of employees by reason of Code Sec. 106(a) (Act Sec. 7001(d)(2) of the Families First Act).

Allocation rules. Qualified health plan expenses must be allocated to qualified sick leave wages in such manner as the Secretary of the Treasury may prescribe. Except as otherwise provided by the Secretary, the allocation will be treated as properly made if made on a pro rata basis among covered employees and pro rata on the basis of periods of coverage (relative to the time periods of leave to which the wages relate). (Act Sec. 7001(d)(3) of the Families First Act).

Example: Assume an employer claims a credit of $5,510 for $5,110 of qualified sick leave wages and $400 of health plan expenses paid during the quarter. The employer has an offsetting income inclusion amount of $5,510, and the employer may deduct $5,110 of qualified sick leave wages and $400 of health plan expenses. (Joint Committee on Taxation Report JCX-10-20, Technical Explanation of Division G, Tax Credits For Paid Sick and Paid Family And Medical Leave, of H.R. 6201, March 17, 2020).

Comment: The IRS has issued numerous FAQs on the COVID-19-related tax credits. The FAQs explain that eligible employers may claim tax credits for qualified leave wages paid to employees on paid sick leave or expanded family and medical leave for reasons related to COVID-19 for leave taken beginning on April 1, 2020, and ending on December 31, 2020. The eligible employers will claim the credits on their federal employment tax returns (e.g., Form 941, *Employer's Quarterly Federal Tax Return*), but they can benefit more quickly from the credits by reducing their federal employment tax deposits. If there are insufficient federal employment taxes to cover the amount of the credits, an eligible employer may request an advance payment of the credits from the IRS by submitting a Form 7200, *Advance Payment of Employer Credits Due to COVID-19*. The eligible employer will account for the amounts received as an advance when it files its Form 941. The IRS expects to begin processing these requests during April 2020.

Eligible employers claiming the credits for qualified leave wages (and allocable qualified health plan expenses and the eligible employer's share of Medicare taxes), must retain records and documentation related to and supporting each employee's leave to substantiate the claim for the credits, and retain the Forms

NEW LAW EXPLAINED

941, *Employer's Quarterly Federal Tax Return,* and 7200, *Advance Payment of Employer Credits Due To COVID-19,* and any other applicable filings made to the IRS requesting the credit.

These, and other FAQs issued by the IRS can be found at https://www.irs.gov/newsroom/covid-19-related-tax-credits-for-required-paid-leave-provided-by-small-and-midsize-businesses-faqs.

▶ **Effective date.** No specific effective date is provided. The provisions are, therefore, considered effective on March 18, 2020, the date of enactment of the Families First Coronavirus Response Act (P.L. 116-127).

Law source: Law at ¶1063.

— Act Sec. 7001 of the Families First Coronavirus Response Act (P.L. 116-127).

¶520 Special Rules for Required Paid Sick Leave Credit

SUMMARY OF NEW LAW

An employer cannot take both the payroll credit allowed for sick leave against the Old-Age, Survivors, and Disability Insurance (OASDI) tax or Railroad Retirement Tax Act (RRTA) for each calendar quarter under the Families First Act and the current credit allowed under Code Sec. 45S. Employers can elect not to participate. The credit does not apply to governments.

BACKGROUND

Under current law, a general business tax credit is not permitted for sick leave wages under Code Sec. 45S. An eligible employer can generally deduct payments of sick leave wages (and any allocable qualified health plan expenses and the employer's share of the Medicare tax on the qualified wages) as ordinary and necessary business expenses in the tax year that these wages are paid or incurred.

NEW LAW EXPLAINED

Special rules for required paid sick leave.—Qualified sick leave wages are not taken into account for purposes of determining a Code Sec. 45S credit (Act Sec. 7001(e)(1) of the Families First Coronavirus Response Act (P.L. 116-127)). There is no double benefit allowed. However, an employer may be able to take a credit under Code Sec. 45S with respect to any additional wages paid, provided the requirements of Code Sec. 45S are met for any additional wages (Joint Committee on Taxation Report JCX-10-20, Technical Explanation of Division G, Tax Credits For Paid Sick and Paid Sick And Medical Leave, of H.R. 6201, March 17, 2020; COVID-19-Related Tax Credits for Required Paid Leave

NEW LAW EXPLAINED

Provided by Small and Midsize Businesses FAQs (https://www.irs.gov/newsroom/covid-19-related-tax-credits-for-required-paid-leave-provided-by-small-and-midsize-businesses-faqs)).

Employer gross income. If an employer claims a credit, the amount claimed is included in the employer's gross income. The credit is not taken into account for purposes of determining any amount allowable as a payroll tax deduction, deduction for qualified family leave wages, or deduction for health plan expenses (Act Sec. 7001(e)(1) of the Families First Act; Joint Committee on Taxation Report JCX-10-20, Technical Explanation of Division G, Tax Credits For Paid Sick and Paid Family And Medical Leave, of H.R. 6201, March 17, 2020).

Employer income tax deduction. In addition, the employer's income tax deduction for any tax imposed by Code Sec. 3111(a) or Code Sec. 3221(a), the employer's share of OASDI or RRTA tax, for such quarter will not be reduced (Act Sec. 7001(e)(1) of the Families First Act; Joint Committee on Taxation Report JCX-10-20, Technical Explanation of Division G, Tax Credits For Paid Sick and Paid Family And Medical Leave, of H.R. 6201, March 17, 2020).

Employer election. An employer may elect, at such time and in such manner as provided by the Secretary of the Treasury (or the Secretary's delegate), to have the payroll credit for required paid sick leave provision not apply to the employer for a calendar quarter (Act Sec. 7001(e)(2) of the Families First Act).

No government credit. Further, the paid sick leave credit does not apply to the federal government, state governments or their agencies. (Act Sec. 7001(e)(4) of the Families First Act).

Application of law. The law provisions apply for the period that begins on a date within 15 days of the date of enactment (March 18, 2020), prescribed by the Secretary of the Treasury (or the Secretary's delegate), and that ends on December 31, 2020. (Act Sec. 7001(g) of the Families First Act). The IRS has determined that the tax credits for qualified sick leave wages and qualified family leave wages required to be paid will apply to wages paid for the period beginning on April 1, 2020, and ending on December 31, 2020 (IRS Notice 2020-21, IRB 2020-16, April 13, 2020).

▶ **Effective date.** No specific effective date is provided. The provisions are, therefore, considered effective on March 18, 2020, the date of enactment of the Families First Coronavirus Response Act (P.L. 116-127).

Law source: Law at ¶1063.

— Act Sec. 7001(e) of the Families First Coronavirus Response Act (P.L. 116-127).

— Act Sec. 7001(g) of the Families First Act.

¶530 Transfers to Federal Old-Age and Survivors Insurance Trust Fund for Sick Leave Credit

SUMMARY OF NEW LAW

Amounts equal to the reduction in revenues to the Treasury by reason of the payroll credit for paid sick leave will be appropriated to the Federal Old-Age and Survivors Insurance Trust Fund and the Federal Disability Insurance Trust Fund.

BACKGROUND

Federal employment taxes are imposed on wages paid to employees and include taxes imposed under the Federal Insurance Contributions Act (FICA), the Federal Unemployment Tax Act (FUTA), and federal personal income tax under the Internal Revenue Code (IRC). In addition, Tier 1 of the Railroad Retirement Tax Act (RRTA) imposes a tax on compensation paid to railroad employees and representatives.

The employee portion of OASDI taxes must be withheld from paychecks and deposited with the federal government by the employer during the quarter, as required by the applicable deposit rules. The employer is liable for the employee portion of OASDI taxes, in addition to its own share, whether or not the employer withholds the amount from the employee's wages.

NEW LAW EXPLAINED

Transfers to federal Old-Age and Survivors Insurance Trust Fund.—Amounts equal to the reduction in revenues to the Treasury by reason of the payroll credit for paid sick leave will be appropriated to the Federal Old-Age and Survivors Insurance Trust Fund and the Federal Disability Insurance Trust Fund established under Section 201 of the Social Security Act (42 U.S.C. 401) and the Social Security Equivalent Benefit Account established under Section 15A(a) of the Railroad Retirement Act of 1974 (45 U.S.C. 231n-1(a)). The amounts appropriated will be transferred from the general fund at such times and in such manner as to replicate to the extent possible the transfers which would have occurred to such Trust Fund or Account had this section not been enacted. (Act Sec. 7001(h) of the Families First Coronavirus Response Act (P.L. 116-127)).

▶ **Effective date.** No specific effective date is provided. The provisions are, therefore, considered effective on March 18, 2020, the date of enactment of the Families First Coronavirus Response Act (P.L. 116-127).

Law source: Law at ¶1063.

— Act Sec. 7001(h) of the Families First Coronavirus Response Act (P.L. 116-127).

¶540 Payroll Credit for Required Paid Family Leave

SUMMARY OF NEW LAW

An employer is allowed a credit against the Old-Age, Survivors, and Disability Insurance (OASDI) tax or Railroad Retirement Tax Act (RRTA) tax imposed on the employer for each calendar quarter in an amount equal to 100% of the qualified family leave wages paid by the employer for the calendar quarter, subject to a few limitations. The credit is refundable and can be obtained in advance.

BACKGROUND

Federal employment taxes are imposed on wages paid to employees and include taxes imposed under the Federal Insurance Contributions Act (FICA), the Federal Unemployment Tax Act (FUTA), and the Internal Revenue Code (IRC). In addition, Tier 1 of the Railroad Retirement Tax Act (RRTA) imposes a tax on compensation paid to railroad employees and representatives.

FICA taxes are comprised of two components: OASDI (Social Security) and HI (hospital insurance or Medicare). The Social Security tax rate is 12.4% with half (6.2%) imposed on the employee (Code Sec. 3101(a)) and the other half (6.2%) imposed on the employer (Code Sec. 3111(a)). The tax is assessed on covered wages up to the Social Security wage base ($137,700 in 2020). The Medicare tax rate for employees (Code Sec. 3101(b)) and employers (Code Sec. 3111(b)) is 1.45% on all of employees' earnings. An additional 0.9% of Medicare taxes are withheld from employees on earnings above $200,000 ($250,000 for joint filers). Individual income tax rates vary under the IRC (Code Sec. 1).

Employers must withhold the employee portion of FICA taxes (Code Sec. 3101) and personal income tax in accordance with IRS withholding tables or computational procedures (Code Sec. 3402) from paychecks and deposit with the federal government as required by the applicable deposit rules. The employer is liable for the employee portion of FICA taxes, in addition to its own share, whether or not the employer withholds the amount from the employee's wages.

Generally, the term "wages" for tax purposes means all remuneration for "employment," including the cash value of all remuneration (including benefits) paid in any medium other than cash, with certain exceptions. Wages includes salaries, vacation allowances, bonuses, deferred compensation, commissions, and fringe benefits. The term "employment" is generally defined as any service, of whatever nature, performed by an employee for the person employing him or her, with certain specific exceptions.

> **Note:** Railroad workers do not participate in the OASDI system, and compensation subject to RRTA tax is exempt from FICA taxes. The RRTA imposes a tax on compensation paid by covered employers to employees in recognition for the performance of services. Employees whose compensation is subject to RRTA are ultimately eligible for railroad retirement benefits that fall under a two-tier

BACKGROUND

structure. Rail employees and employers pay Tier 1 taxes. The Tier 1 tax rates are the same as the FICA rates.

NEW LAW EXPLAINED

Payroll credit for required paid family leave.—An employer is allowed a credit against the employer portion of OASDI (Social Security) tax (Code Sec. 3111(a)) or RRTA (Code Sec. 3221(a)) tax imposed for each calendar quarter in an amount equal to 100% of the qualified family leave wages paid by the employer with respect to that calendar quarter, subject to the limits described below (Act Sec. 7003(a) of the Families First Coronavirus Response Act (P.L. 116-127)). Qualified family leave wages are defined as wages defined in Code Sec. 3121(a) and compensation defined in Code Sec. 3231(e) paid by an employer which are required to be paid by reason of the Emergency Family and Medical Leave Expansion Act (EFMLEA) (Act Sec. 7003(c) of the Families First Act). The credit does not apply to the RRTA Medicare tax.

Payroll credit limitations. The amount of qualified family leave wages that an employer may take into account for an employee has some limitations (Act Sec. 7003(b) of the Families First Act).

The amount of qualified family leave wages taken into account for each employee cannot exceed $200 for any day (or portion thereof) for which the employee is paid qualified family leave wages and $10,000 in the aggregate with respect to all calendar quarters (Act Secs. 7003(b)(1)(A) and (B) of the Families First Act).

Medical expense credit increase. The credit is increased by the amount of the employer's qualified health plan expenses as are properly allocable to the qualified family leave wages for which the credit is allowed (Act Sec. 7003(d) of the Families First Act) (see ¶ 550).

Medicare tax credit increase. In addition, the credit is increased by the amount of the employer's share of Medicare tax (but not for the RRTA Medicare tax) (Act Sec. 7005(b) of the Families First Act) (see ¶ 575).

OASDI and RRTA cap. The credit allowed may not exceed the OASDI tax or RRTA tax imposed on the employer (reduced by any credits allowed for the employment of qualified veterans, the research expenditures of qualified small businesses, and required paid sick leave for that calendar quarter) on the wages paid for all the employer's employees (Act Sec. 7003(b)(2) of the Families First Act).

Credit is refundable and payable in advance. However, if for any calendar quarter the amount of the credit exceeds the OASDI tax or RRTA tax imposed on the employer, as reduced by any credits taken for the employment of qualified veterans, research expenditures of qualified small businesses, and required paid sick leave, the excess is treated as a refundable overpayment (Act Sec. 7003(b)(3) of the Families First Act, as amended by Act Sec. 3606(b)(1)(A) of the Coronavirus Aid, Relief, and Economic Security Act (P.L. 116-136)).

NEW LAW EXPLAINED

Employers can get the payroll tax credit in advance. The Secretary of the Treasury (or the Secretary's delegate) is required to issue forms and instructions as are necessary to allow the advance payment of the credit to be calculated through the end of the most recent payroll period in the quarter (Act Sec. 3606(b)(1)(B) of the CARES Act, adding Act Sec. 7003(b)(3)(B) to the Families First Act). The IRS has issued Form 7200, *Advance Payment of Employer Credits Due to Covid-19*, together with instructions.

Credit mechanics. The IRS has issued several examples of the mechanics for using the credit (IRS News Release IR-2020-57, March 20, 2020; IRS COVID-19-Related Tax Credits for Required Paid Leave Provided by Small and Midsize Businesses FAQs (https://www.irs.gov/newsroom/covid-19-related-tax-credits-for-required-paid-leave-provided-by-small-and-midsize-businesses-faqs, March 31, 2020)).

> **Comment:** Before an advance payment can be received, the employer must retain (use up) all available employment taxes including withheld federal income taxes and the employee and employer share of share of Social Security and Medicare taxes, rather than depositing them with the IRS.

> **Comment:** If the federal employment taxes yet to be deposited are not sufficient to cover the employer's cost of qualified leave wages, plus the allocable qualified health plan expenses and the amount of the employer's share of Medicare tax imposed on those wages, then the employer can file a request for an advance payment from the IRS.

Example 1: An eligible employer pays $10,000 in qualified sick leave wages and qualified family leave wages in Q2 2020. It does not owe the employer's share of Social Security tax on the $10,000, but it will owe $145 for the employer's share of Medicare tax. Its credits equal $10,145, which include the $10,000 in qualified leave wages plus $145 for the eligible employer's share of Medicare tax (this example does not include any qualified health plan expenses allocable to the qualified leave wages). This amount may be applied against any federal employment taxes that the eligible employer is liable for on any wages paid in Q2 2020. Any excess over the federal employment tax liabilities is refunded in accordance with normal procedures. The eligible employer must still withhold the employee's share of Social Security and Medicare taxes on the qualified leave wages paid.

Example 2: An eligible employer paid $5,000 in qualified sick leave wages and qualified family leave wages (and allocable health plan expenses and the eligible employer's share of Medicare tax on the qualified leave wages) and is otherwise required to deposit $8,000 in federal employment taxes, including taxes withheld from all of its employees, for wage payments made during the same quarter as the $5,000 in qualified leave wages. The eligible employer may keep up to $5,000 of the $8,000 of taxes the eligible employer was going to deposit, and it will not owe a penalty for keeping the $5,000. The eligible

NEW LAW EXPLAINED

employer is then only required to deposit the remaining $3,000 on its required deposit date. The eligible employer will later account for the $5,000 it retained when it files Form 941, Employer's Quarterly Federal Tax Return, for the quarter.

Example 3: An eligible employer paid $10,000 in qualified leave wages (and allocable qualified health plan expenses and the eligible employer's share of Medicare tax on the qualified leave wages) and is otherwise required to deposit $8,000 in federal employment taxes, including taxes withheld from all of its employees on wage payments made during the same quarter. The eligible employer can keep the entire $8,000 of taxes that the eligible employer was otherwise required to deposit without penalties as a portion of the credits it is otherwise entitled to claim on the Form 941. The eligible employer may file a request for an advance credit for the remaining $2,000 by completing Form 7200.

Deposit penalty waivers. The Secretary of the Treasury (or the Secretary's delegate) will waive any penalty under Code Sec. 6656 for failure to make a deposit of the OASDI or RRTA taxes if the Secretary determines that such failure was due to the anticipation of the new credit (Act Sec. 3606(c) of the CARES Act, adding Act Sec. 7003(i) to the Families First Act).

Application of law. The law provisions apply for the period that begins on a date within 15 days of the date of enactment (March 18, 2020), prescribed by the Secretary of the Treasury (or the Secretary's delegate), and that ends on December 31, 2020 (Act Sec. 7003(g) of the Families First Act). The IRS has determined that the tax credits for qualified sick leave wages and qualified family leave wages required to be paid will apply to wages paid for the period beginning on April 1, 2020, and ending on December 31, 2020 (IRS Notice 2020-21, IRB 2020-16, April 13, 2020).

Upcoming regulations. The Secretary of the Treasury (or the Secretary's delegate) will be issuing regulations or other guidance to carry out the law including: (1) to prevent the avoidance of the purposes of the limitations; (2) to minimize compliance and record-keeping burdens; (3) providing for waiver of penalties for failure to deposit amounts in anticipation of the allowance of the credit; (4) for recapturing the benefit of credits determined under this provision in cases where there is a subsequent adjustment to the credit; (5) to ensure that the wages taken into account conform with the paid family time required to be provided under the Emergency Family and Medical Leave Expansion Act, and (6) regulations or other guidance to permit the advancement of the credit (Act Sec. 7003(f) of the Families First Act and Act Sec. 3606(b)(2)(C) of the CARES Act, adding Act Sec. 7003(f)(6) to Sec. 7003(f) of the Families First Act).

▶ **Effective date.** No specific effective date is provided. The provisions are, therefore, considered effective on March 18, 2020, the date of enactment of the Families First Coronavirus Response Act (P.L. 116-127). However, the provisions related to overpay-

NEW LAW EXPLAINED

ments and advance payments of refunds are effective on March 27, 2020, the date of enactment of the Coronavirus Aid, Relief, and Economic Security Act (P.L. 116-136).

Law source: Law at ¶1063, ¶1065, and ¶2124.

— Act Sec. 7003 of the Families First Coronavirus Response Act (P.L. 116-127).

— Act Sec. 7005(b) of the Families First Act.

— Act Sec. 3606(b)(1)(A) of the Coronavirus Aid, Relief, and Economic Security Act (P.L. 116-136), amending Act Sec. 7003(b) of the Families First Act.

— Act Sec. 3606(b)(1)(B) of the CARES Act, adding Act Sec. 7003(b)(3)(B) to the Families First Act.

— Act Sec. 3606(b)(2)(C) of the CARES Act, adding Act Sec. 7003(f)(6) to the Families First Act.

— Act Sec. 3606(c) of the CARES Act, adding Act Sec. 7003(i) to the Families First Act.

¶550 Allowance of Required Family Leave Credit for Certain Health Plan Expenses

SUMMARY OF NEW LAW

The amount of the family leave credit will be increased by the amount that the employer's qualified health plan expenses are properly allocable to the qualified family leave wages for which the credit is allowed.

BACKGROUND

Currently, employer-paid premiums for health insurance are exempt from federal income and payroll taxes. Employee-paid premiums are excluded from taxable income.

Generally, the term "group health plan" means an employer plan (including a self-insured plan) or a plan contributed to by an employer to provide health care to the employees. In addition, employer-paid expenses related to health insurance (for employees or for dependents) are 100% tax-deductible as ordinary business expenses.

NEW LAW EXPLAINED

Allowance of credit for certain health plan expenses.—The amount of the family leave credit will be increased by the amount that the employer's qualified health plan expenses are properly allocable to the qualified family leave wages for which the credit is allowed (Act Sec. 7003(d)(1) of the Families First Coronavirus Response Act, P.L. 116-127).

NEW LAW EXPLAINED

Qualified health plan expenses. "Qualified health plan expenses" means amounts paid or incurred by the employer to provide and maintain a group health plan (as defined in Code Sec. 5000(b)(1)), but only to the extent that the amounts are excluded from the gross income of employees by reason of Code Sec. 106(a) (Act Sec. 7003(d)(2) of the Families First Act).

Allocation rules. Qualified health plan expenses will be allocated to qualified family leave wages in such manner as the Secretary of the Treasury may prescribe. Except as otherwise provided by the Secretary, such allocation will be treated as properly made if it is made on a pro rata basis among covered employees and pro rata on the basis of periods of coverage (relative to the time periods of leave to which the wages relate) (Act Sec. 7003(d)(3) of the Families First Act).

> **Comment:** The IRS has issued numerous FAQs on the COVID-19-related tax credits. The FAQs explain that eligible employers may claim tax credits for qualified leave wages paid to employees on paid sick leave or expanded family and medical leave for reasons related to COVID-19 for leave taken beginning on April 1, 2020 and ending on December 31, 2020. Eligible employers will claim the credits on their federal employment tax returns (e.g., Form 941, *Employer's Quarterly Federal Tax Return*), but they can benefit more quickly from the credits by reducing their federal employment tax deposits. If there are insufficient federal employment taxes to cover the amount of the credits, an eligible employer may request an advance payment of the credits from the IRS by submitting a Form 7200, *Advance Payment of Employer Credits Due to COVID-19*. The eligible employer will account for the amounts received as an advance when it files its Form 941. The IRS expects to begin processing these requests during April 2020.
>
> Eligible employers claiming the credits for qualified leave wages (and allocable qualified health plan expenses and the eligible employer's share of Medicare taxes) must retain records and documentation related to and supporting each employee's leave to substantiate the claim for the credits, and retain the Forms 941, *Employer's Quarterly Federal Tax Return*, and 7200, *Advance Payment of Employer Credits Due To COVID-19*, and any other applicable filings made to the IRS requesting the credit.
>
> These, and other FAQs issued by the IRS can be found at https://www.irs.gov/newsroom/covid-19-related-tax-credits-for-required-paid-leave-provided-by-small-and-midsize-businesses-faqs.

▶ **Effective date.** No specific effective date is provided. The provisions are, therefore, considered effective on March 18, 2020, the date of enactment of the Families First Coronavirus Response Act (P.L. 116-127).

Law source: Law at ¶1065.

— Act Sec. 7003(d) of the Families First Coronavirus Response Act (P.L. 116-127).

¶560 Special Rules for Required Paid Family Leave Credit

SUMMARY OF NEW LAW

An employer cannot take both the payroll credit allowed for family leave against the Old-Age, Survivors, and Disability Insurance (OASDI) tax or Railroad Retirement Tax Act (RRTA) for each calendar quarter under the Families First Act and the current credit allowed under Code Sec. 45S. Employers can elect not to participate. The credit does not apply to governments.

BACKGROUND

Currently, a general business tax credit is available for employers for paid leave provided under the Family and Medical Leave Act (FMLA) (Tax Cuts and Jobs Act (P.L. 115-97), adding Code Sec. 45S). An eligible employer is allowed the FMLA credit in an amount equal to the applicable percentage of the wages paid to qualifying employees during the period in which such employees are on leave (see IRS Notice 2018-71, IRB 2018-41, September 24, 2018).

A general business tax credit is available for employers for paid leave provided under the Family and Medical Leave Act (FMLA) (Tax Cuts and Jobs Act (P.L. 115-97), adding Code Sec. 45S). An eligible employer is allowed the FMLA credit in an amount equal to the applicable percentage of the wages paid to qualifying employees during the period in which such employees are on leave (see IRS Notice 2018-71, IRB 2018-41, September 24, 2018). The credit is equal to 12.5% of wages paid to qualifying employees during any period in which such employees are on leave under the FMLA provided that the rate of payment is 50% of the wages normally paid to the employee. The Taxpayer Certainty and Disaster Tax Relief Act of 2019, which was contained in the Further Consolidated Appropriations Act (P.L. 116-94), extended the credit until December 31, 2020.

NEW LAW EXPLAINED

Special rules for required paid family leave credit.—An employer that takes into account qualified leave wages for the applicable paid family leave credit cannot take those wages into account for the employer credit for certain paid family and medical leave under Code Sec. 45S (Act Sec. 7003(e)(1) of the Families First Coronavirus Response Act (P.L. 116-127)). An employer may not claim a credit under Code Sec. 45S for the qualified family leave wages but may be able to take a credit under Code Sec. 45S with respect to any additional wages paid, provided the requirements of Code Sec. 45S are met for any additional wages (Joint Committee on Taxation Report JCX-10-20, Technical Explanation of Division G, Tax Credits For Paid Sick and Paid Family And Medical Leave, of H.R. 6201, March 17, 2020; COVID-19-Related Tax Credits for Required Paid Leave Provided by Small and Midsize Businesses FAQs (https://

NEW LAW EXPLAINED

www.irs.gov/newsroom/covid-19-related-tax-credits-for-required-paid-leave-provided-by-small-and-midsize-businesses-faqs)).

Employer gross income. If an employer claims a credit, the amount claimed is included in the employer's gross income. The credit is not taken into account for purposes of determining any amount allowable as a payroll tax deduction, deduction for qualified sick leave wages, or deduction for health plan expenses (Act Sec. 7003(e)(1) of the Families First Act; Joint Committee on Taxation Report JCX-10-20, Technical Explanation of Division G, Tax Credits For Paid Sick and Paid Sick And Medical Leave, of H.R. 6201, March 17, 2020).

Employer income tax deduction. In addition, the employer's income tax deduction for any tax imposed by Code Sec. 3111(a) or Code Sec. 3221(a), the employer's share of OASDI or RRTA tax, for a quarter will not be reduced (Joint Committee on Taxation Report JCX-10-20, Technical Explanation of Division G, Tax Credits For Paid Sick and Paid Sick And Medical Leave, of H.R. 6201, March 17, 2020).

Employer election. An employer may elect, at such time and in such manner as provided by the Secretary of the Treasury (or the Secretary's delegate), to have the provision not apply to the employer for a calendar quarter (Act Sec. 7003(e)(2) of the Families First Act).

No government credit. Further, the family leave credit does not apply to the federal government, state governments or their political subdivisions, or their respective agencies (Act Sec. 7003(e)(4) of the Families First Act).

Application of law. The provisions apply for the period that begins on a date within 15 days of the date of enactment (March 18, 2020), prescribed by the Secretary of the Treasury (or the Secretary's delegate), and that ends on December 31, 2020 (Act Sec. 7003(g) of the Families First Act). The IRS has determined that the tax credits for qualified sick leave wages and qualified family leave wages required to be paid will apply to wages paid for the period beginning on April 1, 2020, and ending on December 31, 2020 (IRS Notice 2020-21, IRB 2020-16, April 13, 2020).

▶ **Effective date.** No specific effective date is provided. The provisions are, therefore, considered effective on March 18, 2020, the date of enactment of the Families First Coronavirus Response Act (P.L. 116-127).

Law source: Law at ¶1065.

— Act Sec. 7003(e) of the Families First Coronavirus Response Act (P.L. 116-127).

— Act Sec. 7003(g) of the Families First Act.

¶570 Transfers to Federal Old-Age and Survivors Insurance Trust Fund for Family Leave Credit

SUMMARY OF NEW LAW

Amounts equal to the reduction in revenues to the Treasury by reason of the payroll credit for required paid family leave will be appropriated to the Federal Old-Age and Survivors Insurance Trust Fund and the Federal Disability Insurance Trust Fund.

BACKGROUND

Federal employment taxes are imposed on wages paid to employees and include taxes imposed under the Federal Insurance Contributions Act (FICA), the Federal Unemployment Tax Act (FUTA), and federal personal income tax under the Internal Revenue Code (IRC). In addition, Tier 1 of the Railroad Retirement Tax Act (RRTA) imposes a tax on compensation paid to railroad employees and representatives.

The employee portion of OASDI taxes must be withheld from paychecks and deposited with the federal government by the employer during the quarter, as required by the applicable deposit rules. The employer is liable for the employee portion of OASDI taxes, in addition to its own share, whether or not the employer withholds the amount from the employee's wages.

NEW LAW EXPLAINED

Transfers to Federal Old-Age and Survivors Insurance Trust Fund.—Amounts equal to the reduction in revenues to the Treasury by reason of the payroll credit for required paid family leave will be appropriated to the Federal Old-Age and Survivors Insurance Trust Fund and the Federal Disability Insurance Trust Fund established under Section 201 of the Social Security Act (42 U.S.C. 401) and the Social Security Equivalent Benefit Account established under Section 15A(a) of the Railroad Retirement Act of 1974 (45 U.S.C. 231n-1(a)). These appropriated amounts will be transferred from the general fund at such times and in such manner as to replicate to the extent possible the transfers which would have occurred to such Trust Fund or Account had this section not been enacted (Act Sec. 7003(h) of the Families First Coronavirus Response Act (P.L. 116-127)).

▶ **Effective date.** No specific effective date is provided. The provisions are, therefore, considered effective on March 18, 2020, the date of enactment of the Families First Coronavirus Response Act (P.L. 116-127).

Law source: Law at ¶1065.

— Act Sec. 7003(h) of the Families First Coronavirus Response Act (P.L. 116-127).

¶575 Special Rule Related to Tax on Employers

SUMMARY OF NEW LAW

The employer portion of Social Security (FICA) or railroad retirement (RRTA) taxes will not be collected from employers from sick or family leave paid under the Families First Act.

BACKGROUND

Federal employment taxes are imposed on wages paid to employees and include taxes imposed under the Federal Insurance Contributions Act (FICA), the Federal Unemployment Tax Act (FUTA), and the Internal Revenue Code (IRC). In addition, Tier 1 of the Railroad Retirement Tax Act (RRTA) imposes a tax on compensation paid to railroad employees and representatives.

FICA taxes are comprised of two components: OASDI (Social Security) and HI (hospital insurance or Medicare). The Social Security tax rate is 12.4% with half (6.2%) imposed on the employee (Code Sec. 3101(a)) and the other half (6.2%) imposed on the employer (Code Sec. 3111(a)). The tax is assessed on covered wages up to the Social Security wage base ($137,700 in 2020). The Medicare tax rate for employees (Code Sec. 3101(b) and employers (Code Sec. 3111(b)) is 1.45% on all of employees' earnings. An additional 0.9% of Medicare taxes are withheld from employees on earnings above $200,000 ($250,000 for joint filers). Individual income tax rates vary under the IRC (Code Sec. 1).

Employers must withhold the employee portion of FICA taxes (Code Sec. 3101) and personal income tax in accordance with IRS withholding tables or computational procedures (Code Sec. 3402) from paychecks and deposited with the federal government as required by the applicable deposit rules. The employer is liable for the employee portion of FICA taxes, in addition to its own share, whether or not the employer withholds the amount from the employee's wages.

> **Note:** Railroad workers do not participate in the OASDI system, and compensation subject to RRTA tax is exempt from FICA taxes. The RRTA imposes a tax on compensation paid by covered employers to employees in recognition for the performance of services. Employees whose compensation is subject to RRTA are ultimately eligible for railroad retirement benefits that fall under a two-tier structure. Rail employees and employers pay Tier 1 taxes. The Tier 1 tax rates are the same as the FICA rates.

NEW LAW EXPLAINED

Special rule related to tax on employers.— Any wages or compensation required to be paid to employees by reason of the Emergency Family and Medical Leave Expansion Act and the Emergency Paid Sick Leave Act are not considered wages of the employer for purposes of FICA tax or compensation for purposes of RRTA tax. Thus, no federal employment taxes will be collected on such amounts from employers to be contributed

NEW LAW EXPLAINED

to the OASDI or railroad retirement programs (Act Sec. 7005(a) of the Families First Coronavirus Response Act (P.L. 116-127)).

> **Comment:** Although the JCX Committee Report states no federal employment taxes will be collected on such amounts from employers *or employees* to be contributed to the OASDI or railroad retirement funds, the recently released IRS FAQs make it clear that no federal employment taxes will be collected from only the employer portion (IRS COVID-19-Related Tax Credits for Required Paid Leave Provided by Small and Midsize Businesses FAQs (https://www.irs.gov/newsroom/covid-19-related-tax-credits-for-required-paid-leave-provided-by-small-and-midsize-businesses-faqs, March 31, 2020). Questions 55 and 57 of IRS FAQ state:
>
> *55. Should Eligible Employers withhold federal employment taxes on qualified leave wages paid to employees?*
>
> Yes. Qualified leave wages are wages subject to withholding of federal income tax and the employee's share of Social Security and Medicare taxes. Qualified leave wages are also considered wages for purposes of other benefits that the Eligible Employer provides, such as contributions to 401(k) plans.
>
> *57. Are qualified sick leave wages and qualified family leave wages taxable to employees?*
>
> Yes. Under sections 7001(c) and 7003(c) of the FFCRA, qualified leave wages are wages as defined in section 3121(a) of the Internal Revenue Code (the "Code") and compensation as defined in section 3231(e) of the Code, so the employee must pay Social Security and Medicare taxes (and for railroad employees, Tier II of the Railroad Retirement Tax Act tax). In addition, wages are generally compensation for services subject to income tax under section 61 of the Code and federal income tax withholding under section 3402 of the Code unless an exception applies. The FFCRA did not include an exception for qualified leave wages from income.

Allowance of credit for hospital insurance (Medicare). The amount of the credit allowed is increased by the amount of tax imposed by Code Sec. 3111(b) (employer-share of Medicare), which is 1.45%, on qualified sick leave wages or qualified family leave wages (Act Sec. 7005(b)(1) of the Families First Act; Joint Committee on Taxation Report JCX-10-20, Technical Explanation of Division G, Tax Credits for Paid Sick and Paid Sick and Medical Leave, of H.R. 6201, March 17, 2020). (See ¶520 and ¶560).

No double benefit. The no-double-benefit rule applies for purposes of the credit increase (Act Sec. 7005(b)(2) of the Families First Act; Joint Committee on Taxation Report JCX-10-20, Technical Explanation of Division G, Tax Credits for Paid Sick and Paid Sick and Medical Leave, of H.R. 6201, March 17, 2020). (See ¶520 and ¶560).

Transfers to OASDI. Amounts will be transferred to the Federal Old-Age and Survivors Insurance Trust Fund, the Federal Disability Insurance Trust Fund, and the Social Security Equivalent Benefit Account from Treasury's general fund in an amount equal to the reduction in revenues to the Treasury resulting from not treating such paid emergency sick leave and emergency family and medical leave as wages or compensation for employment tax purposes. The amounts are to be transferred from

NEW LAW EXPLAINED

the general fund at such times and in such manner as to replicate, to the extent possible, the transfers which would have occurred to such Trust Fund or Account had the provision not been enacted. (Act Sec. 7005(c) of the Families First Act). (See ¶530 and ¶570).

▶ **Effective date.** No specific effective date is provided. The provisions are, therefore, considered effective on March 18, 2020, the date of enactment of the Families First Coronavirus Response Act (P.L. 116-127).

Law source: Law at ¶1067.

— Act Sec. 7005 of the Families First Coronavirus Response Act (P.L. 116-127).

¶580 Exclusion for Certain Employer Payments of Student Loans

SUMMARY OF NEW LAW

Certain payments made by an employer on a qualified student loan of an employee before January 1, 2021, are excluded from the employee's gross income. The payments can be made to either the employee or a lender to be applied to the employee's student loans and could cover principal or interest.

BACKGROUND

Currently, employers can provide employees with up to $5,250 per employee per year in educational assistance for tuition, fees, and related supplies. Amounts paid by an employer for qualified educational assistance to an employee are excluded from the employee's gross income and are not subject to income tax withholding, Federal Insurance Contributions Act (FICA), or Federal Unemployment Tax Act (FUTA) taxes. The exclusion for employer-provided educational assistance, which had expired and then been extended retroactively by Congress several times over the years, has been made permanent to apply to expenses paid by an employer for both undergraduate and graduate level courses beginning after December 31, 2001.

The term "educational assistance" means the payment, by an employer, of expenses incurred by or on behalf of an employee for education of the employee (including, but not limited to, tuition, fees, and similar payments, books, supplies, and equipment).

NEW LAW EXPLAINED

Certain employer student loan payments excluded from income.—Payments made before January 1, 2021, by an employer to either an employee or a lender to be applied toward an employee's student loans can be excluded from the employee's income in

NEW LAW EXPLAINED

response to the COVID-19 crisis (Code Sec. 127(c)(1)(B), as added by Act Sec. 2206(a) of the Coronavirus Aid, Relief, and Economic Security Act (CARES Act) (P.L. 116-136). The payments can be of principal or interest on any qualified education loan, as defined in Code Sec. 221(d)(1), that is incurred by the employee for the employee's education.

An employer may pay up to $5,250 each tax year toward an employee's student loans, and that amount would be excludable from the employee's income (Code Sec. 127(a)(2)). The $5,250 cap applies to the new benefit for student loan repayment assistance and other educational assistance already provided, such as for tuition, fees, and books. Any excess of benefits is subject to income and employment taxes.

Denial of double benefit. An employee may not take a personal income tax deduction under Code Sec. 221 for student loan interest payments paid by the employer under the new provision that are excluded from the employee's gross income (Code Sec. 221(e), as amended by Act Sec. 2206(b) of the CARES Act).

> **Comment:** Although an employee cannot claim a student loan interest deduction for the payments paid by the employer, an employer can target the benefit by paying the principal and letting the employee pay the interest.

▶ **Effective date.** The provision applies to any student loan payment made by an employer after March 27, 2020, the date of enactment (Act Sec. 2206(c) of the Coronavirus Aid, Relief, and Economic Security Act (P.L. 116-136)).

Law source: Law at ¶2045, ¶5002, and ¶5004.

— Act Sec. 2206 of the Coronavirus Aid, Relief, and Economic Security Act (P.L. 116-136).

— Act Sec. 2206(a) of the CARES Act, amending Code Sec. 127(c)(1).

— Act Sec. 2206(b) of the CARES Act, amending Code Sec. 221(e).

— Act Sec. 2206(c) of the CARES Act, providing the effective date.

¶590 Employee Retention Credit for Employers Subject to Closure Due to COVID-19

SUMMARY OF NEW LAW

To encourage employers to keep employees on their payroll during the COVID-19 crisis, the employee retention credit is a refundable tax credit against the Old-Age, Survivors, and Disability Insurance (OASDI) tax or Railroad Retirement Tax Act (RRTA) tax imposed on the employer for each calendar quarter equal to 50% of the qualified wages an eligible employer pays to employees after March 12, 2020, and before January 1, 2021.

BACKGROUND

The Coronavirus Aid, Relief, and Economic Security Act (P.L. 116-136) is designed to encourage eligible employers to keep employees on their payroll, despite experiencing economic hardship related to COVID-19, with an employee retention tax credit.

Federal employment taxes are imposed on wages paid to employees and include taxes imposed under the Federal Insurance Contributions Act (FICA), the Federal Unemployment Tax Act (FUTA), and the Internal Revenue Code (IRC). In addition, Tier 1 of the Railroad Retirement Tax Act (RRTA) imposes a tax on compensation paid to railroad employees and representatives.

FICA taxes are comprised of two components: OASDI (Social Security) and HI (hospital insurance or Medicare). The Social Security tax rate is 12.4% with half (6.2%) imposed on the employee (Code Sec. 3101(a)) and the other half (6.2%) imposed on the employer (Code Sec. 3111(a)). The tax is assessed on covered wages up to the Social Security wage base ($137,700 in 2020). The Medicare tax rate for employees (Code Sec. 3101(b) and employers (Code Sec. 3111(b)) is 1.45% on all of employees' earnings. An additional 0.9% of Medicare taxes are withheld from employees on earnings above $200,000 ($250,000 for joint filers). Individual income tax rates vary under the IRC (Code Sec. 1).

Employers must withhold the employee portion of FICA taxes (Code Sec. 3101) and personal income tax in accordance with IRS withholding tables or computational procedures (Code Sec. 3402) from paychecks and deposited with the federal government as required by the applicable deposit rules. The employer is liable for the employee portion of FICA taxes, in addition to its own share, whether or not the employer withholds the amount from the employee's wages.

> **Note:** Railroad workers do not participate in the OASDI system, and compensation subject to RRTA tax is exempt from FICA taxes. The RRTA imposes a tax on compensation paid by covered employers to employees in recognition for the performance of services. Employees whose compensation is subject to RRTA are ultimately eligible for railroad retirement benefits that fall under a two-tier structure. Rail employees and employers pay Tier 1 taxes. The Tier 1 tax rates are the same as the FICA rates.

Current retention credits. This is not the first time retention credits have been allowed. Employers whose businesses were destroyed in disaster zones and who were in a federally declared disaster zone can claim an employee retention credit equal to 40% of the wages up to $6,000 paid to each affected employee during the applicable time frame:

- Hurricane Harvey Disaster Zone (August 23, 2017 - December 31, 2017)
- Hurricane Irma Disaster Zone (September 4, 2017 - December 31, 2017)
- Hurricane Maria Disaster Zone (September 16, 2017 - December 31, 2017)
- California Wildfires Disaster Zone (October 8, 2017 -December 31, 2017)
- California Wildfires Disaster Zone (December 4, 2017 -December 31, 2017)
- Employers in qualified 2018 or 2019 Disaster Zones (states and dates differ)

BACKGROUND

Most recently, the Disaster Tax Relief and Airport and Airway Extension Act of 2017 (P.L. 115-63) signed on September 29, 2017, created the employee retention credits for employers affected by Hurricane Harvey, Irma, or Maria.

Employers use Form 5884-A, Employee Retention Credit and Instructions (Rev. March 2020) for these credits. The instructions list all the disaster areas.

NEW LAW EXPLAINED

Employee retention credit for employers subject to closure due to COVID-19.— An employer is allowed a credit against the employer portion of OASDI (Social Security) tax (Code Sec. 3111(a)) or RRTA (Code Sec. 3221(a)) tax imposed for each calendar quarter in an amount equal to 50% of the qualified wages an eligible employer pays to employees, subject to the limits described below (Act Sec. 2301(a) and (c)(1) of the Coronavirus Aid, Relief, and Economic Security Act (P.L. 116-136)).

The employee retention credit applies only to wages paid after March 12, 2020, and before January 1, 2021 (Act Sec. 2301(m) of the CARES Act). Thus, an eligible employer may be able to claim the credit for qualified wages paid as early as March 13, 2020. The credit is not available for wages paid after December 31, 2020 (IRS FAQs: Employee Retention Credit under the CARES Act (https://www.irs.gov/newsroom/faqs-employee-retention-credit-under-the-cares-act)).

Retention credit limitations. The amount of wages that an employer may take into account for an employee has some limitations. The amount of wages for all calendar quarters cannot exceed $10,000 (Act Sec. 2301(b)(1) of the CARES Act).

Wages. The term "wages" means wages as defined in Code Sec. 3121(a) and compensation as defined in Code Sec. 3231(e) (Act Sec. 2301(c)(5) of the CARES Act).

Qualified wages. The definition of qualified wages depends on the average number of full-time employees as defined in Code Sec. 4980H.

If the eligible employer averaged more than 100 full-time employees in 2019, qualified wages are the wages paid to an employee for time that the employee is **not providing services** due to either (1) a full or partial suspension of operations by order of a governmental authority due to COVID-19, or (2) a significant decline in gross receipts (Act Sec. 2301(c)(3)(A)(i) of the CARES Act).

For these employers, qualified wages taken into account for an employee may not exceed what the employee would have been paid for working an equivalent duration during the 30 days immediately preceding the period of economic hardship (Act Sec. 2301(c)(3)(B) of the CARES Act).

Example: An employer's gross receipts were $100,000, $190,000, and $230,000 in the first, second, and third calendar quarters of 2020, respectively. Its gross receipts were $210,000, $230,000, and $250,000 in the first, second, and third calendar quarters of 2019, respectively. Thus, the employer's 2020 first, second,

NEW LAW EXPLAINED

> and third quarter gross receipts were approximately 48%, 83%, and 92% of its 2019 first, second, and third quarter gross receipts, respectively. Accordingly, the employer had a significant decline in gross receipts commencing on the first day of the first calendar quarter of 2020 (the calendar quarter in which gross receipts were less than 50% of the same quarter in 2019) and ending on the first day of the third calendar quarter of 2020 (the quarter following the quarter for which the gross receipts were more than 80% of the same quarter in 2019). Thus, the employer is entitled to a retention credit with respect to the first and second calendar quarters. (IRS FAQs: Employee Retention Credit under the CARES Act, https://www.irs.gov/newsroom/faqs-employee-retention-credit-under-the-cares-act).

If the eligible employer averaged 100 or fewer full-time employees in 2019, qualified wages are the wages paid to **any employee** during any period of economic hardship described in (1) and (2) above (Act Sec. 2301(c)(3)(A)(ii) of the CARES Act).

The same wages cannot be used for both the sick and family leave wages under the Families First Coronavirus Response Act (P.L. 116-127) and the retention credit wages (Act Sec. 2301(c)(3)(A) of the CARES Act).

Eligible employer. An eligible employer is an employer that carried on a trade or business in 2020 and (1) that fully or partially suspends operation during any calendar quarter in 2020 due to orders from an appropriate governmental authority limiting commerce, travel, or group meetings (for commercial, social, religious, or other purposes) due to COVID-19; or (2) whose gross receipts are below 50% of the comparable quarter in 2019. Once the employer's gross receipts go above 80% of a comparable quarter in 2019, it no longer qualifies after the end of that quarter. This applies to each quarter (Act Sec. 2301(c)(2)(A) and (B) of the CARES Act).

For an employer that is a tax-exempt organization, the requirements of carrying on a trade or business during 2020 and suspension of business operations under a governmental order due to COVID-19 apply to all operations of the organization (Act Sec. 2301(c)(2)(C) of the CARES Act).

Aggregation rule. Employers covered by Code Sec. 52(a) or (b) and Code Sec. 414 (m) or (o) will be treated as one employer (Act Sec. 2301(d) of the CARES Act). Rules provided under Code Sec. 51(i)(1) and Code Sec. 280C(a) also apply (Act Sec. 2301(e) of the CARES Act).

No government credit. The credit does not apply to the federal government, state governments, or their agencies (Act Sec. 2301(f) of the CARES Act).

OASDI and RRTA cap. The credit allowed may not exceed the OASDI tax or RRTA tax imposed on the employer, reduced by any credits allowed for the employment of qualified veterans, the research expenditures of qualified small businesses, and the new sick and family leave credits under Act Secs. 7001 and 7003 of the Families First Act for that calendar quarter on the wages paid for all the employer's employees (Act Sec. 2301(b)(2) and (c)(1) of the CARES Act).

NEW LAW EXPLAINED

Medical expense credit increase. The credit is increased by the amount of the employer's qualified health plan expenses as are properly allocable to the qualified wages for which the credit is allowed (Act Sec. 2301(c)(3)(C)(i) of the CARES Act).

Qualified health plan expenses. The term "qualified health plan expenses" means amounts paid or incurred by the employer to provide and maintain a group health plan (as defined in Code Sec. 5000(b)(1)), but only to the extent that such amounts are excluded from the gross income of employees by reason of Code Sec. 106(a) (Act Sec. 2301(c)(3)(C)(ii) of the CARES Act).

Allocation rules. Qualified health plan expenses must be allocated to qualified wages in such manner as the Secretary of the Treasury may prescribe. Except as otherwise provided by the Secretary, the allocation will be treated as properly made if made on the basis of being pro rata among covered employees and pro rata on the basis of periods of coverage (relative to the time periods of leave to which the wages relate) (Act Sec. 2301(c)(3)(C)(iii) of the CARES Act).

Code Sec. 45S credit cannot be included. Any wages taken into account for the employee retention credit cannot be used for the employer credit for certain paid family and medical leave under Code Sec. 45S (Act Sec. 2301(h)(2) of the CARES Act).

No double credit for employees under the Work Opportunity Tax Credit (WOTC). An employee cannot be included for any period with respect to any employer if the employer is allowed a credit under Code Sec. 51 (Act Sec. 2301(h)(1) of the CARES Act).

Employer election. An employer may elect, as provided by the Secretary of the Treasury, to have the employee retention credit not apply to the employer for a calendar quarter (Act Sec. 2301(g) of the CARES Act).

Employers who take small business loans. An employer is not eligible for the employee retention credit if it receives a small business loan under the Paycheck Protection Program of the CARES Act (Act Sec. 2301(j) of the CARES Act).

Credit is refundable and payable in advance. For any calendar quarter, if the amount of the employee retention credit exceeds the OASDI tax or RRTA tax imposed on the employer, as reduced by any credits taken for the employment of qualified veterans and research expenditures of qualified small businesses, and the new sick and family leave credits under Act Secs. 7001 and 7003 of the Families First Act, the excess is treated as a refundable overpayment (Act Sec. 2301(b)(3) of the CARES Act).

Employers can get the payroll tax credit in advance (see IRS Form 7200, *Advance Payment of Employer Credits Due to Covid-19*, and instructions).

> **Comment:** Before an advance payment can be received, the employer must retain (use up) all available employment taxes including withheld federal income taxes and the employee and employer share of share of Social Security and Medicare taxes, rather than depositing them with the IRS.

> **Comment:** If the federal employment taxes yet to be deposited are not sufficient to cover the employer's cost of qualified leave wages, plus the allocable qualified health plan expenses and the amount of the employer's share of Medicare tax

NEW LAW EXPLAINED

imposed on those wages, then the employer can file a request for an advance payment from the IRS.

Credit mechanics. The IRS has issued several examples of the mechanics for using the employee retention credit (IRS FAQs: Employee Retention Credit under the CARES https://www.irs.gov/newsroom/faqs-employee-retention-credit-under-the-cares-act).

Example 1: Eligible employer pays $10,000 in qualified wages to Employee A in Q2 2020. The Employee Retention Credit available to the eligible employer for the qualified wages paid to Employee A is $5,000.

Example 2: Eligible employer pays Employee B $8,000 in qualified wages in Q2 2020 and $8,000 in qualified wages in Q3 2020. The credit available to the eligible employer for the qualified wages paid to Employee B is equal to $4,000 in Q2 and $1,000 in Q3 due to the overall limit of $10,000 on qualified wages per employee for all calendar quarters.

Example 3: Eligible employer pays $10,000 in qualified wages to Employee A in Q2 2020. The Employee Retention Credit available to the eligible employer for the qualified wages paid to Employee A is $5,000. This amount may be applied against the employer share of Social Security taxes that the eligible employer is liable for with respect to all employee wages paid in Q2 2020. Any excess over the employer's share of Social Security taxes is treated as an overpayment and refunded to the eligible employer after offsetting other tax liabilities on the employment tax return and subject to any other offsets under section 6402(a) of the Code.

Example 4: An eligible employer paid $10,000 in qualified wages (including qualified health plan expenses) and is therefore entitled to a $5,000 credit, and is otherwise required to deposit $8,000 in federal employment taxes, including taxes withheld from all of its employees, for wage payments made during the same quarter as the $10,000 in qualified wages. The eligible employer has no paid sick or family leave credits under the FFCRA. The eligible employer may keep up to $5,000 of the $8,000 of taxes the eligible employer was going to deposit, and it will not owe a penalty for keeping the $5,000. The eligible employer is required to deposit only the remaining $3,000 on its required deposit date. The eligible employer will later account for the $5,000 it retained when it files Form 941, Employer's Quarterly Federal Tax Return, for the quarter.

> **Example 5:** An eligible employer paid $20,000 in qualified wages, and is therefore entitled to a credit of $10,000, and is otherwise required to deposit $8,000 in federal employment taxes, including taxes withheld from all of its employees, on wage payments made during the same calendar quarter. The eligible employer has no paid sick or family leave credits under the FFCRA. The eligible employer can keep the entire $8,000 of taxes that the eligible employer was otherwise required to deposit without penalties as a portion of the credits it is otherwise entitled to claim on the Form 941. The eligible employer may file a request for an advance credit for the remaining $2,000 by completing Form 7200.

Deposits penalty waivers. The Secretary of the Treasury (or the Secretary's delegate) will waive any penalty under Code Sec. 6656 for failure to make a deposit of the OASDI or RRTA taxes if the Secretary determines that such failure was due to the anticipation of the retention credit allowed (Act Sec. 2301(k) of the CARES Act).

Upcoming regulations. The Secretary will issue such forms, instructions, regulations, and guidance as are necessary: (1) to allow the advance payment of the credit, (2) to provide for the reconciliation of such advance payment with the amount advanced at the time of filing the return of tax for the applicable calendar quarter or taxable year, (3) to provide for the recapture of the credit if the credit is allowed to a taxpayer which receives a small business loan during a subsequent quarter, (4) with respect to the application of the credit to third party payors (including professional employer organizations, certified professional employer organizations, or agents under Code Sec. 3504 including regulations or guidance allowing such payors to submit documentation necessary to substantiate the eligible employer status of employers that use such payors, and (5) in the case of any employer which was not carrying on a trade or business for all or part of the same calendar quarter in the prior year (Act Sec. 2301(l) of the CARES Act).

Transfers to Federal Old-Age and Survivors Insurance Trust Fund.—Money is appropriated to the Federal Old-Age and Survivors Insurance Trust Fund and the Federal Disability Insurance Trust Fund established under Section 201 of the Social Security Act (42 U.S.C. 401) and the Social Security Equivalent Benefit Account established under Section 15A(a) of the Railroad Retirement Act of 1974 (45 U.S.C. 231n-1(a)) in amounts equal to the reduction in revenues to the Treasury by reason of this section (without regard to this subsection). Amounts appropriated by the preceding sentence will be transferred from the general fund at such times and in such manner as to replicate to the extent possible the transfers which would have occurred to such Trust Fund or Account had this section not been enacted (Act Sec. 2301(i) of the CARES Act).

▶ **Effective date.** No specific effective date is provided. The provisions are, therefore, considered effective on March 27, 2020, the date of enactment of the Coronavirus Aid, Relief, and Economic Security Act (P.L. 116-136).

Law source: Law at ¶2047.

— Act Sec. 2301 of the Coronavirus Aid, Relief, and Economic Security Act (P.L. 116-136).

¶595 Delay of Payment of Employer Payroll Taxes

SUMMARY OF NEW LAW

Employers can defer payment of the employer's share of the Social Security tax that they otherwise are responsible for paying on wages. The deferral applies to taxes normally required to be paid from March 27, 2020, through December 31, 2020. The deferred tax must be paid over two years, with half to be paid by December 31, 2021, and the other half to be paid by December 31, 2022.

BACKGROUND

Generally, employers must deposit federal income tax withheld and both the employer and employee Social Security and Medicare taxes. Employers must use electronic funds transfers (EFT) to make all federal tax deposits. There are two deposit schedules—monthly and semiweekly—for determining when to deposit make deposits. The schedules tell when a deposit is due after a tax liability arises. The tax liability is based on the dates payments were made or wages were paid. Before the beginning of each calendar year, depositors must determine which of the two deposit schedules they are required to use. The deposit schedule is based on the total tax liability reported on Form 941, Employer's Quarterly Federal Tax Return during a lookback period. The rules do not apply to Federal Unemployment Tax Act (FUTA) tax.

The lookback period begins July 1 and ends June 30. If a depositor reported $50,000 or less of taxes for the lookback period, the depositor is a monthly schedule depositor. Those who reported more than $50,000 are semiweekly schedule depositors.

The term "deposit period" refers to the period during which tax liabilities are accumulated for each required deposit due date. For monthly schedule depositors, the deposit period is a calendar month. The deposit periods for semiweekly schedule depositors are Wednesday through Friday and Saturday through Tuesday. For agents with an approved Form 2678, Employer/Payer Appointment of Agent, the deposit rules apply based on the total employment taxes accumulated by the agent for its own employees and on behalf of all employers for whom the agent is authorized to act (Revenue Procedure 2013-39, IRB 2013-52, December 11, 2013).

An employer may hire a certified professional employer organization (CPEO) to handle these duties. The CPEO is generally treated as the sole employer of a work site employee performing services for the customer regarding remuneration that the CPEO paid to the employee (Code Sec. 3511(a)). Solely for purposes of a CPEO's federal employment tax liability and other federal employment tax obligations, the CPEO is considered the employer of any individual (with exceptions) who is performing services covered by a contract meeting the service contract requirements of Code Sec. 7705(e)(2), but only for remuneration that the CPEO paid to the individual (Code Sec. 3511(c)).

NEW LAW EXPLAINED

Delay of payment of employer payroll taxes.— Employers are treated as if the deposits of the employer share of Social Security tax and railroad retirement taxes are on time if they make the deposits by the newly delayed payment dates (Act Sec. 2302(a)(1) of the Coronavirus Aid, Relief, and Economic Security Act (CARES Act) (P.L. 116-136)).

The employer share of Social Security and railroad retirement taxes that would be required to be deposited from March 27, 2020, to December 31, 2020, can be delayed. Half of the taxes are required to be deposited by December 31, 2021. The other half is required to be deposited by December 31, 2022 (Act Sec. 2302(d)(1)-(3) of the CARES Act). It is expected that the IRS will revise Form 941, Employer's Quarterly Federal Tax Return.

> **Comment:** The delay does not include the employee's personal income tax withheld, as there is no reference to Code Sec. 3402. Nor does the law apply to the employer share of Medicare tax (Code Sec. 3111(b)) or the employee share of Social Security tax (Code Sec. 3101(a)) or Medicare tax (Code Sec. 3101(b)).

> **Expert Guidance:** Guinevere Moore, Shareholder at Moore Tax Law Group LLC in Chicago, praises this provision as essentially operating as an interest-free loan to businesses. Thanks to the provision, businesses can keep their Social Security payroll taxes this year—an estimated $300 billion—so they have more cash flow to keep workers and to survive. Note that payroll tax deferral is not available to employers with Paycheck Protection Program (PPP) loans forgiven by the Small Business Administration (SBA) Employers need to consider whether to avail themselves of the payroll tax deferral if they also expect to seek loan forgiveness.

Exception. The deferral does not apply to any taxpayer that has had debt forgiven under Act Sec. 1106 of the CARES Act regarding a loan guaranteed under the Paycheck Protection Program (PPP) of the Small Business Act (15 U.S.C. 636(a)(36)) or debt forgiven under Act Sec. 1109 of the CARES Act (regarding loans under U.S. Treasury Program Management Authority) (Act Sec. 2302(a)(3) of the CARES Act).

Third party liability (agents). Payroll agents are allowed to defer making deposits for an employer if the employer directs the agent to defer payment of any applicable employment taxes during the payroll tax deferral period. However, the employer is still solely liable for the payment before the applicable dates (Act Sec. 2302(c)(1) of the CARES Act).

Certified professional employer organizations. Similarly, a certified professional employer organization that has entered into a service contract with an employer customer is allowed to defer deposits if the employer directs the organization to defer payment of any applicable employment taxes during the payroll tax deferral period. However, the employer is still solely liable for the payment before the applicable dates (Act Sec. 2302(c)(2) of the CARES Act).

NEW LAW EXPLAINED

Trust funds held harmless. The CARES Act appropriates (out of any money in the Treasury not otherwise appropriated) for each fiscal year to the Federal Old-Age and Survivors Insurance Trust Fund and the Federal Disability Insurance Trust and the Social Security Equivalent Benefit Account under the Railroad Retirement Act an amount equal to the reduction in the transfers to the funds for the fiscal year by reason of Section 2302 of the CARES Act. Amounts appropriated are to be transferred at such times and in such manner as to replicate to the extent possible the transfers which would have occurred but for the extension provided by Section 2302 (Act Sec. 2302(e) of the CARES Act).

Regulatory authority. The Secretary of the Treasury is directed to issue regulations or other guidance as necessary to implement Section 2302, including rules for its administration and enforcement (Act Sec. 2302(f) of the CARES Act).

▶ **Effective date.** No specific effective date is provided. The provisions are, therefore, considered effective on March 27, 2020, the date of enactment of the Coronavirus Aid, Relief, and Economic Security Act (P.L. 116-136).

Law source: Law at ¶2048.

— Act Sec. 2302 of the Coronavirus Aid, Relief, and Economic Security Act (P.L. 116-136).

¶597 Temporary Relief for Federal Student Loan Borrowers

SUMMARY OF NEW LAW

Payroll garnishment of wages for the purpose of paying federal student loans that are in default are halted during the period in which the Secretary of Education suspends payments on a loan.

BACKGROUND

Student loan debts owed to partners of the U.S. Department of Education (ED) may be collected through Administrative Wage Garnishment (AWG). The AWG is a process by which federal or state laws grant authority to state or federal agencies to collect for a debt, therefore bypassing the requirement to obtain a garnishment from a court of law. Two federal laws allow for the collection of delinquent student loans. The Higher Education Act (HEA) was amended in 1991 to permit ED and student loan guaranty agencies to administratively collect delinquent student loans. In 1996, Congress passed the Debt Collection Improvement Act (DCIA), which extended AWG to other federal agencies, including ED.

NEW LAW EXPLAINED

NEW LAW EXPLAINED

Suspending involuntary collection.—During the period in which the Secretary of Education suspends payments on a loan under Act Sec. 3513(a) of the Coronavirus Aid, Relief, and Economic Security Act (P.L. 116-136) (March 13, 2020 through September 30, 2020), the Secretary shall also suspend all involuntary collection related to the loan, including wage garnishments authorized under section 488A of the Higher Education Act of 1965 (20 U.S.C. 1095a) or section 3720D of title 31, United States Code regarding wage garnishment (Act Sec. 3513(e)(1) of the CARES Act).

Notice to borrowers. In order to inform borrowers of the actions taken in accordance with this section and ensure an effective transition, the Secretary shall, within 15 days after the date of enactment of the Act (March 27, 2020), notify borrowers whose collections have been suspended of this action being taken (Act Sec. 3513(g)(1) of the CARES Act). Further, beginning on August 1, 2020, the Secretary shall carry out a program to provide not less than six notices by postal mail, telephone, or electronic communication to borrowers indicating when the borrower's normal payment obligations will resume, and that the borrower has the option to enroll in income-driven repayment, including a brief description of such options (Act Sec. 3513(g)(2) of the CARES Act).

> **Comment:** The Federal Student Aid office issued further clarification that the Department of Education will send a letter to human resources departments instructing them to stop wage garnishments for defaulted student loans. If the Department receives funds from a garnishment between March 13, 2020, and Sept. 30, 2020, the garnished wages will be refunded. (https://studentaid.gov/announcements-events/coronavirus.)
>
> Further, according to a release from the Department of Education, the Department will be relying on employers to make the change to borrowers' paychecks, and the Department will monitor employers' compliance with the request to stop wage garnishment. The Department advises that borrowers whose wages continue to be garnished after March 13 should contact their employers' human resources department. (https://www.ed.gov/news/press-releases/secretary-devos-directs-fsa-stop-wage-garnishment-collections-actions-student-loan-borrowers-will-refund-more-18-billion-students-families.)

▶ **Effective date.** No specific effective date is provided. The provisions are, therefore, considered effective on March 27, 2020, the date of enactment of the Coronavirus Aid, Relief, and Economic Security Act (P.L. 116-136).

Law source: Law at ¶2110.

— Act Sec. 3513(e) of the Coronavirus Aid, Relief, and Economic Security Act (P.L. 116-136).

— Act Sec. 3513(g) of the CARES Act.

Chapter 6—Pension Plans Provisions

6

¶600 Coronavirus-Related Distributions from Retirement Plans

SUMMARY OF NEW LAW

The 10-percent additional tax under Code Sec. 72(t) is waived for any qualified coronavirus-related distributions from a retirement plan. Eligible individuals who take such distributions can include them in gross income over a three-year span and have three years to repay the amount.

BACKGROUND

An individual who receives an early distribution from a qualified retirement plan or IRA before turning age 59½ may be required to include at least part of the distribution as income. The taxable amount is generally subject to an additional 10-percent additional tax on that amount, unless the distribution falls under an exception such as the death or disability of the plan participant, or the distribution is eligible to be rolled over to another qualified retirement plan or IRA (Code Sec. 72(t)). The 10-percent additional tax will also not apply to a qualified hurricane distributions from an eligible retirement plan before January 1, 2019, to a individual whose principal place of abode was located in the designated disaster area for Hurricanes Harvey, Irma, or Maria in 2017 and who sustained an economic loss due to the hurricane (Act Secs. 501 and 502(a) of the Disaster Tax Relief and Airport and Airway Extension Act of 2017 (P.L. 115-63)).

BACKGROUND

Relief is sometimes provided from certain natural disasters in the form of qualified disaster distributions and loans for residents in declared disaster areas which allow them to withdraw or borrow up to $100,000 to help them rebuild. Most recently, this relief was extended to any area with respect to which a major disaster was declared, during the period beginning on January 1, 2018, and ending on the date which is 60 days after December 20, 2019, by the President under Section 401 of the Robert T. Stafford Disaster Relief and Emergency Act (Act Secs. 201 and 202, Division Q of Taxpayer Certainty and Disaster Tax Relief Act of 2019 (P.L. 116-94). The incident period of the disaster with respect to the declaration must begin on or before December 20, 2019.

Relief was previously extended to victims of Hurricanes Irma, Harvey, and Maria (P.L. 115-63). Under the relief, affected individuals can receive "qualified hurricane distributions" of up to $100,000 from their employer retirement plan or IRA. These distributions are not subject to the 10-percent additional tax on early distributions, and can either be included in income ratably over a three-year period or, if the amount is recontributed to a plan within three years, excluded from income entirely. Also, individuals who had taken earlier hardship withdrawals to fund a home purchase or construction that was cancelled as a result of a subsequent hurricane can recontribute the withdrawn amount without tax or penalty. The exclusion amounts for loans made from qualified employer plans to hurricane victims for the acquisition of a principal residence and to be paid within five years were increased and the due dates for repayment and the five-year repayment requirement are delayed one year.

Unless the individual elects otherwise, the portion of a qualified hurricane distribution that is includible in income is reported ratably over three years, beginning with the year in which the distribution is received An individual who receives qualified hurricane distributions may recontribute the amount of those distributions to an eligible retirement plan within three years of receiving them. The recontributed amounts are treated as though they were eligible rollover distributions that were transferred in a direct trustee-to-trustee transfer within 60 days, with the result that the original distribution is not subject to tax, and the contributions are not counted against the annual limits. The receiving plan does not have to be the plan from which the funds were withdrawn, but it must be one to which a rollover contribution of the distribution could be made (IRS Pub 976).

NEW LAW EXPLAINED

Relief provided for qualified coronavirus-related distributions.— The 10-percent additional tax under Code Sec. 72(t) is waived for any qualified coronavirus-related distributions made from an eligible retirement plan in response to the COVID-19 (coronavirus) crisis (Act Sec. 2202(a)(1) of the Coronavirus Aid, Relief, and Economic Security (CARES) Act (P.L. 116-136)). The aggregate amount of distributions received by an individual which may be treated as coronavirus-related distributions for any tax year shall not exceed $100,000 (Act Sec. 2202(a)(2)(A) of the CARES Act).

If an individual's total distributions from all plans exceed this amount, a plan will not lose its tax-exempt status merely because it treats such distribution as a qualified

NEW LAW EXPLAINED

coronavirus-related distribution, provided that the aggregate amount of such distributions from all plans maintained by the employer (and any member of any controlled group that includes the employer) do not exceed the $100,000 limit (Act Sec. 2202(a)(2)(B) of the CARES Act). A controlled group for these purposes means any group treated as a single employer under Code Sec. 414(b), (c),(m), or (o) (Act Sec. 2202(a)(2)(C) of the CARES Act).

Expert Guidance: Eugene Kirman, Associate at Agostino & Associates, P.C. in Hackensack, NJ, notes that the temporary relief helps qualified individuals affected by COVID-19 who have retirement accounts by permitting them to take distributions and larger loans. The Act recognizes the vast impact of the disease by defining qualified individuals very broadly and allowing plan administrators to rely on employee certifications. Qualified individuals are individuals and their spouses and dependents diagnosed with COVID-19 disease or SARS-CoV-2 virus, and individuals experiencing adverse financial consequences due to such disease or virus (quarantine, closure, layoff, reduced hours, inability to work due to lack of child care, and other factors as the Secretary determines).

Qualified coronavirus-related distributions. To qualify as a "coronavirus-related distribution", the distribution must be from an eligible retirement plan made on or after March 27, 2020, and before December 31, 2020. In addition, it must be made to an individual:

- who is diagnosed with the virus SARS-CoV-2 or with coronavirus disease 2019 (Covid-19) by a test approved by the Centers for Disease Control and Prevention (CDC);
- whose spouse or dependent (as defined in Code Sec. 152) is diagnosed with such virus or disease by such a test, or
- who experiences adverse financial consequences as a result of the coronavirus (Act Sec. 2202(a)(4)(A)(ii)(III) of the CARES Act).

Expert Guidance: Jim Hamill, Director of Tax Practice at Reynolds, Hix & Co., P.A., in Albuquerque, notes that the special distribution rules apply to any taxpayer who has been personally diagnosed, or who has a spouse or dependent diagnosed, as COVID-19 positive using a CDC-approved test. The difficulty in obtaining a test means that the distribution may be eligible only if the taxpayer satisfies one of the adverse financial result test scenarios. The plan administrator may accept an employee certification of eligibility, but the employee must take particular care to attempt to substantiate eligibility in the absence of a positive test result, and to retain evidence of a positive test otherwise.

"Adverse financial consequences" can include consequences from any of the following:

- being quarantined;

NEW LAW EXPLAINED

- being furloughed or laid off or having work hours reduced due to such virus or disease;
- being unable to work due to lack of child care due to such virus or disease;
- closing or reducing hours of a business owned or operated by the individual due to such virus or disease; or
- other factors as determined by the Secretary of the Treasury (Act Sec. 2202(a)(4)(A)(ii)(III), as amended by the CARES Act).

The administrator of an eligible retirement plan may rely on an employee's certification that the employee satisfies any conditions in determining whether any distribution is a coronavirus-related distribution (Act Sec. 2202(a)(4)(B) of the CARES Act)). An eligible retirement plan includes individual retirement accounts or annuities (IRAs), qualified employer-sponsored retirement plans, 403(a) annuity plans, 403(b) tax-sheltered annuity plans, and 457(b) plans (Act Sec. 2202(a)(4)(C) of the CARES Act)).

Inclusion in gross income over three years; repayment over three years. Unless the individual elects otherwise, the portion of a qualified coronavirus-related distribution that is includible in income is reported ratably over three years, beginning with the year in which the distribution is received (Act Sec. 2202(a)(5)(A) of the CARES Act). If the plan participant dies before all amounts are included in income and the surviving spouse does not acquire the entire interest in the participant's account, the amount is includible in the decendent's income in the tax year of the decedent's death. If the surviving spouse acquires the entire interest, the spouse must include the amount in income (Act Sec. 2202(a)(5)(B) of the CARES Act).

An individual who receives a qualified coronavirus-related distribution may recontribute the amount of those distributions to an eligible retirement plan within three years of receiving them (Act Sec. 2202(a)(3)(A) of the CARES Act). The recontributed amounts are treated as though they were eligible rollover distributions that were transferred in a direct trustee-to-trustee transfer within 60 days, with the result that the original distribution is not subject to tax, and the contributions are not counted against the annual limits. The receiving plan does not have to be the plan from which the funds were withdrawn, but it must be one to which a rollover contribution of the distribution could be made. Rollover treatment is not available for a coronavirus-related distribution to the extent that the distribution is mandatory, such as the distributions required to be made after the owner attains age 70½ (Act Sec. 2202(a)(3)(B) and (a)(3)(C) of the CARES Act).

> **Expert Guidance:** Jim Hamill, Director of Tax Practice at Reynolds, Hix & Co., P.A., in Albuquerque, observes that the ability to use the three-year rollover provision for a coronavirus-related retirement distribution requires that a rollover contribution could otherwise be made. Since only one rollover may be made within each one-year period, a taxpayer who made a rollover within the last year may need to carefully time the 2020 distribution to remain eligible for the three-year rollover.

Expert Guidance: Jim Hamill, Director of Tax Practice at Reynolds, Hix & Co., P.A., in Albuquerque, points out that the 60-day rollover provision for distributions was designed for a world when it was often difficult to do a trustee-to-trustee rollover. The rollover provision was never intended to encourage short-term loans from a retirement account. The three-year rollover rule for coronavirus-related distributions is intended to encourage loans from retirement accounts for those who believe that an economic recovery will allow them to replace the funds.

Other rules for coronavirus-related distribution. Coronavirus-related distributions are exempt from trustee-to-trustee transfer and withholding rules (Code Sec. 401(a)(31), 402(f) and 3405) (Act Sec. 2202(a)(6)(A) of the CARES Act). In addition, qualified distributions are treated as meeting plan distribution requirements of Code Secs. 401(k)(2)(B)(i), 403(b)(7)(A)(i), 403(b)(11), and 457(d)(1)(A) (Act Sec. 2202(a)(6)(B) of the CARES Act).

Expert Guidance: Jim Hamill, Director of Tax Practice at Reynolds, Hix & Co., P.A., in Albuquerque, observes that the IRS will need to clarify certain procedural aspects of the retirement distribution rules. This includes reporting requirements when the taxpayer does not report the distribution in income, even under the three-year spread, because he or she intends a qualified rollover within three years. Presumably failure to complete a three-year rollover will require amended returns for 2020-2022 to include one-third of the distribution in each year. It also includes guidance on how to elect out of the three-year income spread and whether that election is available on an amended return (for example, if the rollover is not completed and the 2020 year is the best year to report the income). Finally, IRS Form 5329, used to report the 10 percent early distribution penalty, will need a new section of the code for COVID-19 distributions.

Plan amendments. A qualified plan will generally be treated as being operating in accordance with its terms if the coronavirus distribution rules apply. Amendment relief is provided to a qualified plan so long as it made on or before the last day of the first plan year beginning on or after January 1, 2022, or such later date as the Secretary of the Treasury may prescribe. In the case of a governmental plan, the date is two years after the date that would otherwise apply (Act Sec. 2202(c) of the CARES Act).

Expert Guidance: Eugene Kirman, Associate at Agostino & Associates, P.C. in Hackensack, NJ, observes that a plan making amendments according to the above by the last day of its first plan year beginning in 2022 (2024 for government plans) is treated as operated in accordance with its terms and does not fail Code Sec. 411(d)(6) or section 204(g) of ERISA if the plan operates, between the amendments' effective date and December 31, 2022, as if the amendments were already in effect.

▶ **Effective date.** No specific effective date is provided by the Act. The amendments made by this act are, therefore, considered effective on March 27, 2020, the date of enactment.

NEW LAW EXPLAINED

Law source: Law at ¶2041.

— Act Sec. 2202(a) and (c) of the Coronavirus Aid, Relief, and Economic Security (CARES) Act (P.L. 116-136).

¶605 Coronavirus-Related Plan Loans from Retirement Plans

SUMMARY OF NEW LAW

The threshold limit on loans from an employer-sponsored retirement plan for a qualified individual affected by the coronavirus is increased to the lesser of $100,000 or 100 percent of the present value (but not less than $10,000) of the plan participant's benefits under the plan.

BACKGROUND

A loan to a participant from a qualified retirement plan is treated as a distribution and included in the participant's gross income unless the loan does not exceed the lesser of $50,000 or 50 percent of the present value (but not less than $10,000) of the plan participant's vested benefits under the plan. The $50,000 limit is reduced by the excess (if any) of: (1) the highest outstanding balance of loans from the plan during the one-year period ending on the day preceding the date of the loan, over (2) the outstanding balance of those loans on the date of the loan (Code Sec. 72(p)). In addition, the loan must be repaid within five years to qualify as an exception to treatment of the loan proceeds as a distribution.

Relief is sometimes provided for natural disasters in the form of qualified disaster distributions and loans for residents in declared disaster areas which allow them to withdraw or borrow up to $100,000 to help them rebuild. Most recently, this relief was extended to any area with respect to which a major disaster was declared, during the period beginning on January 1, 2018, and ending on the date which is 60 days after December 20, 2019, by the President under Section 401 of the Robert T. Stafford Disaster Relief and Emergency Act (Act Secs. 201 and 202, Division Q of Taxpayer Certainty and Disaster Tax Relief Act of 2019 (P.L. 116-94)). The incident period of the disaster with respect to the declaration must begin on or before December 20, 2019.

Relief was previously extended to victims of Hurricanes Harvey, Irma, and Maria (P.L. 115-63. Under the relief, affected individuals can receive "qualified hurricane distributions" of up to $100,000 from their employer retirement plan or IRA. These distributions are not subject to the 10-percent additional tax on early distributions, and can either be included in income ratably over a three-year period or, if the amount is recontributed to a plan within three years, excluded from income entirely. Also, individuals who had taken earlier hardship withdrawals to fund a home purchase or construction that was cancelled as a result of a subsequent hurricane can

BACKGROUND

recontribute the withdrawn amount without tax or penalty. The exclusion amounts for loans made from qualified employer plans to hurricane victims for the acquisition of a principal residence and to be paid within five years were increased and the due dates for repayment and the five-year repayment requirement are delayed one year.

NEW LAW EXPLAINED

Plan loan limit doubled to $100,000.— The threshold limit on loans from a qualified employer plan for a qualified individual is increased to $100,000 or 100 percent of the present value (but not less than $10,000) of the plan participant's benefits under the plan in response to the COVID-19 (coronavirus) crisis (Act Sec. 2202(b)(1) of the Coronavirus Aid, Relief, and Economic Security (CARES) Act (P.L. 116-136)). In addition, if a qualified individual has a loan repayment due date after March 27, 2020, and before December 31, 2020, on an outstanding loan, the payment due date is delayed one year (or, if later, until September 23, 2020, the date which is 180 days after the date of the enactment) (Act Sec. 2202(b)(2) of the CARES Act). Any subsequent repayments with respect to the loan will be adjusted accordingly and the five-year period for repayment is disregarded).

> **Expert Guidance:** Eugene Kirman, Associate at Agostino & Associates, P.C. in Hackensack, NJ, notes that IRA holders cannot take loans and the CARES Act does not change that. So they do not benefit from the Act's loan provisions increasing the limitations.

Qualified individuals. A qualified individual for this purpose is any individual who would qualify for a coronavirus-related distribution (Act Sec. 2202(b)(3) of the CARES Act). Thus, the loan must be made on or after March 27, 2020, and before December 31, 2020, and must be to an individual:

- who is diagnosed with the virus SARS-CoV-2 or with coronavirus disease 2019 (Covid-19) by a test approved by the Centers for Disease Control and Prevention (CDC);
- whose spouse or dependent (as defined in Code Sec. 152) is diagnosed with such virus or disease by such a test; or
- who experiences adverse financial consequences as a result the coronavirus (Act Sec. 2202(a)(4)(A) of the CARES Act).

> **Expert Guidance:** Jim Hamill, Director of Tax Practice at Reynolds, Hix & Co., P.A., in Albuquerque, notes that these special rules apply to any taxpayer who has been personally diagnosed, or who has a spouse or dependent diagnosed, as COVID-19 positive using a CDC-approved test. The difficulty in obtaining a test means that the distribution may be eligible only if the taxpayer satisfies one of the adverse financial result test scenarios. The plan administrator may accept an employee certification of

NEW LAW EXPLAINED

> eligibility, but the employee must take particular care to attempt to substantiate eligibility in the absence of a positive test result, and to retain evidence of a positive test otherwise.

Adverse financial consequences can include consequences from any of the following:

- being quarantined;
- being furloughed or laid off or having work hours reduced due to such virus or disease;
- being unable to work due to lack of child care due to such virus or disease;
- closing or reducing hours of a business owned or operated by the individual due to such virus or disease; or
- other factors as determined by the Secretary of the Treasury (Act Sec. 2202(a)(4)(A)(ii)(III) of the CARES Act).

Plan amendments. A qualified plan will generally be treated as being operating in accordance with its terms if these coronavirus plan rules apply. Amendment relief is provided to a qualified plan so long as it made on or before the last day of the first plan year beginning on or after January 1, 2022, or such later date as the Secretary of the Treasury may prescribe. In the case of a governmental plan, the date is two years after the date that would otherwise apply (Act Sec. 2202(c) of the CARES Act).

> **Expert Guidance:** Eugene Kirman, Associate at Agostino & Associates, P.C. in Hackensack, NJ, observes that a plan making amendments according to the above by the last day of its first plan year beginning in 2022 (2024 for government plans) is treated as operated in accordance with its terms and does not fail Code Sec. 411(d)(6) or section 204(g) of ERISA if the plan operates, between the amendments' effective date and December 31, 2021, as if the amendments were already in effect.

▶ **Effective date.** No specific effective date is provided by the Act. The amendments made by this act are, therefore, considered effective on March 27, 2020, the date of enactment.

Law source: Law at ¶2041.

— Act Sec. 2202(b) and (c) of the Coronavirus Aid, Relief, and Economic Security (CARES) Act (P.L. 116-136).

¶610 Temporary Waiver of Required Minimum Distributions

SUMMARY OF NEW LAW

For the 2020 calendar year, the required minimum distribution (RMD) requirements generally applicable to retirement plans are temporarily suspended with respect to defined contribution retirement plans, including individual retirement accounts (IRAs).

BACKGROUND

Qualified retirement plans, IRAs and other retirement income arrangements qualify for tax-favored status only if they meet the required minimum distribution (RMD) rules contained in Code Sec. 401(a)(9). The rules prevent taxpayers who have no current need for the income derived from the retirement arrangement from extending the tax subsidy for retirement savings indefinitely. They apply to all qualified pension or profit-sharing plans (under Code Sec. 401(a)), qualified annuity plans (under Code Sec. 403(a)), tax-sheltered annuities for employees of charitable organizations and public schools (under Code Sec. 403(b)), eligible deferred compensation plans of government and tax-exempt employers (under Code Sec. 457(b)), traditional individual retirement accounts (IRAs), and Roth IRAs after the death of the account owner.

The RMD rules are implemented through extensive regulations that apply separately to defined contribution plans (Reg. § 1.401(a)(9)-5) and defined benefit plans and annuity contracts (Reg. § 1.401(a)(9)-6). Distributions of benefits from defined contribution arrangements must begin no later than the employee's required beginning date and must be equal to or greater than a specified minimum amount each year. The amount required to be distributed for any year is determined by dividing the balance in the account at the end of the preceding year by a applicable life expectancy period found in tables provided by the IRS.

A participant's required beginning date is generally April 1 of the calendar year following the later of (1) the calendar year in which the participant attains age 70½ prior to 2020 (72 if in 2020 or later) or (2) the calendar year in which the participant retires. However, the required beginning date cannot be delayed until after the participant's retirement if the participant is a five-percent owner of the employer, or if the account is an IRA (Code Sec. 401(a)(9)(C)). A required distribution must be made for the year in which the participant turns 70½ (or 72, if they have not reached 70½ before 2020) or retires and for every year thereafter. The distribution for the first year can be made as late as the required beginning date (April 1 of the following year). For other years, the required distribution must be made during the calendar year.

BACKGROUND

> **Example:** Harold turned 70½ on December 30, 2018, and so was required to take a distribution for 2018 by April 1, 2019, and subsequent RMDs on December 31st annually.

> **Example:** Maude turned 70½ after December 31, 2019, so is not required to take a minimum distribution until age 72. She reaches age 72 on July 1, 2021. She must take her first RMD (for 2021) by April 1, 2022, with subsequent RMDs on December 31st annually thereafter.

Rollovers. Eligible rollover distributions are distributions from tax-favored retirement arrangements that are eligible to be rolled over into another retirement arrangement. An eligible rollover distribution that is in fact rolled over is excluded from the recipient's gross income. Although as a default rule every distribution is an eligible rollover distribution, there are three exceptions: (1) hardship distributions; (2) distributions that are part of a series of substantially equal periodic payments, made not less frequently than annually, for the life or life expectancy of the participant (or of the participant and the participant's designated beneficiary) or for a specified period of more than ten years; and (3) RMDs (Code Sec. 402(c)(4)).

When a plan makes an eligible rollover distribution it is generally required to offer certain options to the recipient and to take certain actions. In particular, a qualified plan must make direct trustee-to-trustee transfers of eligible rollover distributions if the recipient requests one (Code Sec. 401(a)(31)(A)). Also, if a participant is due a mandatory distribution in an amount greater than $1,000, but does not request either a direct payment or a trustee-to-trustee transfer to another plan, the plan must put the distribution into an IRA for the benefit of the participant (Code Sec. 401(a)(31)(B)). If the participant does not elect to have the amount of an eligible rollover distribution transferred directly to another plan, the plan or plan administrator must withhold as taxes 20 percent of the distribution amount (Code Sec. 3405(c)). Finally, before making an eligible rollover distribution, the plan administrator must provide to the participant a written explanation of the participant's rights and of the tax consequences of various choices (Code Sec. 402(f)).

NEW LAW EXPLAINED

Minimum required distribution rules suspended for 2020.—For the 2020 calendar year, the required minimum distribution (RMD) rules do not apply to any:

- qualified defined contribution plan (under Code Sec. 401(a)),
- any defined contribution qualified annuity plan (under Code Sec. 403(a)) or tax-sheltered annuity plan (under Code Sec. 403(b)),
- any defined contribution plan that is an eligible deferred compensation plan of a government employer (under Code Sec. 457(b)), or

NEW LAW EXPLAINED

- any traditional or Roth IRA (under Code Secs. 408 and 408A) (Code Sec. 401(a)(9)(I), as added by the Coronavirus Aid, Relief, and Economic Security (CARES) Act (P.L. 116-136)).

As a result, plan participants and beneficiaries will not be required by law to take RMDs for the year in response to the COVID-19 (coronavirus) crisis. If the participant dies before minimum distributions have begun, and the entire remaining interest must be distributed within five years of the participant's death, then 2020 is excluded from the five-year period (Code Sec. 401(a)(9)(I)(iii)(II), as added by the CARES Act).

> **Caution:** The change in the law suspends, for the 2020 calendar year only, the requirement that covered plans and arrangements contain provisions requiring RMDs. It does not require that any plan or arrangement actually eliminate the plan's distribution requirement for 2020. Plans and arrangements must be formally amended to eliminate the requirement. An amendment will be treated as timely as long as it is made on or before the last day of the first plan year beginning on or after January 1, 2022 (January 1, 2024 for government plans). The plan must operate in accordance with the amendment after its effective date and through the end of 2020 (Act Sec. 2203(c)(2)) of the CARES Act).

Each individual's required beginning date, for purposes of applying the RMD rules in years after 2020, will be determined without regard to the temporary waiver of the requirements (Code Sec. 401(a)(9)(I)(iii)(I), as added by the CARES Act).

> **Expert Guidance:** William D. Elliott, Of Counsel, Elliott, Thomason & Gibson, LLP, in Dallas, notes that the temporary suspension of RMDs for the calendar year 2020 is an important provision. RMDs are based on the recipient's life expectancy and the value of retirement account balances at the end of the previous year. That means an RMD taken in 2020 would be based on account values on December 31, 2019, when the stock markets were nearly 30 percent higher than in mid-March 2020. Further, the effect is to give relief for retirees age 70$^{1}/_{2}$ and older who might be required to sell portfolio securities when the stock market has declined in values.

> **Comment:** Generally, qualified charitable distributions from an IRA that are excluded from the recipient's income count against the recipient's RMD for the year. The suspension of the RMD requirement may therefore lead to a decrease in charitable distributions in 2020.

The first distributions received each year, up to the amount of the individual's RMD, are not eligible rollover distributions; they must be taken into income and cannot be redeposited into another tax-favored retirement account. Distributions in excess of the required minimum generally can be rolled over, as long as they are not hardship distributions or part of a substantially equal series of periodic payments. With RMDs suspended for 2020, additional distributions will qualify as eligible rollover distributions. However, the law provides that these amounts will not be treated as eligible rollover distributions for purposes of the requirements normally imposed on plans making eligible rollover distributions. Thus, a plan will not be required to make direct trustee-to-trustee transfers of eligible rollover distributions on the recipient's

NEW LAW EXPLAINED

request, put a mandatory distribution of more than $1,000 into an IRA for the benefit of the participant, withhold as taxes 20 percent of the distribution amount, or provide to the participant a written explanation of the participant's rights and of the tax consequences of various choices (Code Sec. 402(c)(4), as amended by the CARES Act).

> **Expert Guidance:** Jim Hamill, Director of Tax Practice at Reynolds, Hix & Co., P.A., in Albuquerque, observes that some people without a need for funds may nonetheless take a 2020 distribution as a qualified charitable distribution (QCD). This allows a direct benefit above the new $300 above-the-line charitable deduction allowed to individuals who do not itemize deductions (see ¶115). However the taxpayer could make a QCD less than the RMD due the legislative change.

▶ **Effective date.** The amendments made by this section apply for calendar years beginning after December 31, 2019 (Act Sec. 2203(c)(1) of the Coronavirus Aid, Relief, and Economic Security (CARES) Act (P.L. 116-136)).

Law source: Law at ¶2042, ¶5006, and ¶5007.

— Act Sec. 2203(a) of the Coronavirus Aid, Relief, and Economic Security (CARES) Act (P.L. 116-136), adding Code Sec. 401(a)(9)(I).

— Act Sec. 2203(b), amending Code Sec. 402(c)(4).

— Act Sec. 2203(c), providing the effective date.

¶620 Minimum Funding Rules for Single-Employer Retirement Plans

SUMMARY OF NEW LAW

Minimum required contributions to a single-employer retirement plan otherwise due in calendar year 2020 (including any quarterly contributions) are delayed until January 1, 2021. The amount of each such contribution is increased by any interest accruing for the period between the original due date (without regard to the delay) for the contribution and the payment date. A plan sponsor also may elect to treat the plan's adjusted funding target attainment percentage for the last plan year ending before January 1, 2020, as the adjusted funding target attainment percentage for plan years that include calendar year 2020.

BACKGROUND

A single-employer defined benefit plan is subject to minimum required contribution rules under Code Sec. 430. The minimum required contribution for a plan year generally depends on a comparison of the value of plan assets (reduced by any credit balances) with the plan's funding target. If the value of plan assets is less than the

BACKGROUND

funding target of the plan for the year, then the minimum required contribution for that plan year is the sum of:

- the target normal cost for the plan year;
- the shortfall amortization installments for the plan year; and
- the waiver amortization installments for the plan year).

The minimum required contribution for a plan year must be paid within 8½ months after the close of the plan year (Code Sec. 430(j)). Payments made on a date other than the valuation date for the plan year must be adjusted for interest accruing for the period from the valuation date to the payment date, at the effective interest rate for the plan for the year. Employers maintaining plans that had a funding shortfall for the preceding plan year (i.e., the value of plan assets, as reduced by credit balances, was less than the funding target for the preceding year) must make quarterly contributions to the plan. If the employer fails to pay the full amount of a required quarterly installment, interest is assessed at the plan's effective interest rate plus five percentage points.

Benefit limits apply to plans that have funded target attainment percentage for the preceding year below designated thresholds are deemed to be in "at-risk" status and are subject to increased target liability. The benefit limits on single-employer defined benefit plans are based on the plan's adjusted funding target attainment percentage (AFTAP) (Code Sec. 436(b)). Generally, a plan's funding target attainment percentage is the ratio of the value of plan assets for the plan year (as reduced by any funding standard carryover balance and prefunding balance) to the funding target for the plan year (determined without regard to the plan's at-risk status) (Code Secs. 430(d)(2) and 436(j)(1)).

NEW LAW EXPLAINED

Relief for funding single-employer plans during 2020.—Minimum required contributions under Code Sec. 430(a) and section 303(a) of the Employee Retirement Income Security Act of 1974 (ERISA) (29 U.S.C. 1083(a)) (including any quarterly contributions) otherwise due to single-employer retirement plan during calendar year 2020 are delayed in response to the COVID-19 (coronavirus) crisis (Act Sec. 3608(a) of Coronavirus Aid, Relief, and Economic Security (CARES) Act (P.L. 116-136)). The due date for such contributions is January 1, 2021, and the amount of each required contribution is increased by interest accruing for the period between the original due date (without regard to this delay) for the contribution and the payment date, at the effective rate of interest for the plan for the plan year which includes such payment date.

2019 AFTAP can be used for 2020. A plan sponsor also may elect to treat the plan's adjusted funding target attainment percentage for the last plan year ending before January 1, 2020, as the adjusted funding target attainment percentage for plan years which include calendar year 2020 for purposes of Code Sec. 436 and section 206(g) of ERISA (29 U.S.C. 1056(g)) (Act Sec. 3608(b) of the CARES Act).

NEW LAW EXPLAINED

▶ **Effective date.** No specific effective date is provided by the Act. The amendments made by this act are, therefore, considered effective on March 27, 2020, the date of enactment.

Law source: Law at ¶2126.

— Act Sec. 3608 of Coronavirus Aid, Relief, and Economic Security (CARES) Act (P.L. 116-136)).

¶630 Cooperative and Small Employer Charity (CSEC) Pension Plans

SUMMARY OF NEW LAW

The list of Cooperative and Small Employer Charity (CSEC) pension plans has been amended to add a class of plans belonging to any Code Sec. 501(c)(3) organization in existence since at least 1938 that conducts medical research directly or indirectly through grant making and whose primary exempt purpose is to provide services with respect to mothers and children.

BACKGROUND

The funding rules for defined benefit plans are generally governed by Code Sec. 412 and section 302 of the Employee Retirement Income Security Act of 1974 (ERISA). The Pension Protection Act of 2006 (PPA) (P.L. 109-280) revamped the rules for single-employer plans effective for plan years beginning after 2007. The PPA replaced the old funding standard account rules with minimum funding requirements. The new rules are significantly stricter than the ones they replaced. The PPA retained the old standard account rules for collectively bargained plans ("multiemployer plans").

Effective for plan years beginning after December 31, 2013, eligible cooperative plans and eligible charity plans are permanently relieved from having to comply with the funding rules generally applicable to single-employer plans under the PPA. These plans are treated as a new category of qualified plans referred to as cooperative and small employer charity (CSEC) plans, and have pension funding requirements that are substantially similar to those to which they are currently subject, with some modifications (Code Sec. 433 and section 306 of ERISA, added by the Cooperative and Small Employer Charity Pension Flexibility Act (P.L. 113-97)). Specifically, a CESC pension plan will follow funding provisions in the Code and ERISA that apply substantially similar rules to those that applied under the version of Code Sec. 412 and section 302 prior to amendment by the PPA. Under these provisions, CSEC plans use funding standard accounts and are treated as single employer plans for some purposes.

CSEC plans. A CSEC pension plan is a defined benefit plan (other than a multiemployer plan) that:

BACKGROUND

- is an eligible cooperative plan (as defined in Act Sec. 104 of PPA);
- as of June 25, 2010, was maintained by more than one employer and all employers were Code Sec. 501(c)(3) organizations; or
- as of June 25, 2010, was maintained by an single employer that was a Code Sec. 501(c)(3) organization chartered under part B of subtitle II of title 36, United States Code, whose primary exempt purpose is to provide services with respect to children, and which has employees in at least 40 states (Code Sec. 414(y)(1) and section 210(f)(1) of ERISA).

A Code Sec. 501(c)(3) organization includes corporations, and any community chest, fund, or foundation:

- organized and operated exclusively for religious, charitable, scientific, testing for public safety, literary, or educational purposes, or to foster national or international amateur sports competition (but only if no part of its activities involve the provision of athletic facilities or equipment), or for the prevention of cruelty to children or animals;
- no part of the net earnings of which inures to the benefit of any private shareholder or individual; and
- no substantial part of its activities attempt to influence legislation by propaganda or otherwise (except for certain lobbying activities), and which does not participate in, or intervene in (including the publishing or distributing of statements) any political campaign on behalf of (or in opposition to) any candidate for public office.

NEW LAW EXPLAINED

Certain charity plan added to list of CSEC plans.— A new type of charity plan has been added to the list of Cooperative and Small Employer Charity (CSEC) pension plans. This type of plan includes any plan that as of January 1, 2000, was maintained by an employer that:

- is a Code Sec. 501(c)(3) organization;
- has been in existence since at least 1938;
- conducts medical research directly or indirectly through grant making; and
- has a primary exempt purpose is to provide services with respect to mothers and children (Code Sec. 414(y)(1)(D) and section 210(f)(1)(D) of the Employee Retirement Income Security Act of 1974 (ERISA) (29 U.S.C. 1060(f)(1)), added by the Coronavirus Aid, Relief, and Economic Security (CARES) Act (P.L. 116-136)).

> **Expert Guidance:** William D. Elliott, Of Counsel, Elliott, Thomason & Gibson, LLP, in Dallas, notes that the effect of this provision is to extend the special rules for CSEC pension plan rules to certain charitable employers (who have existed since 1938 and conduct medical research) whose primary purpose is to provide services to mothers and children.

NEW LAW EXPLAINED

> **Comment:** The expansion of the list of CESC pension plans is part of the CARES Act but the change is permanent and not specifically related to providing temporary relief for the COVID-19 (coronavirus) crisis.

▶ **Effective date.** The amendments made by this section apply to plan years beginning after December 31, 2018 (Act Sec. 3609(c)) of the Coronavirus Aid, Relief, and Economic Security (CARES) Act (P.L. 116-136)).

Law source: Law at ¶2127, ¶5008, and ¶6001.

— Act Sec. 3609(a) and (b) of the Coronavirus Aid, Relief, and Economic Security (CARES) Act (P.L. 116-136), adding Code Sec. 414(y)(1)(D) and section 210(f)(1)(D) of the Employee Retirement Income Security Act of 1974 (ERISA) (29 U.S.C. 1060(f)(1)).

— Act Sec. 3609(c), providing the effective date.

¶640 Expansion of Department of Labor Authority to Postpone Certain Deadlines

SUMMARY OF NEW LAW

The Department of Labor has the authority to postpone ERISA compliance deadlines for up to one year in the event of a public health emergency declared by the Secretary of Health and Human Services.

BACKGROUND

The Employee Retirement Income Security Act (ERISA) sets minimum standards for most voluntarily established retirement and health plans in private industry to provide protection for individuals in these plans. The law imposes numerous compliance obligations on such plans, including reporting, disclosure, and funding requirements.

The Victims of Terrorism Tax Relief Act of 2001 (P.L. 107-134) added ERISA Sec. 518, which provides that, in the case of a pension or other employee benefit plan (or any sponsor, administrator, participant, beneficiary, or other person with respect to such plan) affected by a Presidentially declared disaster or a terroristic or military action, the Secretary of Labor may prescribe, by notice or otherwise, a period of up to one year that may be disregarded in determining the date by which any action is required or permitted to be completed under ERISA.

After the terrorist attacks on September 11, 2001, the Department of Labor (DOL) used this authority to extend various deadlines, including the one for filing Form 5500 Annual Return/Report. In more recent years, the DOL has used this authority to provide additional time for employee benefit plans impacted by hurricanes and wildfires to comply with certain deadlines.

NEW LAW EXPLAINED

Authority to postpone deadlines.—The DOL's authority to postpone ERISA deadlines for up to one year is expanded to include a public health emergency declared by the Secretary of Health and Human Services pursuant to Act Sec. 319 of the Public Health Service Act (ERISA Sec. 518, as amended by Act Sec. 3607 of the Coronavirus Aid, Relief, and Economic Security Act (P.L. 116-136)).

▶ **Effective date.** No effective date is provided by the Act. The provision is therefore considered effective on March 27, 2020, the date of enactment of the CARES Act.

Law source: Law at ¶2125 and ¶6002.

— Act Sec. 3607 of the Coronavirus Aid, Relief, and Economic Security Act (P.L. 116-136), amending ERISA Sec. 518.

Chapter 7—Economic Stabilization Provisions

7

¶700 Loans, Loan Guarantees, and Other Investments

SUMMARY OF NEW LAW

The Coronavirus Aid, Relief, and Economic Security Act (CARES Act, P.L. 116-136) authorizes up to $500 billion of funding to provide liquidity to eligible businesses, states, and municipalities experiencing financial distress as a result of the COVID-19 national emergency. The Department of the Treasury may make up to $46 billion in direct loans and loan guarantees to passenger air carriers and related businesses, cargo air carriers, and businesses critical for national security. The Treasury may use the remaining $454 billion for programs established by the Federal Reserve to facilitate direct lending and guarantees and to support lending through banks or other lenders. One of these programs would provide financing to banks and other lenders that make direct low-interest loans to mid-sized businesses.

BACKGROUND

In a March 23, 2020, press release, the Federal Reserve described its actions to support the flow of credit to American families and businesses to limit job and income losses during the coronavirus pandemic. Its actions include:

- establishing new programs that will provide up to $300 billion in new financing (using the Exchange Stabilization Fund, the Treasury will provide $30 billion in equity to these facilities);
- establishing two facilities to support credit to large employers: the Primary Market Corporate Credit Facility for new bond and loan issuance, and the Secondary

BACKGROUND

Market Corporate Credit Facility to provide liquidity for outstanding corporate bonds; and

- establishing a third facility, the Term Asset-Backed Securities Loan Facility, to support the flow of credit to consumers and businesses. This facility will enable the issuance of asset-backed securities backed by student loans, auto loans, credit card loans, loans guaranteed by the Small Business Administration (SBA), and certain other assets.

The Federal Reserve was also expected to announce the establishment of a Main Street Business Lending Program to support lending to eligible small and medium-sized businesses, complementing the SBA's efforts.

Section 4003 of the CARES Act, found in Subtitle A of Title IV, authorizes $500 billion to fund some of the Federal Reserve's programs and facilities and to provide direct loans and loan guarantees to eligible businesses.

NEW LAW EXPLAINED

Loan, loan guarantees, other investments authorized.—The Treasury is authorized to provide up to $46 billion in direct loans and loan guarantees to (Act Sec. 4003(b)(1)-(3) of the Coronavirus Aid, Relief, and Economic Security Act (P.L. 116-136)):

(1) passenger air carriers and specified related businesses—up to $25 billion;

(2) cargo air carriers—up to $4 billion; and

(3) businesses critical to maintaining national security—up to $17 billion.

Up to $454 billion (and any of the allocated $46 billion remaining) is available for loans and loan guarantees to, and other investments in, programs or facilities established by the Federal Reserve for providing liquidity to the financial system that supports lending to eligible businesses, states, or municipalities by (Act Sec. 4003(b)(4) of the CARES Act):

- purchasing obligations or other interests directly from issuers;
- purchasing obligations or other interests in secondary markets or otherwise; or
- making loans, including loans or other advances secured by collateral.

Comment: The CARES Act defines an "eligible business" as an "air carrier or a U.S. business that has not otherwise received adequate economic relief in the form of loans or loan guarantees provided under this Act" (Act Sec. 4002(4) of the CARES Act). Under this definition, air carriers and related businesses, as well as businesses critical to national security, that receive loans or loan guarantees under Section 4003(b)(1)-(3) may also be eligible for liquidity support under Section 4003(b)(4).

Comment: Treasury Secretary Steven Mnuchin has stated that the Federal Reserve could leverage the $454 billion to provide $4 trillion of support ("How the Fed's Magic Money Machine Will Turn $454 Billion Into $4 Trillion," New York Times, March 27, 2020).

NEW LAW EXPLAINED

Interest on loans. The interest rate on Section 4003 loans must be based on the risk and current average yield on outstanding marketable government obligations of comparable maturity (Act Sec. 4003(c)(1)(A) of the CARES Act).

Prohibition on loan forgiveness. The principal of any obligation issued by an eligible business, state, or municipality under Section 4003(b) of the CARES Act may not be reduced by loan forgiveness (Act Sec. 4003(d)(3) of the CARES Act; see also Act Sec. 4029(b)(1)(B) of the CARES Act).

Modification or restructuring. A loan, loan guarantee, or other investment outstanding on December 31, 2020, may be modified, restructured, or otherwise amended, but it may not be extended beyond five years from the initial origination date (Act Sec. 4029(b) of the CARES Act).

Direct Treasury loans and loan guarantees. Treasury loans and loan guarantees to eligible businesses (air carriers and related businesses, and businesses critical to national security) may not exceed five years and must be secured or made at a rate that reflects risk and is not less than the rate for comparable obligations prior to the COVID-19 outbreak (Act Sec. 4003(c)(2)(C), (D) of the CARES Act).

The borrower must (Act Sec. 4003(c)(2)(A), (B), (H), (I) of the CARES Act):

- be an eligible business for which credit is not reasonably available, and the intended obligation must be "prudently incurred";
- certify it is created or organized in the United States or under U.S. law, and it has significant operations in, and a majority of its employees based in, the United States; and
- have incurred or expect to incur "covered losses" that jeopardize its continued operations. "Covered losses" are losses incurred directly or indirectly as a result of coronavirus (Act Sec. 4002(3) of the CARES Act).

In addition (Act Sec. 4003(c)(2)(E)-(G) of the CARES Act):

- the borrower and its affiliates may not repurchase publicly traded stock of the borrower or a parent company until 12 months after the end of the loan or guarantee (unless contractually obligated to do so on March 27, 2020);
- the borrower may not pay dividends or make other capital distributions with respect to its common stock until 12 months after the end of the loan or guarantee; and
- the borrower must maintain at least 90 percent of its March 24, 2020, employment levels until September 30, 2020.

The borrower also must comply with the executive compensation limitations of Section 4004 of the CARES Act (see ¶710).

The Treasury may not issue a loan or loan guarantee to an eligible business unless it receives (Act Sec. 4003(d)(1) of the CARES Act):

- a warrant or equity interest in the business if it has publicly traded stock; or
- for other businesses, a warrant or equity interest in the business or a senior debt instrument issued by the business.

NEW LAW EXPLAINED

No later than 10 days after the March 27, 2020 date of enactment of the CARES Act, the Treasury must publish procedures for application and minimum requirements for loans and loan guarantees (Act Sec. 4003(c)(1)(B) of the CARES Act). On March 30, 2020, the Treasury published "Procedures and Minimum Requirements for Loans to Air Carriers and Eligible Businesses and National Security Businesses under Division A, Title IV, Subtitle A of the Coronavirus Aid, Relief, and Economic Security Act." The guidance provides a list of eligible borrowers and reiterates the eligibility criteria at Section 4003(c)(2). The Treasury noted that the procedures and requirements are preliminary; will be supplemented with additional terms and a loan application form; may be updated, revised, or modified at any time; and may be waived in the Treasury's sole discretion to the extent permitted by law.

Treasury loans and loan guarantees to, and other investments in, Federal Reserve programs and facilities. A program or facility in which the Treasury makes a loan, loan guarantee, or other investment may only purchase obligations or other interests from, or make loans or other advances to, businesses that are created or organized in the United States or under U.S. law, and that have significant operations in, and a majority of employees based in, the United States (Act. Sec. 4003(c)(3)(C) of the CARES Act).

An eligible business (Act Sec. 4003(c)(3)(A)(ii) of the CARES Act):

- may not repurchase its own or a parent company's publicly traded stock until 12 months after the end of the direct loan (unless contractually obligated to do so on March 27, 2020);
- may not pay dividends or make other capital distributions with respect to its common stock until 12 months after the end of the direct loan; and
- must comply with the executive compensation limitations of Section 4004 of the CARES Act (see ¶710).

Federal Reserve programs or facilities must comply with requirements under Section 13(3) of the Federal Reserve Act (12 U.S.C. 343(3)), including requirements regarding loan collateralization, taxpayer protection, and borrower solvency (Act Sec. 4003(c)(3)(B) of the CARES Act).

Mid-size businesses. The Treasury is directed to implement a program or facility that provides financing to banks and other lenders that make direct loans to eligible businesses, including nonprofit organizations, with 500-10,000 employees. The maximum annualized interest rate for such loans may not exceed 2 percent, and no principal or interest is due during the first six months, or longer as the Treasury determines (Act Sec. 4003(c)(3)(D) of the CARES Act).

A mid-size businesses applying for a loan must certify in good faith that (Act Sec. 4003(c)(3)(D)(i)(I), (IV)-(VII) of the CARES Act):

- due to the economic uncertainty, the requested loan is necessary to support ongoing operations;
- it is domiciled in the United States and has significant operations and employees located in the United States;
- it is not a debtor in a bankruptcy proceeding;

NEW LAW EXPLAINED

- it was created or organized in the United States or under U.S. laws, and it has significant operations and a majority of its employees based in the United States; and
- it will not pay any dividends on its common stock or repurchase any of its or a parent company's stock while the loan is outstanding (unless contractually obligated to do so on March 27, 2020).

> **Comment:** Although slightly different, certifications (2) and (4) both ensure the loan applicant's status as a U.S. business.

The business also must certify that it (Act Sec. 4003(c)(3)(D)(i)(II), (III), (VIII)-(X) of the CARES Act):

- will use the funds to retain at least 90 percent of its workforce, at full compensation and benefits, until September 30, 2020;
- intends to reinstate at least 90 percent of its workforce that was employed on February 1, 2020, and to restore all compensation and benefits to employees no later than four months after the COVID-19 emergency ends;
- will not outsource or offshore jobs for the term of the loan and two years after the loan is repaid;
- will not abrogate existing collective bargaining agreements for the term of the loan and two years after the loan is repaid; and
- will remain neutral in any union organizing effort for the term of the loan.

The CARES Act provisions for providing assistance to mid-sized businesses do not limit the Federal Reserve's discretion to establish a Main Street Lending Program or other similar program or facility that supports lending to small and mid-sized businesses (Act Sec. 4003(c)(3)(D)(ii) of the CARES Act).

Lending support to states and municipalities. The Treasury is directed to implement a program or facility that provides liquidity to the financial system that supports lending to states and municipalities (Act Sec. 4003(c)(3)(E) of the CARES Act).

▶ **Effective date.** The Act does not specify an effective date for Section 4003. Accordingly, the section is treated as effective on March 27, 2020, the date of enactment of the CARES Act. The authority to make new loans, loan guarantees, or other investments terminates on December 31, 2020 (Act Sec. 4029(a) of the Coronavirus Aid, Relief, and Economic Security Act (P.L. 116-136)).

Law source: Law at ¶2187, ¶2188, ¶2189, and ¶2214.

— Act Sec. 4002 of the Coronavirus Aid, Relief, and Economic Security Act (P.L. 116-136).

— Act Sec. 4003 of the CARES Act.

— Act Sec. 4004 of the CARES Act.

— Act Sec. 4029 of the CARES Act.

¶710 Limitations on Certain Highly Paid Officer and Employee Compensation

SUMMARY OF NEW LAW

The Secretary of the Treasury may only enter into an agreement to make a loan or loan guarantee to eligible passenger air carriers (and specified related businesses), cargo air carriers, and businesses critical to maintaining national security (as described in Section 4003(b)(1), (2), and (3) of the Coronavirus Aid, Relief, and Economic Security Act (P.L. 116-136)) if the businesses agree to specified limitations on total compensation of certain highly paid officers and employees.

BACKGROUND

An employment agreement between an employer and an executive sets forth the terms of the employment relationship, covering, among other things, compensation arrangements. The compensation (immediate and deferred) may take many forms, including base salaries, bonuses and other incentive compensation, equity, employee retirement and insurance benefits, and severance and change-of-control pay. There are tax consequences for the employer and the executive depending on the type of compensation. Some compensation may be taxable income for the executive and deductible by the employer in a current tax year, and other compensation may be taxable income for the executive in a future tax year and not deductible for the employer until that future tax year.

After passing the Families First Coronavirus Response Act (P.L. 116-127), which attempts to limit the spread of the COVID-19 pandemic and support relief efforts, Congress turned toward stabilizing the economy. Although certain members of Congress wanted to accomplish the stabilization goal by providing various forms of aid to companies, other members wanted to focus more on helping non-executive workers. Ultimately, a bill was passed by Congress that was more worker-first focused while providing distressed businesses access to loans and other economic assistance. In a March 27, 2020, press release covering Nancy Pelosi's speech on the floor of the House of Representatives in support of the CARES Act, Pelosi stated that "[w]e ensured in the bill that any taxpayer dollars given to industry goes first and foremost to workers. Workers' paychecks and benefits, not used to pay CEO bonuses, stocks, fund buybacks or dividends and the rest."

NEW LAW EXPLAINED

Restrictions on certain highly paid officer and employee compensation.—The Treasury Secretary is not allowed to enter into an agreement with an eligible business to make a loan or loan guarantee under Section 4003(b)(1), (2) or (3) of the CARES Act (see ¶700) unless there are restrictions on the compensation of certain highly paid officers and employees (Act Sec. 4004 of the Coronavirus Aid, Relief, and Economic Security Act (P.L. 116-136)).

NEW LAW EXPLAINED

In general, the officer and employee compensation limitations are based on total compensation received in the 2019 calendar year. Specifically, the agreement must provide that, during the period beginning on the date on which the agreement is executed and ending on the date that is one year after the date on which the loan or loan guarantee is no longer outstanding, no officer or employee of the eligible business whose total compensation exceeded $425,000 in calendar-year 2019 (other than an employee whose compensation is determined through an existing collective bargaining agreement entered into prior to March 1, 2020) may receive from the business (a) total compensation that exceeds, during any 12 consecutive months of the covered period, the total compensation received by the officer or employee from the business in calendar year 2019, or (b) severance pay or other benefits upon termination of employment with the business that exceeds twice the maximum total compensation received by the officer or employee from the business in calendar year 2019 (Act Sec. 4004(a)(1) of the CARES Act).

In addition, any agreement between the Secretary and an eligible business receiving a loan or loan guarantee would need to stipulate that between the agreement's execution date and one year after the loan or loan guarantee's termination, any business officer or employee who received more than $3 million in total compensation in calendar year 2019 may not receive (during any 12 consecutive months of that period) more than $3 million, plus one-half of the received calendar year 2019 total compensation that exceeded $3 million (Act Sec. 4004(a)(2) of the CARES Act).

Definitions. For purposes of this section,

- "Coronavirus" means SARS-CoV-2 or another coronavirus with pandemic potential (Act Sec. 4002(2) of the CARES Act).
- "Eligible business" means an air carrier, or a U.S. business that has not otherwise received adequate economic relief in the form of loans or loan guarantees provided under the CARES Act (Act Sec. 4002(4) of the CARES Act).
- "Employee," except where the context otherwise requires, has the meaning given the term in Section 2 of the National Labor Relations Act (29 U.S.C. 152), and includes any individual employed by an employer subject to the Railway Labor Act (45 U.S.C. 151 et seq.) (Act Sec. 4002(5) of the CARES Act).
- "Secretary" means the Secretary of the Treasury, or the designee of the Secretary of the Treasury (Act Sec. 4002(9) of the CARES Act).
- "Total compensation" includes salary, bonuses, awards of stock, and other financial benefits provided by an eligible business to an officer or employee of the eligible business (Act Sec. 4004(b) of the CARES Act).

> **Comment:** Title IV of the CARES Act, which is comprised of Sections 4001-4120, provides $500 billion in emergency relief in order to provide liquidity to eligible businesses, states, municipalities, and Indian tribes related to losses incurred as a result of the COVID-19 pandemic. Section 4003(b)(1)-(3) of the CARES Act (see ¶700) provides a total of $46 billion in funding for relief—in the form of loans or loan guarantees—for passenger air carriers, aviation repair stations, airline ticket

NEW LAW EXPLAINED

agents, cargo air carriers, and "businesses critical to maintaining national security." These loans or loan guarantees are subject to various terms and conditions, including the limitations on certain highly paid officer and employee compensation.

Note that on March 30, 2020, the Treasury Department published guidance, called the "Procedures and Minimum Requirements for Loans to Air Carriers and Eligible Businesses and National Security Businesses under Division A, Title IV, Subtitle A of the Coronavirus Aid, Relief, and Economic Security Act." The Treasury Department explains that the procedures and requirements are preliminary, and may be updated, revised, or modified at any time.

▶ **Effective date.** The Act does not specify an effective date for Section 4004. Accordingly, the section is treated as effective on the March 27, 2020, date of enactment of the CARES Act.

Law source: Law at ¶2187, ¶2188, and ¶2189.

— Act Sec. 4002 of the Coronavirus Aid, Relief, and Economic Security Act (P.L. 116-136).

— Act Sec. 4003 of the CARES Act.

— Act Sec. 4004 of the CARES Act.

¶720 Temporary Sunshine Act Relief

SUMMARY OF NEW LAW

The Board of Governors of the Federal Reserve System may conduct meetings without regard to the Sunshine Act requirements during the covered period for the COVID-19 national emergency if the Chairman of the Board of Governors of the Federal Reserve System determines, in writing, that unusual and exigent circumstances exist.

BACKGROUND

In general, under Section 552b of Title 5, United States Code, every portion of every agency meeting should be open to public observation. Agency meetings are deliberations of at least the number of individual agency members required to take action on behalf of the agency where deliberations determine or result in the joint conduct or disposition of official agency business. There are many exceptions to the open meeting requirement, including, among others, situations where the agency determines that matters are specifically authorized to be kept secret in the interest of national defense or relate to internal agency personnel rules or practices. Also, the exception applies to instances where disclosure of information prematurely would endanger the stability of a financial institution. This is particularly important in cases involving agencies that regulate currencies, securities, commodities or financial institutions.

BACKGROUND

Each federal agency is required to make a public announcement, at least one week before the meeting, of the time, place, and subject matter of the meeting, whether it is open or closed to the public, and the name and phone number of the official designated by the agency to respond to requests for information about the meeting. In addition, Section 552b outlines procedures agencies should use to make transcripts and minutes available to the public.

NEW LAW EXPLAINED

Temporary Federal Reserve Board Sunshine Act relief.—If the Chairman of the Board of Governors of the Federal Reserve System determines, in writing, that unusual and exigent circumstances exist, the Board may conduct meetings without regard to the requirements of Section 552b of Title 5, United States Code, during the period beginning on March 27, 2020, and ending on the earlier of (Act Sec. 4009(a)(1) and (2) of the Coronavirus Aid, Relief, and Economic Security Act (P.L. 116-136)):

(1) the date on which the national emergency concerning the novel coronavirus disease (COVID-19) outbreak declared by the President on March 13, 2020, under the National Emergencies Act (50 U.S.C. 1601 et seq.) terminates; or

(2) December 31, 2020.

For purposes of these provisions, "coronavirus" means SARS-CoV-2 or another coronavirus with pandemic potential (Act Sec. 4002(2) of the CARES Act).

> **Comment:** To help stabilize the economy, the CARES Act allows the federal government to make loans, loan guarantees, and other investments available to distressed businesses (see ¶700). Among other things, the CARES Act provides amounts that are available to make loans and loan guarantees to, and other investments in, programs or facilities established by the Board of Governors of the Federal Reserve System for the purpose of providing liquidity to the financial system that supports the lending and other investments. The provision would allow the Federal Reserve to conduct related discussions without complying with the Sunshine Act.

Records. The Board of Governors of the Federal Reserve System must keep a record of all Board votes and the reasons for the votes during the period described above (Act Sec. 4009(b) of the CARES Act).

► **Effective date.** The provisions are effective on the March 27, 2020, date of enactment of the CARES Act and end on the earlier of the date the COVID-19 national emergency terminates or December 31, 2020 (Act Sec. 4009(a) of the Coronavirus Aid, Relief, and Economic Security Act (P.L. 116-136)).

Law source: Law at ¶2187 and ¶2194.

— Act Sec. 4002 of the Coronavirus Aid, Relief, and Economic Security Act (P.L. 116-136).

— Act Sec. 4009 of the CARES Act.

¶730 Temporary Hiring Flexibility

SUMMARY OF NEW LAW

The Department of Housing and Urban Development, the Securities and Exchange Commission, and the Commodity Futures Trading Commission are granted additional hiring flexibility during the COVID-19 national emergency.

BACKGROUND

Sections 3309-3318 of U.S. Code Title 5 set forth rules for hiring preferences in the competitive civil service.

NEW LAW EXPLAINED

Hiring flexibility granted.—The Coronavirus Aid, Relief, and Economic Security Act (P.L. 116-136) grants the Department of Housing and Urban Development, the Securities and Exchange Commission, and the Commodity Futures Trading Commission additional hiring flexibility upon a determination by the Agency's Secretary that expedited procedures are necessary and appropriate to prevent, prepare for, or respond to COVID-19. Upon such a determination, candidates to fill temporary and term appointments may be recruited and appointed without regard to U.S. Code Title 5, Sections 3309-3318 (Act Sec. 4010(b) of the Coronavirus Aid, Relief, and Economic Security Act (P.L. 116-136)).

The authority to use expedited recruitment and appointment procedures began on March 27, 2020, and ends on the earlier of (Act Sec. 4010(a) of the CARES Act):

(1) the end of the COVID-19 national emergency declared by the President; or

(2) December 31, 2020.

▶ **Effective date.** This section is effective March 27, 2020. It will sunset on the termination date of the national emergency concerning the novel coronavirus disease outbreak that the President declared on March 13, 2020, or December 31, 2020, whichever is earlier (Act Sec. 4010(a) of the Coronavirus Aid, Relief, and Economic Security Act (P.L. 116-136)).

Law source: Law at ¶2195.

— Act Sec. 4010 of the Coronavirus Aid, Relief, and Economic Security Act (P.L. 116-136).

¶740 Credit Protection During COVID-19

SUMMARY OF NEW LAW

The Fair Credit Reporting Act is amended to require data furnishers to report to the credit bureaus that consumers are current on their credit obligations if they enter into an agreement with a consumer affected by COVID-19 to defer, forbear, modify, make

SUMMARY OF NEW LAW

partial payments, or get any other assistance on their loan payments from a financial institution and the consumer fulfills those requirements.

BACKGROUND

A furnisher of information to consumer reporting agencies is under a general obligation to provide accurate information under Fair Credit Reporting Act Section 632(a)(1). A furnisher may, but need not, specify an address for receipt of notices from consumers concerning inaccurate information. If the furnisher specifies an address, then it may not furnish information relating to a consumer to any consumer reporting agency if the furnisher has been notified by the consumer, at the specified address, that the information is inaccurate, and the information is in fact inaccurate. If the furnisher does not specify an address, then it may not furnish any information relating to a consumer to any consumer reporting agency, if it knows or consciously avoids knowing that the information is inaccurate.

NEW LAW EXPLAINED

Reporting information during COVID-19 pandemic.—Section 4021 of the CARES Act amends the Fair Credit Reporting Act to require data furnishers, such as banks, credit card companies, debt collection agencies, and other companies that process financial information, during the COVID-19 pandemic "covered period" to report to the credit bureaus that consumers are current on their credit obligations if they enter into an agreement with a consumer affected by the pandemic to defer, forbear, modify, make partial payments, or get any other assistance on their loan payments from a financial institution and the consumer fulfills those requirements, provided the consumers were current before this period. If the consumer was delinquent before the covered period, then the furnisher shall maintain the delinquent status unless the consumer brings the account or obligation current (Fair Credit Reporting Act Sec. 623(a)(1)(F), as added by Act Sec. 4021 of the Coronavirus Aid, Relief, and Economic Security Act (P.L. 116-136)).

Note: The requirements added by this section do not apply with respect to a credit obligation or account of a consumer that has been "charged-off" (i.e. written off as bad debt).

Accommodation. The term 'accommodation' includes an agreement to defer one or more payments, make a partial payment, forbear any delinquent amounts, modify a loan or contract, or any other assistance or relief granted to a consumer who is affected by the COVID-19 pandemic during the covered period. (FCRA Sec. 623(a)(1)(F), as added by Sec. 4021 of the CARES Act.)

Covered period. The term 'covered period' means the period beginning on January 31, 2020 and ending on the later of 120 days after the March 27, 2020 date of enactment ***or*** 120 days after the date on which the national emergency concerning the COVID-19 outbreak declared by the President on March 13, 2020 terminates. (FCRA Sec. 623(a)(1)(F), as added by Sec. 4021 of the CARES Act.)

NEW LAW EXPLAINED

> **Comment:** In light of the CARES Act relief, the Consumer Financial Protection Bureau (CFPB) provided guidance to credit reporting agencies and information furnishers about CARES Act compliance. The CFPB is encouraging credit reporters and furnishers to continue to furnish information to reporting agencies despite the current crisis. The guidance also indicates that the CFPB expects furnishers to comply with this provision of the CARES Act, and the CFPB will work with furnishers as needed to help them comply. The guidance further noted that although the FRCA generally requires consumer reporting agencies and furnishers to investigate consumer disputes within 30 days of receipt of the consumer's dispute, the timeframe may be extended to 45 days if the consumer provides additional relevant information (CFPB Statement on Supervisory and Enforcement Practices Regarding the Fair Credit Reporting Act and Regulation V in Light of the CARES Act, April 1, 2020).

▶ **Effective date.** The provision is effective on the March 27, 2020 date of enactment of the CARES Act. The relief ends on the later of 120 days after the date of enactment ***or*** 120 days after the date on which the national emergency ends.

Law source: Law at ¶2206 and ¶8001.

— Act Sec. 4021 of the Coronavirus Aid, Relief, and Economic Security Act (P.L. 116-136), adding Section 623(a)(1)(F) of the Fair Credit Reporting Act.

¶750 Protection of Collective Bargaining Agreement

SUMMARY OF NEW LAW

A loan to an air carrier or other eligible business cannot be conditioned on whether that air carrier or eligible business is preparing to enter into negotiations for a collective bargaining agreement regarding pay or other terms and conditions of employment.

BACKGROUND

A collective bargaining agreement is negotiated by employers and employees regarding the terms and conditions of employment, such as rates of pay or hours of employment. The Railway Labor Act provides a large number of procedures designed to promote collective bargaining. The National Labor Relations Act (NLRA) imposes upon employers and unions the duty to bargain collectively in good faith. While the NLRA does not compel the parties to reach an agreement, the good-faith requirement imposes an obligation on both parties to make honest claims. An employer's financial difficulties do not justify a refusal to recognize and bargain with a union.

NEW LAW EXPLAINED

NEW LAW EXPLAINED

Loans cannot be conditioned on negotiations of CBA.— No one acting on behalf of the federal government, including the Treasury Secretary, a department or agency, may condition the issuance of a loan or loan guarantee under Sec. 4003(b)(1), (2), or (3) of the Coronavirus Aid, Relief, and Economic Security Act (P.L. 116-136) (see ¶ 700) to an air carrier or other eligible business on the air carrier's or eligible business's implementation of measures to enter into negotiations with a representative for a certified bargaining agreement under the Railway Labor Act or the National Labor Relations Act regarding pay or other terms and conditions of employment (Act Sec. 4025(a) of the Coronavirus Aid, Relief, and Economic Security Act (P.L. 116-136)).

Definitions. Under Sec. 4002(1) of the CARES Act, the term "air carrier" is defined as having the meaning of that term under section 40102 of Title 49, United States Code. Under Section 4002(4) of the CARES Act, the term "eligible business" means an air carrier or a United States business that has not otherwise received adequate economic relief in the form of loans or loan guarantees provided under the CARES Act. Finally, under Sec. 4002(9) of the CARES Act, the term "Secretary" means the Secretary of Treasury or the designee Secretary of Treasury.

▶ **Effective date.** Takes effect beginning the date on which the air carrier or eligible business is first issued the loan or loan guarantee and ends one year after the date the loan or loan guarantee is no longer outstanding (Act Sec. 4025(b) of the Coronavirus Aid, Relief, and Economic Security Act (P.L. 116-136)).

Law source: Law at ¶2187, ¶2188, and ¶2210.

— Act Sec. 4002 of the Coronavirus Aid, Relief, and Economic Security Act (P.L. 116-136).

— Act Sec. 4025(a) of the CARES Act.

— Act Sec. 4025(b) of the CARES Act, providing the effective date.

Chapter 8—Air Carrier Workers Support

8

¶800 Pandemic Relief for Aviation Workers

SUMMARY OF NEW LAW

The Coronavirus Aid, Relief, and Economic Security (CARES) Act (P.L. 116-136), earmarks $32 billion in financial assistance (*i.e.*, payroll support) to aid the commercial airline industry and its employees affected by travel cutbacks due to the coronavirus pandemic. These funds are in addition to loans and loan guarantees provided to passenger air carriers and businesses critical to maintaining national security provided elsewhere in the statute.

BACKGROUND

Commercial air carriers generally are governed by Title 49, U.S. Code—Transportation and its implementing regulations in Title 14, Code of Federal Regulations. Those provisions are largely applicable based upon the type of operations conducted. For example, the Federal Aviation Administration grants large U.S.-based airlines, regional air carriers, and all-cargo operators the authority to conduct regularly scheduled air service (as opposed to on-demand or chartered service) in the form of an operating certificate issued under 14 C.F.R. Part 121.

Concerns related to the spread of COVID-19 prompted the Trump Administration to ban all commercial flights from mainland China and Hong Kong on January 31, 2020, followed later by similar bans on flights from the Islamic Republic of Iran, Europe, the United Kingdom, and Ireland. U.S. airlines suspended operations to those areas, which gave rise to dramatic reductions in their operating schedules. In addition, air travel within the United States also fell off sharply once several states implemented

BACKGROUND

"stay-home" orders. As a result, thousands of planes have been idled and, with them, the carrier and contractor employees who normally serve those flights.

NEW LAW EXPLAINED

Payroll support.—To preserve aviation jobs and compensate air carrier industry workers, the Secretary (defined under Act Sec. 4111(5) of the CARES Act as "the Secretary of the Treasury") is directed to provide financial assistance to the commercial airline industry to be used exclusively for the continuation of payment of employee wages, salaries, and benefits. Up to $25 billion in the aggregate is available to passenger air carriers, up to $4 billion in the aggregate is available to cargo air carriers, and up to $3 billion in the aggregate is available to airline contractors (Act Sec. 4112 of the Coronavirus Aid, Relief, and Economic Security Act (P.L. 116-136)).

"Contractor" defined. The term "contractor" is defined as a person that performs, under contract with a passenger air carrier conducting operations under 14 C.F.R. Part 121 either: (1) catering functions; (2) functions on the property of an airport that are directly related to the air transportation of persons, property, or mail (including but not limited to the loading and unloading of property on aircraft, assistance to passengers, security, airport ticketing and check-in functions, ground-handling of aircraft, or aircraft cleaning/sanitization functions and waste removal); or (3) a subcontractor that performs those functions (Act Sec. 4111(3) of the CARES Act). "Airline catering services" is defined as "the preparation, assembly, or both, of food, beverages, provisions and related supplies for delivery, and the delivery of such items, directly to aircraft or to a location on or near airport property for subsequent delivery to aircraft" (Act Sec. 4111(2) of the CARES Act).

"Employee" defined. The term "employee" is defined as "an individual, other than a corporate officer, who is employed by an air carrier or a contractor," while "airline catering employee" is defined as "an employee who performs airline catering services" (Act Sec. 4111(4); Act Sec. 4111(1) of the CARES Act). According to guidance issued by the U.S. Department of the Treasury on April 2, 2020, employees will not be included for purposes of the payroll support funds unless they are based in the United States, including its territories and possessions (Q&A: Payroll Support to Air Carriers and Contractors, https://home.treasury.gov/system/files/136/QandA-Payroll-Support-to-Air-Carriers-and-Contractors.pdf).

Administrative expenses. Notwithstanding any other provision of law, the Secretary of the Treasury can use $100 million of the funds made available by Sec. 4120 of the CARES Act for costs and administrative expenses associated with providing financial assistance related to air carrier worker support (Act Sec. 4112(b) of the CARES Act).

▶ **Effective date.** The Act does not specify an effective date. Accordingly, this provision is considered effective on March 27, 2020, the date of enactment of the CARES Act.

Law source: Law at ¶2116 and ¶2217.

— Act Sec. 4111 of the Coronavirus Aid, Relief, and Economic Security Act (P.L. 116-136).

— Act Sec. 4112 of the CARES Act.

¶810 Procedures for Providing Payroll Support

SUMMARY OF NEW LAW

Payroll support funds provided to airlines and airline contractors will be determined based upon the recipients' salaries and benefits incurred during the six-month period between April 1—September 30, 2019, and will be made available under expedited application and payment procedures beginning five days after the enactment of the Coronavirus Aid, Relief, and Economic Security (CARES) Act (P.L. 116-136).

BACKGROUND

Under Title 14, Code of Federal Regulations, Part 241, large certified U.S. air carriers are required to annually file financial and accounting information that includes balance sheet, cash flow, employment, income statement, fuel cost and consumption, aircraft operating expenses, and operating expenses. The data is compiled and maintained by the U.S. Department of Transportation's Bureau of Transportation Statistics. Smaller air carriers and airline contractors are not required to report such information.

NEW LAW EXPLAINED

Awardable amounts.—Financial assistance available under Act Sec. 4112 of the Coronavirus Aid, Relief, and Economic Security (CARES) Act (P.L. 116-136) (see ¶ 800) is available in an amount equal to the salaries and benefits incurred during the six-month period from April 1, 2019, through September 30, 2019, as reported by the air carrier to the U.S. Department of Transportation (pursuant to 14 C.F.R. Part 241) or certified via financial statements or other appropriate data. Smaller air carriers and airline contractors seeking payroll support that do not report Part 241 information must certify—using sworn financial statements or other appropriate data—the amount of wages, salaries, benefits, and other compensation paid to employees over that same time period (Act Sec. 4113(a) of the Coronavirus Aid, Relief, and Economic Security Act (P.L. 116-136)).

Audits. The Department of the Treasury's Inspector General is directed to audit the certifications provided by air carriers and airline contractors requesting financial assistance (Act Sec. 4113(d) of the CARES Act).

Deadlines and procedures. Payroll support funds will be provided in the form, terms, and conditions (including the requirements for audits and the claw-back of any financial assistance provided upon failure by a passenger air carrier, cargo air carrier, or contractor to honor the assurances specified in Act Sec. 4114 of the CARES Act) as deemed appropriate by the Secretary of the Treasury. The Secretary is directed to publish streamlined and expedited procedures for requesting financial assistance within five days of the enactment of the CARES Act and must make initial payments to air

NEW LAW EXPLAINED

carriers and contractors submitting those requests within 10 days of the statute's enactment. The appropriate method for the timely distribution of subsequent payments from the remaining funds available after the initial financial assistance is to be determined by the Secretary (Act Sec. 4113(b) of the CARES Act).

Treasury Department guidance. According guidance issued by the U.S. Department of the Treasury on April 2, 2020, applications currently are being accepted but no longer should be submitted by email (Q&A: Payroll Support to Air Carriers and Contractors, https://home.treasury.gov/system/files/136/QandA-Payroll-Support-to-Air-Carriers-and-Contractors.pdf). Instead, all applicants that have not already submitted an application by email should apply for payroll support via the Department's online application tool at https://forms.treasury.gov/caresact/PayrollSupportRequestForAirCarriers and clicking through the various screens provided therein. While the Department stated that application materials had to be submitted by 5:00 p.m., EDT on April 3, 2020, in order to ensure the most immediate consideration, applications continued to be accepted until 5:00 p.m., EDT on April 27, 2020. Applications submitted after April 3 may receive less immediate consideration, and applications received after April 27, 2020 may or may not be considered at the Department's discretion, subject to the availability of funds.

Reduced payments. The Secretary of the Treasury has the authority to reduce, on a *pro rata* basis, the amounts due to air carriers and contractors under Act Sec. 4112 of the CARES Act in order to address any shortfall in assistance that otherwise would be provided under that section (Act Sec. 4113(c) of the CARES Act).

▶ **Effective date.** The Act does not specify an effective date. Accordingly, this provision is considered effective on March 27, 2020, the date of enactment of the CARES Act.

Law source: Law at ¶2218.

— Act Sec. 4113 of the Coronavirus Aid, Relief, and Economic Security Act (P.L. 116-136).

¶820 Required Assurances

SUMMARY OF NEW LAW

Airlines and airline contractors receiving payroll support funds must agree to refrain from furloughing employees or reducing their pay and benefits through September 30, 2020, as well as from engaging in stock buy-backs through that date and paying dividends or other capital distributions to shareholders.

BACKGROUND

Certificated air carriers are subject to conditions on the company's operations imposed by the U.S. Department of Transportation, such as a limit on the duration of the authority, the quantity, type, or size of aircraft that the carrier can operate, or on

BACKGROUND

the type of service provided. Although the 1978 deregulation of the airline industry gave air carriers almost total freedom to determine which markets to serve domestically and what fares to charge for that service, the Essential Air Service (EAS) program was put into place in order to guarantee that small communities maintain a minimal level of scheduled air service. In that regard, DOT must provide eligible EAS communities with access to the National Air Transportation System, which the Department maintains by subsidizing air carriers to serve approximately 60 communities in Alaska and 115 communities in the lower 48 contiguous states that otherwise would not receive any scheduled air service.

NEW LAW EXPLAINED

In general.—To be eligible for financial assistance under Act Sec. 4112 of the Coronavirus Aid, Relief, and Economic Security (CARES) Act (P.L. 116-136), an air carrier or contractor must enter into an agreement with the Secretary of the Treasury, or otherwise certify in a form and manner prescribed by the Secretary, that the recipient will: (1) refrain from conducting involuntary furloughs or reducing pay rates and benefits until September 30, 2020; (2) through September 30, 2021, ensure that neither the recipient nor any of its affiliates purchase an equity security of the recipient or its parent company that is listed on a national securities exchange; (3) through September 30, 2021, ensure that the recipient will not pay dividends or make other capital distributions with respect to their common stock (or equivalent interest); and (4) meet the requirements of Sections 4115 and 4116 of the CARES Act, relating to protection of collective bargaining agreements and limitations on certain employee compensation, respectively (Act Sec. 4114(a) of the Coronavirus Aid, Relief, and Economic Security Act (P.L. 116-36)).

Service continuation mandate. The Secretary of Transportation can require, to the extent reasonable and practicable, that an air carrier receiving payroll support maintain scheduled air transportation service as she deems necessary to ensure services to any point served by that carrier before March 1, 2020. When considering the authority to require service continuation, the Transportation Secretary must take into consideration the air transportation needs of small and remote communities as well as the need to maintain well-functioning health care supply chains, including medical devices/supplies and pharmaceutical supply chains (Act Sec. 4114(b) of the CARES Act). The U.S. Department of Transportation has detailed those requirements in *Order 2020-3-10*, March 31, 2020.

▶ **Effective date.** The Act does not specify an effective date. Accordingly, this provision is considered effective on March 27, 2020, the date of enactment of the CARES Act. The provision is scheduled to sunset on March 1, 2022 (Act Sec. 4114(b)(3) of the CARES Act).

Law source: Law at ¶2219.

— Act Sec. 4114 of the Coronavirus Aid, Relief, and Economic Security Act (P.L. 116-136).

¶830 Protection of Collective Bargaining Agreements

SUMMARY OF NEW LAW

Payroll support funds to airlines and airline contractors cannot be conditioned upon the recipients' implementation of measures to enter into negotiations with the collective bargaining representatives of their employees regarding wages or other working conditions.

BACKGROUND

Air carriers and the labor unions representing their employees are governed by the Railway Labor Act (RLA), while airline contractors and their employees presumably meet the requirements of, and are thus governed by, the National Labor Relations Act (NLRA). Where the parties have signed a collective bargaining agreement (CBA), both statutes generally bar an employer from making unilateral changes in the wages, hours, or working conditions of the employees subject to that agreement. While employees governed by the NLRA can engage in concerted activity such as work slowdowns, walkouts, and strikes—the RLA prohibits airline employees from striking, substituting instead binding arbitration and mediation for the resolution of labor disputes.

NEW LAW EXPLAINED

In general.—Neither the Secretary of the Treasury nor any other actor, department, or agency of the federal government can condition the issuance of airline industry payroll support on an air carrier's or contractor's implementation of measures to enter into negotiations with the certified bargaining representative of a craft or class of employees of the air carrier or contractor under the Railway Labor Act or the National Labor Relations Act regarding pay or other terms and conditions of employment (Act Sec. 4115(a) of the Coronavirus Aid, Relief, and Economic Security Act (P.L. 116-136)).

Period of effect. The above-mentioned protections are effective with respect to air carriers or airline contractors from the date on which they receive financial assistance under Act Sec. 4112 of the CARES Act and ending on September 30, 2020 (Act Sec. 4115(b) of the CARES Act).

▶ **Effective date.** The Act does not specify an effective date. Accordingly, this provision is considered effective on March 27, 2020, the date of enactment of the CARES Act.

Law source: Law at ¶2220.

— Act Sec. 4115 of the Coronavirus Aid, Relief, and Economic Security Act (P.L. 116-136).

¶840 Limitations on Certain Employee Compensation

SUMMARY OF NEW LAW

Airlines and airline contractors receiving payroll support funds must enter into an agreement with the Secretary of the Treasury that limits the total compensation to be received by corporate officers and employees during any 12-month period between March 24, 2020, and March 24, 2022, to 2019 levels.

BACKGROUND

Like other large, publicly traded companies, U.S. airlines compensate their corporate officers and executives at levels far exceeding those of median employees. According to filings with the U.S. Securities and Exchange Commission, the Chief Executive Officers of the nation's four largest air carriers (Delta, United, American, and Southwest) earned between $7.7 million and $14.9 million in total compensation in 2018.

After the taxpayer-funded bailouts enacted following the 2008 global financial crisis, a report by the New York Attorney General revealed that nine banks that had received loans under the government's Troubled Asset Relief Program (TARP) paid out substantial executive bonuses in the ensuing years, triggering public debate and the appointment by the Obama Administration of a special master in 2009 to oversee compensation given to the 100 highest-paid employees at banks and other firms that had received government bailouts.

NEW LAW EXPLAINED

In general.—To be eligible for financial assistance under Act Sec. 4112 of the Coronavirus Aid, Relief, and Economic Security (CARES) Act (P.L. 116-136), an air carrier or contractor must enter into an agreement with the Secretary of the Treasury which provides that, during the two-year period between March 24, 2020—March 24, 2022, no officer or employee whose total compensation exceeded $425,000 in calendar year 2019 (other than employees whose compensation is determined through an existing collective bargaining agreement entered into prior to March 27, 2020): (1) will receive total compensation during any 12 consecutive months of the two-year period that exceeds the total compensation that he or she had received in calendar year 2019; and (2) will receive severance pay or other benefits upon his or her termination of employment that exceeds twice the maximum total compensation received in calendar year 2019. In addition, no officer or employee whose total compensation exceeded $3 million in calendar year 2019 can receive, during any 12 consecutive months of the two-year period, total compensation exceeding $3 million and 50 percent of the excess over $3 million of the total compensation that he or she had received in calendar year 2019 (Act Sec. 4116(a) of the Coronavirus Aid, Relief, and Economic Security Act (P.L. 116-136)).

NEW LAW EXPLAINED

"Total compensation" defined. The term "total compensation" is defined as including "salary, bonuses, awards of stock, and other financial benefits provided by an air carrier or contractor to an officer or employee" (Act Sec. 4116(b) of the CARES Act).

▶ **Effective date.** The Act does not specify an effective date. Accordingly, this provision is considered effective on March 27, 2020, the date of enactment of the CARES Act.

Law source: Law at ¶2221.

— Act Sec. 4116 of the Coronavirus Aid, Relief, and Economic Security Act (P.L. 116-136).

Families First Coronavirus Response Act, P.L. 116-127

[¶1000]

Introduction

The text of the Families First Coronavirus Response Act (P.L. 116-127) is reproduced below. On March 18, 2020, President Donald Trump signed the bipartisan legislation to provide comprehensive relief to employers and employees impacted by the COVID-19 pandemic. The Families First Act expands the FMLA to include public emergency family and medical leave (by incorporating the Emergency Family and Medical Leave Expansion Act), provides emergency paid sick leave (by incorporating the Emergency Paid Sick Leave Act), provides emergency unemployment insurance, adds health care relief, and provides tax credits to employers for paid sick and paid family and medical leave, among other relief. The Emergency Paid Sick Leave Act was subsequently amended by the Coronavirus Aid, Relief, and Economic Security Act (CARES Act) (P.L. 116-136). Deleted material or the text of the section prior to amendment appears in the amendment notes following each amended provision. *Any changed or added material is set out in italics.* Families First Act sections that were amended by the CARES Act are designated with a caution notation, and a citation to the CARES Act amending section is provided.

[¶1001] SECTION 1. SHORT TITLE.

This Act may be cited as the "Families First Coronavirus Response Act".

[¶1002] SEC. 2. TABLE OF CONTENTS.

The table of contents is as follows:

[¶1003] SEC. 3. REFERENCES.

Except as expressly provided otherwise, any reference to "this Act" contained in any division of this Act shall be treated as referring only to the provisions of that division.

DIVISION A—SECOND CORONAVIRUS PREPAREDNESS AND RESPONSE SUPPLEMENTAL APPROPRIATIONS ACT, 2020

[¶1005] [Introduction]

The following sums are hereby appropriated, out of any money in the Treasury not otherwise appropriated, for the fiscal year ending September 30, 2020, and for other purposes, namely:

TITLE I—DEPARTMENT OF AGRICULTURE

FOOD AND NUTRITION SERVICE

SPECIAL SUPPLEMENTAL NUTRITION PROGRAM FOR WOMEN, INFANTS, AND CHILDREN (WIC)

For an additional amount for the "Special Supplemental Nutrition Program for Women, Infants, and Children", $500,000,000, to remain available through September 30, 2021: *Provided,* That such amount is designated by the Congress as being for an emergency requirement pursuant to section 251(b)(2)(A)(i) of the Balanced Budget and Emergency Deficit Control Act of 1985.

COMMODITY ASSISTANCE PROGRAM

For an additional amount for the "Commodity Assistance Program" for the emergency food assistance program as authorized by section 27(a) of the Food and Nutrition Act of 2008 (7 U.S.C. 2036(a)) and section 204(a)(1) of the Emergency Food Assistance Act of 1983 (7 U.S.C. 7508(a)(1)), $400,000,000, to remain available through September 30, 2021: *Provided,* That of the funds made available, the Secretary may use up to $100,000,000 for costs associated with the distribution of commodities: *Provided further,* That such amount is designated by the Congress as being for an emergency requirement pursuant to section 251(b)(2)(A)(i) of the Balanced Budget and Emergency Deficit Control Act of 1985.

GENERAL PROVISIONS—THIS TITLE

SEC. 1101. (a) PUBLIC HEALTH EMERGENCY.—During fiscal year 2020, in any case in which a school is closed for at least 5 consecutive days during a public health emergency designation during which the school would otherwise be in session, each household containing at least 1 member who is an eligible child attending the school shall be eligible to receive assistance pursuant to a state agency plan approved under subsection (b).

(b) ASSISTANCE.—To carry out this section, the Secretary of Agriculture may approve State agency plans for temporary emergency standards of eligibility and levels of benefits under the Food and Nutrition Act of 2008 (7 U.S.C. 2011 et seq.) for households with eligible children. Plans approved by the Secretary shall provide for supplemental allotments to households receiving benefits under such Act, and issuances to households not already receiving benefits. Such level of benefits shall be determined by the Secretary in an amount not less than the value of meals at the free rate over the course of 5 school days for each eligible child in the household.

(c) MINIMUM CLOSURE REQUIREMENT.—The Secretary of Agriculture shall not provide assistance under this section in the case of a school that is closed for less than 5 consecutive days.

(d) USE OF EBT SYSTEM.—A State agency may provide assistance under this section through the EBT card system established under section 7 of the Food and Nutrition Act of 2008 (7 U.S.C. 2016).

(e) RELEASE OF INFORMATION.—Notwithstanding any other provision of law, the Secretary of Agriculture may authorize State educational agencies and school food authorities administering a school lunch program under the Richard B. Russell National School Lunch Act (42 U.S.C. 1751 et seq.) to release to appropriate officials administering the supplemental nutrition assistance program such information as may be necessary to carry out this section.

(f) WAIVERS.—To facilitate implementation of this section, the Secretary of Agriculture may approve waivers of the limits on certification periods otherwise applicable under section 3(f) of the Food and Nutrition Act of 2008 (7 U.S.C. 2012(f)), reporting requirements otherwise applicable under section 6(c) of such Act (7 U.S.C. 2015(c)), and other administrative requirements otherwise applicable to State agencies under such Act.

(g) AVAILABILITY OF COMMODITIES.—During fiscal year 2020, the Secretary of Agriculture may purchase commodities for emergency distribution in any area of the United States during a public health emergency designation.

(h) DEFINITIONS.—In this section:

(1) The term "eligible child" means a child (as defined in section 12(d) or served under section 11(a)(1) of the Richard B. Russell National School Lunch Act (42 U.S.C. 1760(d), 1759(a)(1)) who, if not for the closure of the school attended by the child during a public health emergency designation and due to concerns about a COVID–19 outbreak, would receive free or reduced price school meals under the Richard B. Russell National School Lunch Act (42 U.S.C. 1751 et seq.) at the school.

(2) The term "public health emergency designation" means the declaration of a public health emergency, based on an outbreak of SARS–CoV–2 or another coronavirus with pandemic potential, by the Secretary of Health and Human Services under section 319 of the Public Health Service Act (42 U.S.C. 247d).

(3) The term "school" has the meaning given the term in section 12(d) of the Richard B. Russell National School Lunch Act (42 U.S.C. 1760(d)).

(i) FUNDING.—There are hereby appropriated to the Secretary of Agriculture such amounts as are necessary to carry out this section: *Provided,* That such amount is designated by the Congress as being for an emergency requirement pursuant to section 251(b)(2)(A)(i) of the Balanced Budget and Emergency Deficit Control Act of 1985.

SEC. 1102. In addition to amounts otherwise made available, $100,000,000, to remain available through September 30, 2021, shall be available for the Secretary of Agriculture to provide grants to the Commonwealth of the Northern Mariana Islands, Puerto Rico, and American Samoa for nutrition assistance in response to a COVID–19 public health emergency: *Provided,* That such amount is designated by the Congress as being for an emergency requirement pursuant to section 251(b)(2)(A)(i) of the Balanced Budget and Emergency Deficit Control Act of 1985.

TITLE II—DEPARTMENT OF DEFENSE

DEFENSE HEALTH PROGRAM

For an additional amount for "Defense Health Program", $82,000,000, to remain available until September 30, 2022, for health services consisting of SARS–CoV–2 or COVID–19 related items and services as described in section 6006(a) of division F of the Families First Coronavirus Response Act (or the administration of such products): *Provided,* That such amount is designated by the Congress as being for an emergency requirement pursuant to section 251(b)(2)(A)(i) of the Balanced Budget and Emergency Deficit Control Act of 1985.

TITLE III—DEPARTMENT OF THE TREASURY

INTERNAL REVENUE SERVICE

TAXPAYER SERVICES

For an additional amount for "Taxpayer Services", $15,000,000, to remain available until September 30, 2022, for the purposes of carrying out the Families First Coronavirus Response Act: *Provided,* That amounts provided under this heading in this Act may be transferred to and merged with "Operations Support": *Provided further,* That such amount is designated by the Congress as being for an emergency requirement pursuant to section 251(b)(2)(A)(i) of the Balanced Budget and Emergency Deficit Control Act of 1985.

TITLE IV—DEPARTMENT OF HEALTH AND HUMAN SERVICES

INDIAN HEALTH SERVICE

INDIAN HEALTH SERVICES

For an additional amount for "Indian Health Services", $64,000,000, to remain available until September 30, 2022, for health services consisting of SARS–CoV–2 or COVID–19 related items and services as described in section 6007 of division F of the Families First Coronavirus Response Act (or the administration of such products): *Provided,* That such amounts shall be allocated at the discretion of the Director of the Indian Health Service: *Provided further,* That such amount is designated by the Congress as being for an emergency requirement pursuant to section 251(b)(2)(A)(i) of the Balanced Budget and Emergency Deficit Control Act of 1985.

TITLE V—DEPARTMENT OF HEALTH AND HUMAN SERVICES

ADMINISTRATION FOR COMMUNITY LIVING

AGING AND DISABILITY SERVICES PROGRAMS

For an additional amount for "Aging and Disability Services Programs", $250,000,000, to remain available until September 30, 2021, for activities authorized under subparts 1 and 2 of part C, of title III, and under title VI, of the Older Americans Act of 1965 ("OAA"), of which $160,000,000 shall be for Home-Delivered Nutrition Services, $80,000,000 shall be for Congregate Nutrition Services, and $10,000,000 shall be for Nutrition Services for Native Americans: *Provided*, That State matching requirements under sections 304(d)(1)(D) and 309(b)(2) of the OAA shall not apply to funds made available under this heading in this Act: *Provided further*, That such amount is designated by the Congress as being for an emergency requirement pursuant to section 251(b)(2)(A)(i) of the Balanced Budget and Emergency Deficit Control Act of 1985.

OFFICE OF THE SECRETARY

PUBLIC HEALTH AND SOCIAL SERVICES EMERGENCY FUND

For an additional amount for "Public Health and Social Services Emergency Fund", $1,000,000,000, to remain available until expended, for activities authorized under section 2812 of the Public Health Service Act (42 U.S.C. 300hh–11), in coordination with the Assistant Secretary for Preparedness and Response and the Administrator of the Centers for Medicare & Medicaid Services, to pay the claims of providers for reimbursement, as described in subsection (a)(3)(D) of such section 2812, for health services consisting of SARS–CoV–2 or COVID–19 related items and services as described in paragraph (1) of section 6001(a) of division F of the Families First Coronavirus Response Act (or the administration of such products) or visits described in paragraph (2) of such section for uninsured individuals: *Provided*, That the term "uninsured individual" in this paragraph means an individual who is not enrolled in—

(1) a Federal health care program (as defined under section 1128B(f) of the Social Security Act (42 U.S.C. 1320a-7b(f)), including an individual who is eligible for medical assistance only because of subsection (a)(10)(A)(ii)(XXIII) of Section 1902 of the Social Security Act; or

(2) a group health plan or health insurance coverage offered by a health insurance issuer in the group or individual market (as such terms are defined in section 2791 of the Public Health Service Act (42 U.S.C. 300gg-91)), or a health plan offered under chapter 89 of title 5, United States Code:

Provided further, That such amount is designated by the Congress as being for an emergency requirement pursuant to section 251(b)(2)(A)(i) of the Balanced Budget and Emergency Deficit Control Act of 1985.

TITLE VI—DEPARTMENT OF VETERANS AFFAIRS

VETERANS HEALTH ADMINISTRATION

MEDICAL SERVICES

For an additional amount for "Medical Services", $30,000,000, to remain available until September 30, 2022, for health services consisting of SARS–CoV–2 or COVID–19 related items and services as described in section 6006(b) of division F of the Families First Coronavirus Response Act (or the administration of such products): *Provided*, That such amount is designated by the Congress as being for an emergency requirement pursuant to section 251(b)(2)(A)(i) of the Balanced Budget and Emergency Deficit Control Act of 1985.

MEDICAL COMMUNITY CARE

For an additional amount for "Medical Community Care", $30,000,000, to remain available until September 30, 2022, for health services consisting of SARS–CoV–2 or COVID–19 related items and services as described in section 6006(b) of division F of the Families First Coronavirus Response Act (or the administration of such products): *Provided*, That such amount is designated by the Congress as being for an emergency requirement pursuant to section 251(b)(2)(A)(i) of the Balanced Budget and Emergency Deficit Control Act of 1985.

TITLE VII—GENERAL PROVISIONS—THIS ACT

SEC. 1701. Not later than 30 days after the date of enactment of this Act, the head of each executive agency that receives funding in this Act shall provide a report detailing the anticipated uses of all such funding to the Committees on Appropriations of the House of Representatives and the Senate: *Provided*, That each report shall include estimated personnel and administrative costs, as well as the total amount of funding apportioned, allotted, obligated, and expended, to date: *Provided* *further,* That each such plan shall be updated and submitted to such Committees every 60 days until all funds are expended or expire.

Sec. 1702. States and local governments receiving funds or assistance pursuant to this division shall ensure the respective State Emergency Operations Center receives regular and real-time reporting on aggregated data on testing and results from State and local public health departments, as determined by the Director of the Centers for Disease Control and Prevention, and that such data is transmitted to the Centers for Disease Control and Prevention.

Sec. 1703. Each amount appropriated or made available by this Act is in addition to amounts otherwise appropriated for the fiscal year involved.

Sec. 1704. No part of any appropriation contained in this Act shall remain available for obligation beyond the current fiscal year unless expressly so provided herein.

Sec. 1705. Unless otherwise provided for by this Act, the additional amounts appropriated by this Act to appropriations accounts shall be available under the authorities and conditions applicable to such appropriations accounts for fiscal year 2020.

Sec. 1706. Each amount designated in this Act by the Congress as being for an emergency requirement pursuant to section 251(b)(2)(A)(i) of the Balanced Budget and Emergency Deficit Control Act of 1985 shall be available (or rescinded or transferred, if applicable) only if the President subsequently so designates all such amounts and transmits such designations to the Congress.

Sec. 1707. Any amount appropriated by this Act, designated by the Congress as an emergency requirement pursuant to section 251(b)(2)(A)(i) of the Balanced Budget and Emergency Deficit Control Act of 1985 and subsequently so designated by the President, and transferred pursuant to transfer authorities provided by this Act shall retain such designation.

This division may be cited as the "Second Coronavirus Preparedness and Response Supplemental Appropriations Act, 2020".

DIVISION B—NUTRITION WAIVERS

TITLE I—MAINTAINING ESSENTIAL ACCESS TO LUNCH FOR STUDENTS ACT

[¶1015] SEC. 2101. SHORT TITLE.

This title may be cited as the "Maintaining Essential Access to Lunch for Students Act" or the "MEALS Act".

[¶1016] SEC. 2102. WAIVER EXCEPTION FOR SCHOOL CLOSURES DUE TO COVID–19.

(a) In General.—The requirements under section 12(l)(1)(A)(iii) of the Richard B. Russell National School Lunch Act (42 U.S.C. 1760(l)(1)(A)(iii)) shall not apply to a qualified COVID–19 waiver.

(b) Allowable Increase in Federal Costs.—Notwithstanding paragraph (4) of section 12(l) of the Richard B. Russell National School Lunch Act (42 U.S.C. 1760(l)), the Secretary of Agriculture may grant a qualified COVID–19 waiver that increases Federal costs.

(c) Termination After Periodic Review.—The requirements under section 12(l)(5) of the Richard B. Russell National School Lunch Act (42 U.S.C. 1760(l)(5)) shall not apply to a qualified COVID–19 waiver.

(d) Qualified COVID–19 Waiver.—In this section, the term "qualified COVID–19 waiver" means a waiver—

(1) requested by a State (as defined in section 12(d)(8) of the Richard B. Russell National School Lunch Act (42 U.S.C. 1760(d)(8))) or eligible service provider under section 12(l) of the Richard B. Russell National School Lunch Act (42 U.S.C. 1760(l)); and

(2) to waive any requirement under such Act (42 U.S.C. 1751 et seq.) or the Child Nutrition Act of 1966 (42 U.S.C. 1771 et seq.), or any regulation issued under either such Act, for purposes of providing meals and meal supplements under such Acts during a school closure due to COVID–19.

TITLE II—COVID—19 CHILD NUTRITION RESPONSE ACT

[¶1018] SEC. 2201. SHORT TITLE.

This title may be cited as the "COVID–19 Child Nutrition Response Act".

[¶1019] SEC. 2202. NATIONAL SCHOOL LUNCH PROGRAM REQUIREMENT WAIVERS ADDRESSING COVID–19.

(a) NATIONWIDE WAIVER.—

(1) IN GENERAL.—Notwithstanding any other provision of law, the Secretary may establish a waiver for all States under section 12(l) of the Richard B. Russell National School Lunch Act (42 U.S.C. 1760(l)), for purposes of—

(A) providing meals and meal supplements under a qualified program; and

(B) carrying out subparagraph (A) with appropriate safety measures with respect to COVID–19, as determined by the Secretary.

(2) STATE ELECTION.—A waiver established under paragraph (1) shall—

(A) notwithstanding paragraph (2) of section 12(l) of the Richard B. Russell National School Lunch Act (42 U.S.C. 1760(l)), apply automatically to any State that elects to be subject to the waiver without further application; and

(B) not be subject to the requirements under paragraph (3) of such section.

(b) CHILD AND ADULT CARE FOOD PROGRAM WAIVER.—Notwithstanding any other provision of law, the Secretary may grant a waiver under section 12(l) of the Richard B. Russell National School Lunch Act (42 U.S.C. 1760(l)) to allow non-congregate feeding under a child and adult care food program under section 17 of the Richard B. Russell National School Lunch Act (42 U.S.C. 1766) if such waiver is for the purposes of—

(1) providing meals and meal supplements under such child and adult care food program; and

(2) carrying out paragraph (1) with appropriate safety measures with respect to COVID–19, as determined by the Secretary.

(c) MEAL PATTERN WAIVER.—Notwithstanding paragraph (4)(A) of section 12(l) of the Richard B. Russell National School Lunch Act (42 U.S.C. 1760(l)) the Secretary may grant a waiver under such section that relates to the nutritional content of meals served if the Secretary determines that—

(1) such waiver is necessary to provide meals and meal supplements under a qualified program; and

(2) there is a supply chain disruption with respect to foods served under such a qualified program and such disruption is due to COVID–19.

(d) REPORTS.—Each State that receives a waiver under subsection (a), (b), or (c), shall, not later than 1 year after the date such State received such waiver, submit a report to the Secretary that includes the following:

(1) A summary of the use of such waiver by the State and eligible service providers.

(2) A description of whether such waiver resulted in improved services to children.

(e) SUNSET.—The authority of the Secretary to establish or grant a waiver under this section shall expire on September 30, 2020.

(f) DEFINITIONS.—In this section:

(1) QUALIFIED PROGRAM.—The term "qualified program" means the following:

(A) The school lunch program under the Richard B. Russell National School Lunch Act (42 U.S.C. 1751 et seq.).

(B) The school breakfast program under section 4 of the Child Nutrition Act of 1966 (42 U.S.C. 1773).

(C) The child and adult care food program under section 17 of the Richard B. Russell National School Lunch Act (42 U.S.C. 1766).

(D) The summer food service program for children under section 13 of the Richard B. Russell National School Lunch Act (42 U.S.C. 1761).

(2) SECRETARY.—The term "Secretary" means the Secretary of Agriculture.

(3) STATE.—The term "State" has the meaning given such term in section 12(d)(8) of the Richard B. Russell National School Lunch Act (42 U.S.C. 1760(d)(8)).

[¶1020] SEC. 2203. PHYSICAL PRESENCE WAIVER UNDER WIC DURING CERTAIN PUBLIC HEALTH EMERGENCIES.

(a) WAIVER AUTHORITY.—

(1) IN GENERAL.—Notwithstanding any other provision of law, the Secretary may grant a request described in paragraph (2) to—

(A) waive the requirement under section 17(d)(3)(C)(i) of the Child Nutrition Act of 1966 (42 U.S.C. 1786(d)(3)(C)(i)); and

(B) defer anthropometric and bloodwork requirements necessary to determine nutritional risk.

(2) REQUEST.—A request described in this paragraph is a request made to the Secretary by a State agency to waive, on behalf of the local agencies served by such State agency, the requirements described in paragraph (1) during any portion of the emergency period (as defined in paragraph (1)(B) of section 1135(g) of the Social Security Act (42 U.S.C. 1320b-5(g)) (beginning on or after the date of the enactment of this section).

(b) REPORTS.—

(1) LOCAL AGENCY REPORTS.—Each local agency that uses a waiver pursuant to subsection (a) shall, not later than 1 year after the date such local agency uses such waiver, submit a report to the State agency serving such local agency that includes the following:

(A) A summary of the use of such waiver by the local agency.

(B) A description of whether such waiver resulted in improved services to women, infants, and children.

(2) STATE AGENCY REPORTS.—Each State agency that receives a waiver under subsection (a) shall, not later than 18 months after the date such State agency received such waiver, submit a report to the Secretary that includes the following:

(A) A summary of the reports received by the State agency under paragraph (1).

(B) A description of whether such waiver resulted in improved services to women, infants, and children.

(c) SUNSET.—The authority under this section shall expire on September 30, 2020.

(d) DEFINITIONS.—In this section:

(1) LOCAL AGENCY.—The term "local agency" has the meaning given the term in section 17(b) of the Child Nutrition Act of 1966 (42 U.S.C. 1786(b)).

(2) NUTRITIONAL RISK.—The term "nutritional risk" has the meaning given the term in section 17(b) of the Child Nutrition Act of 1966 (42 U.S.C. 1786(b)).

(3) SECRETARY.—The term "Secretary" means the Secretary of Agriculture.

(4) STATE AGENCY.—The term "State agency" has the meaning given the term in section 17(b) of the Child Nutrition Act of 1966 (42 U.S.C. 1786(b)).

[¶1021] SEC. 2204. ADMINISTRATIVE REQUIREMENTS WAIVER UNDER WIC.

(a) WAIVER AUTHORITY.—

(1) IN GENERAL.—Notwithstanding any other provision of law, the Secretary of Agriculture may, if requested by a State agency (as defined in section 17(b) of the Child Nutrition Act of 1966 (42 U.S.C. 1786(b)), modify or waive any qualified administrative requirement with respect to such State agency.

(2) QUALIFIED ADMINISTRATIVE REQUIREMENT.—In this section, the term "qualified administrative requirement" means a regulatory requirement issued under section 17 of the Child Nutrition Act of 1966 (42 U.S.C. 1786) that the Secretary of Agriculture determines—

(A) cannot be met by a State agency due to COVID–19; and

(B) the modification or waiver of which is necessary to provide assistance under such section.

(b) STATE AGENCY REPORTS.—Each State agency that receives a waiver under subsection (a)(1) shall, not later than 1 year after the date such State agency received such waiver, submit a report to the Secretary of Agriculture that includes the following:

(1) A summary of the use of such waiver by the State agency.

(2) A description of whether such waiver resulted in improved services to women, infants, and children.

(c) SUNSET.—The authority under this section shall expire on September 30, 2020.

TITLE III—SNAP WAIVERS

[¶1023] SEC. 2301. SNAP FLEXIBILITY FOR LOW-INCOME JOBLESS WORKERS.

(a) Beginning with the first month that begins after the enactment of this Act and for each subsequent month through the end of the month subsequent to the month a public health emergency declaration by the Secretary of Health and Human Services under section 319 of the Public Health Service Act based on an outbreak of coronavirus disease 2019 (COVID–19) is lifted, eligibility for supplemental nutrition assistance program benefits shall not be limited under section 6(o)(2) of the Food and Nutrition Act of 2008 unless an individual does not comply with the requirements of a program offered by the State agency (as defined in section 3 of the Food and Nutrition Act of 2008) that meets the standards of subparagraphs (B) or (C) of such section 6(o)(2).

(b) Beginning on the month subsequent to the month the public health emergency declaration by the Secretary of Health and Human Services under section 319 of the Public Health Service Act based on an outbreak of COVID–19 is lifted for purposes of section 6(o) of the Food and Nutrition Act of 2008, such State agency shall disregard any period during which an individual received benefits under the supplemental nutrition assistance program prior to such month.

[¶1024] SEC. 2302. ADDITIONAL SNAP FLEXIBILITIES IN A PUBLIC HEALTH EMERGENCY.

(a) In the event of a public health emergency declaration by the Secretary of Health and Human Services under section 319 of the Public Health Service Act based on an outbreak of coronavirus disease 2019 (COVID–19) and the issuance of an emergency or disaster declaration by a State based on an outbreak of COVID–19, the Secretary of Agriculture—

(1) shall provide, at the request of a State agency (as defined in section 3 of the Food and Nutrition Act of 2008) that provides sufficient data (as determined by the Secretary through guidance) supporting such request, for emergency allotments to households participating in the supplemental nutrition assistance program under the Food and Nutrition Act of 2008 to address temporary food needs not greater than the applicable maximum monthly allotment for the household size; and

(2) may adjust, at the request of State agencies or by guidance in consultation with one or more State agencies, issuance methods and application and reporting requirements under the Food and Nutrition Act of 2008 to be consistent with what is practicable under actual conditions in affected areas. (In making this adjustment, the Secretary shall consider the availability of offices and personnel in State agencies, any conditions that make reliance on electronic benefit transfer systems described in section 7(h) of the Food and Nutrition Act of 2008 impracticable, any disruptions of transportation and communication facilities, and any health considerations that warrant alternative approaches.)

(b) Not later than 10 days after the date of the receipt or issuance of each document listed in paragraphs (1), (2), or (3) of this subsection, the Secretary of Agriculture shall make publicly available on the website of the Department the following documents:

(1) Any request submitted by State agencies under subsection (a).

(2) The Secretary's approval or denial of each such request.

(3) Any guidance issued under subsection (a)(2).

(c) The Secretary of Agriculture shall, within 18 months after the public health emergency declaration described in subsection (a) is lifted, submit a report to the House and Senate Agriculture Committees with a description of the measures taken to address the food security needs of affected populations during the emergency, any information or data supporting State agency requests, any additional measures that States requested that were not approved, and recommendations for changes to the Secretary's authority under the Food and Nutrition Act of 2008 to assist the Secretary and States and localities in preparations for any future health emergencies.

DIVISION C—EMERGENCY FAMILY AND MEDICAL LEAVE EXPANSION ACT

[¶1026] SEC. 3101. SHORT TITLE.

This Act may be cited as "Emergency Family and Medical Leave Expansion Act".

[¶1027] SEC. 3102. AMENDMENTS TO THE FAMILY AND MEDICAL LEAVE ACT OF 1993.

(a) PUBLIC HEALTH EMERGENCY LEAVE.—

(1) IN GENERAL.—Section 102(a)(1) of the Family and Medical Leave Act of 1993 (29 U.S.C. 2612(a)(1)) is amended by adding at the end the following:

(F) "During the period beginning on the date the Emergency Family and Medical Leave Expansion Act takes effect, and ending on December 31, 2020, because of a qualifying need related to a public health emergency in accordance with section 110.".

(2) PAID LEAVE REQUIREMENT.—Section 102(c) of the Family and Medical Leave Act of 1993 (29 U.S.C. 2612(c)) is amended by striking "under subsection (a)" and inserting "under subsection (a) (other than certain periods of leave under subsection (a)(1)(F))".

(b) REQUIREMENTS.—Title I of the Family and Medical Leave Act of 1993 (29 U.S.C. 2611 et seq.) is amended by adding at the end the following:

SEC. 110. "PUBLIC HEALTH EMERGENCY LEAVE.

(a) "DEFINITIONS.—The following shall apply with respect to leave under section 102(a)(1)(F):

(1) "APPLICATION OF CERTAIN TERMS.—The definitions in section 101 shall apply, except as follows:

(A) "ELIGIBLE EMPLOYEE.—In lieu of the definition in sections 101(2)(A) and 101(2)(B)(ii), the term 'eligible employee' means an employee who has been employed for at least 30 calendar days by the employer with respect to whom leave is requested under section 102(a)(1)(F).

(B) "EMPLOYER THRESHOLD.—Section 101(4)(A)(i) shall be applied by substituting 'fewer than 500 employees' for '50 or more employees for each working day during each of 20 or more calendar workweeks in the current or preceding calendar year'.

(2) "ADDITIONAL DEFINITIONS.—In addition to the definitions described in paragraph (1), the following definitions shall apply with respect to leave under section 102(a)(1)(F):

(A) "QUALIFYING NEED RELATED TO A PUBLIC HEALTH EMERGENCY.—The term 'qualifying need related to a public health emergency', with respect to leave, means the employee is unable to work (or telework) due to a need for leave to care for the son or daughter under 18 years of age of such employee if the school or place of care has been closed, or the child care provider of such son or daughter is unavailable, due to a public health emergency.

(B) "PUBLIC HEALTH EMERGENCY.—The term 'public health emergency' means an emergency with respect to COVID–19 declared by a Federal, State, or local authority.

(C) "CHILD CARE PROVIDER.—The term 'child care provider' means a provider who receives compensation for providing child care services on a regular basis, including an 'eligible child care provider' (as defined in section 658P of the Child Care and Development Block Grant Act of 1990 (42 U.S.C. 9858n)).

(D) "SCHOOL.—The term 'school' means an 'elementary school' or 'secondary school' as such terms are defined in section 8101 of the Elementary and Secondary Education Act of 1965 (20 U.S.C. 7801).

(3) "REGULATORY AUTHORITIES.—The Secretary of Labor shall have the authority to issue regulations for good cause under sections 553(b)(B) and 553(d)(A) of title 5, United States Code—

(A) "to exclude certain health care providers and emergency responders from the definition of eligible employee under section 110(a)(1)(A); and

(B) "to exempt small businesses with fewer than 50 employees from the requirements of section 102(a)(1)(F) when the imposition of such requirements would jeopardize the viability of the business as a going concern.

(b) "RELATIONSHIP TO PAID LEAVE.—

(1) "UNPAID LEAVE FOR INITIAL 10 DAYS.—

(A) "IN GENERAL.—The first 10 days for which an employee takes leave under section 102(a)(1)(F) may consist of unpaid leave.

(B) "EMPLOYEE ELECTION.—An employee may elect to substitute any accrued vacation leave, personal leave, or medical or sick leave for unpaid leave under section 102(a)(1)(F) in accordance with section 102(d)(2)(B).

(2) "PAID LEAVE FOR SUBSEQUENT DAYS.—

(A) "IN GENERAL.—An employer shall provide paid leave for each day of leave under section 102(a)(1)(F) that an employee takes after taking leave under such section for 10 days.

(B) "CALCULATION.—

(i) "IN GENERAL.—Subject to clause (ii), paid leave under subparagraph (A) for an employee shall be calculated based on—

(I) "an amount that is not less than two-thirds of an employee's regular rate of pay (as determined under section 7(e) of the Fair Labor Standards Act of 1938 (29 U.S.C. 207(e)); and

(II) "the number of hours the employee would otherwise be normally scheduled to work (or the number of hours calculated under subparagraph (C)).

(ii) "CLARIFICATION.—In no event shall such paid leave exceed $200 per day and $10,000 in the aggregate.

(C) "VARYING SCHEDULE HOURS CALCULATION.—In the case of an employee whose schedule varies from week to week to such an extent that an employer is unable to determine with certainty the number of hours the employee would have worked if such employee had not taken leave under section 102(a)(1)(F), the employer shall use the following in place of such number:

(i) "Subject to clause (ii), a number equal to the average number of hours that the employee was scheduled per day over the 6-month period ending on the date on which the employee takes such leave, including hours for which the employee took leave of any type.

(ii) "If the employee did not work over such period, the reasonable expectation of the employee at the time of hiring of the average number of hours per day that the employee would normally be scheduled to work.

(c) "NOTICE.—In any case where the necessity for leave under section 102(a)(1)(F) for the purpose described in subsection (a)(2)(A)(iii) is foreseeable, an employee shall provide the employer with such notice of leave as is practicable.

(d) "RESTORATION TO POSITION.—

(1) "IN GENERAL.—Section 104(a)(1) shall not apply with respect to an employee of an employer who employs fewer than 25 employees if the conditions described in paragraph (2) are met.

(2) "CONDITIONS.—The conditions described in this paragraph are the following:

(A) "The employee takes leave under section 102(a)(1)(F).

(B) "The position held by the employee when the leave commenced does not exist due to economic conditions or other changes in operating conditions of the employer—

(i) "that affect employment; and

(ii) "are caused by a public health emergency during the period of leave.

(C) "The employer makes reasonable efforts to restore the employee to a position equivalent to the position the employee held when the leave commenced, with equivalent employment benefits, pay, and other terms and conditions of employment.

(D) "If the reasonable efforts of the employer under subparagraph (C) fail, the employer makes reasonable efforts during the period described in paragraph (3) to contact the employee if an equivalent position described in subparagraph (C) becomes available.

(3) "CONTACT PERIOD.—The period described under this paragraph is the 1-year period beginning on the earlier of—

(A) "the date on which the qualifying need related to a public health emergency concludes; or

(B) "the date that is 12 weeks after the date on which the employee's leave under section 102(a)(1)(F) commences.".

[¶1028] SEC. 3103. EMPLOYMENT UNDER MULTI-EMPLOYER BARGAINING AGREEMENTS.

(a) EMPLOYERS.—An employer signatory to a multiemployer collective bargaining agreement may, consistent with its bargaining obligations and its collective bargaining agreement, fulfill its obligations under section 110(b)(2) of title I of the Family and Medical Leave Act of 1993, as added by the Families First Coronavirus Response Act, by making contributions to a multiemployer fund, plan, or program based on the paid leave each of its employees is entitled to under such section while working under the multiemployer collective bargaining agreement, provided that the fund, plan, or program enables employees to secure pay from such fund, plan, or program based on hours they have worked under the multiemployer collective bargaining agreement for paid leave taken under section 102(a)(1)(F) of title I of the Family and Medical Leave Act of 1993, as added by the Families First Coronavirus Response Act.

(b) EMPLOYEES.—Employees who work under a multiemployer collective bargaining agreement into which their employers make contributions as provided in subsection (a) may secure pay from such fund, plan, or program based on hours they have worked under the multiemployer collective bargaining agreement for paid leave taken under section 102(a)(1)(F) of title I of the Family and Medical Leave Act of 1993, as added by the Families First Coronavirus Response Act.

[¶1029] SEC. 3104. SPECIAL RULE FOR CERTAIN EMPLOYERS.

An employer under 110(a)(B) shall not be subject to section 107(a) for a violation of section 102(a)(1)(F) if the employer does not meet the definition of employer set forth in Section 101(4)(A)(i).

[¶1030] SEC. 3105. SPECIAL RULE FOR HEALTH CARE PROVIDERS AND EMERGENCY RESPONDERS.

An employer of an employee who is a health care provider or an emergency responder may elect to exclude such employee from the application of the provisions in the amendments made under of section 3102 of this Act.

[¶1031] SEC. 3106. EFFECTIVE DATE.

This Act shall take effect not later than 15 days after the date of enactment of this Act.

DIVISION D—EMERGENCY UNEMPLOYMENT INSURANCE STABILIZATION AND ACCESS ACT OF 2020

[¶1033] SEC. 4101. SHORT TITLE.

This division may be cited as the "Emergency Unemployment Insurance Stabilization and Access Act of 2020".

[¶1034] SEC. 4102. EMERGENCY TRANSFERS FOR UNEMPLOYMENT COMPENSATION ADMINISTRATION.

(a) IN GENERAL.—Section 903 of the Social Security Act (42 U.S.C. 1103) is amended by adding at the end the following:

"Emergency Transfers in Fiscal Year 2020 for Administration

(h)(1)(A) "In addition to any other amounts, the Secretary of Labor shall provide for the making of emergency administration grants in fiscal year 2020 to the accounts of the States in the Unemployment Trust Fund, in accordance with succeeding provisions of this subsection.

(B) "The amount of an emergency administration grant with respect to a State shall, as determined by the Secretary of Labor, be equal to the amount obtained by multiplying $1,000,000,000 by the same ratio as would apply under subsection (a)(2)(B) for purposes of determining such State's share of any excess amount (as described in subsection (a)(1)) that would have been subject to transfer to State accounts, as of October 1, 2019, under the provisions of subsection (a).

(C) "Of the emergency administration grant determined under subparagraph (B) with respect to a State—

(i) "not later than 60 days after the date of enactment of this subsection, 50 percent shall be transferred to the account of such State upon a certification by the Secretary of Labor to the Secretary of the Treasury that the State meets the requirements of paragraph (2); and

(ii) "only with respect to a State in which the number of unemployment compensation claims has increased by at least 10 percent over the same quarter in the previous calendar year, the remainder shall be transferred to the account of such State upon a certification by the Secretary of Labor to the Secretary of the Treasury that the State meets the requirements of paragraph (3).

(2) "The requirements of this paragraph with respect to a State are the following:

(A) "The State requires employers to provide notification of the availability of unemployment compensation to employees at the time of separation from employment. Such notification may be based on model notification language issued by the Secretary of Labor.

(B) "The State ensures that applications for unemployment compensation, and assistance with the application process, are accessible in at least two of the following: in-person, by phone, or online.

(C) "The State notifies applicants when an application is received and is being processed, and in any case in which an application is unable to be processed, provides information about steps the applicant can take to ensure the successful processing of the application.

(3) "The requirements of this paragraph with respect to a State are the following:

(A) "The State has expressed its commitment to maintain and strengthen access to the unemployment compensation system, including through initial and continued claims.

(B) "The State has demonstrated steps it has taken or will take to ease eligibility requirements and access to unemployment compensation for claimants, including waiving work search requirements and the waiting week, and non-charging employers directly impacted by COVID–19 due to an illness in the workplace or direction from a public health official to isolate or quarantine workers.

(4) "Any amount transferred to the account of a State under this subsection may be used by such State only for the administration of its unemployment compensation law, including by taking such steps as may be necessary to ensure adequate resources in periods of high demand.

(5) "Not later than 1 year after the date of enactment of the Emergency Unemployment Insurance Stabilization and Access Act of 2020, each State receiving emergency administration grant funding under paragraph (1)(C)(i) shall submit to the Secretary of Labor, the Committee on Ways and Means of the House of Representatives, and the Committee on Finance of the Senate, a report that includes—

(A) "an analysis of the recipiency rate for unemployment compensation in the State as such rate has changed over time;

(B) "a description of steps the State intends to take to increase such recipiency rate.

(6)(A) "Notwithstanding any other provision of law, the Secretary of the Treasury shall transfer from the general fund of the Treasury (from funds not otherwise appropriated) to the employment security administration account (as established by section 901 of the Social Security Act) such sums as the Secretary of Labor estimates to be necessary for purposes of making the transfers described in paragraph (1)(C).

(B) "There are appropriated from the general fund of the Treasury, without fiscal year limitation, the sums referred to in the preceding sentence and such sums shall not be required to be repaid.".

(b) EMERGENCY FLEXIBILITY.—Notwithstanding any other law, if a State modifies its unemployment compensation law and policies with respect to work search, waiting week, good cause, or employer experience rating on an emergency temporary basis as needed to respond to the spread of COVID–19, such modifications shall be disregarded for the purposes of applying section 303 of the Social Security Act and section 3304 of the Internal Revenue Code of 1986 to such State law.

(c) REGULATIONS.—The Secretary of Labor may prescribe any regulations, operating instructions, or other guidance necessary to carry out the amendment made by subsection (a).

[¶1035] SEC. 4103. TEMPORARY ASSISTANCE FOR STATES WITH ADVANCES.

Section 1202(b)(10)(A) of the Social Security Act (42 U.S.C. 1322(b)(10)(A)) is amended by striking "beginning on the date of enactment of this paragraph and ending on December 31, 2010" and inserting "beginning on the date of enactment of the Emergency Unemployment Insurance Stabilization and Access Act of 2020 and ending on December 31, 2020".

[¶1036] SEC. 4104. TECHNICAL ASSISTANCE AND GUIDANCE FOR SHORT-TIME COMPENSATION PROGRAMS.

The Secretary of Labor shall assist States in establishing, implementing, and improving the employer awareness of short-time compensation programs (as defined in section 3306(v) of the Internal Revenue Code of 1986) to help avert layoffs, including by providing technical assistance and guidance.

[¶1037] SEC. 4105. FULL FEDERAL FUNDING OF EXTENDED UNEMPLOYMENT COMPENSATION FOR A LIMITED PERIOD.

(a) IN GENERAL.—In the case of sharable extended compensation and sharable regular compensation paid for weeks of unemployment beginning after the date of the enactment of this section and before December 31, 2020 (and only with respect to States that receive emergency administration grant funding under clauses (i) and (ii) of section 903(h)(1)(C) of the Social Security Act (42 U.S.C. 1102(h)(1)(C))), section 204(a)(1) of the Federal-State Extended Unemployment Compensation Act of 1970 (26 U.S.C. 3304 note) shall be applied by substituting "100 percent of" for "one-half of".

(b) TEMPORARY FEDERAL MATCHING FOR THE FIRST WEEK OF EXTENDED BENEFITS FOR STATES WITH NO WAITING WEEK.—With respect to weeks of unemployment beginning after the date of the enactment of this Act and ending on or before December 31, 2020, subparagraph (B) of section 204(a)(2) of the Federal-State Extended Unemployment Compensation Act of 1970 (26 U.S.C. 3304 note) shall not apply.

(c) DEFINITIONS.—For purposes of this section—

(1) the terms "sharable extended compensation" and "sharable regular compensation" have the respective meanings given such terms under section 204 of the Federal-State Extended Unemployment Compensation Act of 1970; and

(2) the term "week" has the meaning given such term under section 205 of the Federal-State Extended Unemployment Compensation Act of 1970.

(d) REGULATIONS.—The Secretary of Labor may prescribe any operating instructions or regulations necessary to carry out this section.

DIVISION E—EMERGENCY PAID SICK LEAVE ACT

[¶1039] SEC. 5101. SHORT TITLE.

This Act may be cited as the "Emergency Paid Sick Leave Act".

Caution: This section incorporates amendments made by Sec. 3602 of the Coronavirus Aid, Relief, and Economic Security Act (CARES Act) (P.L. 116-136). See ¶2119 for amending section text.

[¶1040] SEC. 5102. PAID SICK TIME REQUIREMENT.

(a) IN GENERAL.—An employer shall provide to each employee employed by the employer paid sick time to the extent that the employee is unable to work (or telework) due to a need for leave because:

(1) The employee is subject to a Federal, State, or local quarantine or isolation order related to COVID–19.

(2) The employee has been advised by a health care provider to self-quarantine due to concerns related to COVID–19.

(3) The employee is experiencing symptoms of COVID–19 and seeking a medical diagnosis.

(4) The employee is caring for an individual who is subject to an order as described in subparagraph (1) or has been advised as described in paragraph (2).

(5) The employee is caring for a son or daughter of such employee if the school or place of care of the son or daughter has been closed, or the child care provider of such son or daughter is unavailable, due to COVID–19 precautions.

(6) The employee is experiencing any other substantially similar condition specified by the Secretary of Health and Human Services in consultation with the Secretary of the Treasury and the Secretary of Labor.

Except that an employer of an employee who is a health care provider or an emergency responder may elect to exclude such employee from the application of this subsection.

(b) DURATION OF PAID SICK TIME.—

(1) IN GENERAL.—An employee shall be entitled to paid sick time for an amount of hours determined under paragraph (2).

(2) AMOUNT OF HOURS.—The amount of hours of paid sick time to which an employee is entitled shall be as follows:

(A) For full-time employees, 80 hours.

(B) For part-time employees, a number of hours equal to the number of hours that such employee works, on average, over a 2-week period.

(3) CARRYOVER.—Paid sick time under this section shall not carry over from 1 year to the next.

(c) EMPLOYER'S TERMINATION OF PAID SICK TIME.—Paid sick time provided to an employee under this Act shall cease beginning with the employee's next scheduled workshift immediately following the termination of the need for paid sick time under subsection (a).

(d) PROHIBITION.—An employer may not require, as a condition of providing paid sick time under this Act, that the employee involved search for or find a replacement employee to cover the hours during which the employee is using paid sick time.

(e) USE OF PAID SICK TIME.—

(1) IN GENERAL.—The paid sick time under subsection (a) shall be available for immediate use by the employee for the purposes described in such subsection, regardless of how long the employee has been employed by an employer.

(2) SEQUENCING.—

(A) IN GENERAL.—An employee may first use the paid sick time under subsection (a) for the purposes described in such subsection.

(B) PROHIBITION.—An employer may not require an employee to use other paid leave provided by the employer to the employee before the employee uses the paid sick time under subsection (a).

(f) LIMITATIONS.—

An employer shall not be required to pay more than either—

(1) $511 per day and $5,110 in the aggregate for each employee, when the employee is taking leave for a reason described in paragraph (1), (2), or (3) of section 5102(a); or

(2) $200 per day and $2,000 in the aggregate for each employee, when the employee is taking leave for a reason described in paragraph (4), (5), or (6) of section 5102(a).

2020 Amendment.—Division A, Title III, Part IV, Subtitle C, Sec. 3602 of P.L. 116-136, effective April 1, 2020, amended section 5102 by adding subsections (f)(1) and (2).

[¶1041] SEC. 5103. NOTICE.

(a) IN GENERAL.—Each employer shall post and keep posted, in conspicuous places on the premises of the employer where notices to employees are customarily posted, a notice, to be prepared or approved by the Secretary of Labor, of the requirements described in this Act.

(b) MODEL NOTICE.—Not later than 7 days after the date of enactment of this Act, the Secretary of Labor shall make publicly available a model of a notice that meets the requirements of subsection (a).

Caution: This section incorporates amendments made by Sec. 3611(8) of the Coronavirus Aid, Relief, and Economic Security Act (CARES Act) (P.L. 116-136). See ¶2129 for amending section text.

[¶1042] SEC. 5104. PROHIBITED ACTS.

It shall be unlawful for any employer to discharge, discipline, or in any other manner discriminate against any employee who—

(1) takes leave in accordance with this Act; *or*

(2) has filed any complaint or instituted or caused to be instituted any proceeding under or related to this Act (including a proceeding that seeks enforcement of this Act), or has testified or is about to testify in any such proceeding.

2020 Amendment.—Division A, Title III, Part IV, Subtitle C, Sec. 3611(8) of P.L. 116-136, effective April 1, 2020, amended section 5104(1) by striking "and" after the semicolon and inserting "or".

Caution: This section incorporates amendments made by Sec. 3611(9) of the Coronavirus Aid, Relief, and Economic Security Act (CARES Act) (P.L. 116-136). See ¶2129 for amending section text.

[¶1043] SEC. 5105. ENFORCEMENT.

(a) UNPAID SICK LEAVE.—An employer who violates section 5102 shall—

(1) be considered to have failed to pay minimum wages in violation of section 6 of the Fair Labor Standards Act of 1938 (29 U.S.C. 206); and

(2) be subject to the penalties described in sections 16 and 17 of such Act (29 U.S.C. 216; 217) with respect to such violation.

(b) UNLAWFUL TERMINATION.—An employer who willfully violates section 5104 shall—

(1) be considered to be in violation of section 15(a)(3) of the Fair Labor Standards Act of 1938 (29 U.S.C. 215(a)(3)); and

(2) be subject to the penalties described in sections 16 and 17 of such Act (29 U.S.C. 216; 217) with respect to such violation.

(c) INVESTIGATION AND COLLECTION OF DATA.—The Secretary of Labor or his designee may investigate and gather data to ensure compliance with this Act in the same manner as authorized by sections 9 and 11 of the Fair Labor Standards Act of 1938 (29 U.S.C. 209; 211).

2020 Amendment.—Division A, Title III, Part IV, Subtitle C, Sec. 3611(9) of P.L. 116-136, effective April 1, 2020, amended section 5105 by adding subsection (c).

[¶1044] SEC. 5106. EMPLOYMENT UNDER MULTI-EMPLOYER BARGAINING AGREEMENTS.

(a) EMPLOYERS.—An employer signatory to a multiemployer collective bargaining agreement may, consistent with its bargaining obligations and its collective bargaining agreement, fulfill its obligations under this Act by making contributions to a multiemployer fund, plan, or program based on the hours of paid sick time each of its employees is entitled to under this Act while working under the multiemployer collective bargaining agreement, provided that the fund, plan, or program enables employees to secure pay from such fund, plan, or program based on hours they have worked under the multiemployer collective bargaining agreement and for the uses specified under section 5102(a).

(b) EMPLOYEES.—Employees who work under a multiemployer collective bargaining agreement into which their employers make contributions as provided in subsection (a) may secure pay from such fund, plan, or program based on hours they have worked under the multiemployer collective bargaining agreement for the uses specified in section 5102(a).

[¶1045] SEC. 5107. RULES OF CONSTRUCTION.

Nothing in this Act shall be construed—

(1) to in any way diminish the rights or benefits that an employee is entitled to under any—

(A) other Federal, State, or local law;

(B) collective bargaining agreement; or

(C) existing employer policy; or

(2) to require financial or other reimbursement to an employee from an employer upon the employee's termination, resignation, retirement, or other separation from employment for paid sick time under this Act that has not been used by such employee.

[¶1046] SEC. 5108. EFFECTIVE DATE.

This Act, and the requirements under this Act, shall take effect not later than 15 days after the date of enactment of this Act.

[¶1047] SEC. 5109. SUNSET.

This Act, and the requirements under this Act, shall expire on December 31, 2020.

»»→ Caution: This section incorporates amendments made by Secs. 3611(5) and (6) of the Coronavirus Aid, Relief, and Economic Security Act (CARES Act) (P.L. 116-136). See ¶2129 for amending section text.

[¶1048] SEC. 5110. DEFINITIONS.

For purposes of the Act:

(1) EMPLOYEE.—The *term* "employee" means an individual who is—

(A)(i) an employee, as defined in section 3(e) of the Fair Labor Standards Act of 1938 (29 U.S.C. 203(e)), who is not covered under subparagraph (E) or (F), including such an employee of the Library of Congress, except that a reference in such section to an employer shall be considered to be a reference to an employer described in clauses (i)(I) and (ii) of *paragraph (2)(A)*; or

(ii) an employee of the Government Accountability Office;

(B) a State employee described in section 304(a) of the Government Employee Rights Act of 1991 (42 U.S.C. 2000e–16c(a));

(C) a covered employee, as defined in section 101 of the Congressional Accountability Act of 1995 (2 U.S.C. 1301), other than an applicant for employment;

(D) a covered employee, as defined in section 411(c) of title 3, United States Code;

(E) a Federal officer or employee covered under subchapter V of chapter 63 of title 5, United States Code; or

(F) any other individual occupying a position in the civil service (as that term is defined in section 2101(1) of title 5, United States Code).

(2) EMPLOYER.—

(A) IN GENERAL.—The term "employer" means a person who is—

(i)(I) a covered employer, as defined in subparagraph (B), who is not covered under subclause (V);

(II) an entity employing a State employee described in section 304(a) of the Government Employee Rights Act of 1991;

(III) an employing office, as defined in section 101 of the Congressional Accountability Act of 1995;

(IV) an employing office, as defined in section 411(c) of title 3, United States Code; or

(V) an Executive Agency as defined in section 105 of title 5, United States Code, and including the U.S. Postal Service and the Postal Regulatory Commission; and

(ii) engaged in commerce (including government), or an industry or activity affecting commerce (including government), as defined in subparagraph (B)(iii).

(B) COVERED EMPLOYER.—

(i) IN GENERAL.—In subparagraph (A)(i)(I), the term "covered employer"—

(I) means any person engaged in commerce or in any industry or activity affecting commerce that—

(aa) in the case of a private entity or individual, employs fewer than 500 employees; and

(bb) in the case of a public agency or any other entity that is not a private entity or individual, employs 1 or more employees;

(II) includes—

(aa) includes any person acting directly or indirectly in the interest of an employer in relation to an employee (within the meaning of such phrase in section 3(d) of the Fair Labor Standards Act of 1938 (29 U.S.C. 203(d)); and

(bb) any successor in interest of an employer;

(III) includes any "public agency", as defined in section 3(x) of the Fair Labor Standards Act of 1938 (29 U.S.C. 203(x)); and

(IV) includes the Government Accountability Office and the Library of Congress.

(ii) PUBLIC AGENCY.—For purposes of *clause (i)(III)*, a public agency shall be considered to be a person engaged in commerce or in an industry or activity affecting commerce.

(iii) DEFINITIONS.—For purposes of this subparagraph:

(I) COMMERCE.—The terms "commerce" and "industry or activity affecting commerce" means any activity, business, or industry in commerce or in which a labor dispute would hinder or obstruct commerce or the free flow of commerce, and include "commerce" and any "industry affecting commerce", as defined in paragraphs (1) and (3) of section 501 of the Labor Management Relations Act of 1947 (29 U.S.C. 142 (1) and (3)).

(II) EMPLOYEE.—The term "employee" has the same meaning given such term in section 3(e) of the Fair Labor Standards Act of 1938 (29 U.S.C. 203(e)).

(III) PERSON.—The term "person" has the same meaning given such term in section 3(a) of the Fair Labor Standards Act of 1938 (29 U.S.C. 203(a)).

(3) FLSA TERMS.—The terms "employ" and "State" have the meanings given such terms in section 3 of the Fair Labor Standards Act of 1938 (29 U.S.C. 203).

(4) FMLA TERMS.—The terms "health care provider" and "son or daughter" have the meanings given such terms in section 101 of the Family and Medical Leave Act of 1993 (29 U.S.C. 2611).

(5) PAID SICK TIME.—

(A) IN GENERAL.—The term "paid sick time" means an increment of compensated leave that—

(i) is provided by an employer for use during an absence from employment for a reason described in any paragraph of section 2(a); and

(ii) is calculated based on the employee's required compensation under subparagraph (B) and the number of hours the employee would otherwise be normally scheduled to work (or the number of hours calculated under subparagraph (C)), except that in no event shall such paid sick time exceed—

(I) $511 per day and $5,110 in the aggregate for a use described in paragraph (1), (2), or (3) of section 5102(a); and

(II) $200 per day and $2,000 in the aggregate for a use described in paragraph (4), (5), or (6) of section 5102(a).

(B) REQUIRED COMPENSATION.—

(i) IN GENERAL.—Subject to subparagraph (A)(ii), the employee's required compensation under this subparagraph shall be not less than the greater of the following:

(I) The employee's regular rate of pay (as determined under section 7(e) of the Fair Labor Standards Act of 1938 (29 U.S.C. 207(e)).

(II) The minimum wage rate in effect under section 6(a)(1) of the Fair Labor Standards Act of 1938 (29 U.S.C. 206(a)(1)).

(III) The minimum wage rate in effect for such employee in the applicable State or locality, whichever is greater, in which the employee is employed.

(ii) SPECIAL RULE FOR CARE OF FAMILY MEMBERS.—Subject to subparagraph (A)(ii), with respect to any paid sick time provided for any use described in paragraph (4), (5), or (6) of section 5102(a), the employee's required compensation under this subparagraph shall be two-thirds of the amount described in clause (B)(i).

(C) VARYING SCHEDULE HOURS CALCULATION.—In the case of a part-time employee described in section 5102(b)(2)(B) whose schedule varies from week to week to such an extent that an employer is unable to determine with certainty the number of hours the employee would have worked if such employee had not taken paid sick time under section 2(a), the employer shall use the following in place of such number:

(i) Subject to clause (ii), a number equal to the average number of hours that the employee was scheduled per day over the 6-month period ending on the date on which the employee takes the paid sick time, including hours for which the employee took leave of any type.

(ii) If the employee did not work over such period, the reasonable expectation of the employee at the time of hiring of the average number of hours per day that the employee would normally be scheduled to work.

(D) GUIDELINES.—Not later than 15 days after the date of the enactment of this Act, the Secretary of Labor shall issue guidelines to assist employers in calculating the amount of paid sick time under subparagraph (A).

(E) REASONABLE NOTICE.—After the first workday (or portion thereof) an employee receives paid sick time under this Act, an employer may require the employee to follow reasonable notice procedures in order to continue receiving such paid sick time.

2020 Amendment.—Division A, Title III, Part IV, Subtitle C, Sec. 3611(5) of P.L. 116-136, effective April 1, 2020, amended section 5110 by: (1) in the matter preceding subparagraph (1)(A), by striking "terms" and inserting "term"; and (2) in subparagraph (1)(A)(i), by striking "paragraph (5)(A)" and inserting "paragraph (2)(A)".

Division A, Title III, Part IV, Subtitle C, Sec. 3611(6) of P.L. 116-136 amended section 5110(2)(B)(ii) striking "clause (i)(IV)" and inserting "clause (i)(III)".

»»→ Caution: This section incorporates amendments made by Sec. 3611(2) of the Coronavirus Aid, Relief, and Economic Security Act (CARES Act) (P.L. 116-136). See ¶2129 for amending section text.

[¶1049] SEC. 5111. REGULATORY AUTHORITIES.

The Secretary of Labor shall have the authority to issue regulations for good cause under sections 553(b)(B) and *553(d)(3)* of title 5, United States Code—

(1) to exclude certain health care providers and emergency responders from the definition of employee under section 5110(1) including by allowing the employer of such health care providers and emergency responders to opt out;

(2) to exempt small businesses with fewer than 50 employees from the requirements of section 5102(a)(5) when the imposition of such requirements would jeopardize the viability of the business as a going concern; and

(3) as necessary, to carry out the purposes of this Act, including to ensure consistency between this Act and Division C and Division G of the Families First Coronavirus Response Act.

2020 Amendment.—Division A, Title III, Part IV, Subtitle C, Sec. 3611(2) of P.L. 116-136, effective April 1, 2020, amended section 5111 by striking "553(d)(A)" and inserting "553(d)(3)".

»»→ Caution: This section incorporates amendments made by Sec. 3604(b) of the Coronavirus Aid, Relief, and Economic Security Act (CARES Act) (P.L. 116-136). See ¶2121 for amending section text.

[¶1050] *SEC. 5112. AUTHORITY TO EXCLUDE CERTAIN EMPLOYEES.*

The Director of the Office of Management and Budget shall have the authority to exclude for good cause from the definition of employee under section 5110(1) certain employees described in subparagraphs (E) and (F) of such section, including by exempting certain United States Government employers covered by section 5110(2)(A)(i)(V) from the requirements of this title with respect to certain categories of Executive Branch employees.

2020 Amendment.—Division A, Title III, Part IV, Subtitle C, Sec. 3604(b) of P.L. 116-136, effective April 1, 2020, added section 5112.

DIVISION F—HEALTH PROVISIONS

[¶1052] SEC. 6001. COVERAGE OF TESTING FOR COVID–19.

(a) IN GENERAL.—A group health plan and a health insurance issuer offering group or individual health insurance coverage (including a grandfathered health plan (as defined in section 1251(e) of the Patient Protection and Affordable Care Act)) shall provide coverage, and shall not impose any cost sharing (including deductibles, copayments, and coinsurance) requirements or prior authorization or other medical management requirements, for the following items and services furnished during any portion of the emergency period defined in paragraph (1)(B) of section 1135(g) of the Social Security Act (42 U.S.C. 1320b-5(g)) beginning on or after the date of the enactment of this Act:

(1) In vitro diagnostic products (as defined in section 809.3(a) of title 21, Code of Federal Regulations) for the detection of SARS–CoV–2 or the diagnosis of the virus that causes COVID–19 that are approved, cleared, or authorized under section 510(k), 513, 515 or 564 of the Federal Food, Drug, and Cosmetic Act, and the administration of such in vitro diagnostic products.

(2) Items and services furnished to an individual during health care provider office visits (which term in this paragraph includes in-person visits and telehealth visits), urgent care center visits, and emergency room visits that result in an order for or administration of an in vitro diagnostic product described in paragraph (1), but only to the extent such items and services relate to the furnishing or administration of such product or to the evaluation of such individual for purposes of determining the need of such individual for such product.

(b) ENFORCEMENT.—The provisions of subsection (a) shall be applied by the Secretary of Health and Human Services, Secretary of Labor, and Secretary of the Treasury to group health plans and health insurance issuers offering group or individual health insurance coverage as if included in the provisions of part A of title XXVII of the Public Health Service Act, part 7 of the Employee Retirement Income Security Act of 1974, and subchapter B of chapter 100 of the Internal Revenue Code of 1986, as applicable.

(c) IMPLEMENTATION.—The Secretary of Health and Human Services, Secretary of Labor, and Secretary of the Treasury may implement the provisions of this section through sub-regulatory guidance, program instruction or otherwise.

(d) TERMS.—The terms "group health plan"; "health insurance issuer"; "group health insurance coverage", and "individual health insurance coverage" have the meanings given such terms in section 2791 of the Public Health Service Act (42 U.S.C. 300gg–91), section 733 of the Employee Retirement Income Security Act of 1974 (29 U.S.C. 1191b), and section 9832 of the Internal Revenue Code of 1986, as applicable.

[¶1053] SEC. 6002. WAIVING COST SHARING UNDER THE MEDICARE PROGRAM FOR CERTAIN VISITS RELATING TO TESTING FOR COVID–19.

(a) IN GENERAL.—Section 1833 of the Social Security Act (42 U.S.C. 1395l) is amended—

(1) in subsection (a)(1)—

(A) by striking "and" before "(CC)"; and

(B) by inserting before the period at the end the following: ", and (DD) with respect to a specified COVID–19 testing-related service described in paragraph (1) of subsection (cc) for which payment may be made under a specified outpatient payment provision described in paragraph (2) of such subsection, the amounts paid shall be 100 percent of the payment amount otherwise recognized under such respective specified outpatient payment provision for such service,";

(2) in subsection (b), in the first sentence—

(A) by striking "and" before "(10)"; and

(B) by inserting before the period at the end the following: ", and (11) such deductible shall not apply with respect to any specified COVID–19 testing-related service described in paragraph (1) of subsection (cc) for which payment may be made under a specified outpatient payment provision described in paragraph (2) of such subsection"; and

(3) by adding at the end the following new subsection:

(cc) "SPECIFIED COVID–19 TESTING-RELATED SERVICES.—For purposes of subsection (a)(1)(DD):

(1) "DESCRIPTION.—

(A) "IN GENERAL.—A specified COVID–19 testing-related service described in this paragraph is a medical visit that—

(i) "is in any of the categories of HCPCS evaluation and management service codes described in subparagraph (B);

(ii) "is furnished during any portion of the emergency period (as defined in section 1135(g)(1)(B)) (beginning on or after the date of enactment of this subsection);

(iii) "results in an order for or administration of a clinical diagnostic laboratory test described in section 1852(a)(1)(B)(iv)(IV); and

(iv) "relates to the furnishing or administration of such test or to the evaluation of such individual for purposes of determining the need of such individual for such test.

(B) "CATEGORIES OF HCPCS CODES.—For purposes of subparagraph (A), the categories of HCPCS evaluation and management services codes are the following:

(i) "Office and other outpatient services.

(ii) "Hospital observation services.

(iii) "Emergency department services.

(iv) "Nursing facility services.

(v) "Domiciliary, rest home, or custodial care services.

(vi) "Home services.

(vii) "Online digital evaluation and management services.

(2) "SPECIFIED OUTPATIENT PAYMENT PROVISION.—A specified outpatient payment provision described in this paragraph is any of the following:

(A) "The hospital outpatient prospective payment system under subsection (t).

(B) "The physician fee schedule under section 1848.

(C) "The prospective payment system developed under section 1834(o).

(D) "Section 1834(g), with respect to an outpatient critical access hospital service.

(E) "The payment basis determined in regulations pursuant to section 1833(a)(3) for rural health clinic services.".

(b) CLAIMS MODIFIER.—The Secretary of Health and Human Services shall provide for an appropriate modifier (or other identifier) to include on claims to identify, for purposes of subparagraph (DD) of section 1833(a)(1), as added by subsection (a), specified COVID–19 testing-related services described in paragraph (1) of section 1833(cc) of the Social Security Act, as added by subsection (a), for which payment may be made under a specified outpatient payment provision described in paragraph (2) of such subsection.

(c) IMPLEMENTATION.—Notwithstanding any other provision of law, the Secretary of Health and Human Services may implement the provisions of, including amendments made by, this section through program instruction or otherwise.

[¶1054] SEC. 6003. COVERAGE OF TESTING FOR COVID–19 AT NO COST SHARING UNDER THE MEDICARE ADVANTAGE PROGRAM.

(a) IN GENERAL.—Section 1852(a)(1)(B) of the Social Security Act (42 U.S.C. 1395w–22(a)(1)(B)) is amended—

(1) in clause (iv)—

(A) by redesignating subclause (IV) as subclause (VI); and

(B) by inserting after subclause (III) the following new subclauses:

(IV) "Clinical diagnostic laboratory test administered during any portion of the emergency period defined in paragraph (1)(B) of section 1135(g) beginning on or after the date of the enactment of the Families First Coronavirus Response Act for the detection of SARS–CoV–2 or the diagnosis of the virus that causes COVID–19 and the administration of such test.

(V) "Specified COVID–19 testing-related services (as described in section 1833(cc)(1)) for which payment would be payable under a specified outpatient payment provision described in section 1833(cc)(2).";

(2) in clause (v), by inserting ", other than subclauses (IV) and (V) of such clause," after "clause (iv)"; and

(3) by adding at the end the following new clause:

(vi) "PROHIBITION OF APPLICATION OF CERTAIN REQUIREMENTS FOR COVID–19 TESTING.—In the case of a product or service described in subclause (IV) or (V), respectively, of clause (iv) that is administered or furnished during any portion of the emergency period described in such subclause beginning on or after the date of the enactment of this clause, an MA plan may not impose any prior authorization or other utilization management requirements with respect to the coverage of such a product or service under such plan.".

(b) IMPLEMENTATION.—Notwithstanding any other provision of law, the Secretary of Health and Human Services may implement the amendments made by this section by program instruction or otherwise.

[¶1055] SEC. 6004. COVERAGE AT NO COST SHARING OF COVID–19 TESTING UNDER MEDICAID AND CHIP.

(a) MEDICAID.—

(1) IN GENERAL.—Section 1905(a)(3) of the Social Security Act (42 U.S.C. 1396d(a)(3)) is amended—

(A) by striking "other laboratory" and inserting "(A) other laboratory";

(B) by inserting "and" after the semicolon; and

(C) by adding at the end the following new subparagraph:

(B) "in vitro diagnostic products (as defined in section 809.3(a) of title 21, Code of Federal Regulations) administered during any portion of the emergency period defined in paragraph (1)(B) of section 1135(g) beginning on or after the date of the enactment of this subparagraph for the detection of SARS–CoV–2 or the diagnosis of the virus that causes COVID–19 that are approved, cleared, or authorized under section 510(k), 513, 515 or 564 of the Federal Food, Drug, and Cosmetic Act, and the administration of such in vitro diagnostic products;".

(2) NO COST SHARING.—

(A) IN GENERAL.—Subsections (a)(2) and (b)(2) of section 1916 of the Social Security Act (42 U.S.C. 1396o) are each amended—

(i) in subparagraph (D), by striking "or" at the end;

(ii) in subparagraph (E), by striking "; and" and inserting a comma; and

(iii) by adding at the end the following new subparagraphs:

(F) "any in vitro diagnostic product described in section 1905(a)(3)(B) that is administered during any portion of the emergency period described in such section beginning on or after the date of the enactment of this subparagraph (and the administration of such product), or

(G) "COVID–19 testing-related services for which payment may be made under the State plan; and".

(B) APPLICATION TO ALTERNATIVE COST SHARING.—Section 1916A(b)(3)(B) of the Social Security Act (42 U.S.C. 1396o–1(b)(3)(B)) is amended by adding at the end the following new clause:

(xi) "Any in vitro diagnostic product described in section 1905(a)(3)(B) that is administered during any portion of the emergency period described in such section beginning on or after the date of the enactment of this clause (and the administration of such product) and any visit described in section 1916(a)(2)(G) that is furnished during any such portion.".

(C) CLARIFICATION.—The amendments made this paragraph shall apply with respect to a State plan of a territory in the same manner as a State plan of one of the 50 States.

(3) STATE OPTION TO PROVIDE COVERAGE FOR UNINSURED INDIVIDUALS.—

(A) IN GENERAL.—Section 1902(a)(10) of the Social Security Act (42 U.S.C. 1396a(a)(10)) is amended—

(i) in subparagraph (A)(ii)—

(I) in subclause (XXI), by striking "or" at the end;

(II) in subclause (XXII), by adding "or" at the end; and

(III) by adding at the end the following new subclause:

(XXIII) "during any portion of the emergency period defined in paragraph (1)(B) of section 1135(g) beginning on or after the date of the enactment of this subclause, who are uninsured individuals (as defined in subsection (ss));"; and

(ii) in the matter following subparagraph (G)—

(I) by striking "and (XVII)" and inserting ", (XVII)"; and

(II) by inserting after "instead of through subclause (VIII)" the following: ", and (XVIII) the medical assistance made available to an uninsured individual (as defined in subsection (ss)) who is eligible for medical assistance only because of subparagraph (A)(ii)(XXIII) shall be limited to medical assistance for any in vitro diagnostic product described in section 1905(a)(3)(B) that is administered during any portion of the emergency period described in such section beginning on or after the date of the enactment of this subclause (and the administration of such product) and any visit described in section 1916(a)(2)(G) that is furnished during any such portion".

(B) RECEIPT AND INITIAL PROCESSING OF APPLICATIONS AT CERTAIN LOCATIONS.—Section 1902(a)(55) of the Social Security Act (42 U.S.C. 1396a(a)(55)) is amended, in the matter preceding subparagraph (A), by striking "or (a)(10)(A)(ii)(IX)" and inserting "(a)(10)(A)(ii)(IX), or (a)(10)(A)(ii)(XXIII)".

(C) UNINSURED INDIVIDUAL DEFINED.—Section 1902 of the Social Security Act (42 U.S.C. 1396a) is amended by adding at the end the following new subsection:

(ss) "UNINSURED INDIVIDUAL DEFINED.—For purposes of this section, the term 'uninsured individual' means, notwithstanding any other provision of this title, any individual who is—

(1) "not described in subsection (a)(10)(A)(i); and

(2) "not enrolled in a Federal health care program (as defined in section 1128B(f)), a group health plan, group or individual health insurance coverage offered by a health insurance issuer (as such terms are defined in section 2791 of the Public Health Service Act), or a health plan offered under chapter 89 of title 5, United States Code.".

(D) FEDERAL MEDICAL ASSISTANCE PERCENTAGE.—Section 1905(b) of the Social Security Act (42 U.S.C. 1396d(b)) is amended by adding at the end the following new sentence: "Notwithstanding the first sentence of this subsection, the Federal medical assistance percentage shall be 100 per centum with respect to (and, notwithstanding any other provision of this title, available for) medical assistance provided to uninsured individuals (as defined in section 1902(ss)) who are eligible for such assistance only on the basis of section 1902(a)(10)(A)(ii)(XXIII) and with respect to expenditures described in section 1903(a)(7) that a State demonstrates to the satisfaction of the Secretary are attributable to administrative costs related to providing for such medical assistance to such individuals under the State plan.".

(b) CHIP.—

(1) IN GENERAL.—Section 2103(c) of the Social Security Act (42 U.S.C. 1397cc(c)) is amended by adding at the end the following paragraph:

(10) "CERTAIN IN VITRO DIAGNOSTIC PRODUCTS FOR COVID–19 TESTING.—The child health assistance provided to a targeted low-income child shall include coverage of any in vitro diagnostic product described in section 1905(a)(3)(B) that is administered during any portion of the emergency period described in such section beginning on or after the date of the enactment of this subparagraph (and the administration of such product).".

(2) COVERAGE FOR TARGETED LOW-INCOME PREGNANT WOMEN.—Section 2112(b)(4) of the Social Security Act (42 U.S.C. 1397ll(b)(4)) is amended by inserting "under section 2103(c)" after "same requirements".

(3) PROHIBITION OF COST SHARING.—Section 2103(e)(2) of the Social Security Act (42 U.S.C. 1397cc(e)(2)) is amended—

(A) in the paragraph header, by inserting ", COVID–19 TESTING," before "OR PREGNANCY-RELATED ASSISTANCE"; and

(B) by striking "category of services described in subsection (c)(1)(D) or" and inserting "categories of services described in subsection (c)(1)(D), in vitro diagnostic products described in subsection (c)(10) (and administration of such products), visits described in section 1916(a)(2)(G), or".

[¶1056] SEC. 6005. TREATMENT OF PERSONAL RESPIRATORY PROTECTIVE DEVICES AS COVERED COUNTERMEASURES.

Section 319F–3(i)(1) of the Public Health Service Act (42 U.S.C. 247d–6d(i)(1)) is amended—

(1) in subparagraph (B), by striking "or" at the end;

(2) in subparagraph (C), by striking the period at the end and inserting "; or"; and

(3) by adding at the end the following new subparagraph:

(D) "a personal respiratory protective device that is—

(i) "approved by the National Institute for Occupational Safety and Health under part 84 of title 42, Code of Federal Regulations (or successor regulations);

(ii) "subject to the emergency use authorization issued by the Secretary on March 2, 2020, or subsequent emergency use authorizations, pursuant to section 564 of the Federal Food, Drug, and Cosmetic Act (authorizing emergency use of personal respiratory protective devices during the COVID–19 outbreak); and

(iii) "used during the period beginning on January 27, 2020, and ending on October 1, 2024, in response to the public health emergency declared on January 31, 2020, pursuant to section 319 as a result of confirmed cases of 2019 Novel Coronavirus (2019-nCoV).".

[¶1057] SEC. 6006. APPLICATION WITH RESPECT TO TRICARE, COVERAGE FOR VETERANS, AND COVERAGE FOR FEDERAL CIVILIANS.

(a) TRICARE.—The Secretary of Defense may not require any copayment or other cost sharing under chapter 55 of title 10, United States Code, for in vitro diagnostic products described in paragraph (1) of section 6001(a) (or the administration of such products) or visits described in paragraph (2) of such section furnished during any portion of the emergency period defined in paragraph (1)(B) of section 1135(g) of the Social Security Act (42 U.S.C. 1320b-5(g)) beginning on or after the date of the enactment of this Act.

(b) VETERANS.—The Secretary of Veterans Affairs may not require any copayment or other cost sharing under chapter 17 of title 38, United States Code, for in vitro diagnostic products described in paragraph (1) of section 6001(a) (or the administration of such products) or visits described in paragraph (2) of such section furnished during any portion of the emergency period defined in paragraph (1)(B) of section 1135(g) of the Social Security Act (42 U.S.C. 1320b-5(g)) beginning on or after the date of the enactment of this Act.

(c) FEDERAL CIVILIANS.—No copayment or other cost sharing may be required for any individual occupying a position in the civil service (as that term is defined in section 2101(1) of title 5, United States Code) enrolled in a health benefits plan, including any plan under chapter 89 of title 5, United States Code, or for any other individual currently enrolled in any plan under chapter 89 of title 5 for in vitro diagnostic products described in paragraph (1) of section 6001(a) (or the administration of such products) or visits described in paragraph (2) of such section furnished during any portion of the emergency period defined in paragraph (1)(B) of section 1135(g) of the Social Security Act (42 U.S.C. 1320b-5(g)) beginning on or after the date of the enactment of this Act.

[¶1058] SEC. 6007. COVERAGE OF TESTING FOR COVID–19 AT NO COST SHARING FOR INDIANS RECEIVING PURCHASED/REFERRED CARE.

The Secretary of Health and Human Services shall cover, without the imposition of any cost sharing requirements, the cost of providing any COVID–19 related items and services as described in paragraph (1) of section 6001(a) (or the administration of such products) or visits described in paragraph (2) of such section furnished during any portion of the emergency period defined in paragraph (1)(B) of section 1135(g) of the Social Security Act (42 U.S.C. 320b-5(g)) beginning on or after the date of the enactment of this Act to Indians (as defined in section 4 of the Indian Health Care Improvement Act (25 U.S.C. 1603)) receiving health services through the Indian Health Service, including through an Urban Indian Organization, regardless of whether such items or services have been authorized under the purchased/referred care system funded by the Indian Health Service or is covered as a health service of the Indian Health Service.

[¶1059] SEC. 6008. TEMPORARY INCREASE OF MEDICAID FMAP.

(a) IN GENERAL.—Subject to subsection (b), for each calendar quarter occurring during the period beginning on the first day of the emergency period defined in paragraph (1)(B) of section 1135(g) of the Social Security Act (42 U.S.C. 1320b-5(g)) and ending on the last day of the calendar quarter in which the last day of such emergency period occurs, the Federal medical assistance percentage determined for each State, including the District of Columbia, American Samoa, Guam, the Commonwealth of the Northern Mariana Islands, Puerto Rico, and the United States Virgin Islands, under section 1905(b) of the Social Security Act (42 U.S.C. 1396d(b)) shall be increased by 6.2 percentage points.

(b) REQUIREMENT FOR ALL STATES.—A State described in subsection (a) may not receive the increase described in such subsection in the Federal medical assistance percentage for such State, with respect to a quarter, if—

(1) eligibility standards, methodologies, or procedures under the State plan of such State under title XIX of the Social Security Act (42 U.S.C. 1396 et seq.) (including any waiver under such title or section 1115 of such Act (42 U.S.C. 1315)) are more restrictive during such quarter than the eligibility standards, methodologies, or procedures, respectively, under such plan (or waiver) as in effect on January 1, 2020;

(2) the amount of any premium imposed by the State pursuant to section 1916 or 1916A of such Act (42 U.S.C. 1396o, 1396o–1) during such quarter, with respect to an individual enrolled under such plan (or waiver), exceeds the amount of such premium as of January 1, 2020;

(3) the State fails to provide that an individual who is enrolled for benefits under such plan (or waiver) as of the date of enactment of this section or enrolls for benefits under such plan (or waiver) during the period beginning on such date of enactment and ending the last day of the month in which the emergency period described in subsection (a) ends shall be treated as eligible for such benefits through the end of the month in which such emergency period ends unless the individual requests a voluntary termination of eligibility or the individual ceases to be a resident of the State; or

(4) the State does not provide coverage under such plan (or waiver), without the imposition of cost sharing, during such quarter for any testing services and treatments for COVID–19, including vaccines, specialized equipment, and therapies.

(c) REQUIREMENT FOR CERTAIN STATES.—Section 1905(cc) of the Social Security Act (42 U.S.C. 1396d(cc)) is amended by striking the period at the end of the subsection and inserting "and section 6008 of the Families First Coronavirus Response Act, except that in applying such treatments to the increases in the Federal medical assistance percentage under section 6008 of the Families First Coronavirus Response Act, the reference to 'December 31, 2009' shall be deemed to be a reference to 'March 11, 2020'.".

[¶1060] SEC. 6009. INCREASE IN MEDICAID ALLOTMENTS FOR TERRITORIES.

Section 1108(g) of the Social Security Act (42 U.S.C. 1308(g)) is amended—

(1) in paragraph (2)—

(A) in subparagraph (B)—

(i) in clause (i), by striking "and" at the end;

(ii) in clause (ii), by striking "for each of fiscal years 2020 through 2021, $126,000,000;" and inserting "for fiscal year 2020, $128,712,500; and"; and

(iii) by adding at the end the following new clause:

(iii) "for fiscal year 2021, $127,937,500;";

(B) in subparagraph (C)—

(i) in clause (i), by striking "and" at the end;

(ii) in clause (ii), by striking "for each of fiscal years 2020 through 2021, $127,000,000;" and inserting "for fiscal year 2020, $130,875,000; and"; and

(iii) by adding at the end the following new clause:

(iii) "for fiscal year 2021, $129,712,500;";

(C) in subparagraph (D)—

(i) in clause (i), by striking "and" at the end;

(ii) in clause (ii), by striking "for each of fiscal years 2020 through 2021, $60,000,000; and" and inserting "for fiscal year 2020, $63,100,000; and"; and

(iii) by adding at the end the following new clause:

(iii) "for fiscal year 2021, $62,325,000; and"; and

(D) in subparagraph (E)—

(i) in clause (i), by striking "and" at the end;

(ii) in clause (ii), by striking "for each of fiscal years 2020 through 2021, $84,000,000." and inserting "for fiscal year 2020, $86,325,000; and"; and

(iii) by adding at the end the following new clause:

(iii) "for fiscal year 2021, $85,550,000."; and

(2) in paragraph (6)(A)—

(A) in clause (i), by striking "$2,623,188,000" and inserting "$2,716,188,000"; and

(B) in clause (ii), by striking "$2,719,072,000" and inserting "$2,809,063,000".

[¶1061] SEC. 6010. CLARIFICATION RELATING TO SECRETARIAL AUTHORITY REGARDING MEDICARE TELEHEALTH SERVICES FURNISHED DURING COVID–19 EMERGENCY PERIOD.

Paragraph (3)(A) of section 1135(g) of the Social Security Act (42 U.S.C. 1320b-5(g)) is amended to read as follows:

(A) "furnished to such individual, during the 3-year period ending on the date such telehealth service was furnished, an item or service that would be considered covered under title XVIII if furnished to an individual entitled to benefits or enrolled under such title; or".

DIVISION G—TAX CREDITS FOR PAID SICK AND PAID FAMILY AND MEDICAL LEAVE

[¶1063] SEC. 7001. PAYROLL CREDIT FOR REQUIRED PAID SICK LEAVE.

(a) IN GENERAL.—In the case of an employer, there shall be allowed as a credit against the tax imposed by section 3111(a) or 3221(a) of the Internal Revenue Code of 1986 for each calendar quarter an amount equal to 100 percent of the qualified sick leave wages paid by such employer with respect to such calendar quarter.

(b) LIMITATIONS AND REFUNDABILITY.—

(1) WAGES TAKEN INTO ACCOUNT.—The amount of qualified sick leave wages taken into account under subsection (a) with respect to any individual shall not exceed $200 ($511 in the case of any day any portion of which is paid sick time described in paragraph (1), (2), or (3) of section 5102(a) of the Emergency Paid Sick Leave Act) for any day (or portion thereof) for which the individual is paid qualified sick leave wages.

(2) OVERALL LIMITATION ON NUMBER OF DAYS TAKEN INTO ACCOUNT.—The aggregate number of days taken into account under paragraph (1) for any calendar quarter shall not exceed the excess (if any) of—

(A) 10, over

(B) the aggregate number of days so taken into account for all preceding calendar quarters.

(3) CREDIT LIMITED TO CERTAIN EMPLOYMENT TAXES.—The credit allowed by subsection (a) with respect to any calendar quarter shall not exceed the tax imposed by section 3111(a) or 3221(a) of such Code for such calendar quarter (reduced by any credits allowed under subsections (e) and (f) of

section 3111 of such Code for such quarter) on the wages paid with respect to the employment of all employees of the employer.

(4) REFUNDABILITY OF EXCESS CREDIT.—

(A) IN GENERAL.—If the amount of the credit under subsection (a) exceeds the limitation of paragraph (3) for any calendar quarter, such excess shall be treated as an overpayment that shall be refunded under sections 6402(a) and 6413(b) of such Code.

(B) TREATMENT OF PAYMENTS.—For purposes of section 1324 of title 31, United States Code, any amounts due to an employer under this paragraph shall be treated in the same manner as a refund due from a credit provision referred to in subsection (b)(2) of such section.

(c) QUALIFIED SICK LEAVE WAGES.—For purposes of this section, the term "qualified sick leave wages" means wages (as defined in section 3121(a) of the Internal Revenue Code of 1986) and compensation (as defined in section 3231(e) of the Internal Revenue Code) paid by an employer which are required to be paid by reason of the Emergency Paid Sick Leave Act.

(d) ALLOWANCE OF CREDIT FOR CERTAIN HEALTH PLAN EXPENSES.—

(1) IN GENERAL.—The amount of the credit allowed under subsection (a) shall be increased by so much of the employer's qualified health plan expenses as are properly allocable to the qualified sick leave wages for which such credit is so allowed.

(2) QUALIFIED HEALTH PLAN EXPENSES.—For purposes of this subsection, the term "qualified health plan expenses" means amounts paid or incurred by the employer to provide and maintain a group health plan (as defined in section 5000(b)(1) of the Internal Revenue Code of 1986), but only to the extent that such amounts are excluded from the gross income of employees by reason of section 106(a) of such Code.

(3) ALLOCATION RULES.—For purposes of this section, qualified health plan expenses shall be allocated to qualified sick leave wages in such manner as the Secretary of the Treasury (or the Secretary's delegate) may prescribe. Except as otherwise provided by the Secretary, such allocation shall be treated as properly made if made on the basis of being pro rata among covered employees and pro rata on the basis of periods of coverage (relative to the time periods of leave to which such wages relate).

(e) SPECIAL RULES.—

(1) DENIAL OF DOUBLE BENEFIT.—For purposes of chapter 1 of such Code, the gross income of the employer, for the taxable year which includes the last day of any calendar quarter with respect to which a credit is allowed under this section, shall be increased by the amount of such credit. Any wages taken into account in determining the credit allowed under this section shall not be taken into account for purposes of determining the credit allowed under section 45S of such Code.

(2) ELECTION NOT TO HAVE SECTION APPLY.—This section shall not apply with respect to any employer for any calendar quarter if such employer elects (at such time and in such manner as the Secretary of the Treasury (or the Secretary's delegate) may prescribe) not to have this section apply.

(3) CERTAIN TERMS.—Any term used in this section which is also used in chapter 21 of such Code shall have the same meaning as when used in such chapter.

(4) CERTAIN GOVERNMENTAL EMPLOYERS.—This credit shall not apply to the Government of the United States, the government of any State or political subdivision thereof, or any agency or instrumentality of any of the foregoing.

(f) REGULATIONS.—The Secretary of the Treasury (or the Secretary's delegate) shall prescribe such regulations or other guidance as may be necessary to carry out the purposes of this section, including—

(1) regulations or other guidance to prevent the avoidance of the purposes of the limitations under this section,

(2) regulations or other guidance to minimize compliance and record-keeping burdens under this section,

(3) regulations or other guidance providing for waiver of penalties for failure to deposit amounts in anticipation of the allowance of the credit allowed under this section,

(4) regulations or other guidance for recapturing the benefit of credits determined under this section in cases where there is a subsequent adjustment to the credit determined under subsection (a), and

(5) regulations or other guidance to ensure that the wages taken into account under this section conform with the paid sick time required to be provided under the Emergency Paid Sick Leave Act.

(g) APPLICATION OF SECTION.—This section shall apply only to wages paid with respect to the period beginning on a date selected by the Secretary of the Treasury (or the Secretary's delegate) which is during the 15-day period beginning on the date of the enactment of this Act, and ending on December 31, 2020.

(h) TRANSFERS TO FEDERAL OLD-AGE AND SURVIVORS INSURANCE TRUST FUND.—There are hereby appropriated to the Federal Old-Age and Survivors Insurance Trust Fund and the Federal Disability Insurance Trust Fund established under section 201 of the Social Security Act (42 U.S.C. 401) and the Social Security Equivalent Benefit Account established under section 15A(a) of the Railroad Retirement Act of 1974 (45 U.S.C. 231n–1(a)) amounts equal to the reduction in revenues to the Treasury by reason of this section (without regard to this subsection). Amounts appropriated by the preceding sentence shall be transferred from the general fund at such times and in such manner as to replicate to the extent possible the transfers which would have occurred to such Trust Fund or Account had this section not been enacted.

[¶1064] SEC. 7002. CREDIT FOR SICK LEAVE FOR CERTAIN SELF-EMPLOYED INDIVIDUALS.

(a) CREDIT AGAINST SELF-EMPLOYMENT TAX.—In the case of an eligible self-employed individual, there shall be allowed as a credit against the tax imposed by subtitle A of the Internal Revenue Code of 1986 for any taxable year an amount equal to the qualified sick leave equivalent amount with respect to the individual.

(b) ELIGIBLE SELF-EMPLOYED INDIVIDUAL.—For purposes of this section, the term "eligible self-employed individual" means an individual who—

(1) regularly carries on any trade or business within the meaning of section 1402 of such Code, and

(2) would be entitled to receive paid leave during the taxable year pursuant to the Emergency Paid Sick Leave Act if the individual were an employee of an employer (other than himself or herself).

(c) QUALIFIED SICK LEAVE EQUIVALENT AMOUNT.—For purposes of this section—

(1) IN GENERAL.—The term "qualified sick leave equivalent amount" means, with respect to any eligible self-employed individual, an amount equal to—

(A) the number of days during the taxable year (but not more than the applicable number of days) that the individual is unable to perform services in any trade or business referred to in section 1402 of such Code for a reason with respect to which such individual would be entitled to receive sick leave as described in subsection (b), multiplied by

(B) the lesser of—

(i) $200 ($511 in the case of any day of paid sick time described in paragraph (1), (2), or (3) of section 5102(a) of the Emergency Paid Sick Leave Act), or

(ii) 67 percent (100 percent in the case of any day of paid sick time described in paragraph (1), (2), or (3) of section 5102(a) of the Emergency Paid Sick Leave Act) of the average daily self-employment income of the individual for the taxable year.

(2) AVERAGE DAILY SELF-EMPLOYMENT INCOME.—For purposes of this subsection, the term "average daily self-employment income" means an amount equal to—

(A) the net earnings from self-employment of the individual for the taxable year, divided by

(B) 260.

(3) APPLICABLE NUMBER OF DAYS.—For purposes of this subsection, the term "applicable number of days" means, with respect to any taxable year, the excess (if any) of 10 days over the number of days taken into account under paragraph (1)(A) in all preceding taxable years.

(d) SPECIAL RULES.—

(1) CREDIT REFUNDABLE.—

(A) IN GENERAL.—The credit determined under this section shall be treated as a credit allowed to the taxpayer under subpart C of part IV of subchapter A of chapter 1 of such Code.

(B) TREATMENT OF PAYMENTS.—For purposes of section 1324 of title 31, United States Code, any refund due from the credit determined under this section shall be treated in the same manner as a refund due from a credit provision referred to in subsection (b)(2) of such section.

(2) DOCUMENTATION.—No credit shall be allowed under this section unless the individual maintains such documentation as the Secretary of the Treasury (or the Secretary's delegate) may prescribe to establish such individual as an eligible self-employed individual.

(3) DENIAL OF DOUBLE BENEFIT.—In the case of an individual who receives wages (as defined in section 3121(a) of the Internal Revenue Code of 1986) or compensation (as defined in section 3231(e) of the Internal Revenue Code) paid by an employer which are required to be paid by reason of the Emergency Paid Sick Leave Act, the qualified sick leave equivalent amount otherwise determined under subsection (c) shall be reduced (but not below zero) to the extent that the sum of the amount described in such subsection and in section 7001(b)(1) exceeds $2,000 ($5,110 in the case of any day any portion of which is paid sick time described in paragraph (1), (2), or (3) of section 5102(a) of the Emergency Paid Sick Leave Act).

(4) CERTAIN TERMS.—Any term used in this section which is also used in chapter 2 of the Internal Revenue Code of 1986 shall have the same meaning as when used in such chapter.

(e) APPLICATION OF SECTION.—Only days occurring during the period beginning on a date selected by the Secretary of the Treasury (or the Secretary's delegate) which is during the 15-day period beginning on the date of the enactment of this Act, and ending on December 31, 2020, may be taken into account under subsection (c)(1)(A).

(f) APPLICATION OF CREDIT IN CERTAIN POSSESSIONS.—

(1) PAYMENTS TO POSSESSIONS WITH MIRROR CODE TAX SYSTEMS.—The Secretary of the Treasury (or the Secretary's delegate) shall pay to each possession of the United States which has a mirror code tax system amounts equal to the loss (if any) to that possession by reason of the application of the provisions of this section. Such amounts shall be determined by the Secretary of the Treasury (or the Secretary's delegate) based on information provided by the government of the respective possession.

(2) PAYMENTS TO OTHER POSSESSIONS.—The Secretary of the Treasury (or the Secretary's delegate) shall pay to each possession of the United States which does not have a mirror code tax system amounts estimated by the Secretary of the Treasury (or the Secretary's delegate) as being equal to the aggregate benefits (if any) that would have been provided to residents of such possession by reason of the provisions of this section if a mirror code tax system had been in effect in such possession. The preceding sentence shall not apply unless the respective possession has a plan, which has been approved by the Secretary of the Treasury (or the Secretary's delegate), under which such possession will promptly distribute such payments to its residents.

(3) MIRROR CODE TAX SYSTEM.—For purposes of this section, the term "mirror code tax system" means, with respect to any possession of the United States, the income tax system of such possession if the income tax liability of the residents of such possession under such system is determined by reference to the income tax laws of the United States as if such possession were the United States.

(4) TREATMENT OF PAYMENTS.—For purposes of section 1324 of title 31, United States Code, the payments under this section shall be treated in the same manner as a refund due from a credit provision referred to in subsection (b)(2) of such section.

(g) REGULATIONS.—The Secretary of the Treasury (or the Secretary's delegate) shall prescribe such regulations or other guidance as may be necessary to carry out the purposes of this section, including—

(1) regulations or other guidance to effectuate the purposes of this Act, and

(2) regulations or other guidance to minimize compliance and record-keeping burdens under this section.

[¶1065] SEC. 7003. PAYROLL CREDIT FOR REQUIRED PAID FAMILY LEAVE.

(a) IN GENERAL.—In the case of an employer, there shall be allowed as a credit against the tax imposed by section 3111(a) or 3221(a) of the Internal Revenue Code of 1986 for each calendar quarter an amount equal to 100 percent of the qualified family leave wages paid by such employer with respect to such calendar quarter.

(b) LIMITATIONS AND REFUNDABILITY.—

(1) WAGES TAKEN INTO ACCOUNT.—The amount of qualified family leave wages taken into account under subsection (a) with respect to any individual shall not exceed—

(A) for any day (or portion thereof) for which the individual is paid qualified family leave wages, $200, and

(B) in the aggregate with respect to all calendar quarters, $10,000.

(2) CREDIT LIMITED TO CERTAIN EMPLOYMENT TAXES.—The credit allowed by subsection (a) with respect to any calendar quarter shall not exceed the tax imposed by section 3111(a) or 3221(a) of such Code for such calendar quarter (reduced by any credits allowed under subsections (e) and (f) of section 3111 of such Code, and section 7001 of this Act, for such quarter) on the wages paid with respect to the employment of all employees of the employer.

(3) REFUNDABILITY OF EXCESS CREDIT.—If the amount of the credit under subsection (a) exceeds the limitation of paragraph (2) for any calendar quarter, such excess shall be treated as an overpayment that shall be refunded under sections 6402(a) and 6413(b) of such Code.

(c) QUALIFIED FAMILY LEAVE WAGES.—For purposes of this section, the term "qualified family leave wages" means wages (as defined in section 3121(a) of such Code) and compensation (as defined in section 3231(e) of the Internal Revenue Code) paid by an employer which are required to be paid by reason of the Emergency Family and Medical Leave Expansion Act (including the amendments made by such Act).

(d) ALLOWANCE OF CREDIT FOR CERTAIN HEALTH PLAN EXPENSES.—

(1) IN GENERAL.—The amount of the credit allowed under subsection (a) shall be increased by so much of the employer's qualified health plan expenses as are properly allocable to the qualified family leave wages for which such credit is so allowed.

(2) QUALIFIED HEALTH PLAN EXPENSES.—For purposes of this subsection, the term "qualified health plan expenses" means amounts paid or incurred by the employer to provide and maintain a group health plan (as defined in section 5000(b)(1) of the Internal Revenue Code of 1986), but only to the extent that such amounts are excluded from the gross income of employees by reason of section 106(a) of such Code.

(3) ALLOCATION RULES.—For purposes of this section, qualified health plan expenses shall be allocated to qualified family leave wages in such manner as the Secretary of the Treasury (or the Secretary's delegate) may prescribe. Except as otherwise provided by the Secretary, such allocation shall be treated as properly made if made on the basis of being pro rata among covered employees and pro rata on the basis of periods of coverage (relative to the time periods of leave to which such wages relate).

(e) SPECIAL RULES.—

(1) DENIAL OF DOUBLE BENEFIT.—For purposes of chapter 1 of such Code, the gross income of the employer, for the taxable year which includes the last day of any calendar quarter with respect to which a credit is allowed under this section, shall be increased by the amount of such credit. Any wages taken into account in determining the credit allowed under this section shall not be taken into account for purposes of determining the credit allowed under section 45S of such Code.

(2) ELECTION NOT TO HAVE SECTION APPLY.—This section shall not apply with respect to any employer for any calendar quarter if such employer elects (at such time and in such manner as the Secretary of the Treasury (or the Secretary's delegate) may prescribe) not to have this section apply.

(3) CERTAIN TERMS.—Any term used in this section which is also used in chapter 21 of such Code shall have the same meaning as when used in such chapter.

(4) CERTAIN GOVERNMENTAL EMPLOYERS.—This credit shall not apply to the Government of the United States, the government of any State or political subdivision thereof, or any agency or instrumentality of any of the foregoing.

(f) REGULATIONS.—The Secretary of the Treasury (or the Secretary's delegate) shall prescribe such regulations or other guidance as may be necessary to carry out the purposes of this section, including—

(1) regulations or other guidance to prevent the avoidance of the purposes of the limitations under this section,

(2) regulations or other guidance to minimize compliance and record-keeping burdens under this section,

(3) regulations or other guidance providing for waiver of penalties for failure to deposit amounts in anticipation of the allowance of the credit allowed under this section,

(4) regulations or other guidance for recapturing the benefit of credits determined under this section in cases where there is a subsequent adjustment to the credit determined under subsection (a), and

(5) regulations or other guidance to ensure that the wages taken into account under this section conform with the paid leave required to be provided under the Emergency Family and Medical Leave Expansion Act (including the amendments made by such Act).

(g) APPLICATION OF SECTION.—This section shall apply only to wages paid with respect to the period beginning on a date selected by the Secretary of the Treasury (or the Secretary's delegate) which is during the 15-day period beginning on the date of the enactment of this Act, and ending on December 31, 2020.

(h) TRANSFERS TO FEDERAL OLD-AGE AND SURVIVORS INSURANCE TRUST FUND.—There are hereby appropriated to the Federal Old-Age and Survivors Insurance Trust Fund and the Federal Disability Insurance Trust Fund established under section 201 of the Social Security Act (42 U.S.C. 401) and the Social Security Equivalent Benefit Account established under section 15A(a) of the Railroad Retirement Act of 1974 (45 U.S.C. 231n–1(a)) amounts equal to the reduction in revenues to the Treasury by reason of this section (without regard to this subsection). Amounts appropriated by the preceding sentence shall be transferred from the general fund at such times and in such manner as to replicate to the extent possible the transfers which would have occurred to such Trust Fund or Account had this section not been enacted.

[¶1066] SEC. 7004. CREDIT FOR FAMILY LEAVE FOR CERTAIN SELF-EMPLOYED INDIVIDUALS.

(a) CREDIT AGAINST SELF-EMPLOYMENT TAX.—In the case of an eligible self-employed individual, there shall be allowed as a credit against the tax imposed by subtitle A of the Internal Revenue Code of 1986 for any taxable year an amount equal to 100 percent of the qualified family leave equivalent amount with respect to the individual.

(b) ELIGIBLE SELF-EMPLOYED INDIVIDUAL.—For purposes of this section, the term "eligible self-employed individual" means an individual who—

(1) regularly carries on any trade or business within the meaning of section 1402 of such Code, and

(2) would be entitled to receive paid leave during the taxable year pursuant to the Emergency Family and Medical Leave Expansion Act if the individual were an employee of an employer (other than himself or herself).

(c) QUALIFIED FAMILY LEAVE EQUIVALENT AMOUNT.—For purposes of this section—

(1) IN GENERAL.—The term "qualified family leave equivalent amount" means, with respect to any eligible self-employed individual, an amount equal to the product of—

(A) the number of days (not to exceed 50) during the taxable year that the individual is unable to perform services in any trade or business referred to in section 1402 of such Code for a reason with respect to which such individual would be entitled to receive paid leave as described in subsection (b), multiplied by

(B) the lesser of—

(i) 67 percent of the average daily self-employment income of the individual for the taxable year, or

(ii) $200.

(2) AVERAGE DAILY SELF-EMPLOYMENT INCOME.—For purposes of this subsection, the term "average daily self-employment income" means an amount equal to—

(A) the net earnings from self-employment income of the individual for the taxable year, divided by

(B) 260.

(d) SPECIAL RULES.—

(1) CREDIT REFUNDABLE.—

(A) IN GENERAL.—The credit determined under this section shall be treated as a credit allowed to the taxpayer under subpart C of part IV of subchapter A of chapter 1 of such Code.

(B) TREATMENT OF PAYMENTS.—For purposes of section 1324 of title 31, United States Code, any refund due from the credit determined under this section shall be treated in the same manner as a refund due from a credit provision referred to in subsection (b)(2) of such section.

(2) DOCUMENTATION.—No credit shall be allowed under this section unless the individual maintains such documentation as the Secretary of the Treasury (or the Secretary's delegate) may prescribe to establish such individual as an eligible self-employed individual.

(3) DENIAL OF DOUBLE BENEFIT.—In the case of an individual who receives wages (as defined in section 3121(a) of the Internal Revenue Code of 1986) or compensation (as defined in section 3231(e) of the Internal Revenue Code) paid by an employer which are required to be paid by reason of the Emergency Family and Medical Leave Expansion Act, the qualified family leave equivalent amount otherwise described in subsection (c) shall be reduced (but not below zero) to the extent that the sum of the amount described in such subsection and in section 7003(b)(1) exceeds $10,000.

(4) CERTAIN TERMS.—Any term used in this section which is also used in chapter 2 of the Internal Revenue Code of 1986 shall have the same meaning as when used in such chapter.

(5) REFERENCES TO EMERGENCY FAMILY AND MEDICAL LEAVE EXPANSION ACT.—Any reference in this section to the Emergency Family and Medical Leave Expansion Act shall be treated as including a reference to the amendments made by such Act.

(e) APPLICATION OF SECTION.—Only days occurring during the period beginning on a date selected by the Secretary of the Treasury (or the Secretary's delegate) which is during the 15-day period beginning on the date of the enactment of this Act, and ending on December 31, 2020, may be taken into account under subsection (c)(1)(A).

(f) APPLICATION OF CREDIT IN CERTAIN POSSESSIONS.—

(1) PAYMENTS TO POSSESSIONS WITH MIRROR CODE TAX SYSTEMS.—The Secretary of the Treasury (or the Secretary's delegate) shall pay to each possession of the United States which has a mirror code tax system amounts equal to the loss (if any) to that possession by reason of the application of the provisions of this section. Such amounts shall be determined by the Secretary of the Treasury (or the Secretary's delegate) based on information provided by the government of the respective possession.

(2) PAYMENTS TO OTHER POSSESSIONS.—The Secretary of the Treasury (or the Secretary's delegate) shall pay to each possession of the United States which does not have a mirror code tax system amounts estimated by the Secretary of the Treasury (or the Secretary's delegate) as being equal to the aggregate benefits (if any) that would have been provided to residents of such possession by reason of the provisions of this section if a mirror code tax system had been in effect in such possession. The preceding sentence shall not apply unless the respective possession has a plan, which has been approved by the Secretary of the Treasury (or the Secretary's delegate), under which such possession will promptly distribute such payments to its residents.

(3) MIRROR CODE TAX SYSTEM.—For purposes of this section, the term "mirror code tax system" means, with respect to any possession of the United States, the income tax system of such possession if the income tax liability of the residents of such possession under such system is determined by reference to the income tax laws of the United States as if such possession were the United States.

(4) TREATMENT OF PAYMENTS.—For purposes of section 1324 of title 31, United States Code, the payments under this section shall be treated in the same manner as a refund due from a credit provision referred to in subsection (b)(2) of such section.

(e) REGULATIONS.—The Secretary of the Treasury (or the Secretary's delegate) shall prescribe such regulations or other guidance as may be necessary to carry out the purposes of this section, including—

(1) regulations or other guidance to prevent the avoidance of the purposes of this Act, and

(2) regulations or other guidance to minimize compliance and record-keeping burdens under this section.

[¶1067] SEC. 7005. SPECIAL RULE RELATED TO TAX ON EMPLOYERS.

(a) IN GENERAL.—Any wages required to be paid by reason of the Emergency Paid Sick Leave Act and the Emergency Family and Medical Leave Expansion Act shall not be considered wages for purposes of section 3111(a) of the Internal Revenue Code of 1986 or compensation for purposes of section 3221(a) of such Code.

(b) ALLOWANCE OF CREDIT FOR HOSPITAL INSURANCE TAXES.—

(1) IN GENERAL.—The credit allowed by section 7001 and the credit allowed by section 7003 shall each be increased by the amount of the tax imposed by section 3111(b) of the Internal Revenue Code of 1986 on qualified sick leave wages, or qualified family leave wages, for which credit is allowed under such section 7001 or 7003 (respectively).

(2) DENIAL OF DOUBLE BENEFIT.—For denial of double benefit with respect to the credit increase under paragraph (1), see sections 7001(e)(1) and 7003(e)(1).

(c) TRANSFERS TO FEDERAL OLD-AGE AND SURVIVORS INSURANCE TRUST FUND.—There are hereby appropriated to the Federal Old-Age and Survivors Insurance Trust Fund and the Federal Disability Insurance Trust Fund established under section 201 of the Social Security Act (42 U.S.C. 401) and the Social Security Equivalent Benefit Account established under section 15A(a) of the Railroad Retirement Act of 1974 (45 U.S.C. 231n–1(a)) amounts equal to the reduction in revenues to the Treasury by reason of this section (without regard to this subsection). Amounts appropriated by the preceding sentence shall be transferred from the general fund at such times and in such manner as to replicate to the extent possible the transfers which would have occurred to such Trust Fund or Account had this section not been enacted.

DIVISION H—BUDGETARY EFFECTS

[¶1069] SEC. 8001. BUDGETARY EFFECTS.

(a) STATUTORY PAYGO SCORECARDS.—The budgetary effects of division B and each succeeding division shall not be entered on either PAYGO scorecard maintained pursuant to section 4(d) of the Statutory Pay-As-You-Go Act of 2010.

(b) SENATE PAYGO SCORECARDS.—The budgetary effects of division B and each succeeding division shall not be entered on any PAYGO scorecard maintained for purposes of section 4106 of H. Con. Res. 71 (115th Congress).

(c) CLASSIFICATION OF BUDGETARY EFFECTS.—Notwithstanding Rule 3 of the Budget Scorekeeping Guidelines set forth in the joint explanatory statement of the committee of conference accompanying Conference Report 105–217 and section 250(c)(8) of the Balanced Budget and Emergency Deficit Control Act of 1985, the budgetary effects of division B and each succeeding division shall not be estimated—

(1) for purposes of section 251 of such Act; and

(2) for purposes of paragraph (4)(C) of section 3 of the Statutory Pay-As-You-Go Act of 2010 as being included in an appropriation Act.

Speaker of the House of Representatives.

Vice President of the United States and President of the Senate.

Coronavirus Aid, Relief, and Economic Security Act (CARES Act), P.L. 116-136

[¶2000]

Introduction

The text of the Coronavirus Aid, Relief, and Economic Security Act (CARES Act) (P.L. 116-136) is reproduced below. On March 27, 2020, President Donald Trump signed the bipartisan legislation that provides measures aimed at stabilizing the economy impacted by the COVID-19 pandemic. The CARES Act provides recovery rebates for individual taxpayers, three new unemployment insurance programs, tax benefits for companies, and payroll relief, and clarifies the emergency paid family leave and paid sick leave provisions in the Families First Coronavirus Response Act, among other relief. On March 24, 2020, the Senate passed the CARES Act by a unanimous vote. On March 27, 2020, the House of Representatives passed the measure by voice vote.

[¶2001] SECTION 1. SHORT TITLE.

This Act may be cited as the "Coronavirus Aid, Relief, and Economic Security Act" or the "CARES Act".

[¶2002] SEC. 2. TABLE OF CONTENTS.

The table of contents for this Act is as follows:

[¶2003] SEC. 3. REFERENCES.

Except as expressly provided otherwise, any reference to "this Act" contained in any division of this Act shall be treated as referring only to the provisions of that division.

DIVISION A—KEEPING WORKERS PAID AND EMPLOYED, HEALTH CARE SYSTEM ENHANCEMENTS, AND ECONOMIC STABILIZATION

TITLE I—KEEPING AMERICAN WORKERS PAID AND EMPLOYED ACT

[¶2006] SEC. 1101. DEFINITIONS.

In this title—

(1) the terms "Administration" and "Administrator" mean the Small Business Administration and the Administrator thereof, respectively; and

(2) the term "small business concern" has the meaning given the term in section 3 of the Small Business Act (15 U.S.C. 636).

[¶2007] SEC. 1102. PAYCHECK PROTECTION PROGRAM.

(a) IN GENERAL.—Section 7(a) of the Small Business Act (15 U.S.C. 636(a)) is amended—

(1) in paragraph (2)—

(A) in subparagraph (A), in the matter preceding clause (i), by striking "and (E)" and inserting "(E), and (F)"; and

(B) by adding at the end the following:

(F) "PARTICIPATION IN THE PAYCHECK PROTECTION PROGRAM.—In an agreement to participate in a loan on a deferred basis under paragraph (36), the participation by the Administration shall be 100 percent."; and

(2) by adding at the end the following:

(36) "PAYCHECK PROTECTION PROGRAM.—

(A) "DEFINITIONS.—In this paragraph—

(i) "the terms 'appropriate Federal banking agency' and 'insured depository institution' have the meanings given those terms in section 3 of the Federal Deposit Insurance Act (12 U.S.C. 1813);

(ii) "the term 'covered loan' means a loan made under this paragraph during the covered period;

(iii) "the term 'covered period' means the period beginning on February 15, 2020 and ending on June 30, 2020;

(iv) "the term 'eligible recipient' means an individual or entity that is eligible to receive a covered loan;

(v) "the term 'eligible self-employed individual' has the meaning given the term in section 7002(b) of the Families First Coronavirus Response Act (Public Law 116–127);

(vi) "the term 'insured credit union' has the meaning given the term in section 101 of the Federal Credit Union Act (12 U.S.C. 1752);

(vii) "the term 'nonprofit organization' means an organization that is described in section 501(c)(3) of the Internal Revenue Code of 1986 and that is exempt from taxation under section 501(a) of such Code;

(viii) "the term 'payroll costs'—

(I) "means—

(aa) "the sum of payments of any compensation with respect to employees that is a—

(AA) "salary, wage, commission, or similar compensation;

(BB) "payment of cash tip or equivalent;

(CC) "payment for vacation, parental, family, medical, or sick leave;

(DD) "allowance for dismissal or separation;

(EE) "payment required for the provisions of group health care benefits, including insurance premiums;

(FF) "payment of any retirement benefit; or

(GG) "payment of State or local tax assessed on the compensation of employees; and

(bb) "the sum of payments of any compensation to or income of a sole proprietor or independent contractor that is a wage, commission, income, net earnings from self-employment, or similar compensation and that is in an amount that is not more than $100,000 in 1 year, as prorated for the covered period; and

(II) "shall not include—

(aa) "the compensation of an individual employee in excess of an annual salary of $100,000, as prorated for the covered period;

(bb) "taxes imposed or withheld under chapters 21, 22, or 24 of the Internal Revenue Code of 1986 during the covered period;

(cc) "any compensation of an employee whose principal place of residence is outside of the United States;

(dd) "qualified sick leave wages for which a credit is allowed under section 7001 of the Families First Coronavirus Response Act (Public Law 116–127); or

(ee) "qualified family leave wages for which a credit is allowed under section 7003 of the Families First Coronavirus Response Act (Public Law 116–127); and

(ix) "the term 'veterans organization' means an organization that is described in section 501(c)(19) of the Internal Revenue Code that is exempt from taxation under section 501(a) of such Code.

(B) "PAYCHECK PROTECTION LOANS.—Except as otherwise provided in this paragraph, the Administrator may guarantee covered loans under the same terms, conditions, and processes as a loan made under this subsection.

(C) "REGISTRATION OF LOANS.—Not later than 15 days after the date on which a loan is made under this paragraph, the Administration shall register the loan using the TIN (as defined in section 7701 of the Internal Revenue Code of 1986) assigned to the borrower.

(D) "INCREASED ELIGIBILITY FOR CERTAIN SMALL BUSINESSES AND ORGANIZATIONS.—

(i) "IN GENERAL.—During the covered period, in addition to small business concerns, any business concern, nonprofit organization, veterans organization, or Tribal business concern described in section 31(b)(2)(C) shall be eligible to receive a covered loan if the business concern, nonprofit organization, veterans organization, or Tribal business concern employs not more than the greater of—

(I) "500 employees; or

(II) "if applicable, the size standard in number of employees established by the Administration for the industry in which the business concern, nonprofit organization, veterans organization, or Tribal business concern operates.

(ii) "INCLUSION OF SOLE PROPRIETORS, INDEPENDENT CONTRACTORS, AND ELIGIBLE SELF-EMPLOYED INDIVIDUALS.—

(I) "IN GENERAL.—During the covered period, individuals who operate under a sole proprietorship or as an independent contractor and eligible self-employed individuals shall be eligible to receive a covered loan.

(II) "DOCUMENTATION.—An eligible self-employed individual, independent contractor, or sole proprietorship seeking a covered loan shall submit such documentation as is necessary to establish such individual as eligible, including payroll tax filings reported to the Internal Revenue Service, Forms 1099–MISC, and income and expenses from the sole proprietorship, as determined by the Administrator and the Secretary.

(iii) "BUSINESS CONCERNS WITH MORE THAN 1 PHYSICAL LOCATION.—During the covered period, any business concern that employs not more than 500 employees per physical location of the business concern and that is assigned a North American Industry Classification System code beginning with 72 at the time of disbursal shall be eligible to receive a covered loan.

(iv) "WAIVER OF AFFILIATION RULES.—During the covered period, the provisions applicable to affiliations under section 121.103 of title 13, Code of Federal Regulations, or any successor regulation, are waived with respect to eligibility for a covered loan for—

(I) "any business concern with not more than 500 employees that, as of the date on which the covered loan is disbursed, is assigned a North American Industry Classification System code beginning with 72;

(II) "any business concern operating as a franchise that is assigned a franchise identifier code by the Administration; and

(III) "any business concern that receives financial assistance from a company licensed under section 301 of the Small Business Investment Act of 1958 (15 U.S.C. 681).

(v) "EMPLOYEE.—For purposes of determining whether a business concern, nonprofit organization, veterans organization, or Tribal business concern described in section 31(b)(2)(C) employs not more than 500 employees under clause (i)(I), the term 'employee' includes individuals employed on a full-time, part-time, or other basis.

(vi) "AFFILIATION.—The provisions applicable to affiliations under section 121.103 of title 13, Code of Federal Regulations, or any successor thereto, shall apply with respect to a nonprofit organization and a veterans organization in the same manner as with respect to a small business concern.

(E) "MAXIMUM LOAN AMOUNT.—During the covered period, with respect to a covered loan, the maximum loan amount shall be the lesser of—

(i)(I) "the sum of—

(aa) "the product obtained by multiplying—

(AA) "the average total monthly payments by the applicant for payroll costs incurred during the 1-year period before the date on which the loan is made, except that, in the case of an applicant that is seasonal employer, as determined by the Administrator, the average total monthly payments for payroll shall be for the 12-week period beginning February 15, 2019, or at the election of the eligible recipient, March 1, 2019, and ending June 30, 2019; by

(BB) "2.5; and

(bb) "the outstanding amount of a loan under subsection (b)(2) that was made during the period beginning on January 31, 2020 and ending on the date on which covered loans are made available to be refinanced under the covered loan; or

(II) "if requested by an otherwise eligible recipient that was not in business during the period beginning on February 15, 2019 and ending on June 30, 2019, the sum of—

(aa) "the product obtained by multiplying—

(AA) "the average total monthly payments by the applicant for payroll costs incurred during the period beginning on January 1, 2020 and ending on February 29, 2020; by

(BB) "2.5; and

(bb) "the outstanding amount of a loan under subsection (b)(2) that was made during the period beginning on January 31, 2020 and ending on the date on which covered loans are made available to be refinanced under the covered loan; or

(ii) "$10,000,000.

(F) "ALLOWABLE USES OF COVERED LOANS.—

(i) "IN GENERAL.—During the covered period, an eligible recipient may, in addition to the allowable uses of a loan made under this subsection, use the proceeds of the covered loan for—

(I) "payroll costs;

(II) "costs related to the continuation of group health care benefits during periods of paid sick, medical, or family leave, and insurance premiums;

(III) "employee salaries, commissions, or similar compensations;

(IV) "payments of interest on any mortgage obligation (which shall not include any prepayment of or payment of principal on a mortgage obligation);

(V) "rent (including rent under a lease agreement);

(VI) "utilities; and

(VII) "interest on any other debt obligations that were incurred before the covered period.

(ii) "DELEGATED AUTHORITY.—

(I) "IN GENERAL.—For purposes of making covered loans for the purposes described in clause (i), a lender approved to make loans under this subsection shall be deemed to have been delegated authority by the Administrator to make and approve covered loans, subject to the provisions of this paragraph.

(II) "CONSIDERATIONS.—In evaluating the eligibility of a borrower for a covered loan with the terms described in this paragraph, a lender shall consider whether the borrower—

(aa) "was in operation on February 15, 2020; and

(bb)(AA) "had employees for whom the borrower paid salaries and payroll taxes; or

(BB) "paid independent contractors, as reported on a Form 1099–MISC.

(iii) "ADDITIONAL LENDERS.—The authority to make loans under this paragraph shall be extended to additional lenders determined by the Administrator and the Secretary of the Treasury to have the necessary qualifications to process, close, disburse and service loans made with the guarantee of the Administration.

(iv) "REFINANCE.—A loan made under subsection (b)(2) during the period beginning on January 31, 2020 and ending on the date on which covered loans are made available may be refinanced as part of a covered loan.

(v) "NONRECOURSE.—Notwithstanding the waiver of the personal guarantee requirement or collateral under subparagraph (J), the Administrator shall have no recourse against any individual shareholder, member, or partner of an eligible recipient of a covered loan for nonpayment of any covered loan, except to the extent that such shareholder, member, or partner uses the covered loan proceeds for a purpose not authorized under clause (i).

(G) "BORROWER REQUIREMENTS.—

(i) "CERTIFICATION.—An eligible recipient applying for a covered loan shall make a good faith certification—

(I) "that the uncertainty of current economic conditions makes necessary the loan request to support the ongoing operations of the eligible recipient;

(II) "acknowledging that funds will be used to retain workers and maintain payroll or make mortgage payments, lease payments, and utility payments;

(III) "that the eligible recipient does not have an application pending for a loan under this subsection for the same purpose and duplicative of amounts applied for or received under a covered loan; and

(IV) "during the period beginning on February 15, 2020 and ending on December 31, 2020, that the eligible recipient has not received amounts under this subsection for the same purpose and duplicative of amounts applied for or received under a covered loan.

(H) "FEE WAIVER.—During the covered period, with respect to a covered loan—

(i) "in lieu of the fee otherwise applicable under paragraph (23)(A), the Administrator shall collect no fee; and

(ii) "in lieu of the fee otherwise applicable under paragraph (18)(A), the Administrator shall collect no fee.

(I) "CREDIT ELSEWHERE.—During the covered period, the requirement that a small business concern is unable to obtain credit elsewhere, as defined in section 3(h), shall not apply to a covered loan.

(J) "WAIVER OF PERSONAL GUARANTEE REQUIREMENT.—During the covered period, with respect to a covered loan—

(i) "no personal guarantee shall be required for the covered loan; and

(ii) "no collateral shall be required for the covered loan.

(K) "MATURITY FOR LOANS WITH REMAINING BALANCE AFTER APPLICATION OF FORGIVENESS.—With respect to a covered loan that has a remaining balance after reduction based on the loan forgiveness amount under section 1106 of the CARES Act—

(i) "the remaining balance shall continue to be guaranteed by the Administration under this subsection; and

(ii) "the covered loan shall have a maximum maturity of 10 years from the date on which the borrower applies for loan forgiveness under that section.

(L) "INTEREST RATE REQUIREMENTS.—A covered loan shall bear an interest rate not to exceed 4 percent.

(M) "LOAN DEFERMENT.—

(i) "DEFINITION OF IMPACTED BORROWER.—

(I) "IN GENERAL.—In this subparagraph, the term 'impacted borrower' means an eligible recipient that—

(aa) "is in operation on February 15, 2020; and

(bb) "has an application for a covered loan that is approved or pending approval on or after the date of enactment of this paragraph.

(II) "PRESUMPTION.—For purposes of this subparagraph, an impacted borrower is presumed to have been adversely impacted by COVID–19.

(ii) "DEFERRAL.—During the covered period, the Administrator shall—

(I) "consider each eligible recipient that applies for a covered loan to be an impacted borrower; and

(II) "require lenders under this subsection to provide complete payment deferment relief for impacted borrowers with covered loans for a period of not less than 6 months, including payment of principal, interest, and fees, and not more than 1 year.

(iii) "SECONDARY MARKET.—During the covered period, with respect to a covered loan that is sold on the secondary market, if an investor declines to approve a deferral requested by a lender under clause (ii), the Administrator shall exercise the authority to purchase the loan so that the impacted borrower may receive a deferral for a period of not less than 6 months, including payment of principal, interest, and fees, and not more than 1 year.

(iv) "GUIDANCE.—Not later than 30 days after the date of enactment of this paragraph, the Administrator shall provide guidance to lenders under this paragraph on the deferment process described in this subparagraph.

(N) "SECONDARY MARKET SALES.—A covered loan shall be eligible to be sold in the secondary market consistent with this subsection. The Administrator may not collect any fee for any guarantee sold into the secondary market under this subparagraph.

(O) "REGULATORY CAPITAL REQUIREMENTS.—

(i) "RISK WEIGHT.—With respect to the appropriate Federal banking agencies or the National Credit Union Administration Board applying capital requirements under their respective risk-based capital requirements, a covered loan shall receive a risk weight of zero percent.

(ii) "TEMPORARY RELIEF FROM TDR DISCLOSURES.—Notwithstanding any other provision of law, an insured depository institution or an insured credit union that modifies a covered loan in relation to COVID–19-related difficulties in a troubled debt restructuring on or after March 13, 2020, shall not be required to comply with the Financial Accounting Standards Board Accounting Standards Codification Subtopic 310–40 ('Receivables –Troubled Debt Restructurings by Creditors') for purposes of compliance with the requirements of the Federal Deposit Insurance Act (12 U.S.C. 1811 et seq.), until such time and under such circumstances as the appropriate Federal banking agency or the National Credit Union Administration Board, as applicable, determines appropriate.

(P) "REIMBURSEMENT FOR PROCESSING.—

(i) "IN GENERAL.—The Administrator shall reimburse a lender authorized to make a covered loan at a rate, based on the balance of the financing outstanding at the time of disbursement of the covered loan, of—

(I) "5 percent for loans of not more than $350,000;

(II) "3 percent for loans of more than $350,000 and less than $2,000,000; and

(III) "1 percent for loans of not less than $2,000,000.

(ii) "FEE LIMITS.—An agent that assists an eligible recipient to prepare an application for a covered loan may not collect a fee in excess of the limits established by the Administrator.

(iii) "TIMING.—A reimbursement described in clause (i) shall be made not later than 5 days after the disbursement of the covered loan.

(iv) "SENSE OF THE SENATE.—It is the sense of the Senate that the Administrator should issue guidance to lenders and agents to ensure that the processing and disbursement of covered loans prioritizes small business concerns and entities in underserved and rural markets, including veterans and members of the military community, small business concerns owned and controlled by socially and economically disadvantaged individuals (as defined in section 8(d)(3)(C)), women, and businesses in operation for less than 2 years.

(Q) "DUPLICATION.—Nothing in this paragraph shall prohibit a recipient of an economic injury disaster loan made under subsection (b)(2) during the period beginning on January 31, 2020 and ending on the date on which covered loans are made available that is for a purpose other than paying payroll costs and other obligations described in subparagraph (F) from receiving assistance under this paragraph.

(R) "WAIVER OF PREPAYMENT PENALTY.—Notwithstanding any other provision of law, there shall be no prepayment penalty for any payment made on a covered loan.".

(b) COMMITMENTS FOR 7(A) LOANS.—During the period beginning on February 15, 2020 and ending on June 30, 2020—

(1) the amount authorized for commitments for general business loans authorized under section 7(a) of the Small Business Act (15 U.S.C. 636(a)), including loans made under paragraph (36) of such section, as added by subsection (a), shall be $349,000,000,000; and

(2) the amount authorized for commitments for such loans under the heading "BUSINESS LOANS PROGRAM ACCOUNT" under the heading "SMALL BUSINESS ADMINISTRATION" under title V of the Consolidated Appropriations Act, 2020 (Public Law 116–93; 133 Stat. 2475) shall not apply.

(c) EXPRESS LOANS.—

(1) IN GENERAL.—Section 7(a)(31)(D) of the Small Business Act (15 U.S.C. 636(a)(31)(D)) is amended by striking "$350,000" and inserting "$1,000,000".

(2) PROSPECTIVE REPEAL.—Effective on January 1, 2021, section 7(a)(31)(D) of the Small Business Act (15 U.S.C. 636(a)(31)(D)) is amended by striking "$1,000,000" and inserting "$350,000".

(d) EXCEPTION TO GUARANTEE FEE WAIVER FOR VETERANS.—Section 7(a)(31)(G) of the Small Business Act (15 U.S.C. 636(a)(31)(G)) is amended—

(1) by striking clause (ii); and

(2) by redesignating clause (iii) as clause (ii).

(e) INTERIM RULE.—On and after the date of enactment of this Act, the interim final rule published by the Administrator entitled "Express Loan Programs: Affiliation Standards" (85 Fed. Reg. 7622 (February 10, 2020)) is permanently rescinded and shall have no force or effect.

[¶2008] SEC. 1103. ENTREPRENEURIAL DEVELOPMENT.

(a) DEFINITIONS.—In this section—

(1) the term "covered small business concern" means a small business concern that has experienced, as a result of COVID–19—

(A) supply chain disruptions, including changes in—

(i) quantity and lead time, including the number of shipments of components and delays in shipments;

(ii) quality, including shortages in supply for quality control reasons; and

(iii) technology, including a compromised payment network;

(B) staffing challenges;

(C) a decrease in gross receipts or customers; or

(D) a closure;

(2) the term "resource partner" means—

(A) a small business development center; and

(B) a women's business center;

(3) the term "small business development center" has the meaning given the term in section 3 of the Small Business Act (15 U.S.C. 632); and

(4) the term "women's business center" means a women's business center described in section 29 of the Small Business Act (15 U.S.C. 656).

(b) EDUCATION, TRAINING, AND ADVISING GRANTS.—

(1) IN GENERAL.—The Administration may provide financial assistance in the form of grants to resource partners to provide education, training, and advising to covered small business concerns.

(2) USE OF FUNDS.—Grants under this subsection shall be used for the education, training, and advising of covered small business concerns and their employees on—

(A) accessing and applying for resources provided by the Administration and other Federal resources relating to access to capital and business resiliency;

(B) the hazards and prevention of the transmission and communication of COVID–19 and other communicable diseases;

(C) the potential effects of COVID–19 on the supply chains, distribution, and sale of products of covered small business concerns and the mitigation of those effects;

(D) the management and practice of telework to reduce possible transmission of COVID–19;

(E) the management and practice of remote customer service by electronic or other means;

(F) the risks of and mitigation of cyber threats in remote customer service or telework practices;

(G) the mitigation of the effects of reduced travel or outside activities on covered small business concerns during COVID–19 or similar occurrences; and

(H) any other relevant business practices necessary to mitigate the economic effects of COVID–19 or similar occurrences.

(3) GRANT DETERMINATION.—

(A) SMALL BUSINESS DEVELOPMENT CENTERS.—The Administration shall award 80 percent of funds authorized to carry out this subsection to small business development centers, which shall be awarded pursuant to a formula jointly developed, negotiated, and agreed upon, with full participation of both parties, between the association formed under section 21(a)(3)(A) of the Small Business Act (15 U.S.C. 648(a)(3)(A)) and the Administration.

(B) WOMEN'S BUSINESS CENTERS.—The Administration shall award 20 percent of funds authorized to carry out this subsection to women's business centers, which shall be awarded pursuant to a process established by the Administration in consultation with recipients of assistance.

(C) NO MATCHING FUNDS REQUIRED.—Matching funds shall not be required for any grant under this subsection.

(4) GOALS AND METRICS.—

(A) IN GENERAL.—Goals and metrics for the funds made available under this subsection shall be jointly developed, negotiated, and agreed upon, with full participation of both parties, between the resource partners and the Administrator, which shall—

(i) take into consideration the extent of the circumstances relating to the spread of COVID–19, or similar occurrences, that affect covered small business concerns located in the areas covered by the resource partner, particularly in rural areas or economically distressed areas;

(ii) generally follow the use of funds outlined in paragraph (2), but shall not restrict the activities of resource partners in responding to unique situations; and

(iii) encourage resource partners to develop and provide services to covered small business concerns.

(B) PUBLIC AVAILABILITY.—The Administrator shall make publicly available the methodology by which the Administrator and resource partners jointly develop the metrics and goals described in subparagraph (A).

(c) RESOURCE PARTNER ASSOCIATION GRANTS.—

(1) IN GENERAL.—The Administrator may provide grants to an association or associations representing resource partners under which the association or associations shall establish a single centralized hub for COVID–19 information, which shall include—

(A) 1 online platform that consolidates resources and information available across multiple Federal agencies for small business concerns related to COVID–19; and

(B) a training program to educate resource partner counselors, members of the Service Corps of Retired Executives established under section 8(b)(1)(B) of the Small Business Act (15 U.S.C. 637(b)(1)(B)), and counselors at veterans business outreach centers described in section 32 of the Small Business Act (15 U.S.C. 657b) on the resources and information described in subparagraph (A).

(2) GOALS AND METRICS.—Goals and metrics for the funds made available under this subsection shall be jointly developed, negotiated, and agreed upon, with full participation of both parties, between the association or associations receiving a grant under this subsection and the Administrator.

(d) REPORT.—Not later than 6 months after the date of enactment of this Act, and annually thereafter, the Administrator shall submit to the Committee on Small Business and Entrepreneurship of the Senate and the Committee on Small Business of the House of Representatives a report that describes—

(1) with respect to the initial year covered by the report—

(A) the programs and services developed and provided by the Administration and resource partners under subsection (b);

(B) the initial efforts to provide those services under subsection (b); and

(C) the online platform and training developed and provided by the Administration and the association or associations under subsection (c); and

(2) with respect to the subsequent years covered by the report—

(A) with respect to the grant program under subsection (b)—

(i) the efforts of the Administrator and resource partners to develop services to assist covered small business concerns;

(ii) the challenges faced by owners of covered small business concerns in accessing services provided by the Administration and resource partners;

(iii) the number of unique covered small business concerns that were served by the Administration and resource partners; and

(iv) other relevant outcome performance data with respect to covered small business concerns, including the number of employees affected, the effect on sales, the disruptions of supply chains, and the efforts made by the Administration and resource partners to mitigate these effects; and

(B) with respect to the grant program under subsection (c)—

(i) the efforts of the Administrator and the association or associations to develop and evolve an online resource for small business concerns; and

(ii) the efforts of the Administrator and the association or associations to develop a training program for resource partner counselors, including the number of counselors trained.

[¶2009] SEC. 1104. STATE TRADE EXPANSION PROGRAM.

(a) IN GENERAL.—Notwithstanding paragraph (3)(C)(iii) of section 22(l) of the Small Business Act (15 U.S.C. 649(l)), for grants under the State Trade Expansion Program under such section 22(l) using amounts made available for fiscal year 2018 or fiscal year 2019, the period of the grant shall continue through the end of fiscal year 2021.

(b) REIMBURSEMENT.—The Administrator shall reimburse any recipient of assistance under section 22(l) of the Small Business Act (15 U.S.C. 649(l)) for financial losses relating to a foreign trade mission or a trade show exhibition that was cancelled solely due to a public health emergency declared due to COVID–19 if the reimbursement does not exceed a recipient's grant funding.

[¶2010] SEC. 1105. WAIVER OF MATCHING FUNDS REQUIREMENT UNDER THE WOMEN'S BUSINESS CENTER PROGRAM.

During the 3-month period beginning on the date of enactment of this Act, the requirement relating to obtaining cash contributions from non-Federal sources under section 29(c)(1) of the Small Business Act (15 U.S.C. 656(c)(1)) is waived for any recipient of assistance under such section 29.

[¶2011] SEC. 1106. LOAN FORGIVENESS.

(a) DEFINITIONS.—In this section—

(1) the term "covered loan" means a loan guaranteed under paragraph (36) of section 7(a) of the Small Business Act (15 U.S.C. 636(a)), as added by section 1102;

(2) the term "covered mortgage obligation" means any indebtedness or debt instrument incurred in the ordinary course of business that—

(A) is a liability of the borrower;

(B) is a mortgage on real or personal property; and

(C) was incurred before February 15, 2020;

(3) the term "covered period" means the 8-week period beginning on the date of the origination of a covered loan;

(4) the term "covered rent obligation" means rent obligated under a leasing agreement in force before February 15, 2020;

(5) the term "covered utility payment" means payment for a service for the distribution of electricity, gas, water, transportation, telephone, or internet access for which service began before February 15, 2020;

(6) the term "eligible recipient" means the recipient of a covered loan;

(7) the term "expected forgiveness amount" means the amount of principal that a lender reasonably expects a borrower to expend during the covered period on the sum of any—

(A) payroll costs;

(B) payments of interest on any covered mortgage obligation (which shall not include any prepayment of or payment of principal on a covered mortgage obligation);

(C) payments on any covered rent obligation; and

(D) covered utility payments; and

(8) the term "payroll costs" has the meaning given that term in paragraph (36) of section 7(a) of the Small Business Act (15 U.S.C. 636(a)), as added by section 1102 of this Act.

(b) FORGIVENESS.—An eligible recipient shall be eligible for forgiveness of indebtedness on a covered loan in an amount equal to the sum of the following costs incurred and payments made during the covered period:

(1) Payroll costs.

(2) Any payment of interest on any covered mortgage obligation (which shall not include any prepayment of or payment of principal on a covered mortgage obligation).

(3) Any payment on any covered rent obligation.

(4) Any covered utility payment.

(c) TREATMENT OF AMOUNTS FORGIVEN.—

(1) IN GENERAL.—Amounts which have been forgiven under this section shall be considered canceled indebtedness by a lender authorized under section 7(a) of the Small Business Act (15 U.S.C. 636(a)).

(2) PURCHASE OF GUARANTEES.—For purposes of the purchase of the guarantee for a covered loan by the Administrator, amounts which are forgiven under this section shall be treated in accordance with the procedures that are otherwise applicable to a loan guaranteed under section 7(a) of the Small Business Act (15 U.S.C. 636(a)).

(3) REMITTANCE.—Not later than 90 days after the date on which the amount of forgiveness under this section is determined, the Administrator shall remit to the lender an amount equal to the amount of forgiveness, plus any interest accrued through the date of payment.

(4) ADVANCE PURCHASE OF COVERED LOAN.—

(A) REPORT.—A lender authorized under section 7(a) of the Small Business Act (15 U.S.C. 636(a)), or, at the discretion of the Administrator, a third party participant in the secondary market, may, report to the Administrator an expected forgiveness amount on a covered loan or on a pool of covered loans of up to 100 percent of the principal on the covered loan or pool of covered loans, respectively.

(B) PURCHASE.—The Administrator shall purchase the expected forgiveness amount described in subparagraph (A) as if the amount were the principal amount of a loan guaranteed under section 7(a) of the Small Business Act 636(a)).

(C) TIMING.—Not later than 15 days after the date on which the Administrator receives a report under subparagraph (A), the Administrator shall purchase the expected forgiveness amount under subparagraph (B) with respect to each covered loan to which the report relates.

(d) LIMITS ON AMOUNT OF FORGIVENESS.—

(1) AMOUNT MAY NOT EXCEED PRINCIPAL.—The amount of loan forgiveness under this section shall not exceed the principal amount of the financing made available under the applicable covered loan.

(2) REDUCTION BASED ON REDUCTION IN NUMBER OF EMPLOYEES.—

(A) IN GENERAL.—The amount of loan forgiveness under this section shall be reduced, but not increased, by multiplying the amount described in subsection (b) by the quotient obtained by dividing—

(i) the average number of full-time equivalent employees per month employed by the eligible recipient during the covered period; by

(ii)(I) at the election of the borrower—

(aa) the average number of full-time equivalent employees per month employed by the eligible recipient during the period beginning on February 15, 2019 and ending on June 30, 2019; or

(bb) the average number of full-time equivalent employees per month employed by the eligible recipient during the period beginning on January 1, 2020 and ending on February 29, 2020; or

(II) in the case of an eligible recipient that is seasonal employer, as determined by the Administrator, the average number of full-time equivalent employees per month employed by the eligible recipient during the period beginning on February 15, 2019 and ending on June 30, 2019.

(B) CALCULATION OF AVERAGE NUMBER OF EMPLOYEES.—For purposes of subparagraph (A), the average number of full-time equivalent employees shall be determined by calculating the average number of full-time equivalent employees for each pay period falling within a month.

(3) REDUCTION RELATING TO SALARY AND WAGES.—

(A) IN GENERAL.—The amount of loan forgiveness under this section shall be reduced by the amount of any reduction in total salary or wages of any employee described in subparagraph (B) during the covered period that is in excess of 25 percent of the total salary or wages of the employee during the most recent full quarter during which the employee was employed before the covered period.

(B) EMPLOYEES DESCRIBED.—An employee described in this subparagraph is any employee who did not receive, during any single pay period during 2019, wages or salary at an annualized rate of pay in an amount more than $100,000.

(4) TIPPED WORKERS.—An eligible recipient with tipped employees described in section 3(m)(2)(A) of the Fair Labor Standards Act of 1938 (29 U.S.C. 203(m)(2)(A)) may receive forgiveness for additional wages paid to those employees.

(5) EXEMPTION FOR RE-HIRES.—

(A) IN GENERAL.—In a circumstance described in subparagraph (B), the amount of loan forgiveness under this section shall be determined without regard to a reduction in the number of full-time equivalent employees of an eligible recipient or a reduction in the salary of 1 or more employees of the eligible recipient, as applicable, during the period beginning on February 15, 2020 and ending on the date that is 30 days after the date of enactment of this Act.

(B) CIRCUMSTANCES.—A circumstance described in this subparagraph is a circumstance—

(i) in which—

(I) during the period beginning on February 15, 2020 and ending on the date that is 30 days after the date of enactment of this Act, there is a reduction, as compared to February 15, 2020, in the number of full-time equivalent employees of an eligible recipient; and

(II) not later than June 30, 2020, the eligible employer has eliminated the reduction in the number of full-time equivalent employees;

(ii) in which—

(I) during the period beginning on February 15, 2020 and ending on the date that is 30 days after the date of enactment of this Act, there is a reduction, as compared to February 15, 2020, in the salary or wages of 1 or more employees of the eligible recipient; and

(II) not later than June 30, 2020, the eligible employer has eliminated the reduction in the salary or wages of such employees; or

(iii) in which the events described in clause (i) and (ii) occur.

(6) EXEMPTIONS.—The Administrator and the Secretary of the Treasury may prescribe regulations granting de minimis exemptions from the requirements under this subsection.

(e) APPLICATION.—An eligible recipient seeking loan forgiveness under this section shall submit to the lender that is servicing the covered loan an application, which shall include—

(1) documentation verifying the number of full-time equivalent employees on payroll and pay rates for the periods described in subsection (d), including—

(A) payroll tax filings reported to the Internal Revenue Service; and

(B) State income, payroll, and unemployment insurance filings;

(2) documentation, including cancelled checks, payment receipts, transcripts of accounts, or other documents verifying payments on covered mortgage obligations, payments on covered lease obligations, and covered utility payments;

(3) a certification from a representative of the eligible recipient authorized to make such certifications that—

(A) the documentation presented is true and correct; and

(B) the amount for which forgiveness is requested was used to retain employees, make interest payments on a covered mortgage obligation, make payments on a covered rent obligation, or make covered utility payments; and

(4) any other documentation the Administrator determines necessary.

(f) PROHIBITION ON FORGIVENESS WITHOUT DOCUMENTATION.—No eligible recipient shall receive forgiveness under this section without submitting to the lender that is servicing the covered loan the documentation required under subsection (e).

(g) DECISION.—Not later than 60 days after the date on which a lender receives an application for loan forgiveness under this section from an eligible recipient, the lender shall issue a decision on the an application.

(h) HOLD HARMLESS.—If a lender has received the documentation required under this section from an eligible recipient attesting that the eligible recipient has accurately verified the payments for payroll costs, payments on covered mortgage obligations, payments on covered lease obligations, or covered utility payments during covered period—

(1) an enforcement action may not be taken against the lender under section 47(e) of the Small Business Act (15 U.S.C. 657t(e)) relating to loan forgiveness for the payments for payroll costs, payments on covered mortgage obligations, payments on covered lease obligations, or covered utility payments, as the case may be; and

(2) the lender shall not be subject to any penalties by the Administrator relating to loan forgiveness for the payments for payroll costs, payments on covered mortgage obligations, payments on covered lease obligations, or covered utility payments, as the case may be.

(i) TAXABILITY.—For purposes of the Internal Revenue Code of 1986, any amount which (but for this subsection) would be includible in gross income of the eligible recipient by reason of forgiveness described in subsection (b) shall be excluded from gross income.

(j) RULE OF CONSTRUCTION.—The cancellation of indebtedness on a covered loan under this section shall not otherwise modify the terms and conditions of the covered loan.

(k) REGULATIONS.—Not later than 30 days after the date of enactment of this Act, the Administrator shall issue guidance and regulations implementing this section.

[¶2012] SEC. 1107. DIRECT APPROPRIATIONS.

(a) IN GENERAL.—There is appropriated, out of amounts in the Treasury not otherwise appropriated, for the fiscal year ending September 30, 2020, to remain available until September 30, 2021, for additional amounts—

(1) $349,000,000,000 under the heading "Small Business Administration—Business Loans Program Account, CARES Act" for the cost of guaranteed loans as authorized under paragraph (36) of section 7(a) of the Small Business Act (15 U.S.C. 636(a)), as added by section 1102(a) of this Act;

(2) $675,000,000 under the heading "Small Business Administration—Salaries and Expenses" for salaries and expenses of the Administration;

(3) $25,000,000 under the heading "Small Business Administration—Office of Inspector General", to remain available until September 30, 2024, for necessary expenses of the Office of Inspector General of the Administration in carrying out the provisions of the Inspector General Act of 1978 (5 U.S.C. App.);

(4) $265,000,000 under the heading "Small Business Administration—Entrepreneurial Development Programs", of which—

(A) $240,000,000 shall be for carrying out section 1103(b) of this Act; and

(B) $25,000,000 shall be for carrying out section 1103(c) of this Act;

(5) $10,000,000 under the heading "Department of Commerce—Minority Business Development Agency" for minority business centers of the Minority Business Development Agency to provide technical assistance to small business concerns;

(6) $10,000,000,000 under the heading "Small Business Administration—Emergency EIDL Grants" shall be for carrying out section 1110 of this Act;

(7) $17,000,000,000 under the heading "Small Business Administration—Business Loans Program Account, CARES Act" shall be for carrying out section 1112 of this Act; and

(8) $25,000,000 under the heading "Department of the Treasury—Departmental Offices—Salaries and Expenses" shall be for carrying out section 1109 of this Act.

(b) SECONDARY MARKET.—During the period beginning on the date of enactment of this Act and ending on September 30, 2021, guarantees of trust certificates authorized by section 5(g) of the Small Business Act (15 U.S.C. 635(g)) shall not exceed a principal amount of $100,000,000,000.

(c) REPORTS.—Not later than 180 days after the date of enactment of this Act, the Administrator shall submit to the Committee on Appropriations of the Senate and the Committee on Appropriations of the House of Representatives a detailed expenditure plan for using the amounts appropriated to the Administration under subsection (a).

[¶2013] SEC. 1108. MINORITY BUSINESS DEVELOPMENT AGENCY.

(a) DEFINITIONS.—In this section—

(1) the term "Agency" means the Minority Business Development Agency of the Department of Commerce;

(2) the term "minority business center" means a Business Center of the Agency;

(3) the term "minority business enterprise" means a for-profit business enterprise—

(A) not less than 51 percent of which is owned by 1 or more socially disadvantaged individuals, as determined by the Agency; and

(B) the management and daily business operations of which are controlled by 1 or more socially disadvantaged individuals, as determined by the Agency; and

(4) the term "minority chamber of commerce" means a chamber of commerce developed specifically to support minority business enterprises.

(b) EDUCATION, TRAINING, AND ADVISING GRANTS.—

(1) IN GENERAL.—The Agency may provide financial assistance in the form of grants to minority business centers and minority chambers of commerce to provide education, training, and advising to minority business enterprises.

(2) USE OF FUNDS.—Grants under this section shall be used for the education, training, and advising of minority business enterprises and their employees on—

(A) accessing and applying for resources provided by the Agency and other Federal resources relating to access to capital and business resiliency;

(B) the hazards and prevention of the transmission and communication of COVID–19 and other communicable diseases;

(C) the potential effects of COVID–19 on the supply chains, distribution, and sale of products of minority business enterprises and the mitigation of those effects;

(D) the management and practice of telework to reduce possible transmission of COVID–19;

(E) the management and practice of remote customer service by electronic or other means;

(F) the risks of and mitigation of cyber threats in remote customer service or telework practices;

(G) the mitigation of the effects of reduced travel or outside activities on minority business enterprises during COVID–19 or similar occurrences; and

(H) any other relevant business practices necessary to mitigate the economic effects of COVID–19 or similar occurrences.

(3) NO MATCHING FUNDS REQUIRED.—Matching funds shall not be required for any grant under this section.

(4) GOALS AND METRICS.—

(A) IN GENERAL.—Goals and metrics for the funds made available under this section shall be jointly developed, negotiated, and agreed upon, with full participation of both parties, between the minority business centers, minority chambers of commerce, and the Agency, which shall—

(i) take into consideration the extent of the circumstances relating to the spread of COVID–19, or similar occurrences, that affect minority business enterprises located in the areas covered by minority business centers and minority chambers of commerce, particularly in rural areas or economically distressed areas;

(ii) generally follow the use of funds outlined in paragraph (2), but shall not restrict the activities of minority business centers and minority chambers of commerce in responding to unique situations; and

(iii) encourage minority business centers and minority chambers of commerce to develop and provide services to minority business enterprises.

(B) PUBLIC AVAILABILITY.—The Agency shall make publicly available the methodology by which the Agency, minority business centers, and minority chambers of commerce jointly develop the metrics and goals described in subparagraph (A).

(c) WAIVERS.—

(1) IN GENERAL.—Notwithstanding any other provision of law or regulation, the Agency may, during the 3-month period that begins on the date of enactment of this Act, waive any matching requirement imposed on a minority business center or a specialty center of the Agency under a cooperative agreement between such a center and the Agency if the applicable center is unable to raise funds, or has suffered a loss of revenue, because of the effects of COVID–19.

(2) REMAINING COMPLIANT.—Notwithstanding any provision of a cooperative agreement between the Agency and a minority business center, if, during the period beginning on the date of enactment of this Act and ending on September 30, 2021, such a center decides not to collect fees because of the economic consequences of COVID–19, the center shall be considered to be in compliance with that agreement if—

(A) the center notifies the Agency with respect to that decision, which the center may provide through electronic mail; and

(B) the Agency, not later than 15 days after the date on which the center provides notice to the Agency under subparagraph (A)—

(i) confirms receipt of the notification under subparagraph (A); and

(ii) accepts the decision of the center.

(d) REPORT.—Not later than 6 months after the date of enactment of this Act, and annually thereafter, the Agency shall submit to the Committee on Small Business and Entrepreneurship and the Committee on Commerce, Science, and Transportation of the Senate and the Committee on Small Business and the Committee on Energy and Commerce of the House of Representatives a report that describes—

(1) with respect to the period covered by the initial report—

(A) the programs and services developed and provided by the Agency, minority business centers, and minority chambers of commerce under subsection (b); and

(B) the initial efforts to provide those services under subsection (b); and

(2) with respect to subsequent years covered by the report—

(A) with respect to the grant program under subsection (b)—

(i) the efforts of the Agency, minority business centers, and minority chambers of commerce to develop services to assist minority business enterprises;

(ii) the challenges faced by owners of minority business enterprises in accessing services provided by the Agency, minority business centers, and minority chambers of commerce;

(iii) the number of unique minority business enterprises that were served by the Agency, minority business centers, or minority chambers of commerce; and

(iv) other relevant outcome performance data with respect to minority business enterprises, including the number of employees affected, the effect on sales, the disruptions of supply chains, and the efforts made by the Agency, minority business centers, and minority chambers of commerce to mitigate these effects.

(e) AUTHORIZATION OF APPROPRIATIONS.—There is authorized to be appropriated $10,000,000 to carry out this section, to remain available until expended.

[¶2014] SEC. 1109. UNITED STATES TREASURY PROGRAM MANAGEMENT AUTHORITY.

(a) DEFINITIONS.—In this section—

(1) the terms "appropriate Federal banking agency" and "insured depository institution" have the meanings given those terms in section 3 of the Federal Deposit Insurance Act (12 U.S.C. 1813);

(2) the term "insured credit union" has the meaning given the term in section 101 of the Federal Credit Union Act (12 U.S.C. 1752); and

(3) the term "Secretary" means the Secretary of the Treasury.

(b) AUTHORITY TO INCLUDE ADDITIONAL FINANCIAL INSTITUTIONS.—The Department of the Treasury, in consultation with the Administrator, and the Chairman of the Farm Credit Administration shall establish criteria for insured depository institutions, insured credit unions, institutions of the Farm Credit System chartered under the Farm Credit Act of 1971 (12 U.S.C. 2001 et seq.), and other lenders that do not already participate in lending under programs of the Administration, to participate in the paycheck protection program to provide loans under this section until the date on which the national emergency declared by the President under the National Emergencies Act (50 U.S.C. 1601 et seq.) with respect to the Coronavirus Disease 2019 (COVID–19) expires.

(c) SAFETY AND SOUNDNESS.—An insured depository institution, insured credit union, institution of the Farm Credit System chartered under the Farm Credit Act of 1971 (12 U.S.C. 2001 et seq.), or other lender may only participate in the program established under this section if participation does not affect the safety and soundness of the institution or lender, as determined by the Secretary in consultation with the appropriate Federal banking agencies or the National Credit Union Administration Board, as applicable.

(d) REGULATIONS FOR LENDERS AND LOANS.—

(1) IN GENERAL.—The Secretary may issue regulations and guidance as necessary to carry out the purposes of this section, including to—

(A) allow additional lenders to originate loans under this section; and

(B) establish terms and conditions for loans under this section, including terms and conditions concerning compensation, underwriting standards, interest rates, and maturity.

(2) REQUIREMENTS.—The terms and conditions established under paragraph (1) shall provide for the following:

(A) A rate of interest that does not exceed the maximum permissible rate of interest available on a loan of comparable maturity under paragraph (36) of section 7(a) of the Small Business Act (15 U.S.C. 636(a)), as added by section 1102 of this Act.

(B) Terms and conditions that, to the maximum extent practicable, are consistent with the terms and conditions required under the following provisions of paragraph (36) of section 7(a) of the Small Business Act (15 U.S.C. 636(a)), as added by section 1102 of this Act:

(i) Subparagraph (D), pertaining to borrower eligibility.

(ii) Subparagraph (E), pertaining to the maximum loan amount.

(iii) Subparagraph (F)(i), pertaining to allowable uses of program loans.

(iv) Subparagraph (H), pertaining to fee waivers.

(v) Subparagraph (M), pertaining to loan deferment.

(C) A guarantee percentage that, to the maximum extent practicable, is consistent with the guarantee percentage required under subparagraph (F) of section 7(a)(2) of the Small Business Act (15 U.S.C. 636(a)(2)), as added by section 1102 of this Act.

(D) Loan forgiveness under terms and conditions that, to the maximum extent practicable, is consistent with the terms and conditions for loan forgiveness under section 1106 of this Act.

(e) ADDITIONAL REGULATIONS GENERALLY.—The Secretary may issue regulations and guidance as necessary to carry out the purposes of this section, including to allow additional lenders to originate loans under this title and to establish terms and conditions such as compensation, underwriting standards, interest rates, and maturity for under this section.

(f) CERTIFICATION.—As a condition of receiving a loan under this section, a borrower shall certify under terms acceptable to the Secretary that the borrower—

(1) does not have an application pending for a loan under section 7(a) of the Small Business Act (15 U.S.C. 636(a)) for the same purpose; and

(2) has not received such a loan during the period beginning on February 15, 2020 and ending on December 31, 2020.

(g) OPT-IN FOR SBA QUALIFIED LENDERS.—Lenders qualified to participate as a lender under 7(a) of the Small Business Act (15 U.S.C. 636(a)) may elect to participate in the paycheck protection program under the criteria, terms, and conditions established under this section. Such participation shall not preclude the lenders from continuing participation as a lender under section 7(a) of the Small Business Act (15 U.S.C. 636(a)).

(h) PROGRAM ADMINISTRATION.—With guidance from the Secretary, the Administrator shall administer the program established under this section, including the making and purchasing of guarantees on loans under the program, until the date on which the national emergency declared by the President under the National Emergencies Act (50 U.S.C. 1601 et seq.) with respect to the Coronavirus Disease 2019 (COVID–19) expires.

(i) CRIMINAL PENALTIES.—A loan under this section shall be deemed to be a loan under the Small Business Act (15 U.S.C. 631 et seq.) for purposes of section 16 of such Act (15 U.S.C. 645).

[¶2015] SEC. 1110. EMERGENCY EIDL GRANTS.

(a) DEFINITIONS.—In this section—

(1) the term "covered period" means the period beginning on January 31, 2020 and ending on December 31, 2020; and

(2) the term "eligible entity" means—

(A) a business with not more than 500 employees;

(B) any individual who operates under a sole proprietorship, with or without employees, or as an independent contractor;

(C) a cooperative with not more than 500 employees;

(D) an ESOP (as defined in section 3 of the Small Business Act (15 U.S.C. 632)) with not more than 500 employees; or

(E) a tribal small business concern, as described in section 31(b)(2)(C) of the Small Business Act (15 U.S.C. 657a(b)(2)(C)), with not more than 500 employees.

(b) ELIGIBLE ENTITIES.—During the covered period, in addition to small business concerns, private nonprofit organizations, and small agricultural cooperatives, an eligible entity shall be eligible for a loan made under section 7(b)(2) of the Small Business Act (15 U.S.C. 636(b)(2)).

(c) TERMS; CREDIT ELSEWHERE.—With respect to a loan made under section 7(b)(2) of the Small Business Act (15 U.S.C. 636(b)(2)) in response to COVID–19 during the covered period, the Administrator shall waive—

(1) any rules related the personal guarantee on advances and loans of not more than $200,000 during the covered period for all applicants;

(2) the requirement that an applicant needs to be in business for the 1-year period before the disaster, except that no waiver may be made for a business that was not in operation on January 31, 2020; and

(3) the requirement in the flush matter following subparagraph (E) of section 7(b)(2) of the Small Business Act (15 U.S.C. 636(b)(2)), as so redesignated by subsection (f) of this section, that an applicant be unable to obtain credit elsewhere.

(d) APPROVAL AND ABILITY TO REPAY FOR SMALL DOLLAR LOANS.—With respect to a loan made under section 7(b)(2) of the Small Business Act (15 U.S.C. 636(b)(2)) in response to COVID–19 during the covered period, the Administrator may—

(1) approve an applicant based solely on the credit score of the applicant and shall not require an applicant to submit a tax return or a tax return transcript for such approval; or

(2) use alternative appropriate methods to determine an applicant's ability to repay.

(e) EMERGENCY GRANT.—

(1) IN GENERAL.—During the covered period, an entity included for eligibility in subsection (b), including small business concerns, private nonprofit organizations, and small agricultural cooperatives, that applies for a loan under section 7(b)(2) of the Small Business Act (15 U.S.C. 636(b)(2)) in

response to COVID–19 may request that the Administrator provide an advance that is, subject to paragraph (3), in the amount requested by such applicant to such applicant within 3 days after the Administrator receives an application from such applicant.

(2) VERIFICATION.—Before disbursing amounts under this subsection, the Administrator shall verify that the applicant is an eligible entity by accepting a self-certification from the applicant under penalty of perjury pursuant to section 1746 of title 28 United States Code.

(3) AMOUNT.—The amount of an advance provided under this subsection shall be not more than $10,000.

(4) USE OF FUNDS.—An advance provided under this subsection may be used to address any allowable purpose for a loan made under section 7(b)(2) of the Small Business Act (15 U.S.C. 636(b)(2)), including—

(A) providing paid sick leave to employees unable to work due to the direct effect of the COVID–19;

(B) maintaining payroll to retain employees during business disruptions or substantial slowdowns;

(C) meeting increased costs to obtain materials unavailable from the applicant's original source due to interrupted supply chains;

(D) making rent or mortgage payments; and

(E) repaying obligations that cannot be met due to revenue losses.

(5) REPAYMENT.—An applicant shall not be required to repay any amounts of an advance provided under this subsection, even if subsequently denied a loan under section 7(b)(2) of the Small Business Act (15 U.S.C. 636(b)(2)).

(6) UNEMPLOYMENT GRANT.—If an applicant that receives an advance under this subsection transfers into, or is approved for, the loan program under section 7(a) of the Small Business Act (15 U.S.C. 636(a)), the advance amount shall be reduced from the loan forgiveness amount for a loan for payroll costs made under such section 7(a).

(7) AUTHORIZATION OF APPROPRIATIONS.—There is authorized to be appropriated to the Administration $10,000,000,000 to carry out this subsection.

(8) TERMINATION.—The authority to carry out grants under this subsection shall terminate on December 31, 2020.

(f) EMERGENCIES INVOLVING FEDERAL PRIMARY RESPONSIBILITY QUALIFYING FOR SBA ASSISTANCE.—Section 7(b)(2) of the Small Business Act (15 U.S.C. 636(b)(2)) is amended—

(1) in subparagraph (A), by striking "or" at the end;

(2) in subparagraph (B), by striking "or" at the end;

(3) in subparagraph (C), by striking "or" at the end;

(4) by redesignating subparagraph (D) as subparagraph (E);

(5) by inserting after subparagraph (C) the following:

(D) "an emergency involving Federal primary responsibility determined to exist by the President under the section 501(b) of the Robert T. Stafford Disaster Relief and Emergency Assistance Act (42 U.S.C. 5191(b)); or"; and

(6) in subparagraph (E), as so redesignated—

(A) by striking "or (C)" and inserting "(C), or (D)";

(B) by striking "disaster declaration" each place it appears and inserting "disaster or emergency declaration";

(C) by striking "disaster has occurred" and inserting "disaster or emergency has occurred";

(D) by striking "such disaster" and inserting "such disaster or emergency"; and

(E) by striking "disaster stricken" and inserting "disaster-or emergency-stricken"; and

(7) in the flush matter following subparagraph (E), as so redesignated, by striking the period at the end and inserting the following: ": Provided further, That for purposes of subparagraph (D), the Administrator shall deem that such an emergency affects each State or subdivision thereof (including counties), and that each State or subdivision has sufficient economic damage to small business

concerns to qualify for assistance under this paragraph and the Administrator shall accept applications for such assistance immediately.".

[¶2016] SEC. 1111. RESOURCES AND SERVICES IN LANGUAGES OTHER THAN ENGLISH.

(a) IN GENERAL.—The Administrator shall provide the resources and services made available by the Administration to small business concerns in the 10 most commonly spoken languages, other than English, in the United States, which shall include Mandarin, Cantonese, Japanese, and Korean.

(b) AUTHORIZATION OF APPROPRIATIONS.—There is authorized to be appropriated to the Administrator $25,000,000 to carry out this section.

[¶2017] SEC. 1112. SUBSIDY FOR CERTAIN LOAN PAYMENTS.

(a) DEFINITION OF COVERED LOAN.—In this section, the term "covered loan" means a loan that is—

(1) guaranteed by the Administration under—

(A) section 7(a) of the Small Business Act (15 U.S.C. 636(a))—

(i) including a loan made under the Community Advantage Pilot Program of the Administration; and

(ii) excluding a loan made under paragraph (36) of such section 7(a), as added by section 1102; or

(B) title V of the Small Business Investment Act of 1958 (15 U.S.C. 695 et seq.); or

(2) made by an intermediary to a small business concern using loans or grants received under section 7(m) of the Small Business Act (15 U.S.C. 636(m)).

(b) SENSE OF CONGRESS.—It is the sense of Congress that—

(1) all borrowers are adversely affected by COVID–19;

(2) relief payments by the Administration are appropriate for all borrowers; and

(3) in addition to the relief provided under this Act, the Administration should encourage lenders to provide payment deferments, when appropriate, and to extend the maturity of covered loans, so as to avoid balloon payments or any requirement for increases in debt payments resulting from deferments provided by lenders during the period of the national emergency declared by the President under the National Emergencies Act (50 U.S.C. 1601 et seq.) with respect to the Coronavirus Disease 2019 (COVID–19).

(c) PRINCIPAL AND INTEREST PAYMENTS.—

(1) IN GENERAL.—The Administrator shall pay the principal, interest, and any associated fees that are owed on a covered loan in a regular servicing status—

(A) with respect to a covered loan made before the date of enactment of this Act and not on deferment, for the 6-month period beginning with the next payment due on the covered loan;

(B) with respect to a covered loan made before the date of enactment of this Act and on deferment, for the 6-month period beginning with the next payment due on the covered loan after the deferment period; and

(C) with respect to a covered loan made during the period beginning on the date of enactment of this Act and ending on the date that is 6 months after such date of enactment, for the 6-month period beginning with the first payment due on the covered loan.

(2) TIMING OF PAYMENT.—The Administrator shall begin making payments under paragraph (1) on a covered loan not later than 30 days after the date on which the first such payment is due.

(3) APPLICATION OF PAYMENT.—Any payment made by the Administrator under paragraph (1) shall be applied to the covered loan such that the borrower is relieved of the obligation to pay that amount.

(d) OTHER REQUIREMENTS.—The Administrator shall—

(1) communicate and coordinate with the Federal Deposit Insurance Corporation, the Office of the Comptroller of the Currency, and State bank regulators to encourage those entities to not require lenders to increase their reserves on account of receiving payments made by the Administrator under subsection (c);

(2) waive statutory limits on maximum loan maturities for any covered loan durations where the lender provides a deferral and extends the maturity of covered loans during the 1-year period following the date of enactment of this Act; and

(3) when necessary to provide more time because of the potential of higher volumes, travel restrictions, and the inability to access some properties during the COVID–19 pandemic, extend lender site visit requirements to—

(A) not more than 60 days (which may be extended at the discretion of the Administration) after the occurrence of an adverse event, other than a payment default, causing a loan to be classified as in liquidation; and

(B) not more than 90 days after a payment default.

(e) RULE OF CONSTRUCTION.—Nothing in this section may be construed to limit the authority of the Administrator to make payments pursuant to subsection (c) with respect to a covered loan solely because the covered loan has been sold in the secondary market.

(f) AUTHORIZATION OF APPROPRIATIONS.—There is authorized to be appropriated to the Administrator $17,000,000,000 to carry out this section.

[¶2018] SEC. 1113. BANKRUPTCY.

(a) SMALL BUSINESS DEBTOR REORGANIZATION.—

(1) IN GENERAL.—Section 1182(1) of title 11, United States Code, is amended to read as follows:

(1) "DEBTOR.—The term 'debtor'—

(A) "subject to subparagraph (B), means a person engaged in commercial or business activities (including any affiliate of such person that is also a debtor under this title and excluding a person whose primary activity is the business of owning single asset real estate) that has aggregate noncontingent liquidated secured and unsecured debts as of the date of the filing of the petition or the date of the order for relief in an amount not more than $7,500,000 (excluding debts owed to 1 or more affiliates or insiders) not less than 50 percent of which arose from the commercial or business activities of the debtor; and

(B) "does not include—

(i) "any member of a group of affiliated debtors that has aggregate noncontingent liquidated secured and unsecured debts in an amount greater than $7,500,000 (excluding debt owed to 1 or more affiliates or insiders);

(ii) "any debtor that is a corporation subject to the reporting requirements under section 13 or 15(d) of the Securities Exchange Act of 1934 (15 U.S.C. 78m, 78o(d)); or

(iii) "any debtor that is an affiliate of an issuer, as defined in section 3 of the Securities Exchange Act of 1934 (15 U.S.C. 78c).".

(2) APPLICABILITY OF CHAPTERS.—Section 103(i) of title 11, United States Code, is amended by striking "small business debtor" and inserting "debtor (as defined in section 1182)".

(3) APPLICATION OF AMENDMENT.—The amendment made by paragraph (1) shall apply only with respect to cases commenced under title 11, United States Code, on or after the date of enactment of this Act.

(4) TECHNICAL CORRECTIONS.—

(A) DEFINITION OF SMALL BUSINESS DEBTOR.—Section 101(51D)(B)(iii) of title 11, United States Code, is amended to read as follows:

(iii) "any debtor that is an affiliate of an issuer (as defined in section 3 of the Securities Exchange Act of 1934 (15 U.S.C. 78c)).".

(B) UNCLAIMED PROPERTY.—Section 347(b) of title 11, United States Code, is amended by striking "1194" and inserting "1191".

(5) SUNSET.—On the date that is 1 year after the date of enactment of this Act, section 1182(1) of title 11, United States Code, is amended to read as follows:

(1) "DEBTOR.—The term 'debtor' means a small business debtor.".

(b) BANKRUPTCY RELIEF.—

(1) IN GENERAL.—

(A) EXCLUSION FROM CURRENT MONTHLY INCOME.—Section 101(10A)(B)(ii) of title 11, United States Code, is amended—

(i) in subclause (III), by striking "; and" and inserting a semicolon;

(ii) in subclause (IV), by striking the period at the end and inserting "; and"; and

(iii) by adding at the end the following:

(V) "Payments made under Federal law relating to the national emergency declared by the President under the National Emergencies Act (50 U.S.C. 1601 et seq.) with respect to the coronavirus disease 2019 (COVID–19).".

(B) CONFIRMATION OF PLAN.—Section 1325(b)(2) of title 11, United States Code, is amended by inserting "payments made under Federal law relating to the national emergency declared by the President under the National Emergencies Act (50 U.S.C. 1601 et seq.) with respect to the coronavirus disease 2019 (COVID–19)," after "other than".

(C) MODIFICATION OF PLAN AFTER CONFIRMATION.—Section 1329 of title 11, United States Code, is amended by adding at end the following:

(d)(1) "Subject to paragraph (3), for a plan confirmed prior to the date of enactment of this subsection, the plan may be modified upon the request of the debtor if—

(A) "the debtor is experiencing or has experienced a material financial hardship due, directly or indirectly, to the coronavirus disease 2019 (COVID–19) pandemic; and

(B) "the modification is approved after notice and a hearing.

(2) "A plan modified under paragraph (1) may not provide for payments over a period that expires more than 7 years after the time that the first payment under the original confirmed plan was due.

(3) "Sections 1322(a), 1322(b), 1323(c), and the requirements of section 1325(a) shall apply to any modification under paragraph (1).".

(D) APPLICABILITY.—

(i) The amendments made by subparagraphs (A) and (B) shall apply to any case commenced before, on, or after the date of enactment of this Act.

(ii) The amendment made by subparagraph (C) shall apply to any case for which a plan has been confirmed under section 1325 of title 11, United States Code, before the date of enactment of this Act.

(2) SUNSET.—

(A) IN GENERAL.—

(i) EXCLUSION FROM CURRENT MONTHLY INCOME.—Section 101(10A)(B)(ii) of title 11, United States Code, is amended—

(I) in subclause (III), by striking the semicolon at the end and inserting "; and";

(II) in subclause (IV), by striking "; and" and inserting a period; and

(III) by striking subclause (V).

(ii) CONFIRMATION OF PLAN.—Section 1325(b)(2) of title 11, United States Code, is amended by striking "payments made under Federal law relating to the national emergency declared by the President under the National Emergencies Act (50 U.S.C. 1601 et seq.) with respect to the coronavirus disease 2019 (COVID–19),".

(iii) MODIFICATION OF PLAN AFTER CONFIRMATION.—Section 1329 of title 11, United States Code, is amended by striking subsection (d).

(B) EFFECTIVE DATE.—The amendments made by subparagraph (A) shall take effect on the date that is 1 year after the date of enactment of this Act.

[¶2019] SEC. 1114. EMERGENCY RULEMAKING AUTHORITY.

Not later than 15 days after the date of enactment of this Act, the Administrator shall issue regulations to carry out this title and the amendments made by this title without regard to the notice requirements under section 553(b) of title 5, United States Code.

TITLE II—ASSISTANCE FOR AMERICAN WORKERS, FAMILIES, AND BUSINESSES

Subtitle A—Unemployment Insurance Provisions

[¶2022] SEC. 2101. SHORT TITLE.

This subtitle may be cited as the "Relief for Workers Affected by Coronavirus Act".

[¶2023] SEC. 2102. PANDEMIC UNEMPLOYMENT ASSISTANCE.

(a) DEFINITIONS.—In this section:

(1) COVID–19.—The term "COVID–19" means the 2019 Novel Coronavirus or 2019-nCoV.

(2) COVID–19 PUBLIC HEALTH EMERGENCY.—The term "COVID–19 public health emergency" means the public health emergency declared by the Secretary of Health and Human Services on January 27, 2020, with respect to the 2019 Novel Coronavirus.

(3) COVERED INDIVIDUAL.—The term "covered individual"—

(A) means an individual who—

(i) is not eligible for regular compensation or extended benefits under State or Federal law or pandemic emergency unemployment compensation under section 2107, including an individual who has exhausted all rights to regular unemployment or extended benefits under State or Federal law or pandemic emergency unemployment compensation under section 2107; and

(ii) provides self-certification that the individual—

(I) is otherwise able to work and available for work within the meaning of applicable State law, except the individual is unemployed, partially unemployed, or unable or unavailable to work because—

(aa) the individual has been diagnosed with COVID–19 or is experiencing symptoms of COVID–19 and seeking a medical diagnosis;

(bb) a member of the individual's household has been diagnosed with COVID–19;

(cc) the individual is providing care for a family member or a member of the individual's household who has been diagnosed with COVID–19;

(dd) a child or other person in the household for which the individual has primary caregiving responsibility is unable to attend school or another facility that is closed as a direct result of the COVID–19 public health emergency and such school or facility care is required for the individual to work;

(ee) the individual is unable to reach the place of employment because of a quarantine imposed as a direct result of the COVID–19 public health emergency;

(ff) the individual is unable to reach the place of employment because the individual has been advised by a health care provider to self-quarantine due to concerns related to COVID–19;

(gg) the individual was scheduled to commence employment and does not have a job or is unable to reach the job as a direct result of the COVID–19 public health emergency;

(hh) the individual has become the breadwinner or major support for a household because the head of the household has died as a direct result of COVID–19;

(ii) the individual has to quit his or her job as a direct result of COVID–19;

(jj) the individual's place of employment is closed as a direct result of the COVID–19 public health emergency; or

(kk) the individual meets any additional criteria established by the Secretary for unemployment assistance under this section; or

(II) is self-employed, is seeking part-time employment, does not have sufficient work history, or otherwise would not qualify for regular unemployment or extended benefits under State or Federal law or pandemic emergency unemployment compensation under section 2107 and meets the requirements of subclause (I); and

(B) does not include—

(i) an individual who has the ability to telework with pay; or

(ii) an individual who is receiving paid sick leave or other paid leave benefits, regardless of whether the individual meets a qualification described in items (aa) through (kk) of subparagraph (A)(i)(I).

(4) SECRETARY.—The term "Secretary" means the Secretary of Labor.

(5) STATE.—The term "State" includes the District of Columbia, the Commonwealth of Puerto Rico, the Virgin Islands, Guam, American Samoa, the Commonwealth of the Northern Mariana Islands, the Federated States of Micronesia, the Republic of the Marshall Islands, and the Republic of Palau.

(b) ASSISTANCE FOR UNEMPLOYMENT AS A RESULT OF COVID–19.—Subject to subsection (c), the Secretary shall provide to any covered individual unemployment benefit assistance while such individual is unemployed, partially unemployed, or unable to work for the weeks of such unemployment with respect to which the individual is not entitled to any other unemployment compensation (as that term is defined in section 85(b) of title 26, United States Code) or waiting period credit.

(c) APPLICABILITY.—

(1) IN GENERAL.—Except as provided in paragraph (2), the assistance authorized under subsection (b) shall be available to a covered individual—

(A) for weeks of unemployment, partial unemployment, or inability to work caused by COVID–19—

(i) beginning on or after January 27, 2020; and

(ii) ending on or before December 31, 2020; and

(B) subject to subparagraph (A)(ii), as long as the covered individual's unemployment, partial unemployment, or inability to work caused by COVID–19 continues.

(2) LIMITATION ON DURATION OF ASSISTANCE.—The total number of weeks for which a covered individual may receive assistance under this section shall not exceed 39 weeks and such total shall include any week for which the covered individual received regular compensation or extended benefits under any Federal or State law, except that if after the date of enactment of this Act, the duration of extended benefits is extended, the 39-week period described in this paragraph shall be extended by the number of weeks that is equal to the number of weeks by which the extended benefits were extended.

(3) ASSISTANCE FOR UNEMPLOYMENT BEFORE DATE OF ENACTMENT.—The Secretary shall establish a process for making assistance under this section available for weeks beginning on or after January 27, 2020, and before the date of enactment of this Act.

(d) AMOUNT OF ASSISTANCE.—

(1) IN GENERAL.—The assistance authorized under subsection (b) for a week of unemployment, partial unemployment, or inability to work shall be—

(A)(i) the weekly benefit amount authorized under the unemployment compensation law of the State where the covered individual was employed, except that the amount may not be less than the minimum weekly benefit amount described in section 625.6 of title 20, Code of Federal Regulations, or any successor thereto; and

(ii) the amount of Federal Pandemic Unemployment Compensation under section 2104; and

(B) in the case of an increase of the weekly benefit amount after the date of enactment of this Act, increased in an amount equal to such increase.

(2) CALCULATIONS OF AMOUNTS FOR CERTAIN COVERED INDIVIDUALS.—In the case of a covered individual who is self-employed, who lives in a territory described in subsection (c) or (d) of section 625.6 of title 20, Code of Federal Regulations, or who would not otherwise qualify for unemployment compensation under State law, the assistance authorized under subsection (b) for a week of unemployment shall be calculated in accordance with section 625.6 of title 20, Code of Federal Regulations, or any successor thereto, and shall be increased by the amount of Federal Pandemic Unemployment Compensation under section 2104.

(3) ALLOWABLE METHODS OF PAYMENT.—Any assistance provided for in accordance with paragraph (1)(A)(ii) shall be payable either—

(A) as an amount which is paid at the same time and in the same manner as the assistance provided for in paragraph (1)(A)(i) is payable for the week involved; or

(B) at the option of the State, by payments which are made separately from, but on the same weekly basis as, any assistance provided for in paragraph (1)(A)(i).

(e) WAIVER OF STATE REQUIREMENT.—Notwithstanding State law, for purposes of assistance authorized under this section, compensation under this Act shall be made to an individual otherwise eligible for such compensation without any waiting period.

(f) AGREEMENTS WITH STATES.—

(1) IN GENERAL.—The Secretary shall provide the assistance authorized under subsection (b) through agreements with States which, in the judgment of the Secretary, have an adequate system for administering such assistance through existing State agencies.

(2) PAYMENTS TO STATES.—There shall be paid to each State which has entered into an agreement under this subsection an amount equal to 100 percent of—

(A) the total amount of assistance provided by the State pursuant to such agreement; and

(B) any additional administrative expenses incurred by the State by reason of such agreement (as determined by the Secretary), including any administrative expenses necessary to facilitate processing of applications for assistance under this section online or by telephone rather than in-person.

(3) TERMS OF PAYMENTS.—Sums payable to any State by reason of such State's having an agreement under this subsection shall be payable, either in advance or by way of reimbursement (as determined by the Secretary), in such amounts as the Secretary estimates the State will be entitled to receive under this subsection for each calendar month, reduced or increased, as the case may be, by any amount by which the Secretary finds that his estimates for any prior calendar month were greater or less than the amounts which should have been paid to the State. Such estimates may be made on the basis of such statistical, sampling, or other method as may be agreed upon by the Secretary and the State agency of the State involved.

(g) FUNDING.—

(1) ASSISTANCE.—

(A) IN GENERAL.—Funds in the extended unemployment compensation account (as established by section 905(a) of the Social Security Act (42 U.S.C. 1105(a)) of the Unemployment Trust Fund (as established by section 904(a) of such Act (42 U.S.C. 1104(a)) shall be used to make payments to States pursuant to subsection (f)(2)(A).

(B) TRANSFER OF FUNDS.—Notwithstanding any other provision of law, the Secretary of the Treasury shall transfer from the general fund of the Treasury (from funds not otherwise appropriated) to the extended unemployment compensation account such sums as the Secretary of Labor estimates to be necessary to make payments described in subparagraph (A). There are appropriated from the general fund of the Treasury, without fiscal year limitation, the sums referred to in the preceding sentence and such sums shall not be required to be repaid.

(2) ADMINISTRATIVE EXPENSES.—

(A) IN GENERAL.—Funds in the employment security administration account (as established by section 901(a) of the Social Security Act (42 U.S.C. 1105(a)) of the Unemployment Trust Fund (as established by section 904(a) of such Act (42 U.S.C. 1104(a)) shall be used to make payments to States pursuant to subsection (f)(2)(B).

(B) TRANSFER OF FUNDS.—Notwithstanding any other provision of law, the Secretary of the Treasury shall transfer from the general fund of the Treasury (from funds not otherwise appropriated) to the employment security administration account such sums as the Secretary of Labor estimates to be necessary to make payments described in subparagraph (A). There are appropriated from the general fund of the Treasury, without fiscal year limitation, the sums referred to in the preceding sentence and such sums shall not be required to be repaid.

(3) CERTIFICATIONS.—The Secretary of Labor shall from time to time certify to the Secretary of the Treasury for payment to each State the sums payable to such State under paragraphs (1) and (2).

(h) RELATIONSHIP BETWEEN PANDEMIC UNEMPLOYMENT ASSISTANCE AND DISASTER UNEMPLOYMENT ASSISTANCE.—Except as otherwise provided in this section or to the extent there is a conflict between this section and section 625 of title 20, Code of Federal Regulations, such section 625 shall apply to this section as if—

(1) the term "COVID–19 public health emergency" were substituted for the term "major disaster" each place it appears in such section 625; and

(2) the term "pandemic" were substituted for the term "disaster" each place it appears in such section 625.

[¶2024] SEC. 2103. EMERGENCY UNEMPLOYMENT RELIEF FOR GOVERNMENTAL ENTITIES AND NONPROFIT ORGANIZATIONS.

(a) FLEXIBILITY IN PAYING REIMBURSEMENT.—The Secretary of Labor may issue clarifying guidance to allow States to interpret their State unemployment compensation laws in a manner that would provide maximum flexibility to reimbursing employers as it relates to timely payment and assessment of penalties and interest pursuant to such State laws.

(b) FEDERAL FUNDING.—Section 903 of the Social Security Act (42 U.S.C. 1103) is amended by adding at the end the following:

"Transfers for Federal Reimbursement of State Unemployment Funds

(i)(1)(A) "In addition to any other amounts, the Secretary of Labor shall provide for the transfer of funds during the applicable period to the accounts of the States in the Unemployment Trust Fund, by transfer from amounts reserved for that purpose in the Federal unemployment account, in accordance with the succeeding provisions of this subsection.

(B) "The amount of funds transferred to the account of a State under subparagraph (A) during the applicable period shall, as determined by the Secretary of Labor, be equal to one-half of the amounts of compensation (as defined in section 3306(h) of the Internal Revenue Code of 1986) attributable under the State law to service to which section 3309(a)(1) of such Code applies that were paid by the State for weeks of unemployment beginning and ending during such period. Such transfers shall be made at such times as the Secretary of Labor considers appropriate.

(C) "Notwithstanding any other law, funds transferred to the account of a State under subparagraph (A) shall be used exclusively to reimburse governmental entities and other organizations described in section 3309(a)(2) of such Code for amounts paid (in lieu of contributions) into the State unemployment fund pursuant to such section.

(D) "For purposes of this paragraph, the term 'applicable period' means the period beginning on March 13, 2020, and ending on December 31, 2020.

(2)(A) "Notwithstanding any other provision of law, the Secretary of the Treasury shall transfer from the general fund of the Treasury (from funds not otherwise appropriated) to the Federal unemployment account such sums as the Secretary of Labor estimates to be necessary for purposes of making the transfers described in paragraph (1).

(B) "There are appropriated from the general fund of the Treasury, without fiscal year limitation, the sums referred to in subparagraph (A) and such sums shall not be required to be repaid.".

[¶2025] SEC. 2104. EMERGENCY INCREASE IN UNEMPLOYMENT COMPENSATION BENEFITS.

(a) FEDERAL-STATE AGREEMENTS.—Any State which desires to do so may enter into and participate in an agreement under this section with the Secretary of Labor (in this section referred to as the "Secretary"). Any State which is a party to an agreement under this section may, upon providing 30 days' written notice to the Secretary, terminate such agreement.

(b) PROVISIONS OF AGREEMENT.—

(1) FEDERAL PANDEMIC UNEMPLOYMENT COMPENSATION.—Any agreement under this section shall provide that the State agency of the State will make payments of regular compensation to individuals in amounts and to the extent that they would be determined if the State law of the State were applied, with respect to any week for which the individual is (disregarding this section) otherwise entitled under the State law to receive regular compensation, as if such State law had been modified in a manner such that the amount of regular compensation (including dependents' allowances) payable for any week shall be equal to—

(A) the amount determined under the State law (before the application of this paragraph), plus

(B) an additional amount of $600 (in this section referred to as "Federal Pandemic Unemployment Compensation").

(2) ALLOWABLE METHODS OF PAYMENT.—Any Federal Pandemic Unemployment Compensation provided for in accordance with paragraph (1) shall be payable either—

(A) as an amount which is paid at the same time and in the same manner as any regular compensation otherwise payable for the week involved; or

(B) at the option of the State, by payments which are made separately from, but on the same weekly basis as, any regular compensation otherwise payable.

(c) NONREDUCTION RULE.—

(1) IN GENERAL.—An agreement under this section shall not apply (or shall cease to apply) with respect to a State upon a determination by the Secretary that the method governing the computation of regular compensation under the State law of that State has been modified in a manner such that the number of weeks (the maximum benefit entitlement), or the average weekly benefit amount, of regular compensation which will be payable during the period of the agreement (determined disregarding any Federal Pandemic Unemployment Compensation) will be less than the number of weeks, or the average weekly benefit amount, of the average weekly benefit amount of regular compensation which would otherwise have been payable during such period under the State law, as in effect on January 1, 2020.

(2) MAXIMUM BENEFIT ENTITLEMENT.—In paragraph (1), the term "maximum benefit entitlement" means the amount of regular unemployment compensation payable to an individual with respect to the individual's benefit year.

(d) PAYMENTS TO STATES.—

(1) IN GENERAL.—

(A) FULL REIMBURSEMENT.—There shall be paid to each State which has entered into an agreement under this section an amount equal to 100 percent of—

(i) the total amount of Federal Pandemic Unemployment Compensation paid to individuals by the State pursuant to such agreement; and

(ii) any additional administrative expenses incurred by the State by reason of such agreement (as determined by the Secretary).

(B) TERMS OF PAYMENTS.—Sums payable to any State by reason of such State's having an agreement under this section shall be payable, either in advance or by way of reimbursement (as determined by the Secretary), in such amounts as the Secretary estimates the State will be entitled to receive under this section for each calendar month, reduced or increased, as the case may be, by any amount by which the Secretary finds that his estimates for any prior calendar month were greater or less than the amounts which should have been paid to the State. Such estimates may be made on the basis of such statistical, sampling, or other method as may be agreed upon by the Secretary and the State agency of the State involved.

(2) CERTIFICATIONS.—The Secretary shall from time to time certify to the Secretary of the Treasury for payment to each State the sums payable to such State under this section.

(3) APPROPRIATION.—There are appropriated from the general fund of the Treasury, without fiscal year limitation, such sums as may be necessary for purposes of this subsection.

(e) APPLICABILITY.—An agreement entered into under this section shall apply to weeks of unemployment—

(1) beginning after the date on which such agreement is entered into; and

(2) ending on or before July 31, 2020.

(f) FRAUD AND OVERPAYMENTS.—

(1) IN GENERAL.—If an individual knowingly has made, or caused to be made by another, a false statement or representation of a material fact, or knowingly has failed, or caused another to fail, to disclose a material fact, and as a result of such false statement or representation or of such nondisclosure such individual has received an amount of Federal Pandemic Unemployment Compensation to which such individual was not entitled, such individual—

(A) shall be ineligible for further Federal Pandemic Unemployment Compensation in accordance with the provisions of the applicable State unemployment compensation law relating to fraud in connection with a claim for unemployment compensation; and

(B) shall be subject to prosecution under section 1001 of title 18, United States Code.

(2) REPAYMENT.—In the case of individuals who have received amounts of Federal Pandemic Unemployment Compensation to which they were not entitled, the State shall require such individuals to repay the amounts of such Federal Pandemic Unemployment Compensation to the State agency, except that the State agency may waive such repayment if it determines that—

(A) the payment of such Federal Pandemic Unemployment Compensation was without fault on the part of any such individual; and

(B) such repayment would be contrary to equity and good conscience.

(3) RECOVERY BY STATE AGENCY.—

(A) IN GENERAL.—The State agency shall recover the amount to be repaid, or any part thereof, by deductions from any Federal Pandemic Unemployment Compensation payable to such individual or from any unemployment compensation payable to such individual under any State or Federal unemployment compensation law administered by the State agency or under any other State or Federal law administered by the State agency which provides for the payment of any assistance or allowance with respect to any week of unemployment, during the 3-year period after the date such individuals received the payment of the Federal Pandemic Unemployment Compensation to which they were not entitled, in accordance with the same procedures as apply to the recovery of overpayments of regular unemployment benefits paid by the State.

(B) OPPORTUNITY FOR HEARING.—No repayment shall be required, and no deduction shall be made, until a determination has been made, notice thereof and an opportunity for a fair hearing has been given to the individual, and the determination has become final.

(4) REVIEW.—Any determination by a State agency under this section shall be subject to review in the same manner and to the same extent as determinations under the State unemployment compensation law, and only in that manner and to that extent.

(g) APPLICATION TO OTHER UNEMPLOYMENT BENEFITS.—Each agreement under this section shall include provisions to provide that the purposes of the preceding provisions of this section shall be applied with respect to unemployment benefits described in subsection (i)(2) to the same extent and in the same manner as if those benefits were regular compensation.

(h) DISREGARD OF ADDITIONAL COMPENSATION FOR PURPOSES OF MEDICAID AND CHIP.—The monthly equivalent of any Federal pandemic unemployment compensation paid to an individual under this section shall be disregarded when determining income for any purpose under the programs established under titles XIX and title XXI of the Social Security Act (42 U.S.C. 1396 et seq., 1397aa et seq.).

(i) DEFINITIONS.—For purposes of this section—

(1) the terms "compensation", "regular compensation", "benefit year", "State", "State agency", "State law", and "week" have the respective meanings given such terms under section 205 of the Federal-State Extended Unemployment Compensation Act of 1970 (26 U.S.C. 3304 note); and

(2) any reference to unemployment benefits described in this paragraph shall be considered to refer to—

(A) extended compensation (as defined by section 205 of the Federal-State Extended Unemployment Compensation Act of 1970);

(B) regular compensation (as defined by section 85(b) of the Internal Revenue Code of 1986) provided under any program administered by a State under an agreement with the Secretary;

(C) pandemic unemployment assistance under section 2102; and

(D) pandemic emergency unemployment compensation under section 2107.

[¶2026] SEC. 2105. TEMPORARY FULL FEDERAL FUNDING OF THE FIRST WEEK OF COMPENSABLE REGULAR UNEMPLOYMENT FOR STATES WITH NO WAITING WEEK.

(a) FEDERAL-STATE AGREEMENTS.—Any State which desires to do so may enter into and participate in an agreement under this section with the Secretary of Labor (in this section referred to as the "Secretary"). Any State which is a party to an agreement under this section may, upon providing 30 days' written notice to the Secretary, terminate such agreement.

(b) REQUIREMENT THAT STATE LAW DOES NOT APPLY A WAITING WEEK.—A State is eligible to enter into an agreement under this section if the State law (including a waiver of State law) provides that compensation is paid to individuals for their first week of regular unemployment without a waiting week. An agreement under this section shall not apply (or shall cease to apply) with respect to a State upon a determination by the Secretary that the State law no longer meets the requirement under the preceding sentence.

(c) PAYMENTS TO STATES.—

(1) FULL REIMBURSEMENT.—There shall be paid to each State which has entered into an agreement under this section an amount equal to 100 percent of—

(A) the total amount of regular compensation paid to individuals by the State for their first week of regular unemployment; and

(B) any additional administrative expenses incurred by the State by reason of such agreement (as determined by the Secretary).

(2) TERMS OF PAYMENTS.—Sums payable to any State by reason of such State's having an agreement under this section shall be payable, either in advance or by way of reimbursement (as determined by the Secretary), in such amounts as the Secretary estimates the State will be entitled to receive under this section for each calendar month, reduced or increased, as the case may be, by any amount by which the Secretary finds that his estimates for any prior calendar month were greater or less than the amounts which should have been paid to the State. Such estimates may be made on the basis of such statistical, sampling, or other method as may be agreed upon by the Secretary and the State agency of the State involved.

(d) FUNDING.—

(1) COMPENSATION.—

(A) IN GENERAL.—Funds in the Federal unemployment account (as established by section 905(g)) of the Unemployment Trust Fund (as established by section 904(a)) shall be used to make payments under subsection (c)(1)(A).

(B) TRANSFER OF FUNDS.—Notwithstanding any other provision of law, the Secretary of the Treasury shall transfer from the general fund of the Treasury (from funds not otherwise appropriated) to the Federal unemployment account such sums as the Secretary of Labor estimates to be necessary to make payments described in subparagraph (A). There are appropriated from the general fund of the Treasury, without fiscal year limitation, the sums referred to in the preceding sentence and such sums shall not be required to be repaid.

(2) ADMINISTRATIVE EXPENSES.—

(A) IN GENERAL.—Funds in the employment security administration account (as established by section 901(a) of the Social Security Act (42 U.S.C. 1105(a)) of the Unemployment Trust Fund (as established by section 904(a) of such Act (42 U.S.C. 1104(a)) shall be used to make payments to States pursuant to subsection (c)(1)(B).

(B) TRANSFER OF FUNDS.—Notwithstanding any other provision of law, the Secretary of the Treasury shall transfer from the general fund of the Treasury (from funds not otherwise appropriated) to the employment security administration account such sums as the Secretary of Labor estimates to be necessary to make payments described in subparagraph (A). There are appropriated from the general fund of the Treasury, without fiscal year limitation, the sums referred to in the preceding sentence and such sums shall not be required to be repaid.

(3) CERTIFICATIONS.—The Secretary shall from time to time certify to the Secretary of the Treasury for payment to each State the sums payable to such State under this section.

(e) APPLICABILITY.—An agreement entered into under this section shall apply to weeks of unemployment—

(1) beginning after the date on which such agreement is entered into; and

(2) ending on or before December 31, 2020.

(f) FRAUD AND OVERPAYMENTS.—The provisions of section 2107(e) shall apply with respect to compensation paid under an agreement under this section to the same extent and in the same manner as in the case of pandemic emergency unemployment compensation under such section.

(g) DEFINITIONS.—For purposes of this section, the terms "regular compensation", "State", "State agency", "State law", and "week" have the respective meanings given such terms under section 205 of the Federal-State Extended Unemployment Compensation Act of 1970 (26 U.S.C. 3304 note).

[¶2027] SEC. 2106. EMERGENCY STATE STAFFING FLEXIBILITY.

Section 4102(b) of the Emergency Unemployment Stabilization and Access Act of 2020 (contained in division D of the Families First Coronavirus Response Act) is amended—

(1) by striking "or employer experience rating" and inserting "employer experience rating, or, subject to the succeeding sentence, personnel standards on a merit basis"; and

(2) by adding at the end the following new sentence: "The emergency flexibility for personnel standards on a merit basis shall only apply through December 31, 2020, and is limited to engaging of temporary staff, rehiring of retirees or former employees on a non-competitive basis, and other temporary actions to quickly process applications and claims.".

[¶2028] SEC. 2107. PANDEMIC EMERGENCY UNEMPLOYMENT COMPENSATION.

(a) FEDERAL-STATE AGREEMENTS.—

(1) IN GENERAL.—Any State which desires to do so may enter into and participate in an agreement under this section with the Secretary of Labor (in this section referred to as the "Secretary"). Any State which is a party to an agreement under this section may, upon providing 30 days' written notice to the Secretary, terminate such agreement.

(2) PROVISIONS OF AGREEMENT.—Any agreement under paragraph (1) shall provide that the State agency of the State will make payments of pandemic emergency unemployment compensation to individuals who—

(A) have exhausted all rights to regular compensation under the State law or under Federal law with respect to a benefit year (excluding any benefit year that ended before July1, 2019);

(B) have no rights to regular compensation with respect to a week under such law or any other State unemployment compensation law or to compensation under any other Federal law;

(C) are not receiving compensation with respect to such week under the unemployment compensation law of Canada; and

(D) are able to work, available to work, and actively seeking work.

(3) EXHAUSTION OF BENEFITS.—For purposes of paragraph (2)(A), an individual shall be deemed to have exhausted such individual's rights to regular compensation under a State law when—

(A) no payments of regular compensation can be made under such law because such individual has received all regular compensation available to such individual based on employment or wages during such individual's base period; or

(B) such individual's rights to such compensation have been terminated by reason of the expiration of the benefit year with respect to which such rights existed.

(4) WEEKLY BENEFIT AMOUNT, ETC.—For purposes of any agreement under this section—

(A) the amount of pandemic emergency unemployment compensation which shall be payable to any individual for any week of total unemployment shall be equal to—

(i) the amount of the regular compensation (including dependents' allowances) payable to such individual during such individual's benefit year under the State law for a week of total unemployment; and

(ii) the amount of Federal Pandemic Unemployment Compensation under section 2104;

(B) the terms and conditions of the State law which apply to claims for regular compensation and to the payment thereof (including terms and conditions relating to availability for work, active search for work, and refusal to accept work) shall apply to claims for pandemic emergency unemployment compensation and the payment thereof, except where otherwise inconsistent with the provisions of this section or with the regulations or operating instructions of the Secretary promulgated to carry out this section;

(C) the maximum amount of pandemic emergency unemployment compensation payable to any individual for whom an pandemic emergency unemployment compensation account is established under subsection (b) shall not exceed the amount established in such account for such individual; and

(D) the allowable methods of payment under section 2104(b)(2) shall apply to payments of amounts described in subparagraph (A)(ii).

(5) COORDINATION RULE.—An agreement under this section shall apply with respect to a State only upon a determination by the Secretary that, under the State law or other applicable rules of such State, the payment of extended compensation for which an individual is otherwise eligible must be deferred until after the payment of any pandemic emergency unemployment compensation under subsection (b) for which the individual is concurrently eligible.

(6) NONREDUCTION RULE.—

(A) IN GENERAL.—An agreement under this section shall not apply (or shall cease to apply) with respect to a State upon a determination by the Secretary that the method governing the computation of regular compensation under the State law of that State has been modified in a manner such that the number of weeks (the maximum benefit entitlement), or the average weekly benefit amount, of regular compensation which will be payable during the period of the agreement will be less than the number of weeks, or the average weekly benefit amount, of the average weekly benefit amount of regular compensation which would otherwise have been payable during such period under the State law, as in effect on January 1, 2020.

(B) MAXIMUM BENEFIT ENTITLEMENT.—In subparagraph (A), the term "maximum benefit entitlement" means the amount of regular unemployment compensation payable to an individual with respect to the individual's benefit year.

(7) ACTIVELY SEEKING WORK.—

(A) IN GENERAL.—Subject to subparagraph (C), for purposes of paragraph (2)(D), the term "actively seeking work" means, with respect to any individual, that such individual—

(i) is registered for employment services in such a manner and to such extent as prescribed by the State agency;

(ii) has engaged in an active search for employment that is appropriate in light of the employment available in the labor market, the individual's skills and capabilities, and includes a number of employer contacts that is consistent with the standards communicated to the individual by the State;

(iii) has maintained a record of such work search, including employers contacted, method of contact, and date contacted; and

(iv) when requested, has provided such work search record to the State agency.

(B) FLEXIBILITY.—Notwithstanding the requirements under subparagraph (A) and paragraph (2)(D), a State shall provide flexibility in meeting such requirements in case of individuals unable to search for work because of COVID–19, including because of illness, quarantine, or movement restriction.

(b) PANDEMIC EMERGENCY UNEMPLOYMENT COMPENSATION ACCOUNT.—

(1) IN GENERAL.—Any agreement under this section shall provide that the State will establish, for each eligible individual who files an application for pandemic emergency unemployment compensation, an pandemic emergency unemployment compensation account with respect to such individual's benefit year.

(2) AMOUNT IN ACCOUNT.—The amount established in an account under subsection (a) shall be equal to 13 times the individual's average weekly benefit amount, which includes the amount of Federal Pandemic Unemployment Compensation under section 2104, for the benefit year.

(3) WEEKLY BENEFIT AMOUNT.—For purposes of this subsection, an individual's weekly benefit amount for any week is the amount of regular compensation (including dependents' allowances) under the State law payable to such individual for such week for total unemployment plus the amount of Federal Pandemic Unemployment Compensation under section 2104.

(c) PAYMENTS TO STATES HAVING AGREEMENTS FOR THE PAYMENT OF PANDEMIC EMERGENCY UNEMPLOYMENT COMPENSATION.—

(1) IN GENERAL.—There shall be paid to each State that has entered into an agreement under this section an amount equal to 100 percent of the pandemic emergency unemployment compensation paid to individuals by the State pursuant to such agreement.

(2) TREATMENT OF REIMBURSABLE COMPENSATION.—No payment shall be made to any State under this section in respect of any compensation to the extent the State is entitled to reimbursement in respect of such compensation under the provisions of any Federal law other than this section or chapter 85 of title 5, United States Code. A State shall not be entitled to any reimbursement under such chapter 85

in respect of any compensation to the extent the State is entitled to reimbursement under this section in respect of such compensation.

(3) DETERMINATION OF AMOUNT.—Sums payable to any State by reason of such State having an agreement under this section shall be payable, either in advance or by way of reimbursement (as may be determined by the Secretary), in such amounts as the Secretary estimates the State will be entitled to receive under this section for each calendar month, reduced or increased, as the case may be, by any amount by which the Secretary finds that the Secretary's estimates for any prior calendar month were greater or less than the amounts which should have been paid to the State. Such estimates may be made on the basis of such statistical, sampling, or other method as may be agreed upon by the Secretary and the State agency of the State involved.

(d) FINANCING PROVISIONS.—

(1) COMPENSATION.—

(A) IN GENERAL.—Funds in the extended unemployment compensation account (as established by section 905(a) of the Social Security Act (42 U.S.C. 1105(a)) of the Unemployment Trust Fund (as established by section 904(a) of such Act (42 U.S.C. 1104(a)) shall be used for the making of payments to States having agreements entered into under this section.

(B) TRANSFER OF FUNDS.—Notwithstanding any other provision of law, the Secretary of the Treasury shall transfer from the general fund of the Treasury (from funds not otherwise appropriated) to the extended unemployment compensation account such sums as the Secretary of Labor estimates to be necessary to make payments described in subparagraph (A). There are appropriated from the general fund of the Treasury, without fiscal year limitation, the sums referred to in the preceding sentence and such sums shall not be required to be repaid.

(2) ADMINISTRATION.—

(A) IN GENERAL.—There are appropriated out of the employment security administration account (as established by section 901(a) of the Social Security Act (42 U.S.C. 1101(a)) of the Unemployment Trust Fund, without fiscal year limitation, such funds as may be necessary for purposes of assisting States (as provided in title III of the Social Security Act (42 U.S.C. 501 et seq.)) in meeting the costs of administration of agreements under this section.

(B) TRANSFER OF FUNDS.—Notwithstanding any other provision of law, the Secretary of the Treasury shall transfer from the general fund of the Treasury (from funds not otherwise appropriated) to the employment security administration account such sums as the Secretary of Labor estimates to be necessary to make payments described in subparagraph (A). There are appropriated from the general fund of the Treasury, without fiscal year limitation, the sums referred to in the preceding sentence and such sums shall not be required to be repaid.

(3) CERTIFICATION.—The Secretary shall from time to time certify to the Secretary of the Treasury for payment to each State the sums payable to such State under this subsection. The Secretary of the Treasury, prior to audit or settlement by the Government Accountability Office, shall make payments to the State in accordance with such certification, by transfers from the extended unemployment compensation account (as so established) to the account of such State in the Unemployment Trust Fund (as so established).

(e) FRAUD AND OVERPAYMENTS.—

(1) IN GENERAL.—If an individual knowingly has made, or caused to be made by another, a false statement or representation of a material fact, or knowingly has failed, or caused another to fail, to disclose a material fact, and as a result of such false statement or representation or of such nondisclosure such individual has received an amount of pandemic emergency unemployment compensation under this section to which such individual was not entitled, such individual—

(A) shall be ineligible for further pandemic emergency unemployment compensation under this section in accordance with the provisions of the applicable State unemployment compensation law relating to fraud in connection with a claim for unemployment compensation; and

(B) shall be subject to prosecution under section 1001 of title 18, United States Code.

(2) REPAYMENT.—In the case of individuals who have received amounts of pandemic emergency unemployment compensation under this section to which they were not entitled, the State shall require such individuals to repay the amounts of such pandemic emergency unemployment compensation to the State agency, except that the State agency may waive such repayment if it determines that—

(A) the payment of such pandemic emergency unemployment compensation was without fault on the part of any such individual; and

(B) such repayment would be contrary to equity and good conscience.

(3) RECOVERY BY STATE AGENCY.—

(A) IN GENERAL.—The State agency shall recover the amount to be repaid, or any part thereof, by deductions from any pandemic emergency unemployment compensation payable to such individual under this section or from any unemployment compensation payable to such individual under any State or Federal unemployment compensation law administered by the State agency or under any other State or Federal law administered by the State agency which provides for the payment of any assistance or allowance with respect to any week of unemployment, during the 3-year period after the date such individuals received the payment of the pandemic emergency unemployment compensation to which they were not entitled, in accordance with the same procedures as apply to the recovery of overpayments of regular unemployment benefits paid by the State.

(B) OPPORTUNITY FOR HEARING.—No repayment shall be required, and no deduction shall be made, until a determination has been made, notice thereof and an opportunity for a fair hearing has been given to the individual, and the determination has become final.

(4) REVIEW.—Any determination by a State agency under this section shall be subject to review in the same manner and to the same extent as determinations under the State unemployment compensation law, and only in that manner and to that extent.

(f) DEFINITIONS.—In this section, the terms "compensation", "regular compensation", "extended compensation", "benefit year", "base period", "State", "State agency", "State law", and "week" have the respective meanings given such terms under section 205 of the Federal-State Extended Unemployment Compensation Act of 1970 (26 U.S.C. 3304 note).

(g) APPLICABILITY.—An agreement entered into under this section shall apply to weeks of unemployment—

(1) beginning after the date on which such agreement is entered into; and

(2) ending on or before December 31, 2020.

[¶2029] SEC. 2108. TEMPORARY FINANCING OF SHORT-TIME COMPENSATION PAYMENTS IN STATES WITH PROGRAMS IN LAW.

(a) PAYMENTS TO STATES.—

(1) IN GENERAL.—Subject to paragraph (3), there shall be paid to a State an amount equal to 100 percent of the amount of short-time compensation paid under a short-time compensation program (as defined in section 3306(v) of the Internal Revenue Code of 1986) under the provisions of the State law.

(2) TERMS OF PAYMENTS.—Payments made to a State under paragraph (1) shall be payable by way of reimbursement in such amounts as the Secretary estimates the State will be entitled to receive under this section for each calendar month, reduced or increased, as the case may be, by any amount by which the Secretary finds that the Secretary's estimates for any prior calendar month were greater or less than the amounts which should have been paid to the State. Such estimates may be made on the basis of such statistical, sampling, or other method as may be agreed upon by the Secretary and the State agency of the State involved.

(3) LIMITATIONS ON PAYMENTS.—

(A) GENERAL PAYMENT LIMITATIONS.—No payments shall be made to a State under this section for short-time compensation paid to an individual by the State during a benefit year in excess of 26 times the amount of regular compensation (including dependents' allowances) under the State law payable to such individual for a week of total unemployment.

(B) EMPLOYER LIMITATIONS.—No payments shall be made to a State under this section for benefits paid to an individual by the State under a short-time compensation program if such individual is employed by the participating employer on a seasonal, temporary, or intermittent basis.

(b) APPLICABILITY.—Payments to a State under subsection (a) shall be available for weeks of unemployment—

(1) beginning on or after the date of the enactment of this Act; and

(2) ending on or before December 31, 2020.

(c) NEW PROGRAMS.—Subject to subsection (b)(2), if at any point after the date of the enactment of this Act the State enacts a State law providing for the payment of short-time compensation under a short-time compensation program that meets the definition of such a program under section 3306(v) of the Internal Revenue Code of 1986, the State shall be eligible for payments under this section after the effective date of such enactment.

(d) FUNDING AND CERTIFICATIONS.—

(1) FUNDING.—There are appropriated, out of moneys in the Treasury not otherwise appropriated, such sums as may be necessary for purposes of carrying out this section.

(2) CERTIFICATIONS.—The Secretary shall from time to time certify to the Secretary of the Treasury for payment to each State the sums payable to such State under this section.

(e) DEFINITIONS.—In this section:

(1) SECRETARY.—The term "Secretary" means the Secretary of Labor.

(2) STATE; STATE AGENCY; STATE LAW.—The terms "State", "State agency", and "State law" have the meanings given those terms in section 205 of the Federal-State Extended Unemployment Compensation Act of 1970 (26 U.S.C. 3304 note).

(f) TECHNICAL CORRECTION TO DEFINITION.—Section 3306(v)(6) of the Internal Revenue Code of 1986 (26 U.S.C. 3306) is amended by striking "Workforce Investment Act of 1998" and inserting "Workforce Innovation and Opportunity Act".

[¶2030] SEC. 2109. TEMPORARY FINANCING OF SHORT-TIME COMPENSATION AGREEMENTS.

(a) FEDERAL-STATE AGREEMENTS.—

(1) IN GENERAL.—Any State which desires to do so may enter into, and participate in, an agreement under this section with the Secretary provided that such State's law does not provide for the payment of short-time compensation under a short-time compensation program (as defined in section 3306(v) of the Internal Revenue Code of 1986).

(2) ABILITY TO TERMINATE.—Any State which is a party to an agreement under this section may, upon providing 30 days' written notice to the Secretary, terminate such agreement.

(b) PROVISIONS OF FEDERAL-STATE AGREEMENT.—

(1) IN GENERAL.—Any agreement under this section shall provide that the State agency of the State will make payments of short-time compensation under a plan approved by the State. Such plan shall provide that payments are made in accordance with the requirements under section 3306(v) of the Internal Revenue Code of 1986.

(2) LIMITATIONS ON PLANS.—

(A) GENERAL PAYMENT LIMITATIONS.—A short-time compensation plan approved by a State shall not permit the payment of short-time compensation to an individual by the State during a benefit year in excess of 26 times the amount of regular compensation (including dependents' allowances) under the State law payable to such individual for a week of total unemployment.

(B) EMPLOYER LIMITATIONS.—A short-time compensation plan approved by a State shall not provide payments to an individual if such individual is employed by the participating employer on a seasonal, temporary, or intermittent basis.

(3) EMPLOYER PAYMENT OF COSTS.—Any short-time compensation plan entered into by an employer must provide that the employer will pay the State an amount equal to one-half of the amount of short-time compensation paid under such plan. Such amount shall be deposited in the State's unemployment fund and shall not be used for purposes of calculating an employer's contribution rate under section 3303(a)(1) of the Internal Revenue Code of 1986.

(c) PAYMENTS TO STATES.—

(1) IN GENERAL.—There shall be paid to each State with an agreement under this section an amount equal to—

(A) one-half of the amount of short-time compensation paid to individuals by the State pursuant to such agreement; and

(B) any additional administrative expenses incurred by the State by reason of such agreement (as determined by the Secretary).

(2) TERMS OF PAYMENTS.—Payments made to a State under paragraph (1) shall be payable by way of reimbursement in such amounts as the Secretary estimates the State will be entitled to receive under this section for each calendar month, reduced or increased, as the case may be, by any amount by which the Secretary finds that the Secretary's estimates for any prior calendar month were greater or less than the amounts which should have been paid to the State. Such estimates may be made on the basis of such statistical, sampling, or other method as may be agreed upon by the Secretary and the State agency of the State involved.

(3) FUNDING.—There are appropriated, out of moneys in the Treasury not otherwise appropriated, such sums as may be necessary for purposes of carrying out this section.

(4) CERTIFICATIONS.—The Secretary shall from time to time certify to the Secretary of the Treasury for payment to each State the sums payable to such State under this section.

(d) APPLICABILITY.—An agreement entered into under this section shall apply to weeks of unemployment—

(1) beginning on or after the date on which such agreement is entered into; and

(2) ending on or before December 31, 2020.

(e) SPECIAL RULE.—If a State has entered into an agreement under this section and subsequently enacts a State law providing for the payment of short-time compensation under a short-time compensation program that meets the definition of such a program under section 3306(v) of the Internal Revenue Code of 1986, the State—

(1) shall not be eligible for payments under this section for weeks of unemployment beginning after the effective date of such State law; and

(2) subject to section 2108(b)(2), shall be eligible to receive payments under section 2108 after the effective date of such State law.

(f) DEFINITIONS.—In this section:

(1) SECRETARY.—The term "Secretary" means the Secretary of Labor.

(2) STATE; STATE AGENCY; STATE LAW.—The terms "State", "State agency", and "State law" have the meanings given those terms in section 205 of the Federal-State Extended Unemployment Compensation Act of 1970 (26 U.S.C. 3304 note).

[¶2031] SEC. 2110. GRANTS FOR SHORT-TIME COMPENSATION PROGRAMS.

(a) GRANTS.—

(1) FOR IMPLEMENTATION OR IMPROVED ADMINISTRATION.—The Secretary shall award grants to States that enact short-time compensation programs (as defined in subsection (i)(2)) for the purpose of implementation or improved administration of such programs.

(2) FOR PROMOTION AND ENROLLMENT.—The Secretary shall award grants to States that are eligible and submit plans for a grant under paragraph (1) for such States to promote and enroll employers in short-time compensation programs (as so defined).

(3) ELIGIBILITY.—

(A) IN GENERAL.—The Secretary shall determine eligibility criteria for the grants under paragraphs (1) and (2).

(B) CLARIFICATION.—A State administering a short-time compensation program that does not meet the definition of a short-time compensation program under section 3306(v) of the Internal Revenue Code of 1986, and a State with an agreement under section 2109, shall not be eligible to receive a grant under this section until such time as the State law of the State provides for payments under a short-time compensation program that meets such definition and such law.

(b) AMOUNT OF GRANTS.—

(1) IN GENERAL.—The maximum amount available for making grants to a State under paragraphs (1) and (2) shall be equal to the amount obtained by multiplying $100,000,000 (less the amount used by the Secretary under subsection (e)) by the same ratio as would apply under subsection (a)(2)(B) of section 903 of the Social Security Act (42 U.S.C. 1103) for purposes of determining such State's share of any excess amount (as described in subsection (a)(1) of such section) that would have been subject to transfer to State accounts, as of October 1, 2019, under the provisions of subsection (a) of such section.

(2) AMOUNT AVAILABLE FOR DIFFERENT GRANTS.—Of the maximum incentive payment determined under paragraph (1) with respect to a State—

(A) one-third shall be available for a grant under subsection (a)(1); and

(B) two-thirds shall be available for a grant under subsection (a)(2).

(c) GRANT APPLICATION AND DISBURSAL.—

(1) APPLICATION.—Any State seeking a grant under paragraph (1) or (2) of subsection (a) shall submit an application to the Secretary at such time, in such manner, and complete with such information as the Secretary may require. In no case may the Secretary award a grant under this section with respect to an application that is submitted after December 31, 2023.

(2) NOTICE.—The Secretary shall, within 30 days after receiving a complete application, notify the State agency of the State of the Secretary's findings with respect to the requirements for a grant under paragraph (1) or (2) (or both) of subsection (a).

(3) CERTIFICATION.—If the Secretary finds that the State law provisions meet the requirements for a grant under subsection (a), the Secretary shall thereupon make a certification to that effect to the Secretary of the Treasury, together with a certification as to the amount of the grant payment to be transferred to the State account in the Unemployment Trust Fund (as established in section 904(a) of the Social Security Act (42 U.S.C. 1104(a))) pursuant to that finding. The Secretary of the Treasury shall make the appropriate transfer to the State account within 7 days after receiving such certification.

(4) REQUIREMENT.—No certification of compliance with the requirements for a grant under paragraph (1) or (2) of subsection (a) may be made with respect to any State whose—

(A) State law is not otherwise eligible for certification under section 303 of the Social Security Act (42 U.S.C. 503) or approvable under section 3304 of the Internal Revenue Code of 1986; or

(B) short-time compensation program is subject to discontinuation or is not scheduled to take effect within 12 months of the certification.

(d) USE OF FUNDS.—The amount of any grant awarded under this section shall be used for the implementation of short-time compensation programs and the overall administration of such programs and the promotion and enrollment efforts associated with such programs, such as through—

(1) the creation or support of rapid response teams to advise employers about alternatives to layoffs;

(2) the provision of education or assistance to employers to enable them to assess the feasibility of participating in short-time compensation programs; and

(3) the development or enhancement of systems to automate—

(A) the submission and approval of plans; and

(B) the filing and approval of new and ongoing short-time compensation claims.

(e) ADMINISTRATION.—The Secretary is authorized to use 0.25 percent of the funds available under subsection (g) to provide for outreach and to share best practices with respect to this section and short-time compensation programs.

(f) RECOUPMENT.—The Secretary shall establish a process under which the Secretary shall recoup the amount of any grant awarded under paragraph (1) or (2) of subsection (a) if the Secretary determines that, during the 5-year period beginning on the first date that any such grant is awarded to the State, the State—

(1) terminated the State's short-time compensation program; or

(2) failed to meet appropriate requirements with respect to such program (as established by the Secretary).

(g) FUNDING.—There are appropriated, out of moneys in the Treasury not otherwise appropriated, to the Secretary, $100,000,000 to carry out this section, to remain available without fiscal year limitation.

(h) REPORTING.—The Secretary may establish reporting requirements for States receiving a grant under this section in order to provide oversight of grant funds.

(i) DEFINITIONS.—In this section:

(1) SECRETARY.—The term "Secretary" means the Secretary of Labor.

(2) SHORT-TIME COMPENSATION PROGRAM.—The term "short-time compensation program" has the meaning given such term in section 3306(v) of the Internal Revenue Code of 1986.

(3) STATE; STATE AGENCY; STATE LAW.—The terms "State", "State agency", and "State law" have the meanings given those terms in section 205 of the Federal-State Extended Unemployment Compensation Act of 1970 (26 U.S.C. 3304 note).

[¶2032] SEC. 2111. ASSISTANCE AND GUIDANCE IN IMPLEMENTING PROGRAMS.

(a) IN GENERAL.—In order to assist States in establishing, qualifying, and implementing short-time compensation programs (as defined in section 3306(v) of the Internal Revenue Code of 1986), the Secretary of Labor (in this section referred to as the "Secretary") shall—

(1) develop model legislative language, or disseminate existing model legislative language, which may be used by States in developing and enacting such programs, and periodically review and revise such model legislative language;

(2) provide technical assistance and guidance in developing, enacting, and implementing such programs; and

(3) establish reporting requirements for States, including reporting on—

(A) the number of estimated averted layoffs;

(B) the number of participating employers and workers; and

(C) such other items as the Secretary of Labor determines are appropriate.

(b) MODEL LANGUAGE AND GUIDANCE.—The model language and guidance developed under subsection (a) shall allow sufficient flexibility by States and participating employers while ensuring accountability and program integrity.

(c) CONSULTATION.—In developing the model legislative language and guidance under subsection (a), and in order to meet the requirements of subsection (b), the Secretary shall consult with employers, labor organizations, State workforce agencies, and other program experts. Existing model legislative language that has been developed through such a consultative process shall be deemed to meet the consultation requirement of this subsection.

(d) REPEAL.—Section 4104 of the Emergency Unemployment Stabilization and Access Act of 2020 (contained in division D of the Families First Coronavirus Response Act) is repealed.

[¶2033] SEC. 2112. WAIVER OF THE 7-DAY WAITING PERIOD FOR BENEFITS UNDER THE RAILROAD UNEMPLOYMENT INSURANCE ACT.

(a) NO WAITING WEEK.—With respect to any registration period beginning after the date of enactment of this Act and ending on or before December 31, 2020, subparagraphs (A)(ii) and (B)(ii) of section 2(a)(1) of the Railroad Unemployment Insurance Act (45 U.S.C. 352(a)(1)) shall not apply.

(b) OPERATING INSTRUCTIONS AND REGULATIONS.—The Railroad Retirement Board may prescribe any operating instructions or regulations necessary to carry out this section.

(c) FUNDING.—Out of any funds in the Treasury not otherwise appropriated, there are appropriated $50,000,000 to cover the costs of additional benefits payable due to the application of subsection (a). Upon the exhaustion of the funds appropriated under this subsection, subsection (a) shall no longer apply with respect to any registration period beginning after the date of exhaustion of funds.

(d) DEFINITION OF REGISTRATION PERIOD.—For purposes of this section, the term "registration period" has the meaning given such term under section 1 of the Railroad Unemployment Insurance Act (45 U.S.C. 351).

[¶2034] SEC. 2113. ENHANCED BENEFITS UNDER THE RAILROAD UNEMPLOYMENT INSURANCE ACT.

Section 2(a) of the Railroad Unemployment Insurance Act (45 U.S.C. §352(a)) is amended by adding at the end the following:

(5)(A) "Notwithstanding paragraph (3), subsection (c)(1)(B), and any other limitation on total benefits in this Act, for registration periods beginning on or after April 1, 2020, but on or before July 31, 2020, a recovery benefit in the amount of $1,200 shall be payable to a qualified employee with respect to any registration period in which the employee received unemployment benefits under paragraph (1)(A), and in any registration period in which the employee did not receive unemployment benefits due to the limitation in subsection (c)(1)(B) or due to reaching the maximum number of days of benefits in the benefit year beginning July 1, 2019, under subsection (c)(1)(A). No recovery benefits shall be payable under this section upon the exhaustion of the funds appropriated under subparagraph (B) for payment of benefits under this subparagraph.

(B) "Out of any funds in the Treasury not otherwise appropriated, there are appropriated $425,000,000 to cover the cost of recovery benefits provided under subparagraph (A), to remain available until expended.".

[¶2035] SEC. 2114. EXTENDED UNEMPLOYMENT BENEFITS UNDER THE RAILROAD UNEMPLOYMENT INSURANCE ACT.

(a) EXTENSION.—Section 2(c)(2)(D)(iii) of the Railroad Unemployment Insurance Act (45 U.S.C. 352(c)(2)(D)(iii) is amended—

(1) by striking "July 1, 2008" and inserting "July 1, 2019";

(2) by striking "June 30, 2013" and inserting "June 30, 2020"; and

(3) by striking "December 31, 2013" and inserting "December 31, 2020".

(b) CLARIFICATION ON AUTHORITY TO USE FUNDS.—Funds appropriated under either the first or second sentence of clause (iv) of section 2(c)(2)(D) of the Railroad Unemployment Insurance Act shall be available to cover the cost of additional extended unemployment benefits provided under such section 2(c)(2)(D) by reason of the amendments made by subsection (a) as well as to cover the cost of such benefits provided under such section 2(c)(2)(D) as in effect on the day before the date of enactment of this Act.

[¶2036] SEC. 2115. FUNDING FOR THE DOL OFFICE OF INSPECTOR GENERAL FOR OVERSIGHT OF UNEMPLOYMENT PROVISIONS.

There are appropriated, out of moneys in the Treasury not otherwise appropriated, to the Office of the Inspector General of the Department of Labor, $25,000,000 to carry out audits, investigations, and other oversight activities authorized under the Inspector General Act of 1978 (5 U.S.C. App.) that are related to the provisions of, and amendments made by, this subtitle, to remain available without fiscal year limitation.

[¶2037] SEC. 2116. IMPLEMENTATION.

(a) NON-APPLICATION OF THE PAPERWORK REDUCTION ACT.—Chapter 35 of title 44, United States Code (commonly referred to as the "Paperwork Reduction Act of 1995"), shall not apply to the provisions of, and the amendments made by, this subtitle.

(b) OPERATING INSTRUCTIONS OR OTHER GUIDANCE.—Notwithstanding any other provision of law, the Secretary of Labor may issue any operating instructions or other guidance necessary to carry out the provisions of, or the amendments made by, this subtitle.

Subtitle B—Rebates and Other Individual Provisions

[¶2039] SEC. 2201. 2020 RECOVERY REBATES FOR INDIVIDUALS.

(a) IN GENERAL.—Subchapter B of chapter 65 of subtitle F of the Internal Revenue Code of 1986 is amended by inserting after section 6427 the following new section:

[¶2040] SEC. 6428. "2020 RECOVERY REBATES FOR INDIVIDUALS.

(a) "IN GENERAL.—In the case of an eligible individual, there shall be allowed as a credit against the tax imposed by subtitle A for the first taxable year beginning in 2020 an amount equal to the sum of—

(1) "$1,200 ($2,400 in the case of eligible individuals filing a joint return), plus

(2) "an amount equal to the product of $500 multiplied by the number of qualifying children (within the meaning of section 24(c)) of the taxpayer.

(b) "TREATMENT OF CREDIT.—The credit allowed by subsection (a) shall be treated as allowed by subpart C of part IV of subchapter A of chapter 1.

(c) "LIMITATION BASED ON ADJUSTED GROSS INCOME.—The amount of the credit allowed by subsection (a) (determined without regard to this subsection and subsection (e)) shall be reduced (but not below zero) by 5 percent of so much of the taxpayer's adjusted gross income as exceeds—

(1) "$150,000 in the case of a joint return,

(2) "$112,500 in the case of a head of household, and

(3) "$75,000 in the case of a taxpayer not described in paragraph (1) or (2).

(d) "ELIGIBLE INDIVIDUAL.—For purposes of this section, the term 'eligible individual' means any individual other than—

(1) "any nonresident alien individual,

(2) "any individual with respect to whom a deduction under section 151 is allowable to another taxpayer for a taxable year beginning in the calendar year in which the individual's taxable year begins, and

(3) "an estate or trust.

(e) "COORDINATION WITH ADVANCE REFUNDS OF CREDIT.—

(1) "IN GENERAL.—The amount of credit which would (but for this paragraph) be allowable under this section shall be reduced (but not below zero) by the aggregate refunds and credits made or allowed to the taxpayer under subsection (f). Any failure to so reduce the credit shall be treated as arising out of a mathematical or clerical error and assessed according to section 6213(b)(1).

(2) "JOINT RETURNS.—In the case of a refund or credit made or allowed under subsection (f) with respect to a joint return, half of such refund or credit shall be treated as having been made or allowed to each individual filing such return.

(f) "ADVANCE REFUNDS AND CREDITS.—

(1) "IN GENERAL.—Subject to paragraph (5), each individual who was an eligible individual for such individual's first taxable year beginning in 2019 shall be treated as having made a payment against the tax imposed by chapter 1 for such taxable year in an amount equal to the advance refund amount for such taxable year.

(2) "ADVANCE REFUND AMOUNT.—For purposes of paragraph (1), the advance refund amount is the amount that would have been allowed as a credit under this section for such taxable year if this section (other than subsection (e) and this subsection) had applied to such taxable year.

(3) "TIMING AND MANNER OF PAYMENTS.—

(A) "TIMING.—The Secretary shall, subject to the provisions of this title, refund or credit any overpayment attributable to this section as rapidly as possible. No refund or credit shall be made or allowed under this subsection after December 31, 2020.

(B) "DELIVERY OF PAYMENTS.—Notwithstanding any other provision of law, the Secretary may certify and disburse refunds payable under this subsection electronically to any account to which the payee authorized, on or after January 1, 2018, the delivery of a refund of taxes under this title or of a Federal payment (as defined in section 3332 of title 31, United States Code).

(C) "WAIVER OF CERTAIN RULES.—Notwithstanding section 3325 of title 31, United States Code, or any other provision of law, with respect to any payment of a refund under this subsection, a disbursing official in the executive branch of the United States Government may modify payment information received from an officer or employee described in section 3325(a)(1)(B) of such title for the purpose of facilitating the accurate and efficient delivery of such payment. Except in cases of fraud or reckless neglect, no liability under sections 3325, 3527, 3528, or 3529 of title 31, United States Code, shall be imposed with respect to payments made under this subparagraph.

(4) "NO INTEREST.—No interest shall be allowed on any overpayment attributable to this section.

(5) "ALTERNATE TAXABLE YEAR.—In the case of an individual who, at the time of any determination made pursuant to paragraph (3), has not filed a tax return for the year described in paragraph (1), the Secretary may—

(A) "apply such paragraph by substituting '2018' for '2019', and

(B) "if the individual has not filed a tax return for such individual's first taxable year beginning in 2018, use information with respect to such individual for calendar year 2019 provided in—

(i) "Form SSA–1099, Social Security Benefit Statement, or

(ii) "Form RRB–1099, Social Security Equivalent Benefit Statement.

(6) "NOTICE TO TAXPAYER.—Not later than 15 days after the date on which the Secretary distributed any payment to an eligible taxpayer pursuant to this subsection, notice shall be sent by mail to such taxpayer's last known address. Such notice shall indicate the method by which such payment was made, the amount of such payment, and a phone number for the appropriate point of contact at the Internal Revenue Service to report any failure to receive such payment.

(g) "IDENTIFICATION NUMBER REQUIREMENT.—

(1) "IN GENERAL.—No credit shall be allowed under subsection (a) to an eligible individual who does not include on the return of tax for the taxable year—

(A) "such individual's valid identification number,

(B) "in the case of a joint return, the valid identification number of such individual's spouse, and

(C) "in the case of any qualifying child taken into account under subsection (a)(2), the valid identification number of such qualifying child.

(2) "VALID IDENTIFICATION NUMBER.—

(A) "IN GENERAL.—For purposes of paragraph (1), the term 'valid identification number' means a social security number (as such term is defined in section 24(h)(7)).

(B) "ADOPTION TAXPAYER IDENTIFICATION NUMBER.—For purposes of paragraph (1)(C), in the case of a qualifying child who is adopted or placed for adoption, the term 'valid identification number' shall include the adoption taxpayer identification number of such child.

(3) "SPECIAL RULE FOR MEMBERS OF THE ARMED FORCES.—Paragraph (1)(B) shall not apply in the case where at least 1 spouse was a member of the Armed Forces of the United States at any time during the taxable year and at least 1 spouse satisfies paragraph (1)(A).

(4) "MATHEMATICAL OR CLERICAL ERROR AUTHORITY.—Any omission of a correct valid identification number required under this subsection shall be treated as a mathematical or clerical error for purposes of applying section 6213(g)(2) to such omission.

(h) "REGULATIONS.—The Secretary shall prescribe such regulations or other guidance as may be necessary to carry out the purposes of this section, including any such measures as are deemed appropriate to avoid allowing multiple credits or rebates to a taxpayer.".

(b) ADMINISTRATIVE AMENDMENTS.—

(1) DEFINITION OF DEFICIENCY.—Section 6211(b)(4)(A) of the Internal Revenue Code of 1986 is amended by striking "and 36B, 168(k)(4)" and inserting "36B, and 6428".

(2) MATHEMATICAL OR CLERICAL ERROR AUTHORITY.—Section 6213(g)(2)(L) of such Code is amended by striking "or 32" and inserting "32, or 6428".

(c) TREATMENT OF POSSESSIONS.—

(1) PAYMENTS TO POSSESSIONS.—

(A) MIRROR CODE POSSESSION.—The Secretary of the Treasury shall pay to each possession of the United States which has a mirror code tax system amounts equal to the loss (if any) to that possession by reason of the amendments made by this section. Such amounts shall be determined by the Secretary of the Treasury based on information provided by the government of the respective possession.

(B) OTHER POSSESSIONS.—The Secretary of the Treasury shall pay to each possession of the United States which does not have a mirror code tax system amounts estimated by the Secretary of the Treasury as being equal to the aggregate benefits (if any) that would have been provided to residents of such possession by reason of the amendments made by this section if a mirror code tax system had been in effect in such possession. The preceding sentence shall not apply unless the respective possession has a plan, which has been approved by the Secretary of the Treasury, under which such possession will promptly distribute such payments to its residents.

(2) COORDINATION WITH CREDIT ALLOWED AGAINST UNITED STATES INCOME TAXES.—No credit shall be allowed against United States income taxes under section 6428 of the Internal Revenue Code of 1986 (as added by this section) to any person—

(A) to whom a credit is allowed against taxes imposed by the possession by reason of the amendments made by this section, or

(B) who is eligible for a payment under a plan described in paragraph (1)(B).

(3) DEFINITIONS AND SPECIAL RULES.—

(A) POSSESSION OF THE UNITED STATES.—For purposes of this subsection, the term "possession of the United States" includes the Commonwealth of Puerto Rico and the Commonwealth of the Northern Mariana Islands.

(B) MIRROR CODE TAX SYSTEM.—For purposes of this subsection, the term "mirror code tax system" means, with respect to any possession of the United States, the income tax system of such possession if the income tax liability of the residents of such possession under such system is determined by reference to the income tax laws of the United States as if such possession were the United States.

(C) TREATMENT OF PAYMENTS.—For purposes of section 1324 of title 31, United States Code, the payments under this subsection shall be treated in the same manner as a refund due from a credit provision referred to in subsection (b)(2) of such section.

(d) EXCEPTION FROM REDUCTION OR OFFSET.—Any credit or refund allowed or made to any individual by reason of section 6428 of the Internal Revenue Code of 1986 (as added by this section) or by reason of subsection (c) of this section shall not be—

(1) subject to reduction or offset pursuant to section 3716 or 3720A of title 31, United States Code,

(2) subject to reduction or offset pursuant to subsection (d), (e), or (f) of section 6402 of the Internal Revenue Code of 1986, or

(3) reduced or offset by other assessed Federal taxes that would otherwise be subject to levy or collection.

(e) PUBLIC AWARENESS CAMPAIGN.—The Secretary of the Treasury (or the Secretary's delegate) shall conduct a public awareness campaign, in coordination with the Commissioner of Social Security and the heads of other relevant Federal agencies, to provide information regarding the availability of the credit and rebate allowed under section 6428 of the Internal Revenue Code of 1986 (as added by this section), including information with respect to individuals who may not have filed a tax return for taxable year 2018 or 2019.

(f) APPROPRIATIONS TO CARRY OUT REBATES.—

(1) IN GENERAL.—Immediately upon the enactment of this Act, the following sums are appropriated, out of any money in the Treasury not otherwise appropriated, for the fiscal year ending September 30, 2020:

(A) DEPARTMENT OF THE TREASURY.—

(i) For an additional amount for "Department of the Treasury—Bureau of the Fiscal Service—Salaries and Expenses", $78,650,000, to remain available until September 30, 2021.

(ii) For an additional amount for "Department of the Treasury—Internal Revenue Service—Taxpayer Services", $293,500,000, to remain available until September 30, 2021.

(iii) For an additional amount for "Department of the Treasury—Internal Revenue Service—Operations Support", $170,000,000, to remain available until September 30, 2021.

(iv) For an additional amount for "Department of Treasury—Internal Revenue Service—Enforcement", $37,200,000, to remain available until September 30, 2021.

Amounts made available in appropriations under clauses (ii), (iii), and (iv) of this subparagraph may be transferred between such appropriations upon the advance notification of the Committees on Appropriations of the House of Representatives and the Senate. Such transfer authority is in addition to any other transfer authority provided by law.

(B) SOCIAL SECURITY ADMINISTRATION.—For an additional amount for "Social Security Administration—Limitation on Administrative Expenses", $38,000,000, to remain available until September 30, 2021.

(2) REPORTS.—No later than 15 days after enactment of this Act, the Secretary of the Treasury shall submit a plan to the Committees on Appropriations of the House of Representatives and the Senate detailing the expected use of the funds provided by paragraph (1)(A). Beginning 90 days after enactment of this Act, the Secretary of the Treasury shall submit a quarterly report to the Committees on Appropriations of the House of Representatives and the Senate detailing the actual expenditure of funds provided by paragraph (1)(A) and the expected expenditure of such funds in the subsequent quarter.

(g) CONFORMING AMENDMENTS.—

(1) Paragraph (2) of section 1324(b) of title 31, United States Code, is amended by inserting "6428," after "54B(h),".

(2) The table of sections for subchapter B of chapter 65 of subtitle F of the Internal Revenue Code of 1986 is amended by inserting after the item relating to section 6427 the following:

"Sec. 6428. 2020 Recovery Rebates for individuals.".

[¶2041] SEC. 2202. SPECIAL RULES FOR USE OF RETIREMENT FUNDS.

(a) TAX-FAVORED WITHDRAWALS FROM RETIREMENT PLANS.—

(1) IN GENERAL.—Section 72(t) of the Internal Revenue Code of 1986 shall not apply to any coronavirus-related distribution.

(2) AGGREGATE DOLLAR LIMITATION.—

(A) IN GENERAL.—For purposes of this subsection, the aggregate amount of distributions received by an individual which may be treated as coronavirus-related distributions for any taxable year shall not exceed $100,000.

(B) TREATMENT OF PLAN DISTRIBUTIONS.—If a distribution to an individual would (without regard to subparagraph (A)) be a coronavirus-related distribution, a plan shall not be treated as violating any requirement of the Internal Revenue Code of 1986 merely because the plan treats such distribution as a coronavirus-related distribution, unless the aggregate amount of such distributions from all plans maintained by the employer (and any member of any controlled group which includes the employer) to such individual exceeds $100,000.

(C) CONTROLLED GROUP.—For purposes of subparagraph (B), the term "controlled group" means any group treated as a single employer under subsection (b), (c), (m), or (o) of section 414 of the Internal Revenue Code of 1986.

(3) AMOUNT DISTRIBUTED MAY BE REPAID.—

(A) IN GENERAL.—Any individual who receives a coronavirus-related distribution may, at any time during the 3-year period beginning on the day after the date on which such distribution was received, make 1 or more contributions in an aggregate amount not to exceed the amount of such distribution to an eligible retirement plan of which such individual is a beneficiary and to which a rollover contribution of such distribution could be made under section 402(c), 403(a)(4), 403(b)(8), 408(d)(3), or 457(e)(16), of the Internal Revenue Code of 1986, as the case may be.

(B) TREATMENT OF REPAYMENTS OF DISTRIBUTIONS FROM ELIGIBLE RETIREMENT PLANS OTHER THAN IRAS.—For purposes of the Internal Revenue Code of 1986, if a contribution is made pursuant to subparagraph (A) with respect to a coronavirus-related distribution from an eligible retirement plan other than an individual retirement plan, then the taxpayer shall, to the extent of the amount of the contribution, be treated as having received the coronavirus-related distribution in an eligible rollover distribution (as defined in section 402(c)(4) of such Code) and as having transferred the amount to the eligible retirement plan in a direct trustee to trustee transfer within 60 days of the distribution.

(C) TREATMENT OF REPAYMENTS OF DISTRIBUTIONS FROM IRAS.—For purposes of the Internal Revenue Code of 1986, if a contribution is made pursuant to subparagraph (A) with respect to a coronavirus-related distribution from an individual retirement plan (as defined by section 7701(a)(37) of such Code), then, to the extent of the amount of the contribution, the coronavirus-related distribution shall be treated as a distribution described in section 408(d)(3) of such Code and as having been transferred to the eligible retirement plan in a direct trustee to trustee transfer within 60 days of the distribution.

(4) DEFINITIONS.—For purposes of this subsection—

(A) CORONAVIRUS-RELATED DISTRIBUTION.—Except as provided in paragraph (2), the term "coronavirus-related distribution" means any distribution from an eligible retirement plan made—

(i) on or after January 1, 2020, and before December 31, 2020,

(ii) to an individual—

(I) who is diagnosed with the virus SARS–CoV–2 or with coronavirus disease 2019 (COVID–19) by a test approved by the Centers for Disease Control and Prevention,

(II) whose spouse or dependent (as defined in section 152 of the Internal Revenue Code of 1986) is diagnosed with such virus or disease by such a test, or

(III) who experiences adverse financial consequences as a result of being quarantined, being furloughed or laid off or having work hours reduced due to such virus or disease, being unable to work due to lack of child care due to such virus or disease, closing or reducing hours of a business owned or operated by the individual due to such virus or disease, or other factors as determined by the Secretary of the Treasury (or the Secretary's delegate).

(B) EMPLOYEE CERTIFICATION.—The administrator of an eligible retirement plan may rely on an employee's certification that the employee satisfies the conditions of subparagraph (A)(ii) in determining whether any distribution is a coronavirus-related distribution.

(C) ELIGIBLE RETIREMENT PLAN.—The term "eligible retirement plan" has the meaning given such term by section 402(c)(8)(B) of the Internal Revenue Code of 1986.

(5) INCOME INCLUSION SPREAD OVER 3-YEAR PERIOD.—

(A) IN GENERAL.—In the case of any coronavirus-related distribution, unless the taxpayer elects not to have this paragraph apply for any taxable year, any amount required to be included in gross income for such taxable year shall be so included ratably over the 3-taxable-year period beginning with such taxable year.

(B) SPECIAL RULE.—For purposes of subparagraph (A), rules similar to the rules of subparagraph (E) of section 408A(d)(3) of the Internal Revenue Code of 1986 shall apply.

(6) SPECIAL RULES.—

(A) EXEMPTION OF DISTRIBUTIONS FROM TRUSTEE TO TRUSTEE TRANSFER AND WITHHOLDING RULES.—For purposes of sections 401(a)(31), 402(f), and 3405 of the Internal Revenue Code of 1986, coronavirus-related distributions shall not be treated as eligible rollover distributions.

(B) CORONAVIRUS-RELATED DISTRIBUTIONS TREATED AS MEETING PLAN DISTRIBUTION REQUIREMENTS.—For purposes of the Internal Revenue Code of 1986, a coronavirus-related distribution shall be treated as meeting the requirements of sections 401(k)(2)(B)(i), 403(b)(7)(A)(i), 403(b)(11), and 457(d)(1)(A) of such Code and section 8433(h)(1) of title 5, United States Code.

(b) LOANS FROM QUALIFIED PLANS.—

(1) INCREASE IN LIMIT ON LOANS NOT TREATED AS DISTRIBUTIONS.—In the case of any loan from a qualified employer plan (as defined under section 72(p)(4) of the Internal Revenue Code of 1986) to a qualified individual made during the 180-day period beginning on the date of the enactment of this Act—

(A) clause (i) of section 72(p)(2)(A) of such Code shall be applied by substituting "$100,000" for "$50,000", and

(B) clause (ii) of such section shall be applied by substituting "the present value of the nonforfeitable accrued benefit of the employee under the plan" for "one-half of the present value of the nonforfeitable accrued benefit of the employee under the plan".

(2) DELAY OF REPAYMENT.—In the case of a qualified individual with an outstanding loan (on or after the date of the enactment of this Act) from a qualified employer plan (as defined in section 72(p)(4) of the Internal Revenue Code of 1986)—

(A) if the due date pursuant to subparagraph (B) or (C) of section 72(p)(2) of such Code for any repayment with respect to such loan occurs during the period beginning on the date of the enactment of this Act and ending on December 31, 2020, such due date shall be delayed for 1 year,

(B) any subsequent repayments with respect to any such loan shall be appropriately adjusted to reflect the delay in the due date under subparagraph (A) and any interest accruing during such delay, and

(C) in determining the 5-year period and the term of a loan under subparagraph (B) or (C) of section 72(p)(2) of such Code, the period described in subparagraph (A) of this paragraph shall be disregarded.

(3) QUALIFIED INDIVIDUAL.—For purposes of this subsection, the term "qualified individual" means any individual who is described in subsection (a)(4)(A)(ii).

(c) PROVISIONS RELATING TO PLAN AMENDMENTS.—

(1) IN GENERAL.—If this subsection applies to any amendment to any plan or annuity contract—

(A) such plan or contract shall be treated as being operated in accordance with the terms of the plan during the period described in paragraph (2)(B)(i), and

(B) except as provided by the Secretary of the Treasury (or the Secretary's delegate), such plan or contract shall not fail to meet the requirements of section 411(d)(6) of the Internal Revenue Code of 1986 and section 204(g) of the Employee Retirement Income Security Act of 1974 by reason of such amendment.

(2) AMENDMENTS TO WHICH SUBSECTION APPLIES.—

(A) IN GENERAL.—This subsection shall apply to any amendment to any plan or annuity contract which is made—

(i) pursuant to any provision of this section, or pursuant to any regulation issued by the Secretary of the Treasury or the Secretary of Labor (or the delegate of either such Secretary) under any provision of this section, and

(ii) on or before the last day of the first plan year beginning on or after January 1, 2022, or such later date as the Secretary of the Treasury (or the Secretary's delegate) may prescribe.

In the case of a governmental plan (as defined in section 414(d) of the Internal Revenue Code of 1986), clause (ii) shall be applied by substituting the date which is 2 years after the date otherwise applied under clause (ii).

(B) CONDITIONS.—This subsection shall not apply to any amendment unless—

(i) during the period—

(I) beginning on the date that this section or the regulation described in subparagraph (A)(i) takes effect (or in the case of a plan or contract amendment not required by this section or such regulation, the effective date specified by the plan), and

(II) ending on the date described in subparagraph (A)(ii) (or, if earlier, the date the plan or contract amendment is adopted),

the plan or contract is operated as if such plan or contract amendment were in effect, and

(ii) such plan or contract amendment applies retroactively for such period.

[¶2042] SEC. 2203. TEMPORARY WAIVER OF REQUIRED MINIMUM DISTRIBUTION RULES FOR CERTAIN RETIREMENT PLANS AND ACCOUNTS.

(a) IN GENERAL.—Section 401(a)(9) of the Internal Revenue Code of 1986 is amended by adding at the end the following new subparagraph:

(I) "TEMPORARY WAIVER OF MINIMUM REQUIRED DISTRIBUTION.—

(i) "IN GENERAL.—The requirements of this paragraph shall not apply for calendar year 2020 to—

(I) "a defined contribution plan which is described in this subsection or in section 403(a) or 403(b),

(II) "a defined contribution plan which is an eligible deferred compensation plan described in section 457(b) but only if such plan is maintained by an employer described in section 457(e)(1)(A), or

(III) "an individual retirement plan.

(ii) "SPECIAL RULE FOR REQUIRED BEGINNING DATES IN 2020.—Clause (i) shall apply to any distribution which is required to be made in calendar year 2020 by reason of—

(I) "a required beginning date occurring in such calendar year, and

(II) "such distribution not having been made before January 1, 2020.

(iii) "SPECIAL RULES REGARDING WAIVER PERIOD.—For purposes of this paragraph—

(I) "the required beginning date with respect to any individual shall be determined without regard to this subparagraph for purposes of applying this paragraph for calendar years after 2020, and

(II) "if clause (ii) of subparagraph (B) applies, the 5-year period described in such clause shall be determined without regard to calendar year 2020.".

(b) ELIGIBLE ROLLOVER DISTRIBUTIONS.—Section 402(c)(4) of the Internal Revenue Code of 1986 is amended by striking "2009" each place it appears in the last sentence and inserting "2020".

(c) EFFECTIVE DATES.—

(1) IN GENERAL.—The amendments made by this section shall apply for calendar years beginning after December 31, 2019.

(2) PROVISIONS RELATING TO PLAN OR CONTRACT AMENDMENTS.—

(A) IN GENERAL.—If this paragraph applies to any plan or contract amendment—

(i) such plan or contract shall not fail to be treated as being operated in accordance with the terms of the plan during the period described in subparagraph (B)(ii) solely because the plan operates in accordance with this section, and

(ii) except as provided by the Secretary of the Treasury (or the Secretary's delegate), such plan or contract shall not fail to meet the requirements of section 411(d)(6) of the Internal Revenue Code of 1986 and section 204(g) of the Employee Retirement Income Security Act of 1974 by reason of such amendment.

(B) AMENDMENTS TO WHICH PARAGRAPH APPLIES.—

(i) IN GENERAL.—This paragraph shall apply to any amendment to any plan or annuity contract which—

(I) is made pursuant to the amendments made by this section, and

(II) is made on or before the last day of the first plan year beginning on or after January 1, 2022.

In the case of a governmental plan, subclause (II) shall be applied by substituting '2024' for '2022'.

(ii) CONDITIONS.—This paragraph shall not apply to any amendment unless during the period beginning on the effective date of the amendment and ending on December 31, 2020, the plan or contract is operated as if such plan or contract amendment were in effect.

[¶2043] SEC. 2204. ALLOWANCE OF PARTIAL ABOVE THE LINE DEDUCTION FOR CHARITABLE CONTRIBUTIONS.

(a) IN GENERAL.—Section 62(a) of the Internal Revenue Code of 1986 is amended by inserting after paragraph (21) the following new paragraph:

(22) "CHARITABLE CONTRIBUTIONS.—In the case of taxable years beginning in 2020, the amount (not to exceed $300) of qualified charitable contributions made by an eligible individual during the taxable year.".

(b) DEFINITIONS.—Section 62 of such Code is amended by adding at the end the following new subsection:

(f) "DEFINITIONS RELATING TO QUALIFIED CHARITABLE CONTRIBUTIONS.—For purposes of subsection (a)(22)—

(1) "ELIGIBLE INDIVIDUAL.—The term 'eligible individual' means any individual who does not elect to itemize deductions.

(2) "QUALIFIED CHARITABLE CONTRIBUTIONS.—The term 'qualified charitable contribution' means a charitable contribution (as defined in section 170(c))—

(A) "which is made in cash,

(B) "for which a deduction is allowable under section 170 (determined without regard to subsection (b) thereof), and

(C) "which is—

(i) "made to an organization described in section 170(b)(1)(A), and

(ii) "not—

(I) "to an organization described in section 509(a)(3), or

(II) "for the establishment of a new, or maintenance of an existing, donor advised fund (as defined in section 4966(d)(2)).

Such term shall not include any amount which is treated as a charitable contribution made in such taxable year by reason of subsection (b)(1)(G)(ii) or (d)(1) of section 170.".

(c) EFFECTIVE DATE.—The amendments made by this section shall apply to taxable years beginning after December 31, 2019.

[¶2044] SEC. 2205. MODIFICATION OF LIMITATIONS ON CHARITABLE CONTRIBUTIONS DURING 2020.

(a) TEMPORARY SUSPENSION OF LIMITATIONS ON CERTAIN CASH CONTRIBUTIONS.—

(1) IN GENERAL.—Except as otherwise provided in paragraph (2), qualified contributions shall be disregarded in applying subsections (b) and (d) of section 170 of the Internal Revenue Code of 1986.

(2) TREATMENT OF EXCESS CONTRIBUTIONS.—For purposes of section 170 of the Internal Revenue Code of 1986—

(A) INDIVIDUALS.—In the case of an individual—

(i) LIMITATION.—Any qualified contribution shall be allowed as a deduction only to the extent that the aggregate of such contributions does not exceed the excess of the taxpayer's contribution base (as defined in subparagraph (H) of section 170(b)(1) of such Code) over the amount of all other charitable contributions allowed under section 170(b)(1) of such Code.

(ii) CARRYOVER.—If the aggregate amount of qualified contributions made in the contribution year (within the meaning of section 170(d)(1) of such Code) exceeds the limitation of clause (i), such excess shall be added to the excess described in section 170(b)(1)(G)(ii).

(B) CORPORATIONS.—In the case of a corporation—

(i) LIMITATION.—Any qualified contribution shall be allowed as a deduction only to the extent that the aggregate of such contributions does not exceed the excess of 25 percent of the taxpayer's taxable income (as determined under paragraph (2) of section 170(b) of such Code) over the amount of all other charitable contributions allowed under such paragraph.

(ii) CARRYOVER.—If the aggregate amount of qualified contributions made in the contribution year (within the meaning of section 170(d)(2) of such Code) exceeds the limitation of clause (i), such excess shall be appropriately taken into account under section 170(d)(2) subject to the limitations thereof.

(3) QUALIFIED CONTRIBUTIONS.—

(A) IN GENERAL.—For purposes of this subsection, the term "qualified contribution" means any charitable contribution (as defined in section 170(c) of the Internal Revenue Code of 1986) if—

(i) such contribution is paid in cash during calendar year 2020 to an organization described in section 170(b)(1)(A) of such Code, and

(ii) the taxpayer has elected the application of this section with respect to such contribution.

(B) EXCEPTION.—Such term shall not include a contribution by a donor if the contribution is—

(i) to an organization described in section 509(a)(3) of the Internal Revenue Code of 1986, or

(ii) for the establishment of a new, or maintenance of an existing, donor advised fund (as defined in section 4966(d)(2) of such Code).

(C) APPLICATION OF ELECTION TO PARTNERSHIPS AND S CORPORATIONS.—In the case of a partnership or S corporation, the election under subparagraph (A)(ii) shall be made separately by each partner or shareholder.

(b) INCREASE IN LIMITS ON CONTRIBUTIONS OF FOOD INVENTORY.—In the case of any charitable contribution of food during 2020 to which section 170(e)(3)(C) of the Internal Revenue Code of 1986 applies, subclauses (I) and (II) of clause (ii) thereof shall each be applied by substituting "25 percent" for "15 percent."

(c) EFFECTIVE DATE.—This section shall apply to taxable years ending after December 31, 2019.

[¶2045] SEC. 2206. EXCLUSION FOR CERTAIN EMPLOYER PAYMENTS OF STUDENT LOANS.

(a) IN GENERAL.—Paragraph (1) of section 127(c) of the Internal Revenue Code of 1986 is amended by striking "and" at the end of subparagraph (A), by redesignating subparagraph (B) as subparagraph (C), and by inserting after subparagraph (A) the following new subparagraph:

(B) "in the case of payments made before January 1, 2021, the payment by an employer, whether paid to the employee or to a lender, of principal or interest on any qualified education loan (as defined in section 221(d)(1)) incurred by the employee for education of the employee, and".

(b) CONFORMING AMENDMENT; DENIAL OF DOUBLE BENEFIT.—The first sentence of paragraph (1) of section 221(e) of the Internal Revenue Code of 1986 is amended by inserting before the period the following: ", or for which an exclusion is allowable under section 127 to the taxpayer by reason of the payment by the taxpayer's employer of any indebtedness on a qualified education loan of the taxpayer".

(c) EFFECTIVE DATE.—The amendments made by this section shall apply to payments made after the date of the enactment of this Act.

Subtitle C—Business Provisions

[¶2047] SEC. 2301. EMPLOYEE RETENTION CREDIT FOR EMPLOYERS SUBJECT TO CLOSURE DUE TO COVID–19.

(a) IN GENERAL.—In the case of an eligible employer, there shall be allowed as a credit against applicable employment taxes for each calendar quarter an amount equal to 50 percent of the qualified wages with respect to each employee of such employer for such calendar quarter.

(b) LIMITATIONS AND REFUNDABILITY.—

(1) WAGES TAKEN INTO ACCOUNT.—The amount of qualified wages with respect to any employee which may be taken into account under subsection (a) by the eligible employer for all calendar quarters shall not exceed $10,000.

(2) CREDIT LIMITED TO EMPLOYMENT TAXES.—The credit allowed by subsection (a) with respect to any calendar quarter shall not exceed the applicable employment taxes (reduced by any credits allowed under subsections (e) and (f) of section 3111 of the Internal Revenue Code of 1986 and sections 7001 and 7003 of the Families First Coronavirus Response Act) on the wages paid with respect to the employment of all the employees of the eligible employer for such calendar quarter.

(3) REFUNDABILITY OF EXCESS CREDIT.—

(A) IN GENERAL.—If the amount of the credit under subsection (a) exceeds the limitation of paragraph (2) for any calendar quarter, such excess shall be treated as an overpayment that shall be refunded under sections 6402(a) and 6413(b) of the Internal Revenue Code of 1986.

(B) TREATMENT OF PAYMENTS.—For purposes of section 1324 of title 31, United States Code, any amounts due to the employer under this paragraph shall be treated in the same manner as a refund due from a credit provision referred to in subsection (b)(2) of such section.

(c) DEFINITIONS.—For purposes of this section—

(1) APPLICABLE EMPLOYMENT TAXES.—The term "applicable employment taxes" means the following:

(A) The taxes imposed under section 3111(a) of the Internal Revenue Code of 1986.

(B) So much of the taxes imposed under section 3221(a) of such Code as are attributable to the rate in effect under section 3111(a) of such Code.

(2) ELIGIBLE EMPLOYER.—

(A) IN GENERAL.—The term "eligible employer" means any employer—

(i) which was carrying on a trade or business during calendar year 2020, and

(ii) with respect to any calendar quarter, for which—

(I) the operation of the trade or business described in clause (i) is fully or partially suspended during the calendar quarter due to orders from an appropriate governmental authority limiting commerce, travel, or group meetings (for commercial, social, religious, or other purposes) due to the coronavirus disease 2019 (COVID–19), or

(II) such calendar quarter is within the period described in subparagraph (B).

(B) SIGNIFICANT DECLINE IN GROSS RECEIPTS.—The period described in this subparagraph is the period—

(i) beginning with the first calendar quarter beginning after December 31, 2019, for which gross receipts (within the meaning of section 448(c) of the Internal Revenue Code of 1986) for the calendar quarter are less than 50 percent of gross receipts for the same calendar quarter in the prior year, and

(ii) ending with the calendar quarter following the first calendar quarter beginning after a calendar quarter described in clause (i) for which gross receipts of such employer are greater than 80 percent of gross receipts for the same calendar quarter in the prior year.

(C) TAX-EXEMPT ORGANIZATIONS.—In the case of an organization which is described in section 501(c) of the Internal Revenue Code of 1986 and exempt from tax under section 501(a) of such Code, clauses (i) and (ii)(I) of subparagraph (A) shall apply to all operations of such organization.

(3) QUALIFIED WAGES.—

(A) IN GENERAL.—The term "qualified wages" means—

(i) in the case of an eligible employer for which the average number of full-time employees (within the meaning of section 4980H of the Internal Revenue Code of 1986) employed by such eligible employer during 2019 was greater than 100, wages paid by such eligible employer with respect to which an employee is not providing services due to circumstances described in subclause (I) or (II) of paragraph (2)(A)(ii), or

(ii) in the case of an eligible employer for which the average number of full-time employees (within the meaning of section 4980H of the Internal Revenue Code of 1986) employed by such eligible employer during 2019 was not greater than 100—

(I) with respect to an eligible employer described in subclause (I) of paragraph (2)(A)(ii), wages paid by such eligible employer with respect to an employee during any period described in such clause, or

(II) with respect to an eligible employer described in subclause (II) of such paragraph, wages paid by such eligible employer with respect to an employee during such quarter.

Such term shall not include any wages taken into account under section 7001 or section 7003 of the Families First Coronavirus Response Act.

(B) LIMITATION.—Qualified wages paid or incurred by an eligible employer described in subparagraph (A)(i) with respect to an employee for any period described in such subparagraph may not exceed the amount such employee would have been paid for working an equivalent duration during the 30 days immediately preceding such period.

(C) ALLOWANCE FOR CERTAIN HEALTH PLAN EXPENSES.—

(i) IN GENERAL.—The term "qualified wages" shall include so much of the eligible employer's qualified health plan expenses as are properly allocable to such wages.

(ii) QUALIFIED HEALTH PLAN EXPENSES.—For purposes of this paragraph, the term "qualified health plan expenses" means amounts paid or incurred by the eligible employer to provide and maintain a group health plan (as defined in section 5000(b)(1) of the Internal Revenue Code of 1986), but only to the extent that such amounts are excluded from the gross income of employees by reason of section 106(a) of such Code.

(iii) ALLOCATION RULES.—For purposes of this paragraph, qualified health plan expenses shall be allocated to qualified wages in such manner as the Secretary may prescribe. Except as otherwise provided by the Secretary, such allocation shall be treated as properly made if made on the basis of being pro rata among employees and pro rata on the basis of periods of coverage (relative to the periods to which such wages relate).

(4) SECRETARY.—The term "Secretary" means the Secretary of the Treasury or the Secretary's delegate.

(5) WAGES.—The term "wages" means wages (as defined in section 3121(a) of the Internal Revenue Code of 1986) and compensation (as defined in section 3231(e) of such Code).

(6) OTHER TERMS.—Any term used in this section which is also used in chapter 21 or 22 of the Internal Revenue Code of 1986 shall have the same meaning as when used in such chapter.

(d) AGGREGATION RULE.—All persons treated as a single employer under subsection (a) or (b) of section 52 of the Internal Revenue Code of 1986, or subsection (m) or (o) of section 414 of such Code, shall be treated as one employer for purposes of this section.

(e) CERTAIN RULES TO APPLY.—For purposes of this section, rules similar to the rules of sections 51(i)(1) and 280C(a) of the Internal Revenue Code of 1986 shall apply.

(f) CERTAIN GOVERNMENTAL EMPLOYERS.—This credit shall not apply to the Government of the United States, the government of any State or political subdivision thereof, or any agency or instrumentality of any of the foregoing.

(g) ELECTION NOT TO HAVE SECTION APPLY.—This section shall not apply with respect to any eligible employer for any calendar quarter if such employer elects (at such time and in such manner as the Secretary may prescribe) not to have this section apply.

(h) SPECIAL RULES.—

(1) EMPLOYEE NOT TAKEN INTO ACCOUNT MORE THAN ONCE.—An employee shall not be included for purposes of this section for any period with respect to any employer if such employer is allowed a credit under section 51 of the Internal Revenue Code of 1986 with respect to such employee for such period.

(2) DENIAL OF DOUBLE BENEFIT.—Any wages taken into account in determining the credit allowed under this section shall not be taken into account for purposes of determining the credit allowed under section 45S of such Code.

(3) THIRD PARTY PAYORS.—Any credit allowed under this section shall be treated as a credit described in section 3511(d)(2) of such Code.

(i) TRANSFERS TO FEDERAL OLD-AGE AND SURVIVORS INSURANCE TRUST FUND.—There are hereby appropriated to the Federal Old-Age and Survivors Insurance Trust Fund and the Federal Disability Insurance Trust Fund established under section 201 of the Social Security Act (42 U.S.C. 401) and the Social Security Equivalent Benefit Account established under section 15A(a) of the Railroad Retirement Act of 1974 (45 U.S.C. 14 231n–1(a)) amounts equal to the reduction in revenues to the Treasury by reason of this section (without regard to this subsection). Amounts appropriated by the preceding sentence shall be transferred from the general fund at such times and in such manner as to replicate to the extent possible the transfers which would have occurred to such Trust Fund or Account had this section not been enacted.

(j) RULE FOR EMPLOYERS TAKING SMALL BUSINESS INTERRUPTION LOAN.—If an eligible employer receives a covered loan under paragraph (36) of section 7(a) of the Small Business Act (15 U.S.C. 636(a)), as added by section 1102 of this Act, such employer shall not be eligible for the credit under this section.

(k) TREATMENT OF DEPOSITS.—The Secretary shall waive any penalty under section 6656 of the Internal Revenue Code of 1986 for any failure to make a deposit of any applicable employment taxes if the Secretary determines that such failure was due to the reasonable anticipation of the credit allowed under this section.

(l) REGULATIONS AND GUIDANCE.—The Secretary shall issue such forms, instructions, regulations, and guidance as are necessary—

(1) to allow the advance payment of the credit under subsection (a), subject to the limitations provided in this section, based on such information as the Secretary shall require,

(2) to provide for the reconciliation of such advance payment with the amount advanced at the time of filing the return of tax for the applicable calendar quarter or taxable year,

(3) to provide for the recapture of the credit under this section if such credit is allowed to a taxpayer which receives a loan described in subsection (j) during a subsequent quarter,

(4) with respect to the application of the credit under subsection (a) to third party payors (including professional employer organizations, certified professional employer organizations, or agents under section 3504 of the Internal Revenue Code of 1986), including regulations or guidance allowing such payors to submit documentation necessary to substantiate the eligible employer status of employers that use such payors, and

(5) for application of subparagraphs (A)(ii)(II) and (B) of subsection (c)(2) in the case of any employer which was not carrying on a trade or business for all or part of the same calendar quarter in the prior year.

(m) APPLICATION.—This section shall only apply to wages paid after March 12, 2020, and before January 1, 2021.

[¶2048] SEC. 2302. DELAY OF PAYMENT OF EMPLOYER PAYROLL TAXES.

(a) IN GENERAL.—

(1) TAXES.—Notwithstanding any other provision of law, the payment for applicable employment taxes for the payroll tax deferral period shall not be due before the applicable date.

(2) DEPOSITS.—Notwithstanding section 6302 of the Internal Revenue Code of 1986, an employer shall be treated as having timely made all deposits of applicable employment taxes that are required to be made (without regard to this section) for such taxes during the payroll tax deferral period if all such deposits are made not later than the applicable date.

(3) EXCEPTION.—This subsection shall not apply to any taxpayer if such taxpayer has had indebtedness forgiven under section 1106 of this Act with respect to a loan under paragraph (36) of section 7(a) of the Small Business Act (15 U.S.C. 636(a)), as added by section 1102 of this Act, or indebtedness forgiven under section 1109 of this Act.

(b) SECA.—

(1) IN GENERAL.—Notwithstanding any other provision of law, the payment for 50 percent of the taxes imposed under section 1401(a) of the Internal Revenue Code of 1986 for the payroll tax deferral period shall not be due before the applicable date.

(2) ESTIMATED TAXES.—For purposes of applying section 6654 of the Internal Revenue Code of 1986 to any taxable year which includes any part of the payroll tax deferral period, 50 percent of the taxes imposed under section 1401(a) of such Code for the payroll tax deferral period shall not be treated as taxes to which such section 6654 applies.

(c) LIABILITY OF THIRD PARTIES.—

(1) ACTS TO BE PERFORMED BY AGENTS.—For purposes of section 3504 of the Internal Revenue Code of 1986, in the case of any person designated pursuant to such section (and any regulations or other guidance issued by the Secretary with respect to such section) to perform acts otherwise required to be performed by an employer under such Code, if such employer directs such person to defer payment of any applicable employment taxes during the payroll tax deferral period under this section, such employer shall be solely liable for the payment of such applicable employment taxes before the applicable date for any wages paid by such person on behalf of such employer during such period.

(2) CERTIFIED PROFESSIONAL EMPLOYER ORGANIZATIONS.—For purposes of section 3511, in the case of a certified professional employer organization (as defined in subsection (a) of section 7705 of the Internal Revenue Code of 1986) that has entered into a service contract described in subsection (e)(2) of such section with a customer, if such customer directs such organization to defer payment of any applicable employment taxes during the payroll tax deferral period under this section, such customer shall, notwithstanding subsections (a) and (c) of section 3511, be solely liable for the payment of such applicable employment taxes before the applicable date for any wages paid by such organization to any work site employee performing services for such customer during such period.

(d) DEFINITIONS.—For purposes of this section—

(1) APPLICABLE EMPLOYMENT TAXES.—The term "applicable employment taxes" means the following:

(A) The taxes imposed under section 3111(a) of the Internal Revenue Code of 1986.

(B) So much of the taxes imposed under section 3211(a) of such Code as are attributable to the rate in effect under section 3111(a) of such Code.

(C) So much of the taxes imposed under section 3221(a) of such Code as are attributable to the rate in effect under section 3111(a) of such Code.

(2) PAYROLL TAX DEFERRAL PERIOD.—The term "payroll tax deferral period" means the period beginning on the date of the enactment of this Act and ending before January 1, 2021.

(3) APPLICABLE DATE.—The term "applicable date" means—

(A) December 31, 2021, with respect to 50 percent of the amounts to which subsection (a) or (b), as the case may be, apply, and

(B) December 31, 2022, with respect to the remaining such amounts.

(4) SECRETARY.—The term "Secretary" means the Secretary of the Treasury (or the Secretary's delegate).

(e) TRUST FUNDS HELD HARMLESS.—There are hereby appropriated (out of any money in the Treasury not otherwise appropriated) for each fiscal year to the Federal Old-Age and Survivors Insurance Trust Fund and the Federal Disability Insurance Trust Fund established under section 201 of the Social Security Act (42 U.S.C. 401) and the Social Security Equivalent Benefit Account established under section 15A(a) of the Railroad Retirement Act of 1974 (45 U.S.C. 231n–1(a)) an amount equal to the reduction in the transfers to such fund for such fiscal year by reason of this section. Amounts appropriated by the preceding sentence shall be transferred from the general fund at such times and in such manner as to replicate to the extent possible the transfers which would have occurred to such Trust Fund had such amendments not been enacted.

(f) REGULATORY AUTHORITY.—The Secretary shall issue such regulations or other guidance as necessary to carry out the purposes of this section, including rules for the administration and enforcement of subsection (c).

[¶2049] SEC. 2303. MODIFICATIONS FOR NET OPERATING LOSSES.

(a) TEMPORARY REPEAL OF TAXABLE INCOME LIMITATION.—

(1) IN GENERAL.—The first sentence of section 172(a) of the Internal Revenue Code of 1986 is amended by striking "an amount equal to" and all that follows and inserting an amount equal to—

(1) "in the case of a taxable year beginning before January 1, 2021, the aggregate of the net operating loss carryovers to such year, plus the net operating loss carrybacks to such year, and

(2) "in the case of a taxable year beginning after December 31, 2020, the sum of—

(A) "the aggregate amount of net operating losses arising in taxable years beginning before January 1, 2018, carried to such taxable year, plus

(B) "the lesser of—

(i) "the aggregate amount of net operating losses arising in taxable years beginning after December 31, 2017, carried to such taxable year, or

(ii) "80 percent of the excess (if any) of—

(I) "taxable income computed without regard to the deductions under this section and sections 199A and 250, over

(II) "the amount determined under subparagraph (A).".

(2) CONFORMING AMENDMENTS.—

(A) Section 172(b)(2)(C) of such Code is amended to read as follows:

(C) "for taxable years beginning after December 31, 2020, be reduced by 20 percent of the excess (if any) described in subsection (a)(2)(B)(ii) for such taxable year.".

(B) Section 172(d)(6)(C) of such Code is amended by striking "subsection (a)(2)" and inserting "subsection (a)(2)(B)(ii)(I)".

(C) Section 860E(a)(3)(B) of such Code is amended by striking all that follows "for purposes of" and inserting "subsection (a)(2)(B)(ii)(I) and the second sentence of subsection (b)(2) of section 172.".

(b) MODIFICATIONS OF RULES RELATING TO CARRYBACKS.—

(1) IN GENERAL.—Section 172(b)(1) of the Internal Revenue Code of 1986 is amended by adding at the end the following new subparagraph:

(D) "SPECIAL RULE FOR LOSSES ARISING IN 2018, 2019, AND 2020.—

(i) "IN GENERAL.—In the case of any net operating loss arising in a taxable year beginning after December 31, 2017, and before January 1, 2021—

(I) "such loss shall be a net operating loss carryback to each of the 5 taxable years preceding the taxable year of such loss, and

(II) "subparagraphs (B) and (C)(i) shall not apply.

(ii) "SPECIAL RULES FOR REITS.—For purposes of this subparagraph—

(I) "IN GENERAL.—A net operating loss for a REIT year shall not be a net operating loss carryback to any taxable year preceding the taxable year of such loss.

(II) "SPECIAL RULE.—In the case of any net operating loss for a taxable year which is not a REIT year, such loss shall not be carried to any preceding taxable year which is a REIT year.

(III) "REIT YEAR.—For purposes of this subparagraph, the term 'REIT year' means any taxable year for which the provisions of part II of subchapter M (relating to real estate investment trusts) apply to the taxpayer.

(iii) "SPECIAL RULE FOR LIFE INSURANCE COMPANIES.—In the case of a life insurance company, if a net operating loss is carried pursuant to clause (i)(I) to a life insurance company taxable year beginning before January 1, 2018, such net operating loss carryback shall be treated in the same manner as an operations loss carryback (within the meaning of section 810 as in effect before its repeal) of such company to such taxable year.

(iv) "RULE RELATING TO CARRYBACKS TO YEARS TO WHICH SECTION 965 APPLIES.—If a net operating loss of a taxpayer is carried pursuant to clause (i)(I) to any taxable year in which an amount is includible in gross income by reason of section 965(a), the taxpayer shall be treated as having made the election under section 965(n) with respect to each such taxable year.

(v) "SPECIAL RULES FOR ELECTIONS UNDER PARAGRAPH (3).—

(I) "SPECIAL ELECTION TO EXCLUDE SECTION 965 YEARS.—If the 5-year carryback period under clause (i)(I) with respect to any net operating loss of a taxpayer includes 1 or more taxable years in which an amount is includible in gross income by reason of section 965(a), the taxpayer may, in lieu of the election otherwise available under paragraph (3), elect under such paragraph to exclude all such taxable years from such carryback period.

(II) "TIME OF ELECTIONS.—An election under paragraph (3) (including an election described in subclause (I)) with respect to a net operating loss arising in a taxable year beginning in 2018 or 2019 shall be made by the due date (including extensions of time) for filing the taxpayer's return for the first taxable year ending after the date of the enactment of this subparagraph.".

(2) CONFORMING AMENDMENT.—Section 172(b)(1)(A) of such Code, as amended by subsection (c)(2), is amended by striking "and (C)(i)" and inserting ", (C)(i), and (D)".

(c) TECHNICAL AMENDMENT RELATING TO SECTION 13302 OF PUBLIC LAW 115–97.—

(1) Section 13302(e) of Public Law 115–97 is amended to read as follows:

(e) "EFFECTIVE DATES.—

(1) "NET OPERATING LOSS LIMITATION.—The amendments made by subsections (a) and (d)(2) shall apply to—

(A) "taxable years beginning after December 31, 2017, and

(B) "taxable years beginning on or before such date to which net operating losses arising in taxable years beginning after such date are carried.

(2) "CARRYOVERS AND CARRYBACKS.—The amendments made by subsections (b), (c), and (d)(1) shall apply to net operating losses arising in taxable years beginning after December 31, 2017.".

(2) Section 172(b)(1)(A) of the Internal Revenue Code of 1986 is amended to read as follows:

(A) "GENERAL RULE.—A net operating loss for any taxable year—

(i) "shall be a net operating loss carryback to the extent provided in subparagraphs (B) and (C)(i), and

(ii) "except as provided in subparagraph (C)(ii), shall be a net operating loss carryover—

(I) "in the case of a net operating loss arising in a taxable year beginning before January 1, 2018, to each of the 20 taxable years following the taxable year of the loss, and

(II) "in the case of a net operating loss arising in a taxable year beginning after December 31, 2017, to each taxable year following the taxable year of the loss.".

(d) EFFECTIVE DATES.—

(1) NET OPERATING LOSS LIMITATION.—The amendments made by subsection (a) shall apply—

(A) to taxable years beginning after December 31, 2017, and

(B) to taxable years beginning on or before December 31, 2017, to which net operating losses arising in taxable years beginning after December 31, 2017, are carried.

(2) CARRYOVERS AND CARRYBACKS.—The amendment made by subsection (b) shall apply to—

(A) net operating losses arising in taxable years beginning after December 31, 2017, and

(B) taxable years beginning before, on, or after such date to which such net operating losses are carried.

(3) TECHNICAL AMENDMENTS.—The amendments made by subsection (c) shall take effect as if included in the provisions of Public Law 115–97 to which they relate.

(4) SPECIAL RULE.—In the case of a net operating loss arising in a taxable year beginning before January 1, 2018, and ending after December 31, 2017—

(A) an application under section 6411(a) of the Internal Revenue Code of 1986 with respect to the carryback of such net operating loss shall not fail to be treated as timely filed if filed not later than the date which is 120 days after the date of the enactment of this Act, and

(B) an election to—

(i) forgo any carryback of such net operating loss,

(ii) reduce any period to which such net operating loss may be carried back, or

(iii) revoke any election made under section 172(b) to forgo any carryback of such net operating loss,

shall not fail to be treated as timely made if made not later than the date which is 120 days after the date of the enactment of this Act.

[¶2050] SEC. 2304. MODIFICATION OF LIMITATION ON LOSSES FOR TAXPAYERS OTHER THAN CORPORATIONS.

(a) IN GENERAL.—Section 461(l)(1) of the Internal Revenue Code of 1986 is amended to read as follows:

(1) "LIMITATION.—In the case of a taxpayer other than a corporation—

(A) "for any taxable year beginning after December 31, 2017, and before January 1, 2026, subsection (j) (relating to limitation on excess farm losses of certain taxpayers) shall not apply, and

(B) "for any taxable year beginning after December 31, 2020, and before January 1, 2026, any excess business loss of the taxpayer for the taxable year shall not be allowed.".

(b) TECHNICAL AMENDMENTS RELATING TO SECTION 11012 OF PUBLIC LAW 115–97.—

(1) Section 461(l)(2) of the Internal Revenue Code of 1986 is amended by striking "a net operating loss carryover to the following taxable year under section 172" and inserting "a net operating loss for the taxable year for purposes of determining any net operating loss carryover under section 172(b) for subsequent taxable years".

(2) Section 461(l)(3)(A) of such Code is amended—

(A) in clause (i), by inserting "and without regard to any deduction allowable under section 172 or 199A" after "under paragraph (1)", and

(B) by adding at the end the following flush sentence:

"Such excess shall be determined without regard to any deductions, gross income, or gains attributable to any trade or business of performing services as an employee.".

(3) Section 461(l)(3) of such Code is amended by redesignating subparagraph (B) as subparagraph (C) and by inserting after subparagraph (A) the following new subparagraph:

(B) "TREATMENT OF CAPITAL GAINS AND LOSSES.—

(i) "LOSSES.—Deductions for losses from sales or exchanges of capital assets shall not be taken into account under subparagraph (A)(i).

(ii) "GAINS.—The amount of gains from sales or exchanges of capital assets taken into account under subparagraph (A)(ii) shall not exceed the lesser of—

(I) "the capital gain net income determined by taking into account only gains and losses attributable to a trade or business, or

(II) "the capital gain net income.".

(c) EFFECTIVE DATES.—

(1) IN GENERAL.—The amendments made by subsection (a) shall apply to taxable years beginning after December 31, 2017.

(2) TECHNICAL AMENDMENTS.—The amendments made by subsection (b) shall take effect as if included in the provisions of Public Law 115–97 to which they relate.

[¶2051] SEC. 2305. MODIFICATION OF CREDIT FOR PRIOR YEAR MINIMUM TAX LIABILITY OF CORPORATIONS.

(a) IN GENERAL.—Section 53(e) of the Internal Revenue Code of 1986 is amended—

(1) by striking "2018, 2019, 2020, or 2021" in paragraph (1) and inserting "2018 or 2019", and

(2) by striking "2021" in paragraph (2) and inserting "2019".

(b) ELECTION TO TAKE ENTIRE REFUNDABLE CREDIT AMOUNT IN 2018.—

(1) IN GENERAL.—Section 53(e) of such Code is amended by adding at the end the following new paragraph:

(5) "SPECIAL RULE.—In the case of a corporation making an election under this paragraph—

(A) "paragraph (1) shall not apply, and

(B) "subsection (c) shall not apply to the first taxable year of such corporation beginning in 2018.".

(c) EFFECTIVE DATE.—The amendments made by this section shall apply to taxable years beginning after December 31, 2017.

(d) SPECIAL RULE.—

(1) IN GENERAL.—For purposes of the Internal Revenue Code of 1986, a credit or refund for which an application described in paragraph (2)(A) is filed shall be treated as made under section 6411 of such Code.

(2) TENTATIVE REFUND.—

(A) APPLICATION.—A taxpayer may file an application for a tentative refund of any amount for which a refund is due by reason of an election under section 53(e)(5) of the Internal Revenue Code of 1986. Such application shall be in such manner and form as the Secretary of the Treasury (or the Secretary's delegate) may prescribe and shall—

(i) be verified in the same manner as an application under section 6411(a) of such Code,

(ii) be filed prior to December 31, 2020, and

(iii) set forth—

(I) the amount of the refundable credit claimed under section 53(e) of such Code for such taxable year,

(II) the amount of the refundable credit claimed under such section for any previously filed return for such taxable year, and

(III) the amount of the refund claimed.

(B) ALLOWANCE OF ADJUSTMENTS.—Within a period of 90 days from the date on which an application is filed under subparagraph (A), the Secretary of the Treasury (or the Secretary's delegate) shall—

(i) review the application,

(ii) determine the amount of the overpayment, and

(iii) apply, credit, or refund such overpayment,

in a manner similar to the manner provided in section 6411(b) of the Internal Revenue Code of 1986.

(C) CONSOLIDATED RETURNS.—The provisions of section 6411(c) of the Internal Revenue Code of 1986 Code shall apply to an adjustment under this paragraph to the same extent and manner as the Secretary of the Treasury (or the Secretary's delegate) may provide.

[¶2052] SEC. 2306. MODIFICATIONS OF LIMITATION ON BUSINESS INTEREST.

(a) IN GENERAL.—Section 163(j) of the Internal Revenue Code of 1986 is amended by redesignating paragraph (10) as paragraph (11) and by inserting after paragraph (9) the following new paragraph:

(10) "SPECIAL RULE FOR TAXABLE YEARS BEGINNING IN 2019 AND 2020.—

(A) "IN GENERAL.—

(i) "IN GENERAL.—Except as provided in clause (ii) or (iii), in the case of any taxable year beginning in 2019 or 2020, paragraph (1)(B) shall be applied by substituting '50 percent' for '30 percent'.

(ii) "SPECIAL RULE FOR PARTNERSHIPS.—In the case of a partnership—

(I) "clause (i) shall not apply to any taxable year beginning in 2019, but

(II) "unless a partner elects not to have this subclause apply, in the case of any excess business interest of the partnership for any taxable year beginning in 2019 which is allocated to the partner under paragraph (4)(B)(i)(II)—

(aa) "50 percent of such excess business interest shall be treated as business interest which, notwithstanding paragraph (4)(B)(ii), is paid or accrued by the partner in the partner's first taxable year beginning in 2020 and which is not subject to the limits of paragraph (1), and

(bb) "50 percent of such excess business interest shall be subject to the limitations of paragraph (4)(B)(ii) in the same manner as any other excess business interest so allocated.

(iii) "ELECTION OUT.—A taxpayer may elect, at such time and in such manner as the Secretary may prescribe, not to have clause (i) apply to any taxable year. Such an election, once made, may be revoked only with the consent of the Secretary. In the case of a partnership, any such election shall be made by the partnership and may be made only for taxable years beginning in 2020.

(B) "ELECTION TO USE 2019 ADJUSTED TAXABLE INCOME FOR TAXABLE YEARS BEGINNING IN 2020.—

(i) "IN GENERAL.—Subject to clause (ii), in the case of any taxable year beginning in 2020, the taxpayer may elect to apply this subsection by substituting the adjusted taxable income of the taxpayer for the last taxable year beginning in 2019 for the adjusted taxable income for such taxable year. In the case of a partnership, any such election shall be made by the partnership.

(ii) "SPECIAL RULE FOR SHORT TAXABLE YEARS.—If an election is made under clause (i) for a taxable year which is a short taxable year, the adjusted taxable income for the taxpayer's last taxable year beginning in 2019 which is substituted under clause (i) shall be equal to the amount which bears the same ratio to such adjusted taxable income determined without regard to this clause as the number of months in the short taxable year bears to 12".

(b) EFFECTIVE DATE.—The amendments made by this section shall apply to taxable years beginning after December 31, 2018.

[¶2053] SEC. 2307. TECHNICAL AMENDMENTS REGARDING QUALIFIED IMPROVEMENT PROPERTY.

(a) IN GENERAL.—Section 168 of the Internal Revenue Code of 1986 is amended—

(1) in subsection (e)—

(A) in paragraph (3)(E), by striking "and" at the end of clause (v), by striking the period at the end of clause (vi) and inserting ", and", and by adding at the end the following new clause:

(vii) "any qualified improvement property.", and

(B) in paragraph (6)(A), by inserting "made by the taxpayer" after "any improvement", and

(2) in the table contained in subsection (g)(3)(B)—

(A) by striking the item relating to subparagraph (D)(v), and

(B) by inserting after the item relating to subparagraph (E)(vi) the following new item:

"(E)(vii) . . . . 20".

(b) EFFECTIVE DATE.—The amendments made by this section shall take effect as if included in section 13204 of Public Law 115–97.

[¶2054] SEC. 2308. TEMPORARY EXCEPTION FROM EXCISE TAX FOR ALCOHOL USED TO PRODUCE HAND SANITIZER.

(a) IN GENERAL.—Section 5214(a) of the Internal Revenue Code of 1986 is amended—

(1) in paragraph (13), by striking the period at the end and inserting "; or", and

(2) by adding at the end the following new paragraph:

(14) "with respect to distilled spirits removed after December 31, 2019, and before January 1, 2021, free of tax for use in or contained in hand sanitizer produced and distributed in a manner consistent with any guidance issued by the Food and Drug Administration that is related to the outbreak of virus SARS–CoV–2 or coronavirus disease 2019 (COVID–19).".

(b) EFFECTIVE DATE.—The amendments made by this section shall apply to distilled spirits removed after December 31, 2019.

(c) APPLICATION OF OTHER LAWS.—Any distilled spirits or product described in paragraph (14) of section 5214(a) of the Internal Revenue Code of 1986 (as added by this section) shall not be subject to any requirements related to labeling or bulk sales under—

(1) section 105 or 106 of the Federal Alcohol Administration Act (27 U.S.C. 205, 206); or

(2) section 204 of the Alcoholic Beverage Labeling Act of 1988 (27 U.S.C. 215).

TITLE III—SUPPORTING AMERICA'S HEALTH CARE SYSTEM IN THE FIGHT AGAINST THE CORONAVIRUS

Subtitle A—Health Provisions

[¶2057] SEC. 3001. SHORT TITLE.

This subtitle may be cited as the "Coronavirus Aid, Relief, and Economic Security Act".

PART I—ADDRESSING SUPPLY SHORTAGES

Subpart A—Medical Product Supplies

[¶2060] SEC. 3101. NATIONAL ACADEMIES REPORT ON AMERICA'S MEDICAL PRODUCT SUPPLY CHAIN SECURITY.

(a) IN GENERAL.—Not later than 60 days after the date of enactment of this Act, the Secretary of Health and Human Services shall enter into an agreement with the National Academies of Sciences, Engineering, and Medicine (referred to in this section as the "National Academies") to examine, and, in a manner that does not compromise national security, report on, the security of the United States medical product supply chain.

(b) PURPOSES.—The report developed under this section shall—

(1) assess and evaluate the dependence of the United States, including the private commercial sector, States, and the Federal Government, on critical drugs and devices that are sourced or manufactured outside of the United States, which may include an analysis of—

(A) the supply chain of critical drugs and devices of greatest priority to providing health care;

(B) any potential public health security or national security risks associated with reliance on critical drugs and devices sourced or manufactured outside of the United States, which may include responses to previous or existing shortages or public health emergencies, such as infectious disease outbreaks, bioterror attacks, and other public health threats;

(C) any existing supply chain information gaps, as applicable; and

(D) potential economic impact of increased domestic manufacturing; and

(2) provide recommendations, which may include a plan to improve the resiliency of the supply chain for critical drugs and devices as described in paragraph (1), and to address any supply vulnerabilities or potential disruptions of such products that would significantly affect or pose a threat to public health security or national security, as appropriate, which may include strategies to—

(A) promote supply chain redundancy and contingency planning;

(B) encourage domestic manufacturing, including consideration of economic impacts, if any;

(C) improve supply chain information gaps;

(D) improve planning considerations for medical product supply chain capacity during public health emergencies; and

(E) promote the accessibility of such drugs and devices.

(c) INPUT.—In conducting the study and developing the report under subsection (b), the National Academies shall—

(1) consider input from the Department of Health and Human Services, the Department of Homeland Security, the Department of Defense, the Department of Commerce, the Department of State, the Department of Veterans Affairs, the Department of Justice, and any other Federal agencies as appropriate; and

(2) consult with relevant stakeholders, which may include conducting public meetings and other forms of engagement, as appropriate, with health care providers, medical professional societies, State-based societies, public health experts, State and local public health departments, State medical boards, patient groups, medical product manufacturers, health care distributors, wholesalers and group purchasing organizations, pharmacists, and other entities with experience in health care and public health, as appropriate.

(d) DEFINITIONS.—In this section, the terms "device" and "drug" have the meanings given such terms in section 201 of the Federal Food, Drug, and Cosmetic Act (21 U.S.C. 321).

[¶2061] SEC. 3102. REQUIRING THE STRATEGIC NATIONAL STOCKPILE TO INCLUDE CERTAIN TYPES OF MEDICAL SUPPLIES.

Section 319F–2(a)(1) of the Public Health Service Act (42 U.S.C. 247d–6b(a)(1)) is amended by inserting "(including personal protective equipment, ancillary medical supplies, and other applicable supplies required for the administration of drugs, vaccines and other biological products, medical devices, and diagnostic tests in the stockpile)" after "other supplies".

[¶2062] SEC. 3103. TREATMENT OF RESPIRATORY PROTECTIVE DEVICES AS COVERED COUNTERMEASURES.

Section 319F–3(i)(1)(D) of the Public Health Service Act (42 U.S.C. 247d–6d(i)(1)(D)) is amended to read as follows:

(D) "a respiratory protective device that is approved by the National Institute for Occupational Safety and Health under part 84 of title 42, Code of Federal Regulations (or any successor regulations), and that the Secretary determines to be a priority for use during a public health emergency declared under section 319.".

Subpart B—Mitigating Emergency Drug Shortages

[¶2064] SEC. 3111. PRIORITIZE REVIEWS OF DRUG APPLICATIONS; INCENTIVES.

Section 506C(g) of the Federal Food, Drug, and Cosmetic Act (21 U.S.C. 356c(g)) is amended—

(1) in paragraph (1), by striking "the Secretary may" and inserting "the Secretary shall, as appropriate";

(2) in paragraph (1), by inserting "prioritize and" before "expedite the review"; and

(3) in paragraph (2), by inserting "prioritize and" before "expedite an inspection".

[¶2065] SEC. 3112. ADDITIONAL MANUFACTURER REPORTING REQUIREMENTS IN RESPONSE TO DRUG SHORTAGES.

(a) EXPANSION TO INCLUDE ACTIVE PHARMACEUTICAL INGREDIENTS.—Subsection (a) of section 506C of the Federal Food, Drug, and Cosmetic Act (21 U.S.C. 356c) is amended—

(1) in paragraph (1)(C), by inserting "or any such drug that is critical to the public health during a public health emergency declared by the Secretary under section 319 of the Public Health Service Act" after "during surgery"; and

(2) in the flush text at the end—

(A) by inserting ", or a permanent discontinuance in the manufacture of an active pharmaceutical ingredient or an interruption in the manufacture of the active pharmaceutical ingredient of such drug that is likely to lead to a meaningful disruption in the supply of the active pharmaceutical ingredient of such drug," before "and the reasons"; and

(B) by adding at the end the following: "Notification under this subsection shall include disclosure of reasons for the discontinuation or interruption, and if applicable, an active pharmaceutical ingredient is a reason for, or risk factor in, such discontinuation or interruption, the source of the active pharmaceutical ingredient and any alternative sources for the active pharmaceutical ingredient known by the manufacturer; whether any associated device used for preparation or administration included in the drug is a reason for, or a risk factor in, such discontinuation or interruption; the expected duration of the interruption; and such other information as the Secretary may require.".

(b) RISK MANAGEMENT.—Section 506C of the Federal Food, Drug, and Cosmetic Act (21 U.S.C. 356c) is amended by adding at the end the following:

(j) "RISK MANAGEMENT PLANS.—Each manufacturer of a drug described in subsection (a) or of any active pharmaceutical ingredient or any associated medical device used for preparation or administration included in the drug, shall develop, maintain, and implement, as appropriate, a redundancy risk management plan that identifies and evaluates risks to the supply of the drug, as applicable, for each establishment in which such drug or active pharmaceutical ingredient of such drug is manufactured. A risk management plan under this section shall be subject to inspection and copying by the Secretary pursuant to an inspection or a request under section 704(a)(4).".

(c) ANNUAL NOTIFICATION.—Section 506E of the Federal Food, Drug, and Cosmetic Act (21 U.S.C. 356e) is amended by adding at the end the following:

(d) "INTERAGENCY NOTIFICATION.—Not later than 180 days after the date of enactment of this subsection, and every 90 days thereafter, the Secretary shall transmit a report regarding the drugs of the current drug shortage list under this section to the Administrator of the Centers for Medicare & Medicaid Services.".

(d) REPORTING AFTER INSPECTIONS.—Section 704(b) of the Federal Food, Drug, and Cosmetic Act (21 U.S.C. 374(b)) is amended—

(1) by redesignating paragraphs (1) and (2) and subparagraphs (A) and (B);

(2) by striking "(b) Upon completion" and inserting "(b)(1) Upon completion"; and

(3) by adding at the end the following:

(2) "In carrying out this subsection with respect to any establishment manufacturing a drug approved under subsection (c) or (j) of section 505 for which a notification has been submitted in accordance with section 506C is, or has been in the last 5 years, listed on the drug shortage list under section 506E, or that is described in section 505(j)(11)(A), a copy of the report shall be sent promptly to

the appropriate offices of the Food and Drug Administration with expertise regarding drug shortages.".

(e) REPORTING REQUIREMENT.—Section 510(j) of the Federal Food, Drug, Cosmetic Act (21 U.S.C. 360(j)) is amended—

(1) by redesignating paragraphs (3) and (4) as paragraphs (4) and (5), respectively; and

(2) by inserting after paragraph (2) the following:

(3)(A) "Each person who registers with the Secretary under this section with regard to a drug shall report annually to the Secretary on the amount of each drug listed under paragraph (1) that was manufactured, prepared, propagated, compounded, or processed by such person for commercial distribution. Such information may be required to be submitted in an electronic format as determined by the Secretary. The Secretary may require that information required to be reported under this paragraph be submitted at the time a public health emergency is declared by the Secretary under section 319 of the Public Health Service Act.

(B) "By order of the Secretary, certain biological products or categories of biological products regulated under section 351 of the Public Health Service Act may be exempt from some or all of the reporting requirements under subparagraph (A), if the Secretary determines that applying such reporting requirements to such biological products or categories of biological products is not necessary to protect the public health.".

(f) CONFIDENTIALITY.—Nothing in the amendments made by this section shall be construed as authorizing the Secretary to disclose any information that is a trade secret or confidential information subject to section 552(b)(4) of title 5, United States Code, or section 1905 of title 18, United States Code.

(g) EFFECTIVE DATE.—The amendments made by this section and section 3111 shall take effect on the date that is 180 days after the date of enactment of this Act.

Subpart C—Preventing Medical Device Shortages

[¶2067] SEC. 3121. DISCONTINUANCE OR INTERRUPTION IN THE PRODUCTION OF MEDICAL DEVICES.

Chapter V of the Federal Food, Drug, and Cosmetic Act (21 U.S.C. 351 et seq.) is amended by inserting after section 506I the following:

[¶2068] SEC. 506J. "DISCONTINUANCE OR INTERRUPTION IN THE PRODUCTION OF MEDICAL DEVICES.

(a) "IN GENERAL.—A manufacturer of a device that—

(1) "is critical to public health during a public health emergency, including devices that are life-supporting, life-sustaining, or intended for use in emergency medical care or during surgery; or

(2) "for which the Secretary determines that information on potential meaningful supply disruptions of such device is needed during, or in advance of, a public health emergency;

shall, during, or in advance of, a public health emergency declared by the Secretary under section 319 of the Public Health Service Act, notify the Secretary, in accordance with subsection (b), of a permanent discontinuance in the manufacture of the device (except for discontinuances as a result of an approved modification of the device) or an interruption of the manufacture of the device that is likely to lead to a meaningful disruption in the supply of that device in the United States, and the reasons for such discontinuance or interruption.

(b) "TIMING.—A notice required under subsection (a) shall be submitted to the Secretary—

(1) "at least 6 months prior to the date of the discontinuance or interruption; or

(2) "if compliance with paragraph (1) is not possible, as soon as practicable.

(c) "DISTRIBUTION.—

(1) "PUBLIC AVAILABILITY.—To the maximum extent practicable, subject to paragraph (2), the Secretary shall distribute, through such means as the Secretary determines appropriate, information on the discontinuance or interruption of the manufacture of devices reported under subsection (a) to

appropriate organizations, including physician, health provider, patient organizations, and supply chain partners, as appropriate and applicable, as described in subsection (g).

(2) "PUBLIC HEALTH EXCEPTION.—The Secretary may choose not to make information collected under this section publicly available pursuant to this section if the Secretary determines that disclosure of such information would adversely affect the public health, such as by increasing the possibility of unnecessary over purchase of product, component parts, or other disruption of the availability of medical products to patients.

(d) "CONFIDENTIALITY.—Nothing in this section shall be construed as authorizing the Secretary to disclose any information that is a trade secret or confidential information subject to section 552(b)(4) of title 5, United States Code, or section 1905 of title 18, United States Code.

(e) "FAILURE TO MEET REQUIREMENTS.—If a person fails to submit information required under subsection (a) in accordance with subsection (b)—

(1) "the Secretary shall issue a letter to such person informing such person of such failure;

(2) "not later than 30 calendar days after the issuance of a letter under paragraph (1), the person who receives such letter shall submit to the Secretary a written response to such letter setting forth the basis for noncompliance and providing information required under subsection (a); and

(3) "not later than 45 calendar days after the issuance of a letter under paragraph (1), the Secretary shall make such letter and any response to such letter under paragraph (2) available to the public on the internet website of the Food and Drug Administration, with appropriate redactions made to protect information described in subsection (d), except that, if the Secretary determines that the letter under paragraph (1) was issued in error or, after review of such response, the person had a reasonable basis for not notifying as required under subsection (a), the requirements of this paragraph shall not apply.

(f) "EXPEDITED INSPECTIONS AND REVIEWS.—If, based on notifications described in subsection (a) or any other relevant information, the Secretary concludes that there is, or is likely to be, a shortage of an device, the Secretary shall, as appropriate—

(1) "prioritize and expedite the review of a submission under section 513(f)(2), 515, review of a notification under section 510(k), or 520(m) for a device that could help mitigate or prevent such shortage; or

(2) "prioritize and expedite an inspection or reinspection of an establishment that could help mitigate or prevent such shortage.

(g) "DEVICE SHORTAGE LIST.—

(1) "ESTABLISHMENT.—The Secretary shall establish and maintain an up-to-date list of devices that are determined by the Secretary to be in shortage in the United States.

(2) "CONTENTS.—For each device included on the list under paragraph (1), the Secretary shall include the following information:

(A) "The category or name of the device in shortage.

(B) "The name of each manufacturer of such device.

(C) "The reason for the shortage, as determined by the Secretary, selecting from the following categories:

(i) "Requirements related to complying with good manufacturing practices.

(ii) "Regulatory delay.

(iii) "Shortage or discontinuance of a component or part.

(iv) "Discontinuance of the manufacture of the device.

(v) "Delay in shipping of the device.

(vi) "Delay in sterilization of the device.

(vii) "Demand increase for the device.

(viii) "Facility closure.

(D) "The estimated duration of the shortage as determined by the Secretary.

(3) "PUBLIC AVAILABILITY.—

(A) "IN GENERAL.—Subject to subparagraphs (B) and (C), the Secretary shall make the information in the list under paragraph (1) publicly available.

(B) "TRADE SECRETS AND CONFIDENTIAL INFORMATION.—Nothing in this subsection shall be construed to alter or amend section 1905 of title 18, United States Code, or section 552(b)(4) of title 5 of such Code.

(C) "PUBLIC HEALTH EXCEPTION.—The Secretary may elect not to make information collected under this subsection publicly available if the Secretary determines that disclosure of such information would adversely affect the public health (such as by increasing the possibility of hoarding or other disruption of the availability of the device to patients).

(h) "RULE OF CONSTRUCTION.—Nothing in this section shall be construed to affect the authority of the Secretary on the date of enactment of this section to expedite the review of devices under section 515 of the Federal Food, Drug, and Cosmetic Act, section 515B of such Act relating to the priority review program for devices, and section 564 of such Act relating to the emergency use authorization authorities.

(i) "DEFINITIONS.—In this section:

(1) "MEANINGFUL DISRUPTION.—The term 'meaningful disruption'—

(A) "means a change in production that is reasonably likely to lead to a reduction in the supply of a device by a manufacturer that is more than negligible and affects the ability of the manufacturer to fill orders or meet expected demand for its product;

(B) "does not include interruptions in manufacturing due to matters such as routine maintenance or insignificant changes in manufacturing so long as the manufacturer expects to resume operations in a short period of time, not to exceed 6 months;

(C) "does not include interruptions in manufacturing of components or raw materials so long as such interruptions do not result in a shortage of the device and the manufacturer expects to resume operations in a reasonable period of time; and

(D) "does not include interruptions in manufacturing that do not lead to a reduction in procedures or diagnostic tests associated with a medical device designed to perform more than one procedure or diagnostic test.

(2) "SHORTAGE.—The term 'shortage', with respect to a device, means a period of time when the demand or projected demand for the device within the United States exceeds the supply of the device.".

PART II—ACCESS TO HEALTH CARE FOR COVID–19 PATIENTS

Subpart A—Coverage of Testing and Preventive Services

[¶2071] SEC. 3201. COVERAGE OF DIAGNOSTIC TESTING FOR COVID–19.

Paragraph (1) of section 6001(a) of division F of the Families First Coronavirus Response Act (Public Law 116–127) is amended to read as follows:

(1) "An in vitro diagnostic test defined in section 809.3 of title 21, Code of Federal Regulations (or successor regulations) for the detection of SARS–CoV–2 or the diagnosis of the virus that causes COVID–19, and the administration of such a test, that—

(A) "is approved, cleared, or authorized under section 510(k), 513, 515, or 564 of the Federal Food, Drug, and Cosmetic Act (21 U.S.C. 360(k), 360c, 360e, 360bbb–3);

(B) "the developer has requested, or intends to request, emergency use authorization under section 564 of the Federal Food, Drug, and Cosmetic Act (21 U.S.C. 360bbb–3), unless and until the emergency use authorization request under such section 564 has been denied or the developer of such test does not submit a request under such section within a reasonable timeframe;

(C) "is developed in and authorized by a State that has notified the Secretary of Health and Human Services of its intention to review tests intended to diagnose COVID–19; or

(D) "other test that the Secretary determines appropriate in guidance.".

[¶2072] SEC. 3202. PRICING OF DIAGNOSTIC TESTING.

(a) REIMBURSEMENT RATES.—A group health plan or a health insurance issuer providing coverage of items and services described in section 6001(a) of division F of the Families First Coronavirus Response Act (Public Law 116–127) with respect to an enrollee shall reimburse the provider of the diagnostic testing as follows:

(1) If the health plan or issuer has a negotiated rate with such provider in effect before the public health emergency declared under section 319 of the Public Health Service Act (42 U.S.C. 247d), such negotiated rate shall apply throughout the period of such declaration.

(2) If the health plan or issuer does not have a negotiated rate with such provider, such plan or issuer shall reimburse the provider in an amount that equals the cash price for such service as listed by the provider on a public internet website, or such plan or issuer may negotiate a rate with such provider for less than such cash price.

(b) REQUIREMENT TO PUBLICIZE CASH PRICE FOR DIAGNOSTIC TESTING FOR COVID–19.—

(1) IN GENERAL.—During the emergency period declared under section 319 of the Public Health Service Act (42 U.S.C. 247d), each provider of a diagnostic test for COVID–19 shall make public the cash price for such test on a public internet website of such provider.

(2) CIVIL MONETARY PENALTIES.—The Secretary of Health and Human Services may impose a civil monetary penalty on any provider of a diagnostic test for COVID–19 that is not in compliance with paragraph (1) and has not completed a corrective action plan to comply with the requirements of such paragraph, in an amount not to exceed $300 per day that the violation is ongoing.

[¶2073] SEC. 3203. RAPID COVERAGE OF PREVENTIVE SERVICES AND VACCINES FOR CORONAVIRUS.

(a) IN GENERAL.—Notwithstanding 2713(b) of the Public Health Service Act (42 U.S.C. 300gg–13), the Secretary of Health and Human Services, the Secretary of Labor, and the Secretary of the Treasury shall require group health plans and health insurance issuers offering group or individual health insurance to cover (without cost-sharing) any qualifying coronavirus preventive service, pursuant to section 2713(a) of the Public Health Service Act (42 U.S.C. 300gg–13(a)) (including the regulations under sections 2590.715–2713 of title 29, Code of Federal Regulations, section 54.9815–2713 of title 26, Code of Federal Regulations, and section 147.130 of title 45, Code of Federal Regulations (or any successor regulations)). The requirement described in this subsection shall take effect with respect to a qualifying coronavirus preventive service on the specified date described in subsection (b)(2).

(b) DEFINITIONS.—For purposes of this section:

(1) QUALIFYING CORONAVIRUS PREVENTIVE SERVICE.—The term "qualifying coronavirus preventive service" means an item, service, or immunization that is intended to prevent or mitigate coronavirus disease 2019 and that is—

(A) an evidence-based item or service that has in effect a rating of "A" or "B" in the current recommendations of the United States Preventive Services Task Force; or

(B) an immunization that has in effect a recommendation from the Advisory Committee on Immunization Practices of the Centers for Disease Control and Prevention with respect to the individual involved.

(2) SPECIFIED DATE.—The term "specified date" means the date that is 15 business days after the date on which a recommendation is made relating to the qualifying coronavirus preventive service as described in such paragraph.

(3) ADDITIONAL TERMS.—In this section, the terms "group health plan", "health insurance issuer", "group health insurance coverage", and "individual health insurance coverage" have the meanings given such terms in section 2791 of the Public Health Service Act (42 U.S.C. 300gg–91), section 733 of the Employee Retirement Income Security Act of 1974 (29 U.S.C. 1191b), and section 9832 of the Internal Revenue Code, as applicable.

Subpart B—Support for Health Care Providers

[¶2075] SEC. 3211. SUPPLEMENTAL AWARDS FOR HEALTH CENTERS.

(a) SUPPLEMENTAL AWARDS.—Section 330(r) of the Public Health Service Act (42 U.S.C. 254b(r)) is amended by adding at the end the following:

(6) "ADDITIONAL AMOUNTS FOR SUPPLEMENTAL AWARDS.—In addition to any amounts made available pursuant to this subsection, section 402A of this Act, or section 10503 of the Patient Protection and Affordable Care Act, there is authorized to be appropriated, and there is appropriated, out of any monies in the Treasury not otherwise appropriated, $1,320,000,000 for fiscal year 2020 for supplemental awards under subsection (d) for the detection of SARS–CoV–2 or the prevention, diagnosis, and treatment of COVID–19.".

(b) APPLICATION OF PROVISIONS.—Amounts appropriated pursuant to the amendment made by subsection (a) for fiscal year 2020 shall be subject to the requirements contained in Public Law 116–94 for funds for programs authorized under sections 330 through 340 of the Public Health Service Act (42 U.S.C. 254 through 256).

[¶2076] SEC. 3212. TELEHEALTH NETWORK AND TELEHEALTH RESOURCE CENTERS GRANT PROGRAMS.

Section 330I of the Public Health Service Act (42 U.S.C. 254c–14) is amended—

(1) in subsection (d)—

(A) in paragraph (1)—

(i) in the matter preceding subparagraph (A), by striking "projects to demonstrate how telehealth technologies can be used through telehealth networks" and inserting "evidence-based projects that utilize telehealth technologies through telehealth networks";

(ii) in subparagraph (A)—

(I) by striking "the quality of" and inserting "access to, and the quality of,"; and

(II) by inserting "and" after the semicolon;

(iii) by striking subparagraph (B);

(iv) by redesignating subparagraph (C) as subparagraph (B); and

(v) in subparagraph (B), as so redesignated, by striking "and patients and their families, for decisionmaking" and inserting ", patients, and their families"; and

(B) in paragraph (2)—

(i) by striking "demonstrate how telehealth technologies can be used" and inserting "support initiatives that utilize telehealth technologies"; and

(ii) by striking ", to establish telehealth resource centers";

(2) in subsection (e), by striking "4 years" and inserting "5 years";

(3) in subsection (f)—

(A) by striking paragraph (2);

(B) in paragraph (1)(B)—

(i) by redesignating clauses (i) through (iii) as paragraphs (1) through (3), respectively, and adjusting the margins accordingly;

(ii) in paragraph (3), as so redesignated by clause (i), by redesignating subclauses (I) through (XII) as subparagraphs (A) through (L), respectively, and adjusting the margins accordingly; and

(iii) by striking "(1) TELEHEALTH NETWORK GRANTS—"and all that follows through "(B) TELEHEALTH NETWORKS—"; and

(C) in paragraph (3)(I), as so redesignated, by inserting "and substance use disorder" after "mental health" each place such term appears;

(4) in subsection (g)(2), by striking "or improve" and inserting "and improve";

(5) by striking subsection (h);

(6) by redesignating subsections (i) through (p) as subsection (h) through (o), respectively;

(7) in subsection (h), as so redesignated—

(A) in paragraph (1)—

(i) in subparagraph (B), by striking "mental health, public health, long-term care, home care, preventive" and inserting "mental health care, public health services, long-term care, home care, preventive care";

(ii) in subparagraph (E), by inserting "and regional" after "local"; and

(iii) by striking subparagraph (F); and

(B) in paragraph (2)(A), by striking "medically underserved areas or" and inserting "rural areas, medically underserved areas, or";

(8) in paragraph (2) of subsection (i), as so redesignated, by striking "ensure that—"and all that follows through the end of subparagraph (B) and inserting "ensure that not less than 50 percent of the funds awarded shall be awarded for projects in rural areas.";

(9) in subsection (j), as so redesignated—

(A) in paragraph (1)(B), by striking "computer hardware and software, audio and video equipment, computer network equipment, interactive equipment, data terminal equipment, and other"; and

(B) in paragraph (2)(F), by striking "health care providers and";

(10) in subsection (k), as so redesignated—

(A) in paragraph (2), by striking "40 percent" and inserting "20 percent"; and

(B) in paragraph (3), by striking "(such as laying cable or telephone lines, or purchasing or installing microwave towers, satellite dishes, amplifiers, or digital switching equipment)";

(11) by striking subsections (q) and (r) and inserting the following:

(p) "REPORT.—Not later than 4 years after the date of enactment of the Coronavirus Aid, Relief, and Economic Security Act, and every 5 years thereafter, the Secretary shall prepare and submit to the Committee on Health, Education, Labor, and Pensions of the Senate and the Committee on Energy and Commerce of the House of Representatives a report on the activities and outcomes of the grant programs under subsection (b).";

(12) by redesignating subsection (s) as subsection (q); and

(13) in subsection (q), as so redesignated, by striking "this section—"and all that follows through the end of paragraph (2) and inserting "this section $29,000,000 for each of fiscal years 2021 through 2025.".

[¶2077] SEC. 3213. RURAL HEALTH CARE SERVICES OUTREACH, RURAL HEALTH NETWORK DEVELOPMENT, AND SMALL HEALTH CARE PROVIDER QUALITY IMPROVEMENT GRANT PROGRAMS.

Section 330A of the Public Health Service Act (42 U.S.C. 254c) is amended—

(1) in subsection (d)(2)—

(A) in subparagraph (A), by striking "essential" and inserting "basic"; and

(B) in subparagraph (B)—

(i) in the matter preceding clause (i), by inserting "to" after "grants"; and

(ii) in clauses (i), (ii), and (iii), by striking "to" each place such term appears;

(2) in subsection (e)—

(A) in paragraph (1)—

(i) by inserting "improving and" after "outreach by";

(ii) by inserting ", through community engagement and evidence-based or innovative, evidence-informed models" before the period of the first sentence; and

(iii) by striking "3 years" and inserting "5 years";

(B) in paragraph (2)—

(i) in the matter preceding subparagraph (A), by inserting "shall" after "entity";

(ii) in subparagraph (A), by striking "shall be a rural public or rural nonprofit private entity" and inserting "be an entity with demonstrated experience serving, or the capacity to serve, rural underserved populations";

(iii) in subparagraphs (B) and (C), by striking "shall" each place such term appears; and

(iv) in subparagraph (B)—

(I) in the matter preceding clause (i), by inserting "that" after "members"; and

(II) in clauses (i) and (ii), by striking "that" each place such term appears; and

(C) in paragraph (3)(C), by striking "the local community or region" and inserting "the rural underserved populations in the local community or region";

(3) in subsection (f)—

(A) in paragraph (1)—

(i) in subparagraph (A)—

(I) in the matter preceding clause (i), by striking "promote, through planning and implementation, the development of integrated health care networks that have combined the functions of the entities participating in the networks" and inserting "plan, develop, and implement integrated health care networks that collaborate"; and

(II) in clause (ii), by striking "essential health care services" and inserting "basic health care services and associated health outcomes"; and

(ii) by amending subparagraph (B) to read as follows:

(B) "GRANT PERIODS.—The Director may award grants under this subsection for periods of not more than 5 years.";

(B) in paragraph (2)—

(i) in the matter preceding subparagraph (A), by inserting "shall" after "entity";

(ii) in subparagraph (A), by striking "shall be a rural public or rural nonprofit private entity" and inserting "be an entity with demonstrated experience serving, or the capacity to serve, rural underserved populations";

(iii) in subparagraph (B)—

(I) in the matter preceding clause (i)—

(aa) by striking "shall"; and

(bb) by inserting "that" after "participants"; and

(II) in clauses (i) and (ii), by striking "that" each place such term appears; and

(iv) in subparagraph (C), by striking "shall"; and

(C) in paragraph (3)—

(i) by amending clause (iii) of subparagraph (C) to read as follows:

(iii) "how the rural underserved populations in the local community or region to be served will benefit from and be involved in the development and ongoing operations of the network;"; and

(ii) in subparagraph (D), by striking "the local community or region" and inserting "the rural underserved populations in the local community or region";

(4) in subsection (g)—

(A) in paragraph (1)—

(i) by inserting ", including activities related to increasing care coordination, enhancing chronic disease management, and improving patient health outcomes" before the period of the first sentence; and

(ii) by striking "3 years" and inserting "5 years";

(B) in paragraph (2)—

(i) in the matter preceding subparagraph (A), by inserting "shall" after "entity";

(ii) in subparagraphs (A) and (B), by striking "shall" each place such term appears; and

(iii) in subparagraph (A)(ii), by inserting "or regional" after "local"; and

(C) in paragraph (3)(D), by striking "the local community or region" and inserting "the rural underserved populations in the local community or region";

(5) in subsection (h)(3), in the matter preceding subparagraph (A), by inserting ", as appropriate," after "the Secretary";

(6) by amending subsection (i) to read as follows:

(i) "REPORT.—Not later than 4 years after the date of enactment of the Coronavirus Aid, Relief, and Economic Security Act, and every 5 years thereafter, the Secretary shall prepare and submit to the Committee on Health, Education, Labor, and Pensions of the Senate and the Committee on Energy and Commerce of the House of Representatives a report on the activities and outcomes of the grant programs under subsections (e), (f), and (g), including the impact of projects funded under such programs on the health status of rural residents with chronic conditions."; and

(7) in subsection (j), by striking "$45,000,000 for each of fiscal years 2008 through 2012" and inserting "$79,500,000 for each of fiscal years 2021 through 2025".

[¶ 2078] SEC. 3214. UNITED STATES PUBLIC HEALTH SERVICE MODERNIZATION.

(a) COMMISSIONED CORPS AND READY RESERVE CORPS.—Section 203 of the Public Health Service Act (42 U.S.C. 204) is amended—

(1) in subsection (a)(1), by striking "a Ready Reserve Corps for service in time of national emergency" and inserting ", for service in time of a public health or national emergency, a Ready Reserve Corps"; and

(2) in subsection (c)—

(A) in the heading, by striking "RESEARCH" and inserting "RESERVE CORPS";

(B) in paragraph (1), by inserting "during public health or national emergencies" before the period;

(C) in paragraph (2)—

(i) in the matter preceding subparagraph (A), by inserting ", consistent with paragraph (1)" after "shall";

(ii) in subparagraph (C), by inserting "during such emergencies" after "members"; and

(iii) in subparagraph (D), by inserting ", consistent with subparagraph (C)" before the period; and

(D) by adding at the end the following:

(3) "STATUTORY REFERENCES TO RESERVE.—A reference in any Federal statute, except in the case of subsection (b), to the 'Reserve Corps' of the Public Health Service or to the 'reserve' of the Public Health Service shall be deemed to be a reference to the Ready Reserve Corps.".

(b) DEPLOYMENT READINESS.—Section 203A(a)(1)(B) of the Public Health Service Act (42 U.S.C. 204a(a)(1)(B)) is amended by striking "Active Reserves" and inserting "Ready Reserve Corps".

(c) RETIREMENT OF COMMISSIONED OFFICERS.—Section 211 of the Public Health Service Act (42 U.S.C. 212) is amended—

(1) by striking "the Service" each place it appears and inserting "the Regular Corps";

(2) in subsection (a)(4), by striking "(in the case of an officer in the Reserve Corps)";

(3) in subsection (c)—

(A) in paragraph (1)—

(i) by striking "or an officer of the Reserve Corps"; and

(ii) by inserting "or under section 221(a)(19)" after "subsection (a)"; and

(B) in paragraph (2), by striking "Regular or Reserve Corps" and inserting "Regular Corps or Ready Reserve Corps"; and

(4) in subsection (f), by striking "the Regular or Reserve Corps of".

(d) RIGHTS, PRIVILEGES, ETC. OF OFFICERS AND SURVIVING BENEFICIARIES.—Section 221 of the Public Health Service Act (42 U.S.C. 213a) is amended—

(1) in subsection (a), by adding at the end the following:

(19) "Chapter 1223, Retired Pay for Non-Regular Service.

(20) "Section 12601, Compensation: Reserve on active duty accepting from any person.

(21) "Section 12684, Reserves: separation for absence without authority or sentence to imprisonment."; and

(2) in subsection (b)—

(A) by striking "Secretary of Health, Education, and Welfare or his designee" and inserting "Secretary of Health and Human Services or the designee of such secretary";

(B) by striking "(b) The authority vested" and inserting the following:

(b)(1) "The authority vested";

(C) by striking "For purposes of" and inserting the following:

(2) "For purposes of"; and

(D) by adding at the end the following:

(3) "For purposes of paragraph (19) of subsection (a), the terms 'Military department', 'Secretary concerned', and 'Armed forces' in such title 10 shall be deemed to include, respectively, the Department of Health and Human Services, the Secretary of Health and Human Services, and the Commissioned Corps.".

(e) TECHNICAL AMENDMENTS.—Title II of the Public Health Service Act (42 U.S.C. 202 et seq.) is amended—

(1) in sections 204 and 207(c), by striking "Regular or Reserve Corps" each place it appears and inserting "Regular Corps or Ready Reserve Corps";

(2) in section 208(a), by striking "Regular and Reserve Corps" each place it appears and inserting "Regular Corps and Ready Reserve Corps"; and

(3) in section 205(c), 206(c), 210, and 219, and in subsections (a), (b), and (d) of section 207, by striking "Reserve Corps" each place it appears and inserting "Ready Reserve Corps".

[¶2079] SEC. 3215. LIMITATION ON LIABILITY FOR VOLUNTEER HEALTH CARE PROFESSIONALS DURING COVID–19 EMERGENCY RESPONSE.

(a) LIMITATION ON LIABILITY.—Except as provided in subsection (b), a health care professional shall not be liable under Federal or State law for any harm caused by an act or omission of the professional in the provision of health care services during the public health emergency with respect to COVID–19 declared by the Secretary of Health and Human Services (referred to in this section as the "Secretary") under section 319 of the Public Health Service Act (42 U.S.C. 247d) on January 31, 2020, if—

(1) the professional is providing health care services in response to such public health emergency, as a volunteer; and

(2) the act or omission occurs—

(A) in the course of providing health care services;

(B) in the health care professional's capacity as a volunteer;

(C) in the course of providing health care services that—

(i) are within the scope of the license, registration, or certification of the volunteer, as defined by the State of licensure, registration, or certification; and

(ii) do not exceed the scope of license, registration, or certification of a substantially similar health professional in the State in which such act or omission occurs; and

(D) in a good faith belief that the individual being treated is in need of health care services.

(b) EXCEPTIONS.—Subsection (a) does not apply if—

(1) the harm was caused by an act or omission constituting willful or criminal misconduct, gross negligence, reckless misconduct, or a conscious flagrant indifference to the rights or safety of the individual harmed by the health care professional; or

(2) the health care professional rendered the health care services under the influence (as determined pursuant to applicable State law) of alcohol or an intoxicating drug.

(c) PREEMPTION.—

(1) IN GENERAL.—This section preempts the laws of a State or any political subdivision of a State to the extent that such laws are inconsistent with this section, unless such laws provide greater protection from liability.

(2) VOLUNTEER PROTECTION ACT.—Protections afforded by this section are in addition to those provided by the Volunteer Protection Act of 1997 (Public Law 105–19).

(d) DEFINITIONS.—In this section—

(1) the term "harm" includes physical, nonphysical, economic, and noneconomic losses;

(2) the term "health care professional" means an individual who is licensed, registered, or certified under Federal or State law to provide health care services;

(3) the term "health care services" means any services provided by a health care professional, or by any individual working under the supervision of a health care professional that relate to—

(A) the diagnosis, prevention, or treatment of COVID–19; or

(B) the assessment or care of the health of a human being related to an actual or suspected case of COVID–19; and

(4) the term "volunteer" means a health care professional who, with respect to the health care services rendered, does not receive compensation or any other thing of value in lieu of compensation, which compensation—

(A) includes a payment under any insurance policy or health plan, or under any Federal or State health benefits program; and

(B) excludes—

(i) receipt of items to be used exclusively for rendering health care services in the health care professional's capacity as a volunteer described in subsection (a)(1); and

(ii) any reimbursement for travel to the site where the volunteer services are rendered and any payments in cash or kind to cover room and board, if services are being rendered more than 75 miles from the volunteer's principal place of residence.

(e) EFFECTIVE DATE.—This section shall take effect upon the date of enactment of this Act, and applies to a claim for harm only if the act or omission that caused such harm occurred on or after the date of enactment.

(f) SUNSET.—This section shall be in effect only for the length of the public health emergency declared by the Secretary of Health and Human Services (referred to in this section as the "Secretary") under section 319 of the Public Health Service Act (42 U.S.C. 247d) on January 31, 2020 with respect to COVID–19.

[¶2080] SEC. 3216. FLEXIBILITY FOR MEMBERS OF NATIONAL HEALTH SERVICE CORPS DURING EMERGENCY PERIOD.

During the public health emergency declared by the Secretary of Health and Human Services under section 319 of the Public Health Service Act (42 U.S.C. 247d) on January 31, 2020, with respect to COVID–19, the Secretary may, notwithstanding section 333 of the Public Health Service Act (42 U.S.C. 254f), assign members of the National Health Service Corps, with the voluntary agreement of such corps members, to provide such health services at such places, and for such number of hours, as the Secretary determines necessary to respond to such emergency, provided that such places are within a reasonable distance of the site to which such members were originally assigned, and the total number of hours required are the same as were required of such members prior to the date of enactment of this Act.

Subpart C—Miscellaneous Provisions

[¶2082] SEC. 3221. CONFIDENTIALITY AND DISCLOSURE OF RECORDS RELATING TO SUBSTANCE USE DISORDER.

(a) CONFORMING CHANGES RELATING TO SUBSTANCE USE DISORDER.—Subsections (a) and (h) of section 543 of the Public Health Service Act (42 U.S.C. 290dd–2) are each amended by striking "substance abuse" and inserting "substance use disorder".

(b) DISCLOSURES TO COVERED ENTITIES CONSISTENT WITH HIPAA.—Paragraph (1) of section 543(b) of the Public Health Service Act (42 U.S.C. 290dd–2(b)) is amended to read as follows:

(1) "CONSENT.—The following shall apply with respect to the contents of any record referred to in subsection (a):

(A) "Such contents may be used or disclosed in accordance with the prior written consent of the patient with respect to whom such record is maintained.

(B) "Once prior written consent of the patient has been obtained, such contents may be used or disclosed by a covered entity, business associate, or a program subject to this section for purposes of treatment, payment, and health care operations as permitted by the HIPAA regulations. Any information so disclosed may then be redisclosed in accordance with the HIPAA regulations. Section 13405(c) of the Health Information Technology and Clinical Health Act (42 U.S.C. 17935(c)) shall apply to all disclosures pursuant to subsection (b)(1) of this section.

(C) "It shall be permissible for a patient's prior written consent to be given once for all such future uses or disclosures for purposes of treatment, payment, and health care operations, until such time as the patient revokes such consent in writing.

(D) "Section 13405(a) of the Health Information Technology and Clinical Health Act (42 U.S.C. 17935(a)) shall apply to all disclosures pursuant to subsection (b)(1) of this section.".

(c) DISCLOSURES OF DE-IDENTIFIED HEALTH INFORMATION TO PUBLIC HEALTH AUTHORITIES.—Paragraph (2) of section 543(b) of the Public Health Service Act (42 U.S.C. 290dd–2(b)), is amended by adding at the end the following:

(D) "To a public health authority, so long as such content meets the standards established in section 164.514(b) of title 45, Code of Federal Regulations (or successor regulations) for creating de-identified information.".

(d) DEFINITIONS.—Section 543 of the Public Health Service Act (42 U.S.C. 290dd–2) is amended by adding at the end the following:

(k) "DEFINITIONS.—For purposes of this section:

(1) "BREACH.—The term 'breach' has the meaning given such term for purposes of the HIPAA regulations.

(2) "BUSINESS ASSOCIATE.—The term 'business associate' has the meaning given such term for purposes of the HIPAA regulations.

(3) "COVERED ENTITY.—The term 'covered entity' has the meaning given such term for purposes of the HIPAA regulations.

(4) "HEALTH CARE OPERATIONS.—The term 'health care operations' has the meaning given such term for purposes of the HIPAA regulations.

(5) "HIPAA REGULATIONS.—The term 'HIPAA regulations' has the meaning given such term for purposes of parts 160 and 164 of title 45, Code of Federal Regulations.

(6) "PAYMENT.—The term 'payment' has the meaning given such term for purposes of the HIPAA regulations.

(7) "PUBLIC HEALTH AUTHORITY.—The term 'public health authority' has the meaning given such term for purposes of the HIPAA regulations.

(8) "TREATMENT.—The term 'treatment' has the meaning given such term for purposes of the HIPAA regulations.

(9) "UNSECURED PROTECTED HEALTH INFORMATION.—The term 'unprotected health information' has the meaning given such term for purposes of the HIPAA regulations.".

(e) USE OF RECORDS IN CRIMINAL, CIVIL, OR ADMINISTRATIVE INVESTIGATIONS, ACTIONS, OR PROCEEDINGS.—Subsection (c) of section 543 of the Public Health Service Act (42 U.S.C. 290dd–2(c)) is amended to read as follows:

(c) "USE OF RECORDS IN CRIMINAL, CIVIL, OR ADMINISTRATIVE CONTEXTS.—Except as otherwise authorized by a court order under subsection (b)(2)(C) or by the consent of the patient, a record referred to in subsection (a), or testimony relaying the information contained therein, may not be disclosed or used in any civil, criminal, administrative, or legislative proceedings conducted by any Federal, State, or local authority, against a patient, including with respect to the following activities:

(1) "Such record or testimony shall not be entered into evidence in any criminal prosecution or civil action before a Federal or State court.

(2) "Such record or testimony shall not form part of the record for decision or otherwise be taken into account in any proceeding before a Federal, State, or local agency.

(3) "Such record or testimony shall not be used by any Federal, State, or local agency for a law enforcement purpose or to conduct any law enforcement investigation.

(4) "Such record or testimony shall not be used in any application for a warrant.".

(f) PENALTIES.—Subsection (f) of section 543 of the Public Health Service Act (42 U.S.C. 290dd–2) is amended to read as follows:

(f) "PENALTIES.—The provisions of sections 1176 and 1177 of the Social Security Act shall apply to a violation of this section to the extent and in the same manner as such provisions apply to a violation of part C of title XI of such Act. In applying the previous sentence—

(1) "the reference to 'this subsection' in subsection (a)(2) of such section 1176 shall be treated as a reference to 'this subsection (including as applied pursuant to section 543(f) of the Public Health Service Act)'; and

(2) "in subsection (b) of such section 1176—

(A) "each reference to 'a penalty imposed under subsection (a)' shall be treated as a reference to 'a penalty imposed under subsection (a) (including as applied pursuant to section 543(f) of the Public Health Service Act)'; and

(B) "each reference to 'no damages obtained under subsection (d)' shall be treated as a reference to 'no damages obtained under subsection (d) (including as applied pursuant to section 543(f) of the Public Health Service Act)'.".

(g) ANTIDISCRIMINATION.—Section 543 of the Public Health Service Act (42 U.S.C. 290dd–2) is amended by inserting after subsection (h) the following:

(i) "ANTIDISCRIMINATION.—

(1) "IN GENERAL.—No entity shall discriminate against an individual on the basis of information received by such entity pursuant to an inadvertent or intentional disclosure of records, or information contained in records, described in subsection (a) in—

(A) "admission, access to, or treatment for health care;

(B) "hiring, firing, or terms of employment, or receipt of worker's compensation;

(C) "the sale, rental, or continued rental of housing;

(D) "access to Federal, State, or local courts; or

(E) "access to, approval of, or maintenance of social services and benefits provided or funded by Federal, State, or local governments.

(2) "RECIPIENTS OF FEDERAL FUNDS.—No recipient of Federal funds shall discriminate against an individual on the basis of information received by such recipient pursuant to an intentional or inadvertent disclosure of such records or information contained in records described in subsection (a) in affording access to the services provided with such funds.".

(h) NOTIFICATION IN CASE OF BREACH.—Section 543 of the Public Health Service Act (42 U.S.C. 290dd–2), as amended by subsection (g), is further amended by inserting after subsection (i) the following:

(j) "NOTIFICATION IN CASE OF BREACH.—The provisions of section 13402 of the HITECH Act (42 U.S.C. 17932) shall apply to a program or activity described in subsection (a), in case of a breach of records described in subsection (a), to the same extent and in the same manner as such provisions apply to a covered entity in the case of a breach of unsecured protected health information.".

(i) REGULATIONS.—

(1) IN GENERAL.—The Secretary of Health and Human Services, in consultation with appropriate Federal agencies, shall make such revisions to regulations as may be necessary for implementing and enforcing the amendments made by this section, such that such amendments shall apply with respect to uses and disclosures of information occurring on or after the date that is 12 months after the date of enactment of this Act.

(2) EASILY UNDERSTANDABLE NOTICE OF PRIVACY PRACTICES.—Not later than 1 year after the date of enactment of this Act, the Secretary of Health and Human Services, in consultation with appropriate legal, clinical, privacy, and civil rights experts, shall update section 164.520 of title 45, Code of Federal Regulations, so that covered entities and entities creating or maintaining the records described in subsection (a) provide notice, written in plain language, of privacy practices regarding patient records referred to in section 543(a) of the Public Health Service Act (42 U.S.C. 290dd–2(a)), including—

(A) a statement of the patient's rights, including self-pay patients, with respect to protected health information and a brief description of how the individual may exercise these rights (as required by subsection (b)(1)(iv) of such section 164.520); and

(B) a description of each purpose for which the covered entity is permitted or required to use or disclose protected health information without the patient's written authorization (as required by subsection (b)(2) of such section 164.520).

(j) RULES OF CONSTRUCTION.—Nothing in this Act or the amendments made by this Act shall be construed to limit—

(1) a patient's right, as described in section 164.522 of title 45, Code of Federal Regulations, or any successor regulation, to request a restriction on the use or disclosure of a record referred to in section 543(a) of the Public Health Service Act (42 U.S.C. 290dd–2(a)) for purposes of treatment, payment, or health care operations; or

(2) a covered entity's choice, as described in section 164.506 of title 45, Code of Federal Regulations, or any successor regulation, to obtain the consent of the individual to use or disclose a record referred to in such section 543(a) to carry out treatment, payment, or health care operation.

(k) SENSE OF CONGRESS.—It is the sense of the Congress that—

(1) any person treating a patient through a program or activity with respect to which the confidentiality requirements of section 543 of the Public Health Service Act (42 U.S.C. 290dd–2) apply is encouraged to access the applicable State-based prescription drug monitoring program when clinically appropriate;

(2) patients have the right to request a restriction on the use or disclosure of a record referred to in section 543(a) of the Public Health Service Act (42 U.S.C. 290dd–2(a)) for treatment, payment, or health care operations;

(3) covered entities should make every reasonable effort to the extent feasible to comply with a patient's request for a restriction regarding such use or disclosure;

(4) for purposes of applying section 164.501 of title 45, Code of Federal Regulations, the definition of health care operations shall have the meaning given such term in such section, except that clause (v) of paragraph (6) shall not apply; and

(5) programs creating records referred to in section 543(a) of the Public Health Service Act (42 U.S.C. 290dd–2(a)) should receive positive incentives for discussing with their patients the benefits to consenting to share such records.

[¶2083] SEC. 3222. NUTRITION SERVICES.

(a) DEFINITIONS.—In this section, the terms "Assistant Secretary", "Secretary", "State agency", and "area agency on aging" have the meanings given the terms in section 102 of the Older Americans Act of 1965 (42 U.S.C. 3002).

(b) NUTRITION SERVICES TRANSFER CRITERIA.—During any portion of the COVID–19 public health emergency declared under section 319 of the Public Health Service Act (42 U.S.C. 247d), the Secretary shall allow a State agency or an area agency on aging, without prior approval, to transfer not more than 100 percent of the funds received by the State agency or area agency on aging, respectively, and attributable to funds appropriated under paragraph (1) or (2) of section 303(b) of the Older Americans Act of 1965 (42 U.S.C. 3023(b)), between subpart 1 and subpart 2 of part C (42 U.S.C. 3030d–2 et seq.) for such use as the State agency or area agency on aging, respectively, considers appropriate to meet the needs of the State or area served.

(c) HOME-DELIVERED NUTRITION SERVICES WAIVER.—For purposes of State agencies' determining the delivery of nutrition services under section 337 of the Older Americans Act of 1965 (42 U.S.C. 3030g), during the period of the COVID–19 public health emergency declared under section 319 of the Public Health Service Act (42 U.S.C. 247d), the same meaning shall be given to an individual who is unable to obtain nutrition because the individual is practicing social distancing due to the emergency as is given to an individual who is homebound by reason of illness.

(d) DIETARY GUIDELINES WAIVER.—To facilitate implementation of subparts 1 and 2 of part C of title III of the Older Americans Act of 1965 (42 U.S.C. 3030d–2 et seq.) during any portion of the COVID–19 public health emergency declared under section 319 of the Public Health Service Act (42 U.S.C. 247d), the Assistant Secretary may waive the requirements for meals provided under those subparts to comply with the requirements of clauses (i) and (ii) of section 339(2)(A) of such Act (42 U.S.C. 3030g–21(2)(A)).

[¶2084] SEC. 3223. CONTINUITY OF SERVICE AND OPPORTUNITIES FOR PARTICIPANTS IN COMMUNITY SERVICE ACTIVITIES UNDER TITLE V OF THE OLDER AMERICANS ACT OF 1965.

To ensure continuity of service and opportunities for participants in community service activities under title V of the Older Americans Act of 1965 (42 U.S.C. 3056 et seq.), the Secretary of Labor—

(1)(A) may allow individuals participating in projects under such title as of March 1, 2020, to extend their participation for a period that exceeds the period described in section 518(a)(3)(B)(i) of such Act (42 U.S.C. 3056p(a)(3)(B)(i)) if the Secretary determines such extension is appropriate due to the effects of the COVID–19 public health emergency declared under section 319 of the Public Health Service Act (42 U.S.C. 247d); and

(B) may increase the average participation cap for eligible individuals applicable to grantees as described in section 502(b)(1)(C) of the Older Americans Act of 1965 (42 U.S.C. 3056(b)(1)(C)) to a cap the Secretary determines is appropriate due to the effects of the COVID–19 public health emergency declared under section 319 of the Public Health Service Act (42 U.S.C. 247d); and

(2) may increase the amount available to pay the authorized administrative costs for a project, described in section 502(c)(3) of the Older Americans Act of 1965 (42 U.S.C. 3056(c)(3)) to an amount not to exceed 20 percent of the grant amount if the Secretary determines that such increase is necessary to adequately respond to the additional administrative needs to respond to the COVID–19 public health emergency declared under section 319 of the Public Health Service Act (42 U.S.C. 247d).

[¶2085] SEC. 3224. GUIDANCE ON PROTECTED HEALTH INFORMATION.

Not later than 180 days after the date of enactment of this Act, the Secretary of Health and Human Services shall issue guidance on the sharing of patients' protected health information pursuant to section 160.103 of title 45, Code of Federal Regulations (or any successor regulations) during the public health emergency declared by the Secretary of Health and Human Services under section 319 of the Public Health Service Act (42 U.S.C. 247d) with respect to COVID–19, during the emergency involving Federal primary responsibility determined to exist by the President under section 501(b) of the Robert T. Stafford Disaster Relief and Emergency Assistance Act (42 U.S.C. 5191(b)) with respect to COVID–19, and during the national emergency declared by the President under the National Emergencies Act (50 U.S.C. 1601 et seq.) with respect to COVID–19. Such guidance shall include information on compliance with the regulations promulgated pursuant to section 264(c) of the Health Insurance Portability and Accountability Act of 1996 (42 U.S.C. 1320d–2 note) and applicable policies, including such policies that may come into effect during such emergencies.

[¶2086] SEC. 3225. REAUTHORIZATION OF HEALTHY START PROGRAM.

Section 330H of the Public Health Service Act (42 U.S.C. 254c–8) is amended—

(1) in subsection (a)—

(A) in paragraph (1), by striking ", during fiscal year 2001 and subsequent years,"; and

(B) in paragraph (2), by inserting "or increasing above the national average" after "areas with high";

(2) in subsection (b)—

(A) in paragraph (1), by striking "consumers of project services, public health departments, hospitals, health centers under section 330" and inserting "participants and former participants of project services, public health departments, hospitals, health centers under section 330, State substance abuse agencies"; and

(B) in paragraph (2)—

(i) in subparagraph (A), by striking "such as low birthweight" and inserting "including poor birth outcomes (such as low birthweight and preterm birth) and social determinants of health";

(ii) by redesignating subparagraph (B) as subparagraph (C);

(iii) by inserting after subparagraph (A), the following:

(B) "Communities with—

(i) "high rates of infant mortality or poor perinatal outcomes; or

(ii) "high rates of infant mortality or poor perinatal outcomes in specific subpopulations within the community."; and

(iv) in subparagraph (C) (as so redesignated)—

(I) by redesignating clauses (i) and (ii) as clauses (ii) and (iii), respectively;

(II) by inserting before clause (ii) (as so redesignated) the following:

(i) "collaboration with the local community in the development of the project;";

(III) in clause (ii) (as so redesignated), by striking "and" at the end;

(IV) in clause (iii) (as so redesignated), by striking the period and inserting "; and"; and

(V) by adding at the end the following:

(iv) "the use and collection of data demonstrating the effectiveness of such program in decreasing infant mortality rates and improving perinatal outcomes, as applicable, or the process by which new applicants plan to collect this data.";

(3) in subsection (c)—

(A) by striking "Recipients of grants" and inserting the following:

(1) "IN GENERAL.—Recipients of grants"; and

(B) by adding at the end the following:

(2) "OTHER PROGRAMS.—The Secretary shall ensure coordination of the program carried out pursuant to this section with other programs and activities related to the reduction of the rate of infant mortality and improved perinatal and infant health outcomes supported by the Department.";

(4) in subsection (e)—

(A) in paragraph (1), by striking "appropriated—"and all that follows through the end and inserting "appropriated $125,500,000 for each of fiscal years 2021 through 2025."; and

(B) in paragraph (2)(B), by adding at the end the following: "Evaluations may also include, to the extent practicable, information related to—

(i) "progress toward achieving any grant metrics or outcomes related to reducing infant mortality rates, improving perinatal outcomes, or reducing the disparity in health status;

(ii) "recommendations on potential improvements that may assist with addressing gaps, as applicable and appropriate; and

(iii) "the extent to which the grantee coordinated with the community in which the grantee is located in the development of the project and delivery of services, including with respect to technical assistance and mentorship programs."; and

(5) by adding at the end the following:

(f) "GAO REPORT.—

(1) "IN GENERAL.—Not later than 4 years after the date of the enactment of this subsection, the Comptroller General of the United States shall conduct an independent evaluation, and submit to the appropriate Committees of Congress a report, concerning the Healthy Start program under this section.

(2) "EVALUATION.—In conducting the evaluation under paragraph (1), the Comptroller General shall consider, as applicable and appropriate, information from the evaluations under subsection (e)(2)(B).

(3) "REPORT.—The report described in paragraph (1) shall review, assess, and provide recommendations, as appropriate, on the following:

(A) "The allocation of Healthy Start program grants by the Health Resources and Services Administration, including considerations made by such Administration regarding disparities in infant mortality or perinatal outcomes among urban and rural areas in making such awards.

(B) "Trends in the progress made toward meeting the evaluation criteria pursuant to subsection (e)(2)(B), including programs which decrease infant mortality rates and improve perinatal outcomes, programs that have not decreased infant mortality rates or improved perinatal outcomes, and programs that have made an impact on disparities in infant mortality or perinatal outcomes.

(C) "The ability of grantees to improve health outcomes for project participants, promote the awareness of the Healthy Start program services, incorporate and promote family participation, facilitate coordination with the community in which the grantee is located, and increase grantee accountability through quality improvement, performance monitoring, evaluation, and the effect such metrics may have toward decreasing the rate of infant mortality and improving perinatal outcomes.

(D) "The extent to which such Federal programs are coordinated across agencies and the identification of opportunities for improved coordination in such Federal programs and activities.".

[¶2087] SEC. 3226. IMPORTANCE OF THE BLOOD SUPPLY.

(a) IN GENERAL.—The Secretary of Health and Human Services (referred to in this section as the "Secretary") shall carry out a national campaign to improve awareness of, and support outreach to the public and health care providers about the importance and safety of blood donation and the need for donations for the blood supply during the public health emergency declared by the Secretary under section 319 of the Public Health Service Act (42 U.S.C. 247d) with respect to COVID–19.

(b) AWARENESS CAMPAIGN.—In carrying out subsection (a), the Secretary may enter into contracts with one or more public or private nonprofit entities, to establish a national blood donation awareness campaign that may include television, radio, internet, and newspaper public service announcements, and other activities to provide for public and professional awareness and education.

(c) CONSULTATION.—In carrying out subsection (a), the Secretary shall consult with the Commissioner of Food and Drugs, the Assistant Secretary for Health, the Director of the Centers for Disease Control and Prevention, the Director of the National Institutes of Health, and the heads of other relevant Federal agencies, and relevant accrediting bodies and representative organizations.

(d) REPORT TO CONGRESS.—Not later than 2 years after the date of enactment of this Act, the Secretary shall submit to the Committee on Health, Education, Labor, and Pensions of the Senate and the Committee on Energy and Commerce of the House of Representatives, a report that shall include—

(1) a description of the activities carried out under subsection (a);

(2) a description of trends in blood supply donations; and

(3) an evaluation of the impact of the public awareness campaign, including any geographic or population variations.

PART III—INNOVATION

[¶2089] SEC. 3301. REMOVING THE CAP ON OTA DURING PUBLIC HEALTH EMERGENCIES.

Section 319L(c)(5)(A) of the Public Health Service Act (42 U.S.C. 247d–7e(c)(5)(A)) is amended—

(1) by redesignating clause (iii) as clause (iv); and

(2) by inserting after clause (ii) the following:

(iii) "AUTHORITY DURING A PUBLIC HEALTH EMERGENCY.—

(I) "IN GENERAL.—Notwithstanding clause (ii), the Secretary, shall, to the maximum extent practicable, use competitive procedures when entering into transactions to carry out projects under this subsection for purposes of a public health emergency declared by the Secretary under section

319. Any such transactions entered into during such public health emergency shall not be terminated solely due to the expiration of such public health emergency, if such public health emergency ends before the completion of the terms of such agreement.

(II) "REPORT.—After the expiration of the public health emergency declared by the Secretary under section 319, the Secretary shall provide a report to the Committee on Health, Education, Labor, and Pensions of the Senate and the Committee on Energy and Commerce of the House of Representatives regarding the use of any funds pursuant to the authority under subclause (I), including any outcomes, benefits, and risks associated with the use of such funds, and a description of the reasons for the use of such authority for the project or projects.".

[¶2089A] SEC. 3302. PRIORITY ZOONOTIC ANIMAL DRUGS.

Chapter V of the Federal Food, Drug, and Cosmetic Act (21 U.S.C. 351 et seq.) is amended by inserting after section 512 the following:

[¶2090] SEC. 512A. "PRIORITY ZOONOTIC ANIMAL DRUGS.

(a) "IN GENERAL.—The Secretary shall, at the request of the sponsor intending to submit an application for approval of a new animal drug under section 512(b)(1) or an application for conditional approval of a new animal drug under section 571, expedite the development and review of such new animal drug if preliminary clinical evidence indicates that the new animal drug, alone or in combination with 1 or more other animal drugs, has the potential to prevent or treat a zoonotic disease in animals, including a vector borne-disease, that has the potential to cause serious adverse health consequences for, or serious or life-threatening diseases in, humans.

(b) "REQUEST FOR DESIGNATION.—The sponsor of a new animal drug may request the Secretary to designate a new animal drug described in subsection (a) as a priority zoonotic animal drug. A request for the designation may be made concurrently with, or at any time after, the opening of an investigational new animal drug file under section 512(j) or the filing of an application under section 512(b)(1) or 571.

(c) "DESIGNATION.—

(1) "IN GENERAL.—Not later than 60 calendar days after the receipt of a request under subsection (b), the Secretary shall determine whether the new animal drug that is the subject of the request meets the criteria described in subsection (a). If the Secretary determines that the new animal drug meets the criteria, the Secretary shall designate the new animal drug as a priority zoonotic animal drug and shall take such actions as are appropriate to expedite the development and review of the application for approval or conditional approval of such new animal drug.

(2) "ACTIONS.—The actions to expedite the development and review of an application under paragraph (1) may include, as appropriate—

(A) "taking steps to ensure that the design of clinical trials is as efficient as practicable, when scientifically appropriate, such as by utilizing novel trial designs or drug development tools (including biomarkers) that may reduce the number of animals needed for studies;

(B) "providing timely advice to, and interactive communication with, the sponsor (which may include meetings with the sponsor and review team) regarding the development of the new animal drug to ensure that the development program to gather the nonclinical and clinical data necessary for approval is as efficient as practicable;

(C) "involving senior managers and review staff with experience in zoonotic or vector-borne disease to facilitate collaborative, cross-disciplinary review, including, as appropriate, across agency centers; and

(D) "implementing additional administrative or process enhancements, as necessary, to facilitate an efficient review and development program.".

PART IV—HEALTH CARE WORKFORCE

[¶2092] SEC. 3401. REAUTHORIZATION OF HEALTH PROFESSIONS WORKFORCE PROGRAMS.

Title VII of the Public Health Service Act (42 U.S.C. 292 et seq.) is amended—

(1) in section 736 (42 U.S.C. 293), by striking subsection (i) and inserting the following:

(i) "AUTHORIZATION OF APPROPRIATIONS.—To carry out this section, there is authorized to be appropriated $23,711,000 for each of fiscal years 2021 through 2025.";

(2) in section 740 (42 U.S.C. 293d)—

(A) in subsection (a), by striking "$51,000,000 for fiscal year 2010, and such sums as may be necessary for each of the fiscal years 2011 through 2014" and inserting "$51,470,000 for each of fiscal years 2021 through 2025";

(B) in subsection (b), by striking "$5,000,000 for each of the fiscal years 2010 through 2014" and inserting "$1,190,000 for each of fiscal years 2021 through 2025";

(C) in subsection (c), by striking "$60,000,000 for fiscal year 2010 and such sums as may be necessary for each of the fiscal years 2011 through 2014" and inserting "$15,000,000 for each of fiscal years 2021 through 2025"; and

(D) in subsection (d), by striking "Not Later than 6 months after the date of enactment of this part, the Secretary shall prepare and submit to the appropriate committees of Congress" and inserting: "Not later than September 30, 2025, and every five years thereafter, the Secretary shall prepare and submit to the Committee on Health, Education, Labor, and Pensions of the Senate, and the Committee on Energy and Commerce of the House of Representatives,";

(3) in section 747 (42 U.S.C. 293k)—

(A) in subsection (a)—

(i) in paragraph (1)(G), by striking "to plan, develop, and operate a demonstration program that provides training" and inserting: "to plan, develop, and operate a program that identifies or develops innovative models of providing care, and trains primary care physicians on such models and"; and

(ii) by adding at the end the following:

(3) "PRIORITIES IN MAKING AWARDS.—In awarding grants or contracts under paragraph (1), the Secretary may give priority to qualified applicants that train residents in rural areas, including for Tribes or Tribal Organizations in such areas.";

(B) in subsection (b)(3)(E), by striking "substance-related disorders" and inserting "substance use disorders"; and

(C) in subsection (c)(1), by striking "$125,000,000 for fiscal year 2010, and such sums as may be necessary for each of fiscal years 2011 through 2014" and inserting "$48,924,000 for each of fiscal years 2021 through 2025";

(4) in section 748 (42 U.S.C. 293k–2)—

(A) in subsection (c)(5), by striking "substance-related disorders" and inserting "substance use disorders"; and

(B) in subsection (f), by striking "$30,000,000 for fiscal year 2010 and such sums as may be necessary for each of fiscal years 2011 through 2015" and inserting "$28,531,000 for each of fiscal years 2021 through 2025";

(5) in section 749(d)(2) (42 U.S.C. 293l(d)(2)), by striking "Committee on Labor and Human Resources of the Senate, and the Committee on Commerce of the House of Representatives" and inserting "Committee on Health, Education, Labor, and Pensions of the Senate, and the Committee on Energy and Commerce of the House of Representatives";

(6) in section 751(j)(1) (42 U.S.C. 294a(j)(1)), by striking "$125,000,000 for each of the fiscal years 2010 through 2014" and inserting "$41,250,000 for each of fiscal years 2021 through 2025";

(7) in section 754(b)(1)(A) (42 U.S.C. 294d(b)(1)(A)), by striking "new and innovative" and inserting "innovative or evidence-based";

(8) in section 755(b)(1)(A) (42 U.S.C. 294e(b)(1)(A)), by striking "the elderly" and inserting "geriatric populations or for maternal and child health";

(9) in section 761(e) (42 U.S.C. 294n(e))—

(A) in paragraph (1)(A), by striking "$7,500,000 for each of fiscal years 2010 through 2014" and inserting "$5,663,000 for each of fiscal years 2021 through 2025"; and

(B) in paragraph (2), by striking "subsection (a)" and inserting "paragraph (1)";

(10) in section 762 (42 U.S.C. 294o)—

(A) in subsection (a)(1), by striking "Committee on Labor and Human Resources" and inserting "Committee on Health, Education, Labor, and Pensions";

(B) in subsection (b)—

(i) in paragraph (2), by striking "Health Care Financing Administration" and inserting "Centers for Medicare & Medicaid Services";

(ii) by redesignating paragraphs (4) through (6) as paragraphs (5) through (7), respectively; and

(iii) by inserting after paragraph (3), the following:

(4) "the Administrator of the Health Resources and Services Administration;";

(C) by striking subsections (i), (j), and (k) and inserting the following:

(i) "REPORTS.—Not later than September 30, 2023, and not less than every 5 years thereafter, the Council shall submit to the Secretary, and to the Committee on Health, Education, Labor, and Pensions of the Senate and the Committee on Energy and Commerce of the House of Representatives, a report on the recommendations described in subsection (a)."; and

(D) by redesignating subsection (l) as subsection (j);

(11) in section 766(b)(1) (42 U.S.C. 295a(b)(1)), by striking "that plans" and all that follows through the period and inserting "that plans, develops, operates, and evaluates projects to improve preventive medicine, health promotion and disease prevention, or access to and quality of health care services in rural or medically underserved communities.";

(12) in section 770(a) (42 U.S.C. 295e(a)), by striking "$43,000,000 for fiscal year 2011, and such sums as may be necessary for each of the fiscal years 2012 through 2015" and inserting "$17,000,000 for each of fiscal years 2021 through 2025"; and

(13) in section 775(e) (42 U.S.C. 295f(e)), by striking "$30,000,000" and all that follows through the period and inserting "such sums as may be necessary for each of fiscal years 2021 through 2025.".

[¶2093] SEC. 3402. HEALTH WORKFORCE COORDINATION.

(a) STRATEGIC PLAN.—

(1) IN GENERAL.—Not later than 1 year after the date of enactment of this Act, the Secretary of Health and Human Services (referred to in this Act as the "Secretary"), in consultation with the Advisory Committee on Training in Primary Care Medicine and Dentistry and the Advisory Council on Graduate Medical Education, shall develop a comprehensive and coordinated plan with respect to the health care workforce development programs of the Department of Health and Human Services, including education and training programs.

(2) REQUIREMENTS.—The plan under paragraph (1) shall—

(A) include performance measures to determine the extent to which the programs described in paragraph (1) are strengthening the Nation's health care system;

(B) identify any gaps that exist between the outcomes of programs described in paragraph (1) and projected health care workforce needs identified in workforce projection reports conducted by the Health Resources and Services Administration;

(C) identify actions to address the gaps described in subparagraph (B); and

(D) identify barriers, if any, to implementing the actions identified under subparagraph (C).

(b) COORDINATION WITH OTHER AGENCIES.—The Secretary shall coordinate with the heads of other Federal agencies and departments that fund or administer health care workforce development programs, including education and training programs, to—

(1) evaluate the performance of such programs, including the extent to which such programs are efficient and effective and are meeting the nation's health workforce needs; and

(2) identify opportunities to improve the quality and consistency of the information collected to evaluate within and across such programs, and to implement such improvements.

(c) REPORT.—Not later than 2 years after the date of enactment of this Act, the Secretary shall submit to the Committee on Health, Education, Labor, and Pensions of the Senate, and the Committee on Energy and Commerce of the House of Representatives, a report describing the plan developed under subsection (a) and actions taken to implement such plan.

[¶2094] SEC. 3403. EDUCATION AND TRAINING RELATING TO GERIATRICS.

Section 753 of the Public Health Service Act (42 U.S.C. 294c) is amended to read as follows:

[¶2095] SEC. 753. "EDUCATION AND TRAINING RELATING TO GERIATRICS.

(a) "GERIATRICS WORKFORCE ENHANCEMENT PROGRAM.—

(1) "IN GENERAL.—The Secretary shall award grants, contracts, or cooperative agreements under this subsection to entities described in paragraph (1), (3), or (4) of section 799B, section 801(2), or section 865(d), or other health professions schools or programs approved by the Secretary, for the establishment or operation of Geriatrics Workforce Enhancement Programs that meet the requirements of paragraph (2).

(2) "REQUIREMENTS.—

(A) "IN GENERAL.—A Geriatrics Workforce Enhancement Program receiving an award under this section shall support the training of health professionals in geriatrics, including traineeships or fellowships. Such programs shall emphasize, as appropriate, patient and family engagement, integration of geriatrics with primary care and other appropriate specialties, and collaboration with community partners to address gaps in health care for older adults.

(B) "ACTIVITIES.—Activities conducted by a program under this section may include the following:

(i) "Clinical training on providing integrated geriatrics and primary care delivery services.

(ii) "Interprofessional training to practitioners from multiple disciplines and specialties, including training on the provision of care to older adults.

(iii) "Establishing or maintaining training-related community-based programs for older adults and caregivers to improve health outcomes for older adults.

(iv) "Providing education on Alzheimer's disease and related dementias to families and caregivers of older adults, direct care workers, and health professions students, faculty, and providers.

(3) "DURATION.—Each grant, contract, or cooperative agreement or contract awarded under paragraph (1) shall be for a period not to exceed 5 years.

(4) "APPLICATIONS.—To be eligible to receive a grant, contract, or cooperative agreement under paragraph (1), an entity described in such paragraph shall submit to the Secretary an application at such time, in such manner, and containing such information as the Secretary may require.

(5) "PROGRAM REQUIREMENTS.—

(A) "IN GENERAL.—In awarding grants, contracts, and cooperative agreements under paragraph (1), the Secretary—

(i) "shall give priority to programs that demonstrate coordination with another Federal or State program or another public or private entity;

(ii) "shall give priority to applicants with programs or activities that are expected to substantially benefit rural or medically underserved populations of older adults, or serve older adults in Indian Tribes or Tribal organizations; and

(iii) "may give priority to any program that—

(I) "integrates geriatrics into primary care practice;

(II) "provides training to integrate geriatric care into other specialties across care settings, including practicing clinical specialists, health care administrators, faculty without backgrounds in geriatrics, and students from all health professions;

(III) "emphasizes integration of geriatric care into existing service delivery locations and care across settings, including primary care clinics, medical homes, Federally qualified health centers, ambulatory care clinics, critical access hospitals, emergency care, assisted living and nursing facilities, and home- and community-based services, which may include adult daycare;

(IV) "supports the training and retraining of faculty, primary care providers, other direct care providers, and other appropriate professionals on geriatrics;

(V) "emphasizes education and engagement of family caregivers on disease management and strategies to meet the needs of caregivers of older adults; or

(VI) "proposes to conduct outreach to communities that have a shortage of geriatric workforce professionals.

(B) "SPECIAL CONSIDERATION.—In awarding grants, contracts, and cooperative agreements under this section, the Secretary shall give special consideration to entities that provide services in areas with a shortage of geriatric workforce professionals.

(6) "PRIORITY.—The Secretary may provide awardees with additional support for activities in areas of demonstrated need, which may include education and training for home health workers, family caregivers, and direct care workers on care for older adults.

(7) "REPORTING.—

(A) "REPORTS FROM ENTITIES.—Each entity awarded a grant, contract, or cooperative agreement under this section shall submit an annual report to the Secretary on the activities conducted under such grant, contract, or cooperative agreement, which may include information on the number of trainees, the number of professions and disciplines, the number of partnerships with health care delivery sites, the number of faculty and practicing professionals who participated in such programs, and other information, as the Secretary may require.

(B) "REPORT TO CONGRESS.—Not later than 4 years after the date of enactment of the Title VII Health Care Workforce Reauthorization Act of 2019 and every 5 years thereafter, the Secretary shall submit to the Committee on Health, Education, Labor, and Pensions of the Senate and the Committee on Energy and Commerce of the House of Representatives a report that provides a summary of the activities and outcomes associated with grants, contracts, and cooperative agreements made under this section. Such reports shall include—

(i) "information on the number of trainees, faculty, and professionals who participated in programs under this section;

(ii) "information on the impact of the program conducted under this section on the health status of older adults, including in areas with a shortage of health professionals; and

(iii) "information on outreach and education provided under this section to families and caregivers of older adults.

(C) "PUBLIC AVAILABILITY.—The Secretary shall make reports submitted under paragraph (B) publically available on the internet website of the Department of Health and Human Services.

(b) "GERIATRIC ACADEMIC CAREER AWARDS.—

(1) "ESTABLISHMENT OF PROGRAM.—The Secretary shall, as appropriate, establish or maintain a program to provide geriatric academic career awards to eligible entities applying on behalf of eligible individuals to promote the career development of such individuals as academic geriatricians or other academic geriatrics health professionals.

(2) "ELIGIBILITY.—

(A) "ELIGIBLE ENTITY.—For purposes of this subsection, the term 'eligible entity' means—

(i) "an entity described in paragraph (1), (3), or (4) of section 799B or section 801(2); or

(ii) "another accredited health professions school or graduate program approved by the Secretary.

(B) "ELIGIBLE INDIVIDUAL.—For purposes of this subsection, the term 'eligible individual' means an individual who—

(i)(I) "is board certified or board eligible in internal medicine, family practice, psychiatry, or licensed dentistry, or has completed required training in a discipline and is employed in an accredited health professions school or graduate program that is approved by the Secretary; or

(II) "has completed an approved fellowship program in geriatrics, or has completed specialty training in geriatrics as required by the discipline and any additional geriatrics training as required by the Secretary; and

(ii) "has a junior, nontenured, faculty appointment at an accredited health professions school or graduate program in geriatrics or a geriatrics health profession.

(C) "CLARIFICATION.—If an eligible individual is promoted during the period of an award under this subsection and thereby no longer meets the criteria of subparagraph (B)(ii), the individual shall continue to be treated as an eligible individual through the term of the award.

(3) "APPLICATION REQUIREMENTS.—In order to receive an award under paragraph (1), an eligible entity, on behalf of an eligible individual, shall—

(A) "submit to the Secretary an application, at such time, in such manner, and containing such information as the Secretary may require;

(B) "provide, in such form and manner as the Secretary may require, assurances that the eligible individual will meet the service requirement described in paragraph (6); and

(C) "provide, in such form and manner as the Secretary may require, assurances that the individual has a full-time faculty appointment in a health professions institution and documented commitment from such eligible entity that the individual will spend 75 percent of the individual's time that is supported by the award on teaching and developing skills in interdisciplinary education in geriatrics.

(4) "EQUITABLE DISTRIBUTION.—In making awards under this subsection, the Secretary shall seek to ensure geographical distribution among award recipients, including among rural or medically underserved areas of the United States.

(5) "AMOUNT AND DURATION.—

(A) "AMOUNT.—The amount of an award under this subsection shall be at least $75,000 for fiscal year 2021, adjusted for subsequent years in accordance with the consumer price index. The Secretary shall determine the amount of an award under this subsection for individuals who are not physicians.

(B) "DURATION.—The Secretary shall make awards under paragraph (1) for a period not to exceed 5 years.

(6) "SERVICE REQUIREMENT.—An individual who receives an award under this subsection shall provide training in clinical geriatrics, including the training of interprofessional teams of health care professionals. The provision of such training shall constitute at least 75 percent of the obligations of such individual under the award.

(c) "NONAPPLICABILITY OF PROVISION.—Notwithstanding any other provision of this title, section 791(a) shall not apply to awards made under this section.

(d) "AUTHORIZATION OF APPROPRIATIONS.—There is authorized to be appropriated $40,737,000 for each of fiscal years 2021 through 2025 for purposes of carrying out this section.".

[¶2096] SEC. 3404. NURSING WORKFORCE DEVELOPMENT.

(a) IN GENERAL.—Title VIII of the Public Health Service Act (42 U.S.C. 296 et seq.) is amended—

(1) in section 801 (42 U.S.C. 296), by adding at the end the following:

(18) "NURSE MANAGED HEALTH CLINIC.—The term 'nurse managed health clinic' means a nurse-practice arrangement, managed by advanced practice nurses, that provides primary care or wellness services to underserved or vulnerable populations and that is associated with a school, college, university or department of nursing, federally qualified health center, or independent nonprofit health or social services agency.";

(2) in section 802(c) (42 U.S.C. 296a(c)), by inserting ", and how such project aligns with the goals in section 806(a)" before the period in the second sentence;

(3) in section 803(b) (42 U.S.C. 296b(b)), by adding at the end the following: "Such Federal funds are intended to supplement, not supplant, existing non-Federal expenditures for such activities.";

(4) in section 806 (42 U.S.C. 296e)—

(A) in subsection (a), by striking "as needed to" and all that follows and inserting the following: "as needed to address national nursing needs, including—

(1) "addressing challenges, including through supporting training and education of nursing students, related to the distribution of the nursing workforce and existing or projected nursing workforce shortages in geographic areas that have been identified as having, or that are projected to have, a nursing shortage;

(2) "increasing access to and the quality of health care services, including by supporting the training of professional registered nurses, advanced practice registered nurses, and advanced education nurses within community based settings and in a variety of health delivery system settings; or

(3) "addressing the strategic goals and priorities identified by the Secretary and that are in accordance with this title.

Contracts may be entered into under this title with public or private entities as determined necessary by the Secretary.";

(B) in subsection (b)(2), by striking "a demonstration" and all that follows and inserting the following: "the reporting of data and information demonstrating that satisfactory progress has been made by the program or project in meeting the performance outcome standards (as described in section 802) of such program or project.";

(C) in subsection (e)(2), by inserting ", and have relevant expertise and experience" before the period at the end of the first sentence; and

(D) by adding at the end the following:

(i) "BIENNIAL REPORT ON NURSING WORKFORCE PROGRAM IMPROVEMENTS.—Not later than September 30, 2020, and biennially thereafter, the Secretary shall submit to the Committee on Health, Education, Labor, and Pensions of the Senate and the Committee on Energy and Commerce of the House of Representatives, a report that contains an assessment of the programs and activities of the Department of Health and Human Services related to enhancing the nursing workforce, including the extent to which programs and activities under this title meet the identified goals and performance measures developed for the respective programs and activities, and the extent to which the Department coordinates with other Federal departments regarding programs designed to improve the nursing workforce.";

(5) in section 811 (42 U.S.C. 296j)—

(A) in subsection (b)—

(i) by striking "Master's" and inserting "graduate"; and

(ii) by inserting "clinical nurse leaders," after "nurse administrators,";

(B) by redesignating subsections (f) and (g) as subsections (g) and (h), respectively; and

(C) by inserting after subsection (e), the following:

(f) "AUTHORIZED CLINICAL NURSE SPECIALIST PROGRAMS.—Clinical nurse specialist programs eligible for support under this section are education programs that—

(1) "provide registered nurses with full-time clinical nurse specialist education; and

(2) "have as their objective the education of clinical nurse specialists who will, upon completion of such a program, be qualified to effectively provide care through the wellness and illness continuum to inpatients and outpatients experiencing acute and chronic illness."; and

(6) in section 831 (42 U.S.C. 296p)—

(A) in the section heading, by striking "**AND QUALITY GRANTS**" and inserting "**QUALITY, AND RETENTION GRANTS**";

(B) in subsection (b)(2), by striking "other high-risk groups such as the elderly, individuals with HIV/AIDS, substance abusers, the homeless, and victims" and inserting "high risk groups, such as the elderly, individuals with HIV/AIDS, individuals with mental health or substance use disorders, individuals who are homeless, and survivors";

(C) in subsection (c)(1)—

(i) in subparagraph (A)—

(I) by striking "advancement for nursing personnel" and inserting the following: "advancement for—

(i) "nursing";

(II) by striking "professional nurses, advanced education nurses, licensed practical nurses, certified nurse assistants, and home health aides" and inserting "professional registered nurses, advanced practice registered nurses, and nurses with graduate nursing education"; and

(III) by adding at the end the following:

(ii) "individuals including licensed practical nurses, licensed vocational nurses, certified nurse assistants, home health aides, diploma degree or associate degree nurses, and other health professionals, such as health aides or community health practitioners certified under the Community Health Aide Program of the Indian Health Service, to become registered nurses with baccalaureate degrees or nurses with graduate nursing education;";

(ii) in subparagraph (B), by striking the period and inserting "; and"; and

(iii) by adding at the end the following:

(C) "developing and implementing internships, accredited fellowships, and accredited residency programs in collaboration with one or more accredited schools of nursing, to encourage the mentoring and development of specialties.";

(D) by striking subsections (e) and (h);

(E) by redesignating subsections (f) and (g), as subsections (e) and (f), respectively;

(F) in subsection (e) (as so redesignated), by striking "The Secretary shall submit to the Congress before the end of each fiscal year" and inserting "As part of the report on nursing workforce programs described in section 806(i), the Secretary shall include"; and

(G) in subsection (f) (as so redesignated), by striking "a school of nursing, as defined in section 801(2),," and inserting "an accredited school of nursing, as defined in section 801(2), a health care facility, including federally qualified health centers or nurse-managed health clinics, or a partnership of such a school and facility";

(7) by striking section 831A (42 U.S.C. 296p–1);

(8) in section 846 (42 U.S.C. 297n)—

(A) by striking the last sentence of subsection (a);

(B) in subsection (b)(1), by striking "he began such practice" and inserting "the individual began such practice"; and

(C) in subsection (i), by striking "FUNDING" in the subsection heading and all that follows through "paragraph (1)" in paragraph (2), and inserting the following: "ALLOCATIONS.—Of the amounts appropriated under section 871(b),";

(9) in section 846A (42 U.S.C. 247n–1), by striking subsection (f);

(10) in section 847 (42 U.S.C. 297o), by striking subsection (g);

(11) in section 851 (42 U.S.C. 297t)—

(A) in subsection (b)(1)(A)(iv), by striking "and nurse anesthetists" and inserting "nurse anesthetists, and clinical nurse specialists";

(B) in subsection (d)(3)—

(i) by striking "3 years after the date of enactment of this section" and inserting "2 years after the date of enactment of the Title VIII Nursing Reauthorization Act";

(ii) by striking "Labor and Human Resources" and inserting "Health, Education, Labor, and Pensions"; and

(iii) by inserting "Energy and" before "Commerce"; and

(C) in subsection (g), by striking "under this title" and inserting "for carrying out parts B, C, and D";

(12) by striking sections 861 and 862 (42 U.S.C. 297w and 297x); and

(13) in section 871 (42 U.S.C. 298d)—

(A) by striking "For the purpose of" and inserting the following:

(a) "IN GENERAL.—For the purpose of";

(B) by striking "$338,000,000 for fiscal year 2010, and such sums as may be necessary for each of the fiscal years 2011 through 2016" and inserting "$137,837,000 for each of fiscal years 2021 through 2025"; and

(C) by adding at the end the following:

(b) "PART E.—For the purpose of carrying out part E, there are authorized to be appropriated $117,135,000 for each of the fiscal years 2021 through 2025.".

(b) EVALUATION AND REPORT ON NURSE LOAN REPAYMENT PROGRAMS.—

(1) EVALUATION.—The Comptroller General shall conduct an evaluation of the nurse loan repayment programs administered by the Health Resources and Services Administration. Such evaluation shall include—

(A) the manner in which payments are made under such programs;

(B) the existing oversight functions necessary to ensure the proper use of such programs, including payments made as part of such programs;

(C) the identification of gaps, if any, in oversight functions; and

(D) information on the number of nurses assigned to facilities pursuant to such programs, including the type of facility to which nurses are assigned and the impact of modifying the eligibility requirements for programs under section 846 of the Public Health Service Act (42 U.S.C. 297n), such as the impact on entities to which nurses had previously been assigned prior to fiscal year 2019 (such as federally qualified health centers and facilities affiliated with the Indian Health Service).

(2) REPORT.—Not later than 18 months after the enactment of this Act, the Comptroller General shall submit to the Committee on Health, Education, Labor, and Pensions of the Senate and the Committee on Energy and Commerce of the House of Representatives, a report on the evaluation under paragraph (1), which may include recommendations to improve relevant nursing workforce loan repayment programs.

Subtitle B—Education Provisions

[¶2098] SEC. 3501. SHORT TITLE.

This subtitle may be cited as the "COVID–19 Pandemic Education Relief Act of 2020".

[¶2099] SEC. 3502. DEFINITIONS.

(a) DEFINITIONS.—In this subtitle:

(1) CORONAVIRUS.—The term "coronavirus" has the meaning given the term in section 506 of the Coronavirus Preparedness and Response Supplemental Appropriations Act, 2020 (Public Law 116–123).

(2) FOREIGN INSTITUTION.—The term "foreign institution" means an institution of higher education located outside the United States that is described in paragraphs (1)(C) and (2) of section 102(a) of the Higher Education Act of 1965 (20 U.S.C. 1002(a)).

(3) INSTITUTION OF HIGHER EDUCATION.—The term "institution of higher education" has the meaning of the term under section 102 of the Higher Education Act of 1965 (20 U.S.C. 1002).

(4) QUALIFYING EMERGENCY.—The term "qualifying emergency" means—

(A) a public health emergency related to the coronavirus declared by the Secretary of Health and Human Services pursuant to section 319 of the Public Health Service Act (42 U.S.C. 247d);

(B) an event related to the coronavirus for which the President declared a major disaster or an emergency under section 401 or 501, respectively, of the Robert T. Stafford Disaster Relief and Emergency Assistance Act (42 U.S.C. 5170 and 5191); or

(C) a national emergency related to the coronavirus declared by the President under section 201 of the National Emergencies Act (50 U.S.C. 1601 et seq.).

(5) SECRETARY.—The term "Secretary" means the Secretary of Education.

[¶2100] SEC. 3503. CAMPUS-BASED AID WAIVERS.

(a) WAIVER OF NON-FEDERAL SHARE REQUIREMENT.—Notwithstanding sections 413C(a)(2) and 443(b)(5) of the Higher Education Act of 1965 (20 U.S.C. 1070b–2(a)(2) and 1087–53(b)(5)), with respect to funds made available for award years 2019–2020 and 2020–2021, the Secretary shall waive the requirement that a participating institution of higher education provide a non-Federal share to match Federal funds provided to the institution for the programs authorized pursuant to subpart 3 of part A and part C of title IV of the Higher Education Act of 1965 (20 U.S.C. 1070b et seq. and 1087–51 et seq.) for all awards made under such programs during such award years, except nothing in this subsection shall affect the non-Federal share requirement under section 443(c)(3) that applies to private for-profit organizations.

(b) AUTHORITY TO REALLOCATE.—Notwithstanding sections 413D, 442, and 488 of the Higher Education Act of 1965 (20 U.S.C. 1070b–3, 1087–52, and 1095), during a period of a qualifying emergency, an institution may transfer up to 100 percent of the institution's unexpended allotment under section 442 of such Act to the institution's allotment under section 413D of such Act, but may not transfer any funds from the institution's unexpended allotment under section 413D of such Act to the institution's allotment under section 442 of such Act.

[¶2101] SEC. 3504. USE OF SUPPLEMENTAL EDUCATIONAL OPPORTUNITY GRANTS FOR EMERGENCY AID.

(a) IN GENERAL.—Notwithstanding section 413B of the Higher Education Act of 1965 (20 U.S.C. 1070b–1), an institution of higher education may reserve any amount of an institution's allocation under subpart 3 of part A of title IV of the Higher Education Act of 1965 (20 U.S.C. 1070b et seq.) for a fiscal year to award, in such fiscal year, emergency financial aid grants to assist undergraduate or graduate students for unexpected expenses and unmet financial need as the result of a qualifying emergency.

(b) DETERMINATIONS.—In determining eligibility for and awarding emergency financial aid grants under this section, an institution of higher education may—

(1) waive the amount of need calculation under section 471 of the Higher Education Act of 1965 (20 U.S.C. 1087kk);

(2) allow for a student affected by a qualifying emergency to receive funds in an amount that is not more than the maximum Federal Pell Grant for the applicable award year; and

(3) utilize a contract with a scholarship-granting organization designated for the sole purpose of accepting applications from or disbursing funds to students enrolled in the institution of higher education, if such scholarship-granting organization disburses the full allocated amount provided to the institution of higher education to the recipients.

(c) SPECIAL RULE.—Any emergency financial aid grants to students under this section shall not be treated as other financial assistance for the purposes of section 471 of the Higher Education Act of 1965 (20 U.S.C. 1087kk).

[¶2102] SEC. 3505. FEDERAL WORK-STUDY DURING A QUALIFYING EMERGENCY.

(a) IN GENERAL.—In the event of a qualifying emergency, an institution of higher education participating in the program under part C of title IV of the Higher Education Act of 1965 (20 U.S.C. 1087–51 et seq.) may make payments under such part to affected work-study students, for the period of time (not to exceed one academic year) in which affected students were unable to fulfill the students' work-study obligation for all or part of such academic year due to such qualifying emergency, as follows:

(1) Payments may be made under such part to affected work-study students in an amount equal to or less than the amount of wages such students would have been paid under such part had the students been able to complete the work obligation necessary to receive work study funds, as a one time grant or as multiple payments.

(2) Payments shall not be made to any student who was not eligible for work study or was not completing the work obligation necessary to receive work study funds under such part prior to the occurrence of the qualifying emergency.

(3) Any payments made to affected work-study students under this subsection shall meet the matching requirements of section 443 of the Higher Education Act of 1965 (20 U.S.C. 1087–53), unless such matching requirements are waived by the Secretary.

(b) DEFINITION OF AFFECTED WORK-STUDY STUDENT.—In this section, the term "affected work-study student" means a student enrolled at an eligible institution participating in the program under part C of title IV of the Higher Education Act of 1965 (20 U.S.C. 1087–51 et seq.) who—

(1) received a work-study award under section 443 of the Higher Education Act of 1965 (20 U.S.C. 1087–53) for the academic year during which a qualifying emergency occurred;

(2) earned Federal work-study wages from such eligible institution for such academic year; and

(3) was prevented from fulfilling the student's work-study obligation for all or part of such academic year due to such qualifying emergency.

[¶2103] SEC. 3506. ADJUSTMENT OF SUBSIDIZED LOAN USAGE LIMITS.

Notwithstanding section 455(q)(3) of the Higher Education Act of 1965 (20 U.S.C. 1087e(q)(3)), the Secretary shall exclude from a student's period of enrollment for purposes of loans made under part D of title IV of the Higher Education Act of 1965 (20 U.S.C. 1087a et seq.) any semester (or the equivalent) that the student does not complete due to a qualifying emergency, if the Secretary is able to administer such policy in a manner that limits complexity and the burden on the student.

[¶2104] SEC. 3507. EXCLUSION FROM FEDERAL PELL GRANT DURATION LIMIT.

The Secretary shall exclude from a student's Federal Pell Grant duration limit under section 401(c)(5) of the Higher Education Act of 1965 (2 U.S.C. 1070a(c)(5)) any semester (or the equivalent) that the student does not complete due to a qualifying emergency if the Secretary is able to administer such policy in a manner that limits complexity and the burden on the student.

[¶2105] SEC. 3508. INSTITUTIONAL REFUNDS AND FEDERAL STUDENT LOAN FLEXIBILITY.

(a) INSTITUTIONAL WAIVER.—

(1) IN GENERAL.—The Secretary shall waive the institutional requirement under section 484B of the Higher Education Act of 1965 (20 U.S.C. 1091b) with respect to the amount of grant or loan assistance (other than assistance received under part C of title IV of such Act) to be returned under such section if a recipient of assistance under title IV of the Higher Education Act of 1965 (20 U.S.C. 1070 et seq.) withdraws from the institution of higher education during the payment period or period of enrollment as a result of a qualifying emergency.

(2) WAIVERS.—The Secretary shall require each institution using a waiver relating to the withdrawal of recipients under this subsection to report the number of such recipients, the amount of grant or loan assistance (other than assistance received under part C of title IV of such Act) associated with each such recipient, and the total amount of grant or loan assistance (other than assistance received under part C of title IV of such Act) for which each institution has not returned assistance under title IV to the Secretary.

(b) STUDENT WAIVER.—The Secretary shall waive the amounts that students are required to return under section 484B of the Higher Education Act of 1965 (20 U.S.C. 1091b) with respect to Federal Pell Grants or other grant assistance if the withdrawals on which the returns are based, are withdrawals by students who withdrew from the institution of higher education as a result of a qualifying emergency.

(c) CANCELING LOAN OBLIGATION.—Notwithstanding any other provision of the Higher Education Act of 1965 (20 U.S.C. 1001 et seq.), the Secretary shall cancel the borrower's obligation to repay the entire portion of a loan made under part D of title IV of such Act (20 U.S.C. 1087a et seq.) associated with a payment period for a recipient of such loan who withdraws from the institution of higher education during the payment period as a result of a qualifying emergency.

(d) APPROVED LEAVE OF ABSENCE.—Notwithstanding any other provision of the Higher Education Act of 1965 (20 U.S.C. 1001 et seq.), for purposes of receiving assistance under title IV of the Higher Education Act of 1965 (20 U.S.C. 1070 et seq.), an institution of higher education may, as a result of a qualifying emergency, provide a student with an approved leave of absence that does not require the student to return at the same point in the academic program that the student began the leave of absence if the student returns within the same semester (or the equivalent).

[¶2106] SEC. 3509. SATISFACTORY ACADEMIC PROGRESS.

Notwithstanding section 484 of the Higher Education Act of 1965 (20 U.S.C. 1091), in determining whether a student is maintaining satisfactory academic progress for purposes of title IV of the Higher Education Act of 1965 (20 U.S.C. 1070 et seq.), an institution of higher education may, as a result of a qualifying emergency, exclude from the quantitative component of the calculation any attempted credits that were not completed by such student without requiring an appeal by such student.

[¶2107] SEC. 3510. CONTINUING EDUCATION AT AFFECTED FOREIGN INSTITUTIONS.

(a) IN GENERAL.—Notwithstanding section 481(b) of the Higher Education Act of 1965 (20 U.S.C. 1088(b)), with respect to a foreign institution, in the case of a public health emergency, major disaster or emergency, or national emergency declared by the applicable government authorities in the country in which the foreign institution is located, the Secretary may permit any part of an otherwise eligible program to be offered via distance education for the duration of such emergency or disaster and the following payment period for purposes of title IV of the Higher Education Act of 1965 (20 U.S.C. 1070 et seq.).

(b) ELIGIBILITY.—An otherwise eligible program that is offered in whole or in part through distance education by a foreign institution between March 1, 2020, and the date of enactment of this Act shall be deemed eligible for the purposes of part D of title IV of the Higher Education Act of 1965 (20 U.S.C. 1087a et seq.) for the duration of the qualifying emergency and the following payment period for purposes of title IV of the Higher Education Act of 1965 (20 U.S.C. 1070 et seq.). An institution of higher education that uses the authority provided in the previous sentence shall report such use to the Secretary—

(1) for the 2019–2020 award year, not later than June 30, 2020; and

(2) for an award year subsequent to the 2019–2020 award year, not later than 30 days after such use.

(c) REPORT.—Not later than 180 days after the date of enactment of this Act, and every 180 days thereafter for the duration of the qualifying emergency and the following payment period, the Secretary shall submit to the authorizing committees (as defined in section 103 of the Higher Education Act of 1965 (20 U.S.C. 1003)) a report that identifies each foreign institution that carried out a distance education program authorized under this section.

(d) WRITTEN ARRANGEMENTS.—

(1) IN GENERAL.—Notwithstanding section 102 of the Higher Education Act of 1965 (20 U.S.C. 1002), for the duration of a qualifying emergency and the following payment period, the Secretary may allow a foreign institution to enter into a written arrangement with an institution of higher education located in the United States that participates in the Federal Direct Loan Program under part D of title IV of the Higher Education Act of 1965 (20 U.S.C. 1087a et seq.) for the purpose of allowing a student of the foreign institution who is a borrower of a loan made under such part to take courses from the institution of higher education located in the United States.

(2) FORM OF ARRANGEMENTS.—

(A) PUBLIC OR OTHER NONPROFIT INSTITUTIONS.—A foreign institution that is a public or other nonprofit institution may enter into a written arrangement under subsection (a) only with an institution of higher education described in section 101 of such Act (20 U.S.C. 1001).

(B) OTHER INSTITUTIONS.—A foreign institution that is a graduate medical school, nursing school, or a veterinary school and that is not a public or other nonprofit institution may enter into a written arrangement under subsection (a) with an institution of higher education described in section 101 or section 102 of such Act (20 U.S.C. 1001 and 1002).

(3) REPORT ON USE.—An institution of higher education that uses the authority described in paragraph (2) shall report such use to the Secretary—

(A) for the 2019–2020 award year, not later than June 30, 2020; and

(B) for an award year subsequent to the 2019–2020 award year, not later than 30 days after such use.

(4) REPORT FROM THE SECRETARY.—Not later than 180 days after the date of enactment of this Act, and every 180 days thereafter for the duration of the qualifying emergency and the following payment period, the Secretary shall submit to the authorizing committees (as defined in section 103 of the Higher Education Act of 1965 (20 U.S.C. 1003)) a report that identifies each foreign institution that entered into a written arrangement authorized under subsection (a).

[¶2108] SEC. 3511. NATIONAL EMERGENCY EDUCATIONAL WAIVERS.

(a) IN GENERAL.—Notwithstanding any other provision of law, the Secretary may, upon the request of a State educational agency or Indian tribe, waive any statutory or regulatory provision described under paragraphs (1) and (2) of subsection (b), and upon the request of a local educational agency, waive any statutory or regulatory provision described under paragraph (2) of subsection (b), if the Secretary determines that such a waiver is necessary and appropriate due to the emergency involving Federal primary responsibility determined to exist by the President under the section 501(b) of the Robert T. Stafford Disaster Relief and Emergency Assistance Act (42 U.S.C. 5191(b)) with respect to the Coronavirus Disease 2019 (COVID–19).

(b) APPLICABLE PROVISIONS OF LAW.—

(1) STREAMLINED WAIVERS.—The Secretary shall create an expedited application process to request a waiver and the Secretary may waive any statutory or regulatory requirements for a State educational agency (related to assessments, accountability, and reporting requirements related to assessments and accountability), if the Secretary determines that such a waiver is necessary and appropriate as described in subsection (a), under the following provisions of law:

(A) The following provisions under section 1111 of the Elementary and Secondary Education Act of 1965 (20 U.S.C. 6311):

(i) Paragraphs (2) and (3) of subsection (b).

(ii) Subsection (c)(4).

(iii) Subparagraphs (C) and (D) of subsection (d)(2).

(iv) The following provisions under subsection (h) of such section 1111:

(I) Clauses (i), (ii), (iii)(I), (iv), (v), (vi), (vii), and (xi) of paragraph (1)(C).

(II) Paragraph (2)(C) with respect to the waived requirements under subclause (I).

(III) Clauses (i) and (ii) of paragraph (2)(C).

(B) Section 421(b) of the General Education Provisions Act (20 U.S.C. 1225(b)).

(2) STATE AND LOCALLY-REQUESTED WAIVERS.—For a State educational agency, local educational agency, or Indian tribe that receives funds under a program authorized under the Elementary and Secondary Education Act of 1965 (20 U.S.C. 6301 et seq.) that requests a waiver under subsection (c), the Secretary may waive statutory and regulatory requirements under any of the following provisions of such Act:

(A) Section 1114(a)(1).

(B) Section 1118(a) and section 8521.

(C) Section 1127.

(D) Section 4106(d).

(E) Subparagraphs (C), (D), and (E) of section 4106(e)(2).

(F) Section 4109(b).

(G) The definition under section 8101(42) for purposes of the Elementary and Secondary Education Act of 1965 (20 U.S.C. 6301 et seq.).

(3) APPLICABILITY TO CHARTER SCHOOLS.—Any waivers issued by the Secretary under this section shall be implemented, as applicable—

(A) for all public schools, including public charter schools within the boundaries of the recipient of the waiver;

(B) in accordance with State charter school law; and

(C) pursuant to section 1111(c)(5) of the Elementary and Secondary Education Act of 1965 (20 U.S.C. 6311(c)(5)).

(4) LIMITATION.—Nothing in this section shall be construed to allow the Secretary to waive any statutory or regulatory requirements under applicable civil rights laws.

(5) ACCOUNTABILITY AND IMPROVEMENT.—Any school located in a State that receives a waiver under paragraph (1) and that is identified for comprehensive support and improvement, targeted support and improvement, or additional targeted support in the 2019–2020 school year under section 1111(c)(4)(D) or section 1111(d)(2) of the Elementary and Secondary Education Act of 1965 (20 U.S.C. 6311(c)(4)(D) or (d)(2)) shall maintain that identification status in the 2020–2021 school year and continue to receive supports and interventions consistent with the school's support and improvement plan in the 2020–2021 school year.

(c) STATE AND LOCAL REQUESTS FOR WAIVERS.—

(1) IN GENERAL.—A State educational agency, local educational agency, or Indian tribe that desires a waiver from any statutory or regulatory provision described under subsection (b)(2), may submit a waiver request to the Secretary in accordance with this subsection.

(2) REQUESTS SUBMITTED.—A request for a waiver under this subsection shall—

(A) identify the Federal programs affected by the requested waiver;

(B) describe which Federal statutory or regulatory requirements are to be waived;

(C) describe how the emergency involving Federal primary responsibility determined to exist by the President under the section 501(b) of the Robert T. Stafford Disaster Relief and Emergency Assistance Act (42 U.S.C. 5191(b)) with respect to the Coronavirus Disease 2019 (COVID–19) prevents or otherwise restricts the ability of the State, State educational agency, local educational agency, Indian tribe, or school to comply with such statutory or regulatory requirements; and

(D) provide an assurance that the State educational agency, local educational agency, or Indian tribe will work to mitigate any negative effects, if any, that may occur as a result of the requested waiver.

(3) SECRETARY APPROVAL.—

(A) IN GENERAL.—Except as provided under subparagraph (B), the Secretary shall approve or disapprove a waiver request submitted under paragraph (1) not more than 30 days after the date on which such request is submitted.

(B) EXCEPTIONS.—The Secretary may disapprove a waiver request submitted under paragraph (1), only if the Secretary determines that—

(i) the waiver request does not meet the requirements of this section;

(ii) the waiver is not permitted pursuant to subsection (b)(2); or

(iii) the description required under paragraph (2)(C) provides insufficient information to demonstrate that the waiving of such requirements is necessary or appropriate consistent with subsection (a).

(4) DURATION.—A waiver approved by the Secretary under this section may be for a period not to exceed the 2019–2020 academic year, except to carry out full implementation of any maintenance of effort waivers granted during the 2019–2020 academic year.

(d) REPORTING AND PUBLICATION.—

(1) PUBLIC NOTICE.—A State educational agency, Indian Tribe, or local educational agency requesting a waiver under subsection (b)(2) shall provide the public and all local educational agencies in the State with notice of, and the opportunity to comment on, the request by posting information regarding the waiver request and the process for commenting on the State website.

(2) NOTIFYING CONGRESS.—Not later than 7 days after granting a waiver under this section, the Secretary shall notify the Committee on Health, Education, Labor, and Pensions of the Senate, the Committee on Appropriations of the Senate, the Committee on Education and Labor of the House of Representatives, and the Committee on Appropriations of the House of Representatives of such waiver.

(3) PUBLICATION.—Not later than 30 days after granting a waiver under this section, the Secretary shall publish a notice of the Secretary's decision (including which waiver was granted and the reason for granting the waiver) in the Federal Register and on the website of the Department of Education.

(4) REPORT.—Not later than 30 days after the date of enactment of this Act, the Secretary shall prepare and submit a report to the Committee on Health, Education, Labor, and Pensions and the

Committee on Appropriations of the Senate, and the Committee on Education and Labor and the Committee on Appropriations of the House of Representatives, with recommendations on any additional waivers under the Individuals with Disabilities Education Act (20 U.S.C. 1401 et seq.), the Rehabilitation Act of 1973 (29 U.S.C. 701 et seq.), the Elementary and Secondary Education Act of 1965 (20 U.S.C. 6301 et seq.), and the Carl D. Perkins Career and Technical Education Act of 2006 (20 U.S.C. 2301 et seq.) the Secretary believes are necessary to be enacted into law to provide limited flexibility to States and local educational agencies to meet the needs of students during the emergency involving Federal primary responsibility determined to exist by the President under section 501(b) of the Robert T. Stafford Disaster Relief and Emergency Assistance Act (42 U.S.C. 5191(b)) with respect to the Coronavirus Disease 2019 (COVID–19).

(e) TERMS.—In this section, the term "State educational agency" includes the Bureau of Indian Education, and the term "local educational agency" includes Bureau of Indian Education funded schools operated pursuant to a grant under the Tribally Controlled Schools Act of 1988 (25 U.S.C. 2501 et seq.), or a contract under the Indian Self-Determination and Education Assistance Act (25 U.S.C. 5301 et seq.).

[¶2109] SEC. 3512. HBCU CAPITAL FINANCING.

(a) DEFERMENT PERIOD.—

(1) IN GENERAL.—Notwithstanding any provision of title III of the Higher Education Act of 1965 (20 U.S.C. 1051 et seq.), or any regulation promulgated under such title, the Secretary may grant a deferment, for the duration of a qualifying emergency, to an institution that has received a loan under part D of title III of such Act (20 U.S.C. 1066 et seq.).

(2) TERMS.—During the deferment period granted under this subsection—

(A) the institution shall not be required to pay any periodic installment of principal or interest required under the loan agreement for such loan; and

(B) the Secretary shall make principal and interest payments otherwise due under the loan agreement.

(3) CLOSING.—At the closing of a loan deferred under this subsection, terms shall be set under which the institution shall be required to repay the Secretary for the payments of principal and interest made by the Secretary during the deferment, on a schedule that begins upon repayment to the lender in full on the loan agreement, except in no case shall repayment be required to begin before the date that is 1 full fiscal year after the date that is the end of the qualifying emergency.

(b) TERMINATION DATE.—

(1) IN GENERAL.—The authority provided under this section to grant a loan deferment under subsection (a) shall terminate on the date on which the qualifying emergency is no longer in effect.

(2) DURATION.—Any provision of a loan agreement or insurance agreement modified by the authority under this section shall remain so modified for the duration of the period covered by the loan agreement or insurance agreement.

(c) REPORT.—Not later than 180 days after the date of enactment of this Act, and every 180 days thereafter during the period beginning on the first day of the qualifying emergency and ending on September 30 of the fiscal year following the end of the qualifying emergency, the Secretary shall submit to the authorizing committees (as defined in section 103 of the Higher Education Act of 1965 (20 U.S.C. 1003)) a report that identifies each institution that received assistance under this section.

(d) FUNDING.—There is hereby appropriated, out of any money in the Treasury not otherwise appropriated, $62,000,000 to carry out this section.

[¶2110] SEC. 3513. TEMPORARY RELIEF FOR FEDERAL STUDENT LOAN BORROWERS.

(a) IN GENERAL.—The Secretary shall suspend all payments due for loans made under part D and part B (that are held by the Department of Education) of title IV of the Higher Education Act of 1965 (20 U.S.C. 1087a et seq.; 1071 et seq.) through September 30, 2020.

(b) NO ACCRUAL OF INTEREST.—Notwithstanding any other provision of the Higher Education Act of 1965 (20 U.S.C. 1001 et seq.), interest shall not accrue on a loan described under subsection (a) for which payment was suspended for the period of the suspension.

(c) Consideration of Payments.—Notwithstanding any other provision of the Higher Education Act of 1965 (20 U.S.C. 1001 et seq.), the Secretary shall deem each month for which a loan payment was suspended under this section as if the borrower of the loan had made a payment for the purpose of any loan forgiveness program or loan rehabilitation program authorized under part D or B of title IV of the Higher Education Act of 1965 (20 U.S.C. 1087a et seq.; 1071 et seq.) for which the borrower would have otherwise qualified.

(d) Reporting to Consumer Reporting Agencies.—During the period in which the Secretary suspends payments on a loan under subsection (a), the Secretary shall ensure that, for the purpose of reporting information about the loan to a consumer reporting agency, any payment that has been suspended is treated as if it were a regularly scheduled payment made by a borrower.

(e) Suspending Involuntary Collection.—During the period in which the Secretary suspends payments on a loan under subsection (a), the Secretary shall suspend all involuntary collection related to the loan, including—

(1) a wage garnishment authorized under section 488A of the Higher Education Act of 1965 (20 U.S.C. 1095a) or section 3720D of title 31, United States Code;

(2) a reduction of tax refund by amount of debt authorized under section 3720A of title 31, United States Code, or section 6402(d) of the Internal Revenue Code of 1986;

(3) a reduction of any other Federal benefit payment by administrative offset authorized under section 3716 of title 31, United States Code (including a benefit payment due to an individual under the Social Security Act or any other provision described in subsection (c)(3)(A)(i) of such section); and

(4) any other involuntary collection activity by the Secretary.

(f) Waivers.—In carrying out this section, the Secretary may waive the application of—

(1) subchapter I of chapter 35 of title 44, United States Code (commonly known as the "Paperwork Reduction Act");

(2) the master calendar requirements under section 482 of the Higher Education Act of 1965 (20 U.S.C. 1089);

(3) negotiated rulemaking under section 492 of the Higher Education Act of 1965 (20 U.S.C. 1098a); and

(4) the requirement to publish the notices related to the system of records of the agency before implementation required under paragraphs (4) and (11) of section 552a(e) of title 5, United States Code (commonly known as the "Privacy Act of 1974"), except that the notices shall be published not later than 180 days after the date of enactment of this Act.

(g) Notice to Borrowers and Transition Period.—To inform borrowers of the actions taken in accordance with this section and ensure an effective transition, the Secretary shall—

(1) not later than 15 days after the date of enactment of this Act, notify borrowers—

(A) of the actions taken in accordance with subsections (a) and (b) for whom payments have been suspended and interest waived;

(B) of the actions taken in accordance with subsection (e) for whom collections have been suspended;

(C) of the option to continue making payments toward principal; and

(D) that the program under this section is a temporary program.

(2) beginning on August 1, 2020, carry out a program to provide not less than 6 notices by postal mail, telephone, or electronic communication to borrowers indicating—

(A) when the borrower's normal payment obligations will resume; and

(B) that the borrower has the option to enroll in income-driven repayment, including a brief description of such options.

[¶2111] SEC. 3514. PROVISIONS RELATED TO THE CORPORATION FOR NATIONAL AND COMMUNITY SERVICE.

(a) Accrual of Service Hours.—

(1) Accrual through other service hours.—

(A) IN GENERAL.—Notwithstanding any other provision of the Domestic Volunteer Service Act of 1973 (42 U.S.C. 4950 et seq.) or the National and Community Service Act of 1990 (42 U.S.C. 12501 et seq.), the Corporation for National and Community Service shall allow an individual described in subparagraph (B) to accrue other service hours that will count toward the number of hours needed for the individual's education award.

(B) AFFECTED INDIVIDUALS.—Subparagraph (A) shall apply to any individual serving in a position eligible for an educational award under subtitle D of title I of the National and Community Service Act of 1990 (42 U.S.C. 12601 et seq.)—

(i) who is performing limited service due to COVID–19; or

(ii) whose position has been suspended or placed on hold due to COVID–19.

(2) PROVISIONS IN CASE OF EARLY EXIT.—In any case where an individual serving in a position eligible for an educational award under subtitle D of title I of the National and Community Service Act of 1990 (42 U.S.C. 12601 et seq.) was required to exit the position early at the direction of the Corporation for National and Community Service, the Chief Executive Officer of the Corporation for National and Community Service may—

(A) deem such individual as having met the requirements of the position; and

(B) award the individual the full value of the educational award under such subtitle for which the individual would otherwise have been eligible.

(b) AVAILABILITY OF FUNDS.—Notwithstanding any other provision of law, all funds made available to the Corporation for National and Community Service under any Act, including the amounts appropriated to the Corporation under the headings "OPERATING EXPENSES", "SALARIES AND EXPENSES", and "OFFICE OF THE INSPECTOR GENERAL" under the heading "CORPORATION FOR NATIONAL AND COMMUNITY SERVICE" under title IV of Division A of the Further Consolidated Appropriations Act, 2020 (Public Law 116–94), shall remain available for the fiscal year ending September 30, 2021.

(c) NO REQUIRED RETURN OF GRANT FUNDS.—Notwithstanding section 129(l)(3)(A)(i) of the National and Community Service Act of 1990 (42 U.S.C. 12581(l)(3)(A)(i)), the Chief Executive Officer of the Corporation for National and Community Service may permit fixed-amount grant recipients under such section 129(l) to maintain a pro rata amount of grant funds, at the discretion of the Corporation for National and Community Service, for participants who exited, were suspended, or are serving in a limited capacity due to COVID–19, to enable the grant recipients to maintain operations and to accept participants.

(d) EXTENSION OF TERMS AND AGE LIMITS.—Notwithstanding any other provision of law, the Corporation for National and Community Service may extend the term of service (for a period not to exceed the 1-year period immediately following the end of the national emergency) or waive any upper age limit (except in no case shall the maximum age exceed 26 years of age) for national service programs carried out by the National Civilian Community Corps under subtitle E of title I of the National and Community Service Act of 1990 (42 U.S.C. 12611 et seq.), and the participants in such programs, for the purposes of—

(1) addressing disruptions due to COVID–19; and

(2) minimizing the difficulty in returning to full operation due to COVID–19 on such programs and participants.

[¶2112] SEC. 3515. WORKFORCE RESPONSE ACTIVITIES.

(a) ADMINISTRATIVE COSTS.—Notwithstanding section 128(b)(4) of the Workforce Innovation Opportunity Act (29 U.S.C. 3163(b)(4)), of the total amount allocated to a local area (including the total amount allotted to a single State local area) under subtitle B of title I of such Act (29 U.S.C. 3151 et seq.) for program year 2019, not more than 20 percent of the total amount may be used for the administrative costs of carrying out local workforce investment activities under chapter 2 or chapter 3 of subtitle B of title I of such Act, if the portion of the total amount that exceeds 10 percent of the total amount is used to respond to a qualifying emergency.

(b) RAPID RESPONSE ACTIVITIES.—

(1) STATEWIDE RAPID RESPONSE.—Of the funds reserved by a Governor for program year 2019 for statewide activities under section 128(a) of the Workforce Innovation and Opportunity Act (29 U.S.C. 3163(a)) that remain unobligated, such funds may be used for statewide rapid response activities as

described in section 134(a)(2)(A) of such Act (29 U.S.C. 3174(a)(2)(A)) for responding to a qualifying emergency.

(2) LOCAL BOARDS.—Of the funds reserved by a Governor for program year 2019 under section 133(a)(2) of such Act (29 U.S.C. 3173(a)(2)) that remain unobligated, such funds may be released within 30 days after the date of enactment of this Act to the local boards most impacted by the coronavirus at the determination of the Governor for rapid response activities related to responding to a qualifying emergency.

(c) DEFINITIONS.—Except as otherwise provided, the terms in this section have the meanings given the terms in section 3 of the Workforce Innovation and Opportunity Act (29 U.S.C. 3102).

[¶2113] SEC. 3516. TECHNICAL AMENDMENTS.

(a) IN GENERAL.—

(1) Section 6103(a)(3) of the Internal Revenue Code of 1986, as amended by the FUTURE Act (Public Law 116–91), is further amended by striking "(13), (16)" and inserting "(13)(A), (13)(B), (13)(C), (13)(D)(i), (16)".

(2) Section 6103(p)(3)(A) of such Code, as so amended, is further amended by striking "(12)," and inserting "(12), (13)(A), (13)(B), (13)(C), (13)(D)(i)".

(3) Section 6103(p)(4) of such Code, as so amended, is further amended by striking "(13) or (16)" each place it appears and inserting "(13), or (16)".

(4) Section 6103(p)(4) of such Code, as so amended and as amended by paragraph (3), is further amended by striking "(13)" each place it appears and inserting "(13)(A), (13)(B), (13)(C), (13)(D)(i)".

(5) Section 6103(l)(13)(C)(ii) of such Code, as added by the FUTURE Act (Public Law 116–91), is amended by striking "section 236A(e)(4)" and inserting "section 263A(e)(4)".

(b) EFFECTIVE DATE.—The amendments made by this section shall apply as if included in the enactment of the FUTURE Act (Public Law 116–91).

[¶2114] SEC. 3517. WAIVER AUTHORITY AND REPORTING REQUIREMENT FOR INSTITUTIONAL AID.

(a) WAIVER AUTHORITY.—Notwithstanding any other provision of the Higher Education Act of 1965 (U.S.C. 1001 et seq.), unless enacted with specific reference to this section, for any institution of higher education that was receiving assistance under title III, title V, or subpart 4 of part A of title VII of such Act (20 U.S.C. 1051 et seq.; 1101 et seq.; 1136a et seq.) at the time of a qualifying emergency, the Secretary may, for the period beginning on the first day of the qualifying emergency and ending on September 30 of the fiscal year following the end of the qualifying emergency—

(1) waive—

(A) the eligibility data requirements set forth in section 391(d) and 521(e) of the Higher Education Act of 1965 (20 U.S.C. 1068(d); 1103(e));

(B) the wait-out period set forth in section 313(d) of the Higher Education Act of 1965 (20 U.S.C. 1059(d));

(C) the allotment requirements under paragraphs (2) and (3) of subsection 318(e) of the Higher Education Act of 1965 (20 U.S.C. 1059e(e)), and the reference to "the academic year preceding the beginning of that fiscal year" under such section 318(e)(1);

(D) the allotment requirements under subsections (b), (c), and (g) of section 324 of the Higher Education Act of 1965 (20 U.S.C. 1063), the reference to "the end of the school year preceding the beginning of that fiscal year" under such section 324(a), and the reference to "the academic year preceding such fiscal year" under such section 324(h);

(E) subparagraphs (A), (C), (D), and (E) of section 326(f)(3) of the Higher Education Act of 1965 (20 U.S.C. 1063b(f)(3)), and references to "previous year" under such section 326(f)(3)(B);

(F) subparagraphs (A), (C), (D), and (E) of section 723(f)(3) and subparagraphs (A), (C), (D), and (E) of section 724(f)(3) of the Higher Education Act of 1965 (20 U.S.C. 1136a(f)(3); 1136b(f)(3)), and references to "previous academic year" under subparagraph (B) of such sections 723(f)(3) and 724(f)(3); and

(G) the allotment restriction set forth in section 318(d)(4) and section 323(c)(2) of the Higher Education Act of 1965 (20 U.S.C. 1059e(d)(4); 1062(c)(2)); and

(2) waive or modify any statutory or regulatory provision to ensure that institutions that were receiving assistance under title III, title V, or subpart 4 of part A of title VII of such Act (20 U.S.C. 1051 et seq.; 1101 et seq.; 1136a et seq.) at the time of a qualifying emergency are not adversely affected by any formula calculation for fiscal year 2020 and for the period beginning on the first day of the qualifying emergency and ending on September 30 of the fiscal year following the end of the qualifying emergency, as necessary.

(b) USE OF UNEXPENDED FUNDS.—Any funds paid to an institution under title III, title V, or subpart 4 of part A of title VII of the Higher Education Act of 1965 (20 U.S.C. 1051 et seq.; 1101 et seq.; 1136a et seq.) and not expended or used for the purposes for which the funds were paid to the institution during the 5-year period following the date on which the funds were first paid to the institution, may be carried over and expended during the succeeding 5-year period.

(c) REPORT.—Not later than 180 days after the date of enactment of this Act, and every 180 days thereafter for the period beginning on the first day of the qualifying emergency and ending on September 30 of the fiscal year following the end of the qualifying emergency, the Secretary shall submit to the authorizing committees (as defined in section 103 of the Higher Education Act of 1965 (20 U.S.C. 1003)) a report that identifies each institution that received a waiver or modification under this section.

[¶2115] SEC. 3518. AUTHORIZED USES AND OTHER MODIFICATIONS FOR GRANTS.

(a) IN GENERAL.—The Secretary is authorized to modify the required and allowable uses of funds for grants awarded under part A or B of title III, chapter I or II of subpart 2 of part A of title IV, title V, or subpart 4 of part A of title VII of the Higher Education Act of 1965 (20 U.S.C. 1057 et seq.; 1060 et seq.; 1070a–11 et seq.; 1070a–21 et seq.; 1101 et seq.; 1136a et seq.) to an institution of higher education or other grant recipient (not including individual recipients of Federal student financial assistance), at the request of an institution of higher education or other recipient of a grant (not including individual recipients of Federal student financial assistance) as a result of a qualifying emergency, for the period beginning on the first day of the qualifying emergency and ending on September 30 of the fiscal year following the end of the qualifying emergency.

(b) MATCHING REQUIREMENT MODIFICATIONS.—Notwithstanding any other provision of the Higher Education Act of 1965 (20 U.S.C. 1001 et seq.), the Secretary is authorized to modify any Federal share or other financial matching requirement for a grant awarded on a competitive basis or a grant awarded under part A or B of title III or subpart 4 of part A of title VII of the Higher Education Act of 1965 (20 U.S.C. 1057 et seq.; 1060 et seq.; 1136a et seq.) at the request of an institution of higher education or other grant recipient as a result of a qualifying emergency, for the period beginning on the first day of the qualifying emergency and ending on September 30 of the fiscal year following the end of the qualifying emergency.

(c) REPORTS.—Not later than 180 days after the date of enactment of this Act, and every 180 days thereafter for the duration of the period beginning on the first day of the qualifying emergency and ending on September 30 of the fiscal year following the end of the qualifying emergency, the Secretary shall submit to the authorizing committees (as defined in section 103 of the Higher Education Act of 1965 (20 U.S.C. 1003)) a report that identifies each institution of higher education or other grant recipient that received a modification under this section.

[¶2116] SEC. 3519. SERVICE OBLIGATIONS FOR TEACHERS.

(a) TEACH GRANTS.—For the purpose of section 420N of the Higher Education Act of 1965 (20 U.S.C. 1070g–2), during a qualifying emergency, the Secretary—

(1) may modify the categories of extenuating circumstances under which a recipient of a grant under subpart 9 of part A of title IV of the Higher Education Act of 1965 (20 U.S.C. 1070g et seq.) who is unable to fulfill all or part of the recipient's service obligation may be excused from fulfilling that portion of the service obligation; and

(2) shall consider teaching service that, as a result of a qualifying emergency, is part-time or temporarily interrupted, to be full-time service and to fulfill the service obligations under such section 420N.

(b) TEACHER LOAN FORGIVENESS.—Notwithstanding section 428J or 460 of the Higher Education Act of 1965 (20 U.S.C. 1078–10; 1087j), the Secretary shall waive the requirements under such sections that years of teaching service shall be consecutive if—

(1) the teaching service of a borrower is temporarily interrupted due to a qualifying emergency; and

(2) after the temporary interruption due to a qualifying emergency, the borrower resumes teaching service and completes a total of 5 years of qualifying teaching service under such sections, including qualifying teaching service performed before, during, and after such qualifying emergency.

Subtitle C—Labor Provisions

[¶2118] SEC. 3601. LIMITATION ON PAID LEAVE.

Section 110(b)(2)(B) of the Family and Medical Leave Act of 1993 (as added by the Emergency Family and Medical Leave Expansion Act) is amended by striking clause (ii) and inserting the following:

(ii) "LIMITATION.—An employer shall not be required to pay more than $200 per day and $10,000 in the aggregate for each employee for paid leave under this section.".

[¶2119] SEC. 3602. EMERGENCY PAID SICK LEAVE ACT LIMITATION.

Section 5102 of the Emergency Paid Sick Leave Act (division E of the Families First Coronavirus Response Act) is amended by adding at the end the following:

(f) "LIMITATIONS.—An employer shall not be required to pay more than either—

(1) "$511 per day and $5,110 in the aggregate for each employee, when the employee is taking leave for a reason described in paragraph (1), (2), or (3) of section 5102(a); or

(2) "$200 per day and $2,000 in the aggregate for each employee, when the employee is taking leave for a reason described in paragraph (4), (5), or (6) of section 5102(a).".

[¶2120] SEC. 3603. UNEMPLOYMENT INSURANCE.

Section 903(h)(2)(B) of the Social Security Act (42 U.S.C. 1103(h)(2)(B)), as added by section 4102 of the Emergency Unemployment Insurance Stabilization and Access Act of 2020, is amended to read as follows:

(B) "The State ensures that applications for unemployment compensation, and assistance with the application process, are accessible, to the extent practicable in at least two of the following: in person, by phone, or online.".

[¶2121] SEC. 3604. OMB WAIVER OF PAID FAMILY AND PAID SICK LEAVE.

(a) FAMILY AND MEDICAL LEAVE ACT OF 1993.—Section 110(a) of title I of the Family and Medical Leave Act of 1993 (29 U.S.C. 2611 et seq.) (as added by division C of the Families First Coronavirus Response Act) is amended by adding at the end the following new paragraph:

(4) "The Director of the Office of Management and Budget shall have the authority to exclude for good cause from the requirements under subsection (b) certain employers of the United States Government with respect to certain categories of Executive Branch employees.".

(b) EMERGENCY PAID SICK LEAVE ACT.—The Emergency Paid Sick Leave Act (division E of the Families First Coronavirus Response Act) is amended by adding at the end the following new section:

[¶2122] SEC. 5112. "AUTHORITY TO EXCLUDE CERTAIN EMPLOYEES.

"The Director of the Office of Management and Budget shall have the authority to exclude for good cause from the definition of employee under section 5110(1) certain employees described in subparagraphs (E) and (F) of such section, including by exempting certain United States Government employers covered by section 5110(2)(A)(i)(V) from the requirements of this title with respect to certain categories of Executive Branch employees.".

[¶2123] SEC. 3605. PAID LEAVE FOR REHIRED EMPLOYEES.

Section 110(a)(1)(A) of the Family and Medical Leave Act of 1993, as added by section 3102 of the Emergency Family and Medical Leave Expansion Act, is amended to read as follows:

(A) "ELIGIBLE EMPLOYEE.—

(i) "IN GENERAL.—In lieu of the definition in sections 101(2)(A) and 101(2)(B)(ii), the term 'eligible employee' means an employee who has been employed for at least 30 calendar days by the employer with respect to whom leave is requested under section 102(a)(1)(F).

(ii) "RULE REGARDING REHIRED EMPLOYEES.—For purposes of clause (i), the term 'employed for at least 30 calendar days', used with respect to an employee and an employer described in clause (i), includes an employee who was laid off by that employer not earlier than March 1, 2020, had worked for the employer for not less than 30 of the last 60 calendar days prior to the employee's layoff, and was rehired by the employer.".

[¶2124] SEC. 3606. ADVANCE REFUNDING OF CREDITS.

(a) PAYROLL CREDIT FOR REQUIRED PAID SICK LEAVE.—Section 7001 of division G of the Families First Coronavirus Response Act is amended—

(1) in subsection (b)(4)(A)—

(A) by striking "(a) In general.—If the amount" and inserting "(A)(i) Credit is refundable.—If the amount"; and

(B) by adding at the end the following:

(ii) "ADVANCING CREDIT.—In anticipation of the credit, including the refundable portion under clause (i), the credit may be advanced, according to forms and instructions provided by the Secretary, up to an amount calculated under subsection (a), subject to the limits under subsection (b), both calculated through the end of the most recent payroll period in the quarter.";

(2) in subsection (f)—

(A) in paragraph (4), by striking ", and" and inserting a comma;

(B) in paragraph (5), by striking the period at the end and inserting ", and"; and

(C) by adding at the end the following:

(6) "regulations or other guidance to permit the advancement of the credit determined under subsection (a)."; and

(3) by inserting after subsection (h) the following new subsection:

(i) "TREATMENT OF DEPOSITS.—The Secretary of the Treasury (or the Secretary's delegate) shall waive any penalty under section 6656 of the Internal Revenue Code of 1986 for any failure to make a deposit of the tax imposed by section 3111(a) or 3221(a) of such Code if the Secretary determines that such failure was due to the anticipation of the credit allowed under this section.".

(b) PAYROLL CREDIT FOR REQUIRED PAID FAMILY LEAVE.—Section 7003 of division G of the Families First Coronavirus Response Act is amended—

(1) in subsection (b)(3)—

(A) by striking "if the amount" and inserting "(a) credit is refundable.—If the amount"; and

(B) by adding at the end the following:

(B) "ADVANCING CREDIT.—In anticipation of the credit, including the refundable portion under subparagraph (A), the credit may be advanced, according to forms and instructions provided by the Secretary, up to an amount calculated under subsection (a), subject to the limits under subsection (b), both calculated through the end of the most recent payroll period in the quarter.";

(2) in subsection (f)—

(A) in paragraph (4), by striking ", and" and inserting a comma;

(B) in paragraph (5), by striking the period at the end and inserting ", and"; and

(C) by adding at the end the following:

(6) "regulations or other guidance to permit the advancement of the credit determined under subsection (a)."; and

(c) by inserting after subsection (h) the following new subsection:

(i) "Treatment of Deposits.—The Secretary of the Treasury (or the Secretary's delegate) shall waive any penalty under section 6656 of the Internal Revenue Code of 1986 for any failure to make a deposit of the tax imposed by section 3111(a) or 3221(a) of such Code if the Secretary determines that such failure was due to the anticipation of the credit allowed under this section.".

[¶2125] SEC. 3607. EXPANSION OF DOL AUTHORITY TO POSTPONE CERTAIN DEADLINES.

Section 518 of the Employee Retirement Income Security Act of 1974 (29 U.S.C. 1148) is amended by striking "or a terroristic or military action (as defined in section 692(c)(2) of such Code), the Secretary may" and inserting "a terroristic or military action (as defined in section 692(c)(2) of such Code), or a public health emergency declared by the Secretary of Health and Human Services pursuant to section 319 of the Public Health Service Act, the Secretary may".

[¶2126] SEC. 3608. SINGLE-EMPLOYER PLAN FUNDING RULES.

(a) Delay in Payment of Minimum Required Contributions.—In the case of any minimum required contribution (as determined under section 430(a) of the Internal Revenue Code of 1986 and section 303(a) of the Employee Retirement Income Security Act of 1974 (29 U.S.C. 1083(a))) which (but for this section) would otherwise be due under section 430(j) of such Code (including quarterly contributions under paragraph (3) thereof) and section 303(j) of such Act (29 U.S.C. 1083(j)) (including quarterly contributions under paragraph (3) thereof) during calendar year 2020—

(1) the due date for such contributions shall be January 1, 2021, and

(2) the amount of each such minimum required contribution shall be increased by interest accruing for the period between the original due date (without regard to this section) for the contribution and the payment date, at the effective rate of interest for the plan for the plan year which includes such payment date.

(b) Benefit Restriction Status.—For purposes of section 436 of the Internal Revenue Code of 1986 and section 206(g) of the Employee Retirement Income Security Act of 1974 (29 U.S.C. 1056(g)), a plan sponsor may elect to treat the plan's adjusted funding target attainment percentage for the last plan year ending before January 1, 2020, as the adjusted funding target attainment percentage for plan years which include calendar year 2020.

[¶2127] SEC. 3609. APPLICATION OF COOPERATIVE AND SMALL EMPLOYER CHARITY PENSION PLAN RULES TO CERTAIN CHARITABLE EMPLOYERS WHOSE PRIMARY EXEMPT PURPOSE IS PROVIDING SERVICES WITH RESPECT TO MOTHERS AND CHILDREN.

(a) Employee Retirement Income Security Act of 1974.—Section 210(f)(1) of the Employee Retirement Income Security Act of 1974 (29 U.S.C. 1060(f)(1)) is amended—

(1) by striking "or" at the end of subparagraph (B);

(2) by striking the period at the end of subparagraph (C)(iv) and inserting "; or"; and

(3) by inserting after subparagraph (C) the following new subparagraph:

(D) "that, as of January 1, 2000, was maintained by an employer—

(i) "described in section 501(c)(3) of the Internal Revenue Code of 1986,

(ii) "who has been in existence since at least 1938,

(iii) "who conducts medical research directly or indirectly through grant making, and

(iv) "whose primary exempt purpose is to provide services with respect to mothers and children.".

(b) Internal Revenue Code of 1986.—Section 414(y)(1) of the Internal Revenue Code of 1986 is amended—

(1) by striking "or" at the end of subparagraph (B);

(2) by striking the period at the end of subparagraph (C)(iv) and inserting "; or"; and

(3) by inserting after subparagraph (C) the following new subparagraph:

(D) "that, as of January 1, 2000, was maintained by an employer—

(i) "described in section 501(c)(3),

(ii) "who has been in existence since at least 1938,

(iii) "who conducts medical research directly or indirectly through grant making, and

(iv) "whose primary exempt purpose is to provide services with respect to mothers and children.".

(c) EFFECTIVE DATE.—The amendments made by this section shall apply to plan years beginning after December 31, 2018.

[¶2128] SEC. 3610. FEDERAL CONTRACTOR AUTHORITY.

Notwithstanding any other provision of law, and subject to the availability of appropriations, funds made available to an agency by this Act or any other Act may be used by such agency to modify the terms and conditions of a contract, or other agreement, without consideration, to reimburse at the minimum applicable contract billing rates not to exceed an average of 40 hours per week any paid leave, including sick leave, a contractor provides to keep its employees or subcontractors in a ready state, including to protect the life and safety of Government and contractor personnel, but in no event beyond September 30, 2020. Such authority shall apply only to a contractor whose employees or subcontractors cannot perform work on a site that has been approved by the Federal Government, including a federally-owned or leased facility or site, due to facility closures or other restrictions, and who cannot telework because their job duties cannot be performed remotely during the public health emergency declared on January 31, 2020 for COVID–19: Provided, That the maximum reimbursement authorized by this section shall be reduced by the amount of credit a contractor is allowed pursuant to division G of Public Law 116–127 and any applicable credits a contractor is allowed under this Act.

[¶2129] SEC. 3611. TECHNICAL CORRECTIONS.

(1) Section 110(a)(3) of the Family and Medical Leave Act of 1993 (as added by the Emergency and Medical Leave Expansion Act) is amended by striking "553(d)(A)" and inserting "553(d)(3)".

(2) Section 5111 of the Emergency Paid Sick Leave Act (division E of the Families First Coronavirus Response Act) is amended by striking "553(d)(A)" and inserting "553(d)(3)".

(3) Section 110(c) of the Family and Medical Leave Act of 1993 (as added by the Emergency and Medical Leave Expansion Act) is amended by striking "subsection (a)(2)(A)(iii)" and inserting "subsection (a)(2)(A)".

(4) Section 3104 of the Emergency Family and Medical Leave Expansion Act (division C of the Families First Coronavirus Response Act) is amended—

(A) by striking "110(a)(B)" and inserting "section 110(a)(1)(B) of the Family and Medical Leave Act of 1993"; and

(B) by striking "section 107(a) for a violation of section 102(a)(1)(F) if the employer does not meet the definition of employer set forth in Section 101(4)(A)(i)" and inserting "section 107(a) of such Act for a violation of section 102(a)(1)(F) of such Act if the employer does not meet the definition of employer set forth in section 101(4)(A)(i) of such Act".

(5) Section 5110(1) of the Emergency Paid Sick Leave Act (division E of the Families First Coronavirus Response Act) is amended—

(A) in the matter preceding subparagraph (A), by striking "terms" and inserting "term"; and

(B) in subparagraph (A)(i), by striking "paragraph (5)(A)" and inserting "paragraph (2)(A)".

(6) Section 5110(2)(B)(ii) of the Emergency Paid Sick Leave Act (division E of the Families First Coronavirus Response Act) is amended by striking "clause (i)(IV)" and inserting "clause (i)(III)".

(7) Section 110(a)(3) of the Family and Medical Leave Act of 1993 (as added by the Emergency and Medical Leave Expansion Act) is amended—

(A) by striking "and" after the semicolon at the end of subparagraph (A);

(B) by striking the period at end of subparagraph (B) and inserting "; and"; and

(C) by adding at the end the following:

(C) "as necessary to carry out the purposes of this Act, including to ensure consistency between this Act and Division E and Division G of the Families First Coronavirus Response Act.".

(8) Section 5104(1) of the Emergency Paid Sick Leave Act (division E of the Families First Coronavirus Response Act) is amended by striking "and" after the semicolon and inserting "or".

(9) Section 5105 of the Emergency Paid Sick Leave Act (division E of the Families First Coronavirus Response Act) is amended by adding at the end the following:

(c) "INVESTIGATIONS AND COLLECTION OF DATA.—The Secretary of Labor or his designee may investigate and gather data to ensure compliance with this Act in the same manner as authorized by sections 9 and 11 of the Fair Labor Standards Act of 1938 (29 U.S.C. 209; 211).".

Subtitle D—Finance Committee

[¶2131] SEC. 3701. EXEMPTION FOR TELEHEALTH SERVICES.

(a) IN GENERAL.—Paragraph (2) of section 223(c) of the Internal Revenue Code of 1986 is amended by adding at the end the following new subparagraph:

(E) "SAFE HARBOR FOR ABSENCE OF DEDUCTIBLE FOR TELEHEALTH.—In the case of plan years beginning on or before December 31, 2021, a plan shall not fail to be treated as a high deductible health plan by reason of failing to have a deductible for telehealth and other remote care services.".

(b) CERTAIN COVERAGE DISREGARDED.—Clause (ii) of section 223(c)(1)(B) of the Internal Revenue Code of 1986 is amended by striking "or long-term care" and inserting "long-term care, or (in the case of plan years beginning on or before December 31, 2021) telehealth and other remote care".

(c) EFFECTIVE DATE.—The amendments made by this section shall take effect on the date of the enactment of this Act.

[¶2132] SEC. 3702. INCLUSION OF CERTAIN OVER-THE-COUNTER MEDICAL PRODUCTS AS QUALIFIED MEDICAL EXPENSES.

(a) HSAS.—Section 223(d)(2) of the Internal Revenue Code of 1986 is amended—

(1) by striking the last sentence of subparagraph (A) and inserting the following: "For purposes of this subparagraph, amounts paid for menstrual care products shall be treated as paid for medical care."; and

(2) by adding at the end the following new subparagraph:

(D) "MENSTRUAL CARE PRODUCT.—For purposes of this paragraph, the term 'menstrual care product' means a tampon, pad, liner, cup, sponge, or similar product used by individuals with respect to menstruation or other genital-tract secretions.".

(b) ARCHER MSAS.—Section 220(d)(2)(A) of such Code is amended by striking the last sentence and inserting the following: "For purposes of this subparagraph, amounts paid for menstrual care products (as defined in section 223(d)(2)(D)) shall be treated as paid for medical care.".

(c) HEALTH FLEXIBLE SPENDING ARRANGEMENTS AND HEALTH REIMBURSEMENT ARRANGEMENTS.—Section 106 of such Code is amended by striking subsection (f) and inserting the following new subsection:

(f) "REIMBURSEMENTS FOR MENSTRUAL CARE PRODUCTS.—For purposes of this section and section 105, expenses incurred for menstrual care products (as defined in section 223(d)(2)(D)) shall be treated as incurred for medical care.".

(d) EFFECTIVE DATES.—

(1) DISTRIBUTIONS FROM SAVINGS ACCOUNTS.—The amendment made by subsections (a) and (b) shall apply to amounts paid after December 31, 2019.

(2) REIMBURSEMENTS.—The amendment made by subsection (c) shall apply to expenses incurred after December 31, 2019.

[¶2133] SEC. 3703. INCREASING MEDICARE TELEHEALTH FLEXIBILITIES DURING EMERGENCY PERIOD.

Section 1135 of the Social Security Act (42 U.S.C. 1320b–5) is amended—

(1) in subsection (b)(8), by striking "to an individual by a qualified provider (as defined in subsection (g)(3))" and all that follows through the period and inserting ", the requirements of section 1834(m)."; and

(2) in subsection (g), by striking paragraph (3).

[¶2134] SEC. 3704. ENHANCING MEDICARE TELEHEALTH SERVICES FOR FEDERALLY QUALIFIED HEALTH CENTERS AND RURAL HEALTH CLINICS DURING EMERGENCY PERIOD.

Section 1834(m) of the Social Security Act (42 U.S.C. 1395m(m)) is amended—

(1) in the first sentence of paragraph (1), by striking "The Secretary" and inserting "Subject to paragraph (8), the Secretary";

(2) in paragraph (2)(A), by striking "The Secretary" and inserting "Subject to paragraph (8), the Secretary";

(3) in paragraph (4)—

(A) in subparagraph (A), by striking "The term" and inserting "Subject to paragraph (8), the term"; and

(B) in subparagraph (F)(i), by striking "The term" and inserting "Subject to paragraph (8), the term"; and

(4) by adding at the end the following new paragraph:

(8) "ENHANCING TELEHEALTH SERVICES FOR FEDERALLY QUALIFIED HEALTH CENTERS AND RURAL HEALTH CLINICS DURING EMERGENCY PERIOD.—

(A) "IN GENERAL.—During the emergency period described in section 1135(g)(1)(B)—

(i) "the Secretary shall pay for telehealth services that are furnished via a telecommunications system by a Federally qualified health center or a rural health clinic to an eligible telehealth individual enrolled under this part notwithstanding that the Federally qualified health center or rural clinic providing the telehealth service is not at the same location as the beneficiary;

(ii) "the amount of payment to a Federally qualified health center or rural health clinic that serves as a distant site for such a telehealth service shall be determined under subparagraph (B); and

(iii) "for purposes of this subsection—

(I) "the term 'distant site' includes a Federally qualified health center or rural health clinic that furnishes a telehealth service to an eligible telehealth individual; and

(II) "the term 'telehealth services' includes a rural health clinic service or Federally qualified health center service that is furnished using telehealth to the extent that payment codes corresponding to services identified by the Secretary under clause (i) or (ii) of paragraph (4)(F) are listed on the corresponding claim for such rural health clinic service or Federally qualified health center service.

(B) "SPECIAL PAYMENT RULE.—

(i) "IN GENERAL.—The Secretary shall develop and implement payment methods that apply under this subsection to a Federally qualified health center or rural health clinic that serves as a distant site that furnishes a telehealth service to an eligible telehealth individual during such emergency period. Such payment methods shall be based on payment rates that are similar to the national average payment rates for comparable telehealth services under the physician fee schedule under section 1848. Notwithstanding any other provision of law, the Secretary may implement such payment methods through program instruction or otherwise.

(ii) "EXCLUSION FROM FQHC PPS CALCULATION AND RHC AIR CALCULATION.—Costs associated with telehealth services shall not be used to determine the amount of payment for Federally qualified health center services under the prospective payment system under section 1834(o) or for rural health clinic services under the methodology for all-inclusive rates (established by the Secretary) under section 1833(a)(3).".

[¶2135] SEC. 3705. TEMPORARY WAIVER OF REQUIREMENT FOR FACE-TO-FACE VISITS BETWEEN HOME DIALYSIS PATIENTS AND PHYSICIANS.

Section 1881(b)(3)(B) of the Social Security Act (42 U.S.C. 1395rr(b)(3)(B)) is amended—

(1) in clause (i), by striking "clause (ii)" and inserting "clauses (ii) and (iii)";

(2) in clause (ii), in the matter preceding subclause (I), by striking "Clause (i)" and inserting "Except as provided in clause (iii), clause (i)"; and

(3) by adding at the end the following new clause:

(iii) "The Secretary may waive the provisions of clause (ii) during the emergency period described in section 1135(g)(1)(B).".

[¶2136] SEC. 3706. USE OF TELEHEALTH TO CONDUCT FACE-TO-FACE ENCOUNTER PRIOR TO RECERTIFICATION OF ELIGIBILITY FOR HOSPICE CARE DURING EMERGENCY PERIOD.

Section 1814(a)(7)(D)(i) of the Social Security Act (42 U.S.C. 1395f(a)(7(D)(i)) is amended—

(1) by striking "a hospice" and inserting "(I) subject to subclause (II), a hospice"; and

(2) by inserting after subclause (I), as added by paragraph (1), the following new subclause:

(II) "during the emergency period described in section 1135(g)(1)(B), a hospice physician or nurse practitioner may conduct a face-to-face encounter required under this clause via telehealth, as determined appropriate by the Secretary; and".

[¶2137] SEC. 3707. ENCOURAGING USE OF TELECOMMUNICATIONS SYSTEMS FOR HOME HEALTH SERVICES FURNISHED DURING EMERGENCY PERIOD.

With respect to home health services (as defined in section 1861(m) of the Social Security Act (42 U.S.C. 1395x(m)) that are furnished during the emergency period described in section 1135(g)(1)(B) of such Act (42 U.S.C. 1320b–5(g)(1)(B)), the Secretary of Health and Human Services shall consider ways to encourage the use of telecommunications systems, including for remote patient monitoring as described in section 409.46(e) of title 42, Code of Federal Regulations (or any successor regulations) and other communications or monitoring services, consistent with the plan of care for the individual, including by clarifying guidance and conducting outreach, as appropriate.

[¶2138] SEC. 3708. IMPROVING CARE PLANNING FOR MEDICARE HOME HEALTH SERVICES.

(a) PART A PROVISIONS.—Section 1814(a) of the Social Security Act (42 U.S.C. 1395f(a)) is amended—

(1) in paragraph (2)—

(A) in the matter preceding subparagraph (A), by inserting ", a nurse practitioner or clinical nurse specialist (as such terms are defined in section 1861(aa)(5)) who is working in accordance with State law, or a physician assistant (as defined in section 1861(aa)(5)) who is working in accordance with State law, who is" after "in the case of services described in subparagraph (C), a physician"; and

(B) in subparagraph (C)—

(i) by inserting ", a nurse practitioner, a clinical nurse specialist, or a physician assistant (as the case may be)" after "physician" the first 2 times it appears; and

(ii) by striking ", and, in the case of a certification made by a physician" and all that follows through "face-to-face encounter" and inserting ", and, in the case of a certification made by a physician after January 1, 2010, or by a nurse practitioner, clinical nurse specialist, or physician assistant (as the case may be) after a date specified by the Secretary (but in no case later than the date that is 6 months after the date of the enactment of the CARES Act), prior to making such certification a physician, nurse practitioner, clinical nurse specialist, or physician assistant must document that a physician, nurse practitioner, clinical nurse specialist, certified nurse-midwife (as defined in section 1861(gg)) as authorized by State law, or physician assistant has had a face-to-face encounter";

(2) in the third sentence—

(A) by striking "physician certification" and inserting "certification";

(B) by inserting "(or in the case of regulations to implement the amendments made by section 3708 of the CARES Act, the Secretary shall prescribe regulations, which shall become effective no later than 6 months after the date of the enactment of such Act)" after "1981"; and

(C) by striking "a physician who" and inserting "a physician, nurse practitioner, clinical nurse specialist, or physician assistant who";

(3) in the fourth sentence, by inserting ", nurse practitioner, clinical nurse specialist, or physician assistant" after "physician"; and

(4) in the fifth sentence—

(A) by inserting "or no later than 6 months after the date of the enactment of the CARES Act for purposes of documentation for certification and recertification made under paragraph (2) by a nurse practitioner, clinical nurse specialist, or physician assistant," after "January 1, 2019"; and

(B) by inserting ", nurse practitioner, clinical nurse specialist, or physician assistant" after "of the physician".

(b) PART B PROVISIONS.—Section 1835(a) of the Social Security Act (42 U.S.C. 1395n(a)) is amended—

(1) in paragraph (2)—

(A) in the matter preceding subparagraph (A), by inserting ", a nurse practitioner or clinical nurse specialist (as those terms are defined in section 1861(aa)(5)) who is working in accordance with State law, or a physician assistant (as defined in section 1861(aa)(5)) who is working in accordance with State law, who is" after "in the case of services described in subparagraph (A), a physician"; and

(B) in subparagraph (A)—

(i) in each of clauses (ii) and (iii) of subparagraph (A) by inserting ", a nurse practitioner, a clinical nurse specialist, or a physician assistant (as the case may be)" after "physician"; and

(ii) in clause (iv), by striking "after January 1, 2010" and all that follows through "face-to-face encounter" and inserting "made by a physician after January 1, 2010, or by a nurse practitioner, clinical nurse specialist, or physician assistant (as the case may be) after a date specified by the Secretary (but in no case later than the date that is 6 months after the date of the enactment of the CARES Act), prior to making such certification a physician, nurse practitioner, clinical nurse specialist, or physician assistant must document that a physician, nurse practitioner, clinical nurse specialist, certified nurse-midwife (as defined in section 1861(gg)) as authorized by State law, or physician assistant has had a face-to-face encounter";

(2) in the third sentence, by inserting ", nurse practitioner, clinical nurse specialist, or physician assistant (as the case may be)" after physician;

(3) in the fourth sentence—

(A) by striking "physician certification" and inserting "certification";

(B) by inserting "(or in the case of regulations to implement the amendments made by section 3708 of the CARES Act the Secretary shall prescribe regulations which shall become effective no later than 6 months after the enactment of such Act)" after "1981"; and

(C) by striking "a physician who" and inserting "a physician, nurse practitioner, clinical nurse specialist, or physician assistant who";

(4) in the fifth sentence, by inserting ", nurse practitioner, clinical nurse specialist, or physician assistant" after "physician"; and

(5) in the sixth sentence—

(A) by inserting "or no later than 6 months after the date of the enactment of the CARES Act for purposes of documentation for certification and recertification made under paragraph (2) by a nurse practitioner, clinical nurse specialist, or physician assistant," after "January 1, 2019"; and

(B) by inserting ", nurse practitioner, clinical nurse specialist, or physician assistant" after "of the physician".

(c) DEFINITION PROVISIONS.—

(1) HOME HEALTH SERVICES.—Section 1861(m) of the Social Security Act (42 U.S.C. 1395x(m)) is amended—

(A) in the matter preceding paragraph (1)—

(i) by inserting ", a nurse practitioner or a clinical nurse specialist (as those terms are defined in subsection (aa)(5)), or a physician assistant (as defined in subsection (aa)(5))" after "physician" the first place it appears; and

(ii) by inserting ", a nurse practitioner, a clinical nurse specialist, or a physician assistant" after "physician" the second place it appears; and

(B) in paragraph (3), by inserting ", a nurse practitioner, a clinical nurse specialist, or a physician assistant" after "physician".

(2) HOME HEALTH AGENCY.—Section 1861(o)(2) of the Social Security Act (42 U.S.C. 1395x(o)(2)) is amended—

(A) by inserting ", nurse practitioners or clinical nurse specialists (as those terms are defined in subsection (aa)(5)), certified nurse-midwives (as defined in subsection (gg)), or physician assistants (as defined in subsection (aa)(5))" after "physicians"; and

(B) by inserting ", nurse practitioner, clinical nurse specialist, certified nurse-midwife, physician assistant," after "physician".

(3) COVERED OSTEOPOROSIS DRUG.—Section 1861(kk)(1) of the Social Security Act (42 U.S.C. 1395x(kk)(1)) is amended by inserting ", nurse practitioner or clinical nurse specialist (as those terms are defined in subsection (aa)(5)), certified nurse-midwife (as defined in subsection (gg)), or physician assistant (as defined in subsection (aa)(5))" after "attending physician".

(d) HOME HEALTH PROSPECTIVE PAYMENT SYSTEM PROVISIONS.—Section 1895 of the Social Security Act (42 U.S.C. 1395fff) is amended—

(1) in subsection (c)(1)—

(A) by striking "(provided under section 1842(r))"; and

(B) by inserting "the nurse practitioner or clinical nurse specialist (as those terms are defined in section 1861(aa)(5)), or the physician assistant (as defined in section 1861(aa)(5))" after "physician"; and

(2) in subsection (e)—

(A) in paragraph (1)(A), by inserting "a nurse practitioner or clinical nurse specialist, or a physician assistant" after "physician"; and

(B) in paragraph (2)—

(i) in the heading, by striking "PHYSICIAN CERTIFICATION" and inserting "RULE OF CONSTRUCTION REGARDING REQUIREMENT FOR CERTIFICATION"; and

(ii) by striking "physician".

(e) APPLICATION TO MEDICAID.—The amendments made under this section shall apply under title XIX of the Social Security Act in the same manner and to the same extent as such requirements apply under title XVIII of such Act or regulations promulgated thereunder.

(f) EFFECTIVE DATE.—The Secretary of Health and Human Services shall prescribe regulations to apply the amendments made by this section to items and services furnished, which shall become effective no later than 6 months after the date of the enactment of this legislation. The Secretary shall promulgate an interim final rule if necessary, to comply with the required effective date.

[¶2139] SEC. 3709. ADJUSTMENT OF SEQUESTRATION.

(a) TEMPORARY SUSPENSION OF MEDICARE SEQUESTRATION.—During the period beginning on May 1, 2020 and ending on December 31, 2020, the Medicare programs under title XVIII of the Social Security Act (42 U.S.C. 1395 et seq.) shall be exempt from reduction under any sequestration order issued before, on, or after the date of enactment of this Act.

(b) EXTENSION OF DIRECT SPENDING REDUCTIONS THROUGH FISCAL YEAR 2030.—Section 251A(6) of the Balanced Budget and Emergency Deficit Control Act of 1985 (2 U.S.C. 901a(6)) is amended—

(1) in subparagraph (B), in the matter preceding clause (i), by striking "through 2029" and inserting "through 2030"; and

(2) in subparagraph (C), in the matter preceding clause (i), by striking "fiscal year 2029" and inserting "fiscal year 2030".

[¶2140] SEC. 3710. MEDICARE HOSPITAL INPATIENT PROSPECTIVE PAYMENT SYSTEM ADD-ON PAYMENT FOR COVID–19 PATIENTS DURING EMERGENCY PERIOD.

(a) IN GENERAL.—Section 1886(d)(4)(C) of the Social Security Act (42 U.S.C. 1395ww(d)(4)(C)) is amended by adding at the end the following new clause:

(iv)(I) "For discharges occurring during the emergency period described in section 1135(g)(1)(B), in the case of a discharge of an individual diagnosed with COVID–19, the Secretary shall increase the weighting factor that would otherwise apply to the diagnosis-related group to which the discharge is assigned by 20 percent. The Secretary shall identify a discharge of such an individual through the use of diagnosis codes, condition codes, or other such means as may be necessary.

(II) "Any adjustment under subclause (I) shall not be taken into account in applying budget neutrality under clause (iii)

(III) "In the case of a State for which the Secretary has waived all or part of this section under the authority of section 1115A, nothing in this section shall preclude such State from implementing an adjustment similar to the adjustment under subclause (I).".

(b) IMPLEMENTATION.—Notwithstanding any other provision of law, the Secretary may implement the amendment made by subsection (a) by program instruction or otherwise.

[¶2141] SEC. 3711. INCREASING ACCESS TO POST-ACUTE CARE DURING EMERGENCY PERIOD.

(a) WAIVER OF IRF 3-HOUR RULE.—With respect to inpatient rehabilitation services furnished by a rehabilitation facility described in section 1886(j)(1) of the Social Security Act (42 U.S.C. 1395ww(j)(1)) during the emergency period described in section 1135(g)(1)(B) of the Social Security Act (42 U.S.C. 1320b–5(g)(1)(B)), the Secretary of Health and Human Services shall waive section 412.622(a)(3)(ii) of title 42, Code of Federal Regulations (or any successor regulations), relating to the requirement that patients of an inpatient rehabilitation facility receive at least 15 hours of therapy per week.

(b) WAIVER OF SITE-NEUTRAL PAYMENT RATE PROVISIONS FOR LONG-TERM CARE HOSPITALS.—With respect to inpatient hospital services furnished by a long-term care hospital described in section 1886(d)(1)(B)(iv) of the Social Security Act (42 U.S.C. 1395ww(d)(1)(B)(iv)) during the emergency period described in section 1135(g)(1)(B) of the Social Security Act (42 U.S.C. 1320b–5(g)(1)(B)), the Secretary of Health and Human Services shall waive the following provisions of section 1886(m)(6) of such Act (42 U.S.C. 1395ww(m)(6)):

(1) LTCH 50-PERCENT RULE.—Subparagraph (C)(ii) of such section, relating to the payment adjustment for long-term care hospitals that do not have a discharge payment percentage for the period that is at least 50 percent.

(2) SITE-NEUTRAL IPPS PAYMENT RATE.—Subparagraph (A)(i) of such section, relating to the application of the site-neutral payment rate (and payment shall be made to a long-term care hospital without regard to such section) for a discharge if the admission occurs during such emergency period and is in response to the public health emergency described in such section 1135(g)(1)(B).

[¶2142] SEC. 3712. REVISING PAYMENT RATES FOR DURABLE MEDICAL EQUIPMENT UNDER THE MEDICARE PROGRAM THROUGH DURATION OF EMERGENCY PERIOD.

(a) RURAL AND NONCONTIGUOUS AREAS.—The Secretary of Health and Human Services shall implement section 414.210(g)(9)(iii) of title 42, Code of Federal Regulations (or any successor regulation), to apply the transition rule described in such section to all applicable items and services furnished in rural areas and noncontiguous areas (as such terms are defined for purposes of such section) as planned through December 31, 2020, and through the duration of the emergency period described in section 1135(g)(1)(B) of the Social Security Act (42 U.S.C. 1320b–5(g)(1)(B)), if longer.

(b) AREAS OTHER THAN RURAL AND NONCONTIGUOUS AREAS.—With respect to items and services furnished on or after the date that is 30 days after the date of the enactment of this Act, the Secretary of Health and Human Services shall apply section 414.210(g)(9)(iv) of title 42, Code of Federal Regulations (or any successor regulation), as if the reference to "dates of service from June 1, 2018 through December 31, 2020, based on the fee schedule amount for the area is equal to 100 percent of the adjusted payment amount established under this section" were instead a reference to "dates of service from March 6, 2020, through the remainder of the duration of the emergency period described in section 1135(g)(1)(B) of the Social Security Act (42 U.S.C. 1320b–5(g)(1)(B)), based on the fee schedule amount for the area is equal to 75 percent of the adjusted payment amount established under this section and 25 percent of the unadjusted fee schedule amount".

[¶2143] SEC. 3713. COVERAGE OF THE COVID–19 VACCINE UNDER PART B OF THE MEDICARE PROGRAM WITHOUT ANY COST-SHARING.

(a) MEDICAL AND OTHER HEALTH SERVICES.—Section 1861(s)(10)(A) of the Social Security Act (42 U.S.C. 1395x(s)(10)(A)) is amended by inserting ", and COVID–19 vaccine and its administration" after "influenza vaccine and its administration".

(b) PART B DEDUCTIBLE.—The first sentence of section 1833(b) of the Social Security Act (42 U.S.C. 1395l(b)) is amended—

(1) in paragraph (10), by striking "and" at the end; and

(2) in paragraph (11), by striking the period at the end and inserting ", and (12) such deductible shall not apply with respect a COVID–19 vaccine and its administration described in section 1861(s)(10)(A).".

(c) MEDICARE ADVANTAGE.—Section 1852(a)(1)(B) of the Social Security Act (42 U.S.C. 1395w–22(a)(1)(B)) is amended—

(1) in clause (iv)—

(A) by redesignating subclause (VI) as subclause (VII); and

(B) by inserting after subclause (V) the following new subclause:

(VI) "A COVID–19 vaccine and its administration described in section 1861(s)(10)(A)."; and

(2) in clause (v), by striking "subclauses (IV) and (V)" inserting "subclauses (IV), (V), and (VI)".

(d) EFFECTIVE DATE.—The amendments made by this section shall take effect on the date of enactment of this Act and shall apply with respect to a COVID–19 vaccine beginning on the date that such vaccine is licensed under section 351 of the Public Health Service Act (42 U.S.C. 262).

(e) IMPLEMENTATION.—Notwithstanding any other provision of law, the Secretary may implement the provisions of, and the amendments made by, this section by program instruction or otherwise.

[¶2144] SEC. 3714. REQUIRING MEDICARE PRESCRIPTION DRUG PLANS AND MA–PD PLANS TO ALLOW DURING THE COVID–19 EMERGENCY PERIOD FOR FILLS AND REFILLS OF COVERED PART D DRUGS FOR UP TO A 3-MONTH SUPPLY.

(a) IN GENERAL.—Section 1860D–4(b) of the Social Security Act (42 U.S.C. 1395w–104(b)) is amended by adding at the end the following new paragraph:

(4) "ENSURING ACCESS DURING COVID–19 PUBLIC HEALTH EMERGENCY PERIOD.—

(A) "IN GENERAL.—During the emergency period described in section 1135(g)(1)(B), subject to subparagraph (B), a prescription drug plan or MA–PD plan shall, notwithstanding any cost and utilization management, medication therapy management, or other such programs under this part, permit a part D eligible individual enrolled in such plan to obtain in a single fill or refill, at the option of such individual, the total day supply (not to exceed a 90-day supply) prescribed for such individual for a covered part D drug.

(B) "SAFETY EDIT EXCEPTION.—A prescription drug plan or MA–PD plan may not permit a part D eligible individual to obtain a single fill or refill inconsistent with an applicable safety edit.".

(b) IMPLEMENTATION.—Notwithstanding any other provision of law, the Secretary of Health and Human Services may implement the amendment made by this section by program instruction or otherwise.

[¶2144A] SEC. 3715. PROVIDING HOME AND COMMUNITY-BASED SERVICES IN ACUTE CARE HOSPITALS.

Section 1902(h) of the Social Security Act (42 U.S.C. 1396a(h)) is amended—

(1) by inserting "(1)" after "(h)";

(2) by inserting ", home and community-based services provided under subsection (c), (d), or (i) of section 1915 or under a waiver or demonstration project under section 1115, self-directed personal assistance services provided pursuant to a written plan of care under section 1915(j), and home and community-based attendant services and supports under section 1915(k)" before the period; and

(3) by adding at the end the following:

(2) "Nothing in this title, title XVIII, or title XI shall be construed as prohibiting receipt of any care or services specified in paragraph (1) in an acute care hospital that are—

(A) "identified in an individual's person-centered service plan (or comparable plan of care);

(B) "provided to meet needs of the individual that are not met through the provision of hospital services;

(C) "not a substitute for services that the hospital is obligated to provide through its conditions of participation or under Federal or State law, or under another applicable requirement; and

(D) "designed to ensure smooth transitions between acute care settings and home and community-based settings, and to preserve the individual's functional abilities.".

[¶2144B] SEC. 3716. CLARIFICATION REGARDING UNINSURED INDIVIDUALS.

Subsection (ss) of section 1902 of the Social Security Act (42 U.S.C. 1396a), as added by section 6004(a)(3)(C) of the Families First Coronavirus Response Act, is amended—

(1) in paragraph (1), by inserting "(excluding subclause (VIII) of such subsection if the individual is a resident of a State which does not furnish medical assistance to individuals described in such subclause)" before the semicolon; and

(2) in paragraph (2), by inserting ", except that individuals who are eligible for medical assistance under subsection (a)(10)(A)(ii)(XII), subsection (a)(10)(A)(ii)(XVIII), subsection (a)(10)(A)(ii)(XXI), or subsection (a)(10)(C) (but only to the extent such an individual is considered to not have minimum essential coverage under section 5000A(f)(1) of the Internal Revenue Code of 1986), or who are described in subsection (l)(1)(A) and are eligible for medical assistance only because of subsection (a)(10)(A)(i)(IV) or (a)(10)(A)(ii)(IX) and whose eligibility for such assistance is limited by the State under clause (VII) in the matter following subsection (a)(10)(G), shall not be treated as enrolled in a Federal health care program for purposes of this paragraph" before the period at the end.

[¶2145] SEC. 3717. CLARIFICATION REGARDING COVERAGE OF COVID–19 TESTING PRODUCTS.

Subparagraph (B) of section 1905(a)(3) of the Social Security Act (42 U.S.C. 1396d(a)(3)), as added by section 6004(a)(1)(C) of the Families First Coronavirus Response Act (Public Law 116–127), is amended by striking "that are approved, cleared, or authorized under section 510(k), 513, 515 or 564 of the Federal Food, Drug, and Cosmetic Act".

[¶2146] SEC. 3718. AMENDMENTS RELATING TO REPORTING REQUIREMENTS WITH RESPECT TO CLINICAL DIAGNOSTIC LABORATORY TESTS.

(a) Revised Reporting Period for Reporting of Private Sector Payment Rates for Establishment of Medicare Payment Rates.—Section 1834A(a)(1)(B) of the Social Security Act (42 U.S.C. 1395m–1(a)(1)(B)) is amended—

(1) in clause (i), by striking "December 31, 2020" and inserting "December 31, 2021"; and

(2) in clause (ii)—

(A) by striking "January 1, 2021" and inserting "January 1, 2022"; and

(B) by striking "March 31, 2021" and inserting "March 31, 2022".

(b) Revised Phase-In of Reductions From Private Payor Rate Implementation.—Section 1834A(b)(3) of the Social Security Act (42 U.S.C. 1395m–1(b)(3)) is amended—

(1) in subparagraph (A), by striking "through 2023" and inserting "through 2024"; and

(2) in subparagraph (B)—

(A) in clause (i), by striking "and" at the end;

(B) by redesignating clause (ii) as clause (iii);

(C) by inserting after clause (i) the following new clause:

(ii) "for 2021, 0 percent; and"; and

(D) in clause (iii), as redesignated by subparagraph (B), by striking "2021 through 2023" and inserting "2022 through 2024".

[¶2147] SEC. 3719. EXPANSION OF THE MEDICARE HOSPITAL ACCELERATED PAYMENT PROGRAM DURING THE COVID–19 PUBLIC HEALTH EMERGENCY.

Section 1815 of the Social Security Act (42 U.S.C. 1395g) is amended—

(1) in subsection (e)(3), by striking "In the case" and inserting "Subject to subsection (f), in the case"; and

(2) by adding at the end the following new subsection:

(f)(1) "During the emergency period described in section 1135(g)(1)(B), the Secretary shall expand the program under subsection (e)(3) pursuant to paragraph (2).

(2) "In expanding the program under subsection (e)(3), the following shall apply:

(A)(i) "In addition to the hospitals described in subsection (e)(3), the following hospitals shall be eligible to participate in the program:

(I) "Hospitals described in clause (iii) of section 1886(d)(1)(B).

(II) "Hospitals described in clause (v) of such section.

(III) "Critical access hospitals (as defined in section 1861(mm)(1)).

(ii) "Subject to appropriate safeguards against fraud, waste, and abuse, upon a request of a hospital described in clause (i), the Secretary shall provide accelerated payments under the program to such hospital.

(B) "Upon the request of the hospital, the Secretary may do any of the following:

(i) "Make accelerated payments on a periodic or lump sum basis.

(ii) "Increase the amount of payment that would otherwise be made to hospitals under the program up to 100 percent (or, in the case of critical access hospitals, up to 125 percent).

(iii) "Extend the period that accelerated payments cover so that it covers up to a 6-month period.

(C) "Upon the request of the hospital, the Secretary shall do the following:

(i) "Provide up to 120 days before claims are offset to recoup the accelerated payment.

(ii) "Allow not less than 12 months from the date of the first accelerated payment before requiring that the outstanding balance be paid in full.

(3) "Nothing in this subsection shall preclude the Secretary from carrying out the provisions described in clauses (i), (ii), and (iii) of paragraph (2)(B) and clauses (i) and (ii) of paragraph (2)(C) under the program under subsection (e)(3) after the period for which this subsection applies.

(4) "Notwithstanding any other provision of law, the Secretary may implement the provisions of this subsection by program instruction or otherwise.".

[¶2148] SEC. 3720. DELAYING REQUIREMENTS FOR ENHANCED FMAP TO ENABLE STATE LEGISLATION NECESSARY FOR COMPLIANCE.

Section 6008 of the Families First Coronavirus Response Act is amended by adding at the end the following new subsection:

(d) "DELAY IN APPLICATION OF PREMIUM REQUIREMENT.—During the 30 day period beginning on the date of enactment of this Act, a State shall not be ineligible for the increase to the Federal medical assistance percentage of the State described in subsection (a) on the basis that the State imposes a premium that violates the requirement of subsection (b)(2) if such premium was in effect on the date of enactment of this Act.".

Subtitle E—Health and Human Services Extenders

PART I—MEDICARE PROVISIONS

[¶2151] SEC. 3801. EXTENSION OF THE WORK GEOGRAPHIC INDEX FLOOR UNDER THE MEDICARE PROGRAM.

Section 1848(e)(1)(E) of the Social Security Act (42 U.S.C. 1395w–4(e)(1)(E)) is amended by striking "May 23, 2020" and inserting "December 1, 2020".

[¶2152] SEC. 3802. EXTENSION OF FUNDING FOR QUALITY MEASURE ENDORSEMENT, INPUT, AND SELECTION.

(a) IN GENERAL.—Section 1890(d)(2) of the Social Security Act (42 U.S.C. 1395aaa(d)(2)) is amended—

(1) in the first sentence, by striking "and $4,830,000 for the period beginning on October 1, 2019, and ending on May 22, 2020" and inserting "$20,000,000 for fiscal year 2020, and for the period beginning on October 1, 2020, and ending on November 30, 2020, the amount equal to the pro rata portion of the amount appropriated for such period for fiscal year 2020"; and

(2) in the third sentence, by striking "and 2019 and for the period beginning on October 1, 2019, and ending on May 22, 2020" and inserting ", 2019, and 2020, and for the period beginning on October 1, 2020, and ending on November 30, 2020,".

(b) EFFECTIVE DATE.—The amendments made by subsection (a) shall take effect as if included in the enactment of the Further Consolidated Appropriations Act, 2020 (Public Law 116–94).

[¶2153] SEC. 3803. EXTENSION OF FUNDING OUTREACH AND ASSISTANCE FOR LOW-INCOME PROGRAMS.

(a) FUNDING EXTENSIONS.—

(1) ADDITIONAL FUNDING FOR STATE HEALTH INSURANCE PROGRAMS.—Subsection (a)(1)(B) of section 119 of the Medicare Improvements for Patients and Providers Act of 2008 (42 U.S.C. 1395b–3 note), as amended by section 3306 of the Patient Protection and Affordable Care Act (Public Law 111–148), section 610 of the American Taxpayer Relief Act of 2012 (Public Law 112–240), section 1110 of the Pathway for SGR Reform Act of 2013 (Public Law 113–67), section 110 of the Protecting Access to Medicare Act of 2014 (Public Law 113–93), section 208 of the Medicare Access and CHIP Reauthorization Act of 2015 (Public Law 114–10), section 50207 of division E of the Bipartisan Budget Act of 2018 (Public Law 115–123), section 1402 of division B of the Continuing Appropriations Act, 2020, and Health Extenders Act of 2019 (Public Law 116–59), section 1402 of division B of the Further Continuing Appropriations Act, 2020, and Further Health Extenders Act of 2019 (Public Law 116–69), and section 103 of division N of the Further Consolidated Appropriations Act, 2020 (Public Law 116–94) is amended by striking clauses (x) through (xii) and inserting the following new clauses:

(x) "for fiscal year 2020, of $13,000,000; and

(xi) "for the period beginning on October 1, 2020, and ending on November 30, 2020, the amount equal to the pro rata portion of the amount appropriated for such period for fiscal year 2020.".

(2) ADDITIONAL FUNDING FOR AREA AGENCIES ON AGING.—Subsection (b)(1)(B) of such section 119, as so amended, is amended by striking clauses (x) through (xii) and inserting the following new clauses:

(x) "for fiscal year 2020, of $7,500,000; and

(xi) "for the period beginning on October 1, 2020, and ending on November 30, 2020, the amount equal to the pro rata portion of the amount appropriated for such period for fiscal year 2020.".

(3) ADDITIONAL FUNDING FOR AGING AND DISABILITY RESOURCE CENTERS.—Subsection (c)(1)(B) of such section 119, as so amended, is amended by striking clauses (x) through (xii) and inserting the following new clauses:

(x) "for fiscal year 2020, of $5,000,000; and

(xi) "for the period beginning on October 1, 2020, and ending on November 30, 2020, the amount equal to the pro rata portion of the amount appropriated for such period for fiscal year 2020.".

(4) ADDITIONAL FUNDING FOR CONTRACT WITH THE NATIONAL CENTER FOR BENEFITS AND OUTREACH ENROLLMENT.—Subsection (d)(2) of such section 119, as so amended, is amended by striking clauses (x) through (xii) and inserting the following new clauses:

(x) "for fiscal year 2020, of $12,000,000; and

(xi) "for the period beginning on October 1, 2020, and ending on November 30, 2020, the amount equal to the pro rata portion of the amount appropriated for such period for fiscal year 2020.".

(b) EFFECTIVE DATE.—The amendments made by subsection (a) shall take effect as if included in the enactment of the Further Consolidated Appropriations Act, 2020 (Public Law 116–94).

PART II—MEDICAID PROVISIONS

[¶2155] SEC. 3811. EXTENSION OF THE MONEY FOLLOWS THE PERSON REBALANCING DEMONSTRATION PROGRAM.

Section 6071(h) of the Deficit Reduction Act of 2005 (42 U.S.C. 1396a note) is amended—

(1) in paragraph (1), by striking subparagraph (G) and inserting the following:

(G) "subject to paragraph (3), $337,500,000 for the period beginning on January 1, 2020, and ending on September 30, 2020; and

(H) "subject to paragraph (3), for the period beginning on October 1, 2020, and ending on November 30, 2020, the amount equal to the pro rata portion of the amount appropriated for such period for fiscal year 2020."; and

(2) in paragraph (3), by striking "and (G)" and inserting ", (G), and (H)".

[¶2156] SEC. 3812. EXTENSION OF SPOUSAL IMPOVERISHMENT PROTECTIONS.

(a) IN GENERAL.—Section 2404 of Public Law 111–148 (42 U.S.C. 1396r–5 note) is amended by striking "May 22, 2020" and inserting "November 30, 2020".

(b) RULE OF CONSTRUCTION.—Nothing in section 2404 of Public Law 111–148 (42 U.S.C. 1396r–5 note) or section 1902(a)(17) or 1924 of the Social Security Act (42 U.S.C. 1396a(a)(17), 1396r–5) shall be construed as prohibiting a State from—

(1) applying an income or resource disregard under a methodology authorized under section 1902(r)(2) of such Act (42 U.S.C. 1396a(r)(2))—

(A) to the income or resources of an individual described in section 1902(a)(10)(A)(ii)(VI) of such Act (42 U.S.C. 1396a(a)(10)(A)(ii)(VI)) (including a disregard of the income or resources of such individual's spouse); or

(B) on the basis of an individual's need for home and community-based services authorized under subsection (c), (d), (i), or (k) of section 1915 of such Act (42 U.S.C. 1396n) or under section 1115 of such Act (42 U.S.C. 1315); or

(2) disregarding an individual's spousal income and assets under a plan amendment to provide medical assistance for home and community-based services for individuals by reason of being determined eligible under section 1902(a)(10)(C) of such Act (42 U.S.C. 1396a(a)(10)(C)) or by reason of section 1902(f) of such Act (42 U.S.C. 1396a(f)) or otherwise on the basis of a reduction of income based on costs incurred for medical or other remedial care under which the State disregarded the income and assets of the individual's spouse in determining the initial and ongoing financial eligibility of an individual for such services in place of the spousal impoverishment provisions applied under section 1924 of such Act (42 U.S.C. 1396r–5).

[¶2157] SEC. 3813. DELAY OF DSH REDUCTIONS.

Section 1923(f)(7)(A) of the Social Security Act (42 U.S.C. 1396r–4(f)(7)(A)) is amended—

(1) in clause (i), in the matter preceding subclause (I), by striking "May 23, 2020, and ending September 30, 2020, and for each of fiscal years 2021" and inserting "December 1, 2020, and ending September 30, 2021, and for each of fiscal years 2022"; and

(2) in clause (ii)—

(A) in subclause (I), by striking "May 23, 2020, and ending September 30, 2020" and inserting "December 1, 2020, and ending September 30, 2021"; and

(B) in subclause (II), by striking "2021" and inserting "2022".

[¶2158] SEC. 3814. EXTENSION AND EXPANSION OF COMMUNITY MENTAL HEALTH SERVICES DEMONSTRATION PROGRAM.

(a) IN GENERAL.—Section 223(d) of the Protecting Access to Medicare Act of 2014 (42 U.S.C. 1396a note) is amended—

(1) in paragraph (3)—

(A) by striking "Not more than" and inserting "Subject to paragraph (8), not more than"; and

(B) by striking "May 22, 2020" and inserting "November 30, 2020"; and

(2) by adding at the end the following new paragraph:

(8) "ADDITIONAL PROGRAMS.—

(A) "IN GENERAL.—Not later than 6 months after the date of enactment of this paragraph, in addition to the 8 States selected under paragraph (1), the Secretary shall select 2 States to participate in 2-year demonstration programs that meet the requirements of this subsection.

(B) "SELECTION OF STATES.—

(i) "IN GENERAL.—Subject to clause (ii), in selecting States under this paragraph, the Secretary—

(I) "shall select States that—

(aa) "were awarded planning grants under subsection (c); and

(bb) "applied to participate in the demonstration programs under this subsection under paragraph (1) but, as of the date of enactment of this paragraph, were not selected to participate under paragraph (1); and

(II) "shall use the results of the Secretary's evaluation of each State's application under paragraph (1) to determine which States to select, and shall not require the submission of any additional application.

(C) "REQUIREMENTS FOR SELECTED STATES.—Prior to services being delivered under the demonstration authority in a State selected under this paragraph, the State shall—

(i) "submit a plan to monitor certified community behavioral health clinics under the demonstration program to ensure compliance with certified community behavioral health criteria during the demonstration period; and

(ii) "commit to collecting data, notifying the Secretary of any planned changes that would deviate from the prospective payment system methodology outlined in the State's demonstration application, and obtaining approval from the Secretary for any such change before implementing the change.".

(b) LIMITATION.—Section 223(d)(5) of the Protecting Access to Medicare Act of 2014 (42 U.S.C. 1396a note) is amended—

(1) in subparagraph (B), in the matter preceding clause (i), by striking "The Federal matching" and inserting "Subject to subparagraph (C)(iii), the Federal matching"; and

(2) in subparagraph (C), by adding at the end the following new clause:

(iii) "PAYMENTS FOR AMOUNTS EXPENDED AFTER 2019.—The Federal matching percentage applicable under subparagraph (B) to amounts expended by a State participating in the demonstration program under this subsection shall—

(I) "in the case of a State participating in the demonstration program as of January 1, 2020, apply to amounts expended by the State during the 8 fiscal quarter period (or any portion of such period) that begins on January 1, 2020; and

(II) "in the case of a State selected to participate in the demonstration program under paragraph (8), during first 8 fiscal quarter period (or any portion of such period) that the State participates in a demonstration program.".

(c) GAO STUDY AND REPORT ON THE COMMUNITY AND MENTAL HEALTH SERVICES DEMONSTRATION PROGRAM.—

(1) IN GENERAL.—Not later than 18 months after the date of the enactment of this Act, the Comptroller General of the United States shall submit to the Committee on Energy and Commerce of the House of Representatives and the Committee on Finance of the Senate a report on the community and mental health services demonstration program conducted under section 223 of the Protecting Access to Medicare Act of 2014 (42 U.S.C. 1396a note) (referred to in this subsection as the "demonstration program").

(2) CONTENT OF REPORT.—The report required under paragraph (1) shall include the following information:

(A) Information on States' experiences participating in the demonstration program, including the extent to which States—

(i) measure the effects of access to certified community behavioral health clinics on patient health and cost of care, including—

(I) engagement in treatment for behavioral health conditions;

(II) relevant clinical outcomes, to the extent collected;

(III) screening and treatment for comorbid medical conditions; and

(IV) use of crisis stabilization, emergency department, and inpatient care.

(B) Information on Federal efforts to evaluate the demonstration program, including—

(i) quality measures used to evaluate the program;

(ii) assistance provided to States on data collection and reporting;

(iii) assessments of the reliability and usefulness of State-submitted data; and

(iv) the extent to which such efforts provide information on the relative quality, scope, and cost of services as compared with services not provided under the demonstration program, and in comparison to Medicaid beneficiaries with mental illness and substance use disorders not served under the demonstration program.

(C) Recommendations for improvements to the following:

(i) The reporting, accuracy, and validation of encounter data.

(ii) Accuracy in payments to certified community behavioral health clinics under State plans or waivers under title XIX of the Social Security Act (42 U.S.C. 1396 et seq.).

PART III—HUMAN SERVICES AND OTHER HEALTH PROGRAMS

[¶2160] SEC. 3821. EXTENSION OF SEXUAL RISK AVOIDANCE EDUCATION PROGRAM.

Section 510 of the Social Security Act (42 U.S.C. 710) is amended—

(1) in subsection (a)—

(A) in paragraph (1), in the matter preceding subparagraph (A)—

(i) by striking "and 2019 and for the period beginning October 1, 2019, and ending May 22, 2020" and inserting "through 2020 and for the period beginning October 1, 2020, and ending November 30, 2020"; and

(ii) by striking "fiscal year 2020" and inserting "fiscal year 2021"

(B) in paragraph (2)(A)—

(i) by striking "and 2019 and for the period beginning October 1, 2019, and ending May 22, 2020" and inserting "through 2020 and for the period beginning October 1, 2020, and ending November 30, 2020"; and

(ii) by striking "fiscal year 2020" and inserting "fiscal year 2021"; and

(2) in subsection (f)(1), by striking "and 2019 and $48,287,671 for the period beginning October 1, 2019, and ending May 22, 2020" and inserting "through 2020, and for the period beginning on October 1, 2020, and ending on November 30, 2020, the amount equal to the pro rata portion of the amount appropriated for such period for fiscal year 2020".

[¶2161] SEC. 3822. EXTENSION OF PERSONAL RESPONSIBILITY EDUCATION PROGRAM.

Section 513 of the Social Security Act (42 U.S.C. 713) is amended—

(1) in subsection (a)—

(A) in paragraph (1)—

(i) in subparagraph (A), in the matter preceding clause (i), by striking "2019 and for the period beginning October 1, 2019, and ending May 22, 2020" and inserting "2020 and for the period beginning October 1, 2020, and ending November 30, 2020"; and

(ii) in subparagraph (B)(i), by striking by striking "October 1, 2019, and ending May 22, 2020" and inserting "October 1, 2020, and ending November 30, 2020";

(2) in paragraph (4)(A), by striking "2019" each place it appears and inserting "2020"; and

(3) in subsection (f), by striking "2019 and $48,287,671 for the period beginning October 1, 2019, and ending May 22, 2020" and inserting "2020, and for the period beginning on October 1, 2020, and ending on November 30, 2020, the amount equal to the pro rata portion of the amount appropriated for such period for fiscal year 2020".

[¶2162] SEC. 3823. EXTENSION OF DEMONSTRATION PROJECTS TO ADDRESS HEALTH PROFESSIONS WORKFORCE NEEDS.

Activities authorized by section 2008 of the Social Security Act shall continue through November 30, 2020, in the manner authorized for fiscal year 2019, and out of any money in the Treasury of the United States not otherwise appropriated, there are hereby appropriated such sums as may be necessary for such purpose. Grants and payments may be made pursuant to this authority through the date so specified at the pro rata portion of the total amount authorized for such activities in fiscal year 2019.

[¶2163] SEC. 3824. EXTENSION OF THE TEMPORARY ASSISTANCE FOR NEEDY FAMILIES PROGRAM AND RELATED PROGRAMS.

Activities authorized by part A of title IV and section 1108(b) of the Social Security Act shall continue through November 30, 2020, in the manner authorized for fiscal year 2019, and out of any money in the Treasury of the United States not otherwise appropriated, there are hereby appropriated such sums as may be necessary for such purpose.

PART IV—PUBLIC HEALTH PROVISIONS

[¶2165] SEC. 3831. EXTENSION FOR COMMUNITY HEALTH CENTERS, THE NATIONAL HEALTH SERVICE CORPS, AND TEACHING HEALTH CENTERS THAT OPERATE GME PROGRAMS.

(a) COMMUNITY HEALTH CENTERS.—Section 10503(b)(1)(F) of the Patient Protection and Affordable Care Act (42 U.S.C. 254b–2(b)(1)(F)) is amended by striking "and $2,575,342,466 for the period beginning on October 1, 2019, and ending on May 22, 2020" and inserting "$4,000,000,000 for fiscal year 2020, and $668,493,151 for the period beginning on October 1, 2020, and ending on November 30, 2020".

(b) NATIONAL HEALTH SERVICE CORPS.—Section 10503(b)(2) of the Patient Protection and Affordable Care Act (42 U.S.C. 254b–2(b)(2)) is amended—

(1) in subparagraph (F), by striking "and" at the end; and

(2) by striking subparagraph (G) and inserting the following:

(G) "$310,000,000 for fiscal year 2020; and

(H) "$51,808,219 for the period beginning on October 1, 2020, and ending on November 30, 2020.".

(c) TEACHING HEALTH CENTERS THAT OPERATE GRADUATE MEDICAL EDUCATION PROGRAMS.—Section 340H(g)(1) of the Public Health Service Act (42 U.S.C. 256h(g)(1)) is amended by striking "and 2019, and $81,445,205 for the period beginning on October 1, 2019, and ending on May 22, 2020" and inserting "through fiscal year 2020, and $21,141,096 for the period beginning on October 1, 2020, and ending on November 30, 2020".

(d) APPLICATION OF PROVISIONS.—Amounts appropriated pursuant to the amendments made by this section for fiscal year 2020 and for the period beginning on October 1, 2020, and ending on November 30, 2020, shall be subject to the requirements contained in Public Law 116–94 for funds for programs authorized under sections 330 through 340 of the Public Health Service Act (42 U.S.C. 254 through 256).

(e) CONFORMING AMENDMENT.—Paragraph (4) of section 3014(h) of title 18, United States Code, as amended by section 401(e) of division N of Public Law 116–94, is amended by striking "section 401(d) of division N of the Further Consolidated Appropriations Act, 2020" and inserting "section 3831 of the CARES Act".

[¶2166] SEC. 3832. DIABETES PROGRAMS.

(a) TYPE I.—Section 330B(b)(2)(D) of the Public Health Service Act (42 U.S.C. 254c–2(b)(2)(D)) is amended by striking "and 2019, and $96,575,342 for the period beginning on October 1, 2019, and ending on May 22, 2020" and inserting "through 2020, and $25,068,493 for the period beginning on October 1, 2020, and ending on November 30, 2020".

(b) INDIANS.—Section 330C(c)(2)(D) of the Public Health Service Act (42 U.S.C. 254c–3(c)(2)(D)) is amended by striking "and 2019, and $96,575,342 for the period beginning on October 1, 2019, and ending on May 22, 2020" and inserting "through 2020, and $25,068,493 for the period beginning on October 1, 2020, and ending on November 30, 2020".

PART V—MISCELLANEOUS PROVISIONS

[¶2168] SEC. 3841. PREVENTION OF DUPLICATE APPROPRIATIONS FOR FISCAL YEAR 2020.

Expenditures made under any provision of law amended in this title pursuant to the amendments made by the Continuing Appropriations Act, 2020, and Health Extenders Act of 2019 (Public Law 116–59), the Further Continuing Appropriations Act, 2020, and Further Health Extenders Act of 2019 (Public Law 116–69), and the Further Consolidated Appropriations Act, 2020 (Public Law 116–94) for fiscal year 2020 shall be charged to the applicable appropriation or authorization provided by the amendments made by this title to such provision of law for such fiscal year.

Subtitle F—Over-the-Counter Drugs

PART I—OTC DRUG REVIEW

[¶2171] SEC. 3851. REGULATION OF CERTAIN NONPRESCRIPTION DRUGS THAT ARE MARKETED WITHOUT AN APPROVED DRUG APPLICATION.

(a) IN GENERAL.—Chapter V of the Federal Food, Drug, and Cosmetic Act is amended by inserting after section 505F of such Act (21 U.S.C. 355g) the following:

[¶2172] SEC. 505G. "REGULATION OF CERTAIN NONPRESCRIPTION DRUGS THAT ARE MARKETED WITHOUT AN APPROVED DRUG APPLICATION.

(a) "NONPRESCRIPTION DRUGS MARKETED WITHOUT AN APPROVED APPLICATION.—Nonprescription drugs marketed without an approved drug application under section 505, as of the date of the enactment of this section, shall be treated in accordance with this subsection.

(1) "DRUGS SUBJECT TO A FINAL MONOGRAPH; CATEGORY I DRUGS SUBJECT TO A TENTATIVE FINAL MONOGRAPH.—A drug is deemed to be generally recognized as safe and effective under section 201(p)(1), not a new drug under section 201(p), and not subject to section 503(b)(1), if—

(A) "the drug is—

(i) "in conformity with the requirements for nonprescription use of a final monograph issued under part 330 of title 21, Code of Federal Regulations (except as provided in paragraph (2)), the general requirements for nonprescription drugs, and conditions or requirements under subsections (b), (c), and (k); and

(ii) "except as permitted by an order issued under subsection (b) or, in the case of a minor change in the drug, in conformity with an order issued under subsection (c), in a dosage form that, immediately prior to the date of the enactment of this section, has been used to a material extent and for a material time under section 201(p)(2); or

(B) "the drug is—

(i) "classified in category I for safety and effectiveness under a tentative final monograph that is the most recently applicable proposal or determination issued under part 330 of title 21, Code of Federal Regulations;

(ii) "in conformity with the proposed requirements for nonprescription use of such tentative final monograph, any applicable subsequent determination by the Secretary, the general requirements for nonprescription drugs, and conditions or requirements under subsections (b), (c), and (k); and

(iii) "except as permitted by an order issued under subsection (b) or, in the case of a minor change in the drug, in conformity with an order issued under subsection (c), in a dosage form that, immediately prior to the date of the enactment of this section, has been used to a material extent and for a material time under section 201(p)(2).

(2) "TREATMENT OF SUNSCREEN DRUGS.—With respect to sunscreen drugs subject to this section, the applicable requirements in terms of conformity with a final monograph, for purposes of paragraph (1)(A)(i), shall be the requirements specified in part 352 of title 21, Code of Federal Regulations, as published on May 21, 1999, beginning on page 27687 of volume 64 of the Federal Register, except that the applicable requirements governing effectiveness and labeling shall be those specified in section 201.327 of title 21, Code of Federal Regulations.

(3) "CATEGORY III DRUGS SUBJECT TO A TENTATIVE FINAL MONOGRAPH; CATEGORY I DRUGS SUBJECT TO PROPOSED MONOGRAPH OR ADVANCE NOTICE OF PROPOSED RULEMAKING.—A drug that is not described in paragraph (1), (2), or (4) is not required to be the subject of an application approved under section 505, and is not subject to section 503(b)(1), if—

(A) "the drug is—

(i) "classified in category III for safety or effectiveness in the preamble of a proposed rule establishing a tentative final monograph that is the most recently applicable proposal or determination for such drug issued under part 330 of title 21, Code of Federal Regulations;

(ii) "in conformity with—

(I) "the conditions of use, including indication and dosage strength, if any, described for such category III drug in such preamble or in an applicable subsequent proposed rule;

(II) "the proposed requirements for drugs classified in such tentative final monograph in category I in the most recently proposed rule establishing requirements related to such tentative final monograph and in any final rule establishing requirements that are applicable to the drug; and

(III) "the general requirements for nonprescription drugs and conditions or requirements under subsection (b) or (k); and

(iii) "in a dosage form that, immediately prior to the date of the enactment of this section, had been used to a material extent and for a material time under section 201(p)(2); or

(B) "the drug is—

(i) "classified in category I for safety and effectiveness under a proposed monograph or advance notice of proposed rulemaking that is the most recently applicable proposal or determination for such drug issued under part 330 of title 21, Code of Federal Regulations;

(ii) "in conformity with the requirements for nonprescription use of such proposed monograph or advance notice of proposed rulemaking, any applicable subsequent determination by the Secretary, the general requirements for nonprescription drugs, and conditions or requirements under subsection (b) or (k); and

(iii) "in a dosage form that, immediately prior to the date of the enactment of this section, has been used to a material extent and for a material time under section 201(p)(2).

(4) "CATEGORY II DRUGS DEEMED NEW DRUGS.—A drug that is classified in category II for safety or effectiveness under a tentative final monograph or that is subject to a determination to be not

generally recognized as safe and effective in a proposed rule that is the most recently applicable proposal issued under part 330 of title 21, Code of Federal Regulations, shall be deemed to be a new drug under section 201(p), misbranded under section 502(ee), and subject to the requirement for an approved new drug application under section 505 beginning on the day that is 180 calendar days after the date of the enactment of this section, unless, before such day, the Secretary determines that it is in the interest of public health to extend the period during which the drug may be marketed without such an approved new drug application.

(5) "DRUGS NOT GRASE DEEMED NEW DRUGS.—A drug that the Secretary has determined not to be generally recognized as safe and effective under section 201(p)(1) under a final determination issued under part 330 of title 21, Code of Federal Regulations, shall be deemed to be a new drug under section 201(p), misbranded under section 502(ee), and subject to the requirement for an approved new drug application under section 505.

(6) "OTHER DRUGS DEEMED NEW DRUGS.—Except as provided in subsection (m), a drug is deemed to be a new drug under section 201(p) and misbranded under section 502(ee) if the drug—

(A) "is not subject to section 503(b)(1); and

(B) "is not described in paragraph (1), (2), (3), (4), or (5), or subsection (b)(1)(B).

(b) "ADMINISTRATIVE ORDERS.—

(1) "IN GENERAL.—

(A) "DETERMINATION.—The Secretary may, on the initiative of the Secretary or at the request of one or more requestors, issue an administrative order determining whether there are conditions under which a specific drug, a class of drugs, or a combination of drugs, is determined to be—

(i) "not subject to section 503(b)(1); and

(ii) "generally recognized as safe and effective under section 201(p)(1).

(B) "EFFECT.—A drug or combination of drugs shall be deemed to not require approval under section 505 if such drug or combination of drugs—

(i) "is determined by the Secretary to meet the conditions specified in clauses (i) and (ii) of subparagraph (A);

(ii) "is marketed in conformity with an administrative order under this subsection;

(iii) "meets the general requirements for nonprescription drugs; and

(iv) "meets the requirements under subsections (c) and (k).

(C) "STANDARD.—The Secretary shall find that a drug is not generally recognized as safe and effective under section 201(p)(1) if—

(i) "the evidence shows that the drug is not generally recognized as safe and effective under section 201(p)(1); or

(ii) "the evidence is inadequate to show that the drug is generally recognized as safe and effective under section 201(p)(1).

(2) "ADMINISTRATIVE ORDERS INITIATED BY THE SECRETARY.—

(A) "IN GENERAL.—In issuing an administrative order under paragraph (1) upon the Secretary's initiative, the Secretary shall—

(i) "make reasonable efforts to notify informally, not later than 2 business days before the issuance of the proposed order, the sponsors of drugs who have a listing in effect under section 510(j) for the drugs or combination of drugs that will be subject to the administrative order;

(ii) "after any such reasonable efforts of notification—

(I) "issue a proposed administrative order by publishing it on the website of the Food and Drug Administration and include in such order the reasons for the issuance of such order; and

(II) "publish a notice of availability of such proposed order in the Federal Register;

(iii) "except as provided in subparagraph (B), provide for a public comment period with respect to such proposed order of not less than 45 calendar days; and

(iv) "if, after completion of the proceedings specified in clauses (i) through (iii), the Secretary determines that it is appropriate to issue a final administrative order—

(I) "issue the final administrative order, together with a detailed statement of reasons, which order shall not take effect until the time for requesting judicial review under paragraph (3)(D)(ii) has expired;

(II) "publish a notice of such final administrative order in the Federal Register;

(III) "afford requestors of drugs that will be subject to such order the opportunity for formal dispute resolution up to the level of the Director of the Center for Drug Evaluation and Research, which initially must be requested within 45 calendar days of the issuance of the order, and, for subsequent levels of appeal, within 30 calendar days of the prior decision; and

(IV) "except with respect to drugs described in paragraph (3)(B), upon completion of the formal dispute resolution procedure, inform the persons which sought such dispute resolution of their right to request a hearing.

(B) "EXCEPTIONS.—When issuing an administrative order under paragraph (1) on the Secretary's initiative proposing to determine that a drug described in subsection (a)(3) is not generally recognized as safe and effective under section 201(p)(1), the Secretary shall follow the procedures in subparagraph (A), except that—

(i) "the proposed order shall include notice of—

(I) "the general categories of data the Secretary has determined necessary to establish that the drug is generally recognized as safe and effective under section 201(p)(1); and

(II) "the format for submissions by interested persons;

(ii) "the Secretary shall provide for a public comment period of no less than 180 calendar days with respect to such proposed order, except when the Secretary determines, for good cause, that a shorter period is in the interest of public health; and

(iii) "any person who submits data in such comment period shall include a certification that the person has submitted all evidence created, obtained, or received by that person that is both within the categories of data identified in the proposed order and relevant to a determination as to whether the drug is generally recognized as safe and effective under section 201(p)(1).

(3) "HEARINGS; JUDICIAL REVIEW.—

(A) "IN GENERAL.—Only a person who participated in each stage of formal dispute resolution under subclause (III) of paragraph (2)(A)(iv) of an administrative order with respect to a drug may request a hearing concerning a final administrative order issued under such paragraph with respect to such drug. If a hearing is sought, such person must submit a request for a hearing, which shall be based solely on information in the administrative record, to the Secretary not later than 30 calendar days after receiving notice of the final decision of the formal dispute resolution procedure.

(B) "NO HEARING REQUIRED WITH RESPECT TO ORDERS RELATING TO CERTAIN DRUGS.—

(i) "IN GENERAL.—The Secretary shall not be required to provide notice and an opportunity for a hearing pursuant to paragraph (2)(A)(iv) if the final administrative order involved relates to a drug—

(I) "that is described in subsection (a)(3)(A); and

(II) "with respect to which no human or non-human data studies relevant to the safety or effectiveness of such drug have been submitted to the administrative record since the issuance of the most recent tentative final monograph relating to such drug.

(ii) "HUMAN DATA STUDIES AND NON-HUMAN DATA DEFINED.—In this subparagraph:

(I) "The term 'human data studies' means clinical trials of safety or effectiveness (including actual use studies), pharmacokinetics studies, or bioavailability studies.

(II) "The term 'non-human data' means data from testing other than with human subjects which provides information concerning safety or effectiveness.

(C) "HEARING PROCEDURES.—

(i) "DENIAL OF REQUEST FOR HEARING.—If the Secretary determines that information submitted in a request for a hearing under subparagraph (A) with respect to a final administrative order issued under paragraph (2)(A)(iv) does not identify the existence of a genuine and substantial question of material fact, the Secretary may deny such request. In making such a determination, the Secretary may consider only information and data that are based on relevant and reliable scientific principles and methodologies.

(ii) "SINGLE HEARING FOR MULTIPLE RELATED REQUESTS.—If more than one request for a hearing is submitted with respect to the same administrative order under subparagraph (A), the Secretary may direct that a single hearing be conducted in which all persons whose hearing requests were granted may participate.

(iii) "PRESIDING OFFICER.—The presiding officer of a hearing requested under subparagraph (A) shall—

(I) "be designated by the Secretary;

(II) "not be an employee of the Center for Drug Evaluation and Research; and

(III) "not have been previously involved in the development of the administrative order involved or proceedings relating to that administrative order.

(iv) "RIGHTS OF PARTIES TO HEARING.—The parties to a hearing requested under subparagraph (A) shall have the right to present testimony, including testimony of expert witnesses, and to cross-examine witnesses presented by other parties. Where appropriate, the presiding officer may require that cross-examination by parties representing substantially the same interests be consolidated to promote efficiency and avoid duplication.

(v) "FINAL DECISION.—

(I) "At the conclusion of a hearing requested under subparagraph (A), the presiding officer of the hearing shall issue a decision containing findings of fact and conclusions of law. The decision of the presiding officer shall be final.

(II) "The final decision may not take effect until the period under subparagraph (D)(ii) for submitting a request for judicial review of such decision expires.

(D) "JUDICIAL REVIEW OF FINAL ADMINISTRATIVE ORDER.—

(i) "IN GENERAL.—The procedures described in section 505(h) shall apply with respect to judicial review of final administrative orders issued under this subsection in the same manner and to the same extent as such section applies to an order described in such section except that the judicial review shall be taken by filing in an appropriate district court of the United States in lieu of the appellate courts specified in such section.

(ii) "PERIOD TO SUBMIT A REQUEST FOR JUDICIAL REVIEW.—A person eligible to request a hearing under this paragraph and seeking judicial review of a final administrative order issued under this subsection shall file such request for judicial review not later than 60 calendar days after the latest of—

(I) "the date on which notice of such order is published;

(II) "the date on which a hearing with respect to such order is denied under subparagraph (B) or (C)(i);

(III) "the date on which a final decision is made following a hearing under subparagraph (C)(v); or

(IV) "if no hearing is requested, the date on which the time for requesting a hearing expires.

(4) "EXPEDITED PROCEDURE WITH RESPECT TO ADMINISTRATIVE ORDERS INITIATED BY THE SECRETARY.—

(A) "IMMINENT HAZARD TO THE PUBLIC HEALTH.—

(i) "IN GENERAL.—In the case of a determination by the Secretary that a drug, class of drugs, or combination of drugs subject to this section poses an imminent hazard to the public health, the Secretary, after first making reasonable efforts to notify, not later than 48 hours before issuance of such order under this subparagraph, sponsors who have a listing in effect under section 510(j) for such drug or combination of drugs—

(I) "may issue an interim final administrative order for such drug, class of drugs, or combination of drugs under paragraph (1), together with a detailed statement of the reasons for such order;

(II) "shall publish in the Federal Register a notice of availability of any such order; and

(III) "shall provide for a public comment period of at least 45 calendar days with respect to such interim final order.

(ii) "NONDELEGATION.—The Secretary may not delegate the authority to issue an interim final administrative order under this subparagraph.

(B) "SAFETY LABELING CHANGES.—

(i) "IN GENERAL.—In the case of a determination by the Secretary that a change in the labeling of a drug, class of drugs, or combination of drugs subject to this section is reasonably expected to mitigate a significant or unreasonable risk of a serious adverse event associated with use of the drug, the Secretary may—

(I) "make reasonable efforts to notify informally, not later than 48 hours before the issuance of the interim final order, the sponsors of drugs who have a listing in effect under section 510(j) for such drug or combination of drugs;

(II) "after reasonable efforts of notification, issue an interim final administrative order in accordance with paragraph (1) to require such change, together with a detailed statement of the reasons for such order;

(III) "publish in the Federal Register a notice of availability of such order; and

(IV) "provide for a public comment period of at least 45 calendar days with respect to such interim final order.

(ii) "CONTENT OF ORDER.—An interim final order issued under this subparagraph with respect to the labeling of a drug may provide for new warnings and other information required for safe use of the drug.

(C) "EFFECTIVE DATE.—An order under subparagraph (A) or (B) shall take effect on a date specified by the Secretary.

(D) "FINAL ORDER.—After the completion of the proceedings in subparagraph (A) or (B), the Secretary shall—

(i) "issue a final order in accordance with paragraph (1);

(ii) "publish a notice of availability of such final administrative order in the Federal Register; and

(iii) "afford sponsors of such drugs that will be subject to such an order the opportunity for formal dispute resolution up to the level of the Director of the Center for Drug Evaluation and Research, which must initially be within 45 calendar days of the issuance of the order, and for subsequent levels of appeal, within 30 calendar days of the prior decision.

(E) "HEARINGS.—A sponsor of a drug subject to a final order issued under subparagraph (D) and that participated in each stage of formal dispute resolution under clause (iii) of such subparagraph may request a hearing on such order. The provisions of subparagraphs (A), (B), and (C) of paragraph (3), other than paragraph (3)(C)(v)(II), shall apply with respect to a hearing on such order in the same manner and to the same extent as such provisions apply with respect to a hearing on an administrative order issued under paragraph (2)(A)(iv).

(F) "TIMING.—

(i) "FINAL ORDER AND HEARING.—The Secretary shall—

(I) "not later than 6 months after the date on which the comment period closes under subparagraph (A) or (B), issue a final order in accordance with paragraph (1); and

(II) "not later than 12 months after the date on which such final order is issued, complete any hearing under subparagraph (E).

(ii) "DISPUTE RESOLUTION REQUEST.—The Secretary shall specify in an interim final order issued under subparagraph (A) or (B) such shorter periods for requesting dispute resolution under subparagraph (D)(iii) as are necessary to meet the requirements of this subparagraph.

(G) "JUDICIAL REVIEW.—A final order issued pursuant to subparagraph (F) shall be subject to judicial review in accordance with paragraph (3)(D).

(5) "ADMINISTRATIVE ORDER INITIATED AT THE REQUEST OF A REQUESTOR.—

(A) "IN GENERAL.—In issuing an administrative order under paragraph (1) at the request of a requestor with respect to certain drugs, classes of drugs, or combinations of drugs—

(i) "the Secretary shall, after receiving a request under this subparagraph, determine whether the request is sufficiently complete and formatted to permit a substantive review;

(ii) "if the Secretary determines that the request is sufficiently complete and formatted to permit a substantive review, the Secretary shall—

(I) "file the request; and

(II) "initiate proceedings with respect to issuing an administrative order in accordance with paragraphs (2) and (3); and

(iii) "except as provided in paragraph (6), if the Secretary determines that a request does not meet the requirements for filing or is not sufficiently complete and formatted to permit a substantive review, the requestor may demand that the request be filed over protest, and the Secretary shall initiate proceedings to review the request in accordance with paragraph (2)(A).

(B) "REQUEST TO INITIATE PROCEEDINGS.—

(i) "IN GENERAL.—A requestor seeking an administrative order under paragraph (1) with respect to certain drugs, classes of drugs, or combinations of drugs, shall submit to the Secretary a request to initiate proceedings for such order in the form and manner as specified by the Secretary. Such requestor may submit a request under this subparagraph for the issuance of an administrative order—

(I) "determining whether a drug is generally recognized as safe and effective under section 201(p)(1), exempt from section 503(b)(1), and not required to be the subject of an approved application under section 505; or

(II) "determining whether a change to a condition of use of a drug is generally recognized as safe and effective under section 201(p)(1), exempt from section 503(b)(1), and not required to be the subject of an approved application under section 505, if, absent such a changed condition of use, such drug is—

(aa) "generally recognized as safe and effective under section 201(p)(1) in accordance with subsection (a)(1), (a)(2), or an order under this subsection; or

(bb) "subject to subsection (a)(3), but only if such requestor initiates such request in conjunction with a request for the Secretary to determine whether such drug is generally recognized as safe and effective under section 201(p)(1), which is filed by the Secretary under subparagraph (A)(ii).

(ii) "EXCEPTION.—The Secretary is not required to complete review of a request for a change described in clause (i)(II) if the Secretary determines that there is an inadequate basis to find the drug is generally recognized as safe and effective under section 201(p)(1) under paragraph (1) and issues a final order announcing that determination.

(iii) "WITHDRAWAL.—The requestor may withdraw a request under this paragraph, according to the procedures set forth pursuant to subsection (d)(2)(B). Notwithstanding any other provision of this section, if such request is withdrawn, the Secretary may cease proceedings under this subparagraph.

(C) "EXCLUSIVITY.—

(i) "IN GENERAL.—A final administrative order issued in response to a request under this section shall have the effect of authorizing solely the order requestor (or the licensees, assignees, or successors in interest of such requestor with respect to the subject of such order), for a period of 18 months following the effective date of such final order and beginning on the date the requestor may lawfully market such drugs pursuant to the order, to market drugs—

(I) "incorporating changes described in clause (ii); and

(II) "subject to the limitations under clause (iv).

(ii) "CHANGES DESCRIBED.—A change described in this clause is a change subject to an order specified in clause (i), which—

(I) "provides for a drug to contain an active ingredient (including any ester or salt of the active ingredient) not previously incorporated in a drug described in clause (iii); or

(II) "provides for a change in the conditions of use of a drug, for which new human data studies conducted or sponsored by the requestor (or for which the requestor has an exclusive right of reference) were essential to the issuance of such order.

(iii) "DRUGS DESCRIBED.—The drugs described in this clause are drugs—

(I) "specified in subsection (a)(1), (a)(2), or (a)(3);

(II) "subject to a final order issued under this section;

(III) "subject to a final sunscreen order (as defined in section 586(2)(A)); or

(IV) "described in subsection (m)(1), other than drugs subject to an active enforcement action under chapter III of this Act.

(iv) "LIMITATIONS ON EXCLUSIVITY.—

(I) "IN GENERAL.—Only one 18-month period under this subparagraph shall be granted, under each order described in clause (i), with respect to changes (to the drug subject to such order) which are either—

(aa) "changes described in clause (ii)(I), relating to active ingredients; or

(bb) "changes described in clause (ii)(II), relating to conditions of use.

(II) "NO EXCLUSIVITY ALLOWED.—No exclusivity shall apply to changes to a drug which are—

(aa) "the subject of a Tier 2 OTC monograph order request (as defined in section 744L);

(bb) "safety-related changes, as defined by the Secretary, or any other changes the Secretary considers necessary to assure safe use; or

(cc) "changes related to methods of testing safety or efficacy.

(v) "NEW HUMAN DATA STUDIES DEFINED.—In this subparagraph, the term 'new human data studies' means clinical trials of safety or effectiveness (including actual use studies), pharmacokinetics studies, or bioavailability studies, the results of which—

(I) "have not been relied on by the Secretary to support—

(aa) "a proposed or final determination that a drug described in subclause (I), (II), or (III) of clause (iii) is generally recognized as safe and effective under section 201(p)(1); or

(bb) "approval of a drug that was approved under section 505; and

(II) "do not duplicate the results of another study that was relied on by the Secretary to support—

(aa) "a proposed or final determination that a drug described in subclause (I), (II), or (III) of clause (iii) is generally recognized as safe and effective under section 201(p)(1); or

(bb) "approval of a drug that was approved under section 505.

(vi) "NOTIFICATION OF DRUG NOT AVAILABLE FOR SALE.—A requestor that is granted exclusivity with respect to a drug under this subparagraph shall notify the Secretary in writing within 1 year of the issuance of the final administrative order if the drug that is the subject of such order will not be available for sale within 1 year of the date of issuance of such order. The requestor shall include with such notice the—

(I) "identity of the drug by established name and by proprietary name, if any;

(II) "strength of the drug;

(III) "date on which the drug will be available for sale, if known; and

(IV) "reason for not marketing the drug after issuance of the order.

(6) "INFORMATION REGARDING SAFE NONPRESCRIPTION MARKETING AND USE AS CONDITION FOR FILING A GENERALLY RECOGNIZED AS SAFE AND EFFECTIVE REQUEST.—

(A) "IN GENERAL.—In response to a request under this section that a drug described in subparagraph (B) be generally recognized as safe and effective, the Secretary—

(i) "may file such request, if the request includes information specified under subparagraph (C) with respect to safe nonprescription marketing and use of such drug; or

(ii) "if the request fails to include information specified under subparagraph (C), shall refuse to file such request and require that nonprescription marketing of the drug be pursuant to a new drug application as described in subparagraph (D).

(B) "DRUG DESCRIBED.—A drug described in this subparagraph is a nonprescription drug which contains an active ingredient not previously incorporated in a drug—

(i) "specified in subsection (a)(1), (a)(2), or (a)(3);

(ii) "subject to a final order under this section; or

(iii) "subject to a final sunscreen order (as defined in section 586(2)(A)).

(C) "INFORMATION DEMONSTRATING PRIMA FACIE SAFE NONPRESCRIPTION MARKETING AND USE.—Information specified in this subparagraph, with respect to a request described in subparagraph (A)(i), is—

(i) "information sufficient for a prima facie demonstration that the drug subject to such request has a verifiable history of being marketed and safely used by consumers in the United States as a nonprescription drug under comparable conditions of use;

(ii) "if the drug has not been previously marketed in the United States as a nonprescription drug, information sufficient for a prima facie demonstration that the drug was marketed and safely used under comparable conditions of marketing and use in a country listed in section 802(b)(1)(A) or designated by the Secretary in accordance with section 802(b)(1)(B)—

(I) "for such period as needed to provide reasonable assurances concerning the safe nonprescription use of the drug; and

(II) "during such time was subject to sufficient monitoring by a regulatory body considered acceptable by the Secretary for such monitoring purposes, including for adverse events associated with nonprescription use of the drug; or

(iii) "if the Secretary determines that information described in clause (i) or (ii) is not needed to provide a prima facie demonstration that the drug can be safely marketed and used as a nonprescription drug, such other information the Secretary determines is sufficient for such purposes.

(D) "MARKETING PURSUANT TO NEW DRUG APPLICATION.—In the case of a request described in subparagraph (A)(ii), the drug subject to such request may be resubmitted for filing only if—

(i) "the drug is marketed as a nonprescription drug, under conditions of use comparable to the conditions specified in the request, for such period as the Secretary determines appropriate (not to exceed 5 consecutive years) pursuant to an application approved under section 505; and

(ii) "during such period, 1,000,000 retail packages of the drug, or an equivalent quantity as determined by the Secretary, were distributed for retail sale, as determined in such manner as the Secretary finds appropriate.

(E) "RULE OF APPLICATION.—Except in the case of a request involving a drug described in section 586(9), as in effect on January 1, 2017, if the Secretary refuses to file a request under this paragraph, the requestor may not file such request over protest under paragraph (5)(A)(iii).

(7) "PACKAGING.—An administrative order issued under paragraph (2), (4)(A), or (5) may include requirements for the packaging of a drug to encourage use in accordance with labeling. Such requirements may include unit dose packaging, requirements for products intended for use by pediatric populations, requirements to reduce risk of harm from unsupervised ingestion, and other appropriate requirements. This paragraph does not authorize the Food and Drug Administration to require standards or testing procedures as described in part 1700 of title 16, Code of Federal Regulations.

(8) "FINAL AND TENTATIVE FINAL MONOGRAPHS FOR CATEGORY I DRUGS DEEMED FINAL ADMINISTRATIVE ORDERS.—

(A) "IN GENERAL.—A final monograph or tentative final monograph described in subparagraph (B) shall be deemed to be a final administrative order under this subsection and may be amended, revoked, or otherwise modified in accordance with the procedures of this subsection.

(B) "MONOGRAPHS DESCRIBED.—For purposes of subparagraph (A), a final monograph or tentative final monograph is described in this subparagraph if it—

(i) "establishes conditions of use for a drug described in paragraph (1) or (2) of subsection (a); and

(ii) "represents the most recently promulgated version of such conditions, including as modified, in whole or in part, by any proposed or final rule.

(C) "DEEMED ORDERS INCLUDE HARMONIZING TECHNICAL AMENDMENTS.—The deemed establishment of a final administrative order under subparagraph (A) shall be construed to include any technical amendments to such order as the Secretary determines necessary to ensure that such order is appropriately harmonized, in terms of terminology or cross-references, with the applicable provisions of this Act (and regulations thereunder) and any other orders issued under this section.

(c) "PROCEDURE FOR MINOR CHANGES.—

(1) "IN GENERAL.—Minor changes in the dosage form of a drug that is described in paragraph (1) or (2) of subsection (a) or the subject of an order issued under subsection (b) may be made by a requestor without the issuance of an order under subsection (b) if—

(A) "the requestor maintains such information as is necessary to demonstrate that the change—

(i) "will not affect the safety or effectiveness of the drug; and

(ii) "will not materially affect the extent of absorption or other exposure to the active ingredient in comparison to a suitable reference product; and

(B) "the change is in conformity with the requirements of an applicable administrative order issued by the Secretary under paragraph (3).

(2) "ADDITIONAL INFORMATION.—

(A) "ACCESS TO RECORDS.—A sponsor shall submit records requested by the Secretary relating to such a minor change under section 704(a)(4), within 15 business days of receiving such a request, or such longer period as the Secretary may provide.

(B) "INSUFFICIENT INFORMATION.—If the Secretary determines that the information contained in such records is not sufficient to demonstrate that the change does not affect the safety or effectiveness of the drug or materially affect the extent of absorption or other exposure to the active ingredient, the Secretary—

(i) "may so inform the sponsor of the drug in writing; and

(ii) "if the Secretary so informs the sponsor, shall provide the sponsor of the drug with a reasonable opportunity to provide additional information.

(C) "FAILURE TO SUBMIT SUFFICIENT INFORMATION.—If the sponsor fails to provide such additional information within a time prescribed by the Secretary, or if the Secretary determines that such additional information does not demonstrate that the change does not—

(i) "affect the safety or effectiveness of the drug; or

(ii) "materially affect the extent of absorption or other exposure to the active ingredient in comparison to a suitable reference product,

the drug as modified is a new drug under section 201(p) and shall be deemed to be misbranded under section 502(ee).

(3) "DETERMINING WHETHER A CHANGE WILL AFFECT SAFETY OR EFFECTIVENESS.—

(A) "IN GENERAL.—The Secretary shall issue one or more administrative orders specifying requirements for determining whether a minor change made by a sponsor pursuant to this subsection will affect the safety or effectiveness of a drug or materially affect the extent of absorption or other exposure to an active ingredient in the drug in comparison to a suitable reference product, together with guidance for applying those orders to specific dosage forms.

(B) "STANDARD PRACTICES.—The orders and guidance issued by the Secretary under subparagraph (A) shall take into account relevant public standards and standard practices for evaluating the quality of drugs, and may take into account the special needs of populations, including children.

(d) "CONFIDENTIALITY OF INFORMATION SUBMITTED TO THE SECRETARY.—

(1) "IN GENERAL.—Subject to paragraph (2), any information, including reports of testing conducted on the drug or drugs involved, that is submitted by a requestor in connection with proceedings on an order under this section (including any minor change under subsection (c)) and is a trade secret or confidential information subject to section 552(b)(4) of title 5, United States Code, or section 1905 of title 18, United States Code, shall not be disclosed to the public unless the requestor consents to that disclosure.

(2) "PUBLIC AVAILABILITY.—

(A) "IN GENERAL.—Except as provided in subparagraph (B), the Secretary shall—

(i) "make any information submitted by a requestor in support of a request under subsection (b)(5)(A) available to the public not later than the date on which the proposed order is issued; and

(ii) "make any information submitted by any other person with respect to an order requested (or initiated by the Secretary) under subsection (b), available to the public upon such submission.

(B) "LIMITATIONS ON PUBLIC AVAILABILITY.—Information described in subparagraph (A) shall not be made public if—

(i) "the information pertains to pharmaceutical quality information, unless such information is necessary to establish standards under which a drug is generally recognized as safe and effective under section 201(p)(1);

(ii) "the information is submitted in a requestor-initiated request, but the requestor withdraws such request, in accordance with withdrawal procedures established by the Secretary, before the Secretary issues the proposed order;

(iii) "the Secretary requests and obtains the information under subsection (c) and such information is not submitted in relation to an order under subsection (b); or

(iv) "the information is of the type contained in raw datasets.

(e) "UPDATES TO DRUG LISTING INFORMATION.—A sponsor who makes a change to a drug subject to this section shall submit updated drug listing information for the drug in accordance with section 510(j) within 30 calendar days of the date when the drug is first commercially marketed, except that a sponsor who was the order requestor with respect to an order subject to subsection (b)(5)(C) (or a licensee, assignee, or successor in interest of such requestor) shall submit updated drug listing information on or before the date when the drug is first commercially marketed.

(f) "APPROVALS UNDER SECTION 505.—The provisions of this section shall not be construed to preclude a person from seeking or maintaining the approval of an application for a drug under sections 505(b)(1), 505(b)(2), and 505(j). A determination under this section that a drug is not subject to section 503(b)(1), is generally recognized as safe and effective under section 201(p)(1), and is not a new drug under section 201(p) shall constitute a finding that the drug is safe and effective that may be relied upon for purposes of an application under section 505(b)(2), so that the applicant shall be required to submit for purposes of such application only information needed to support any modification of the drug that is not covered by such determination under this section.

(g) "PUBLIC AVAILABILITY OF ADMINISTRATIVE ORDERS.—The Secretary shall establish, maintain, update (as determined necessary by the Secretary but no less frequently than annually), and make publicly available, with respect to orders issued under this section—

(1) "a repository of each final order and interim final order in effect, including the complete text of the order; and

(2) "a listing of all orders proposed and under development under subsection (b)(2), including—

(A) "a brief description of each such order; and

(B) "the Secretary's expectations, if resources permit, for issuance of proposed orders over a 3-year period.

(h) "DEVELOPMENT ADVICE TO SPONSORS OR REQUESTORS.—The Secretary shall establish procedures under which sponsors or requestors may meet with appropriate officials of the Food and Drug Administration to obtain advice on the studies and other information necessary to support submissions under this section and other matters relevant to the regulation of nonprescription drugs and the development of new nonprescription drugs under this section.

(i) "PARTICIPATION OF MULTIPLE SPONSORS OR REQUESTORS.—The Secretary shall establish procedures to facilitate efficient participation by multiple sponsors or requestors in proceedings under this section, including provision for joint meetings with multiple sponsors or requestors or with organizations nominated by sponsors or requestors to represent their interests in a proceeding.

(j) "ELECTRONIC FORMAT.—All submissions under this section shall be in electronic format.

(k) "EFFECT ON EXISTING REGULATIONS GOVERNING NONPRESCRIPTION DRUGS.—

(1) "REGULATIONS OF GENERAL APPLICABILITY TO NONPRESCRIPTION DRUGS.—Except as provided in this subsection, nothing in this section supersedes regulations establishing general requirements for nonprescription drugs, including regulations of general applicability contained in parts 201, 250, and 330 of title 21, Code of Federal Regulations, or any successor regulations. The Secretary shall establish or modify such regulations by means of rulemaking in accordance with section 553 of title 5, United States Code.

(2) "REGULATIONS ESTABLISHING REQUIREMENTS FOR SPECIFIC NONPRESCRIPTION DRUGS.—

(A) "The provisions of section 310.545 of title 21, Code of Federal Regulations, as in effect on the day before the date of the enactment of this section, shall be deemed to be a final order under subsection (b).

(B) "Regulations in effect on the day before the date of the enactment of this section, establishing requirements for specific nonprescription drugs marketed pursuant to this section (including such requirements in parts 201 and 250 of title 21, Code of Federal Regulations), shall be deemed to be final orders under subsection (b), only as they apply to drugs—

(i) "subject to paragraph (1), (2), (3), or (4) of subsection (a); or

(ii) "otherwise subject to an order under this section.

(3) "WITHDRAWAL OF REGULATIONS.—The Secretary shall withdraw regulations establishing final monographs and the procedures governing the over-the-counter drug review under part 330 and other relevant parts of title 21, Code of Federal Regulations (as in effect on the day before the date of the enactment of this section), or make technical changes to such regulations to ensure conformity with appropriate terminology and cross references. Notwithstanding subchapter II of chapter 5 of title 5, United States Code, any such withdrawal or technical changes shall be made without public notice and comment and shall be effective upon publication through notice in the Federal Register (or upon such date as specified in such notice).

(l) "GUIDANCE.—The Secretary shall issue guidance that specifies—

(1) "the procedures and principles for formal meetings between the Secretary and sponsors or requestors for drugs subject to this section;

(2) "the format and content of data submissions to the Secretary under this section;

(3) "the format of electronic submissions to the Secretary under this section;

(4) "consolidated proceedings for appeal and the procedures for such proceedings where appropriate; and

(5) "for minor changes in drugs, recommendations on how to comply with the requirements in orders issued under subsection (c)(3).

(m) "RULE OF CONSTRUCTION.—

(1) "IN GENERAL.—This section shall not affect the treatment or status of a nonprescription drug—

(A) "that is marketed without an application approved under section 505 as of the date of the enactment of this section;

(B) "that is not subject to an order issued under this section; and

(C) "to which paragraph (1), (2), (3), (4), or (5) of subsection (a) do not apply.

(2) "TREATMENT OF PRODUCTS PREVIOUSLY FOUND TO BE SUBJECT TO TIME AND EXTENT REQUIREMENTS.—

(A) "Notwithstanding subsection (a), a drug described in subparagraph (B) may only be lawfully marketed, without an application approved under section 505, pursuant to an order issued under this section.

(B) "A drug described in this subparagraph is a drug which, prior to the date of the enactment of this section, the Secretary determined in a proposed or final rule to be ineligible for review under the OTC drug review (as such phrase 'OTC drug review' was used in section 330.14 of title 21, Code of Federal Regulations, as in effect on the day before the date of the enactment of this section).

(3) "PRESERVATION OF AUTHORITY.—

(A) "Nothing in paragraph (1) shall be construed to preclude or limit the applicability of any provision of this Act other than this section.

(B) "Nothing in subsection (a) shall be construed to prohibit the Secretary from issuing an order under this section finding a drug to be not generally recognized as safe and effective under section 201(p)(1), as the Secretary determines appropriate.

(n) "INVESTIGATIONAL NEW DRUGS.—A drug is not subject to this section if an exemption for investigational use under section 505(i) is in effect for such drug.

(o) "INAPPLICABILITY OF PAPERWORK REDUCTION ACT.—Chapter 35 of title 44, United States Code, shall not apply to collections of information made under this section.

(p) "INAPPLICABILITY OF NOTICE AND COMMENT RULEMAKING AND OTHER REQUIREMENTS.—The requirements of subsection (b) shall apply with respect to orders issued under this section instead of the requirements of subchapter II of chapter 5 of title 5, United States Code.

(q) "DEFINITIONS.—In this section:

(1) "The term 'nonprescription drug' refers to a drug not subject to the requirements of section 503(b)(1).

(2) "The term 'sponsor' refers to any person marketing, manufacturing, or processing a drug that—

(A) "is listed pursuant to section 510(j); and

(B) "is or will be subject to an administrative order under this section of the Food and Drug Administration.

(3) "The term 'requestor' refers to any person or group of persons marketing, manufacturing, processing, or developing a drug.".

(b) GAO STUDY.—Not later than 4 years after the date of enactment of this Act, the Comptroller General of the United States shall submit a study to the Committee on Energy and Commerce of the House of Representatives and the Committee on Health, Education, Labor, and Pensions of the Senate addressing the effectiveness and overall impact of exclusivity under section 505G of the Federal Food, Drug, and Cosmetic Act, as added by subsection (a), and section 586C of such Act (21 U.S.C. 360fff–3), including the impact of such exclusivity on consumer access. Such study shall include—

(1) an analysis of the impact of exclusivity under such section 505G for nonprescription drug products, including—

(A) the number of nonprescription drug products that were granted exclusivity and the indication for which the nonprescription drug products were determined to be generally recognized as safe and effective;

(B) whether the exclusivity for such drug products was granted for—

(i) a new active ingredient (including any ester or salt of the active ingredient); or

(ii) changes in the conditions of use of a drug, for which new human data studies conducted or sponsored by the requestor were essential;

(C) whether, and to what extent, the exclusivity impacted the requestor's or sponsor's decision to develop the drug product;

(D) an analysis of the implementation of the exclusivity provision in such section 505G, including—

(i) the resources used by the Food and Drug Administration;

(ii) the impact of such provision on innovation, as well as research and development in the nonprescription drug market;

(iii) the impact of such provision on competition in the nonprescription drug market;

(iv) the impact of such provision on consumer access to nonprescription drug products;

(v) the impact of such provision on the prices of nonprescription drug products; and

(vi) whether the administrative orders initiated by requestors under such section 505G have been sufficient to encourage the development of nonprescription drug products that would likely not be otherwise developed, or developed in as timely a manner; and

(E) whether the administrative orders initiated by requestors under such section 505G have been sufficient incentive to encourage innovation in the nonprescription drug market; and

(2) an analysis of the impact of exclusivity under such section 586C for sunscreen ingredients, including—

(A) the number of sunscreen ingredients that were granted exclusivity and the specific ingredient that was determined to be generally recognized as safe and effective;

(B) whether, and to what extent, the exclusivity impacted the requestor's or sponsor's decision to develop the sunscreen ingredient;

(C) whether, and to what extent, the sunscreen ingredient granted exclusivity had previously been available outside of the United States;

(D) an analysis of the implementation of the exclusivity provision in such section 586C, including—

(i) the resources used by the Food and Drug Administration;

(ii) the impact of such provision on innovation, as well as research and development in the sunscreen market;

(iii) the impact of such provision on competition in the sunscreen market;

(iv) the impact of such provision on consumer access to sunscreen products;

(v) the impact of such provision on the prices of sunscreen products; and

(vi) whether the administrative orders initiated by requestors under such section 505G have been utilized by sunscreen ingredient sponsors and whether such process has been sufficient to encourage the development of sunscreen ingredients that would likely not be otherwise developed, or developed in as timely a manner; and

(E) whether the administrative orders initiated by requestors under such section 586C have been sufficient incentive to encourage innovation in the sunscreen market.

(c) CONFORMING AMENDMENT.—Section 751(d)(1) of the Federal Food, Drug, and Cosmetic Act (21 U.S.C. 379r(d)(1)) is amended—

(1) in the matter preceding subparagraph (A)—

(A) by striking "final regulation promulgated" and inserting "final order under section 505G"; and

(B) by striking "and not misbranded"; and

(2) in subparagraph (A), by striking "regulation in effect" and inserting "regulation or order in effect".

[¶2173] SEC. 3852. MISBRANDING.

Section 502 of the Federal Food, Drug, and Cosmetic Act (21 U.S.C. 352) is amended by adding at the end the following:

(ee) "If it is a nonprescription drug that is subject to section 505G, is not the subject of an application approved under section 505, and does not comply with the requirements under section 505G.

(ff) "If it is a drug and it was manufactured, prepared, propagated, compounded, or processed in a facility for which fees have not been paid as required by section 744M.".

[¶2174] SEC. 3853. DRUGS EXCLUDED FROM THE OVER-THE-COUNTER DRUG REVIEW.

(a) IN GENERAL.—Nothing in this Act (or the amendments made by this Act) shall apply to any nonprescription drug (as defined in section 505G(q) of the Federal Food, Drug, and Cosmetic Act, as added by section 3851 of this subtitle) which was excluded by the Food and Drug Administration from the Over-the-Counter Drug Review in accordance with the paragraph numbered 25 on page 9466 of volume 37 of the Federal Register, published on May 11, 1972.

(b) RULE OF CONSTRUCTION.—Nothing in this section shall be construed to preclude or limit the applicability of any other provision of the Federal Food, Drug, and Cosmetic Act (21 U.S.C. 301 et seq.).

[¶2175] SEC. 3854. TREATMENT OF SUNSCREEN INNOVATION ACT.

(a) REVIEW OF NONPRESCRIPTION SUNSCREEN ACTIVE INGREDIENTS.—

(1) APPLICABILITY OF SECTION 505G FOR PENDING SUBMISSIONS.—

(A) IN GENERAL.—A sponsor of a nonprescription sunscreen active ingredient or combination of nonprescription sunscreen active ingredients that, as of the date of enactment of this Act, is subject to a proposed sunscreen order under section 586C of the Federal Food, Drug, and Cosmetic Act (21 U.S.C. 360fff–3) may elect, by means of giving written notification to the Secretary of Health and Human Services within 180 calendar days of the enactment of this Act, to transition into the review of such ingredient or combination of ingredients pursuant to the process set out in section 505G of the Federal Food, Drug, and Cosmetic Act, as added by section 3851 of this subtitle.

(B) ELECTION EXERCISED.—Upon receipt by the Secretary of Health and Human Services of a timely notification under subparagraph (A)—

(i) the proposed sunscreen order involved is deemed to be a request for an order under subsection (b) of section 505G of the Federal Food, Drug, and Cosmetic Act, as added by section 3851 of this subtitle; and

(ii) such order is deemed to have been accepted for filing under subsection (b)(6)(A)(i) of such section 505G.

(C) ELECTION NOT EXERCISED.—If a notification under subparagraph (A) is not received by the Secretary of Health and Human Services within 180 calendar days of the date of enactment of this Act, the review of the proposed sunscreen order described in subparagraph (A)—

(i) shall continue under section 586C of the Federal Food, Drug, and Cosmetic Act (21 U.S.C. 360fff–3); and

(ii) shall not be eligible for review under section 505G, added by section 3851 of this subtitle.

(2) DEFINITIONS.—In this subsection, the terms "sponsor", "nonprescription", "sunscreen active ingredient", and "proposed sunscreen order" have the meanings given to those terms in section 586 of the Federal Food, Drug, and Cosmetic Act (21 U.S.C. 360fff).

(b) AMENDMENTS TO SUNSCREEN PROVISIONS.—

(1) FINAL SUNSCREEN ORDERS.—Paragraph (3) of section 586C(e) of the Federal Food, Drug, and Cosmetic Act (21 U.S.C. 360fff–3(e)) is amended to read as follows:

(3) "RELATIONSHIP TO ORDERS UNDER SECTION 505G.—A final sunscreen order shall be deemed to be a final order under section 505G.".

(2) MEETINGS.—Paragraph (7) of section 586C(b) of the Federal Food, Drug, and Cosmetic Act (21 U.S.C. 360fff–3(b)) is amended—

(A) by striking "A sponsor may request" and inserting the following:

(A) "IN GENERAL.—A sponsor may request"; and

(B) by adding at the end the following:

(B) "CONFIDENTIAL MEETINGS.—A sponsor may request one or more confidential meetings with respect to a proposed sunscreen order, including a letter deemed to be a proposed sunscreen order under paragraph (3), to discuss matters relating to data requirements to support a general recognition of safety and effectiveness involving confidential information and public information related to such proposed sunscreen order, as appropriate. The Secretary shall convene a confidential meeting with such sponsor in a reasonable time period. If a sponsor requests more than one confidential meeting for the same proposed sunscreen order, the Secretary may refuse to grant an additional confidential meeting request if the Secretary determines that such additional confidential meeting is not reasonably necessary for the sponsor to advance its proposed sunscreen order, or if the request for a confidential meeting fails to include sufficient information upon which to base a substantive discussion. The Secretary shall publish a post-meeting summary of each confidential meeting under this subparagraph that does not disclose confidential commercial information or trade secrets. This subparagraph does not authorize the disclosure of confidential commercial information or trade secrets subject to 552(b)(4) of title 5, United States Code, or section 1905 of title 18, United States Code.".

(3) EXCLUSIVITY.—Section 586C of the Federal Food, Drug, and Cosmetic Act (21 U.S.C. 360fff–3) is amended by adding at the end the following:

(f) "EXCLUSIVITY.—

(1) "IN GENERAL.—A final sunscreen order shall have the effect of authorizing solely the order requestor (or the licensees, assignees, or successors in interest of such requestor with respect to the subject of such request and listed under paragraph (5)) for a period of 18 months, to market a sunscreen ingredient under this section incorporating changes described in paragraph (2) subject to the limitations under paragraph (4), beginning on the date the requestor (or any licensees, assignees, or successors in interest of such requestor with respect to the subject of such request and listed under paragraph (5)) may lawfully market such sunscreen ingredient pursuant to the order.

(2) "CHANGES DESCRIBED.—A change described in this paragraph is a change subject to an order specified in paragraph (1) that permits a sunscreen to contain an active sunscreen ingredient not previously incorporated in a marketed sunscreen listed in paragraph (3).

(3) "MARKETED SUNSCREEN.—The marketed sunscreen ingredients described in this paragraph are sunscreen ingredients—

(A) "marketed in accordance with a final monograph for sunscreen drug products set forth at part 352 of title 21, Code of Federal Regulations (as published at 64 Fed. Reg. 27687); or

(B) "marketed in accordance with a final order issued under this section.

(4) "LIMITATIONS ON EXCLUSIVITY.—Only one 18-month period may be granted per ingredient under paragraph (1).

(5) "LISTING OF LICENSEES, ASSIGNEES, OR SUCCESSORS IN INTEREST.—Requestors shall submit to the Secretary at the time when a drug subject to such request is introduced or delivered for introduction into interstate commerce, a list of licensees, assignees, or successors in interest under paragraph (1).".

(4) SUNSET PROVISION.—Subchapter I of chapter V of the Federal Food, Drug, and Cosmetic Act (21 U.S.C. 360fff et seq.) is amended by adding at the end the following:

[¶2175A] SEC. 586H. "SUNSET.

"This subchapter shall cease to be effective at the end of fiscal year 2022.".

(5) TREATMENT OF FINAL SUNSCREEN ORDER.—The Federal Food, Drug, and Cosmetic Act is amended by striking section 586E of such Act (21 U.S.C. 360fff–5).

(c) TREATMENT OF AUTHORITY REGARDING FINALIZATION OF SUNSCREEN MONOGRAPH.—

(1) IN GENERAL.—

(A) REVISION OF FINAL SUNSCREEN ORDER.—The Secretary of Health and Human Services (referred to in this subsection as the "Secretary") shall amend and revise the final administrative order concerning nonprescription sunscreen (referred to in this subsection as the "sunscreen order") for which the content, prior to the date of enactment of this Act, was represented by the final monograph for sunscreen drug products set forth in part 352 of title 21, Code of Federal Regulations (as in effect on May 21, 1999).

(B) ISSUANCE OF REVISED SUNSCREEN ORDER; EFFECTIVE DATE.—A revised sunscreen order described in subparagraph (A) shall be—

(i) issued in accordance with the procedures described in section 505G(b)(2) of the Federal Food, Drug, and Cosmetic Act;

(ii) issued in proposed form not later than 18 months after the date of enactment of this Act; and

(iii) issued by the Secretary at least 1 year prior to the effective date of the revised order.

(2) REPORTS.—If a revised sunscreen order issued under paragraph (1) does not include provisions related to the effectiveness of various sun protection factor levels, and does not address all dosage forms known to the Secretary to be used in sunscreens marketed in the United States without a new drug application approved under section 505 of the Federal Food, Drug, and Cosmetic Act (21 U.S.C. 355), the Secretary shall submit a report to the Committee on Energy and Commerce of the House of Representatives and the Committee on Health, Education, Labor, and Pensions of the Senate on the rationale for omission of such provisions from such order, and a plan and timeline to compile any information necessary to address such provisions through such order.

(d) TREATMENT OF NON-SUNSCREEN TIME AND EXTENT APPLICATIONS.—

(1) IN GENERAL.—Any application described in section 586F of the Federal Food, Drug, and Cosmetic Act (21 U.S.C. 360fff–6) that was submitted to the Secretary pursuant to section 330.14 of title 21, Code of Federal Regulations, as such provisions were in effect immediately prior to the date of enactment date of this Act, shall be extinguished as of such date of enactment, subject to paragraph (2).

(2) ORDER REQUEST.—Nothing in paragraph (1) precludes the submission of an order request under section 505G(b) of the Federal Food, Drug, and Cosmetic Act, as added by section 3851 of this subtitle, with respect to a drug that was the subject of an application extinguished under paragraph (1).

[¶2176] SEC. 3855. ANNUAL UPDATE TO CONGRESS ON APPROPRIATE PEDIATRIC INDICATION FOR CERTAIN OTC COUGH AND COLD DRUGS.

(a) IN GENERAL.—Subject to subsection (c), the Secretary of Health and Human Services shall, beginning not later than 1 year after the date of enactment of this Act, annually submit to the Committee on Energy and Commerce of the House of Representatives and the Committee on Health, Education, Labor, and Pensions of the Senate a letter describing the progress of the Food and Drug Administration—

(1) in evaluating the cough and cold monograph described in subsection (b) with respect to children under age 6; and

(2) as appropriate, revising such cough and cold monograph to address such children through the order process under section 505G(b) of the Federal Food, Drug, and Cosmetic Act, as added by section 3851 of this subtitle.

(b) COUGH AND COLD MONOGRAPH DESCRIBED.—The cough and cold monograph described in this subsection consists of the conditions under which nonprescription drugs containing antitussive, expectorant, nasal decongestant, or antihistamine active ingredients (or combinations thereof) are generally recognized as safe and effective, as specified in part 341 of title 21, Code of Federal Regulations (as in effect immediately prior to the date of enactment of this Act), and included in an order deemed to be established under section 505G(b) of the Federal Food, Drug, and Cosmetic Act, as added by section 3851 of this subtitle.

(c) DURATION OF AUTHORITY.—The requirement under subsection (a) shall terminate as of the date of a letter submitted by the Secretary of Health and Human Services pursuant to such subsection in which the Secretary indicates that the Food and Drug Administration has completed its evaluation and revised, in a final order, as applicable, the cough and cold monograph as described in subsection (a)(2).

[¶2177] SEC. 3856. TECHNICAL CORRECTIONS.

(a) IMPORTS AND EXPORTS.—Section 801(e)(4)(E)(iii) of the Federal Food, Drug, and Cosmetic Act (21 U.S.C. 381(e)(4)(E)(iii)) is amended by striking "subparagraph" each place such term appears and inserting "paragraph".

(b) FDA REAUTHORIZATION ACT OF 2017.—

(1) IN GENERAL.—Section 905(b)(4) of the FDA Reauthorization Act of 2017 (Public Law 115–52) is amended by striking "Section 744H(e)(2)(B)" and inserting "Section 744H(f)(2)(B)".

(2) EFFECTIVE DATE.—The amendment made by paragraph (1) shall take effect as of the enactment of the FDA Reauthorization Act of 2017 (Public Law 115–52).

PART II—USER FEES

[¶2179] SEC. 3861. FINDING.

The Congress finds that the fees authorized by the amendments made in this part will be dedicated to OTC monograph drug activities, as set forth in the goals identified for purposes of part 10 of subchapter C of chapter VII of the Federal Food, Drug, and Cosmetic Act, in the letters from the Secretary of Health and Human Services to the Chairman of the Committee on Health, Education, Labor, and Pensions of the Senate and the Chairman of the Committee on Energy and Commerce of the House of Representatives, as set forth in the Congressional Record.

[¶2180] SEC. 3862. FEES RELATING TO OVER-THE-COUNTER DRUGS.

Subchapter C of chapter VII of the Federal Food, Drug, and Cosmetic Act (21 U.S.C. 379f et seq.) is amended by inserting after part 9 the following:

"PART 10—FEES RELATING TO OVER-THE-COUNTER DRUGS

[¶2181] SEC. 744L. "DEFINITIONS.

"In this part:

(1) "The term 'affiliate' means a business entity that has a relationship with a second business entity if, directly or indirectly—

(A) "one business entity controls, or has the power to control, the other business entity; or

(B) "a third party controls, or has power to control, both of the business entities.

(2) "The term 'contract manufacturing organization facility' means an OTC monograph drug facility where neither the owner of such manufacturing facility nor any affiliate of such owner or facility sells the OTC monograph drug produced at such facility directly to wholesalers, retailers, or consumers in the United States.

(3) "The term 'costs of resources allocated for OTC monograph drug activities' means the expenses in connection with OTC monograph drug activities for—

(A) "officers and employees of the Food and Drug Administration, contractors of the Food and Drug Administration, advisory committees, and costs related to such officers, employees, and committees and costs related to contracts with such contractors;

(B) "management of information, and the acquisition, maintenance, and repair of computer resources;

(C) "leasing, maintenance, renovation, and repair of facilities and acquisition, maintenance, and repair of fixtures, furniture, scientific equipment, and other necessary materials and supplies; and

(D) "collecting fees under section 744M and accounting for resources allocated for OTC monograph drug activities.

(4) "The term 'FDA establishment identifier' is the unique number automatically generated by Food and Drug Administration's Field Accomplishments and Compliance Tracking System (FACTS) (or any successor system).

(5) "The term 'OTC monograph drug' means a nonprescription drug without an approved new drug application which is governed by the provisions of section 505G.

(6) "The term 'OTC monograph drug activities' means activities of the Secretary associated with OTC monograph drugs and inspection of facilities associated with such products, including the following activities:

(A) "The activities necessary for review and evaluation of OTC monographs and OTC monograph order requests, including—

(i) "orders proposing or finalizing applicable conditions of use for OTC monograph drugs;

(ii) "orders affecting status regarding general recognition of safety and effectiveness of an OTC monograph ingredient or combination of ingredients under specified conditions of use;

(iii) "all OTC monograph drug development and review activities, including intra-agency collaboration;

(iv) "regulation and policy development activities related to OTC monograph drugs;

(v) "development of product standards for products subject to review and evaluation;

(vi) "meetings referred to in section 505G(i);

(vii) "review of labeling prior to issuance of orders related to OTC monograph drugs or conditions of use; and

(viii) "regulatory science activities related to OTC monograph drugs.

(B) "Inspections related to OTC monograph drugs.

(C) "Monitoring of clinical and other research conducted in connection with OTC monograph drugs.

(D) "Safety activities with respect to OTC monograph drugs, including—

(i) "collecting, developing, and reviewing safety information on OTC monograph drugs, including adverse event reports;

(ii) "developing and using improved adverse event data-collection systems, including information technology systems; and

(iii) "developing and using improved analytical tools to assess potential safety risks, including access to external databases.

(E) "Other activities necessary for implementation of section 505G.

(7) "The term 'OTC monograph order request' means a request for an order submitted under section 505G(b)(5).

(8) "The term 'Tier 1 OTC monograph order request' means any OTC monograph order request not determined to be a Tier 2 OTC monograph order request.

(9)(A) "The term 'Tier 2 OTC monograph order request' means, subject to subparagraph (B), an OTC monograph order request for—

(i) "the reordering of existing information in the drug facts label of an OTC monograph drug;

(ii) "the addition of information to the other information section of the drug facts label of an OTC monograph drug, as limited by section 201.66(c)(7) of title 21, Code of Federal Regulations (or any successor regulations);

(iii) "modification to the directions for use section of the drug facts label of an OTC monograph drug, if such changes conform to changes made pursuant to section 505G(c)(3)(A);

(iv) "the standardization of the concentration or dose of a specific finalized ingredient within a particular finalized monograph;

(v) "a change to ingredient nomenclature to align with nomenclature of a standards-setting organization; or

(vi) "addition of an interchangeable term in accordance with section 330.1 of title 21, Code of Federal Regulations (or any successor regulations).

(B) "The Secretary may, based on program implementation experience or other factors found appropriate by the Secretary, characterize any OTC monograph order request as a Tier 2 OTC monograph order request (including recharacterizing a request from Tier 1 to Tier 2) and publish such determination in a proposed order issued pursuant to section 505G.

(10)(A) "The term 'OTC monograph drug facility' means a foreign or domestic business or other entity that—

(i) "is—

(I) "under one management, either direct or indirect; and

(II) "at one geographic location or address engaged in manufacturing or processing the finished dosage form of an OTC monograph drug;

(ii) "includes a finished dosage form manufacturer facility in a contractual relationship with the sponsor of one or more OTC monograph drugs to manufacture or process such drugs; and

(iii) "does not include a business or other entity whose only manufacturing or processing activities are one or more of the following: production of clinical research supplies, testing, or placement of outer packaging on packages containing multiple products, for such purposes as creating multipacks, when each monograph drug product contained within the overpackaging is already in a final packaged form prior to placement in the outer overpackaging.

(B) "For purposes of subparagraph (A)(i)(II), separate buildings or locations within close proximity are considered to be at one geographic location or address if the activities conducted in such buildings or locations are—

(i) "closely related to the same business enterprise;

(ii) "under the supervision of the same local management; and

(iii) "under a single FDA establishment identifier and capable of being inspected by the Food and Drug Administration during a single inspection.

(C) "If a business or other entity would meet criteria specified in subparagraph (A), but for being under multiple management, the business or other entity is deemed to constitute multiple facilities, one per management entity, for purposes of this paragraph.

(11) "The term 'OTC monograph drug meeting' means any meeting regarding the content of a proposed OTC monograph order request.

(12) "The term 'person' includes an affiliate of a person.

(13) "The terms 'requestor' and 'sponsor' have the meanings given such terms in section 505G.

[¶2182] SEC. 744M. "AUTHORITY TO ASSESS AND USE OTC MONOGRAPH FEES.

(a) "Types of Fees.—Beginning with fiscal year 2021, the Secretary shall assess and collect fees in accordance with this section as follows:

(1) "Facility fee.—

(A) "In general.—Each person that owns a facility identified as an OTC monograph drug facility on December 31 of the fiscal year or at any time during the preceding 12-month period shall be assessed an annual fee for each such facility as determined under subsection (c).

(B) "Exceptions.—

(i) "Facilities that cease activities.—A fee shall not be assessed under subparagraph (A) if the identified OTC monograph drug facility—

(I) "has ceased all activities related to OTC monograph drugs prior to December 31 of the year immediately preceding the applicable fiscal year; and

(II) "has updated its registration to reflect such change under the requirements for drug establishment registration set forth in section 510.

(ii) "Contract manufacturing organizations.—The amount of the fee for a contract manufacturing organization facility shall be equal to two-thirds of the amount of the fee for an OTC monograph drug facility that is not a contract manufacturing organization facility.

(C) "Amount.—The amount of fees established under subparagraph (A) shall be established under subsection (c).

(D) "Due date.—

(i) "For first program year.—For fiscal year 2021, the facility fees required under subparagraph (A) shall be due on the later of—

(I) "the first business day of July of 2020; or

(II) "45 calendar days after publication of the Federal Register notice provided for under subsection (c)(4)(A).

(ii) "SUBSEQUENT FISCAL YEARS.—For each fiscal year after fiscal year 2021, the facility fees required under subparagraph (A) shall be due on the later of—

(I) "the first business day of June of such year; or

(II) "the first business day after the enactment of an appropriations Act providing for the collection and obligation of fees under this section for such year.

(2) "OTC MONOGRAPH ORDER REQUEST FEE.—

(A) "IN GENERAL.—Each person that submits an OTC monograph order request shall be subject to a fee for an OTC monograph order request. The amount of such fee shall be—

(i) "for a Tier 1 OTC monograph order request, $500,000, adjusted for inflation for the fiscal year (as determined under subsection (c)(1)(B)); and

(ii) "for a Tier 2 OTC monograph order request, $100,000, adjusted for inflation for the fiscal year (as determined under subsection (c)(1)(B)).

(B) "DUE DATE.—The OTC monograph order request fees required under subparagraph (A) shall be due on the date of submission of the OTC monograph order request.

(C) "EXCEPTION FOR CERTAIN SAFETY CHANGES.—A person who is named as the requestor in an OTC monograph order shall not be subject to a fee under subparagraph (A) if the Secretary finds that the OTC monograph order request seeks to change the drug facts labeling of an OTC monograph drug in a way that would add to or strengthen—

(i) "a contraindication, warning, or precaution;

(ii) "a statement about risk associated with misuse or abuse; or

(iii) "an instruction about dosage and administration that is intended to increase the safe use of the OTC monograph drug.

(D) "REFUND OF FEE IF ORDER REQUEST IS RECATEGORIZED AS A TIER 2 OTC MONOGRAPH ORDER REQUEST.—If the Secretary determines that an OTC monograph request initially characterized as Tier 1 shall be re-characterized as a Tier 2 OTC monograph order request, and the requestor has paid a Tier 1 fee in accordance with subparagraph (A)(i), the Secretary shall refund the requestor the difference between the Tier 1 and Tier 2 fees determined under subparagraphs (A)(i) and (A)(ii), respectively.

(E) "REFUND OF FEE IF ORDER REQUEST REFUSED FOR FILING OR WITHDRAWN BEFORE FILING.—The Secretary shall refund 75 percent of the fee paid under subparagraph (B) for any order request which is refused for filing or was withdrawn before being accepted or refused for filing.

(F) "FEES FOR ORDER REQUESTS PREVIOUSLY REFUSED FOR FILING OR WITHDRAWN BEFORE FILING.—An OTC monograph order request that was submitted but was refused for filing, or was withdrawn before being accepted or refused for filing, shall be subject to the full fee under subparagraph (A) upon being resubmitted or filed over protest.

(G) "REFUND OF FEE IF ORDER REQUEST WITHDRAWN.—If an order request is withdrawn after the order request was filed, the Secretary may refund the fee or a portion of the fee if no substantial work was performed on the order request after the application was filed. The Secretary shall have the sole discretion to refund a fee or a portion of the fee under this subparagraph. A determination by the Secretary concerning a refund under this subparagraph shall not be reviewable.

(3) "REFUNDS.—

(A) "IN GENERAL.—Other than refunds provided pursuant to any of subparagraphs (D) through (G) of paragraph (2), the Secretary shall not refund any fee paid under paragraph (1) except as provided in subparagraph (B).

(B) "DISPUTES CONCERNING FEES.—To qualify for the return of a fee claimed to have been paid in error under paragraph (1) or (2), a person shall submit to the Secretary a written request justifying such return within 180 calendar days after such fee was paid.

(4) "NOTICE.—Within the timeframe specified in subsection (c), the Secretary shall publish in the Federal Register the amount of the fees under paragraph (1) for such fiscal year.

(b) "FEE REVENUE AMOUNTS.—

(1) "FISCAL YEAR 2021.—For fiscal year 2021, fees under subsection (a)(1) shall be established to generate a total facility fee revenue amount equal to the sum of—

(A) "the annual base revenue for fiscal year 2021 (as determined under paragraph (3));

(B) "the dollar amount equal to the operating reserve adjustment for the fiscal year, if applicable (as determined under subsection (c)(2)); and

(C) "additional direct cost adjustments (as determined under subsection (c)(3)).

(2) "SUBSEQUENT FISCAL YEARS.—For each of the fiscal years 2022 through 2025, fees under subsection (a)(1) shall be established to generate a total facility fee revenue amount equal to the sum of—

(A) "the annual base revenue for the fiscal year (as determined under paragraph (3));

(B) "the dollar amount equal to the inflation adjustment for the fiscal year (as determined under subsection (c)(1));

(C) "the dollar amount equal to the operating reserve adjustment for the fiscal year, if applicable (as determined under subsection (c)(2));

(D) "additional direct cost adjustments (as determined under subsection (c)(3)); and

(E) "additional dollar amounts for each fiscal year as follows:

(i) "$7,000,000 for fiscal year 2022.

(ii) "$6,000,000 for fiscal year 2023.

(iii) "$7,000,000 for fiscal year 2024.

(iv) "$3,000,000 for fiscal year 2025.

(3) "ANNUAL BASE REVENUE.—For purposes of paragraphs (1)(A) and (2)(A), the dollar amount of the annual base revenue for a fiscal year shall be—

(A) "for fiscal year 2021, $8,000,000; and

(B) "for fiscal years 2022 through 2025, the dollar amount of the total revenue amount established under this subsection for the previous fiscal year, not including any adjustments made under subsection (c)(2) or (c)(3).

(c) "ADJUSTMENTS; ANNUAL FEE SETTING.—

(1) "INFLATION ADJUSTMENT.—

(A) "IN GENERAL.—For purposes of subsection (b)(2)(B), the dollar amount of the inflation adjustment to the annual base revenue for fiscal year 2022 and each subsequent fiscal year shall be equal to the product of—

(i) "such annual base revenue for the fiscal year under subsection (b)(2); and

(ii) "the inflation adjustment percentage under subparagraph (C).

(B) "OTC MONOGRAPH ORDER REQUEST FEES.—For purposes of subsection (a)(2), the dollar amount of the inflation adjustment to the fee for OTC monograph order requests for fiscal year 2022 and each subsequent fiscal year shall be equal to the product of—

(i) "the applicable fee under subsection (a)(2) for the preceding fiscal year; and

(ii) "the inflation adjustment percentage under subparagraph (C).

(C) "INFLATION ADJUSTMENT PERCENTAGE.—The inflation adjustment percentage under this subparagraph for a fiscal year is equal to—

(i) "for each of fiscal years 2022 and 2023, the average annual percent change that occurred in the Consumer Price Index for urban consumers (Washington-Baltimore, DC–MD–VA–WV; Not Seasonally Adjusted; All items; Annual Index) for the first 3 years of the preceding 4 years of available data; and

(ii) "for each of fiscal years 2024 and 2025, the sum of—

(I) "the average annual percent change in the cost, per full-time equivalent position of the Food and Drug Administration, of all personnel compensation and benefits paid with respect to such positions for the first 3 years of the preceding 4 fiscal years, multiplied by the proportion of personnel compensation and benefits costs to total costs of OTC monograph drug activities for the first 3 years of the preceding 4 fiscal years; and

(II) "the average annual percent change that occurred in the Consumer Price Index for urban consumers (Washington-Baltimore, DC–MD–VA–WV; Not Seasonally Adjusted; All items; Annual Index) for the first 3 years of the preceding 4 years of available data multiplied by the proportion of all costs other than personnel compensation and benefits costs to total costs of OTC monograph drug activities for the first 3 years of the preceding 4 fiscal years.

(2) "OPERATING RESERVE ADJUSTMENT.—

(A) "IN GENERAL.—For fiscal year 2021 and subsequent fiscal years, for purposes of subsections (b)(1)(B) and (b)(2)(C), the Secretary may, in addition to adjustments under paragraph (1), further increase the fee revenue and fees if such an adjustment is necessary to provide operating reserves of carryover user fees for OTC monograph drug activities for not more than the number of weeks specified in subparagraph (B).

(B) "NUMBER OF WEEKS.—The number of weeks specified in this subparagraph is—

(i) "3 weeks for fiscal year 2021;

(ii) "7 weeks for fiscal year 2022;

(iii) "10 weeks for fiscal year 2023;

(iv) "10 weeks for fiscal year 2024; and

(v) "10 weeks for fiscal year 2025.

(C) "DECREASE.—If the Secretary has carryover balances for such process in excess of 10 weeks of the operating reserves referred to in subparagraph (A), the Secretary shall decrease the fee revenue and fees referred to in such subparagraph to provide for not more than 10 weeks of such operating reserves.

(D) "RATIONALE FOR ADJUSTMENT.—If an adjustment under this paragraph is made, the rationale for the amount of the increase or decrease (as applicable) in fee revenue and fees shall be contained in the annual Federal Register notice under paragraph (4) establishing fee revenue and fees for the fiscal year involved.

(3) "ADDITIONAL DIRECT COST ADJUSTMENT.—The Secretary shall, in addition to adjustments under paragraphs (1) and (2), further increase the fee revenue and fees for purposes of subsection (b)(2)(D) by an amount equal to—

(A) "$14,000,000 for fiscal year 2021;

(B) "$7,000,000 for fiscal year 2022;

(C) "$4,000,000 for fiscal year 2023;

(D) "$3,000,000 for fiscal year 2024; and

(E) "$3,000,000 for fiscal year 2025.

(4) "ANNUAL FEE SETTING.—

(A) "FISCAL YEAR 2021.—The Secretary shall, not later than the second Monday in May of 2020—

(i) "establish OTC monograph drug facility fees for fiscal year 2021 under subsection (a), based on the revenue amount for such year under subsection (b) and the adjustments provided under this subsection; and

(ii) "publish fee revenue, facility fees, and OTC monograph order requests in the Federal Register.

(B) "SUBSEQUENT FISCAL YEARS.—The Secretary shall, for each fiscal year that begins after September 30, 2021, not later than the second Monday in March that precedes such fiscal year—

(i) "establish for such fiscal year, based on the revenue amounts under subsection (b) and the adjustments provided under this subsection—

(I) "OTC monograph drug facility fees under subsection (a)(1); and

(II) "OTC monograph order request fees under subsection (a)(2); and

(ii) "publish such fee revenue amounts, facility fees, and OTC monograph order request fees in the Federal Register.

(d) "IDENTIFICATION OF FACILITIES.—Each person that owns an OTC monograph drug facility shall submit to the Secretary the information required under this subsection each year. Such information shall, for each fiscal year—

(1) "be submitted as part of the requirements for drug establishment registration set forth in section 510; and

(2) "include for each such facility, at a minimum, identification of the facility's business operation as that of an OTC monograph drug facility.

(e) "EFFECT OF FAILURE TO PAY FEES.—

(1) "OTC MONOGRAPH DRUG FACILITY FEE.—

(A) "IN GENERAL.—Failure to pay the fee under subsection (a)(1) within 20 calendar days of the due date as specified in subparagraph (D) of such subsection shall result in the following:

(i) "The Secretary shall place the facility on a publicly available arrears list.

(ii) "All OTC monograph drugs manufactured in such a facility or containing an ingredient manufactured in such a facility shall be deemed misbranded under section 502(ff).

(B) "APPLICATION OF PENALTIES.—The penalties under this paragraph shall apply until the fee established by subsection (a)(1) is paid.

(2) "ORDER REQUESTS.—An OTC monograph order request submitted by a person subject to fees under subsection (a) shall be considered incomplete and shall not be accepted for filing by the Secretary until all fees owed by such person under this section have been paid.

(3) "MEETINGS.—A person subject to fees under this section shall be considered ineligible for OTC monograph drug meetings until all such fees owed by such person have been paid.

(f) "CREDITING AND AVAILABILITY OF FEES.—

(1) "IN GENERAL.—Fees authorized under subsection (a) shall be collected and available for obligation only to the extent and in the amount provided in advance in appropriations Acts. Such fees are authorized to remain available until expended. Such sums as may be necessary may be transferred from the Food and Drug Administration salaries and expenses appropriation account without fiscal year limitation to such appropriation account for salaries and expenses with such fiscal year limitation. The sums transferred shall be available solely for OTC monograph drug activities.

(2) "COLLECTIONS AND APPROPRIATION ACTS.—

(A) "IN GENERAL.—Subject to subparagraph (C), the fees authorized by this section shall be collected and available in each fiscal year in an amount not to exceed the amount specified in appropriation Acts, or otherwise made available for obligation, for such fiscal year.

(B) "USE OF FEES AND LIMITATION.—The fees authorized by this section shall be available to defray increases in the costs of the resources allocated for OTC monograph drug activities (including increases in such costs for an additional number of full-time equivalent positions in the Department of Health and Human Services to be engaged in such activities), only if the Secretary allocates for such purpose an amount for such fiscal year (excluding amounts from fees collected under this section) no less than $12,000,000, multiplied by the adjustment factor applicable to the fiscal year involved under subsection (c)(1).

(C) "COMPLIANCE.—The Secretary shall be considered to have met the requirements of subparagraph (B) in any fiscal year if the costs funded by appropriations and allocated for OTC monograph drug activities are not more than 15 percent below the level specified in such subparagraph.

(D) "PROVISION FOR EARLY PAYMENTS IN SUBSEQUENT YEARS.—Payment of fees authorized under this section for a fiscal year (after fiscal year 2021), prior to the due date for such fees, may be accepted by the Secretary in accordance with authority provided in advance in a prior year appropriations Act.

(3) "AUTHORIZATION OF APPROPRIATIONS.—For each of the fiscal years 2021 through 2025, there is authorized to be appropriated for fees under this section an amount equal to the total amount of fees assessed for such fiscal year under this section.

(g) "COLLECTION OF UNPAID FEES.—In any case where the Secretary does not receive payment of a fee assessed under subsection (a) within 30 calendar days after it is due, such fee shall be treated as a claim of the United States Government subject to subchapter II of chapter 37 of title 31, United States Code.

(h) "CONSTRUCTION.—This section may not be construed to require that the number of full-time equivalent positions in the Department of Health and Human Services, for officers, employers, and advisory committees not engaged in OTC monograph drug activities, be reduced to offset the number of officers, employees, and advisory committees so engaged.

[¶2183] SEC. 744N. "REAUTHORIZATION; REPORTING REQUIREMENTS.

(a) "PERFORMANCE REPORT.—Beginning with fiscal year 2021, and not later than 120 calendar days after the end of each fiscal year thereafter for which fees are collected under this part, the Secretary shall prepare and submit to the Committee on Energy and Commerce of the House of Representatives and the Committee on Health, Education, Labor, and Pensions of the Senate a report concerning the progress of the Food and Drug Administration in achieving the goals identified in the letters described in section 3861(b) of the CARES Act during such fiscal year and the future plans of the Food and Drug Administration for meeting such goals.

(b) "FISCAL REPORT.—Not later than 120 calendar days after the end of fiscal year 2021 and each subsequent fiscal year for which fees are collected under this part, the Secretary shall prepare and submit to the Committee on Energy and Commerce of the House of Representatives and the Committee on Health, Education, Labor, and Pensions of the Senate a report on the implementation of the authority for such fees during such fiscal year and the use, by the Food and Drug Administration, of the fees collected for such fiscal year.

(c) "PUBLIC AVAILABILITY.—The Secretary shall make the reports required under subsections (a) and (b) available to the public on the internet website of the Food and Drug Administration.

(d) "REAUTHORIZATION.—

(1) "CONSULTATION.—In developing recommendations to present to the Congress with respect to the goals described in subsection (a), and plans for meeting the goals, for OTC monograph drug activities for the first 5 fiscal years after fiscal year 2025, and for the reauthorization of this part for such fiscal years, the Secretary shall consult with—

(A) "the Committee on Energy and Commerce of the House of Representatives;

(B) "the Committee on Health, Education, Labor, and Pensions of the Senate;

(C) "scientific and academic experts;

(D) "health care professionals;

(E) "representatives of patient and consumer advocacy groups; and

(F) "the regulated industry.

(2) "PUBLIC REVIEW OF RECOMMENDATIONS.—After negotiations with the regulated industry, the Secretary shall—

(A) "present the recommendations developed under paragraph (1) to the congressional committees specified in such paragraph;

(B) "publish such recommendations in the Federal Register;

(C) "provide for a period of 30 calendar days for the public to provide written comments on such recommendations;

(D) "hold a meeting at which the public may present its views on such recommendations; and

(E) "after consideration of such public views and comments, revise such recommendations as necessary.

(3) "TRANSMITTAL OF RECOMMENDATIONS.—Not later than January 15, 2025, the Secretary shall transmit to the Congress the revised recommendations under paragraph (2), a summary of the views and comments received under such paragraph, and any changes made to the recommendations in response to such views and comments.".

TITLE IV—ECONOMIC STABILIZATION AND ASSISTANCE TO SEVERELY DISTRESSED SECTORS OF THE UNITED STATES ECONOMY

Subtitle A—Coronavirus Economic Stabilization Act of 2020

[¶2186] SEC. 4001. SHORT TITLE.

This subtitle may be cited as the "Coronavirus Economic Stabilization Act of 2020".

[¶2187] SEC. 4002. DEFINITIONS.

In this subtitle:

(1) AIR CARRIER.—The term "air carrier" has the meaning such term has under section 40102 of title 49, United States Code.

(2) CORONAVIRUS.—The term "coronavirus" means SARS–CoV–2 or another coronavirus with pandemic potential.

(3) COVERED LOSS.—The term "covered loss" includes losses incurred directly or indirectly as a result of coronavirus, as determined by the Secretary.

(4) ELIGIBLE BUSINESS.—The term "eligible business" means—

(A) an air carrier; or

(B) a United States business that has not otherwise received adequate economic relief in the form of loans or loan guarantees provided under this Act.

(5) EMPLOYEE.—Except where the context otherwise requires, the term "employee"—

(A) has the meaning given the term in section 2 of the National Labor Relations Act (29 U.S.C. 152); and

(B) includes any individual employed by an employer subject to the Railway Labor Act (45 U.S.C. 151 et seq.).

(6) EQUITY SECURITY; EXCHANGE.—The terms "equity security" and "exchange" have the meanings given the terms in section 3(a) of the Securities Exchange Act of 1934 (15 U.S.C. 78c(a)).

(7) MUNICIPALITY.—The term "municipality" includes—

(A) a political subdivision of a State, and

(B) an instrumentality of a municipality, a State, or a political subdivision of a State.

(8) NATIONAL SECURITIES EXCHANGE.—The term "national securities exchange" means an exchange registered as a national securities exchange under section 6 of the Securities Exchange Act of 1934 (15 U.S.C. 78f).

(9) SECRETARY.—The term "Secretary" means the Secretary of the Treasury, or the designee of the Secretary of the Treasury.

(10) STATE.—The term "State" means—

(A) any of the several States;

(B) the District of Columbia;

(C) any of the territories and possessions of the United States;

(D) any bi-State or multi-State entity; and

(E) any Indian Tribe.

[¶2188] SEC. 4003. EMERGENCY RELIEF AND TAXPAYER PROTECTIONS.

(a) IN GENERAL.—Notwithstanding any other provision of law, to provide liquidity to eligible businesses, States, and municipalities related to losses incurred as a result of coronavirus, the Secretary is authorized to make loans, loan guarantees, and other investments in support of eligible businesses, States, and municipalities that do not, in the aggregate, exceed $500,000,000,000 and provide the subsidy amounts necessary for such loans, loan guarantees, and other investments in accordance with the provisions of the Federal Credit Reform Act of 1990 (2 U.S.C. 661 et seq.).

(b) LOANS, LOAN GUARANTEES, AND OTHER INVESTMENTS.—Loans, loan guarantees, and other investments made pursuant to subsection (a) shall be made available as follows:

(1) Not more than $25,000,000,000 shall be available to make loans and loan guarantees for passenger air carriers, eligible businesses that are certified under part 145 of title 14, Code of Federal Regulations, and approved to perform inspection, repair, replace, or overhaul services, and ticket agents (as defined in section 40102 of title 49, United States Code).

(2) Not more than $4,000,000,000 shall be available to make loans and loan guarantees for cargo air carriers.

(3) Not more than $17,000,000,000 shall be available to make loans and loan guarantees for businesses critical to maintaining national security.

(4) Not more than the sum of $454,000,000,000 and any amounts available under paragraphs (1), (2), and (3) that are not used as provided under those paragraphs shall be available to make loans and loan guarantees to, and other investments in, programs or facilities established by the Board of Governors of the Federal Reserve System for the purpose of providing liquidity to the financial system that supports lending to eligible businesses, States, or municipalities by—

(A) purchasing obligations or other interests directly from issuers of such obligations or other interests;

(B) purchasing obligations or other interests in secondary markets or otherwise; or

(C) making loans, including loans or other advances secured by collateral.

(c) TERMS AND CONDITIONS.—

(1) IN GENERAL.—

(A) FORMS; TERMS AND CONDITIONS.—A loan, loan guarantee, or other investment by the Secretary shall be made under this section in such form and on such terms and conditions and contain such covenants, representations, warranties, and requirements (including requirements for audits) as the Secretary determines appropriate. Any loans made by the Secretary under this section shall be at a rate determined by the Secretary based on the risk and the current average yield on outstanding marketable obligations of the United States of comparable maturity.

(B) PROCEDURES.—As soon as practicable, but in no case later than 10 days after the date of enactment of this Act, the Secretary shall publish procedures for application and minimum requirements, which may be supplemented by the Secretary in the Secretary's discretion, for making loans, loan guarantees, or other investments under paragraphs (1), (2) and (3) of subsection (b).

(2) LOANS AND LOAN GUARANTEES.—The Secretary may enter into agreements to make loans or loan guarantees to 1 or more eligible businesses under paragraphs (1), (2) and (3) of subsection (b) if the Secretary determines that, in the Secretary's discretion—

(A) the applicant is an eligible business for which credit is not reasonably available at the time of the transaction;

(B) the intended obligation by the applicant is prudently incurred;

(C) the loan or loan guarantee is sufficiently secured or is made at a rate that—

(i) reflects the risk of the loan or loan guarantee; and

(ii) is to the extent practicable, not less than an interest rate based on market conditions for comparable obligations prevalent prior to the outbreak of the coronavirus disease 2019 (COVID–19);

(D) the duration of the loan or loan guarantee is as short as practicable and in any case not longer than 5 years;

(E) the agreement provides that, until the date 12 months after the date the loan or loan guarantee is no longer outstanding, neither the eligible business nor any affiliate of the eligible business may purchase an equity security that is listed on a national securities exchange of the eligible business or any parent company of the eligible business, except to the extent required under a contractual obligation in effect as of the date of enactment of this Act;

(F) the agreement provides that, until the date 12 months after the date the loan or loan guarantee is no longer outstanding, the eligible business shall not pay dividends or make other capital distributions with respect to the common stock of the eligible business;

(G) the agreement provides that, until September 30, 2020, the eligible business shall maintain its employment levels as of March 24, 2020, to the extent practicable, and in any case shall not reduce its employment levels by more than 10 percent from the levels on such date;

(H) the agreement includes a certification by the eligible business that it is created or organized in the United States or under the laws of the United States and has significant operations in and a majority of its employees based in the United States; and

(I) for purposes of a loan or loan guarantee under paragraphs (1), (2), and (3) of subsection (b), the eligible business must have incurred or is expected to incur covered losses such that the continued operations of the business are jeopardized, as determined by the Secretary.

(3) FEDERAL RESERVE PROGRAMS OR FACILITIES.—

(A) TERMS AND CONDITIONS.—

(i) DEFINITION.—In this paragraph, the term "direct loan" means a loan under a bilateral loan agreement that is —

(I) entered into directly with an eligible business as borrower; and

(II) not part of a syndicated loan, a loan originated by a financial institution in the ordinary course of business, or a securities or capital markets transaction.

(ii) RESTRICTIONS.—The Secretary may make a loan, loan guarantee, or other investment under subsection (b)(4) as part of a program or facility that provides direct loans only if the applicable eligible businesses agree—

(I) until the date 12 months after the date on which the direct loan is no longer outstanding, not to repurchase an equity security that is listed on a national securities exchange of the eligible business or any parent company of the eligible business while the direct loan is outstanding, except to the extent required under a contractual obligation that is in effect as of the date of enactment of this Act;

(II) until the date 12 months after the date on which the direct loan is no longer outstanding, not to pay dividends or make other capital distributions with respect to the common stock of the eligible business; and

(III) to comply with the limitations on compensation set forth in section 4004.

(iii) WAIVER.—The Secretary may waive the requirement under clause (ii) with respect to any program or facility upon a determination that such waiver is necessary to protect the interests of the Federal Government. If the Secretary exercises a waiver under this clause, the Secretary shall make himself available to testify before the Committee on Banking, Housing, and Urban Affairs of the Senate and the Committee on Financial Services of the House of Representatives regarding the reasons for the waiver.

(B) FEDERAL RESERVE ACT TAXPAYER PROTECTIONS AND OTHER REQUIREMENTS APPLY.—For the avoidance of doubt, any applicable requirements under section 13(3) of the Federal Reserve Act (12 U.S.C. 343(3)), including requirements relating to loan collateralization, taxpayer protection, and borrower solvency, shall apply with respect to any program or facility described in subsection (b)(4).

(C) UNITED STATES BUSINESSES.—A program or facility in which the Secretary makes a loan, loan guarantee, or other investment under subsection (b)(4) shall only purchase obligations or other interests (other than securities that are based on an index or that are based on a diversified pool of securities) from, or make loans or other advances to, businesses that are created or organized in the United States or under the laws of the United States and that have significant operations in and a majority of its employees based in the United States.

(D) ASSISTANCE FOR MID-SIZED BUSINESSES.—

(i) IN GENERAL.—Without limiting the terms and conditions of the programs and facilities that the Secretary may otherwise provide financial assistance to under subsection (b)(4), the Secretary shall endeavor to seek the implementation of a program or facility described in subsection (b)(4) that provides financing to banks and other lenders that make direct loans to eligible businesses including, to the extent practicable, nonprofit organizations, with between 500 and 10,000 employees, with such direct loans being subject to an annualized interest rate that is not higher than 2 percent per annum. For the first 6 months after any such direct loan is made, or for such longer period as the Secretary may determine in his discretion, no principal or interest shall be due and payable. Any eligible borrower applying for a direct loan under this program shall make a good-faith certification that—

(I) the uncertainty of economic conditions as of the date of the application makes necessary the loan request to support the ongoing operations of the recipient;

(II) the funds it receives will be used to retain at least 90 percent of the recipient's workforce, at full compensation and benefits, until September 30, 2020;

(III) the recipient intends to restore not less than 90 percent of the workforce of the recipient that existed as of February 1, 2020, and to restore all compensation and benefits to the workers of the recipient no later than 4 months after the termination date of the public health emergency declared by the Secretary of Health and Human Services on January 31, 2020, under section 319 of the Public Health Services Act (42 U.S.C. 247d) in response to COVID–19;

(IV) the recipient is an entity or business that is domiciled in the United States with significant operations and employees located in the United States;

(V) the recipient is not a debtor in a bankruptcy proceeding;

(VI) the recipient is created or organized in the United States or under the laws of the United States and has significant operations in and a majority of its employees based in the United States;

(VII) the recipient will not pay dividends with respect to the common stock of the eligible business, or repurchase an equity security that is listed on a national securities exchange of the recipient or any parent company of the recipient while the direct loan is outstanding, except to the extent required under a contractual obligation that is in effect as of the date of enactment of this Act;

(VIII) the recipient will not outsource or offshore jobs for the term of the loan and 2 years after completing repayment of the loan;

(IX) the recipient will not abrogate existing collective bargaining agreements for the term of the loan and 2 years after completing repayment of the loan; and

(X) that the recipient will remain neutral in any union organizing effort for the term of the loan.

(ii) MAIN STREET LENDING PROGRAM.—Nothing in this subparagraph shall limit the discretion of the Board of Governors of the Federal Reserve System to establish a Main Street Lending Program or other similar program or facility that supports lending to small and mid-sized businesses on such terms and conditions as the Board may set consistent with section 13(3) of the Federal Reserve Act (12 U.S.C. 343(3)), including any such program in which the Secretary makes a loan, loan guarantee, or other investment under subsection (b)(4).

(E) GOVERNMENT PARTICIPANTS.—The Secretary shall endeavor to seek the implementation of a program or facility in accordance with subsection (b)(4) that provides liquidity to the financial system that supports lending to States and municipalities.

(d) FINANCIAL PROTECTION OF GOVERNMENT.—

(1) WARRANT OR SENIOR DEBT INSTRUMENT.—The Secretary may not issue a loan to, or a loan guarantee for, an eligible business under paragraph (1), (2), or (3) of subsection (b) unless—

(A)(i) the eligible business has issued securities that are traded on a national securities exchange; and

(ii) the Secretary receives a warrant or equity interest in the eligible business; or

(B) in the case of any eligible business other than an eligible business described in subparagraph (A), the Secretary receives, in the discretion of the Secretary—

(i) a warrant or equity interest in the eligible business; or

(ii) a senior debt instrument issued by the eligible business.

(2) TERMS AND CONDITIONS.—The terms and conditions of any warrant, equity interest, or senior debt instrument received under paragraph (1) shall be set by the Secretary and shall meet the following requirements:

(A) PURPOSES.—Such terms and conditions shall be designed to provide for a reasonable participation by the Secretary, for the benefit of taxpayers, in equity appreciation in the case of a warrant or other equity interest, or a reasonable interest rate premium, in the case of a debt instrument.

(B) AUTHORITY TO SELL, EXERCISE, OR SURRENDER.—For the primary benefit of taxpayers, the Secretary may sell, exercise, or surrender a warrant or any senior debt instrument received under this subsection. The Secretary shall not exercise voting power with respect to any shares of common stock acquired under this section.

(C) SUFFICIENCY.—If the Secretary determines that the eligible business cannot feasibly issue warrants or other equity interests as required by this subsection, the Secretary may accept a senior debt instrument in an amount and on such terms as the Secretary deems appropriate.

(3) PROHIBITION ON LOAN FORGIVENESS.—The principal amount of any obligation issued by an eligible business, State, or municipality under a program described in subsection (b) shall not be reduced through loan forgiveness.

(e) DEPOSIT OF PROCEEDS.—Amounts collected under subsection (b) shall be deposited in the following order of priority:

(1) Into the financing accounts established under section 505 of the Federal Credit Reform Act of 1990 (2 U.S.C. 661d) to implement this subtitle, up to an amount equal to the sum of—

(A) the amount transferred from the appropriation made under section 4027 to the financing accounts; and

(B) the amount necessary to repay any amount lent from the Treasury to such financing accounts.

(2) After the deposits specified in paragraph (1) of this subsection have been made, into the Federal Old-Age and Survivors Insurance Trust Fund established under section 201(a) of the Social Security Act (42 U.S.C. 401).

(f) ADMINISTRATIVE PROVISIONS.—Notwithstanding any other provision of law, the Secretary may use not greater than $100,000,000 of the funds made available under section 4027 to pay costs and administrative expenses associated with the loans, loan guarantees, and other investments authorized under this section. The Secretary is authorized to take such actions as the Secretary deems necessary to carry out the authorities in this subtitle, including, without limitation—

(1) using direct hiring authority to hire employees to administer this subtitle;

(2) entering into contracts, including contracts for services authorized by this subtitle;

(3) establishing vehicles that are authorized, subject to supervision by the Secretary, to purchase, hold, and sell assets and issue obligations; and

(4) issuing such regulations and other guidance as may be necessary or appropriate to carry out the authorities or purposes of this subtitle.

(g) FINANCIAL AGENTS.—The Secretary is authorized to designate financial institutions, including but not limited to, depositories, brokers, dealers, and other institutions, as financial agents of the United States. Such institutions shall—

(1) perform all reasonable duties the Secretary determines necessary to respond to the coronavirus; and

(2) be paid for such duties using appropriations available to the Secretary to reimburse financial institutions in their capacity as financial agents of the United States.

(h) LOANS MADE BY OR GUARANTEED BY THE DEPARTMENT OF THE TREASURY TREATED AS INDEBTEDNESS FOR TAX PURPOSES.—

(1) IN GENERAL.—Any loan made by or guaranteed by the Department of the Treasury under this section shall be treated as indebtedness for purposes of the Internal Revenue Code of 1986, shall be treated as issued for its stated principal amount, and stated interest on such loans shall be treated as qualified stated interest.

(2) REGULATIONS OR GUIDANCE.—The Secretary of the Treasury (or the Secretary's delegate) shall prescribe such regulations or guidance as may be necessary or appropriate to carry out the purposes of this section, including guidance providing that the acquisition of warrants, stock options, common or preferred stock or other equity under this section does not result in an ownership change for purposes of section 382 of the Internal Revenue Code of 1986.

[¶2189] SEC. 4004. LIMITATION ON CERTAIN EMPLOYEE COMPENSATION.

(a) IN GENERAL.—The Secretary may only enter into an agreement with an eligible business to make a loan or loan guarantee under paragraph (1), (2) or (3) of section 4003(b) if such agreement provides that, during the period beginning on the date on which the agreement is executed and ending on the date that is 1 year after the date on which the loan or loan guarantee is no longer outstanding—

(1) no officer or employee of the eligible business whose total compensation exceeded $425,000 in calendar year 2019 (other than an employee whose compensation is determined through an existing collective bargaining agreement entered into prior to March 1, 2020)—

(A) will receive from the eligible business total compensation which exceeds, during any 12 consecutive months of such period, the total compensation received by the officer or employee from the eligible business in calendar year 2019; or

(B) will receive from the eligible business severance pay or other benefits upon termination of employment with the eligible business which exceeds twice the maximum total compensation received by the officer or employee from the eligible business in calendar year 2019; and

(2) no officer or employee of the eligible business whose total compensation exceeded $3,000,000 in calendar year 2019 may receive during any 12 consecutive months of such period total compensation in excess of the sum of—

(A) $3,000,000; and

(B) 50 percent of the excess over $3,000,000 of the total compensation received by the officer or employee from the eligible business in calendar year 2019.

(b) TOTAL COMPENSATION DEFINED.—In this section, the term "total compensation" includes salary, bonuses, awards of stock, and other financial benefits provided by an eligible business to an officer or employee of the eligible business.

[¶2190] SEC. 4005. CONTINUATION OF CERTAIN AIR SERVICE.

The Secretary of Transportation is authorized to require, to the extent reasonable and practicable, an air carrier receiving loans and loan guarantees under section 4003 to maintain scheduled air transportation service as the Secretary of Transportation deems necessary to ensure services to any point served by that carrier before March 1, 2020. When considering whether to exercise the authority granted by this section, the Secretary of Transportation shall take into consideration the air transportation needs of small and remote communities and the need to maintain well-functioning health care and pharmaceutical supply chains, including for medical devices and supplies. The authority under this section, including any requirement issued by the Secretary under this section, shall terminate on March 1, 2022.

[¶2191] SEC. 4006. COORDINATION WITH SECRETARY OF TRANSPORTATION.

In implementing this subtitle with respect to air carriers, the Secretary shall coordinate with the Secretary of Transportation.

[¶2192] SEC. 4007. SUSPENSION OF CERTAIN AVIATION EXCISE TAXES.

(a) TRANSPORTATION BY AIR.—In the case of any amount paid for transportation by air (including any amount treated as paid for transportation by air by reason of section 4261(e)(3) of the Internal Revenue Code of 1986) during the excise tax holiday period, no tax shall be imposed under section 4261 or 4271 of such Code. The preceding sentence shall not apply to amounts paid on or before the date of the enactment of this Act.

(b) USE OF KEROSENE IN COMMERCIAL AVIATION.—In the case of kerosene used in commercial aviation (as defined in section 4083 of the Internal Revenue Code of 1986) during the excise tax holiday period—

(1) no tax shall be imposed on such kerosene under—

(A) section 4041(c) of the Internal Revenue Code of 1986, or

(B) section 4081 of such Code (other than at the rate provided in subsection (a)(2)(B) thereof), and

(2) section 6427(l) of such Code shall be applied—

(A) by treating such use as a nontaxable use, and

(B) without regard to paragraph (4)(A)(ii) thereof.

(c) EXCISE TAX HOLIDAY PERIOD.—For purposes of this section, the term "excise tax holiday period" means the period beginning after the date of the enactment of this section and ending before January 1, 2021.

[¶2193] SEC. 4008. DEBT GUARANTEE AUTHORITY.

(a) Section 1105 of the Dodd-Frank Wall Street Reform and Consumer Protection Act (12 U.S.C. 5612) is amended—

(1) in subsection (f)—

(A) by inserting "in noninterest-bearing transaction accounts" after "institutions"; and

(B) by striking "shall not" and inserting "may"; and

(2) by adding at the end the following:

(h) "APPROVAL OF GUARANTEE PROGRAM DURING THE COVID–19 CRISIS.—

(1) "IN GENERAL.—For purposes of the congressional joint resolution of approval provided for in subsections (c)(1) and (2) and (d), notwithstanding any other provision of this section, the Federal Deposit Insurance Corporation is approved upon enactment of this Act to establish a program provided for in subsection (a), provided that any such program and any such guarantee shall terminate not later than December 31, 2020.

(2) "MAXIMUM AMOUNT.—Any debt guarantee program authorized by this subsection shall include a maximum amount of outstanding debt that is guaranteed.".

(b) FEDERAL CREDIT UNION TRANSACTION ACCOUNT GUARANTEES.—Notwithstanding any other provision of law and in coordination with the Federal Deposit Insurance Corporation, the National Credit Union Administration Board may by a vote of the Board increase to unlimited, or such lower amount as the Board approves, the share insurance coverage provided by the National Credit Union Share Insurance Fund on any noninterest-bearing transaction account in any federally insured credit union without exception, provided that any such increase shall terminate not later than December 31, 2020.

[¶2194] SEC. 4009. TEMPORARY GOVERNMENT IN THE SUNSHINE ACT RELIEF.

(a) IN GENERAL.—Except as provided in subsection (b), notwithstanding any other provision of law, if the Chairman of the Board of Governors of the Federal Reserve System determines, in writing, that unusual and exigent circumstances exist, the Board may conduct meetings without regard to the requirements of section 552b of title 5, United States Code, during the period beginning on the date of enactment of this Act and ending on the earlier of—

(1) the date on which the national emergency concerning the novel coronavirus disease (COVID–19) outbreak declared by the President on March 13, 2020 under the National Emergencies Act (50 U.S.C. 1601 et seq.) terminates; or

(2) December 31, 2020.

(b) RECORDS.—The Board of Governors of the Federal Reserve System shall keep a record of all Board votes and the reasons for such votes during the period described in subsection (a).

[¶2195] SEC. 4010. TEMPORARY HIRING FLEXIBILITY.

(a) DEFINITION.—In this section, the term "covered period" means the period beginning on the date of enactment of this Act and ending on the sooner of—

(1) the termination date of the national emergency concerning the novel coronavirus disease (COVID–19) outbreak declared by the President on March 13, 2020 under the National Emergencies Act (50 U.S.C. 1601 et seq.); or

(2) December 31, 2020.

(b) AUTHORITY.—During the covered period, the Secretary of Housing and Urban Development, the Securities and Exchange Commission, and the Commodity Futures Trading Commission may, without regard to sections 3309 through 3318 of title 5, United States Code, recruit and appoint candidates to fill temporary and term appointments within their respective agencies upon a determination that those expedited procedures are necessary and appropriate to enable the respective agencies to prevent, prepare for, or respond to COVID–19.

[¶2196] SEC. 4011. TEMPORARY LENDING LIMIT WAIVER.

(a) IN GENERAL.—Section 5200 of the Revised Statutes of the United States (12 U.S.C. 84) is amended—

(1) in subsection (c)(7)—

(A) by inserting "any nonbank financial company (as that term is defined in section 102 of the Financial Stability Act of 2010 (12 U.S.C. 5311))," after "Loans or extensions of credit to"; and

(B) by striking "financial institution or to" and inserting "financial institution, or to"; and

(2) in subsection (d), by adding at the end of paragraph (1) the following: "The Comptroller of the Currency may, by order, exempt any transaction or series of transactions from the requirements of this section upon a finding by the Comptroller that such exemption is in the public interest and consistent with the purposes of this section.".

(b) EFFECTIVE PERIOD.—This section, and the amendments made by this section, shall be effective during the period beginning on the date of enactment of this Act and ending on the sooner of—

(1) the termination date of the national emergency concerning the novel coronavirus disease (COVID–19) outbreak declared by the President on March 13, 2020 under the National Emergencies Act (50 U.S.C. 1601 et seq.); or

(2) December 31, 2020.

[¶2197] SEC. 4012. TEMPORARY RELIEF FOR COMMUNITY BANKS.

(a) DEFINITIONS.—In this section—

(1) the term "appropriate Federal banking agency" has the meaning given the term in section 2 of the Economic Growth, Regulatory Relief, and Consumer Protection Act (12 U.S.C. 5365 note); and

(2) the terms "Community Bank Leverage Ratio" and "qualifying community bank" have the meanings given the terms in section 201(a) of the Economic Growth, Regulatory Relief, and Consumer Protection Act (12 U.S.C. 5371 note).

(b) INTERIM RULE.—

(1) IN GENERAL.—Notwithstanding any other provision of law or regulation, the appropriate Federal banking agencies shall issue an interim final rule that provides that, for the purposes of section 201 of the Economic Growth, Regulatory Relief, and Consumer Protection Act (12 U.S.C. 5371 note)—

(A) the Community Bank Leverage Ratio shall be 8 percent; and

(B) a qualifying community bank that falls below the Community Bank Leverage Ratio established under subparagraph (A) shall have a reasonable grace period to satisfy the Community Bank Leverage Ratio.

(2) EFFECTIVE PERIOD.—The interim rule issued under paragraph (1) shall be effective during the period beginning on the date on which the appropriate Federal banking agencies issue the rule and ending on the sooner of—

(A) the termination date of the national emergency concerning the novel coronavirus disease (COVID–19) outbreak declared by the President on March 13, 2020 under the National Emergencies Act (50 U.S.C. 1601 et seq.); or

(B) December 31, 2020.

(c) GRACE PERIOD.—During a grace period described in subsection (b)(1)(B), a qualifying community bank to which the grace period applies may continue to be treated as a qualifying community bank and shall be presumed to satisfy the capital and leverage requirements described in section 201(c) of the Economic Growth, Regulatory Relief, and Consumer Protection Act (12 U.S.C. 5371 note).

[¶2198] SEC. 4013. TEMPORARY RELIEF FROM TROUBLED DEBT RESTRUCTURINGS.

(a) DEFINITIONS.—In this section:

(1) APPLICABLE PERIOD.—The term "applicable period" means the period beginning on March 1, 2020 and ending on the earlier of December 31, 2020, or the date that is 60 days after the date on

which the national emergency concerning the novel coronavirus disease (COVID–19) outbreak declared by the President on March 13, 2020 under the National Emergencies Act (50 U.S.C. 1601 et seq.) terminates.

(2) APPROPRIATE FEDERAL BANKING AGENCY.—The term "appropriate Federal banking agency"—

(A) has the meaning given the term in section 3 of the Federal Deposit Insurance Act (12 U.S.C. 1813); and

(B) includes the National Credit Union Administration.

(b) SUSPENSION.—

(1) IN GENERAL.—During the applicable period, a financial institution may elect to—

(A) suspend the requirements under United States generally accepted accounting principles for loan modifications related to the coronavirus disease 2019 (COVID–19) pandemic that would otherwise be categorized as a troubled debt restructuring; and

(B) suspend any determination of a loan modified as a result of the effects of the coronavirus disease 2019 (COVID–19) pandemic as being a troubled debt restructuring, including impairment for accounting purposes.

(2) APPLICABILITY.—Any suspension under paragraph (1)—

(A) shall be applicable for the term of the loan modification, but solely with respect to any modification, including a forbearance arrangement, an interest rate modification, a repayment plan, and any other similar arrangement that defers or delays the payment of principal or interest, that occurs during the applicable period for a loan that was not more than 30 days past due as of December 31, 2019; and

(B) shall not apply to any adverse impact on the credit of a borrower that is not related to the coronavirus disease 2019 (COVID–19) pandemic.

(c) DEFERENCE.—The appropriate Federal banking agency of the financial institution shall defer to the determination of the financial institution to make a suspension under this section.

(d) RECORDS.—For modified loans for which suspensions under subsection (a) apply—

(1) financial institutions should continue to maintain records of the volume of loans involved; and

(2) the appropriate Federal banking agencies may collect data about such loans for supervisory purposes.

[¶2199] SEC. 4014. OPTIONAL TEMPORARY RELIEF FROM CURRENT EXPECTED CREDIT LOSSES.

(a) DEFINITIONS.—In this section:

(1) APPROPRIATE FEDERAL BANKING AGENCY.—The term "appropriate Federal banking agency"—

(A) has the meaning given the term in section 3 of the Federal Deposit Insurance Act (12 U.S.C. 1813); and

(B) includes the National Credit Union Administration.

(2) INSURED DEPOSITORY INSTITUTION.—The term "insured depository institution"—

(A) has the meaning given the term in section 3 of the Federal Deposit Insurance Act (12 U.S.C. 1813); and

(B) includes a credit union.

(b) TEMPORARY RELIEF FROM CECL STANDARDS.—Notwithstanding any other provision of law, no insured depository institution, bank holding company, or any affiliate thereof shall be required to comply with the Financial Accounting Standards Board Accounting Standards Update No. 2016–13 ("Measurement of Credit Losses on Financial Instruments"), including the current expected credit losses methodology for estimating allowances for credit losses, during the period beginning on the date of enactment of this Act and ending on the earlier of—

(1) the date on which the national emergency concerning the novel coronavirus disease (COVID–19) outbreak declared by the President on March 13, 2020 under the National Emergencies Act (50 U.S.C. 1601 et seq.) terminates; or

(2) December 31, 2020.

[¶2200] SEC. 4015. NON-APPLICABILITY OF RESTRICTIONS ON ESF DURING NATIONAL EMERGENCY.

(a) IN GENERAL.—Section 131 of the Emergency Economic Stabilization Act of 2008 (12 U.S.C. 5236) shall not apply during the period beginning on the date of enactment of this Act and ending on December 31, 2020. Any guarantee established as a result of the application of subsection (a) shall—

(1) be limited to a guarantee of the total value of a shareholder's account in a participating fund as of the close of business on the day before the announcement of the guarantee; and

(2) terminate not later than December 31, 2020.

(b) DIRECT APPROPRIATION.—Upon the expiration of the period described in subsection (a), there is appropriated, out of amounts in the Treasury not otherwise appropriated, such sums as may be necessary to reimburse the fund established under section 5302(a)(1) of title 31, United States Code, for any funds that are used for the Treasury Money Market Funds Guaranty Program for the United States money market mutual fund industry to the extent a claim payment made exceeds the balance of fees collected by the fund.

[¶2201] SEC. 4016. TEMPORARY CREDIT UNION PROVISIONS.

(a) IN GENERAL.—

(1) DEFINITIONS.—Section 302(1) of the Federal Credit Union Act (12 U.S.C. 1795a(1)) is amended, in the matter preceding subparagraph (A), by striking "primarily serving natural persons".

(2) MEMBERSHIP.—Section 304(b)(2) of the Federal Credit Union Act (12 U.S.C. 1795c(b)(2)) is amended by striking "all those credit unions" and inserting "such credit unions as the Board may in its discretion determine".

(3) EXTENSIONS OF CREDIT.—Section 306(a)(1) of the Federal Credit Union Act (12 U.S.C. 1795e(a)(1)) is amended, in the second sentence, by striking "the intent of which is to expand credit union portfolios" and inserting "without first having obtained evidence from the applicant that the applicant has made reasonable efforts to first use primary sources of liquidity of the applicant, including balance sheet and market funding sources, to address the liquidity needs of the applicant".

(4) POWERS OF THE BOARD.—Section 307(a)(4)(A) of the Federal Credit Union Act (12 U.S.C. 1795f(a)(4)(A)) is amended by inserting ", provided that, the total face value of such obligations shall not exceed 16 times the subscribed capital stock and surplus of the Facility for the period beginning on the date of enactment of the Coronavirus Economic Stabilization Act of 2020 and ending on December 31, 2020" after "Facility".

(b) SUNSET.—

(1) IN GENERAL.—

(A) DEFINITIONS.—Section 302(1) of the Federal Credit Union Act (12 U.S.C. 1795a(1)) is amended, in the matter preceding subparagraph (A), by inserting "primarily serving natural persons" after "credit unions".

(B) MEMBERSHIP.—Section 304(b)(2) of the Federal Credit Union Act (12 U.S.C. 1795c(b)(2)) is amended by striking "such credit unions as the Board may in its discretion determine" and inserting "all those credit unions".

(C) EXTENSIONS OF CREDIT.—Section 306(a)(1) of the Federal Credit Union Act (12 U.S.C. 1795e(a)(1)) is amended, in the second sentence, by striking "without first having obtained evidence from the applicant that the applicant has made reasonable efforts to first use primary sources of liquidity of the applicant, including balance sheet and market funding sources, to address the liquidity needs of the applicant" and inserting "the intent of which is to expand credit union portfolios".

(2) EFFECTIVE DATE.—The amendments made by paragraph (1) shall take effect on December 31, 2020.

[¶2202] SEC. 4017. INCREASING ACCESS TO MATERIALS NECESSARY FOR NATIONAL SECURITY AND PANDEMIC RECOVERY.

Notwithstanding any other provision of law—

(1) during the 2-year period beginning on the date of enactment of this Act, the requirements described in sections 303(a)(6)(C) and 304(e) of the Defense Production Act of 1950 (50 U.S.C. 4533(a)(6)(C), 4534(e)) shall not apply; and

(2) during the 1-year period beginning on the date of enactment of this Act, the requirements described in sections 302(d)(1) and 303 (a)(6)(B) of the Defense Production Act of 1950 (50 U.S.C. 4532(d)(1), 4533(a)(6)(B)) shall not apply.

[¶2203] SEC. 4018. SPECIAL INSPECTOR GENERAL FOR PANDEMIC RECOVERY.

(a) OFFICE OF INSPECTOR GENERAL.—There is hereby established within the Department of the Treasury the Office of the Special Inspector General for Pandemic Recovery.

(b) APPOINTMENT OF INSPECTOR GENERAL; REMOVAL.—

(1) IN GENERAL.—The head of the Office of the Special Inspector General for Pandemic Recovery shall be the Special Inspector General for Pandemic Recovery (referred to in this section as the "Special Inspector General"), who shall be appointed by the President, by and with the advice and consent of the Senate.

(2) NOMINATION.—The nomination of the Special Inspector General shall be made on the basis of integrity and demonstrated ability in accounting, auditing, financial analysis, law, management analysis, public administration, or investigations. The nomination of an individual as Special Inspector General shall be made as soon as practicable after any loan, loan guarantee, or other investment is made under section 4003.

(3) REMOVAL.—The Special Inspector General shall be removable from office in accordance with the provisions of section 3(b) of the Inspector General Act of 1978 (5 U.S.C. App.).

(4) POLITICAL ACTIVITY.—For purposes of section 7324 of title 5, United States Code, the Special Inspector General shall not be considered an employee who determines policies to be pursued by the United States in the nationwide administration of Federal law.

(5) BASIC PAY.—The annual rate of basic pay of the Special Inspector General shall be the annual rate of basic pay for an Inspector General under section 3(e) of the Inspector General Act of 1978 (5 U.S.C. App.).

(c) DUTIES.—

(1) IN GENERAL.—It shall be the duty of the Special Inspector General to, in accordance with section 4(b)(1) of the Inspector General Act of 1978 (5 U.S.C. App.), conduct, supervise, and coordinate audits and investigations of the making, purchase, management, and sale of loans, loan guarantees, and other investments made by the Secretary of the Treasury under any program established by the Secretary under this Act, and the management by the Secretary of any program established under this Act, including by collecting and summarizing the following information:

(A) A description of the categories of the loans, loan guarantees, and other investments made by the Secretary.

(B) A listing of the eligible businesses receiving loan, loan guarantees, and other investments made under each category described in subparagraph (A).

(C) An explanation of the reasons the Secretary determined it to be appropriate to make each loan or loan guarantee under this Act, including a justification of the price paid for, and other financial terms associated with, the applicable transaction.

(D) A listing of, and detailed biographical information with respect to, each person hired to manage or service each loan, loan guarantee, or other investment made under section 4003.

(E) A current, as of the date on which the information is collected, estimate of the total amount of each loan, loan guarantee, and other investment made under this Act that is outstanding, the amount of interest and fees accrued and received with respect to each loan or loan guarantee, the total amount of matured loans, the type and amount of collateral, if any, and any losses or gains, if any, recorded or accrued for each loan, loan guarantee, or other investment.

(2) MAINTENANCE OF SYSTEMS.—The Special Inspector General shall establish, maintain, and oversee such systems, procedures, and controls as the Special Inspector General considers appropriate to discharge the duties of the Special Inspector General under paragraph (1).

(3) ADDITIONAL DUTIES AND RESPONSIBILITIES.—In addition to the duties described in paragraphs (1) and (2), the Special Inspector General shall also have the duties and responsibilities of inspectors general under the Inspector General Act of 1978 (5 U.S.C. App.).

(d) POWERS AND AUTHORITIES.—

(1) IN GENERAL.—In carrying out the duties of the Special Inspector General under subsection (c), the Special Inspector General shall have the authorities provided in section 6 of the Inspector General Act of 1978 (5 U.S.C. App.).

(2) TREATMENT OF OFFICE.—The Office of the Special Inspector General for Pandemic Recovery shall be considered to be an office described in section 6(f)(3) of the Inspector General Act of 1978 (5 U.S.C. App.) and shall be exempt from an initial determination by the Attorney General under section 6(f)(2) of that Act.

(e) PERSONNEL, FACILITIES, AND OTHER RESOURCES.—

(1) APPOINTMENT OF OFFICERS AND EMPLOYEES.—The Special Inspector General may select, appoint, and employ such officers and employees as may be necessary for carrying out the duties of the Special Inspector General, subject to the provisions of title 5, United States Code, governing appointments in the competitive service, and the provisions of chapter 51 and subchapter III of chapter 53 of that title, relating to classification and General Schedule pay rates.

(2) EXPERTS AND CONSULTANTS.—The Special Inspector General may obtain services as authorized under section 3109 of title 5, United States Code, at daily rates not to exceed the equivalent rate prescribed for grade GS–15 of the General Schedule by section 5332 of that title.

(3) CONTRACTS.—The Special Inspector General may enter into contracts and other arrangements for audits, studies, analyses, and other services with public agencies and with private persons, and make such payments as may be necessary to carry out the duties of the Inspector General.

(4) REQUESTS FOR INFORMATION.—

(A) IN GENERAL.—Upon request of the Special Inspector General for information or assistance from any department, agency, or other entity of the Federal Government, the head of that department, agency, or entity shall, to the extent practicable and not in contravention of any existing law, furnish that information or assistance to the Special Inspector General, or an authorized designee.

(B) REFUSAL TO PROVIDE REQUESTED INFORMATION.—Whenever information or assistance requested by the Special Inspector General is, in the judgment of the Special Inspector General, unreasonably refused or not provided, the Special Inspector General shall report the circumstances to the appropriate committees of Congress without delay.

(f) REPORTS.—

(1) QUARTERLY REPORTS.—

(A) IN GENERAL.—Not later than 60 days after the date on which the Special Inspector General is confirmed, and once every calendar quarter thereafter, the Special Inspector General shall submit to the appropriate committees of Congress a report summarizing the activities of the Special Inspector General during the 3-month period ending on the date on which the Special Inspector General submits the report.

(B) CONTENTS.—Each report submitted under subparagraph (A) shall include, for the period covered by the report, a detailed statement of all loans, loan guarantees, other transactions, obligations, expenditures, and revenues associated with any program established by the Secretary under section 4003, as well as the information collected under subsection (c)(1).

(2) RULE OF CONSTRUCTION.—Nothing in this subsection may be construed to authorize the public disclosure of information that is—

(A) specifically prohibited from disclosure by any other provision of law;

(B) specifically required by Executive order to be protected from disclosure in the interest of national defense or national security or in the conduct of foreign affairs; or

(C) a part of an ongoing criminal investigation.

(g) FUNDING.—

(1) IN GENERAL.—Of the amounts made available to the Secretary under section 4027, $25,000,000 shall be made available to the Special Inspector General to carry out this section.

(2) AVAILABILITY.—The amounts made available to the Special Inspector General under paragraph (1) shall remain available until expended.

(h) TERMINATION.—The Office of the Special Inspector General shall terminate on the date 5 years after the enactment of this Act.

(i) COUNCIL OF THE INSPECTORS GENERAL ON INTEGRITY AND EFFICIENCY.—The Special Inspector General shall be a member of the Council of the Inspectors General on Integrity and Efficiency established under section 11 of the Inspector General Act of 1978 (5 U.S.C. App.) until the date of termination of the Office of the Special Inspector General.

(j) CORRECTIVE RESPONSES TO AUDIT PROBLEMS.—The Secretary shall—

(1) take action to address deficiencies identified by a report or investigation of the Special Inspector General; or

(2) with respect to a deficiency identified under paragraph (1), certify to the Committee on Banking, Housing, and Urban Affairs of the Senate, the Committee on Finance of the Senate, the Committee on Financial Services of the House of Representatives, and the Committee on Ways and Means of the House of Representatives that no action is necessary or appropriate.

[¶2204] SEC. 4019. CONFLICTS OF INTEREST.

(a) DEFINITIONS.—In this section:

(1) CONTROLLING INTEREST.—The term "controlling interest" means owning, controlling, or holding not less than 20 percent, by vote or value, of the outstanding amount of any class of equity interest in an entity.

(2) COVERED ENTITY.—The term "covered entity" means an entity in which a covered individual directly or indirectly holds a controlling interest. For the purpose of determining whether an entity is a covered entity, the securities owned, controlled, or held by 2 or more individuals who are related as described in paragraph (3)(B) shall be aggregated.

(3) COVERED INDIVIDUAL.—The term "covered individual" means—

(A) the President, the Vice President, the head of an Executive department, or a Member of Congress; and

(B) the spouse, child, son-in-law, or daughter-in-law, as determined under applicable common law, of an individual described in subparagraph (A).

(4) EXECUTIVE DEPARTMENT.—The term "Executive department" has the meaning given the term in section 101 of title 5, United States Code.

(5) MEMBER OF CONGRESS.—The term "member of Congress" means a member of the Senate or House of Representatives, a Delegate to the House of Representatives, and the Resident Commissioner from Puerto Rico.

(6) EQUITY INTEREST.—The term "equity interest" means—

(A) a share in an entity, without regard to whether the share is—

(i) transferable; or

(ii) classified as stock or anything similar;

(B) a capital or profit interest in a limited liability company or partnership; or

(C) a warrant or right, other than a right to convert, to purchase, sell, or subscribe to a share or interest described in subparagraph (A) or (B), respectively.

(b) PROHIBITION.—Notwithstanding any other provision of this subtitle, no covered entity may be eligible for any transaction described in section 4003.

(c) REQUIREMENT.—The principal executive officer and the principal financial officer, or individuals performing similar functions, of an entity seeking to enter a transaction under section 4003 shall, before that transaction is approved, certify to the Secretary and the Board of Governors of the Federal Reserve System that the entity is eligible to engage in that transaction, including that the entity is not a covered entity.

[¶2205] SEC. 4020. CONGRESSIONAL OVERSIGHT COMMISSION.

(a) ESTABLISHMENT.—There is hereby established the Congressional Oversight Commission (hereafter in this section referred to as the "Oversight Commission") as an establishment in the legislative branch.

(b) DUTIES.—

(1) IN GENERAL.—The Oversight Commission shall—

(A) conduct oversight of the implementation of this subtitle by the Department of the Treasury and the Board of Governors of the Federal Reserve System, including efforts of the Department and the Board to provide economic stability as a result of the coronavirus disease 2019 (COVID–19) pandemic of 2020;

(B) submit to Congress reports under paragraph (2); and

(C) review the implementation of this subtitle by the Federal Government.

(2) REGULAR REPORTS.—

(A) IN GENERAL.—Reports of the Oversight Commission shall include the following:

(i) The use by the Secretary and the Board of Governors of the Federal Reserve System of authority under this subtitle, including with respect to the use of contracting authority and administration of the provisions of this subtitle.

(ii) The impact of loans, loan guarantees, and investments made under this subtitle on the financial well-being of the people of the United States and the United States economy, financial markets, and financial institutions.

(iii) The extent to which the information made available on transactions under this subtitle has contributed to market transparency.

(iv) The effectiveness of loans, loan guarantees, and investments made under this subtitle of minimizing long-term costs to the taxpayers and maximizing the benefits for taxpayers.

(B) TIMING.—The reports required under this paragraph shall be submitted not later than 30 days after the first exercise by the Secretary and the Board of Governors of the Federal Reserve System of the authority under this subtitle and every 30 days thereafter.

(c) MEMBERSHIP.—

(1) IN GENERAL.—The Oversight Commission shall consist of 5 members as follows:

(A) 1 member appointed by the Speaker of the House of Representatives.

(B) 1 member appointed by the minority leader of the House of Representatives.

(C) 1 member appointed by the majority leader of the Senate.

(D) 1 member appointed by the minority leader of the Senate.

(E) 1 member appointed as Chairperson by the Speaker of the House of Representatives and the majority leader of the Senate, after consultation with the minority leader of the Senate and the minority leader of the House of Representatives

(2) PAY.—Each member of the Oversight Commission shall be paid at a rate equal to the daily equivalent of the annual rate of basic pay for level I of the Executive Schedule for each day (including travel time) during which such member is engaged in the actual performance of duties vested in the Oversight Commission.

(3) PROHIBITION OF COMPENSATION OF FEDERAL EMPLOYEES.—Members of the Oversight Commission who are full-time officers or employees of the United States may not receive additional pay, allowances, or benefits by reason of their service on the Oversight Commission.

(4) TRAVEL EXPENSES.—Each member shall receive travel expenses, including per diem in lieu of subsistence, in accordance with applicable provisions under subchapter I of chapter 57 of title 5, United States Code.

(5) QUORUM.—Four members of the Oversight Commission shall constitute a quorum but a lesser number may hold hearings.

(6) VACANCIES.—A vacancy on the Oversight Commission shall be filled in the manner in which the original appointment was made.

(7) MEETINGS.—The Oversight Commission shall meet at the call of the Chairperson or a majority of its members.

(d) STAFF.—

(1) IN GENERAL.—The Oversight Commission may appoint and fix the pay of any personnel as the Oversight Commission considers appropriate.

(2) EXPERTS AND CONSULTANTS.—The Oversight Commission may procure temporary and intermittent services under section 3109(b) of title 5, United States Code.

(3) STAFF OF AGENCIES.—Upon request of the Oversight Commission, the head of any Federal department or agency may detail, on a reimbursable basis, any of the personnel of that department or agency to the Oversight Commission to assist it in carrying out its duties under the this subtitle.

(e) POWERS.—

(1) HEARINGS AND EVIDENCE.—The Oversight Commission, or any subcommittee or member thereof, may, for the purpose of carrying out this section hold hearings, sit and act at times and places, take testimony, and receive evidence as the Oversight Commission considers appropriate and may administer oaths or affirmations to witnesses appearing before it.

(2) CONTRACTING.—The Oversight Commission may, to such extent and in such amounts as are provided in appropriation Acts, enter into contracts to enable the Oversight Commission to discharge its duties under this section.

(3) POWERS OF MEMBERS AND AGENTS.—Any member or agent of the Oversight Commission may, if authorized by the Oversight Commission, take any action which the Oversight Commission is authorized to take by this section.

(4) OBTAINING OFFICIAL DATA.—The Oversight Commission may secure directly from any department or agency of the United States information necessary to enable it to carry out this section. Upon request of the Chairperson of the Oversight Commission, the head of that department or agency shall furnish that information to the Oversight Commission.

(5) REPORTS.—The Oversight Commission shall receive and consider all reports required to be submitted to the Oversight Commission under this subtitle.

(f) TERMINATION.—The Oversight Commission shall terminate on September 30, 2025.

(g) FUNDING FOR EXPENSES.—

(1) AUTHORIZATION OF APPROPRIATIONS.—There is authorized to be appropriated to the Oversight Commission such sums as may be necessary for any fiscal year, half of which shall be derived from the applicable account of the House of Representatives, and half of which shall be derived from the contingent fund of the Senate.

(2) REIMBURSEMENT OF AMOUNTS.—An amount equal to the expenses of the Oversight Commission shall be promptly transferred by the Secretary and the Board of Governors of the Federal Reserve System, from time to time upon the presentment of a statement of such expenses by the Chairperson of the Oversight Commission, from funds made available to the Secretary under this subtitle to the applicable fund of the House of Representatives and the contingent fund of the Senate, as appropriate, as reimbursement for amounts expended from such account and fund under paragraph (1).

[¶2206] SEC. 4021. CREDIT PROTECTION DURING COVID–19.

Section 623(a)(1) of the Fair Credit Reporting Act (15 U.S.C. 1681s–2(a)(1)) is amended by adding at the end the following:

(F) "REPORTING INFORMATION DURING COVID–19 PANDEMIC.—

(i) "DEFINITIONS.—In this subsection:

(I) "ACCOMMODATION.—The term 'accommodation' includes an agreement to defer 1 or more payments, make a partial payment, forbear any delinquent amounts, modify a loan or contract, or any other assistance or relief granted to a consumer who is affected by the coronavirus disease 2019 (COVID–19) pandemic during the covered period.

(II) "COVERED PERIOD.—The term 'covered period' means the period beginning on January 31, 2020 and ending on the later of—

(aa) "120 days after the date of enactment of this subparagraph; or

(bb) "120 days after the date on which the national emergency concerning the novel coronavirus disease (COVID–19) outbreak declared by the President on March 13, 2020 under the National Emergencies Act (50 U.S.C. 1601 et seq.) terminates.

(ii) "REPORTING.—Except as provided in clause (iii), if a furnisher makes an accommodation with respect to 1 or more payments on a credit obligation or account of a consumer, and the consumer makes the payments or is not required to make 1 or more payments pursuant to the accommodation, the furnisher shall—

(I) "report the credit obligation or account as current; or

(II) "if the credit obligation or account was delinquent before the accommodation—

(aa) "maintain the delinquent status during the period in which the accommodation is in effect; and

(bb) "if the consumer brings the credit obligation or account current during the period described in item (aa), report the credit obligation or account as current.

(iii) "EXCEPTION.—Clause (ii) shall not apply with respect to a credit obligation or account of a consumer that has been charged-off.".

[¶2207] SEC. 4022. FORECLOSURE MORATORIUM AND CONSUMER RIGHT TO REQUEST FORBEARANCE.

(a) DEFINITIONS.—In this section:

(1) COVID–19 EMERGENCY.—The term "COVID–19 emergency" means the national emergency concerning the novel coronavirus disease (COVID–19) outbreak declared by the President on March 13, 2020 under the National Emergencies Act (50 U.S.C. 1601 et seq.).

(2) FEDERALLY BACKED MORTGAGE LOAN.—The term "Federally backed mortgage loan" includes any loan which is secured by a first or subordinate lien on residential real property (including individual units of condominiums and cooperatives) designed principally for the occupancy of from 1- to 4-families that is—

(A) insured by the Federal Housing Administration under title II of the National Housing Act (12 U.S.C. 1707 et seq.);

(B) insured under section 255 of the National Housing Act (12 U.S.C. 1715z–20);

(C) guaranteed under section 184 or 184A of the Housing and Community Development Act of 1992 (12 U.S.C. 1715z–13a, 1715z–13b);

(D) guaranteed or insured by the Department of Veterans Affairs;

(E) guaranteed or insured by the Department of Agriculture;

(F) made by the Department of Agriculture; or

(G) purchased or securitized by the Federal Home Loan Mortgage Corporation or the Federal National Mortgage Association.

(b) FORBEARANCE.—

(1) IN GENERAL.—During the covered period, a borrower with a Federally backed mortgage loan experiencing a financial hardship due, directly or indirectly, to the COVID–19 emergency may request forbearance on the Federally backed mortgage loan, regardless of delinquency status, by—

(A) submitting a request to the borrower's servicer; and

(B) affirming that the borrower is experiencing a financial hardship during the COVID–19 emergency.

(2) DURATION OF FORBEARANCE.—Upon a request by a borrower for forbearance under paragraph (1), such forbearance shall be granted for up to 180 days, and shall be extended for an additional period of up to 180 days at the request of the borrower, provided that, at the borrower's request, either the initial or extended period of forbearance may be shortened.

(3) ACCRUAL OF INTEREST OR FEES.—During a period of forbearance described in this subsection, no fees, penalties, or interest beyond the amounts scheduled or calculated as if the borrower made all

contractual payments on time and in full under the terms of the mortgage contract, shall accrue on the borrower's account.

(c) REQUIREMENTS FOR SERVICERS.—

(1) IN GENERAL.—Upon receiving a request for forbearance from a borrower under subsection (b), the servicer shall with no additional documentation required other than the borrower's attestation to a financial hardship caused by the COVID–19 emergency and with no fees, penalties, or interest (beyond the amounts scheduled or calculated as if the borrower made all contractual payments on time and in full under the terms of the mortgage contract) charged to the borrower in connection with the forbearance, provide the forbearance for up to 180 days, which may be extended for an additional period of up to 180 days at the request of the borrower, provided that, the borrower's request for an extension is made during the covered period, and, at the borrower's request, either the initial or extended period of forbearance may be shortened.

(2) FORECLOSURE MORATORIUM.—Except with respect to a vacant or abandoned property, a servicer of a Federally backed mortgage loan may not initiate any judicial or non-judicial foreclosure process, move for a foreclosure judgment or order of sale, or execute a foreclosure-related eviction or foreclosure sale for not less than the 60-day period beginning on March 18, 2020.

[¶ 2208] SEC. 4023. FORBEARANCE OF RESIDENTIAL MORTGAGE LOAN PAYMENTS FOR MULTIFAMILY PROPERTIES WITH FEDERALLY BACKED LOANS.

(a) IN GENERAL.—During the covered period, a multifamily borrower with a Federally backed multifamily mortgage loan experiencing a financial hardship due, directly or indirectly, to the COVID–19 emergency may request a forbearance under the terms set forth in this section.

(b) REQUEST FOR RELIEF.—A multifamily borrower with a Federally backed multifamily mortgage loan that was current on its payments as of February 1, 2020, may submit an oral or written request for forbearance under subsection (a) to the borrower's servicer affirming that the multifamily borrower is experiencing a financial hardship during the COVID–19 emergency.

(c) FORBEARANCE PERIOD.—

(1) IN GENERAL.—Upon receipt of an oral or written request for forbearance from a multifamily borrower, a servicer shall—

(A) document the financial hardship;

(B) provide the forbearance for up to 30 days; and

(C) extend the forbearance for up to 2 additional 30 day periods upon the request of the borrower provided that, the borrower's request for an extension is made during the covered period, and, at least 15 days prior to the end of the forbearance period described under subparagraph (B).

(2) RIGHT TO DISCONTINUE.—A multifamily borrower shall have the option to discontinue the forbearance at any time.

(d) RENTER PROTECTIONS DURING FORBEARANCE PERIOD.—A multifamily borrower that receives a forbearance under this section may not, for the duration of the forbearance—

(1) evict or initiate the eviction of a tenant from a dwelling unit located in or on the applicable property solely for nonpayment of rent or other fees or charges; or

(2) charge any late fees, penalties, or other charges to a tenant described in paragraph (1) for late payment of rent.

(e) NOTICE.—A multifamily borrower that receives a forbearance under this section—

(1) may not require a tenant to vacate a dwelling unit located in or on the applicable property before the date that is 30 days after the date on which the borrower provides the tenant with a notice to vacate; and

(2) may not issue a notice to vacate under paragraph (1) until after the expiration of the forbearance.

(f) DEFINITIONS.—In this section:

(1) APPLICABLE PROPERTY.—The term "applicable property", with respect to a Federally backed multifamily mortgage loan, means the residential multifamily property against which the mortgage loan is secured by a lien.

(2) FEDERALLY BACKED MULTIFAMILY MORTGAGE LOAN.—The term "Federally backed multifamily mortgage loan" includes any loan (other than temporary financing such as a construction loan) that—

(A) is secured by a first or subordinate lien on residential multifamily real property designed principally for the occupancy of 5 or more families, including any such secured loan, the proceeds of which are used to prepay or pay off an existing loan secured by the same property; and

(B) is made in whole or in part, or insured, guaranteed, supplemented, or assisted in any way, by any officer or agency of the Federal Government or under or in connection with a housing or urban development program administered by the Secretary of Housing and Urban Development or a housing or related program administered by any other such officer or agency, or is purchased or securitized by the Federal Home Loan Mortgage Corporation or the Federal National Mortgage Association.

(3) MULTIFAMILY BORROWER.—the term "multifamily borrower" means a borrower of a residential mortgage loan that is secured by a lien against a property comprising 5 or more dwelling units.

(4) COVID–19 EMERGENCY.—The term "COVID–19 emergency" means the national emergency concerning the novel coronavirus disease (COVID–19) outbreak declared by the President on March 13, 2020 under the National Emergencies Act (50 U.S.C. 1601 et seq.).

(5) COVERED PERIOD.—The term "covered period" means the period beginning on the date of enactment of this Act and ending on the sooner of—

(A) the termination date of the national emergency concerning the novel coronavirus disease (COVID–19) outbreak declared by the President on March 13, 2020 under the National Emergencies Act (50 U.S.C. 1601 et seq.); or

(B) December 31, 2020.

[¶2209] SEC. 4024. TEMPORARY MORATORIUM ON EVICTION FILINGS.

(a) DEFINITIONS.—In this section:

(1) COVERED DWELLING.—The term "covered dwelling" means a dwelling that—

(A) is occupied by a tenant—

(i) pursuant to a residential lease; or

(ii) without a lease or with a lease terminable under State law; and

(B) is on or in a covered property.

(2) COVERED PROPERTY.—The term "covered property" means any property that—

(A) participates in—

(i) a covered housing program (as defined in section 41411(a) of the Violence Against Women Act of 1994 (34 U.S.C. 12491(a))); or

(ii) the rural housing voucher program under section 542 of the Housing Act of 1949 (42 U.S.C. 1490r); or

(B) has a—

(i) Federally backed mortgage loan; or

(ii) Federally backed multifamily mortgage loan.

(3) DWELLING.—The term "dwelling"—

(A) has the meaning given the term in section 802 of the Fair Housing Act (42 U.S.C. 3602); and

(B) includes houses and dwellings described in section 803(b) of such Act (42 U.S.C. 3603(b)).

(4) FEDERALLY BACKED MORTGAGE LOAN.—The term "Federally backed mortgage loan" includes any loan (other than temporary financing such as a construction loan) that—

(A) is secured by a first or subordinate lien on residential real property (including individual units of condominiums and cooperatives) designed principally for the occupancy of from 1 to 4 families, including any such secured loan, the proceeds of which are used to prepay or pay off an existing loan secured by the same property; and

(B) is made in whole or in part, or insured, guaranteed, supplemented, or assisted in any way, by any officer or agency of the Federal Government or under or in connection with a housing or urban development program administered by the Secretary of Housing and Urban Development or a housing or related program administered by any other such officer or agency, or is purchased or securitized by the Federal Home Loan Mortgage Corporation or the Federal National Mortgage Association.

(5) FEDERALLY BACKED MULTIFAMILY MORTGAGE LOAN.—The term "Federally backed multifamily mortgage loan" includes any loan (other than temporary financing such as a construction loan) that—

(A) is secured by a first or subordinate lien on residential multifamily real property designed principally for the occupancy of 5 or more families, including any such secured loan, the proceeds of which are used to prepay or pay off an existing loan secured by the same property; and

(B) is made in whole or in part, or insured, guaranteed, supplemented, or assisted in any way, by any officer or agency of the Federal Government or under or in connection with a housing or urban development program administered by the Secretary of Housing and Urban Development or a housing or related program administered by any other such officer or agency, or is purchased or securitized by the Federal Home Loan Mortgage Corporation or the Federal National Mortgage Association.

(b) MORATORIUM.—During the 120-day period beginning on the date of enactment of this Act, the lessor of a covered dwelling may not—

(1) make, or cause to be made, any filing with the court of jurisdiction to initiate a legal action to recover possession of the covered dwelling from the tenant for nonpayment of rent or other fees or charges; or

(2) charge fees, penalties, or other charges to the tenant related to such nonpayment of rent.

(c) NOTICE.—The lessor of a covered dwelling unit—

(1) may not require the tenant to vacate the covered dwelling unit before the date that is 30 days after the date on which the lessor provides the tenant with a notice to vacate; and

(2) may not issue a notice to vacate under paragraph (1) until after the expiration of the period described in subsection (b).

[¶2210] SEC. 4025. PROTECTION OF COLLECTIVE BARGAINING AGREEMENT.

(a) IN GENERAL.—Neither the Secretary, nor any other actor, department, or agency of the Federal Government, shall condition the issuance of a loan or loan guarantee under paragraph (1), (2), or (3) of section 4003(b) of this subtitle on an air carrier's or eligible business's implementation of measures to enter into negotiations with the certified bargaining representative of a craft or class of employees of the air carrier or eligible business under the Railway Labor Act (45 U.S.C. 151 et seq.) or the National Labor Relations Act (29 U.S.C. 151 et seq.), regarding pay or other terms and conditions of employment.

(b) PERIOD OF EFFECT.—With respect to an air carrier or eligible business to which the loan or loan guarantee is provided under this subtitle, this section shall be in effect with respect to the air carrier or eligible business beginning on the date on which the air carrier or eligible business is first issued such loan or loan guarantee and ending on the date that is 1 year after the loan or loan guarantee is no longer outstanding.

[¶2211] SEC. 4026. REPORTS.

(a) DISCLOSURE OF TRANSACTIONS.—Not later than 72 hours after any transaction by the Secretary under paragraph (1), (2), or (3) of section 4003(b), the Secretary shall publish on the website of the Department of the Treasury—

(1) a plain-language description of the transaction, including the date of application, date of application approval, and identity of the counterparty;

(2) the amount of the loan or loan guarantee;

(3) the interest rate, conditions, and any other material or financial terms associated with the transaction, if applicable; and

(4) a copy of the relevant and final term sheet, if applicable, and contract or other relevant documentation regarding the transaction.

(b) REPORTS.—

(1) TO CONGRESS.—

(A) IN GENERAL.—In addition to such reports as are required under section 5302(c) of title 31, United States Code, not later than 7 days after the Secretary makes any loan or loan guarantee under paragraph (1), (2), or (3) of section 4003(b), the Secretary shall submit to the Chairmen and Ranking Members of the Committee on Banking, Housing, and Urban Affairs and the Committee on Finance of the Senate and the Chairmen and Ranking Members of the Committee on Financial Services and the Committee on Ways and Means of the House of Representatives a report summarizing—

(i) an overview of actions taken by the Secretary under paragraph (1), (2) or (3) of section 4003(b) during such period;

(ii) the actual obligation, expenditure, and disbursements of the funds during such period; and

(iii) a detailed financial statement with respect to the exercise of authority under paragraph (1), (2) or (3) of section 4003(b) showing—

(I) all loans and loan guarantees made, renewed, or restructured;

(II) all transactions during such period, including the types of parties involved;

(III) the nature of the assets purchased;

(IV) a description of the vehicles established to exercise such authority; and

(V) any or all repayment activity, delinquencies or defaults on loans and loan guarantees issued under paragraph (1), (2) or (3) of section 4003(b).

(B) PUBLICATION.—Not later than 7 days after the date on which the Secretary submits a report under subparagraph (A) to the committees of Congress described in such subparagraph, the Secretary shall publish such report on the website of the Department of the Treasury.

(C) 30-DAY REPORTS.—Every 30 days during such time as a loan or loan guarantee under paragraph (1), (2), or (3) of section 4003(b) is outstanding, the Secretary shall publish on the website of the Department of the Treasury a report summarizing the information set forth in subparagraph (A).

(2) BOARD OF GOVERNORS.—

(A) IN GENERAL.—With respect to any program or facility described in paragraph (4) of section 4003(b), the Board of Governors of the Federal Reserve System shall provide to the Committee on Banking, Housing, and Urban Affairs of the Senate and the Committee on Financial Services of the House of Representatives such reports as are required to be provided under section 13(3) of the Federal Reserve Act (12 U.S.C. 343(3))—

(i) not later than 7 days after the Board authorizes a new facility or other financial assistance in accordance with section 13(3)(C)(i) of the Federal Reserve Act (12 U.S.C. 343(3)(C)(i)); and

(ii) once every 30 days with respect to outstanding loans or financial assistance in accordance with section 13(3)(C)(ii) of the Federal Reserve Act (12 U.S.C. 343(3)(C)(ii)).

(B) PUBLICATION.—Not later than 7 days after the Board of Governors of the Federal Reserve System submits a report under subparagraph (A) to the committees of Congress described in subparagraph (A), the Board shall publish on its website such report.

(c) TESTIMONY.—The Secretary and the Chairman of the Board of Governors of the Federal Reserve System shall testify, on a quarterly basis, before the Committee on Banking, Housing, and Urban Affairs of the Senate and the Committee on Financial Services of the House of Representatives regarding the obligations of the Department of the Treasury and the Federal Reserve System, and transactions entered into, under this Act.

(d) PROGRAM DESCRIPTIONS.—The Secretary shall post on the website of the Department of the Treasury all criteria, guidelines, eligibility requirements, and application materials for the making of any loan or loan guarantee under paragraph (1), (2), or (3) of section 4003(b).

(e) ADMINISTRATIVE CONTRACTS.—Not later than 24 hours after the Secretary enters into a contract in connection with the administration of any loan or loan guarantee authorized to be made under paragraph (1), (2), or (3) of section 4003(b), the Secretary shall post on the website of the Department of the Treasury a copy of the contract.

(f) GOVERNMENT ACCOUNTABILITY OFFICE.—

(1) STUDY.—The Comptroller General of the United States shall conduct a study on the loans, loan guarantees, and other investments provided under section 4003.

(2) REPORT.—Not later than 9 months after the date of enactment of this Act, and annually thereafter through the year succeeding the last year for which loans, loan guarantees, or other investments made under section 4003 are outstanding, the Comptroller General shall submit to the Committee on Financial Services, the Committee on Transportation and Infrastructure, the Committee on Appropriations, and the Committee on the Budget of the House of Representatives and the Committee on Banking, Housing, and Urban Affairs, the Committee on Commerce, Science, and Transportation, the Committee on Appropriations, and the Committee on the Budget of the Senate a report on the loans, loan guarantees, and other investments made under section 4003.

[¶2212] SEC. 4027. DIRECT APPROPRIATION.

(a) IN GENERAL.—Notwithstanding any other provision of law, there is appropriated, out of amounts in the Treasury not otherwise appropriated, to the fund established under section 5302(a)(1) of title 31, United States Code, $500,000,000,000 to carry out this subtitle.

(b) TECHNICAL AND CONFORMING AMENDMENT.—Section 5302(a) of title 31, United States Code, is amended—

(1) by striking "and" before "section 3"; and

(2) by inserting "and the Coronavirus Economic Stabilization Act of 2020," before "and for investing".

(c) CLARIFICATION.—

(1) IN GENERAL.—On or after January 1, 2021, any remaining funds made available under section 4003(b) may be used only for—

(A) modifications, restructurings, or other amendments of loans, loan guarantees, or other investments in accordance with section 4029(b)(1); and

(B) exercising any options, warrants, or other investments made prior to January 1, 2021; and

(C) paying costs and administrative expenses as provided in section 4003(f).

(2) DEFICIT REDUCTION.—On January 1, 2026, any funds described in paragraph (1) that are remaining shall be transferred to the general fund of the Treasury to be used for deficit reduction.

[¶2213] SEC. 4028. RULE OF CONSTRUCTION.

Nothing in this subtitle shall be construed to allow the Secretary to provide relief to eligible businesses, States, and municipalities except in the form of loans, loan guarantees, and other investments as provided in this subtitle and under terms and conditions that are in the interest of the Federal Government.

[¶2214] SEC. 4029. TERMINATION OF AUTHORITY.

(a) IN GENERAL.—Except as provided in subsection (b), on December 31, 2020, the authority provided under this subtitle to make new loans, loan guarantees, or other investments shall terminate.

(b) OUTSTANDING.—

(1) IN GENERAL.—Except as provided in paragraph (2), any loan, loan guarantee, or other investment outstanding on the date described in subsection (a)—

(A) may be modified, restructured, or otherwise amended; and

(B) may not be forgiven.

(2) DURATION.—The duration of any loan or loan guarantee made under section 4003(b)(1) that is modified, restructured, or otherwise amended under paragraph (1) shall not be extended beyond 5 years from the initial origination date of the loan or loan guarantee.

Subtitle B—Air Carrier Worker Support

[¶2216] SEC. 4111. DEFINITIONS.

Unless otherwise specified, the terms in section 40102(a) of title 49, United States Code, shall apply to this subtitle, except that—

(1) the term "airline catering employee" means an employee who performs airline catering services;

(2) the term "airline catering services" means preparation, assembly, or both, of food, beverages, provisions and related supplies for delivery, and the delivery of such items, directly to aircraft or to a location on or near airport property for subsequent delivery to aircraft;

(3) the term "contractor" means—

(A) a person that performs, under contract with a passenger air carrier conducting operations under part 121 of title 14, Code of Federal Regulations—

(i) catering functions; or

(ii) functions on the property of an airport that are directly related to the air transportation of persons, property, or mail, including but not limited to the loading and unloading of property on aircraft; assistance to passengers under part 382 of title 14, Code of Federal Regulations; security; airport ticketing and check-in functions; ground-handling of aircraft; or aircraft cleaning and sanitization functions and waste removal; or

(B) a subcontractor that performs such functions;

(4) the term "employee" means an individual, other than a corporate officer, who is employed by an air carrier or a contractor; and

(5) the term "Secretary" means the Secretary of the Treasury.

[¶2217] SEC. 4112. PANDEMIC RELIEF FOR AVIATION WORKERS.

(a) Financial Assistance for Employee Wages, Salaries, and Benefits.—Notwithstanding any other provision of law, to preserve aviation jobs and compensate air carrier industry workers, the Secretary shall provide financial assistance that shall exclusively be used for the continuation of payment of employee wages, salaries, and benefits to—

(1) passenger air carriers, in an aggregate amount up to $25,000,000,000;

(2) cargo air carriers, in the aggregate amount up to $4,000,000,000; and

(3) contractors, in an aggregate amount up to $3,000,000,000.

(b) Administrative Expenses.—Notwithstanding any other provision of law, the Secretary, may use $100,000,000 of the funds made available under section 4120(a) for costs and administrative expenses associated with providing financial assistance under this subtitle.

[¶2218] SEC. 4113. PROCEDURES FOR PROVIDING PAYROLL SUPPORT.

(a) Awardable Amounts.—The Secretary shall provide financial assistance under this subtitle—

(1) to an air carrier in an amount equal to the salaries and benefits reported by the air carrier to the Department of Transportation pursuant to part 241 of title 14, Code of Federal Regulations, for the period from April 1, 2019, through September 30, 2019; and

(2) to an air carrier that does not transmit reports under such part 241, in an amount that such air carrier certifies, using sworn financial statements or other appropriate data, as the amount of wages, salaries, benefits, and other compensation that such air carrier paid the employees of such air carrier during the period from April 1, 2019, through September 30, 2019; and

(3) to a contractor, in an amount that the contractor certifies, using sworn financial statements or other appropriate data, as the amount of wages, salaries, benefits, and other compensation that such contractor paid the employees of such contractor during the period from April 1, 2019, through September 30, 2019.

(b) Deadlines and Procedures.—

(1) In general.—

(A) Forms; terms and conditions.—Financial assistance provided to an air carrier or contractor under this subtitle shall be in such form, on such terms and conditions (including requirements for audits and the clawback of any financial assistance provided upon failure by a passenger air carrier, cargo air carrier, or contractor to honor the assurances specified in section 4114), as the Secretary determines appropriate.

(B) Procedures.—The Secretary shall publish streamlined and expedited procedures not later than 5 days after the date of enactment of this Act for air carriers and contractors to submit requests for financial assistance under this subtitle.

(2) DEADLINE FOR IMMEDIATE PAYROLL ASSISTANCE.—Not later than 10 days after the date of enactment of this Act, the Secretary shall make initial payments to air carriers and contractors that submit requests for financial assistance approved by to the Secretary.

(3) SUBSEQUENT PAYMENTS.—The Secretary shall determine an appropriate method for timely distribution of payments to air carriers and contractors with approved requests for financial assistance from any funds remaining available after providing initial financial assistance payments under paragraph (2).

(c) PRO RATA AUTHORITY.—The Secretary shall have the authority to reduce, on a pro rata basis, the amounts due to air carriers and contractors under the applicable paragraph of section 4112 in order to address any shortfall in assistance that would otherwise be provided under such section.

(d) AUDITS.—The Inspector General of the Department of the Treasury shall audit certifications made under subsection (a).

[¶2219] SEC. 4114. REQUIRED ASSURANCES.

(a) IN GENERAL.—To be eligible for financial assistance under this subtitle, an air carrier or contractor shall enter into an agreement with the Secretary, or otherwise certify in such form and manner as the Secretary shall prescribe, that the air carrier or contractor shall—

(1) refrain from conducting involuntary furloughs or reducing pay rates and benefits until September 30, 2020;

(2) through September 30, 2021, ensure that neither the air carrier or contractor nor any affiliate of the air carrier or contractor may, in any transaction, purchase an equity security of the air carrier or contractor or the parent company of the air carrier or contractor that is listed on a national securities exchange;

(3) through September 30, 2021, ensure that the air carrier or contractor shall not pay dividends, or make other capital distributions, with respect to the common stock (or equivalent interest) of the air carrier or contractor; and

(4) meet the requirements of sections 4115 and 4116.

(b) DEPARTMENT OF TRANSPORTATION AUTHORITY TO CONDITION ASSISTANCE ON CONTINUATION OF SERVICE.—

(1) IN GENERAL.—The Secretary of Transportation is authorized to require, to the extent reasonable and practicable, an air carrier provided financial assistance under this subtitle to maintain scheduled air transportation service, as the Secretary of Transportation deems necessary, to ensure services to any point served by that carrier before March 1, 2020.

(2) REQUIRED CONSIDERATIONS.—When considering whether to exercise the authority provided by this section, the Secretary of Transportation shall take into consideration the air transportation needs of small and remote communities and the need to maintain well-functioning health care supply chains, including medical devices and supplies, and pharmaceutical supply chains.

(3) SUNSET.—The authority provided under this subsection shall terminate on March 1, 2022, and any requirements issued by the Secretary of Transportation under this subsection shall cease to apply after that date.

[¶2220] SEC. 4115. PROTECTION OF COLLECTIVE BARGAINING AGREEMENT.

(a) IN GENERAL.—Neither the Secretary, nor any other actor, department, or agency of the Federal Government, shall condition the issuance of financial assistance under this subtitle on an air carrier's or contractor's implementation of measures to enter into negotiations with the certified bargaining representative of a craft or class of employees of the air carrier or contractor under the Railway Labor Act (45 U.S.C. 151 et seq.) or the National Labor Relations Act (29 U.S.C. 151 et seq.), regarding pay or other terms and conditions of employment.

(b) PERIOD OF EFFECT.—With respect to an air carrier or contractor to which financial assistance is provided under this subtitle, this section shall be in effect with respect to the air carrier or contractor beginning on the date on which the air carrier or contractor is first issued such financial assistance and ending on September 30, 2020.

[¶2221] SEC. 4116. LIMITATION ON CERTAIN EMPLOYEE COMPENSATION.

(a) IN GENERAL.—The Secretary may only provide financial assistance under this subtitle to an air carrier or contractor after such carrier or contractor enters into an agreement with the Secretary which provides that, during the 2-year period beginning March 24, 2020, and ending March 24, 2022, no officer or employee of the air carrier or contractor whose total compensation exceeded $425,000 in calendar year 2019 (other than an employee whose compensation is determined through an existing collective bargaining agreement entered into prior to enactment of this Act)—

(1) will receive from the air carrier or contractor total compensation which exceeds, during any 12 consecutive months of such 2-year period, the total compensation received by the officer or employee from the air carrier or contractor in calendar year 2019;

(2) will receive from the air carrier or contractor severance pay or other benefits upon termination of employment with the air carrier or contractor which exceeds twice the maximum total compensation received by the officer or employee from the air carrier or contractor in calendar year 2019; and

(3) no officer or employee of the eligible business whose total compensation exceeded $3,000,000 in calendar year 2019 may receive during any 12 consecutive months of such period total compensation in excess of the sum of—

(A) $3,000,000; and

(B) 50 percent of the excess over $3,000,000 of the total compensation received by the officer or employee from the eligible business in calendar year 2019.

(b) TOTAL COMPENSATION DEFINED.—In this section, the term "total compensation" includes salary, bonuses, awards of stock, and other financial benefits provided by an air carrier or contractor to an officer or employee of the air carrier or contractor.

[¶2222] SEC. 4117. TAX PAYER PROTECTION.

The Secretary may receive warrants, options, preferred stock, debt securities, notes, or other financial instruments issued by recipients of financial assistance under this subtitle which, in the sole determination of the Secretary, provide appropriate compensation to the Federal Government for the provision of the financial assistance.

[¶2223] SEC. 4118. REPORTS.

(a) REPORT.—Not later than November 1, 2020, the Secretary shall submit to the Committee on Transportation and Infrastructure and the Committee on Financial Services of the House of Representatives and the Committee on Commerce, Science, and Transportation and the Committee on Banking, Housing, and Urban Affairs of the Senate a report on the financial assistance provided to air carriers and contractors under this subtitle, including a description of any financial assistance provided.

(b) UPDATE.—Not later than the last day of the 1-year period following the date of enactment of this Act, the Secretary shall update and submit to the Committee on Transportation and the Committee on Financial Services and Infrastructure of the House of Representatives and the Committee on Commerce, Science, and Transportation and the Committee on Banking, Housing, and Urban Affairs of the Senate the report described in subsection (a).

[¶2224] SEC. 4119. COORDINATION.

In implementing this subtitle the Secretary shall coordinate with the Secretary of Transportation.

[¶2225] SEC. 4120. DIRECT APPROPRIATION.

Notwithstanding any other provision of law, there is appropriated, out of amounts in the Treasury not otherwise appropriated, $32,000,000,000 to carry out this subtitle.

TITLE V—CORONAVIRUS RELIEF FUNDS

[¶2226] SEC. 5001. CORONAVIRUS RELIEF FUND.

(a) IN GENERAL.—The Social Security Act (42 U.S.C. 301 et seq.) is amended by inserting after title V the following:

"TITLE VI—CORONAVIRUS RELIEF FUND

[¶2227] SEC. 601. "CORONAVIRUS RELIEF FUND.

(a) "APPROPRIATION.—

(1) "IN GENERAL.—Out of any money in the Treasury of the United States not otherwise appropriated, there are appropriated for making payments to States, Tribal governments, and units of local government under this section, $150,000,000,000 for fiscal year 2020.

(2) "RESERVATION OF FUNDS.—Of the amount appropriated under paragraph (1), the Secretary shall reserve—

(A) "$3,000,000,000 of such amount for making payments to the District of Columbia, the Commonwealth of Puerto Rico, the United States Virgin Islands, Guam, the Commonwealth of the Northern Mariana Islands, and American Samoa; and

(B) "$8,000,000,000 of such amount for making payments to Tribal governments.

(b) "AUTHORITY TO MAKE PAYMENTS.—

(1) "IN GENERAL.—Subject to paragraph (2), not later than 30 days after the date of enactment of this section, the Secretary shall pay each State and Tribal government, and each unit of local government that meets the condition described in paragraph (2), the amount determined for the State, Tribal government, or unit of local government, for fiscal year 2020 under subsection (c).

(2) "DIRECT PAYMENTS TO UNITS OF LOCAL GOVERNMENT.—If a unit of local government of a State submits the certification required by subsection (e) for purposes of receiving a direct payment from the Secretary under the authority of this paragraph, the Secretary shall reduce the amount determined for that State by the relative unit of local government population proportion amount described in subsection (c)(5) and pay such amount directly to such unit of local government.

(c) "PAYMENT AMOUNTS.—

(1) "IN GENERAL.—Subject to paragraph (2), the amount paid under this section for fiscal year 2020 to a State that is 1 of the 50 States shall be the amount equal to the relative population proportion amount determined for the State under paragraph (3) for such fiscal year.

(2) "MINIMUM PAYMENT.—

(A) "IN GENERAL.—No State that is 1 of the 50 States shall receive a payment under this section for fiscal year 2020 that is less than $1,250,000,000.

(B) "PRO RATA ADJUSTMENTS.—The Secretary shall adjust on a pro rata basis the amount of the payments for each of the 50 States determined under this subsection without regard to this subparagraph to the extent necessary to comply with the requirements of subparagraph (A).

(3) "RELATIVE POPULATION PROPORTION AMOUNT.—For purposes of paragraph (1), the relative population proportion amount determined under this paragraph for a State for fiscal year 2020 is the product of—

(A) "the amount appropriated under paragraph (1) of subsection (a) for fiscal year 2020 that remains after the application of paragraph (2) of that subsection; and

(B) "the relative State population proportion (as defined in paragraph (4)).

(4) "RELATIVE STATE POPULATION PROPORTION DEFINED.—For purposes of paragraph (3)(B), the term 'relative State population proportion' means, with respect to a State, the quotient of—

(A) "the population of the State; and

(B) "the total population of all States (excluding the District of Columbia and territories specified in subsection (a)(2)(A)).

(5) "RELATIVE UNIT OF LOCAL GOVERNMENT POPULATION PROPORTION AMOUNT.—For purposes of subsection (b)(2), the term 'relative unit of local government population proportion amount' means, with respect to a unit of local government and a State, the amount equal to the product of—

(A) "45 percent of the amount of the payment determined for the State under this subsection (without regard to this paragraph); and

(B) "the amount equal to the quotient of—

(i) "the population of the unit of local government; and

(ii) "the total population of the State in which the unit of local government is located.

(6) "DISTRICT OF COLUMBIA AND TERRITORIES.—The amount paid under this section for fiscal year 2020 to a State that is the District of Columbia or a territory specified in subsection (a)(2)(A) shall be the amount equal to the product of—

(A) "the amount set aside under subsection (a)(2)(A) for such fiscal year; and

(B) "each such District's and territory's share of the combined total population of the District of Columbia and all such territories, as determined by the Secretary.

(7) "TRIBAL GOVERNMENTS.—From the amount set aside under subsection (a)(2)(B) for fiscal year 2020, the amount paid under this section for fiscal year 2020 to a Tribal government shall be the amount the Secretary shall determine, in consultation with the Secretary of the Interior and Indian Tribes, that is based on increased expenditures of each such Tribal government (or a tribally-owned entity of such Tribal government) relative to aggregate expenditures in fiscal year 2019 by the Tribal government (or tribally-owned entity) and determined in such manner as the Secretary determines appropriate to ensure that all amounts available under subsection (a)(2)(B) for fiscal year 2020 are distributed to Tribal governments.

(8) "DATA.—For purposes of this subsection, the population of States and units of local governments shall be determined based on the most recent year for which data are available from the Bureau of the Census.

(d) "USE OF FUNDS.—A State, Tribal government, and unit of local government shall use the funds provided under a payment made under this section to cover only those costs of the State, Tribal government, or unit of local government that—

(1) "are necessary expenditures incurred due to the public health emergency with respect to the Coronavirus Disease 2019 (COVID–19);

(2) "were not accounted for in the budget most recently approved as of the date of enactment of this section for the State or government; and

(3) "were incurred during the period that begins on March 1, 2020, and ends on December 30, 2020.

(e) "CERTIFICATION.—In order to receive a payment under this section, a unit of local government shall provide the Secretary with a certification signed by the Chief Executive for the unit of local government that the local government's proposed uses of the funds are consistent with subsection (d).

(f) "INSPECTOR GENERAL OVERSIGHT; RECOUPMENT.—

(1) "OVERSIGHT AUTHORITY.—The Inspector General of the Department of the Treasury shall conduct monitoring and oversight of the receipt, disbursement, and use of funds made available under this section.

(2) "RECOUPMENT.—If the Inspector General of the Department of the Treasury determines that a State, Tribal government, or unit of local government has failed to comply with subsection (d), the amount equal to the amount of funds used in violation of such subsection shall be booked as a debt of such entity owed to the Federal Government. Amounts recovered under this subsection shall be deposited into the general fund of the Treasury.

(3) "APPROPRIATION.—Out of any money in the Treasury of the United States not otherwise appropriated, there are appropriated to the Office of the Inspector General of the Department of the Treasury, $35,000,000 to carry out oversight and recoupment activities under this subsection. Amounts appropriated under the preceding sentence shall remain available until expended.

(4) "AUTHORITY OF INSPECTOR GENERAL.—Nothing in this subsection shall be construed to diminish the authority of any Inspector General, including such authority as provided in the Inspector General Act of 1978 (5 U.S.C. App.).

(g) "DEFINITIONS.—In this section:

(1) "INDIAN TRIBE.—The term 'Indian Tribe' has the meaning given that term in section 4(e) of the Indian Self-Determination and Education Assistance Act (25 U.S.C. 5304(e)).

(2) "LOCAL GOVERNMENT.—The term 'unit of local government' means a county, municipality, town, township, village, parish, borough, or other unit of general government below the State level with a population that exceeds 500,000.

(3) "SECRETARY.—The term 'Secretary' means the Secretary of the Treasury.

(4) "STATE.—The term 'State' means the 50 States, the District of Columbia, the Commonwealth of Puerto Rico, the United States Virgin Islands, Guam, the Commonwealth of the Northern Mariana Islands, and American Samoa.

(5) "TRIBAL GOVERNMENT.—The term 'Tribal government' means the recognized governing body of an Indian Tribe.".

(b) APPLICATION OF PROVISIONS.—Amounts appropriated for fiscal year 2020 under section 601(a)(1) of the Social Security Act (as added by subsection (a)) shall be subject to the requirements contained in Public Law 116–94 for funds for programs authorized under sections 330 through 340 of the Public Health Service Act (42 U.S.C. 254 through 256).

TITLE VI—MISCELLANEOUS PROVISIONS

[¶2229] SEC. 6001. COVID–19 BORROWING AUTHORITY FOR THE UNITED STATES POSTAL SERVICE.

(a) DEFINITIONS.—In this section—

(1) the term "COVID–19 emergency" means the emergency involving Federal primary responsibility determined to exist by the President under section 501(b) of the Robert T. Stafford Disaster Relief and Emergency Assistance Act (42 U.S.C. 5191(b)) with respect to the Coronavirus Disease 2019 (COVID–19); and

(2) the term "Postal Service" means the United States Postal Service.

(b) ADDITIONAL BORROWING AUTHORITY.—Notwithstanding section 2005 of title 39, United States Code, or any other provision of law, if the Postal Service determines that, due to the COVID–19 emergency, the Postal Service will not be able to fund operating expenses without borrowing money—

(1) the Postal Service may borrow money from the Treasury in an amount not to exceed $10,000,000,000—

(A) to be used for such operating expenses; and

(B) which may not be used to pay any outstanding debt of the Postal Service; and

(2) the Secretary of the Treasury may lend up to the amount described in paragraph (1) at the request of the Postal Service, upon terms and conditions mutually agreed upon by the Secretary and the Postal Service.

(c) PRIORITIZATION OF DELIVERY FOR MEDICAL PURPOSES DURING COVID–19 EMERGENCY.—Notwithstanding any other provision of law, during the COVID–19 emergency, the Postal Service—

(1) shall prioritize delivery of postal products for medical purposes; and

(2) may establish temporary delivery points, in such form and manner as the Postal Service determines necessary, to protect employees of the Postal Service and individuals receiving deliveries from the Postal Service.

[¶2230] SEC. 6002. EMERGENCY DESIGNATION.

(a) IN GENERAL.—The amounts provided under this division are designated as an emergency requirement pursuant to section 4(g) of the Statutory Pay-As-You-Go Act of 2010 (2 U.S.C. 933(g)).

(b) DESIGNATION IN SENATE.—In the Senate, this division is designated as an emergency requirement pursuant to section 4112(a) of H. Con. Res. 71 (115th Congress), the concurrent resolution on the budget for fiscal year 2018.

DIVISION B—EMERGENCY APPROPRIATIONS FOR CORONAVIRUS HEALTH RESPONSE AND AGENCY OPERATIONS

The following sums are hereby are appropriated, out of any money in the Treasury not otherwise appropriated, for the fiscal year ending September 30, 2020, and for other purposes, namely:

TITLE I AGRICULTURAL PROGRAMS

Office of the Secretary

For an additional amount for the "Office of the Secretary", $9,500,000,000, to remain available until expended, to prevent, prepare for, and respond to coronavirus by providing support for agricultural producers impacted by coronavirus, including producers of specialty crops, producers that supply local food systems, including farmers markets, restaurants, and schools, and livestock producers, including dairy producers: Provided, That such amount is designated by the Congress as being for an emergency requirement pursuant to section 251(b)(2)(A)(i) of the Balanced Budget and Emergency Deficit Control Act of 1985.

Office of Inspector General

For an additional amount for "Office of Inspector General", $750,000, to remain available until September 30, 2021, to prevent, prepare for, and respond to coronavirus, domestically or internationally: Provided, That the funding made available under this heading in this Act shall be used for conducting audits and investigations of projects and activities carried out with funds made available in this Act to the Department of Agriculture to prevent, prepare for, and respond to coronavirus, domestically or internationally: Provided further, That such amount is designated by the Congress as being for an emergency requirement pursuant to section 251(b)(2)(A)(i) of the Balanced Budget and Emergency Deficit Control Act of 1985.

Animal and Plant Health Inspection Service

SALARIES AND EXPENSES

For an additional amount for "Salaries and Expenses", $55,000,000, to remain available until September 30, 2021, to prevent, prepare for, and respond to coronavirus, domestically or internationally, including for necessary expenses for salary costs associated with the Agriculture Quarantine and Inspection Program: Provided, That such amount is designated by the Congress as being for an emergency requirement pursuant to section 251(b)(2)(A)(i) of the Balanced Budget and Emergency Deficit Control Act of 1985.

Agricultural Marketing Service

MARKETING SERVICES

For an additional amount for "Marketing Services", $45,000,000, to remain available until September 30, 2021, to prevent, prepare for, and respond to coronavirus, domestically or internationally, including necessary expenses for salary costs associated with commodity grading, inspection, and audit activities: Provided, That such amount is designated by the Congress as being for an emergency requirement pursuant to section 251(b)(2)(A)(i) of the Balanced Budget and Emergency Deficit Control Act of 1985.

Food Safety and Inspection Service

For an additional amount for "Food Safety and Inspection Service", $33,000,000, to remain available until September 30, 2021, to prevent, prepare for, and respond to coronavirus, domestically or internationally, including for support of temporary and intermittent workers, relocation of inspectors, and, notwithstanding 21 U.S.C. 468, 695 and 1053 and 7 U.S.C. 2219a, costs of overtime inspectors under the Federal Meat Inspection Act, the Poultry Products Inspection Act, and the Egg Products Inspection Act: Provided, That such amount is designated by the Congress as being for an emergency requirement pursuant to section 251(b)(2)(A)(i) of the Balanced Budget and Emergency Deficit Control Act of 1985.

FARM PRODUCTION AND CONSERVATION PROGRAMS

Farm Service Agency

For an additional amount for "Salaries and Expenses", $3,000,000, to remain available until September 30, 2021, to prevent, prepare for, and respond to coronavirus, domestically or internationally, including necessary expenses to hire temporary staff and overtime expenses: Provided, That

such amount is designated by the Congress as being for an emergency requirement pursuant to section 251(b)(2)(A)(i) of the Balanced Budget and Emergency Deficit Control Act of 1985.

RURAL DEVELOPMENT PROGRAMS

RURAL BUSINESS—COOPERATIVE SERVICE

RURAL BUSINESS PROGRAM ACCOUNT

For an additional amount for "Rural Business Program Account", $20,500,000, to remain available until September 30, 2021, to prevent, prepare for, and respond to coronavirus, for the cost of loans for rural business development programs authorized by section 310B and described in subsection (g) of section 310B of the Consolidated Farm and Rural Development Act:Provided, That such amount is designated by the Congress as being for an emergency requirement pursuant to section 251(b)(2)(A)(i) of the Balanced Budget and Emergency Deficit Control Act of 1985.

RURAL UTILITIES SERVICE

DISTANCE LEARNING, TELEMEDICINE, AND BROADBAND PROGRAM

For an additional amount for "Distance Learning, Telemedicine, and Broadband Program", $25,000,000, to remain available until expended, to prevent, prepare for, and respond to coronavirus, domestically or internationally, for telemedicine and distance learning services in rural areas, as authorized by 7 U.S.C. 950aaa et seq.: Provided, That such amount is designated by the Congress as being for an emergency requirement pursuant to section 251(b)(2)(A)(i) of the Balanced Budget and Emergency Deficit Control Act of 1985.

DOMESTIC FOOD PROGRAMS

FOOD AND NUTRITION SERVICE

CHILD NUTRITION PROGRAMS

For an additional amount for "Child Nutrition Programs", $8,800,000,000 to remain available until September 30, 2021, to prevent, prepare for, and respond to coronavirus, domestically or internationally: Provided, That such amount is designated by the Congress as being for an emergency requirement pursuant to section 251(b)(2)(A)(i) of the Balanced Budget and Emergency Deficit Control Act of 1985.

SUPPLEMENTAL NUTRITION ASSISTANCE PROGRAM

For an additional amount for "Supplemental Nutrition Assistance Program", $15,810,000,000, to remain available until September 30, 2021, to prevent, prepare for, and respond to coronavirus, domestically or internationally: Provided, That of the amount provided under this heading in this Act, $15,510,000,000 shall be placed in a contingency reserve to be allocated as the Secretary deems necessary to support participation should cost or participation exceed budget estimates to prevent, prepare for, and respond to coronavirus: Provided further, That of the amount provided under this heading in this Act, $100,000,000 shall be for the food distribution program on Indian reservations program as authorized by Section 4(b) of the Food and Nutrition Act of 2008 (7 U.S.C. 2013) and Section 4(a) of the Agriculture and Consumer Protection Act of 1973 (7 U.S.C. 1431) to prevent, prepare for, and respond to coronavirus, of which $50,000,000 shall be for facility improvements and equipment upgrades and of which $50,000,000 shall be for the costs relating to additional food purchases: Provided further, That of the amount provided under this heading in this Act, $200,000,000 to remain available through September 30, 2021, shall be available for the Secretary of Agriculture to provide grants to the Commonwealth of the Northern Mariana Islands, Puerto Rico, and American Samoa for nutrition assistance to prevent, prepare for, and respond to coronavirus, domestically or internationally: Provided further, That such amount is designated by the Congress as being for an emergency requirement pursuant to section 251(b)(2)(A)(i) of the Balanced Budget and Emergency Deficit Control Act of 1985.

COMMODITY ASSISTANCE PROGRAM

For an additional amount for "Commodity Assistance Program", $450,000,000, to remain available through September 30, 2021, to prevent, prepare for, and respond to coronavirus, domestically or internationally, for the emergency food assistance program as authorized by section 27(a) of the Food and Nutrition Act of 2008 (7 U.S.C. 2036(a)) and section 204(a)(1) of the Emergency Food Assistance Act of 1983 (7 U.S.C. 7508(a)(1)): Provided, That of the funds made available, the Secretary may use up to $150,000,000 for costs associated with the distribution of commodities: Provided further, That

such amount is designated by the Congress as being for an emergency requirement pursuant to section 251(b)(2)(A)(i) of the Balanced Budget and Emergency Deficit Control Act of 1985.

FOREIGN ASSISTANCE AND RELATED PROGRAMS

FOREIGN AGRICULTURAL SERVICE

SALARIES AND EXPENSES

For an additional amount for "Salaries and Expenses", $4,000,000, to remain available until September 30, 2021, to prevent, prepare for, and respond to coronavirus, domestically or internationally, including necessary expenses to relocate employees and their dependents back from overseas posts: Provided, That such amount is designated by the Congress as being for an emergency requirement pursuant to section 251(b)(2)(A)(i) of the Balanced Budget and Emergency Deficit Control Act of 1985.

RELATED AGENCIES AND FOOD AND DRUG ADMINISTRATION

DEPARTMENT OF HEALTH AND HUMAN SERVICES

FOOD AND DRUG ADMINISTRATION

SALARIES AND EXPENSES

For an additional amount for "Salaries and Expenses", $80,000,000, to remain available until expended, to prevent, prepare for, and respond to coronavirus, domestically or internationally, including funds for the development of necessary medical countermeasures and vaccines, advanced manufacturing for medical products, the monitoring of medical product supply chains, and related administrative activities: Provided, That such amount is designated by the Congress as being for an emergency requirement pursuant to section 251(b)(2)(A)(i) of the Balanced Budget and Emergency Deficit Control Act of 1985.

GENERAL PROVISIONS—THIS TITLE

(INCLUDING TRANSFER OF FUNDS)

SEC. 11001. Of the funds made available to the Rural Development mission area in this title, and in addition to funds otherwise made available for such purpose, not more than 3 percent may be used for administrative costs to carry out loan, loan guarantee and grant activities funded in this title to prevent, prepare for, and respond to coronavirus, domestically or internationally: Provided, That such funds shall be transferred to, and merged with, the appropriation for "Rural Development, Salaries and Expenses" and, once transferred, shall be used only to prevent, prepare for, and respond to coronavirus, domestically or internationally: Provided further, that this transfer authority is in addition to any other transfer authority provided by law.

COMMODITY CREDIT CORPORATION

REIMBURSEMENT OF PRESENT NET REALIZED LOSSES

SEC. 11002. Of the amounts provided in the Further Consolidated Appropriations Act, 2020 (Public Law 116–94) under the heading "Commodity Credit Corporation Fund—Reimbursement for Net Realized Losses", $14,000,000,000, may be used, prior to the completion of the report described in 15 U.S.C. 713a–11, to reimburse the Commodity Credit Corporation for net realized losses sustained, but not previously reimbursed, as reflected in the June 2020 report of its financial condition: Provided, That such amount is designated by the Congress as being for an emergency requirement pursuant to section 251(b)(2)(A)(i) of the Balanced Budget and Emergency Deficit Control Act of 1985.

SEC. 11003. The Secretary may extend the term of a marketing assistance loan authorized by section 1201 of the Agricultural Act of 2014 (7 U.S.C. 9033) for any loan commodity to 12 months: Provided, That the authority made available pursuant to this section shall expire on September 30, 2020: Provided further, That the amount provided by this section is designated by the Congress as being for an emergency requirement pursuant to section 251(b)(2)(A)(i) of the Balanced Budget and Emergency Deficit Control Act of 1985.

SEC. 11004. For an additional amount for grants under the pilot program established under section 779 of Public Law 115–141, to prevent, prepare for, and respond to coronavirus, $100,000,000, to remain available until September 30, 2021: Provided, That at least 90 percent of the households to be served by a project receiving a grant shall be in a rural area without sufficient access to broadband: Provided further, That for purposes of such pilot program, a rural area without sufficient access to broadband shall be defined as 10 Mbps downstream and 1 Mbps upstream, and such definition shall be reevaluated and redefined, as necessary, on an annual basis by the Secretary of Agriculture:

Provided further, That an entity to which a grant is made under the pilot program shall not use a grant to overbuild or duplicate broadband expansion efforts made by any entity that has received a broadband loan from the Rural Utilities Service: Provided further, That priority consideration for grants shall be given to previous applicants now eligible as a result of adjusted eligibility requirements: Provided further, That such amount is designated by the Congress as being for an emergency requirement pursuant to section 251(b)(2)(A)(i) of the Balanced Budget and Emergency Deficit Control Act of 1985.

TITLE II DEPARTMENT OF COMMERCE

Economic Development Administration

ECONOMIC DEVELOPMENT ASSISTANCE PROGRAMS

(INCLUDING TRANSFERS OF FUNDS)

Pursuant to section 703 of the Public Works and Economic Development Act (42 U.S.C. 3233), for an additional amount for "Economic Development Assistance Programs", $1,500,000,000, to remain available until September 30, 2022, to prevent, prepare for, and respond to coronavirus, domestically or internationally, including for necessary expenses for responding to economic injury as a result of coronavirus: Provided, That such amount shall be for economic adjustment assistance as authorized by section 209 of the Public Works and Economic Development Act of 1965 (42 U.S.C. 3149): Provided further, That within the amount appropriated under this heading in this Act, up to 2 percent of funds may be transferred to the "Salaries and Expenses" account for administration and oversight activities related to preventing, preparing for, and responding to coronavirus: Provided further, That the Secretary of Commerce is authorized to appoint and fix the compensation of such temporary personnel as may be necessary to implement the requirements under this heading in this Act to prevent, prepare for, and respond to coronavirus, without regard to the provisions of title 5, United States Code, governing appointments in competitive service: Provided further, That the Secretary of Commerce is authorized to appoint such temporary personnel, after serving continuously for 2 years, to positions in the Economic Development Administration in the same manner that competitive service employees with competitive status are considered for transfer, reassignment, or promotion to such positions and an individual appointed under this provision shall become a career-conditional employee, unless the employee has already completed the service requirements for career tenure: Provided further, That within the amount appropriated under this heading in this Act, $3,000,000 shall be transferred to the "Office of Inspector General" account for carrying out investigations and audits related to the funding provided to prevent, prepare for, and respond to coronavirus under this heading in this Act: Provided further, That such amount is designated by the Congress as being for an emergency requirement pursuant to section 251(b)(2)(A)(i) of the Balanced Budget and Emergency Deficit Control Act of 1985.

National Institute of Standards and Technology

SCIENTIFIC AND TECHNICAL RESEARCH AND SERVICES

For an additional amount for "Scientific and Technical Research and Services", $6,000,000, to remain available until September, 30, 2021, to prevent, prepare for, and respond to coronavirus, domestically or internationally, by supporting continuity of operations, including measurement science to support viral testing and biomanufacturing: Provided, That such amount is designated by the Congress as being for an emergency requirement pursuant to section 251(b)(2)(A)(i) of the Balanced Budget and Emergency Deficit Control Act of 1985.

INDUSTRIAL TECHNOLOGY SERVICES

For an additional amount for "Industrial Technology Services", $60,000,000, to remain available until September 30, 2021, to prevent, prepare for, and respond to coronavirus, domestically or internationally: Provided, That of the amount provided under this heading in this Act, $50,000,000 shall be for the Hollings Manufacturing Extension Partnership to assist manufacturers to prevent, prepare for, and respond to coronavirus and $10,000,000 shall be for the National Network for Manufacturing Innovation (also known as "Manufacturing USA") to prevent, prepare for, and respond to coronavirus, including to support development and manufacturing of medical countermeasures and biomedical equipment and supplies: Provided further, That none of the funds provided under this heading in this Act shall be subject to cost share requirements under 15 U.S.C. 278k(e)(2) or 15 U.S.C. 278s(e)(7)(A): Provided further, That such amount is designated by the

Congress as being for an emergency requirement pursuant to section 251(b)(2)(A)(i) of the Balanced Budget and Emergency Deficit Control Act of 1985.

NATIONAL OCEANIC AND ATMOSPHERIC ADMINISTRATION

OPERATIONS, RESEARCH, AND FACILITIES

For an additional amount for "Operations, Research, and Facilities", $20,000,000, to remain available until September, 30, 2021, to prevent, prepare for, and respond to coronavirus, domestically or internationally, by supporting continuity of operations, including National Weather Service life and property related operations: Provided, That such amount is designated by the Congress as being for an emergency requirement pursuant to section 251(b)(2)(A)(i) of the Balanced Budget and Emergency Deficit Control Act of 1985.

DEPARTMENT OF JUSTICE

GENERAL ADMINISTRATION

JUSTICE INFORMATION SHARING TECHNOLOGY

For an additional amount for "Justice Information Sharing Technology", $2,000,000, to remain available until expended, to prevent, prepare for, and respond to coronavirus, domestically or internationally, including the impact of coronavirus on the work of the Department of Justice: Provided, That such amount is designated by the Congress as being for an emergency requirement pursuant to section 251(b)(2)(A)(i) of the Balanced Budget and Emergency Deficit Control Act of 1985.

OFFICE OF INSPECTOR GENERAL

For an additional amount for "Office of Inspector General", $2,000,000, to remain available until expended to prevent, prepare for, and respond to coronavirus, domestically or internationally, including the impact of coronavirus on the work of the Department of Justice and to carry out investigations and audits related to the funding made available for the Department of Justice in this Act: Provided, That such amount is designated by the Congress as being for an emergency requirement pursuant to section 251(b)(2)(A)(i) of the Balanced Budget and Emergency Deficit Control Act of 1985.

LEGAL ACTIVITIES

SALARIES AND EXPENSES, UNITED STATES ATTORNEYS

For an additional amount for "Salaries and Expenses, United States Attorneys", $3,000,000, to prevent, prepare for, and respond to coronavirus, domestically or internationally, including the impact of coronavirus on the work of the Department of Justice: Provided, That such amount is designated by the Congress as being for an emergency requirement pursuant to section 251(b)(2)(A)(i) of the Balanced Budget and Emergency Deficit Control Act of 1985.

UNITED STATES MARSHALS SERVICE

SALARIES AND EXPENSES

For an additional amount for "United States Marshals Service, Salaries and Expenses", $15,000,000, to prevent, prepare for, and respond to coronavirus, domestically or internationally, including the impact of coronavirus on the work of the Department of Justice: Provided, That such amount is designated by the Congress as being for an emergency requirement pursuant to section 251(b)(2)(A)(i) of the Balanced Budget and Emergency Deficit Control Act of 1985.

FEDERAL BUREAU OF INVESTIGATION

SALARIES AND EXPENSES

For an additional amount for "Federal Bureau of Investigation, Salaries and Expenses", $20,000,000, to prevent, prepare for, and respond to coronavirus, domestically or internationally, including the impact of coronavirus on the work of the Department of Justice: Provided, That such amount is designated by the Congress as being for an emergency requirement pursuant to section 251(b)(2)(A)(i) of the Balanced Budget and Emergency Deficit Control Act of 1985.

DRUG ENFORCEMENT ADMINISTRATION

SALARIES AND EXPENSES

For an additional amount for "Drug Enforcement Administration, Salaries and Expenses", $15,000,000, to prevent, prepare for, and respond to coronavirus, domestically or internationally, including the impact of coronavirus on the work of the Department of Justice: Provided, That such amount is designated by the Congress as being for an emergency requirement pursuant to section 251(b)(2)(A)(i) of the Balanced Budget and Emergency Deficit Control Act of 1985.

FEDERAL PRISON SYSTEM

SALARIES AND EXPENSES

For an additional amount for "Federal Prison System, Salaries and Expenses", $100,000,000, to prevent, prepare for, and respond to coronavirus, domestically or internationally, including the impact of coronavirus on the work of the Department of Justice: Provided, That such amount is designated by the Congress as being for an emergency requirement pursuant to section 251(b)(2)(A)(i) of the Balanced Budget and Emergency Deficit Control Act of 1985.

STATE AND LOCAL LAW ENFORCEMENT ACTIVITIES

OFFICE OF JUSTICE PROGRAMS

STATE AND LOCAL LAW ENFORCEMENT ASSISTANCE

For an additional amount for "State and Local Law Enforcement Assistance", $850,000,000, to remain available until expended, to prevent, prepare for, and respond to coronavirus, domestically or internationally, to be awarded pursuant to the formula allocation (adjusted in proportion to the relative amounts statutorily designated therefor) that was used in fiscal year 2019 for the Edward Byrne Memorial Justice Assistance Grant program as authorized by subpart 1 of part E of title I of the Omnibus Crime Control and Safe Streets Acts of 1968 ("1968 Act"): Provided, That the allocation provisions under sections 505(a) through (e) and the special rules for Puerto Rico under section 505(g), and section 1001(c), of the 1968 Act, shall not apply to the amount provided under this heading in this Act: Provided further, That awards hereunder, shall not be subject to restrictions or special conditions that are the same as (or substantially similar to) those, imposed on awards under such subpart in fiscal year 2018, that forbid interference with Federal law enforcement: Provided further, That such amount is designated by the Congress as being for an emergency requirement pursuant to section 251(b)(2)(A)(i) of the Balanced Budget and Emergency Deficit Control Act of 1985.

SCIENCE

NATIONAL AERONAUTICS AND SPACE ADMINISTRATION

SAFETY, SECURITY AND MISSION SERVICES

For an additional amount for "Safety, Security and Mission Services", $60,000,000, to remain available until September 30, 2021, to prevent, prepare for, and respond to coronavirus, domestically or internationally: Provided, That such amount is designated by the Congress as being for an emergency requirement pursuant to section 251(b)(2)(A)(i) of the Balanced Budget and Emergency Deficit Control Act of 1985.

NATIONAL SCIENCE FOUNDATION

RESEARCH AND RELATED ACTIVITIES

For an additional amount for "Research and Related Activities", $75,000,000, to remain available until September 30, 2021, to prevent, prepare for, and respond to coronavirus, domestically or internationally, including to fund research grants and other necessary expenses: Provided, That such amount is designated by the Congress as being for an emergency requirement pursuant to section 251(b)(2)(A)(i) of the Balanced Budget and Emergency Deficit Control Act of 1985.

AGENCY OPERATIONS AND AWARD MANAGEMENT

For an additional amount for "Agency Operations and Award Management", $1,000,000, to prevent, prepare for, and respond to coronavirus, domestically or internationally, including to administer research grants and other necessary expenses: Provided, That such amount is designated by the Congress as being for an emergency requirement pursuant to section 251(b)(2)(A)(i) of the Balanced Budget and Emergency Deficit Control Act of 1985.

RELATED AGENCIES

LEGAL SERVICES CORPORATION

PAYMENT TO THE LEGAL SERVICES CORPORATION

For an additional amount for "Payment to the Legal Services Corporation", $50,000,000, to prevent, prepare for, and respond to coronavirus, domestically or internationally: Provided, That none of the funds appropriated under this heading in this Act to the Legal Services Corporation shall be expended for any purpose prohibited or limited by, or contrary to any of the provisions of, sections 501, 502, 503, 504, 505, and 506 of Public Law 105–119, and all funds appropriated in this Act to the Legal Services Corporation shall be subject to the same terms and conditions set forth in such sections, except that all references in sections 502 and 503 to 1997 and 1998 shall be deemed to refer instead to 2019 and 2020, respectively, and except that sections 501 and 503 of Public Law 104–134 (referenced by Public Law 105–119) shall not apply to the amount made available under this heading: Provided further, That for the purposes of this Act, the Legal Services Corporation shall be considered an agency of the United States Government: Provided further, That such amount is designated by the Congress as being for an emergency requirement pursuant to section 251(b)(2)(A)(i) of the Balanced Budget and Emergency Deficit Control Act of 1985.

GENERAL PROVISIONS—THIS TITLE

SEC. 12001. Amounts provided by the Consolidated Appropriations Act, 2020, (Public Law 116–93) for the Hollings Manufacturing Extension Partnership under the heading "National Institute of Standards and Technology—Industrial Technology Services" shall not be subject to cost share requirements under 15 U.S.C. 278k(e)(2): Provided, That the authority made available pursuant to this section shall be elective for any Manufacturing Extension Partnership Center that also receives funding from a State that is conditioned upon the application of a Federal cost sharing requirement.

SEC. 12002. (a) Funds appropriated in this title for the National Science Foundation may be made available to restore amounts, either directly or through reimbursement, for obligations incurred by the National Science Foundation for research grants and other necessary expenses to prevent, prepare for, and respond to coronavirus, domestically or internationally, prior to the date of enactment of this Act.

(b) Grants or cooperative agreements made by the National Science Foundation under this title, to carry out research grants and other necessary expenses to prevent, prepare for, and respond to coronavirus, domestically or internationally, shall include amounts to reimburse costs for these purposes incurred between January 20, 2020, and the date of issuance of such grants or agreements.

BUREAU OF PRISONS

SEC. 12003. (a) DEFINITIONS.—In this section—

(1) the term "Bureau" means the Bureau of Prisons;

(2) the term "covered emergency period" means the period beginning on the date on which the President declared a national emergency under the National Emergencies Act (50 U.S.C. 1601 et seq.) with respect to the Coronavirus Disease 2019 (COVID–19) and ending on the date that is 30 days after the date on which the national emergency declaration terminates; and

(3) the term "Secretary" means the Secretary of Health and Human Services.

(b) SUPPLY OF PERSONAL PROTECTIVE EQUIPMENT AND TEST KITS TO BUREAU OF PRISONS; HOME CONFINEMENT AUTHORITY.—

(1) PERSONAL PROTECTIVE EQUIPMENT AND TEST KITS.—

(A) FINDINGS.—Congress finds the following:

(i) There is an urgent need for personal protective equipment and test kits to the Bureau based on the density of the inmate population, the high traffic, the high volume of inmates, the high rate of turnover of inmates and personnel, and the number of high-security areas, within the facilities of the Bureau.

(ii) The inability of the Bureau to secure the purchase of infectious disease personal protective equipment and related supplies now and in the future is a vulnerability.

(iii) The Bureau is currently competing in and engaging the same landscape of vendors as all other Federal agencies and private entities.

(iv) The ability of the Bureau to purchase needed equipment and supplies is currently subject to an individual manufacturer's specific recognition of the Bureau as a priority and subsequent allocation of the inventory of the manufacturer to the Bureau.

(B) CONSIDERATION.—The Secretary shall appropriately consider, relative to other priorities of the Department of Health and Human Services for high-risk and high-need populations, the distribution of infectious disease personal protective equipment and COVID–19 test kits to the Bureau for use by inmates and personnel of the Bureau.

(2) HOME CONFINEMENT AUTHORITY.—During the covered emergency period, if the Attorney General finds that emergency conditions will materially affect the functioning of the Bureau, the Director of the Bureau may lengthen the maximum amount of time for which the Director is authorized to place a prisoner in home confinement under the first sentence of section 3624(c)(2) of title 18, United States Code, as the Director determines appropriate.

(c) VIDEO VISITATION.—

(1) IN GENERAL.—During the covered emergency period, if the Attorney General finds that emergency conditions will materially affect the functioning of the Bureau, the Director of the Bureau shall promulgate rules regarding the ability of inmates to conduct visitation through video teleconferencing and telephonically, free of charge to inmates, during the covered emergency period.

(2) EXEMPTION FROM NOTICE-AND-COMMENT RULEMAKING REQUIREMENTS.—Section 553 of title 5, United States Code, shall not apply to the promulgation of rules under paragraph (1) of this subsection.

(d) EMERGENCY REQUIREMENT.—The amount provided by this section is designated by the Congress as being for an emergency requirement pursuant to section 251(b)(2)(A)(i) of the Balanced Budget and Emergency Deficit Control Act of 1985.

TEMPORARY AUTHORITY OF DIRECTOR OF THE USPTO DURING THE COVID–19 EMERGENCY.

SEC. 12004. (a) IN GENERAL.—During the emergency period described in subsection (e), the Director may toll, waive, adjust, or modify, any timing deadline established by title 35, United States Code, the Trademark Act, section 18 of the Leahy-Smith America Invents Act (35 U.S.C. 321 note), or regulations promulgated thereunder, in effect during such period, if the Director determines that the emergency related to such period—

(1) materially affects the functioning of the Patent and Trademark Office;

(2) prejudices the rights of applicants, registrants, patent owners, or others appearing before the Office; or

(3) prevents applicants, registrants, patent owners, or others appearing before the Office from filing a document or fee with the Office.

(b) PUBLIC NOTICE.—If the Director determines that tolling, waiving, adjusting, or modifying a timing deadline under subsection (a) is appropriate, the Director shall publish publicly a notice to such effect.

(c) STATEMENT REQUIRED.—Not later than 20 days after the Director tolls, waives, adjusts, or modifies a timing deadline under subsection (a) and such toll, waiver, adjustment, or modification is in effect for a consecutive or cumulative period exceeding 120 days, the Director shall submit to Congress a statement describing the action taken, relevant background, and rationale for the period of tolling, waiver, adjustment, or modification.

(d) OTHER LAWS.—Notwithstanding section 301 of the National Emergencies Act (50 U.S.C. 1631), the authority of the Director under subsection (a) is not contingent on a specification made by the President under such section or any other requirement under that Act (other than the emergency declaration under section 201(a) of such Act (50 U.S.C. 1621(a))). The authority described in this section supersedes the authority of title II of the National Emergencies Act (50 U.S.C. 1621 et seq.).

(e) EMERGENCY PERIOD.—The emergency period described in this subsection includes the duration of the portion of the emergency declared by the President pursuant to the National Emergencies Act on March 13, 2020, as a result of the COVID–19 outbreak (and any renewal thereof) beginning on or after the date of the enactment of this section and the 60 day period following such duration.

(f) RULE OF CONSTRUCTION.—Nothing in this section may be construed as limiting other statutory authorities the Director may have to grant relief regarding filings or deadlines.

(g) SUNSET.—Notwithstanding subsection (a), the authorities provided under this section shall expire upon the expiration of the 2-year period after the date of the enactment of this section.

(h) DEFINITIONS.—In this section:

(1) DIRECTOR.—The term "Director" means the Under Secretary of Commerce for Intellectual Property and Director of the United States Patent and Trademark Office.

(2) TRADEMARK ACT.—The term "Trademark Act" means the Act entitled "An Act to provide for the registration and protection of trademarks used in commerce, to carry out the provisions of certain international conventions, and for other purposes", approved July 5, 1946 (15 U.S.C. 1051 et seq.).

(i) EMERGENCY REQUIREMENT.—The amount provided by this section is designated by the Congress as being for an emergency requirement pursuant to section 251(b)(2)(A)(i) of the Balanced Budget and Emergency Deficit Control Act of 1985.

ASSISTANCE TO FISHERY PARTICIPANTS

SEC. 12005. (a) IN GENERAL.—The Secretary of Commerce is authorized to provide assistance to Tribal, subsistence, commercial, and charter fishery participants affected by the novel coronavirus (COVID–19), which may include direct relief payments.

(b) FISHERY PARTICIPANTS.—For the purposes of this section, "fishery participants" include Tribes, persons, fishing communities, aquaculture businesses not otherwise eligible for assistance under part 1416 of title 7 of the Code of Federal Regulations for losses related to COVID–19, processors, or other fishery-related businesses, who have incurred, as a direct or indirect result of the coronavirus pandemic—

(1) economic revenue losses greater than 35 percent as compared to the prior 5-year average revenue; or

(2) any negative impacts to subsistence, cultural, or ceremonial fisheries.

(c) ROLLING BASIS.—Funds may be awarded under this section on a rolling basis, and within a fishing season, to ensure rapid delivery of funds during the COVID–19 pandemic.

(d) APPROPRIATIONS.—In addition to funds that are otherwise made available to assist fishery participants under this Act, there are authorized to be appropriated, and there are appropriated, $300,000,000, to remain available until September 30, 2021, to carry out this section, of which up to 2 percent may be used for administration and oversight activities.

(e) EMERGENCY REQUIREMENT.—The amount provided by this section is designated by the Congress as being for an emergency requirement pursuant to section 251(b)(2)(A)(i) of the Balanced Budget and Emergency Deficit Control Act of 1985.

TITLE III DEPARTMENT OF DEFENSE MILITARY PERSONNEL

NATIONAL GUARD PERSONNEL, ARMY

For an additional amount for "National Guard Personnel, Army", $746,591,000, to prevent, prepare for, and respond to coronavirus, domestically or internationally: Provided, That such amount is designated by the Congress as being for an emergency requirement pursuant to section 251(b)(2)(A)(i) of the Balanced Budget and Emergency Deficit Control Act of 1985.

NATIONAL GUARD PERSONNEL, AIR FORCE

For an additional amount for "National Guard Personnel, Air Force", $482,125,000, to prevent, prepare for, and respond to coronavirus, domestically or internationally: Provided, That such amount is designated by the Congress as being for an emergency requirement pursuant to section 251(b)(2)(A)(i) of the Balanced Budget and Emergency Deficit Control Act of 1985.

OPERATION AND MAINTENANCE

OPERATION AND MAINTENANCE, ARMY

For an additional amount for "Operation and Maintenance, Army", $160,300,000, to prevent, prepare for, and respond to coronavirus, domestically or internationally: Provided, That such amount is designated by the Congress as being for an emergency requirement pursuant to section 251(b)(2)(A)(i) of the Balanced Budget and Emergency Deficit Control Act of 1985.

OPERATION AND MAINTENANCE, NAVY

For an additional amount for "Operation and Maintenance, Navy", $360,308,000, to prevent, prepare for, and respond to coronavirus, domestically or internationally: Provided, That such amount is designated by the Congress as being for an emergency requirement pursuant to section 251(b)(2)(A)(i) of the Balanced Budget and Emergency Deficit Control Act of 1985.

OPERATION AND MAINTENANCE, MARINE CORPS

For an additional amount for "Operation and Maintenance, Marine Corps", $90,000,000, to prevent, prepare for, and respond to coronavirus, domestically or internationally: Provided, That

such amount is designated by the Congress as being for an emergency requirement pursuant to section 251(b)(2)(A)(i) of the Balanced Budget and Emergency Deficit Control Act of 1985.

Operation and Maintenance, Air Force

For an additional amount for "Operation and Maintenance, Air Force", $155,000,000, to prevent, prepare for, and respond to coronavirus, domestically or internationally: Provided, That such amount is designated by the Congress as being for an emergency requirement pursuant to section 251(b)(2)(A)(i) of the Balanced Budget and Emergency Deficit Control Act of 1985.

Operation and Maintenance, Army Reserve

For an additional amount for "Operation and Maintenance, Army Reserve", $48,000,000, to prevent, prepare for, and respond to coronavirus, domestically or internationally: Provided, That such amount is designated by the Congress as being for an emergency requirement pursuant to section 251(b)(2)(A)(i) of the Balanced Budget and Emergency Deficit Control Act of 1985.

Operation and Maintenance, Army National Guard

For an additional amount for "Operation and Maintenance, Army National Guard", $186,696,000, to prevent, prepare for, and respond to coronavirus, domestically or internationally: Provided, That such amount is designated by the Congress as being for an emergency requirement pursuant to section 251(b)(2)(A)(i) of the Balanced Budget and Emergency Deficit Control Act of 1985.

Operation and Maintenance, Air National Guard

For an additional amount for "Operation and Maintenance, Air National Guard", $75,754,000, to prevent, prepare for, and respond to coronavirus, domestically or internationally: Provided, That such amount is designated by the Congress as being for an emergency requirement pursuant to section 251(b)(2)(A)(i) of the Balanced Budget and Emergency Deficit Control Act of 1985.

Operation and Maintenance, Defense-Wide

For an additional amount for "Operation and Maintenance, Defense-Wide", $827,800,000, to prevent, prepare for, and respond to coronavirus, domestically or internationally: Provided, That such amount is designated by the Congress as being for an emergency requirement pursuant to section 251(b)(2)(A)(i) of the Balanced Budget and Emergency Deficit Control Act of 1985.

PROCUREMENT

Defense Production Act Purchases

For an additional amount for "Defense Production Act Purchases", $1,000,000,000, to remain available until expended, to prevent, prepare for, and respond to coronavirus, domestically or internationally: Provided, That for the two-year period beginning with the date of enactment of this Act, the requirements described in Section 301(a)(3)(A) and 302(c)(1) of Public Law 81–774, shall be waived: Provided further, That such amount is designated by the Congress as being for an emergency requirement pursuant to section 251(b)(2)(A)(i) of the Balanced Budget and Emergency Deficit Control Act of 1985.

REVOLVING AND MANAGEMENT FUNDS

Defense Working Capital Funds

For an additional amount for "Defense Working Capital Funds", $1,450,000,000, to prevent, position, prepare for, and respond to coronavirus, domestically or internationally: Provided, That of the amount provided under this heading in this Act, $475,000,000 shall be for the Navy Working Capital Fund, $475,000,000 shall be for the Air Force Working Capital Fund, and $500,000,000 shall be for the Defense-Wide Working Capital Fund: Provided further, That such amount is designated by the Congress as being for an emergency requirement pursuant to section 251(b)(2)(A)(i) of the Balanced Budget and Emergency Deficit Control Act of 1985.

OTHER DEPARTMENT OF DEFENSE PROGRAMS

Defense Health Program

For an additional amount for "Defense Health Program", $3,805,600,000, of which $3,390,600,000 shall be for operation and maintenance, and $415,000,000 shall be for research, development, test and evaluation, to remain available until September 30, 2021, to prevent, prepare for, and respond to coronavirus, domestically or internationally: Provided, That, notwithstanding that one percent of funding for operation and maintenance under this heading in Public Law 116–93 shall remain available for obligation until September 30, 2021, funding for operation and maintenance made available under this heading in this Act shall only be available through September 30, 2020: Provided further, That such amount is designated by the Congress as being for an emergency requirement pursuant to section 251(b)(2)(A)(i) of the Balanced Budget and Emergency Deficit Control Act of 1985.

OFFICE OF THE INSPECTOR GENERAL

For an additional amount for "Office of the Inspector General", $20,000,000, to prevent, prepare for, and respond to coronavirus, domestically or internationally: Provided, That the funding made available under this heading in this Act shall be used for conducting audits and investigations of projects and activities carried out with funds made available in this Act to the Department of Defense to prevent, prepare for, and respond to coronavirus, domestically or internationally: Provided further, That such amount is designated by the Congress as being for an emergency requirement pursuant to section 251(b)(2)(A)(i) of the Balanced Budget and Emergency Deficit Control Act of 1985.

GENERAL PROVISIONS—THIS TITLE

SEC. 13001. Funds appropriated by this title may be transferred to, and merged with, other applicable appropriations of the Department of Defense, except for "Drug Interdiction and Counter-Drug Activities, Defense", for expenses incurred in preventing, preparing for, or responding to coronavirus, including expenses of the Department of Defense incurred in support of other Federal Departments and agencies, and State, local, and Indian tribal governments, to be merged with and to be available for the same purposes, and for the same time period, as the appropriation or fund to which transferred: Provided, That upon a determination that all or part of the funds transferred pursuant to this section that are not necessary for the purposes provided herein, such funds shall be transferred back to the original appropriation: Provided further, That the transfer authority provided by this section is in addition to any other transfer authority provided by law.

SEC. 13002. For an additional amount for "Defense Health Program", $1,095,500,000, which shall be for operation and maintenance, and of which $1,095,500,000 may be available for contracts entered into under the TRICARE program: Provided, That, notwithstanding that one percent of funding for operation and maintenance under this heading in Public Law 116–93 shall remain available for obligation until September 30, 2021, funding for operation and maintenance made available under this heading in this section shall only be available through September 30, 2020: Provided further, That such amount is designated by the Congress as being for an emergency requirement pursuant to section 251(b)(2)(A)(i) of the Balanced Budget and Emergency Deficit Control Act of 1985.

SEC. 13003. (a) Notwithstanding section 2208(l)(3) of title 10, United States Code, during fiscal year 2020, the total amount of the advance billings rendered or imposed for all working-capital funds of the Department of Defense may exceed the amount otherwise specified in such section.

(b) In this section, the term "advance billing" has the meaning given that term in section 2208(l)(4) of title 10, United States Code.

SEC. 13004. (a) Section 2326(b)(3) of title 10, United States Code, shall not apply to any undefinitized contract action of the Department of Defense related to the national emergency for the Coronavirus Disease 2019 (COVID–19).

(b) In this section, the term "undefinitized contract action" has the meaning given that term in section 2326(j)(6) of title 10, United States Code.

SEC. 13005. (a) The head of an agency may waive the provisions of section 2326(b) of title 10, United States Code, with respect to a contract of such agency if the head of the agency determines that the waiver is necessary due to the national emergency for the Coronavirus Disease 2019 (COVID–19).

(b) In this section, the term "head of an agency" has the meaning given that term in section 2302(2) of title 10, United States Code.

SEC. 13006. (a) Notwithstanding paragraph (3) of section 2371b(a) of title 10, United States Code, the authority of a senior procurement executive or director of the Defense Advanced Research Projects Agency or Missile Defense Agency under paragraph (2)(A) of such section, and the authority of the Under Secretaries of Defense under paragraph (2)(B) of such section, for any transaction related to the national emergency for the Coronavirus Disease 2019 (COVID–19) may be delegated to such officials in the Department of Defense as the Secretary of Defense shall specify for purposes of this section.

(b)(1) Notwithstanding clause (ii) of section 2371b(a)(2)(B) of title 10, United States Code, no advance notice to Congress is required under that clause for transitions described in that section that are related to the national emergency for the Coronavirus Disease 2019 (COVID–19).

(2) In the event a transaction covered by paragraph (1) is carried out, the Under Secretary of Defense for Research and Engineering or the Under Secretary of Defense for Acquisition and Sustainment, as applicable, shall submit to the congressional defense committees a notice on the carrying out of such transaction as soon as is practicable after the commencement of the carrying out of such transaction.

(3) In this subsection, the term "congressional defense committees" has the meaning given such term in section 101(a)(16) of title 10, United States Code.

Sec. 13007. (a) The President may extend the appointment of the Chief of Army Reserve as prescribed in section 7038(c) of title 10, United States Code, for the incumbent in that position as of the date of the enactment of this Act until the date of the appointment of the successor to such incumbent, notwithstanding any limitation otherwise imposed on such term by such section 7038(c).

(b) The President may extend the appointment of the Chief of Navy Reserve as prescribed in section 8083(c) of title 10, United States Code, for the incumbent in that position as of the date of the enactment of this Act until the date of the appointment of the successor to such incumbent, notwithstanding any limitation otherwise imposed on such term by such section 8083(c).

(c) The President may extend the appointment of the Chief of Staff of the Air Force prescribed in section 9033(a)(1) of title 10, United States Code, for the incumbent in that position as of the date of the enactment of this Act until the date of the appointment of the successor to such incumbent, notwithstanding any limitation otherwise imposed on such term by such section 9033(a)(1).

(d) The President may extend the appointment of the Chief of Space Operations, as prescribed in section 9082(a)(2) of title 10, United States Code, for the incumbent in that position as of the date of the enactment of this Act until the date of the appointment of the successor to such incumbent, notwithstanding any limitation otherwise imposed on such term by such section 9082(a)(2).

(e) The President may extend the appointment of the Chief of the National Guard Bureau as prescribed in section 10502(b) of title 10, United States Code, for the incumbent in that position as of the date of the enactment of this Act until the date of the appointment of the successor to such incumbent, notwithstanding any limitation otherwise imposed on such term by such section 10502(b).

(f) The President may extend the appointment of Director, Army National Guard and Director, Air National Guard as prescribed in section 10506(a)(3)(D) of title 10, United States Code, for the incumbent in such position as of the date of the enactment of this Act until the date of the appointment of the successor to such incumbent, notwithstanding any limitation otherwise imposed on such term by such section 10506(a)(3)(D).

(g) Notwithstanding paragraph (4) of section 10505(a) of title 10, United States Code, the Secretary of Defense may waive the limitations in paragraphs (2) and (3) of that section for a period of not more than 270 days.

(h)(1) The President may delegate the exercise of the authorities in subsections (a) through (f) to the Secretary of Defense.

(2) The Secretary of Defense may not redelegate the exercise of any authority delegated to the Secretary pursuant to paragraph (1), and may not delegate the exercise of the authority in subsection (g).

TITLE IV CORPS OF ENGINEERS—CIVIL DEPARTMENT OF THE ARMY OPERATION AND MAINTENANCE

For an additional amount for "Operation and Maintenance", $50,000,000, to remain available until September 30, 2021, to prevent, prepare for, and respond to coronavirus, domestically or internationally: Provided, That such amount is designated by the Congress as being for an emergency requirement pursuant to section 251(b)(2)(A)(i) of the Balanced Budget and Emergency Deficit Control Act of 1985.

EXPENSES

For an additional amount for "Expenses", $20,000,000, to remain available until September 30, 2021, to prevent, prepare for, and respond to coronavirus, domestically or internationally: Provided,

That such amount is designated by the Congress as being for an emergency requirement pursuant to section 251(b)(2)(A)(i) of the Balanced Budget and Emergency Deficit Control Act of 1985.

DEPARTMENT OF THE INTERIOR

Bureau of Reclamation

WATER AND RELATED RESOURCES

(INCLUDING TRANSFER OF FUNDS)

For an additional amount for "Water and Related Resources", $12,500,000, to remain available until September 30, 2021, to prevent, prepare for, and respond to coronavirus, domestically or internationally: Provided, That $500,000 of the funds provided under this heading in this Act shall be transferred to the "Central Utah Project Completion Account" to prevent, prepare for, and respond to coronavirus: Provided further, That such amount is designated by the Congress as being for an emergency requirement pursuant to section 251(b)(2)(A)(i) of the Balanced Budget and Emergency Deficit Control Act of 1985.

POLICY AND ADMINISTRATION

For an additional amount for "Policy and Administration", $8,100,000, to remain available until September 30, 2021, to prevent, prepare for, and respond to coronavirus, domestically or internationally: Provided, That such amount is designated by the Congress as being for an emergency requirement pursuant to section 251(b)(2)(A)(i) of the Balanced Budget and Emergency Deficit Control Act of 1985.

DEPARTMENT OF ENERGY

ENERGY PROGRAMS

Science

For an additional amount for "Science", $99,500,000, to remain available until September 30, 2021, to prevent, prepare for, and respond to coronavirus, domestically or internationally, for necessary expenses related to providing support and access to scientific user facilities in the Office of Science and National Nuclear Security Administration, including equipment, enabling technologies, and personnel associated with the operations of those scientific user facilities: Provided, That such amount is designated by the Congress as being for an emergency requirement pursuant to section 251(b)(2)(A)(i) of the Balanced Budget and Emergency Deficit Control Act of 1985.

Departmental Administration

(INCLUDING TRANSFER OF FUNDS)

For an additional amount for "Departmental Administration", $28,000,000, to remain available until September 30, 2021, to prevent, prepare for, and respond to coronavirus, domestically or internationally, including for necessary expenses related to supporting remote access for personnel: Provided, That funds appropriated under this heading in this Act may be transferred to, and merged with, other appropriation accounts of the Department of Energy to prevent, prepare for, and respond to coronavirus, including for necessary expenses related to supporting remote access for personnel: Provided further, That such amount is designated by the Congress as being for an emergency requirement pursuant to section 251(b)(2)(A)(i) of the Balanced Budget and Emergency Deficit Control Act of 1985.

INDEPENDENT AGENCIES

Nuclear Regulatory Commission

SALARIES AND EXPENSES

For an additional amount for "Salaries and Expenses", $3,300,000, to remain available until September 30, 2021, to prevent, prepare for, and respond to coronavirus, domestically or internationally: Provided, That, notwithstanding 42 U.S.C. 2214, such amount shall not be derived from fee revenue: Provided further, That such amount is designated by the Congress as being for an emergency requirement pursuant to section 251(b)(2)(A)(i) of the Balanced Budget and Emergency Deficit Control Act of 1985.

GENERAL PROVISIONS—THIS TITLE

Sec. 14001. Funds appropriated in this title may be made available to restore amounts, either directly or through reimbursement, for obligations incurred to prevent, prepare for, and respond to coronavirus prior to the date of enactment of this Act.

SEC. 14002. (a) Section 404 of the Bipartisan Budget Act of 2015 (42 U.S.C. 6239 note) is amended—

(1) in subsection (e), by striking "2020" and inserting "2022"; and

(2) in subsection (g), by striking "2020" and inserting "2022".

(b) Title III of division C of the Further Consolidated Appropriations Act, 2020 (Public Law 116–94) is amended in the matter under the heading "Department of Energy—Energy Programs—Strategic Petroleum Reserve" by striking the three provisos before the final period and inserting the following:

"Provided, That, as authorized by section 404 of the Bipartisan Budget Act of 2015 (Public Law 114–74; 42 U.S.C. 6239 note), the Secretary of Energy shall draw down and sell not to exceed a total of $450,000,000 of crude oil from the Strategic Petroleum Reserve in fiscal year 2020, fiscal year 2021, or fiscal year 2022: Provided further, That the proceeds from such drawdown and sale shall be deposited into the 'Energy Security and Infrastructure Modernization Fund' during the fiscal year in which the sale occurs and shall be made available in such fiscal year, to remain available until expended, for necessary expenses to carry out the Life Extension II project for the Strategic Petroleum Reserve".

(c) The amount provided by this section is designated by the Congress as being for an emergency requirement pursuant to section 251(b)(2)(A)(i) of the Balanced Budget and Emergency Deficit Control Act of 1985.

SEC. 14003. Any discretionary appropriation for the Corps of Engineers derived from the Harbor Maintenance Trust Fund (not to exceed the total amount deposited in the Harbor Maintenance Trust Fund in the prior fiscal year) shall be subtracted from the estimate of discretionary budget authority and outlays for any estimate of an appropriations Act under the Congressional Budget and Impoundment Control Act of 1974 or the Balanced Budget and Emergency Deficit Control Act of 1985: Provided, That the modifications described in this section shall not take effect until the earlier of January 1, 2021 or the date of enactment of legislation authorizing the development of water resources and shall remain in effect thereafter.

SEC. 14004. Section 14321(a)(2)(B)(ii) of title 40, United States Code, is amended by inserting ", except that a discretionary grant to respond to economic distress directly related to the impacts of the Coronavirus Disease 2019 (COVID–19) shall not be included in such aggregate amount" before the period at the end.

TITLE V DEPARTMENT OF THE TREASURY

INTERNAL REVENUE SERVICE

ADMINISTRATIVE PROVISION—INTERNAL REVENUE SERVICE

(INCLUDING TRANSFER OF FUNDS)

SEC. 15001. In addition to the amounts otherwise available to the Internal Revenue Service in fiscal year 2020, $250,000,000, to remain available until September 30, 2021, shall be available to prevent, prepare for, and respond to coronavirus, domestically or internationally, including costs associated with the extended filing season and implementation of the Families First Coronavirus Response Act: Provided, That such funds may be transferred by the Commissioner to the "Taxpayer Services," "Enforcement," or "Operations Support" accounts of the Internal Revenue Service for an additional amount to be used solely to prevent, prepare for, and respond to coronavirus, domestically or internationally: Provided further, That the Committees on Appropriations of the House of Representatives and the Senate shall be notified in advance of any such transfer: Provided further, That such transfer authority is in addition to any other transfer authority provided by law: Provided further, That not later than 30 days after the date of enactment of this Act, the Commissioner shall submit to the Committees on Appropriations of the House of Representatives and the Senate a spending plan for such funds: Provided further, That such amount is designated by the Congress as being for an emergency requirement pursuant to section 251(b)(2)(A)(i) of the Balanced Budget and Emergency Deficit Control Act of 1985.

THE JUDICIARY

SUPREME COURT OF THE UNITED STATES

SALARIES AND EXPENSES

For an additional amount for "Salaries and Expenses", $500,000, to prevent, prepare for, and respond to coronavirus, domestically or internationally: Provided, That such amount is designated by the Congress as being for an emergency requirement pursuant to section 251(b)(2)(A)(i) of the Balanced Budget and Emergency Deficit Control Act of 1985.

COURTS OF APPEALS, DISTRICT COURTS, AND OTHER JUDICIAL SERVICES

SALARIES AND EXPENSES

For an additional amount for "Salaries and Expenses", $6,000,000, to prevent, prepare for, and respond to coronavirus, domestically or internationally: Provided, That such amount is designated by the Congress as being for an emergency requirement pursuant to section 251(b)(2)(A)(i) of the Balanced Budget and Emergency Deficit Control Act of 1985.

DEFENDER SERVICES

For an additional amount for "Defender Services", $1,000,000, to remain available until expended, to prevent, prepare for, and respond to coronavirus, domestically or internationally: Provided, That such amount is designated by the Congress as being for an emergency requirement pursuant to section 251(b)(2)(A)(i) of the Balanced Budget and Emergency Deficit Control Act of 1985.

ADMINISTRATIVE PROVISION—THE JUDICIARY

VIDEO TELECONFERENCING FOR CRIMINAL PROCEEDINGS

SEC. 15002. (a) DEFINITION.—In this section, the term "covered emergency period" means the period beginning on the date on which the President declared a national emergency under the National Emergencies Act (50 U.S.C. 1601 et seq.) with respect to the Coronavirus Disease 2019 (COVID–19) and ending on the date that is 30 days after the date on which the national emergency declaration terminates.

(b) VIDEO TELECONFERENCING FOR CRIMINAL PROCEEDINGS.—

(1) IN GENERAL.—Subject to paragraphs (3), (4), and (5), if the Judicial Conference of the United States finds that emergency conditions due to the national emergency declared by the President under the National Emergencies Act (50 U.S.C. 1601 et seq.) with respect to the Coronavirus Disease 2019 (COVID–19) will materially affect the functioning of either the Federal courts generally or a particular district court of the United States, the chief judge of a district court covered by the finding (or, if the chief judge is unavailable, the most senior available active judge of the court or the chief judge or circuit justice of the circuit that includes the district court), upon application of the Attorney General or the designee of the Attorney General, or on motion of the judge or justice, may authorize the use of video teleconferencing, or telephone conferencing if video teleconferencing is not reasonably available, for the following events:

(A) Detention hearings under section 3142 of title 18, United States Code.

(B) Initial appearances under Rule 5 of the Federal Rules of Criminal Procedure.

(C) Preliminary hearings under Rule 5.1 of the Federal Rules of Criminal Procedure.

(D) Waivers of indictment under Rule 7(b) of the Federal Rules of Criminal Procedure.

(E) Arraignments under Rule 10 of the Federal Rules of Criminal Procedure.

(F) Probation and supervised release revocation proceedings under Rule 32.1 of the Federal Rules of Criminal Procedure.

(G) Pretrial release revocation proceedings under section 3148 of title 18, United States Code.

(H) Appearances under Rule 40 of the Federal Rules of Criminal Procedure.

(I) Misdemeanor pleas and sentencings as described in Rule 43(b)(2) of the Federal Rules of Criminal Procedure.

(J) Proceedings under chapter 403 of title 18, United States Code (commonly known as the "Federal Juvenile Delinquency Act"), except for contested transfer hearings and juvenile delinquency adjudication or trial proceedings.

(2) FELONY PLEAS AND SENTENCING.—

(A) IN GENERAL.—Subject to paragraphs (3), (4), and (5), if the Judicial Conference of the United States finds that emergency conditions due to the national emergency declared by the President under the National Emergencies Act (50 U.S.C. 1601 et seq.) with respect to the Coronavirus Disease 2019 (COVID–19) will materially affect the functioning of either the Federal courts generally or a particular district court of the United States, the chief judge of a district court covered by the finding (or, if the chief judge is unavailable, the most senior available active judge of the court or the chief judge or circuit justice of the circuit that includes the district court) specifically finds, upon application of the Attorney General or the designee of the Attorney General, or on motion of the judge or justice, that felony pleas under Rule 11 of the Federal Rules of Criminal Procedure and felony sentencings under Rule 32 of the Federal Rules of Criminal Procedure cannot be conducted in person without seriously jeopardizing public health and safety, and the district judge in a particular case finds for specific reasons that the plea or sentencing in that case cannot be further delayed without serious harm to the interests of justice, the plea or sentencing in that case may be conducted by video teleconference, or by telephone conference if video teleconferencing is not reasonably available.

(B) APPLICABILITY TO JUVENILES.—The video teleconferencing and telephone conferencing authority described in subparagraph (A) shall apply with respect to equivalent plea and sentencing, or disposition, proceedings under chapter 403 of title 18, United States Code (commonly known as the "Federal Juvenile Delinquency Act").

(3) REVIEW.—

(A) IN GENERAL.—On the date that is 90 days after the date on which an authorization for the use of video teleconferencing or telephone conferencing under paragraph (1) or (2) is issued, if the emergency authority has not been terminated under paragraph (5), the chief judge of the district court (or, if the chief judge is unavailable, the most senior available active judge of the court or the chief judge or circuit justice of the circuit that includes the district court) to which the authorization applies shall review the authorization and determine whether to extend the authorization.

(B) ADDITIONAL REVIEW.—If an authorization is extended under subparagraph (A), the chief judge of the district court (or, if the chief judge is unavailable, the most senior available active judge of the court or the chief judge or circuit justice of the circuit that includes the district court) to which the authorization applies shall review the extension of authority not less frequently than once every 90 days until the earlier of—

(i) the date on which the chief judge (or other judge or justice) determines the authorization is no longer warranted; or

(ii) the date on which the emergency authority is terminated under paragraph (5).

(4) CONSENT.—Video teleconferencing or telephone conferencing authorized under paragraph (1) or (2) may only take place with the consent of the defendant, or the juvenile, after consultation with counsel.

(5) TERMINATION OF EMERGENCY AUTHORITY.—The authority provided under paragraphs (1), (2), and (3), and any specific authorizations issued under those paragraphs, shall terminate on the earlier of—

(A) the last day of the covered emergency period; or

(B) the date on which the Judicial Conference of the United States finds that emergency conditions due to the national emergency declared by the President under the National Emergencies Act (50 U.S.C. 1601 et seq.) with respect to the Coronavirus Disease 2019 (COVID–19) no longer materially affect the functioning of either the Federal courts generally or the district court in question.

(6) NATIONAL EMERGENCIES GENERALLY.—The Judicial Conference of the United States and the Supreme Court of the United States shall consider rule amendments under chapter 131 of title 28, United States Code (commonly known as the "Rules Enabling Act"), that address emergency measures that may be taken by the Federal courts when the President declares a national emergency under the National Emergencies Act (50 U.S.C. 1601 et seq.).

(7) RULE OF CONSTRUCTION.—Nothing in this subsection shall obviate a defendant's right to counsel under the Sixth Amendment to the Constitution of the United States, any Federal statute, or the Federal Rules of Criminal Procedure.

(c) The amount provided by this section is designated by the Congress as being for an emergency requirement pursuant to section 251(b)(2)(A)(i) of the Balanced Budget and Emergency Deficit Control Act of 1985.

DISTRICT OF COLUMBIA

FEDERAL FUNDS

FEDERAL PAYMENT FOR EMERGENCY PLANNING AND SECURITY COSTS IN THE DISTRICT OF COLUMBIA

For an additional amount for "Federal Payment for Emergency Planning and Security Costs in the District of Columbia", $5,000,000, to remain available until expended, to prevent, prepare for, and respond to coronavirus, domestically or internationally: Provided, That such amount is designated by the Congress as being for an emergency requirement pursuant to section 251(b)(2)(A)(i) of the Balanced Budget and Emergency Deficit Control Act of 1985.

INDEPENDENT AGENCIES

Election Assistance Commission

ELECTION SECURITY GRANTS

For an additional amount for "Election Security Grants", $400,000,000, to prevent, prepare for, and respond to coronavirus, domestically or internationally, for the 2020 Federal election cycle: Provided, That a State receiving a payment with funds provided under this heading in this Act shall provide to the Election Assistance Commission, within 20 days of each election in the 2020 Federal election cycle in that State, a report that includes a full accounting of the State's uses of the payment and an explanation of how such uses allowed the State to prevent, prepare for, and respond to coronavirus: Provided further, That, within 3 days of its receipt of a report required in the preceding proviso, the Election Assistance Commission will transmit the report to the Committee on Appropriations and the Committee on House Administration of the House of Representatives and the Committee on Appropriations and the Committee on Rules and Administration of the Senate: Provided further, That not later than 30 days after the date of enactment of this Act, the Election Assistance Commission shall make the payments to States under this heading: Provided further, That any portion of a payment made to a State with funds provided under this heading in this Act which is unobligated on December 31, 2020 shall be returned to the Treasury: Provided further, That such amount is designated by the Congress as being for an emergency requirement pursuant to section 251(b)(2)(A)(i) of the Balanced Budget and Emergency Deficit Control Act of 1985.

Federal Communications Commission

SALARIES AND EXPENSES

For an additional amount for "Salaries and Expenses", $200,000,000, to remain available until expended, to prevent, prepare for, and respond to coronavirus, domestically or internationally, including to support efforts of health care providers to address coronavirus by providing telecommunications services, information services, and devices necessary to enable the provision of telehealth services during an emergency period, as defined in section 1135(g)(1) of the Social Security Act (42 U.S.C. 1320b–5(g)(1)): Provided, That the Federal Communications Commission may rely on the rules of the Commission under part 54 of title 47, Code of Federal Regulations, in administering the amount provided under the heading in this Act if the Commission determines that such administration is in the public interest: Provided further, That such amount is designated by the Congress as being for an emergency requirement pursuant to section 251(b)(2)(A)(i) of the Balanced Budget and Emergency Deficit Control Act of 1985.

General Services Administration

REAL PROPERTY ACTIVITIES

FEDERAL BUILDINGS FUND

(INCLUDING TRANSFERS OF FUNDS)

For an additional amount to be deposited in the "Federal Buildings Fund", $275,000,000, to remain available until expended, to prevent, prepare for, and respond to coronavirus, domestically or internationally: Provided, That the amount provided under this heading in this Act may be used to reimburse the Fund for obligations incurred for this purpose prior to the date of the enactment of this Act: Provided further, That such amount may be transferred to, and merged with, accounts within the Federal Buildings Fund in amounts necessary to cover costs incurred to prevent, prepare for, and respond to coronavirus, domestically or internationally: Provided further, That the Administrator of General Services shall notify the Committees on Appropriations of the House of Representatives and the Senate quarterly on the obligations and expenditures of the funds provided by this Act by account of the Federal Buildings Fund: Provided further, That funds made available to the Administrator in this or any previous Act shall not be subject to section 3307 of title 40, United States Code, for the acquisition of space necessary to prevent, prepare for, or respond to coronavirus, domestically or internationally: Provided further, That no action taken by the Administrator to acquire real property and interests in real property or to improve real property in response to coronavirus shall be deemed a Federal action or undertaking and subject to review under the National Environmental Policy Act of 1969, as amended (42 U.S.C. 4321 et seq.), or the National Historic Preservation Act of 1966, as amended (54 U.S.C. 300101 et seq.), respectively: Provided further, That such amount is designated by the Congress as being for an emergency requirement pursuant to section 251(b)(2)(A)(i) of the Balanced Budget and Emergency Deficit Control Act of 1985.

GENERAL ACTIVITIES

FEDERAL CITIZEN SERVICES FUND

(INCLUDING TRANSFER OF FUNDS)

For an additional amount to be deposited in the "Federal Citizen Services Fund", $18,650,000, to remain available until expended, to prevent, prepare for, and respond to coronavirus, domestically or internationally: Provided, That such amount is designated by the Congress as being for an emergency requirement pursuant to section 251(b)(2)(A)(i) of the Balanced Budget and Emergency Deficit Control Act of 1985.

WORKING CAPITAL FUND

For an additional amount for "Working Capital Fund", $1,500,000, to remain available until expended, to prevent, prepare for, and respond to coronavirus, domestically or internationally: Provided, That such amount is designated by the Congress as being for an emergency requirement pursuant to section 251(b)(2)(A)(i) of the Balanced Budget and Emergency Deficit Control Act of 1985.

ADMINISTRATIVE PROVISION—GENERAL SERVICES ADMINISTRATION

SEC. 15003. Notwithstanding 41 U.S.C. 3304(a)(7)(B), the Administrator, when making a determination that use of noncompetitive procedures is necessary for public interest in accordance with 41 U.S.C. 3304(a)(7)(A) in response to a public health emergency declaration by the Secretary of Health and Human Services under section 319 of the Public Health Service Act (42 U.S.C. 247(d)), is required to notify Congress in writing of that determination not less than 3 days prior to the award of the contract.

NATIONAL ARCHIVES AND RECORDS ADMINISTRATION

OPERATING EXPENSES

For an additional amount for "Operating Expenses", $8,100,000, to remain available until September 30, 2021, to prevent, prepare for, and respond to coronavirus, domestically or internationally: Provided, That the amount provided under this heading in this Act may be used to provide expenses of the Federal Records Center Program for preventing, preparing for, and responding to coronavirus, domestically or internationally: Provided further, That such amount is designated by the Congress as being for an emergency requirement pursuant to section 251(b)(2)(A)(i) of the Balanced Budget and Emergency Deficit Control Act of 1985.

OFFICE OF PERSONNEL MANAGEMENT

SALARIES AND EXPENSES

For an additional amount for "Salaries and Expenses", $12,100,000, to remain available until September 30, 2021, to prevent, prepare for, and respond to coronavirus, domestically or internationally, including technologies for digital case management, short-term methods to allow electronic submissions of retirement application packages in support of paper-based business operations, and increased telecommunications: Provided, That such amount is designated by the Congress as being for an emergency requirement pursuant to section 251(b)(2)(A)(i) of the Balanced Budget and Emergency Deficit Control Act of 1985.

PANDEMIC RESPONSE ACCOUNTABILITY COMMITTEE

For an additional amount for "Pandemic Response Accountability Committee", $80,000,000, to remain available until expended, to promote transparency and support oversight of funds provided in this Act to prevent, prepare for, and respond to coronavirus, domestically or internationally: Provided, That such amount is designated by the Congress as being for an emergency requirement pursuant to section 251(b)(2)(A)(i) of the Balanced Budget and Emergency Deficit Control Act of 1985.

SMALL BUSINESS ADMINISTRATION

DISASTER LOANS PROGRAM ACCOUNT

(INCLUDING TRANSFERS OF FUNDS)

For an additional amount for the "Disaster Loans Program Account", $562,000,000, to remain available until expended, to prevent, prepare for, and respond to coronavirus, domestically or internationally, for the cost of direct loans authorized by section 7(b) of the Small Business Act and for administrative expenses to carry out the disaster loan program authorized by section 7(b) of the Small Business Act: Provided, That the amounts provided under this heading in this Act may be transferred to, and merged with, "Small Business Administration—Salaries and Expenses" to prevent, prepare for, and respond to coronavirus, domestically or internationally: Provided further, That such amount is designated by the Congress as being for an emergency requirement pursuant to section 251(b)(2)(A)(i) of the Balanced Budget and Emergency Deficit Control Act of 1985.

GENERAL PROVISIONS—THIS TITLE

PANDEMIC RESPONSE ACCOUNTABILITY COMMITTEE

SEC. 15010. (a) In this section—

(1) the term "agency" has the meaning given the term in section 551 of title 5, United States Code;

(2) the term "appropriate congressional committees" means—

(A) the Committees on Appropriations of the Senate and the House of Representatives;

(B) the Committee on Homeland Security and Governmental Affairs of the Senate;

(C) the Committee on Oversight and Reform of the House of Representatives; and

(D) any other relevant congressional committee of jurisdiction;

(3) the term "Chairperson" means the Chairperson of the Committee;

(4) the term "Council" means the Council of the Inspectors General on Integrity and Efficiency established under section 11 of the Inspector General Act of 1978 (5 U.S.C. App);

(5) the term "Committee" means the Pandemic Response Accountability Committee established under subsection (b);

(6) the term "covered funds" means any funds, including loans, that are made available in any form to any non-Federal entity, not including an individual, under—

(A) this Act;

(B) the Coronavirus Preparedness and Response Supplemental Appropriations Act, 2020 (Public Law 116–123);

(C) the Families First Coronavirus Response Act (Public Law 116–127); or

(D) any other Act primarily making appropriations for the Coronavirus response and related activities; and

(7) the term "Coronavirus response" means the Federal Government's response to the nationwide public health emergency declared by the Secretary of Health and Human Services, retroactive to January 27, 2020, pursuant to section 319 of the Public Health Service Act (42 U.S.C. 247d), as a result of confirmed cases of the novel coronavirus (COVID–19) in the United States.

(b) There is established within the Council the Pandemic Response Accountability Committee to promote transparency and conduct and support oversight of covered funds and the Coronavirus response to—

(1) prevent and detect fraud, waste, abuse, and mismanagement; and

(2) mitigate major risks that cut across program and agency boundaries.

(c)(1) The Chairperson of the Committee shall be selected by the Chairperson of the Council from among Inspectors General described in subparagraphs (B), (C), and (D) of paragraph (2) with experience managing oversight of large organizations and expenditures.

(2) The members of the Committee shall include—

(A) the Chairperson;

(B) the Inspectors General of the Departments of Defense, Education, Health and Human Services, Homeland Security, Justice, Labor, and the Treasury;

(C) the Inspector General of the Small Business Administration;

(D) the Treasury Inspector General for Tax Administration; and

(E) any other Inspector General, as designated by the Chairperson from any agency that expends or obligates covered funds or is involved in the Coronavirus response.

(3)(A) There shall be an Executive Director and a Deputy Executive Director of the Committee.

(B)(i)(I) Not later than 30 days after the date of enactment of this Act, the Executive Director of the Committee shall be appointed by the Chairperson of the Council, in consultation with the majority leader of the Senate, the Speaker of the House of Representatives, the minority leader of the Senate, and the minority leader of the House of Representatives.

(II) Not later than 90 days after the date of enactment of this Act, the Deputy Executive Director of the Committee shall be appointed by the Chairperson of the Council, in consultation with the majority leader of the Senate, the Speaker of the House of Representatives, the minority leader of the Senate, the minority leader of the House of Representatives, and the Executive Director of the Committee.

(ii) The Executive Director and the Deputy Executive Director of the Committee shall—

(I) have demonstrated ability in accounting, auditing, and financial analysis;

(II) have experience managing oversight of large organizations and expenditures; and

(III) be full-time employees of the Committee.

(C) The Executive Director of the Committee shall—

(i) report directly to the Chairperson;

(ii) appoint staff of the Committee, subject to the approval of the Chairperson, consistent with subsection (f);

(iii) supervise and coordinate Committee functions and staff; and

(iv) perform any other duties assigned to the Executive Director by the Committee.

(4)(A) Members of the Committee may not receive additional compensation for services performed.

(B) The Executive Director and Deputy Executive Director of the Committee shall be compensated at the rate of basic pay prescribed for level IV of the Executive Schedule under section 5315 of title 5, United States Code.

(d)(1)(A) The Committee shall conduct and coordinate oversight of covered funds and the Coronavirus response and support Inspectors General in the oversight of covered funds and the Coronavirus response in order to—

(i) detect and prevent fraud, waste, abuse, and mismanagement; and

(ii) identify major risks that cut across programs and agency boundaries.

(B) The functions of the Committee shall include—

(i) developing a strategic plan to ensure coordinated, efficient, and effective comprehensive oversight by the Committee and Inspectors General over all aspects of covered funds and the Coronavirus response;

(ii) auditing or reviewing covered funds, including a comprehensive audit and review of charges made to Federal contracts pursuant to authorities provided in the Coronavirus Aid, Relief, and Economic Security Act, to determine whether wasteful spending, poor contract or grant management, or other abuses are occurring and referring matters the Committee considers appropriate for investigation to the Inspector General for the agency that disbursed the covered funds, including conducting randomized audits to identify fraud;

(iii) reviewing whether the reporting of contracts and grants using covered funds meets applicable standards and specifies the purpose of the contract or grant and measures of performance;

(iv) reviewing the economy, efficiency, and effectiveness in the administration of, and the detection of fraud, waste, abuse, and mismanagement in, Coronavirus response programs and operations;

(v) reviewing whether competition requirements applicable to contracts and grants using covered funds have been satisfied;

(vi) serving as a liaison to the Director of the Office of Management and Budget, the Secretary of the Treasury, and other officials responsible for implementing the Coronavirus response;

(vii) reviewing whether there are sufficient qualified acquisition, grant, and other applicable personnel overseeing covered funds and the Coronavirus response;

(viii) reviewing whether personnel whose duties involve the Coronavirus response or acquisitions or grants made with covered funds or are otherwise related to the Coronavirus response receive adequate training, technology support, and other resources;

(ix) reviewing whether there are appropriate mechanisms for interagency collaboration relating to the oversight of covered funds and the Coronavirus response, including coordinating and collaborating to the extent practicable with State and local government entities;

(x) expeditiously reporting to the Attorney General any instance in which the Committee has reasonable grounds to believe there has been a violation of Federal criminal law; and

(xi) coordinating and supporting Inspectors General on matters related to oversight of covered funds and the Coronavirus response.

(2)(A)(i) The Committee shall submit to the President and Congress, including the appropriate congressional committees, management alerts on potential management, risk, and funding problems that require immediate attention.

(ii) The Committee shall submit to Congress such other reports or provide such periodic updates on the work of the Committee as the Committee considers appropriate on the use of covered funds and the Coronavirus response.

(B) The Committee shall submit biannual reports to the President and Congress, including the appropriate congressional committees, and may submit additional reports as appropriate—

(i) summarizing the findings of the Committee; and

(ii) identifying and quantifying the impact of any tax expenditures or credits authorized under this Act to the extent practicable.

(C)(i) All reports submitted under this paragraph shall be made publicly available and posted on the website established under subsection (g).

(ii) Any portion of a report submitted under this paragraph may be redacted when made publicly available, if that portion would disclose information that is not subject to disclosure under sections 552 and 552a of title 5, United States Code, or is otherwise prohibited from disclosure by law.

(3)(A) The Committee shall make recommendations to agencies on measures to prevent or address fraud, waste, abuse and mismanagement, and to mitigate risks that cut across programs and agency boundaries, relating to covered funds and the Coronavirus response.

(B) Not later than 30 days after receipt of a recommendation under subparagraph (A), an agency shall submit a report to the President and the appropriate congressional committees on—

(i) whether the agency agrees or disagrees with the recommendations; and

(ii) any actions the agency will take to implement the recommendations, which shall also be included in the report required under section 2(b) of the GAO–IG Act (31 U.S.C. 1105 note).

(e)(1) The Committee shall conduct audits and reviews of programs, operations, and expenditures relating to covered funds and the Coronavirus response and coordinate on such activities with the Inspector General of the relevant agency to avoid unnecessary duplication and overlap of work.

(2) The Committee may—

(A) conduct its own independent investigations, audits, and reviews relating to covered funds or the Coronavirus response;

(B) collaborate on audits and reviews relating to covered funds with any Inspector General of an agency; and

(C) provide support to relevant agency Inspectors General in conducting investigations, audits, and reviews relating to the covered funds and Coronavirus response.

(3)(A) In conducting and supporting investigations, audits, and reviews under this subsection, the Committee—

(i) shall have the authorities provided under section 6 of the Inspector General Act of 1978 (5 U.S.C. App.);

(ii) may issue subpoenas to compel the testimony of persons who are not Federal officers or employees; and

(iii) may enforce such subpoenas in the event of a refusal to obey by order of any appropriate United States district court as provided for under section 6 of the Inspector General Act of 1978 (5 U.S.C. App).

(B) The Committee shall carry out the powers under paragraphs (1) and (2) in accordance with section 4(b)(1) of the Inspector General Act of 1978 (5 U.S.C. App.).

(C) Whenever information or assistance requested by the Committee or an Inspector General is unreasonably refused or not provided, the Committee shall immediately report the circumstances to the appropriate congressional committees.

(D) The Committee shall leverage existing information technology resources within the Council, such as oversight.gov, to carry out the duties of the Committee.

(4)(A) The Committee may hold public hearings and Committee personnel may conduct necessary inquiries.

(B) The head of each agency shall make all officers and employees of that agency available to provide testimony to the Committee and Committee personnel.

(C) The Committee may issue subpoenas to compel the testimony of persons who are not Federal officers or employees at such public hearings, which may be enforced in the same manner as provided for subpoenas under section 6 of the Inspector General Act of 1978 (5 U.S.C. App.).

(5) The Committee may enter into contracts to enable the Committee to discharge its duties, including contracts and other arrangements for audits, studies, analyses, and other services with public agencies and with private persons, and make such payments as may be necessary to carry out the duties of the Committee.

(6) The Committee may establish subcommittees to facilitate the ability of the Committee to discharge its duties.

(7) The Committee may transfer funds appropriated to the Committee for expenses to support administrative support services and audits, reviews, or other activities related to oversight by the Committee of covered funds or the Coronavirus response to any Office of the Inspector General or the General Services Administration.

(f)(1)(A)(i) Subject to subparagraph (B), the Committee may exercise the authorities of subsections (b) through (i) of section 3161 of title 5, United States Code (without regard to subsection (a) of that section) to carry out the functions of the Committee under this section.

(ii) For purposes of exercising the authorities described under clause (i), the term "Chairperson" shall be substituted for the term "head of a temporary organization".

(iii) In exercising the authorities described in clause (i), the Chairperson shall consult with members of the Committee.

(iv) In addition to the authority provided by section 3161(c) of title 5, United States Code, upon the request of an Inspector General, the Committee may detail, on a nonreimbursable basis, any personnel of the Council to that Inspector General to assist in carrying out any audit, review, or investigation pertaining to the oversight of covered funds or the Coronavirus response.

(B) In exercising the employment authorities under section 3161(b) of title 5, United States Code, as provided under subparagraph (A) of this paragraph—

(i) section 3161(b)(2) of that title (relating to periods of appointments) shall not apply; and

(ii) no period of appointment may exceed the date on which the Committee terminates.

(C)(i) A person employed by the Committee shall acquire competitive status for appointment to any position in the competitive service for which the employee possesses the required qualifications upon the completion of 2 years of continuous service as an employee under this subsection.

(ii) No person who is first employed as described in clause (i) more than 2 years after the date of enactment of this Act may acquire competitive status under clause (i).

(2)(A) The Committee may employ annuitants covered by section 9902(g) of title 5, United States Code, for purposes of the oversight of covered funds or the Coronavirus response.

(B) The employment of annuitants under this paragraph shall be subject to the provisions of section 9902(g) of title 5, United States Code, as if the Committee was the Department of Defense.

(3) Upon request of the Committee for information or assistance from any agency or other entity of the Federal Government, the head of such entity shall, insofar as is practicable and not in contravention of any existing law, and consistent with section 6 of the Inspector General Act of 1978 (5 U.S.C. App.), furnish such information or assistance to the Committee, or an authorized designee, including an Inspector General designated by the Chairperson.

(4) Any Inspector General responsible for conducting oversight related to covered funds or the Coronavirus response may, consistent with the duties, responsibilities, policies, and procedures of the Inspector General, provide information requested by the Committee or an Inspector General on the Committee relating to the responsibilities of the Committee.

(g)(1)(A) Not later than 30 days after the date of enactment of this Act, the Committee shall establish and maintain a user-friendly, public-facing website to foster greater accountability and transparency in the use of covered funds and the Coronavirus response, which shall have a uniform resource locator that is descriptive and memorable.

(B) The Committee shall leverage existing information technology and resources, such as oversight.gov, to the greatest extent practicable to meet the requirements under this section.

(2) The website established and maintained under paragraph (1) shall be a portal or gateway to key information relating to the oversight of covered funds and the Coronavirus response and provide connections to other Government websites with related information.

(3) In establishing and maintaining the website under paragraph (1), the Committee shall ensure the following:

(A) The website shall provide materials and information explaining the Coronavirus response and how covered funds are being used. The materials shall be easy to understand and regularly updated.

(i) The website shall provide accountability information, including findings from Inspectors General, including any progress reports, audits, inspections, or other reports, including reports from or links to reports on the website of the Government Accountability Office.

(ii) The website shall provide data on relevant operational, economic, financial, grant, subgrant, contract, and subcontract information in user-friendly visual presentations to enhance public awareness of the use of covered funds and the Coronavirus response.

(iii) The website shall provide detailed data on any Federal Government awards that expend covered funds, including a unique trackable identification number for each project, information about the process that was used to award the covered funds, and for any covered funds over $150,000, a detailed explanation of any associated agreement, where applicable.

(iv) The website shall include downloadable, machine-readable, open format reports on covered funds obligated by month to each State and congressional district, where applicable.

(v) The website shall provide a means for the public to give feedback on the performance of any covered funds and of the Coronavirus response, including confidential feedback.

(vi) The website shall include detailed information on Federal Government awards that expend covered funds, including data elements required under the Federal Funding Accountability and Transparency Act of 2006 (31 U.S.C. 6101 note), allowing aggregate reporting on awards below $50,000, as prescribed by the Director of the Office of Management and Budget.

(vii) The website shall provide a link to estimates of the jobs sustained or created by this Act to the extent practicable.

(viii) The website shall include appropriate links to other government websites with information concerning covered funds and the Coronavirus response, including Federal agency and State websites.

(ix) The website shall include a plan from each Federal agency for using covered funds.

(x) The website shall provide information on Federal allocations of mandatory and other entitlement programs by State, county, or other geographical unit related to covered funds or the Coronavirus response.

(xi) The website shall present the data such that funds subawarded by recipients are not double counted in search results, data visualizations, or other reports.

(xii) The website shall include all recommendations made to agencies relating to covered funds and the Coronavirus response, as well as the status of each recommendation.

(xiii) The website shall be enhanced and updated as necessary to carry out the purposes of this section.

(4) The Committee may exclude posting contractual or other information on the website on a case-by-case basis when necessary to protect national security or to protect information that is not subject to disclosure under sections 552 and 552a of title 5, United States Code.

(h)(1) Nothing in this section shall affect the independent authority of an Inspector General to determine whether to conduct an audit or investigation of covered funds or the Coronavirus response.

(2) If the Committee requests that an Inspector General of an agency conduct or refrain from conducting an audit or investigation and the Inspector General rejects the request in whole or in part, the Inspector General shall, not later than 30 days after rejecting the request, submit a report to the Committee, the head of the applicable agency, and the appropriate congressional committees, that states the reasons that the Inspector General has rejected the request in whole or in part.

(i) The Committee shall coordinate its oversight activities with the Comptroller General of the United States and State auditors.

(j) For the purposes of carrying out the mission of the Committee under this section, there are authorized to be appropriated such sums as may be necessary to carry out the duties and functions of the Committee.

(k) The Committee shall terminate on September 30, 2025.

REPORTING ON USE OF FUNDS

SEC. 15011. (a) In this section—

(1) the terms "agency", "appropriate congressional committees", "Committee", "covered funds", and "Coronavirus response" have the meanings given those terms in section 15010;

(2) the term "covered recipient"—

(A) means any entity that receives large covered funds; and

(B) includes any State, the District of Columbia, and any territory or possession of the United States; and

(3) the term "large covered funds" means covered funds that amount to more than $150,000.

(b)(1)(A) On a monthly basis until September 30, 2021, each agency shall report to the Director of the Office of Management and Budget, the Bureau of Fiscal Service in the Department of the Treasury, the Committee, and the appropriate congressional committees on any obligation or expenditure of large covered funds, including loans and awards.

(B) Not later than 90 days after the date of enactment of this Act, each agency shall submit to the Committee a plan describing how the agency will use covered funds.

(2) Not later than 10 days after the end of each calendar quarter, each covered recipient shall submit to the agency and the Committee a report that contains—

(A) the total amount of large covered funds received from the agency;

(B) the amount of large covered funds received that were expended or obligated for each project or activity;

(C) a detailed list of all projects or activities for which large covered funds were expended or obligated, including—

(i) the name of the project or activity;

(ii) a description of the project or activity; and

(iii) the estimated number of jobs created or retained by the project or activity, where applicable; and

(D) detailed information on any level of subcontracts or subgrants awarded by the covered recipient or its subcontractors or subgrantees, to include the data elements required to comply with the Federal Funding Accountability and Transparency Act of 2006 (31 U.S.C. 6101 note) allowing aggregate reporting on awards below $50,000 or to individuals, as prescribed by the Director of the Office of Management and Budget.

(3) Not later than 30 days after the end of each calendar quarter, the Committee, in consultation with the agency that made large covered funds available to any covered recipient shall make the information in reports submitted under paragraph (2) publicly available by posting the information on the website established under section 15010(g).

(4)(A) Each agency, in coordination with the Committee and the Director of the Office of Management and Budget shall provide user-friendly means for covered recipients to meet requirements of this subsection.

(B) Federal agencies may use existing mechanisms to ensure that information under this subsection is reported accurately.

(c)(1) The Director of the Office of Management and Budget, in consultation with the Secretary of the Treasury, the Administrator of the Small Business Administration, and the Chairperson of the Council of Economic Advisors, shall submit to the appropriate congressional committees and publicly release on the website established under section 15010(g) quarterly reports that detail the impact of programs funded through large covered funds on employment, estimated economic growth, and other key economic indicators, including information about impacted industries.

(2)(A) The first report submitted under paragraph (1) shall be submitted not later than 45 days after the end of the first full quarter following the date of enactment of this Act.

(B) The last report required to be submitted under paragraph (1) shall apply to the quarter in which the Committee terminates.

TITLE VI DEPARTMENT OF HOMELAND SECURITY

Management Directorate

OPERATIONS AND SUPPORT

For an additional amount for "Operations and Support", $178,300,000, to remain available until September 30, 2021, to prevent, prepare for, and respond to coronavirus, domestically or internationally, which shall be for the purchase of personal protective equipment and sanitization materials: Provided, That funds provided under this heading in this Act may be transferred by the Secretary of Homeland Security between appropriations in the Department only for the purchase of personal protective equipment and sanitization materials to prevent, prepare for, and respond to coronavirus, domestically or internationally: Provided further, That none of the funds made available under this heading may be transferred pursuant to the authority in section 503 of the Department of Homeland Security Appropriations Act, 2020: Provided further, That the Department shall provide notice of any transfer to the Committees on Appropriations of the Senate and the House of Representatives not later than 5 days after executing such transfer: Provided further, That such amount is designated by the Congress as being for an emergency requirement pursuant to section 251(b)(2)(A)(i) of the Balanced Budget and Emergency Deficit Control Act of 1985.

Transportation Security Administration

OPERATIONS AND SUPPORT

For an additional amount for "Operations and Support", $100,000,000, to remain available until September 30, 2021, to prevent, prepare for, and respond to coronavirus, domestically or internationally, which shall be for cleaning and sanitization at checkpoints and other airport common areas; overtime and travel costs; and explosive detection materials: Provided, That such amount is designated by the Congress as being for an emergency requirement pursuant to section 251(b)(2)(A)(i) of the Balanced Budget and Emergency Deficit Control Act of 1985.

United States Coast Guard

OPERATIONS AND SUPPORT

For an additional amount for "Operations and Support", $140,800,000, to remain available until September 30, 2021, to prevent, prepare for, and respond to coronavirus, domestically or internationally, which shall be for mobilization of reservists and increasing the capability and capacity of Coast Guard information technology systems and infrastructure: Provided, That such amount is designated by the Congress as being for an emergency requirement pursuant to section 251(b)(2)(A)(i) of the Balanced Budget and Emergency Deficit Control Act of 1985.

CYBERSECURITY AND INFRASTRUCTURE SECURITY AGENCY

OPERATIONS AND SUPPORT

For an additional amount for "Operations and Support", $9,100,000, to remain available until September 30, 2021, to prevent, prepare for, and respond to coronavirus, domestically or internationally, which shall be for support of interagency critical infrastructure coordination and related activities: Provided, That such amount is designated by the Congress as being for an emergency requirement pursuant to section 251(b)(2)(A)(i) of the Balanced Budget and Emergency Deficit Control Act of 1985.

FEDERAL EMERGENCY MANAGEMENT AGENCY

OPERATIONS AND SUPPORT

For an additional amount for "Operations and Support", $44,987,000, to remain available until September 30, 2021, to prevent, prepare for, and respond to coronavirus, domestically or internationally, which shall be for enhancements to information technology and for facilities support: Provided, That such amount is designated by the Congress as being for an emergency requirement pursuant to section 251(b)(2)(A)(i) of the Balanced Budget and Emergency Deficit Control Act of 1985.

DISASTER RELIEF FUND

For an additional amount for "Disaster Relief Fund", $45,000,000,000, to remain available until expended: Provided, That of the amount provided under this heading in this Act, $25,000,000,000 shall be for major disasters declared pursuant to the Robert T. Stafford Disaster Relief and Emergency Assistance Act (42 U.S.C. 5121 et seq.): Provided further, That of the amount provided under this heading in this Act, $15,000,000,000 may be used for all purposes authorized under such Act and may be used in addition to amounts designated by the Congress as being for disaster relief pursuant to section 251(b)(2)(D) of the Balanced Budget and Emergency Deficit Control Act of 1985: Provided further, That every 30 days the Administrator shall provide the Committees on Appropriations of the Senate and the House of Representatives both projected and actual costs for funds provided under this heading for major disasters and any other expenses: Provided further, That of the amounts provided under this heading, $3,000,000 shall be transferred to "Office of Inspector General" and shall remain available until expended for oversight of activities supported by funds provided under this heading: Provided further, That such amount is designated by the Congress as being for an emergency requirement pursuant to section 251(b)(2)(A)(i) of the Balanced Budget and Emergency Deficit Control Act of 1985.

FEDERAL ASSISTANCE

For an additional amount for "Federal Assistance", $400,000,000, to remain available until September 30, 2021, to prevent, prepare for, and respond to coronavirus, domestically or internationally: Provided, That of the amount provided under this heading in this Act, $100,000,000 shall be for Assistance to Firefighter Grants for the purchase of personal protective equipment and related supplies, including reimbursements; $100,000,000 shall be for Emergency Management Performance Grants; and $200,000,000 shall be for the Emergency Food and Shelter Program: Provided further, That such amount is designated by the Congress as being for an emergency requirement pursuant to section 251(b)(2)(A)(i) of the Balanced Budget and Emergency Deficit Control Act of 1985.

GENERAL PROVISIONS—THIS TITLE

SEC. 16001. Notwithstanding any other provision of law, funds made available under each heading in this title, except for "Federal Emergency Management Agency—Disaster Relief Fund", shall only be used for the purposes specifically described under that heading.

SEC. 16002. Notwithstanding any other provision of law, any amounts appropriated for "Federal Emergency Management Agency—Disaster Relief Fund" in this Act are available only for the purposes for which they were appropriated.

SEC. 16003. (a) PREMIUM PAY AUTHORITY.—If services performed during fiscal year 2020 are determined by the head of the agency to be primarily related to preparation, prevention, or response to coronavirus, any premium pay that is funded, either directly or through reimbursement, by the Federal Emergency Management Agency shall be exempted from the aggregate of basic pay and premium pay calculated under section 5547(a) of title 5, United States Code, and any other provision of law limiting the aggregate amount of premium pay payable on a biweekly or calendar year basis.

(b) OVERTIME AUTHORITY.—Any overtime that is funded for such services described in subsection (a), either directly or through reimbursement, by the Federal Emergency Management Agency shall be exempted from any annual limit on the amount of overtime payable in a calendar or fiscal year.

(c) APPLICABILITY OF AGGREGATE LIMITATION ON PAY.—In determining whether an employee's pay exceeds the applicable annual rate of basic pay payable under section 5307 of title 5, United States Code, the head of an Executive agency shall not include pay exempted under this section.

(d) LIMITATION OF PAY AUTHORITY.—Pay exempted from otherwise applicable limits under subsection (a) shall not cause the aggregate pay earned for the calendar year in which the exempted pay is earned to exceed the rate of basic pay payable for a position at level II of the Executive Schedule under section 5313 of title 5, United States Code.

(e) EFFECTIVE DATE.—This section shall take effect as if enacted on January 1, 2020.

SEC. 16004. (a) Amounts provided for "Coast Guard—Operations and Support" in the Consolidated Appropriations Act, 2020 (Public Law 116–93) may be available for pay and benefits of Coast Guard Yard and Vessel Documentation personnel, Non-Appropriated Funds personnel, and for Morale, Welfare and Recreation Programs.

(b) No amounts may be used under this section from amounts that were designated by the Congress for Overseas Contingency Operations/Global War on Terrorism pursuant to the Concurrent Resolution on the Budget or the Balanced Budget and Emergency Deficit Control Act of 1985.

SEC. 16005. (a) Notwithstanding any other provision of law regarding the licensure of health-care providers, a health-care professional described in subsection (b) may practice the health profession or professions of the health-care professional at any location in any State, the District of Columbia, or Commonwealth, territory, or possession of the United States, or any location designated by the Secretary, regardless of where such health-care professional or the patient is located, so long as the practice is within the scope of the authorized Federal duties of such health-care professional.

(b) DEFINITION.—As used in this section, the term "health-care professional" means an individual (other than a member of the Coast Guard, a civilian employee of the Coast Guard, member of the Public Health Service who is assigned to the Coast Guard, or an individual with whom the Secretary, pursuant to 10 U.S.C. 1091, has entered into a personal services contract to carry out health care responsibilities of the Secretary at a medical treatment facility of the Coast Guard) who—

(1) is—

(A) an employee of the Department of Homeland Security,

(B) a detailee to the Department from another Federal agency,

(C) a personal services contractor of the Department, or

(D) hired under a Contract for Services;

(2) performs health care services as part of duties of the individual in that capacity;

(3) has a current, valid, and unrestricted equivalent license certification that is—

(A) issued by a State, the District of Columbia, or a Commonwealth, territory, or possession of the United States; and

(B) for the practice of medicine, osteopathic medicine, dentistry, nursing, emergency medical services, or another health profession; and

(4) is not affirmatively excluded from practice in the licensing or certifying jurisdiction or in any other jurisdiction.

(c) Subsection (a) shall apply during the incident period of the emergency declared by the President on March 13, 2020, pursuant to section 501(b) of the Robert T. Stafford Disaster Relief and Emergency Assistance Act (42 U.S.C. 5121(b)), and to any subsequent major declaration under section 401 of such Act that supersedes such emergency declaration.

SEC. 16006. The Secretary of Homeland Security, under the authority granted under section 205(b) of the REAL ID Act of 2005 (Public Law 109–13; 49 U.S.C. 30301 note) shall extend the deadline by which States are required to meet the driver license and identification card issuance requirements under section 202(a)(1) of such Act until not earlier than September 30, 2021.

SEC. 16007. Section 5 of the Protecting and Securing Chemical Facilities from Terrorist Attacks Act of 2014 (Public Law 113–254; 6 U.S.C. 621 note) is amended by striking "the date that is 5 years and 3 months after the effective date of this Act" and inserting "July 23, 2020": Provided, That the amount provided by this section is designated by the Congress as being for an emergency requirement pursuant to section 251(b)(2)(A)(i) of the Balanced Budget and Emergency Deficit Control Act of 1985.

TITLE VII DEPARTMENT OF THE INTERIOR

INDIAN AFFAIRS

BUREAU OF INDIAN AFFAIRS

OPERATION OF INDIAN PROGRAMS

(INCLUDING TRANSFERS OF FUNDS)

For an additional amount for "Operation of Indian Programs", $453,000,000, to remain available until September 30, 2021, to prevent, prepare for, and respond to coronavirus, domestically or internationally, including, but not limited to, funds for public safety and justice programs, executive direction to carry out deep cleaning of facilities, purchase of personal protective equipment, purchase of information technology to improve teleworking capability, welfare assistance and social services programs (including assistance to individuals), and assistance to tribal governments, including tribal governments who participate in the "Small and Needy" program: Provided, That amounts received from funds provided under this heading in this Act for welfare assistance programs shall not be included in the statutory maximum for welfare assistance funds included in Public Law 116–94, the Further Consolidated Appropriations Act, 2020: Provided further, That assistance received from funds provided under this heading in this Act shall not be included in the calculation of funds received by those tribal governments who participate in the "Small and Needy" program: Provided further, That of the amounts provided under this heading in this Act, not less than $400,000,000 shall be made available to meet the direct needs of tribes: Provided further, That amounts provided under this heading in this Act may be made available for distribution through tribal priority allocations for tribal response and capacity building activities: Provided further, That funds provided under this heading in this Act, if transferred to tribes and tribal organizations under the Indian Self-Determination and Education Assistance Act, will be transferred on a one-time basis and that these non-recurring funds are not part of the amount required by 25 U.S.C. § 5325: Provided further, That such amount is designated by the Congress as being for an emergency requirement pursuant to section 251(b)(2)(A)(i) of the Balanced Budget and Emergency Deficit Control Act of 1985.

BUREAU OF INDIAN EDUCATION

OPERATION OF INDIAN EDUCATION PROGRAMS

For an additional amount for "Operation of Indian Education Programs", $69,000,000, to remain available until September 30, 2021, to prevent, prepare for, and respond to coronavirus, domestically or internationally, including, but not limited to, funding for tribal colleges and universities, salaries, transportation, and information technology: Provided, That of the amounts provided in this paragraph, not less than $20,000,000 shall be for tribal colleges and universities: Provided further, That such amount is designated by the Congress as being for an emergency requirement pursuant to section 251(b)(2)(A)(i) of the Balanced Budget and Emergency Deficit Control Act of 1985.

DEPARTMENTAL OFFICES

OFFICE OF THE SECRETARY

DEPARTMENTAL OPERATIONS

(INCLUDING TRANSFERS OF FUNDS)

For an additional amount for "Departmental Operations", $158,400,000, to remain available until September 30, 2021, to prevent, prepare for, and respond to coronavirus, domestically or internationally, including, but not limited to, funds for purchasing equipment and supplies to disinfect and clean buildings and public areas, supporting law enforcement and emergency management operations, biosurveillance of wildlife and environmental persistence studies, employee overtime and special pay expenses, and other response, mitigation, or recovery activities: Provided, That funds appropriated under this heading in this Act shall be used to absorb increased operational costs necessary to prevent, prepare for, and respond to coronavirus, domestically or internationally: Provided further, That the Secretary of the Interior may transfer the funds provided under this heading in this Act to any other account in the Department to prevent, prepare for, and respond to coronavirus, domestically or internationally, and may expend such funds directly or through cooperative agreements: Provided further, That the Secretary shall provide a monthly report to the Committees on Appropriations of the House of Representatives and the Senate detailing the allocation and obligation of these funds by account, beginning not later than 90 days after enactment of this Act: Provided further, That as soon as practicable after the date of enactment of this Act, the Secretary shall transfer $1,000,000 to the Office of the Inspector General, "Salaries and Expenses" account for oversight activities related to the implementation of programs, activities or projects funded herein: Provided further, That such amount is designated by the Congress as being for an emergency requirement pursuant to section 251(b)(2)(A)(i) of the Balanced Budget and Emergency Deficit Control Act of 1985.

Insular Affairs

ASSISTANCE TO TERRITORIES

For an additional amount for "Assistance to Territories", $55,000,000, to remain available until September 30, 2021, to prevent, prepare for, and respond to coronavirus, domestically or internationally, for general technical assistance: Provided, That such amount is designated by the Congress as being for an emergency requirement pursuant to section 251(b)(2)(A)(i) of the Balanced Budget and Emergency Deficit Control Act of 1985.

ENVIRONMENTAL PROTECTION AGENCY

Science and Technology

For an additional amount for "Science and Technology", $2,250,000, to remain available until September 30, 2021, to prevent, prepare for, and respond to coronavirus, domestically or internationally: Provided, That of the amount provided under this heading in this Act, $750,000 shall be for necessary expenses for cleaning and disinfecting equipment or facilities of, or for use by, the Environmental Protection Agency, and $1,500,000 shall be for research on methods to reduce the risks from environmental transmission of coronavirus via contaminated surfaces or materials: Provided further, That such amount is designated by the Congress as being for an emergency requirement pursuant to section 251(b)(2)(A)(i) of the Balanced Budget and Emergency Deficit Control Act of 1985.

Environmental Programs and Management

For an additional amount for "Environmental Programs and Management", $3,910,000, to remain available until September 30, 2021, to prevent, prepare for, and respond to coronavirus, domestically or internationally: Provided, That of the amount provided under this heading in this Act, $2,410,000 shall be for necessary expenses for cleaning and disinfecting equipment or facilities of, or for use by, the Environmental Protection Agency, and operational continuity of Environmental Protection Agency programs and related activities, and $1,500,000 shall be for expediting registration and other actions related to pesticides to address coronavirus: Provided further, That such amount is designated by the Congress as being for an emergency requirement pursuant to section 251(b)(2)(A)(i) of the Balanced Budget and Emergency Deficit Control Act of 1985.

Buildings and Facilities

For an additional amount for "Buildings and Facilities", $300,000, to remain available until September 30, 2021, to prevent, prepare for, and respond to coronavirus, domestically or internationally: Provided, That the funds provided under this heading in this Act shall be for necessary expenses for cleaning and disinfecting equipment or facilities of, or for use by, the Environmental Protection Agency: Provided further, That such amount is designated by the Congress as being for an emergency requirement pursuant to section 251(b)(2)(A)(i) of the Balanced Budget and Emergency Deficit Control Act of 1985.

Hazardous Substance Superfund

For an additional amount for "Hazardous Substance Superfund", $770,000, to remain available until September 30, 2021, to prevent, prepare for, and respond to coronavirus, domestically or internationally: Provided, That the funds provided under this heading in this Act shall be for necessary expenses for cleaning and disinfecting equipment or facilities of, or for use by, the Environmental Protection Agency: Provided further, That such amount is designated by the Congress as being for an emergency requirement pursuant to section 251(b)(2)(A)(i) of the Balanced Budget and Emergency Deficit Control Act of 1985.

RELATED AGENCIES

DEPARTMENT OF AGRICULTURE

Forest Service

FOREST AND RANGELAND RESEARCH

For an additional amount for "Forest and Rangeland Research", $3,000,000, to remain available until September 30, 2021, to prevent, prepare for, and respond to coronavirus, domestically or internationally, including for the reestablishment of abandoned or failed experiments associated with employee restrictions due to the coronavirus outbreak: Provided, That amounts provided under this heading in this Act shall be allocated at the discretion of the Chief of the Forest Service: Provided further, That such amount is designated by the Congress as being for an emergency requirement pursuant to section 251(b)(2)(A)(i) of the Balanced Budget and Emergency Deficit Control Act of 1985.

NATIONAL FOREST SYSTEM

For an additional amount for "National Forest System", $34,000,000, to remain available until September 30, 2021, to prevent, prepare for, and respond to coronavirus, domestically or internationally, including for cleaning and disinfecting of public recreation amenities and for personal protective equipment and baseline health testing for first responders: Provided, That amounts provided under this heading in this Act shall be allocated at the discretion of the Chief of the Forest Service: Provided further, That such amount is designated by the Congress as being for an emergency requirement pursuant to section 251(b)(2)(A)(i) of the Balanced Budget and Emergency Deficit Control Act of 1985.

CAPITAL IMPROVEMENT AND MAINTENANCE

For an additional amount for "Capital Improvement and Maintenance", $26,800,000, to remain available until September 30, 2021, to prevent, prepare for, and respond to coronavirus, domestically or internationally, including for janitorial services: Provided, That amounts provided under this heading in this Act shall be allocated at the discretion of the Chief of the Forest Service: Provided further, That such amount is designated by the Congress as being for an emergency requirement pursuant to section 251(b)(2)(A)(i) of the Balanced Budget and Emergency Deficit Control Act of 1985.

WILDLAND FIRE MANAGEMENT

For an additional amount for "Wildland Fire Management", $7,000,000, to remain available until September 30, 2021, to prevent, prepare for, and respond to coronavirus, domestically or internationally, including for personal protective equipment and baseline health testing for first responders: Provided, That amounts provided under this heading in this Act shall be allocated at the discretion of the Chief of the Forest Service: Provided further, That such amount is designated by the Congress as being for an emergency requirement pursuant to section 251(b)(2)(A)(i) of the Balanced Budget and Emergency Deficit Control Act of 1985.

DEPARTMENT OF HEALTH AND HUMAN SERVICES

INDIAN HEALTH SERVICE

INDIAN HEALTH SERVICES

(INCLUDING TRANSFERS OF FUNDS)

For an additional amount for "Indian Health Services", $1,032,000,000, to remain available until September 30, 2021, to prevent, prepare for, and respond to coronavirus, domestically or internationally, including for public health support, electronic health record modernization, telehealth and other information technology upgrades, Purchased/Referred Care, Catastrophic Health Emergency Fund, Urban Indian Organizations, Tribal Epidemiology Centers, Community Health Representatives, and other activities to protect the safety of patients and staff: Provided, That of the amount provided under this heading in this Act, up to $65,000,000 is for electronic health record stabilization and support, including for planning and tribal consultation: Provided further, That of amounts provided under this heading in this Act, not less than $450,000,000 shall be distributed through IHS directly operated programs and to tribes and tribal organizations under the Indian Self-Determination and Education Assistance Act and through contracts or grants with urban Indian organizations under title V of the Indian Health Care Improvement Act: Provided further, That any amounts provided in this paragraph not allocated pursuant to the preceding proviso shall be allocated at the discretion of the Director of the Indian Health Service: Provided further, That of the funds provided herein, up to $125,000,000 may be transferred to and merged with the "Indian Health Service, Indian Health Facilities" appropriation at the discretion of the Director for the purposes specified in this Act: Provided further, That amounts provided under this heading in this Act, if transferred to tribes and tribal organizations under the Indian Self-Determination and Education Assistance Act, will be transferred on a one-time basis and that these non-recurring funds are not part of the amount required by 25 U.S.C. § 5325, and that such amounts may only be used for the purposes identified under this heading notwithstanding any other provision of law: Provided further, That such amount is designated by the Congress as being for an emergency requirement pursuant to section 251(b)(2)(A)(i) of the Balanced Budget and Emergency Deficit Control Act of 1985.

AGENCY FOR TOXIC SUBSTANCES AND DISEASE REGISTRY

TOXIC SUBSTANCES AND ENVIRONMENTAL PUBLIC HEALTH

For an additional amount for "Toxic Substances and Environmental Public Health", $12,500,000, to remain available until September 30, 2021, to prevent, prepare for, and respond to coronavirus, domestically or internationally: Provided, That $7,500,000 of the funds provided under this heading in this Act shall be for necessary expenses of the Geospatial Research, Analysis and Services Program to support spatial analysis and Geographic Information System mapping of infectious disease hot spots, including cruise ships: Provided further, That $5,000,000 of the funds provided under this heading in this Act shall be for necessary expenses for awards to Pediatric Environmental Health Specialty Units and state health departments to provide guidance and outreach on safe practices for disinfection for home, school, and daycare facilities: Provided further, That such amount is designated by the Congress as being for an emergency requirement pursuant to section 251(b)(2)(A)(i) of the Balanced Budget and Emergency Deficit Control Act of 1985.

OTHER RELATED AGENCIES

INSTITUTE OF AMERICAN INDIAN AND ALASKA NATIVE CULTURE AND ARTS DEVELOPMENT

PAYMENT TO THE INSTITUTE

For an additional amount for "Payment to the Institute", $78,000, to remain available until September 30, 2021, to prevent, prepare for, and respond to coronavirus, domestically or internationally: Provided, That such amount is designated by the Congress as being for an emergency requirement pursuant to section 251(b)(2)(A)(i) of the Balanced Budget and Emergency Deficit Control Act of 1985.

SMITHSONIAN INSTITUTION

SALARIES AND EXPENSES

For an additional amount for "Salaries and Expenses", $7,500,000, to remain available until September 30, 2021, to prevent, prepare for, and respond to coronavirus, domestically or internationally, including funding for deep cleaning, security, information technology, and staff overtime: Provided, That such amount is designated by the Congress as being for an emergency requirement pursuant to section 251(b)(2)(A)(i) of the Balanced Budget and Emergency Deficit Control Act of 1985.

JOHN F. KENNEDY CENTER FOR THE PERFORMING ARTS

OPERATIONS AND MAINTENANCE

For an additional amount for "Operations and Maintenance", $25,000,000, to remain available until September 30, 2021, to prevent, prepare for, and respond to coronavirus, domestically or internationally, including funding for deep cleaning and information technology to improve telework capability and for operations and maintenance requirements related to the consequences of coronavirus: Provided, That notwithstanding the provisions of 20 U.S.C. 76h et seq., funds provided under this heading in this Act shall be made available to cover operating expenses required to ensure the continuity of the John F. Kennedy Center for the Performing Arts and its affiliates, including for employee compensation and benefits, grants, contracts, payments for rent or utilities, fees for artists or performers, information technology, and other administrative expenses: Provided further, That no later than October 31, 2020, the Board of Trustees of the Center shall submit a report to the Committees on Appropriations of the House of Representatives and Senate that includes a detailed explanation of the distribution of the funds provided herein: Provided further, That such amount is designated by the Congress as being for an emergency requirement pursuant to section 251(b)(2)(A)(i) of the Balanced Budget and Emergency Deficit Control Act of 1985.

NATIONAL FOUNDATION ON THE ARTS AND HUMANITIES

NATIONAL ENDOWMENT FOR THE ARTS

GRANTS AND ADMINISTRATION

For an additional amount for "Grants and Administration", $75,000,000, to remain available until September 30, 2021, to prevent, prepare for, and respond to coronavirus, domestically or internationally, to be distributed in grants: Provided, That such funds are available under the same terms and conditions as grant funding appropriated to this heading in Public Law 116–94: Provided further, That 40 percent of such funds shall be distributed to State arts agencies and regional arts organizations and 60 percent of such funds shall be for direct grants: Provided further, That notwithstanding any other provision of law, such funds may also be used by the recipients of such grants for purposes of the general operations of such recipients: Provided further, That the matching requirements under subsections (e), (g)(4)(A), and (p)(3) of section 5 of the National Foundation on the Arts and Humanities Act of 1965 (20 U.S.C. 954) may be waived with respect to such grants: Provided further, That such amount is designated by the Congress as being for an emergency requirement pursuant to section 251(b)(2)(A)(i) of the Balanced Budget and Emergency Deficit Control Act of 1985.

NATIONAL ENDOWMENT FOR THE HUMANITIES

GRANTS AND ADMINISTRATION

For an additional amount for "Grants and Administration", $75,000,000, to remain available until September 30, 2021, to prevent, prepare for, and respond to coronavirus, domestically or internationally, to be distributed in grants: Provided, That such funds are available under the same terms and conditions as grant funding appropriated to this heading in Public Law 116–94: Provided further, That 40 percent of such funds shall be distributed to state humanities councils and 60 percent of such funds shall be for direct grants: Provided further, That notwithstanding any other provision of law, such funds may also be used by the recipients of such grants for purposes of the general operations of such recipients: Provided further, That the matching requirements under subsection (h)(2)(A) of section 7 of the National Foundation on the Arts and Humanities Act of 1965 may be waived with respect to such grants: Provided further, That such amount is designated by the Congress as being for an emergency requirement pursuant to section 251(b)(2)(A)(i) of the Balanced Budget and Emergency Deficit Control Act of 1985.

TITLE VIII DEPARTMENT OF LABOR

EMPLOYMENT AND TRAINING ADMINISTRATION

TRAINING AND EMPLOYMENT SERVICES

For an additional amount for "Training and Employment Services", $345,000,000, to remain available through September 30, 2022, to prevent, prepare for, and respond to coronavirus, domestically or internationally, for necessary expenses for the dislocated workers assistance national reserve: Provided, That the funds provided under this heading in this Act may be used to replace grant funds previously obligated to the impacted areas: Provided further, That such amount is designated by the Congress as being for an emergency requirement pursuant to section 251(b)(2)(A)(i) of the Balanced Budget and Emergency Deficit Control Act of 1985.

DEPARTMENTAL MANAGEMENT

SALARIES AND EXPENSES

(INCLUDING TRANSFER OF FUNDS)

For an additional amount for "Departmental Management", $15,000,000, to remain available through September 30, 2022, to prevent, prepare for, and respond to coronavirus, including to enforce worker protection laws and regulations, and to oversee and coordinate activities related to division C, division D, division E, and division F of Public Law 116–127: Provided, That the Secretary of Labor may transfer the amounts provided under this heading in this Act as necessary to "Employee Benefits Security Administration", "Wage and Hour Division", "Occupational Safety and Health Administration", and "Employment and Training Administration—Program Administration" to prevent, prepare for, and respond to coronavirus, including for enforcement, oversight, and coordination activities in those accounts: Provided further, That of the amount provided under this heading in this Act, $1,000,000, to remain available until expended, shall be transferred to "Office of Inspector General" for oversight of activities related to Public Law 116–127 and for oversight activities supported with funds appropriated to the Department of Labor to prevent, prepare for, and respond to coronavirus: Provided further, That 15 days prior to transferring any funds pursuant to the previous provisos under the heading in this Act, the Secretary shall provide to the Committees on Appropriations of the House of Representatives and the Senate an operating plan describing the planned uses of each amount proposed to be transferred: Provided further, That such amount is designated by the Congress as being for an emergency requirement pursuant to section 251(b)(2)(A)(i) of the Balanced Budget and Emergency Deficit Control Act of 1985.

DEPARTMENT OF HEALTH AND HUMAN SERVICES

CENTERS FOR DISEASE CONTROL AND PREVENTION

CDC–WIDE ACTIVITIES AND PROGRAM SUPPORT

(INCLUDING TRANSFER OF FUNDS)

For an additional amount for "CDC-Wide Activities and Program Support", $4,300,000,000, to remain available until September 30, 2024, to prevent, prepare for, and respond to coronavirus, domestically or internationally: Provided, That not less than $1,500,000,000 of the amount provided under this heading in this Act shall be for grants to or cooperative agreements with States, localities, territories, tribes, tribal organizations, urban Indian health organizations, or health service providers to tribes, including to carry out surveillance, epidemiology, laboratory capacity, infection control, mitigation, communications, and other preparedness and response activities: Provided further, That every grantee that received a Public Health Emergency Preparedness grant for fiscal year 2019 shall receive not less than 100 percent of that grant level from funds provided in the first proviso under this heading in this Act: Provided further, That of the amount in the first proviso, not less than $125,000,000 shall be allocated to tribes, tribal organizations, urban Indian health organizations, or health service providers to tribes: Provided further, That the Director of the Centers for Disease Control and Prevention ("CDC") may satisfy the funding thresholds outlined in the preceding two provisos by making awards through other grant or cooperative agreement mechanisms: Provided further, That of the amount provided under this heading in this Act, not less than $500,000,000 shall be for global disease detection and emergency response: Provided further, That of the amount provided under this heading in this Act, not less than $500,000,000 shall be for public health data surveillance and analytics infrastructure modernization: Provided further, That CDC shall report to the Committees on Appropriations of the House of Representatives and the Senate on the development of a public health surveillance and data collection system for coronavirus within 30 days of enactment of this Act: Provided further, That of the amount provided under this heading in this Act, $300,000,000 shall be transferred to and merged with amounts in the Infectious Diseases Rapid Response Reserve Fund ("Reserve Fund"), established by section 231 of division B of Public Law 115–245: Provided further, That the Secretary of Health and Human Services, in consultation with the Director of the CDC, shall provide a report to the Committees on Appropriations of the House of Representatives and the Senate every 14 days, for one year from the date from any such declaration or determination described in the third proviso of section 231 of division B of Public Law 115–245, that details commitment and obligation information for the Reserve Fund during the prior two weeks, as long as such report would detail obligations in excess of $5,000,000, and upon the request by such Committees: Provided further, That funds appropriated under this heading in this Act may be used for grants for the rent, lease, purchase, acquisition, construction, alteration, or renovation of non-federally owned facilities to improve preparedness and response capability at the State and local level: Provided further, That funds provided under this heading in this Act may be used for purchase and insurance of official motor vehicles in foreign countries: Provided further, That such amount is designated by the Congress as being for an emergency requirement pursuant to section 251(b)(2)(A)(i) of the Balanced Budget and Emergency Deficit Control Act of 1985.

NATIONAL INSTITUTES OF HEALTH

NATIONAL HEART, LUNG, AND BLOOD INSTITUTE

For an additional amount for "National Heart, Lung, and Blood Institute", $103,400,000, to remain available until September 30, 2024, to prevent, prepare for, and respond to coronavirus, domestically or internationally: Provided, That such amount is designated by the Congress as being for an emergency requirement pursuant to section 251(b)(2)(A)(i) of the Balanced Budget and Emergency Deficit Control Act of 1985.

NATIONAL INSTITUTE OF ALLERGY AND INFECTIOUS DISEASES

For an additional amount for "National Institute of Allergy and Infectious Diseases", $706,000,000, to remain available until September 30, 2024, to prevent, prepare for, and respond to coronavirus, domestically or internationally: Provided, That not less than $156,000,000 of the amounts provided under this heading in this Act shall be provided for the study of, construction of, demolition of, renovation of, and acquisition of equipment for, vaccine and infectious diseases research facilities of or used by NIH, including the acquisition of real property: Provided further, That such amount is designated by the Congress as being for an emergency requirement pursuant to section 251(b)(2)(A)(i) of the Balanced Budget and Emergency Deficit Control Act of 1985.

NATIONAL INSTITUTE OF BIOMEDICAL IMAGING AND BIOENGINEERING

For an additional amount for "National Institute of Biomedical Imaging and Bioengineering", $60,000,000, to remain available until September 30, 2024, to prevent, prepare for, and respond to coronavirus, domestically or internationally: Provided, That such amount is designated by the Congress as being for an emergency requirement pursuant to section 251(b)(2)(A)(i) of the Balanced Budget and Emergency Deficit Control Act of 1985.

NATIONAL LIBRARY OF MEDICINE

For an additional amount for "National Library of Medicine", $10,000,000, to remain available until September 30, 2024, to prevent, prepare for, and respond to coronavirus, domestically or internationally: Provided, That such amount is designated by the Congress as being for an emergency requirement pursuant to section 251(b)(2)(A)(i) of the Balanced Budget and Emergency Deficit Control Act of 1985.

NATIONAL CENTER FOR ADVANCING TRANSLATIONAL SCIENCES

For an additional amount for "National Center for Advancing Translational Sciences", $36,000,000, to remain available until September 30, 2024, to prevent, prepare for, and respond to coronavirus, domestically or internationally: Provided, That such amount is designated by the Congress as being for an emergency requirement pursuant to section 251(b)(2)(A)(i) of the Balanced Budget and Emergency Deficit Control Act of 1985.

OFFICE OF THE DIRECTOR

For an additional amount for "Office of the Director", $30,000,000, to remain available until September 30, 2024, to prevent, prepare for, and respond to coronavirus, domestically or internationally: Provided, That these funds shall be available for the Common Fund established under section 402A(c)(1) of the PHS Act: Provided further, That such amount is designated by the Congress as being for an emergency requirement pursuant to section 251(b)(2)(A)(i) of the Balanced Budget and Emergency Deficit Control Act of 1985.

SUBSTANCE ABUSE AND MENTAL HEALTH SERVICES ADMINISTRATION

HEALTH SURVEILLANCE AND PROGRAM SUPPORT

For an additional amount for "Heath Surveillance and Program Support", $425,000,000, to remain available through September 30, 2021, to prevent, prepare for, and respond to coronavirus, domestically or internationally: Provided, That of the amount appropriated under this heading in this Act, not less than $250,000,000 is available for Certified Community Behavioral Health Clinic Expansion Grant program: Provided further, That of the amount appropriated under this heading in this Act, not less than $50,000,000 shall be available for suicide prevention programs: Provided further, That of the amount appropriated under this heading in this Act, not less than $100,000,000 is available for activities authorized under section 501(o) of the Public Health Service Act: Provided further, That of the funding made available under this heading in this Act, not less than $15,000,000 shall be allocated to tribes, tribal organizations, urban Indian health organizations, or health or behavioral health service providers to tribes: Provided further, That such amount is designated by the Congress as being for an emergency requirement pursuant to section 251(b)(2)(A)(i) of the Balanced Budget and Emergency Deficit Control Act of 1985.

CENTERS FOR MEDICARE & MEDICAID SERVICES

PROGRAM MANAGEMENT

For an additional amount for "Program Management", $200,000,000, to remain available through September 30, 2023, to prevent, prepare for, and respond to coronavirus, domestically and internationally: Provided, That of the amount appropriated under this heading in this Act, not less than $100,000,000 shall be available for necessary expenses of the survey and certification program, prioritizing nursing home facilities in localities with community transmission of coronavirus: Provided further, That such amount is designated by the Congress as being for an emergency requirement pursuant to section 251(b)(2)(A)(i) of the Balanced Budget and Emergency Deficit Control Act of 1985.

ADMINISTRATION FOR CHILDREN AND FAMILIES

LOW INCOME HOME ENERGY ASSISTANCE

For an additional amount for "Low Income Home Energy Assistance", $900,000,000, to remain available through September 30, 2021, to prevent, prepare for, or respond to coronavirus, domestically or internationally, for making payments under subsection (b) of section 2602 of the Low-Income

Home Energy Assistance Act of 1981 (42 U.S.C. 8621 et seq.): Provided, That of the amount provided under this heading in this Act, $225,000,000 shall be allocated as though the total appropriation for such payments for fiscal year 2020 was less than $1,975,000,000: Provided further, That section 2607(b)(2)(B) of such Act (42 U.S.C. 8626(b)(2)(B)) shall not apply to funds made available under this heading in this Act in fiscal year 2020: Provided further, That such amount is designated by the Congress as being for an emergency requirement pursuant to section 251(b)(2)(A)(i) of the Balanced Budget and Emergency Deficit Control Act of 1985.

PAYMENTS TO STATES FOR THE CHILD CARE AND DEVELOPMENT BLOCK GRANT

For an additional amount for "Payments to States for the Child Care and Development Block Grant", $3,500,000,000, to remain available through September 30, 2021, to prevent, prepare for, and respond to coronavirus, domestically or internationally, including for federal administrative expenses, which shall be used to supplement, not supplant State, Territory, and Tribal general revenue funds for child care assistance for low-income families within the United States (including territories) without regard to requirements in sections 658E(c)(3)(D)–(E) or 658G of the Child Care and Development Block Grant Act: Provided, That funds provided under this heading in this Act may be used to provide continued payments and assistance to child care providers in the case of decreased enrollment or closures related to coronavirus, and to assure they are able to remain open or reopen as appropriate and applicable: Provided further, That States, Territories, and Tribes are encouraged to place conditions on payments to child care providers that ensure that child care providers use a portion of funds received to continue to pay the salaries and wages of staff: Provided further, That the Secretary shall remind States that CCDBG State plans do not need to be amended prior to utilizing existing authorities in the CCDBG Act for the purposes provided herein: Provided further, That States, Territories, and Tribes are authorized to use funds appropriated under this heading in this Act to provide child care assistance to health care sector employees, emergency responders, sanitation workers, and other workers deemed essential during the response to coronavirus by public officials, without regard to the income eligibility requirements of section 658P(4) of such Act: Provided further, That funds appropriated under this heading in this Act shall be available to eligible child care providers under section 658P(6) of the CCDBG Act, even if such providers were not receiving CCDBG assistance prior to the public health emergency as a result of the coronavirus, for the purposes of cleaning and sanitation, and other activities necessary to maintain or resume the operation of programs: Provided further, That payments made under this heading in this Act may be obligated in this fiscal year or the succeeding two fiscal years: Provided further, That funds appropriated under this heading in this Act may be made available to restore amounts, either directly or through reimbursement, for obligations incurred to prevent, prepare for, and respond to coronavirus, domestically or internationally, prior to the date of enactment of this Act: Provided further, That such amount is designated by the Congress as being for an emergency requirement pursuant to section 251(b)(2)(A)(i) of the Balanced Budget and Emergency Deficit Control Act of 1985.

CHILDREN AND FAMILIES SERVICES PROGRAMS

For an additional amount for "Children and Families Services Programs", $1,874,000,000, to remain available through September 30, 2021, to prevent, prepare for, and respond to coronavirus, domestically or internationally, which shall be used as follows: (1) $1,000,000,000 for carrying out activities under sections 674 through 679 of the Community Services Block Grant Act, including for federal administrative expenses, and of which no part shall be subject to section 674(b)(3) of such Act: Provided, That to the extent Community Services Block Grant funds are distributed as grant funds by a State to an eligible entity as provided under such Act, and have not been expended by such entity, they shall remain with such entity for carryover into the next two fiscal years for expenditure by such entity consistent with program purpose: Provided further, That for services furnished under such Act during fiscal years 2020 and 2021, States may apply the last sentence of section 673(2) of such Act by substituting "200 percent" for "125 percent"; (2) $750,000,000 for making payments under the Head Start Act, including for Federal administrative expenses, and allocated in an amount that bears the same ratio to such portion as the number of enrolled children served by the agency involved bears to the number of enrolled children by all Head Start agencies: Provided further, That none of the funds appropriated in this paragraph shall be included in the calculation of the "base grant" in subsequent fiscal years, as such term is defined in sections 640(a)(7)(A), 641A(h)(1)(B), or 645(d)(3) of the Head Start Act: Provided further, That funds appropriated in this paragraph are not subject to the allocation requirements of section 640(a) of the Head Start Act: Provided further, That up to $500,000,000 shall be available for the purpose of operating supplemental summer programs through non-competitive grant supplements to existing grantees determined to be most ready to operate those programs by the Office of Head Start; (3) $2,000,000 for the National Domestic Violence Hotline as authorized by section 303(b) of the Family Violence Prevention and Services Act: Provided further, That the Secretary may make such funds available for providing hotline services remotely; (4) $45,000,000 for Family Violence Prevention and Services formula grants as authorized by section 303(a) of the Family Violence and Prevention and Services Act with such funds available to grantees without regard to matching requirements under section 306(c)(4) of such Act: Provided further, That the Secretary may make such funds available for providing temporary housing and assistance to victims of family, domestic, and dating violence; (5) $25,000,000 for carrying out activities under the Runaway and Homeless Youth Act: Provided further, That such amounts shall be used to supplement, not supplant, existing funds and shall be available without regard to matching requirements; (6) $45,000,000 shall be used for child welfare services as authorized by subpart 1 of part B of title IV of the Social Security Act (other than sections 426, 427, and 429 of such subpart), with such funds available to grantees without regard to matching requirements under section 424(a) of that Act or any applicable reductions in federal financial participation under section 424(f) of that Act; and (7) $7,000,000 for Federal administrative expenses: Provided further, That funds appropriated under this heading in this Act may be made available to restore amounts, either directly or through reimbursement, for obligations incurred to prevent, prepare for, and respond to coronavirus, domestically or internationally, prior to the date of enactment of this Act: Provided further, That such amount is designated by the Congress as being for an emergency requirement pursuant to section 251(b)(2)(A)(i) of the Balanced Budget and Emergency Deficit Control Act of 1985.

Administration for Community Living

AGING AND DISABILITY SERVICES PROGRAMS

For an additional amount for "Aging and Disability Services Programs", $955,000,000, to remain available until September 30, 2021, to prevent, prepare for, and respond to coronavirus, domestically or internationally: Provided, That of the amount made available under this heading in this Act to prevent, prepare for, and respond to coronavirus, $820,000,000 shall be for activities authorized under the Older Americans Act of 1965 ("OAA"), including $200,000,000 for supportive services under part B of title III; $480,000,000 for nutrition services under subparts 1 and 2 of part C of title III; $20,000,000 for nutrition services under title VI; $100,000,000 for support services for family caregivers under part E of title III; and $20,000,000 for elder rights protection activities, including the long-term ombudsman program under title VII of such Act: Provided further, That of the amount made available under this heading in this Act, $50,000,000 shall be for aging and disability resource centers authorized in sections 202(b) and 411 of the OAA to prevent, prepare for, and respond to coronavirus: Provided further, That of the amount made available under this heading in this Act to prevent, prepare for, and respond to coronavirus, $85,000,000 shall be available for centers for independent living that have received grants funded under part C of chapter I of title VII of the Rehabilitation Act of 1973: Provided further, That to facilitate State use of funds provided under this heading in this Act, matching requirements under sections 304(d)(1)(D) and 373(g)(2) of the OAA shall not apply to funds made available under this heading in this Act: Provided further, That the transfer authority under section 308(b)(4)(A) of the OAA shall apply to funds made available under this heading in this Act by substituting "100 percent" for "40 percent": Provided further, That the State Long-Term Care Ombudsman shall have continuing direct access (or other access through the use of technology) to residents of long-term care facilities during any portion of the public health emergency relating to coronavirus beginning on the date of enactment of this Act and ending on September 30, 2020, to provide services described in section 712(a)(3)(B) of the OAA: Provided further, That such amount is designated by the Congress as being for an emergency requirement pursuant to section 251(b)(2)(A)(i) of the Balanced Budget and Emergency Deficit Control Act of 1985.

Office of the Secretary

PUBLIC HEALTH AND SOCIAL SERVICES EMERGENCY FUND

(including transfer of funds)

For an additional amount for "Public Health and Social Services Emergency Fund", $27,014,500,000, to remain available until September 30, 2024, to prevent, prepare for, and respond to coronavirus, domestically or internationally, including the development of necessary countermeasures and vaccines, prioritizing platform-based technologies with U.S.-based manufacturing capabilities, the purchase of vaccines, therapeutics, diagnostics, necessary medical supplies, as well as medical surge capacity, addressing blood supply chain, workforce modernization, telehealth access and infrastructure, initial advanced manufacturing, novel dispensing, enhancements to the U.S.

Commissioned Corps, and other preparedness and response activities: Provided, That funds appropriated under this paragraph in this Act may be used to develop and demonstrate innovations and enhancements to manufacturing platforms to support such capabilities: Provided further, That the Secretary of Health and Human Services shall purchase vaccines developed using funds made available under this paragraph in this Act to respond to an outbreak or pandemic related to coronavirus in quantities determined by the Secretary to be adequate to address the public health need: Provided further, That products purchased by the Federal government with funds made available under this paragraph in this Act, including vaccines, therapeutics, and diagnostics, shall be purchased in accordance with Federal Acquisition Regulation guidance on fair and reasonable pricing: Provided further, That the Secretary may take such measures authorized under current law to ensure that vaccines, therapeutics, and diagnostics developed from funds provided in this Act will be affordable in the commercial market: Provided further, That in carrying out the previous proviso, the Secretary shall not take actions that delay the development of such products: Provided further, That products purchased with funds appropriated under this paragraph in this Act may, at the discretion of the Secretary of Health and Human Services, be deposited in the Strategic National Stockpile under section 319F–2 of the Public Health Service Act: Provided further, That of the amount appropriated under this paragraph in this Act, not more than $16,000,000,000 shall be for the Strategic National Stockpile under section 319F–2(a) of such Act: Provided further, That funds appropriated under this paragraph in this Act may be transferred to, and merged with, the fund authorized by section 319F–4, the Covered Countermeasure Process Fund, of the Public Health Service Act: Provided further, That of the amount appropriated under this paragraph in this Act, not less than $250,000,000 shall be available for grants to or cooperative agreements with entities that are either grantees or sub-grantees of the Hospital Preparedness Program authorized in section 319C–2 of the Public Health Service Act or that meet such other criteria as the Secretary may prescribe, with such awards issued under such section or section 311 of such Act: Provided further, That of the amount provided under this paragraph in this Act, not less than $3,500,000,000 shall be available to the Biomedical Advanced Research and Development Authority for necessary expenses of manufacturing, production, and purchase, at the discretion of the Secretary, of vaccines, therapeutics, diagnostics, and small molecule active pharmaceutical ingredients, including the development, translation, and demonstration at scale of innovations in manufacturing platforms: Provided further, That funds in the previous proviso may be used for the construction or renovation of U.S.-based next generation manufacturing facilities, other than facilities owned by the United States Government: Provided further, That of the amount appropriated under this paragraph in this Act, funds may be used to reimburse the Department of Veterans Affairs for expenses incurred by the Veterans Health Administration to prevent, prepare for, and respond to coronavirus, and to provide medical care for such purposes to individuals not otherwise eligible for care: Provided further, That funds used for the preceding proviso shall be made available to reimburse the Department of Veterans Affairs only if the Secretary of Health and Human Services certifies to the Committees on Appropriations of the House of Representatives and the Senate that funds available for assignments under Public Law 93–288, as amended, are insufficient and such funds are necessary to reimburse the Department of Veterans Affairs for expenses incurred to provide health care to civilians: Provided further, That the Secretary shall notify the Committees on Appropriations of the House of Representatives and the Senate not less than 3 days prior to such certification: Provided further, That of the amounts appropriated under this paragraph in this Act, not more than $289,000,000 may be transferred as necessary to other federal agencies for necessary expenses related to medical care that are incurred to prevent, prepare for, and respond to coronavirus for persons eligible for treatment pursuant to section 322 of the Public Health Service Act, as amended, as determined by the Secretary of the recipient agency: Provided further, That of the amount appropriated under this paragraph in this Act, $1,500,000 shall be available for the Secretary to enter into an agreement with the National Academies of Sciences, Engineering, and Medicine not later than 60 days after the date of enactment of this Act to examine, and, in a manner that does not compromise national security, report on, the security of the United States medical product supply chain: Provided further, That funds appropriated under this paragraph in this Act may be used for grants for the construction, alteration, or renovation of non-federally owned facilities to improve preparedness and response capability at the State and local level: Provided further, That funds appropriated under this paragraph in this Act may be used for the construction, alteration, or renovation of non-federally owned facilities for the production of vaccines, therapeutics, and diagnostics where the Secretary determines that such a contract is necessary to secure sufficient amounts of such supplies: Provided further, That such amount is designated by the

Congress as being for an emergency requirement pursuant to section 251(b)(2)(A)(i) of the Balanced Budget and Emergency Deficit Control Act of 1985.

For an additional amount for the "Public Health and Social Services Emergency Fund", $275,000,000, to remain available until September 30, 2022, to prevent, prepare for, and respond to coronavirus, domestically or internationally: Provided, That $90,000,000 of the funds appropriated under this paragraph shall be transferred to "Health Resources and Services Administration—Ryan White HIV/AIDS Program" to remain available until September 30, 2022 for modifications to existing contracts, and supplements to existing grants and cooperative agreements under parts A, B, C, D, and section 2692(a) of title XXVI of the Public Health Service Act (referred to as "PHS" Act) to respond to coronavirus, domestically or internationally: Provided further, That supplements made in the preceding proviso shall be awarded using a data-driven methodology determined by the Secretary: Provided further, That sections 2604(c), 2612(b), and 2651(c) of the PHS Act shall not apply to funds under this paragraph: Provided further, That $5,000,000 of the funds appropriated under this paragraph shall be transferred to "Health Resources and Services Administration—Health Care Systems" to remain available until September 30, 2022, for activities under sections 1271 and 1273 of the PHS Act to improve the capacity of poison control centers to respond to increased calls: Provided further, That $180,000,000 of the funds appropriated under this paragraph shall be transferred to "Health Resources and Services Administration—Rural Health" to remain available until September 30, 2022, to carry out telehealth and rural health activities under sections 330A and 330I of the PHS Act and sections 711 and 1820 of the Social Security Act to prevent, prepare for, and respond to coronavirus, domestically or internationally: Provided further, That of the funding in the previous proviso, no less than $15,000,000 shall be allocated to tribes, tribal organizations, urban Indian health organizations, or health service providers to tribes: Provided further, That section 1820(g)(3)(A), section 1820(g)(3)(D) and section 1820(g)(3)(E) of such Act shall not apply to funds in the preceding two provisos: Provided further, That funds appropriated under this heading in this Act may be made available to restore amounts, either directly or through reimbursement, for obligations incurred to prevent, prepare for, and respond to coronavirus, domestically or internationally, prior to the date of enactment of this Act: Provided further, That for the purposes of any funding provided for fiscal year 2020 for the Health Centers Program pursuant to section 330 of the PHS Act (42 U.S.C. 254b), maintaining or increasing health center capacity and staffing levels during a public health emergency related to coronavirus shall be deemed a cost of prevention, diagnosis, and treatment of coronavirus: Provided further, That such amount is designated by the Congress as being for an emergency requirement pursuant to section 251(b)(2)(A)(i) of the Balanced Budget and Emergency Deficit Control Act of 1985.

For an additional amount for "Public Health and Social Services Emergency Fund", $100,000,000,000, to remain available until expended, to prevent, prepare for, and respond to coronavirus, domestically or internationally, for necessary expenses to reimburse, through grants or other mechanisms, eligible health care providers for health care related expenses or lost revenues that are attributable to coronavirus: Provided, That these funds may not be used to reimburse expenses or losses that have been reimbursed from other sources or that other sources are obligated to reimburse: Provided further, That recipients of payments under this paragraph shall submit reports and maintain documentation as the Secretary determines are needed to ensure compliance with conditions that are imposed by this paragraph for such payments, and such reports and documentation shall be in such form, with such content, and in such time as the Secretary may prescribe for such purpose: Provided further, That "eligible health care providers" means public entities, Medicare or Medicaid enrolled suppliers and providers, and such for-profit entities and not-for-profit entities not otherwise described in this proviso as the Secretary may specify, within the United States (including territories), that provide diagnoses, testing, or care for individuals with possible or actual cases of COVID–19: Provided further, That the Secretary of Health and Human Services shall, on a rolling basis, review applications and make payments under this paragraph in this Act: Provided further, That funds appropriated under this paragraph in this Act shall be available for building or construction of temporary structures, leasing of properties, medical supplies and equipment including personal protective equipment and testing supplies, increased workforce and trainings, emergency operation centers, retrofitting facilities, and surge capacity: Provided further, That, in this paragraph, the term "payment" means a pre-payment, prospective payment, or retrospective payment, as determined appropriate by the Secretary: Provided further, That payments under this paragraph shall be made in consideration of the most efficient payment systems practicable to provide emergency payment: Provided further, That to be eligible for a payment under this paragraph, an eligible health care provider shall submit to the Secretary of Health and Human Services an application that includes a statement justifying the need of the provider for the payment and the eligible health care provider shall have a valid tax identification number: Provided further, That, not later than 3 years after final payments are made under this paragraph, the Office of Inspector General of the Department of Health and Human Services shall transmit a final report on audit findings with respect to this program to the Committees on Appropriations of the House of Representatives and the Senate: Provided further, That nothing in this section limits the authority of the Inspector General or the Comptroller General to conduct audits of interim payments at an earlier date: Provided further, That not later than 60 days after the date of enactment of this Act, the Secretary of Health and Human Services shall provide a report to the Committees on Appropriations of the House of Representatives and the Senate on obligation of funds, including obligations to such eligible health care providers summarized by State of the payment receipt: Provided further, That such reports shall be updated and submitted to such Committees every 60 days until funds are expended: Provided further, That such amount is designated by the Congress as being for an emergency requirement pursuant to section 251(b)(2)(A)(i) of the Balanced Budget and Emergency Deficit Control Act of 1985.

DEPARTMENT OF EDUCATION

EDUCATION STABILIZATION FUND

For an additional amount for "Education Stabilization Fund", $30,750,000,000, to remain available through September 30, 2021, to prevent, prepare for, and respond to coronavirus, domestically or internationally: Provided, That such amount is designated by the Congress as being for an emergency requirement pursuant to section 251(b)(2)(A)(i) of the Balanced Budget and Emergency Deficit Control Act of 1985.

GENERAL PROVISIONS

EDUCATION STABILIZATION FUND

SEC. 18001. (a) ALLOCATIONS.—From the amount made available under this heading in this Act to carry out the Education Stabilization Fund, the Secretary shall first allocate—

(1) not more than 1/2 of 1 percent to the outlying areas on the basis of their respective needs, as determined by the Secretary, in consultation with the Secretary of the Interior;

(2) one-half of 1 percent for the Secretary of Interior, in consultation with the Secretary of Education, for programs operated or funded by the Bureau of Indian Education; and

(3) 1 percent for grants to States with the highest coronavirus burden to support activities under this heading in this Act, for which the Secretary shall issue a notice inviting applications not later than 30 days of enactment of this Act and approve or deny applications not later than 30 days after receipt.

(b) RESERVATIONS.—After carrying out subsection (a), the Secretary shall reserve the remaining funds made available as follows:

(1) 9.8 percent to carry out section 18002 of this title.

(2) 43.9 percent to carry out section 18003 of this title.

(3) 46.3 percent to carry out section 18004 of this title.

GOVERNOR'S EMERGENCY EDUCATION RELIEF FUND

SEC. 18002. (a) GRANTS.—From funds reserved under section 18001(b)(1) of this title, the Secretary shall make Emergency Education Relief grants to the Governor of each State with an approved application. The Secretary shall issue a notice inviting applications not later than 30 days of enactment of this Act and shall approve or deny applications not later than 30 days after receipt.

(b) ALLOCATIONS.—The amount of each grant under subsection (a) shall be allocated by the Secretary to each State as follows:

(1) 60 percent on the basis of their relative population of individuals aged 5 through 24.

(2) 40 percent on the basis of their relative number of children counted under section 1124(c) of the Elementary and Secondary Education Act of 1965 (referred to under this heading as "ESEA").

(c) USES OF FUNDS.—Grant funds awarded under subsection (b) may be used to—

(1) provide emergency support through grants to local educational agencies that the State educational agency deems have been most significantly impacted by coronavirus to support the ability of such local educational agencies to continue to provide educational services to their students and to support the on-going functionality of the local educational agency;

(2) provide emergency support through grants to institutions of higher education serving students within the State that the Governor determines have been most significantly impacted by coronavirus to support the ability of such institutions to continue to provide educational services and support the on-going functionality of the institution; and

(3) provide support to any other institution of higher education, local educational agency, or education related entity within the State that the Governor deems essential for carrying out emergency educational services to students for authorized activities described in section 18003(d)(1) of this title or the Higher Education Act, the provision of child care and early childhood education, social and emotional support, and the protection of education-related jobs.

(d) REALLOCATION.—Each Governor shall return to the Secretary any funds received under this section that the Governor does not award within one year of receiving such funds and the Secretary shall reallocate such funds to the remaining States in accordance with subsection (b).

ELEMENTARY AND SECONDARY SCHOOL EMERGENCY RELIEF FUND

SEC. 18003. (a) GRANTS.—From funds reserved under section 18001(b)(2) of this title, the Secretary shall make elementary and secondary school emergency relief grants to each State educational agency with an approved application. The Secretary shall issue a notice inviting applications not later than 30 days of enactment of this Act and approve or deny applications not later than 30 days after receipt.

(b) ALLOCATIONS TO STATES.—The amount of each grant under subsection (a) shall be allocated by the Secretary to each State in the same proportion as each State received under part A of title I of the ESEA of 1965 in the most recent fiscal year.

(c) SUBGRANTS TO LOCAL EDUCATIONAL AGENCIES.—Each State shall allocate not less than 90 percent of the grant funds awarded to the State under this section as subgrants to local educational agencies (including charter schools that are local educational agencies) in the State in proportion to the amount of funds such local educational agencies and charter schools that are local educational agencies received under part A of title I of the ESEA of 1965 in the most recent fiscal year.

(d) USES OF FUNDS.—A local educational agency that receives funds under this title may use the funds for any of the following:

(1) Any activity authorized by the ESEA of 1965, including the Native Hawaiian Education Act and the Alaska Native Educational Equity, Support, and Assistance Act (20 U.S.C. 6301 et seq.), the Individuals with Disabilities Education Act (20 U.S.C. 1400 et seq.) ("IDEA"), the Adult Education and Family Literacy Act (20 U.S.C. 1400 et seq.), the Carl D. Perkins Career and Technical Education Act of 2006 (20 U.S.C. 2301 et seq.) ("the Perkins Act"), or subtitle B of title VII of the McKinney-Vento Homeless Assistance Act (42 U.S.C. 11431 et seq.).

(2) Coordination of preparedness and response efforts of local educational agencies with State, local, Tribal, and territorial public health departments, and other relevant agencies, to improve coordinated responses among such entities to prevent, prepare for, and respond to coronavirus.

(3) Providing principals and others school leaders with the resources necessary to address the needs of their individual schools.

(4) Activities to address the unique needs of low-income children or students, children with disabilities, English learners, racial and ethnic minorities, students experiencing homelessness, and foster care youth, including how outreach and service delivery will meet the needs of each population.

(5) Developing and implementing procedures and systems to improve the preparedness and response efforts of local educational agencies.

(6) Training and professional development for staff of the local educational agency on sanitation and minimizing the spread of infectious diseases.

(7) Purchasing supplies to sanitize and clean the facilities of a local educational agency, including buildings operated by such agency.

(8) Planning for and coordinating during long-term closures, including for how to provide meals to eligible students, how to provide technology for online learning to all students, how to provide guidance for carrying out requirements under the Individuals with Disabilities Education Act (20 U.S.C. 1401 et seq.) and how to ensure other educational services can continue to be provided consistent with all Federal, State, and local requirements.

(9) Purchasing educational technology (including hardware, software, and connectivity) for students who are served by the local educational agency that aids in regular and substantive educational interaction between students and their classroom instructors, including low-income students and students with disabilities, which may include assistive technology or adaptive equipment.

(10) Providing mental health services and supports.

(11) Planning and implementing activities related to summer learning and supplemental after-school programs, including providing classroom instruction or online learning during the summer months and addressing the needs of low-income students, students with disabilities, English learners, migrant students, students experiencing homelessness, and children in foster care.

(12) Other activities that are necessary to maintain the operation of and continuity of services in local educational agencies and continuing to employ existing staff of the local educational agency.

(e) STATE FUNDING.—With funds not otherwise allocated under subsection (c), a State may reserve not more than 1/2 of 1 percent for administrative costs and the remainder for emergency needs as determined by the state educational agency to address issues responding to coronavirus, which may be addressed through the use of grants or contracts.

(f) REALLOCATION.—A State shall return to the Secretary any funds received under this section that the State does not award within 1 year of receiving such funds and the Secretary shall reallocate such funds to the remaining States in accordance with subsection (b).

HIGHER EDUCATION EMERGENCY RELIEF FUND

SEC. 18004. (a) IN GENERAL.—The Secretary shall allocate funding under this section as follows:

(1) 90 percent to each institution of higher education to prevent, prepare for, and respond to coronavirus, by apportioning it—

(A) 75 percent according to the relative share of full-time equivalent enrollment of Federal Pell Grant recipients who are not exclusively enrolled in distance education courses prior to the coronavirus emergency; and

(B) 25 percent according to the relative share of full-time equivalent enrollment of students who were not Federal Pell Grant recipients who are not exclusively enrolled in distance education courses prior to the coronavirus emergency.

(2) 7.5 percent for additional awards under parts A and B of title III, parts A and B of title V, and subpart 4 of part A of title VII of the Higher Education Act to address needs directly related to coronavirus, that shall be in addition to awards made in section 18004(a)(1) of this title, and allocated by the Secretary proportionally to such programs based on the relative share of funding appropriated to such programs in the Further Consolidated Appropriations Act, 2020 (Public Law 116–94) and which may be used to defray expenses (including lost revenue, reimbursement for expenses already incurred, technology costs associated with a transition to distance education, faculty and staff trainings, payroll) incurred by institutions of higher education and for grants to students for any component of the student's cost of attendance (as defined under section 472 of the Higher Education Act), including food, housing, course materials, technology, health care, and child care.

(3) 2.5 percent for part B of title VII of the Higher Education Act for institutions of higher education that the Secretary determines have the greatest unmet needs related to coronavirus, which may be used to defray expenses (including lost revenue, reimbursement for expenses already incurred, technology costs associated with a transition to distance education, faculty and staff trainings, payroll) incurred by institutions of higher education and for grants to students for any component of the student's cost of attendance (as defined under section 472 of the Higher Education Act), including food, housing, course materials, technology, health care, and child care.

(b) DISTRIBUTION.—The funds made available to each institution under subsection (a)(1) shall be distributed by the Secretary using the same systems as the Secretary otherwise distributes funding to each institution under title IV of the Higher Education Act of 1965 (20 U.S.C. 1001 et seq.).

(c) USES OF FUNDS.—Except as otherwise specified in subsection (a), an institution of higher education receiving funds under this section may use the funds received to cover any costs associated with significant changes to the delivery of instruction due to the coronavirus, so long as such costs do not include payment to contractors for the provision of pre-enrollment recruitment activities; endowments; or capital outlays associated with facilities related to athletics, sectarian instruction, or religious worship. Institutions of higher education shall use no less than 50 percent of such funds to provide emergency financial aid grants to students for expenses related to the disruption of campus operations due to coronavirus (including eligible expenses under a student's cost of attendance, such as food, housing, course materials, technology, health care, and child care).

(d) SPECIAL PROVISIONS.—(1) In awarding grants under section 18004(a)(3) of this title, the Secretary shall give priority to any institution of higher education that is not otherwise eligible for funding under paragraphs (1) and (2) of section 18004(a) of this title of at least $500,000 and demonstrates significant unmet needs related to expenses associated with coronavirus.

(2) A Historically Black College and University or a Minority Serving Institution may use prior awards provided under titles III, V, and VII of the Higher Education Act to prevent, prepare for, and respond to coronavirus.

(e) REPORT.—An institution receiving funds under this section shall submit a report to the Secretary, at such time and in such manner as the Secretary may require, that describes the use of funds provided under this section.

ASSISTANCE TO NON-PUBLIC SCHOOLS

SEC. 18005. (a) IN GENERAL.—A local educational agency receiving funds under sections 18002 or 18003 of this title shall provide equitable services in the same manner as provided under section 1117 of the ESEA of 1965 to students and teachers in non-public schools, as determined in consultation with representatives of non-public schools.

(b) PUBLIC CONTROL OF FUNDS.—The control of funds for the services and assistance provided to a non-public school under subsection (a), and title to materials, equipment, and property purchased with such funds, shall be in a public agency, and a public agency shall administer such funds, materials, equipment, and property and shall provide such services (or may contract for the provision of such services with a public or private entity).

CONTINUED PAYMENT TO EMPLOYEES

SEC. 18006. A local educational agency, State, institution of higher education, or other entity that receives funds under "Education Stabilization Fund", shall to the greatest extent practicable, continue to pay its employees and contractors during the period of any disruptions or closures related to coronavirus.

DEFINITIONS

SEC. 18007. Except as otherwise provided in sections 18001–18006 of this title, as used in such sections—

(1) the terms "elementary education" and "secondary education" have the meaning given such terms under State law;

(2) the term "institution of higher education" has the meaning given such term in title I of the Higher Education Act of 1965 (20 U.S.C. 1001 et seq.);

(3) the term "Secretary" means the Secretary of Education;

(4) the term "State" means each of the 50 States, the District of Columbia, and the Commonwealth of Puerto Rico;

(5) the term "cost of attendance" has the meaning given such term in section 472 of the Higher Education Act of 1965.

(6) the term "Non-public school" means a non-public elementary and secondary school that (A) is accredited, licensed, or otherwise operates in accordance with State law; and (B) was in existence prior to the date of the qualifying emergency for which grants are awarded under this section;

(7) the term "public school" means a public elementary or secondary school; and

(8) any other term used that is defined in section 8101 of the Elementary and Secondary Education Act of 1965 (20 U.S.C. 7801) shall have the meaning given the term in such section.

MAINTENANCE OF EFFORT

SEC. 18008. (a) A State's application for funds to carry out sections 18002 or 18003 of this title shall include assurances that the State will maintain support for elementary and secondary education, and State support for higher education (which shall include State funding to institutions of higher education and state need-based financial aid, and shall not include support for capital projects or for research and development or tuition and fees paid by students) in fiscal years 2020 and 2021 at least at the levels of such support that is the average of such State's support for elementary and secondary education and for higher education provided in the 3 fiscal years preceding the date of enactment of this Act.

(b) The secretary may waive the requirement in subsection (a) for the purpose of relieving fiscal burdens on States that have experienced a precipitous decline in financial resources.

SAFE SCHOOLS AND CITIZENSHIP EDUCATION

For an additional amount for "Safe Schools and Citizenship Education", $100,000,000, to remain available through September 30, 2021, to prevent, prepare for, and respond to coronavirus, domestically or internationally, to supplement funds otherwise available for "Project SERV", including to help elementary, secondary and postsecondary schools clean and disinfect affected schools, and assist in counseling and distance learning and associated costs: Provided, That such amount is designated by the Congress as being for an emergency requirement pursuant to section 251(b)(2)(A)(i) of the Balanced Budget and Emergency Deficit Control Act of 1985.

GALLAUDET UNIVERSITY

For an additional amount for "Gallaudet University", $7,000,000, to remain available through September 30, 2021, to prevent, prepare for, and respond to coronavirus, domestically or internationally, including to help defray the expenses directly caused by coronavirus and to enable grants to students for expenses directly related to coronavirus and the disruption of university operations: Provided, That such amount is designated by the Congress as being for an emergency requirement pursuant to section 251(b)(2)(A)(i) of the Balanced Budget and Emergency Deficit Control Act of 1985.

Student Aid Administration

For an additional amount for "Student Aid Administration", $40,000,000, to remain available through September 30, 2021, to prevent, prepare for, and respond to coronavirus, domestically or internationally, for carrying out part D of title I, and subparts 1, 3, 9 and 10 of part A, and parts B, C, D, and E of title IV of the HEA, and subpart 1 of part A of title VII of the Public Health Service Act: Provided, That such amount is designated by the Congress as being for an emergency requirement pursuant to section 251(b)(2)(A)(i) of the Balanced Budget and Emergency Deficit Control Act of 1985.

Howard University

For an additional amount for "Howard University", $13,000,000, to remain available through September 30, 2021, to prevent, prepare for, and respond to coronavirus, domestically or internationally, including to help defray the expenses directly caused by coronavirus and to enable grants to students for expenses directly related to coronavirus and the disruption of university operations: Provided, That such amount is designated by the Congress as being for an emergency requirement pursuant to section 251(b)(2)(A)(i) of the Balanced Budget and Emergency Deficit Control Act of 1985.

Departmental Management

PROGRAM ADMINISTRATION

For an additional amount for "Program Administration", $8,000,000, to remain available through September 30, 2021 to prevent, prepare for, and respond to coronavirus, domestically or internationally: Provided, That such amount is designated by the Congress as being for an emergency requirement pursuant to section 251(b)(2)(A)(i) of the Balanced Budget and Emergency Deficit Control Act of 1985.

OFFICE OF THE INSPECTOR GENERAL

For an additional amount for "Office of the Inspector General", $7,000,000, to remain available through September 30, 2022, to prevent, prepare for, and respond to coronavirus, domestically or internationally, including for salaries and expenses necessary for oversight and audit of programs, grants, and projects funded in this Act to respond to coronavirus: Provided, That such amount is designated by the Congress as being for an emergency requirement pursuant to section 251(b)(2)(A)(i) of the Balanced Budget and Emergency Deficit Control Act of 1985.

Corporation for Public Broadcasting

For an additional amount for "Corporation for Public Broadcasting", $75,000,000, to remain available through September 30, 2021, to prevent, prepare for, and respond to coronavirus, including for fiscal stabilization grants to public telecommunications entities, as defined by 47 U.S.C. 397(12), with no deduction for administrative or other costs of the Corporation, to maintain programming and services and preserve small and rural stations threatened by declines in non-Federal revenues:

Provided, That such amount is designated by the Congress as being for an emergency requirement pursuant to section 251(b)(2)(A)(i) of the Balanced Budget and Emergency Deficit Control Act of 1985.

INSTITUTE OF MUSEUM AND LIBRARY SERVICES

OFFICE OF MUSEUM AND LIBRARY SERVICES: GRANTS AND ADMINISTRATION

For an additional amount for "Institute of Museum and Library Services", $50,000,000, to remain available until September 30, 2021, to prevent, prepare for, and respond to coronavirus, including grants to States, territories and tribes to expand digital network access, purchase internet accessible devices, and provide technical support services: Provided, That any matching funds requirements for States, tribes, libraries, and museums are waived for grants provided with funds made available under this heading in this Act: Provided further, That such amount is designated by the Congress as being for an emergency requirement pursuant to section 251(b)(2)(A)(i) of the Balanced Budget and Emergency Deficit Control Act of 1985.

RAILROAD RETIREMENT BOARD

LIMITATION ON ADMINISTRATION

For an additional amount for the "Railroad Retirement Board", $5,000,000, to remain available until September 30, 2021, to prevent, prepare for, and respond to coronavirus, including the purchase of information technology equipment to improve the mobility of the workforce and provide for additional hiring or overtime hours as needed to administer the Railroad Unemployment Insurance Act: Provided, That such amount is designated by the Congress as being for an emergency requirement pursuant to section 251(b)(2)(A)(i) of the Balanced Budget and Emergency Deficit Control Act of 1985.

SOCIAL SECURITY ADMINISTRATION

LIMITATION ON ADMINISTRATIVE EXPENSES

For an additional amount for "Limitation on Administrative Expenses", $300,000,000, to remain available through September 30, 2021 to prevent, prepare for, and respond to coronavirus, domestically or internationally, including paying the salaries and benefits of all employees affected as a result of office closures, telework, phone and communication services for employees, overtime costs, and supplies, and for resources necessary for processing disability and retirement workloads and backlogs: Provided, That such amount is designated by the Congress as being for an emergency requirement pursuant to section 251(b)(2)(A)(i) of the Balanced Budget and Emergency Deficit Control Act of 1985.

GENERAL PROVISIONS—THIS TITLE

(INCLUDING TRANSFER OF FUNDS)

SEC. 18108. Funds appropriated by this title may be used by the Secretary of the Department of Health and Human Services to appoint, without regard to the provisions of sections 3309 through 3319 of title 5 of the United States Code, candidates needed for positions to perform critical work relating to coronavirus for which—

(1) public notice has been given; and

(2) the Secretary of Health and Human Services has determined that such a public health threat exists.

SEC. 18109. Funds made available by this title may be used to enter into contracts with individuals for the provision of personal services (as described in section 104 of part 37 of title 48, Code of Federal Regulations (48 CFR 37.104)) to support the prevention of, preparation for, or response to coronavirus, domestically and internationally, subject to prior notification to the Committees on Appropriations of the House of Representatives and the Senate: Provided, That such individuals may not be deemed employees of the United States for the purpose of any law administered by the Office of Personnel Management: Provided further, That the authority made available pursuant to this section shall expire on September 30, 2024.

SEC. 18110. (a) If services performed by an employee during fiscal year 2020 are determined by the head of the agency to be primarily related to preparation, prevention, or response to coronavirus, any premium pay for such services shall be disregarded in calculating the aggregate of such employee's basic pay and premium pay for purposes of a limitation under section 5547(a) of title 5, United States Code, or under any other provision of law, whether such employee's pay is paid on a biweekly or calendar year basis.

(b) Any overtime pay for such services shall be disregarded in calculating any annual limit on the amount of overtime pay payable in a calendar or fiscal year.

(c) With regard to such services, any pay that is disregarded under either subsection (a) or (b) shall be disregarded in calculating such employee's aggregate pay for purposes of the limitation in section 5307 of such title 5.

(d)(1) Pay that is disregarded under subsection (a) or (b) shall not cause the aggregate of the employee's basic pay and premium pay for the applicable calendar year to exceed the rate of basic pay payable for a position at level II of the Executive Schedule under section 5313 of title 5, United States Code, as in effect at the end of such calendar year.

(2) For purposes of applying this subsection to an employee who would otherwise be subject to the premium pay limits established under section 5547 of title 5, United States Code, "premium pay" means the premium pay paid under the provisions of law cited in section 5547(a).

(3) For purposes of applying this subsection to an employee under a premium pay limit established under an authority other than section 5547 of title 5, United States Code, the agency responsible for administering such limit shall determine what payments are considered premium pay.

(e) This section shall take effect as if enacted on February 2, 2020.

(f) If application of this section results in the payment of additional premium pay to a covered employee of a type that is normally creditable as basic pay for retirement or any other purpose, that additional pay shall not—

(1) be considered to be basic pay of the covered employee for any purpose; or

(2) be used in computing a lump-sum payment to the covered employee for accumulated and accrued annual leave under section 5551 or section 5552 of title 5, United States Code.

SEC. 18111. Funds appropriated by this title to the heading "Department of Health and Human Services" may be transferred to, and merged with, other appropriation accounts under the headings "Centers for Disease Control and Prevention", "Public Health and Social Services Emergency Fund", "Administration for Children and Families", "Administration for Community Living", and "National Institutes of Health" to prevent, prepare for, and respond to coronavirus following consultation with the Office of Management and Budget: Provided, That the Committees on Appropriations of the House of Representatives and the Senate shall be notified 10 days in advance of any such transfer: Provided further, That, upon a determination that all or part of the funds transferred from an appropriation by this title are not necessary, such amounts may be transferred back to that appropriation: Provided further, That none of the funds made available by this title may be transferred pursuant to the authority in section 205 of division A of Public Law 116–94 or section 241(a) of the PHS Act.

SEC. 18112. Not later than 30 days after the date of enactment of this Act, the Secretary of Health and Human Services shall provide a detailed spend plan of anticipated uses of funds made available to the Department of Health and Human Services in this Act, including estimated personnel and administrative costs, to the Committees on Appropriations of the House of Representatives and the Senate: Provided, That such plans shall be updated and submitted to such Committees every 60 days until September 30, 2024: Provided further, That the spend plans shall be accompanied by a listing of each contract obligation incurred that exceeds $5,000,000 which has not previously been reported, including the amount of each such obligation.

SEC. 18113. Of the funds appropriated by this title under the heading "Public Health and Social Services Emergency Fund", up to $4,000,000 shall be transferred to, and merged with, funds made available under the heading "Office of the Secretary, Office of Inspector General", and shall remain available until expended, for oversight of activities supported with funds appropriated to the Department of Health and Human Services to prevent, prepare for, and respond to coronavirus, domestically or internationally: Provided, That the Inspector General of the Department of Health and Human Services shall consult with the Committees on Appropriations of the House of Representatives and the Senate prior to obligating such funds: Provided further, That the transfer authority provided by this section is in addition to any other transfer authority provided by law.

SEC. 18114. (a) Funds appropriated in title III of the Coronavirus Preparedness and Response Supplemental Appropriations Act, 2020 (Public Law 116–123) shall be paid to the "Department of Homeland Security—Countering Weapons of Mass Destruction Office—Federal Assistance" account for costs incurred, including to reimburse costs incurred prior to the enactment of this Act, under other transaction authority and related to screening for coronavirus, domestically or internationally.

(b) The term coronavirus has the meaning given the term in section 506 of the Coronavirus Preparedness and Response Supplemental Appropriations Act, 2020.

(c) The amounts repurposed in this section that were previously designated by the Congress as an emergency requirement pursuant to the Balanced Budget and Emergency Deficit Control Act of 1985 are designated by the Congress as an emergency requirement pursuant to section 251(b)(2)(A)(i) of the Balanced Budget and Emergency Deficit Control Act of 1985.

SEC. 18115. (a) IN GENERAL.—Every laboratory that performs or analyzes a test that is intended to detect SARS–CoV–2 or to diagnose a possible case of COVID–19 shall report the results from each such test, to the Secretary of Health and Human Services in such form and manner, and at such timing and frequency, as the Secretary may prescribe until the end of the Secretary's Public Health Emergency declaration with respect to COVID–19 or any extension of such declaration.

(b) LABORATORIES COVERED.—The Secretary may prescribe which laboratories must submit reports pursuant to this section.

(c) IMPLEMENTATION.—The Secretary may make prescriptions under this section by regulation, including by interim final rule, or by guidance, and may issue such regulations or guidance without regard to the procedures otherwise required by section 553 of title 5, United States Code.

(d) REPEALER.—Section 1702 of division A of the Families First Coronavirus Response Act is repealed.

TITLE IX LEGISLATIVE BRANCH SENATE

CONTINGENT EXPENSES OF THE SENATE

SERGEANT AT ARMS AND DOORKEEPER OF THE SENATE

For an additional amount for "Sergeant at Arms and Doorkeeper of the Senate", $1,000,000, to remain available until expended, to prevent, prepare for, and respond to coronavirus, domestically or internationally: Provided, That such amount is designated by the Congress as being for an emergency requirement pursuant to section 251(b)(2)(A)(i) of the Balanced Budget and Emergency Deficit Control Act of 1985.

MISCELLANEOUS ITEMS

For an additional amount for "Miscellaneous Items", $9,000,000, to remain available until expended, to prevent, prepare for, and respond to coronavirus, domestically or internationally, subject to approval by the Committee on Appropriations of the Senate and the Senate Committee on Rules and Administration: Provided, That such amount is designated by the Congress as being for an emergency requirement pursuant to section 251(b)(2)(A)(i) of the Balanced Budget and Emergency Deficit Control Act of 1985.

HOUSE OF REPRESENTATIVES

SALARIES AND EXPENSES

For an additional amount for "Salaries and Expenses", $25,000,000, to remain available until September 30, 2021, except that $5,000,000 shall remain available until expended, to prevent, prepare for, and respond to coronavirus, domestically or internationally, to be allocated in accordance with a spend plan submitted to the Committee on Appropriations of the House of Representatives by the Chief Administrative Officer and approved by such Committee: Provided, That such amount is designated by the Congress as being for an emergency requirement pursuant to section 251(b)(2)(A)(i) of the Balanced Budget and Emergency Deficit Control Act of 1985.

JOINT ITEMS

OFFICE OF THE ATTENDING PHYSICIAN

For an additional amount for "Office of the Attending Physician", $400,000, to remain available until expended, to prevent, prepare for, and respond to coronavirus, domestically or internationally: Provided, That such amount is designated by the Congress as being for an emergency requirement pursuant to section 251(b)(2)(A)(i) of the Balanced Budget and Emergency Deficit Control Act of 1985.

CAPITOL POLICE

SALARIES

For an additional amount for "Salaries", $12,000,000, to remain available until September 30, 2021, to prevent, prepare for, and respond to coronavirus, domestically or internationally: Provided, That the Capitol Police may transfer amounts appropriated under this heading in this Act to "General Expenses" without the approval requirement of 2 U.S.C. 1907(a): Provided further, That such amount is designated by the Congress as being for an emergency requirement pursuant to section 251(b)(2)(A)(i) of the Balanced Budget and Emergency Deficit Control Act of 1985.

ARCHITECT OF THE CAPITOL

CAPITAL CONSTRUCTION AND OPERATIONS

For an additional amount for "Capital Construction and Operations", $25,000,000, to remain available until September 30, 2021, to prevent, prepare for, and respond to coronavirus, domestically or internationally, including to purchase and distribute cleaning and sanitation products throughout all facilities and grounds under the care of the Architect of the Capitol, wherever located, and any related services and operational costs: Provided, That the Architect of the Capitol shall provide a report within 30 days enactment of this Act, and every 30 days thereafter, to the Committees on Appropriations of the Senate and House of Representatives, the Senate Committee on Rules and Administration, and the Committee on House Administration on expenditure of funds from amounts appropriated under this heading in this Act: Provided further, That this amount shall be in addition to any other funds available for such purposes in appropriations Acts for the legislative branch: Provided further, That such amount is designated by the Congress as being for an emergency requirement pursuant to section 251(b)(2)(A)(i) of the Balanced Budget and Emergency Deficit Control Act of 1985.

LIBRARY OF CONGRESS

SALARIES AND EXPENSES

For an additional amount for "Salaries and Expenses", $700,000, to remain available until September 30, 2020, to prevent, prepare for, and respond to coronavirus, domestically or internationally, to be made available to the Little Scholars Child Development Center, subject to approval by the Committees on Appropriations of the Senate and House of Representatives, the Senate Committee on Rules and Administration, and the Committee on House Administration: Provided, That such amount is designated by the Congress as being for an emergency requirement pursuant to section 251(b)(2)(A)(i) of the Balanced Budget and Emergency Deficit Control Act of 1985.

GOVERNMENT ACCOUNTABILITY OFFICE

SALARIES AND EXPENSES

For an additional amount for "Salaries and Expenses", $20,000,000, to remain available until expended, to prevent, prepare for, and respond to coronavirus, domestically or internationally, for audits and investigations and for reimbursement of the Tiny Findings Child Development Center for salaries for employees, as authorized by this Act: Provided, That not later than 90 days after the date of enactment of this Act, the Government Accountability Office shall submit to the Committees on Appropriations of the House of Representatives and the Senate a spend plan specifying funding estimates and a timeline for such audits and investigations: Provided further, That $600,000 shall be made available to the Tiny Findings Child Development Center, subject to approval by the Committees on Appropriations of the Senate and House of Representatives, the Senate Committee on Rules and Administration, and the Committee on House Administration: Provided further, That such amount is designated by the Congress as being for an emergency requirement pursuant to section 251(b)(2)(A)(i) of the Balanced Budget and Emergency Deficit Control Act of 1985.

GENERAL PROVISIONS—THIS TITLE

SOURCE OF FUNDS USED FOR PAYMENT OF SALARIES AND EXPENSES OF SENATE EMPLOYEE CHILD CARE CENTER

SEC. 19001. The Secretary of the Senate shall reimburse the Senate Employee Child Care Center for personnel costs incurred starting on April 1, 2020, for employees of such Center who have been ordered to cease working due to measures taken in the Capitol complex to combat coronavirus, not to exceed $84,000 per month, from amounts in the appropriations account "Miscellaneous Items" within the contingent fund of the Senate.

SOURCE OF FUNDS USED FOR PAYMENT OF SALARIES AND EXPENSES OF HOUSE OF REPRESENTATIVES CHILD CARE CENTER

SEC. 19002. (a) AUTHORIZING USE OF REVOLVING FUND OR APPROPRIATED FUNDS.—Section 312(d)(3)(A) of the Legislative Branch Appropriations Act, 1992 (2 U.S.C. 2062(d)(3)(A)) is amended—

(1) in subparagraph (A), by striking the period at the end and inserting the following: ", and, at the option of the Chief Administrative Officer during an emergency situation, the payment of the salary of other employees of the Center."; and

(2) by adding at the end the following new subparagraph:

(C) "During an emergency situation, the payment of such other expenses for activities carried out under this section as the Chief Administrative Officer determines appropriate.".

(b) EFFECTIVE DATE.—The amendment made by subsection (a) shall apply with respect to fiscal year 2020 and each succeeding fiscal year.

PAYMENTS TO ENSURE CONTINUING AVAILABILITY OF GOODS AND SERVICES DURING THE CORONAVIRUS EMERGENCY

SEC. 19003. (a) AUTHORIZATION TO MAKE PAYMENTS.—Notwithstanding any other provision of law and subject to subsection (b), during an emergency situation, the Chief Administrative Officer of the House of Representatives may make payments under contracts with vendors providing goods and services to the House in amounts and under terms and conditions other than those provided under the contract in order to ensure that those goods and services remain available to the House throughout the duration of the emergency.

(b) CONDITIONS.—

(1) APPROVAL REQUIRED.—The Chief Administrative Officer may not make payments under the authority of subsection (a) without the approval of the Committee on House Administration of the House of Representatives.

(2) AVAILABILITY OF APPROPRIATIONS.—The authority of the Chief Administrative Officer to make payments under the authority of subsection (a) is subject to the availability of appropriations to make such payments.

(c) APPLICABILITY.—This section shall apply with respect to fiscal year 2020 and each succeeding fiscal year.

SOURCE OF FUNDS USED FOR PAYMENT OF SALARIES AND EXPENSES OF LITTLE SCHOLARS CHILD DEVELOPMENT CENTER

SEC. 19004. The Library of Congress shall reimburse Little Scholars Child Development Center for salaries for employees incurred from April 1, 2020, to September 30, 2020, for employees of such Center who have been ordered to cease working due to measures taken in the Capitol complex to combat coronavirus, not to exceed $113,000 per month, from amounts in the appropriations account "Library of Congress—Salaries and Expenses".

AUTHORIZING PAYMENTS UNDER SERVICE CONTRACTS DURING THE CORONAVIRUS EMERGENCY

SEC. 19005. (a) AUTHORIZING PAYMENTS.—Notwithstanding section 3324(a) of title 31, United States Code, or any other provision of law and subject to subsection (b), if the employees of a contractor with a service contract with the Architect of the Capitol are furloughed or otherwise unable to work during closures, stop work orders, or reductions in service arising from or related to the impacts of coronavirus, the Architect of the Capitol may continue to make the payments provided for under the contract for the weekly salaries and benefits of such employees for not more than 16 weeks.

(b) AVAILABILITY OF APPROPRIATIONS.—The authority of the Architect of the Capitol to make payments under the authority of subsection (a) is subject to the availability of appropriations to make such payments.

(c) REGULATIONS.—The Architect of the Capitol shall promulgate such regulations as may be necessary to carry out this section.

MASS MAILINGS AS FRANKED MAIL

SEC. 19006. (a) WAIVER.—Section 3210(a)(6)(D) of title 39, United States Code, is amended by striking the period at the end of the first sentence and inserting the following: ", and in the case of the Commission, to waive this paragraph in the case of mailings sent in response to or to address threats to life safety.".

(b) EFFECTIVE DATE.—The amendments made by this subsection shall apply with respect to mailings sent on or after the date of the enactment of this Act.

TECHNICAL CORRECTION

SEC. 19007. In the matter preceding the first proviso under the heading "Library of Congress—Salaries and Expenses" in division E of the Further Consolidated Appropriations Act, 2020 (Public Law 116–94), strike "$504,164,000" and insert "$510,164,000".

CONFORMING AMENDMENT

[¶2240] SEC. 19008. Section 110(a)(1)(A) of the Family and Medical Leave Act of 1993 (as added by section 3102 of the Families First Coronavirus Response Act (Public Law 116–127)) is amended—

(1) by inserting before "In lieu of" the following:

(i) "IN GENERAL.—"; and

(2) by adding at the end the following:

(ii) "SPECIAL RULE.—For purposes of applying section 102(a)(1)(F) and this section under the Congressional Accountability Act of 1995, in lieu of the definition in section 202(a)(2)(B) of that Act (2 U.S.C. 1312(a)(2)(B)), the term 'eligible employee' means a covered employee (as defined in section 101 of that Act (2 U.S.C. 1301)) who has been employed for at least 30 calendar days by the employing office (as so defined) with respect to whom leave is requested under section 102(a)(1)(F).".

SOURCE OF FUNDS USED FOR PAYMENT OF SALARIES AND EXPENSES OF TINY FINDINGS CHILD DEVELOPMENT CENTER

SEC. 19009. The Government Accountability Office may reimburse the Tiny Findings Child Development Center for salaries for employees incurred from April 1, 2020, to September 30, 2020, for employees of such Center who have been ordered to cease working due to measures taken in the Capitol complex to combat coronavirus, not to exceed $100,000 per month, from amounts in the appropriations account "Government Accountability Office—Salaries and Expenses".

OVERSIGHT AND AUDIT AUTHORITY

SEC. 19010. (a) DEFINITIONS.—In this section—

(1) the term "appropriate congressional committees" means—

(A) the Committee on Appropriations of the Senate;

(B) the Committee on Homeland Security and Governmental Affairs of the Senate;

(C) the Committee on Health, Education, Labor, and Pensions of the Senate;

(D) the Committee on Appropriations of the House of Representatives;

(E) the Committee on Homeland Security of the House of Representatives;

(F) the Committee on Oversight and Reform of the House of Representatives; and

(G) the Committee on Energy and Commerce of the House of Representatives; and

(2) the term "Comptroller General" means the Comptroller General of the United States.

(b) AUTHORITY.—The Comptroller General shall conduct monitoring and oversight of the exercise of authorities, or the receipt, disbursement, and use of funds made available, under this Act or any other Act to prepare for, respond to, and recover from the Coronavirus 2019 pandemic and the effect of the pandemic on the health, economy, and public and private institutions of the United States, including public health and homeland security efforts by the Federal Government and the use of selected funds under this or any other Act related to the Coronavirus 2019 pandemic and a comprehensive audit and review of charges made to Federal contracts pursuant to authorities provided in the Coronavirus Aid, Relief, and Economic Security Act.

(c) BRIEFINGS AND REPORTS.—In conducting monitoring and oversight under subsection (b), the Comptroller General shall—

(1) during the period beginning on the date of enactment of this Act and ending on the date on which the national emergency declared by the President under the National Emergencies Act (50 U.S.C. 1601 et seq.) with respect to the Coronavirus Disease 2019 (COVID–19) expires, offer regular briefings on not less frequently than a monthly basis to the appropriate congressional committees regarding Federal public health and homeland security efforts;

(2) publish reports regarding the ongoing monitoring and oversight efforts, which, along with any audits and investigations conducted by the Comptroller General, shall be submitted to the appropriate congressional committees and posted on the website of the Government Accountability Office—

(A) not later than 90 days after the date of enactment of this Act, and every other month thereafter until the date that is 1 year after the date of enactment of this Act; and

(B) after the period described in subparagraph (A), on a periodic basis; and

(3) submit to the appropriate congressional committees additional reports as warranted by the findings of the monitoring and oversight activities of the Comptroller General.

(d) ACCESS TO INFORMATION.—

(1) RIGHT OF ACCESS.—In conducting monitoring and oversight activities under this section, the Comptroller General shall have access to records, upon request, of any Federal, State, or local agency, contractor, grantee, recipient, or subrecipient pertaining to any Federal effort or assistance of any type related to the Coronavirus 2019 pandemic under this Act or any other Act, including private entities receiving such assistance.

(2) COPIES.—The Comptroller General may make and retain copies of any records accessed under paragraph (1) as the Comptroller General determines appropriate.

(3) INTERVIEWS.—In addition to such other authorities as are available, the Comptroller General or a designee of the Comptroller General may interview Federal, State, or local officials, contractor staff, grantee staff, recipients, or subrecipients pertaining to any Federal effort or assistance of any type related to the Coronavirus 2019 pandemic under this or any other Act, including private entities receiving such assistance.

(4) INSPECTION OF FACILITIES.—As determined necessary by the Comptroller General, the Government Accountability Office may inspect facilities at which Federal, State, or local officials, contractor staff, grantee staff, or recipients or subrecipients carry out their responsibilities related to the Coronavirus 2019 pandemic.

(5) ENFORCEMENT.—Access rights under this subsection shall be subject to enforcement consistent with section 716 of title 31, United States Code.

(e) RELATIONSHIP TO EXISTING AUTHORITY.—Nothing in this section shall be construed to limit, amend, supersede, or restrict in any manner any existing authority of the Comptroller General.

NATIONAL EMERGENCY RELIEF AUTHORITY FOR THE REGISTER OF COPYRIGHTS

SEC. 19011. (a) AMENDMENT.—Chapter 7 of title 17, United States Code, is amended by adding at the end the following:

[¶ 2240A] SEC. 710. "Emergency relief authority

(a) "EMERGENCY ACTION.—If, on or before December 31, 2021, the Register of Copyrights determines that a national emergency declared by the President under the National Emergencies Act (50 U.S.C. 1601 et seq.) generally disrupts or suspends the ordinary functioning of the copyright system under this title, or any component thereof, including on a regional basis, the Register may, on a temporary basis, toll, waive, adjust, or modify any timing provision (including any deadline or effective period, except as provided in subsection (c)) or procedural provision contained in this title or chapters II or III of title 37, Code of Federal Regulations, for no longer than the Register reasonably determines to be appropriate to mitigate the impact of the disruption caused by the national emergency. In taking such action, the Register shall consider the scope and severity of the particular national emergency, and its specific effect with respect to the particular provision, and shall tailor any remedy accordingly.

(b) "NOTICE AND EFFECT.—Any action taken by the Register in response to a national emergency pursuant to subsection (a) shall not be subject to section 701(e) or subchapter II of chapter 5 of title 5, United States Code, and chapter 7 of title 5, United States Code. The provision of general public notice detailing the action being taken by the Register in response to the national emergency under subsection (a) is sufficient to effectuate such action. The Register may make such action effective both prospectively and retroactively in relation to a particular provision as the Register determines to be appropriate based on the timing, scope, and nature of the public emergency, but any action by the Register may only be retroactive with respect to a deadline that has not already passed before the declaration described in subsection (a).

(c) "STATEMENT REQUIRED.—Except as provided in subsection (d), not later than 20 days after taking any action that results in a provision being modified for a cumulative total of longer than 120 days, the Register shall submit to Congress a statement detailing the action taken, the relevant background, and rationale for the action.

(d) "EXCEPTIONS.—The authority of the Register to act under subsection (a) does not extend provisions under this title requiring the commencement of an action or proceeding in Federal court within a specified period of time, except that if the Register adjusts the license availability date defined in section 115(e)(15), such adjustment shall not affect the ability to commence actions for any claim of infringement of exclusive rights provided by paragraphs (1) and (3) of section 106 against a digital music provider arising from the unauthorized reproduction or distribution of a musical work by such digital music provider in the course of engaging in covered activities that accrued after January 1, 2018, provided that such action is commenced within the time periods prescribed under section 115(d)(10)(C)(i) or 115(d)(10)(C)(ii) as calculated from the adjusted license availability date. If the Register adjusts the license availability date, the Register must provide the statement to Congress under subsection (c) at the same time as the public notice of such adjustment with a detailed explanation of why such adjustment is needed.

(e) "COPYRIGHT TERM EXCEPTION.—The authority of the Register to act under subsection (a) does not extend to provisions under chapter 3, except section 304(c), or section 1401(a)(2).

(f) "OTHER LAWS.—Notwithstanding section 301 of the National Emergencies Act (50 U.S.C. 1631), the authority of the Register under subsection (a) is not contingent on a specification made by the President under such section or any other requirement under that Act (other than the emergency declaration under section 201(a) of such Act (50 U.S.C. 1621(a))). The authority described in this section supersedes the authority of title II of the National Emergencies Act (50 U.S.C. 1621 et seq.).".

(b) TECHNICAL AND CONFORMING AMENDMENT.—The table of sections for chapter 7 of title 17, United States Code, is amended by adding at the end the following:

"710. Emergency relief authority.".

(c) EMERGENCY REQUIREMENT.—The amount provided by this section is designated by the Congress as being for an emergency requirement pursuant to section 251(b)(2)(A)(i) of the Balanced Budget and Emergency Deficit Control Act of 1985.

TITLE X DEPARTMENT OF VETERANS AFFAIRS

VETERANS BENEFITS ADMINISTRATION

GENERAL OPERATING EXPENSES, VETERANS BENEFITS ADMINISTRATION

For an additional amount for "General Operating Expenses, Veterans Benefits Administration", $13,000,000, to remain available until September 30, 2021, to prevent, prepare for, and respond to coronavirus, domestically or internationally: Provided, That such amount is designated by the Congress as being for an emergency requirement pursuant to section 251(b)(2)(A)(i) of the Balanced Budget and Emergency Deficit Control Act of 1985.

VETERANS HEALTH ADMINISTRATION

MEDICAL SERVICES

For an additional amount for "Medical Services", $14,432,000,000, to remain available until September 30, 2021, to prevent, prepare for, and respond to coronavirus, domestically or internationally, including related impacts on health care delivery, and for support to veterans who are homeless or at risk of becoming homeless: Provided, That such amount is designated by the Congress as being for an emergency requirement pursuant to section 251(b)(2)(A)(i) of the Balanced Budget and Emergency Deficit Control Act of 1985.

MEDICAL COMMUNITY CARE

For an additional amount for "Medical Community Care", $2,100,000,000, to remain available until September 30, 2021, to prevent, prepare for, and respond to coronavirus, domestically or internationally, including related impacts on health care delivery: Provided, That such amount is designated by the Congress as being for an emergency requirement pursuant to section 251(b)(2)(A)(i) of the Balanced Budget and Emergency Deficit Control Act of 1985.

MEDICAL SUPPORT AND COMPLIANCE

For an additional amount for "Medical Support and Compliance", $100,000,000, to remain available until September 30, 2021, to prevent, prepare for, and respond to coronavirus, domestically or internationally, including related impacts on health care delivery: Provided, That such amount is designated by the Congress as being for an emergency requirement pursuant to section 251(b)(2)(A)(i) of the Balanced Budget and Emergency Deficit Control Act of 1985.

MEDICAL FACILITIES

For an additional amount for "Medical Facilities", $606,000,000, to remain available until September 30, 2021, to prevent, prepare for, and respond to coronavirus, domestically or internationally, including related impacts on health care delivery: Provided, That such amount is designated by the Congress as being for an emergency requirement pursuant to section 251(b)(2)(A)(i) of the Balanced Budget and Emergency Deficit Control Act of 1985.

DEPARTMENTAL ADMINISTRATION

GENERAL ADMINISTRATION

For an additional amount for "General Administration", $6,000,000, to remain available until September 30, 2021, to prevent, prepare for, and respond to coronavirus, domestically or internationally: Provided, That such amount is designated by the Congress as being for an emergency requirement pursuant to section 251(b)(2)(A)(i) of the Balanced Budget and Emergency Deficit Control Act of 1985.

INFORMATION TECHNOLOGY SYSTEMS

For an additional amount for "Information Technology Systems", $2,150,000,000, to remain available until September 30, 2021, to prevent, prepare for, and respond to coronavirus, domestically or internationally, including related impacts on health care delivery: Provided, That the Secretary shall transmit to the Committees on Appropriations of both Houses of Congress a spend plan detailing the allocation of such funds between pay and associated costs, operations and maintenance, and information technology systems development: Provided further, That after such transmittal is provided, funds may only be reprogrammed among the three subaccounts referenced in the previous proviso after the Secretary of Veterans Affairs submits notice to the Committees on Appropriations of both Houses of Congress: Provided further, That such amount is designated by the Congress as being for an emergency requirement pursuant to section 251(b)(2)(A)(i) of the Balanced Budget and Emergency Deficit Control Act of 1985.

OFFICE OF INSPECTOR GENERAL

For an additional amount for "Office of Inspector General", $12,500,000, to remain available until September 30, 2022, to prevent, prepare for, and respond to coronavirus, domestically or internationally, for oversight and audit of programs, activities, grants and projects funded under this title: Provided, That such amount is designated by the Congress as being for an emergency requirement pursuant to section 251(b)(2)(A)(i) of the Balanced Budget and Emergency Deficit Control Act of 1985.

GRANTS FOR CONSTRUCTION OF STATE EXTENDED CARE FACILITIES

For an additional amount for "Grants for Construction of State Extended Care Facilities", $150,000,000, to remain available until September 30, 2021, to prevent, prepare for, and respond to coronavirus, domestically or internationally, including to modify or alter existing hospital, nursing home, and domiciliary facilities in State homes: Provided, That such amount is designated by the Congress as being for an emergency requirement pursuant to section 251(b)(2)(A)(i) of the Balanced Budget and Emergency Deficit Control Act of 1985.

RELATED AGENCIES

ARMED FORCES RETIREMENT HOME TRUST FUND

For an additional amount for the "Armed Forces Retirement Home Trust Fund", $2,800,000, to remain available until September 30, 2021, to prevent, prepare for, and respond to coronavirus, to be paid from funds available in the Armed Forces Retirement Home Trust Fund: Provided, That of the amounts made available under this heading from funds available in the Armed Forces Retirement Home Trust Fund, $2,800,000 shall be paid from the general fund of the Treasury to the Trust Fund: Provided further, That the Chief Executive Officer of the Armed Forces Retirement Home shall submit to the Committees on Appropriations of both Houses of Congress monthly reports detailing obligations, expenditures, and planned activities: Provided further, That such amount is designated by the Congress as being for an emergency requirement pursuant to section 251(b)(2)(A)(i) of the Balanced Budget and Emergency Deficit Control Act of 1985.

GENERAL PROVISIONS—THIS TITLE

(INCLUDING TRANSFER OF FUNDS)

SEC. 20001. Amounts made available for the Department of Veterans Affairs in this title, under the "Medical Services", "Medical Community Care", "Medical Support and Compliance", and "Medical Facilities" accounts may be transferred among the accounts to prevent, prepare for, and respond to coronavirus, domestically and internationally: Provided, That any transfers among the "Medical Services", "Medical Community Care", "Medical Support and Compliance", and "Medical Facilities" accounts of 2 percent or less of the total amount appropriated to an account in this title may take place subject to notification from the Secretary of Veterans Affairs to the Committees on Appropriations of both Houses of Congress of the amount and purpose of the transfer: Provided further, That any transfers among the "Medical Services", "Medical Community Care", "Medical Support and Compliance", and "Medical Facilities" accounts in excess of 2 percent of the total amount appropriated to an account in this title, or exceeding a cumulative 2 percent for all of the funds provided in this title, may take place only after the Secretary requests from the Committees on Appropriations of both Houses of Congress the authority to make the transfer and an approval is issued.

SEC. 20002. For all of the funds appropriated in this title the Secretary of Veterans Affairs shall submit to the Committees on Appropriations of both Houses of Congress monthly reports detailing obligations, expenditures, and planned activities.

PUBLIC HEALTH EMERGENCY

SEC. 20003. In this title, the term "public health emergency" means an emergency with respect to COVID–19 declared by a Federal, State, or local authority.

SHORT-TERM AGREEMENTS OR CONTRACTS WITH TELECOMMUNICATIONS PROVIDERS TO EXPAND TELEMENTAL HEALTH SERVICES FOR ISOLATED VETERANS DURING A PUBLIC HEALTH EMERGENCY

SEC. 20004. (a) IN GENERAL.—Notwithstanding any other provision of law, the Secretary of Veterans Affairs may enter into short-term agreements or contracts with telecommunications companies to provide temporary, complimentary or subsidized, fixed and mobile broadband services for the purposes of providing expanded mental health services to isolated veterans through telehealth or VA Video Connect during a public health emergency.

(b) ELIGIBILITY.—

(1) IN GENERAL.—The Secretary may expand eligibility for services described in subsection (a) from the Department of Veterans Affairs to include veterans already receiving care from the Department who may not be eligible for mental health services or other health care services delivered through telehealth or VA Video Connect.

(2) PRIORITY.—For purposes of expanding eligibility under paragraph (1), the Secretary shall prioritize—

(A) veterans who are in unserved and underserved areas;

(B) veterans who reside in rural and highly rural areas, as defined in the Rural-Urban Commuting Areas coding system of the Department of Agriculture;

(C) low-income veterans; and

(D) any other veterans that the Secretary considers to be at a higher risk for suicide and mental health concerns during isolation periods due to a public health emergency.

(c) DEFINITIONS.—In this section:

(1) TELEHEALTH.—

(A) IN GENERAL.—The term "telehealth" means the use of electronic information and telecommunications technologies to support and promote long-distance clinical health care, patient and professional health-related education, public health, and health administration.

(B) TECHNOLOGIES.—For purposes of subparagraph (A), telecommunications technologies include videoconferencing, the internet, streaming media, and terrestrial and wireless communications.

(2) VA VIDEO CONNECT.—The term "VA Video Connect" means the program of the Department of Veterans Affairs to connect veterans with their health care team from anywhere, using encryption to ensure a secure and private session.

TREATMENT OF STATE HOMES DURING PUBLIC HEALTH EMERGENCY

SEC. 20005. (a) WAIVER OF OCCUPANCY RATE REQUIREMENTS.—During a public health emergency, occupancy rate requirements for State homes for purposes of receiving per diem payments set forth in section 51.40(c) of title 38, Code of Federal Regulations, or successor regulations, shall not apply.

(b) WAIVER OF VETERAN PERCENTAGE REQUIREMENTS.—During a public health emergency, the veteran percentage requirements for State homes set forth in section 51.210(d) of title 38, Code of Regulations, or successor regulations, and in agreements for grants to construct State homes, shall not apply.

(c) PROVISION OF MEDICINE, EQUIPMENT, AND SUPPLIES.—

(1) IN GENERAL.—During a public health emergency, the Secretary of Veterans Affairs may provide to State homes medicines, personal protective equipment, medical supplies, and any other equipment, supplies, and assistance available to the Department of Veterans Affairs.

(2) PROVISION OF EQUIPMENT.—Personal protective equipment may be provided under paragraph (1) through the All Hazards Emergency Cache of the Department of Veterans Affairs or any other source available to the Department.

(d) DEFINITIONS.—In this section:

(1) PERSONAL PROTECTIVE EQUIPMENT.—The term "personal protective equipment" means any protective equipment required to prevent the wearer from contracting COVID–19, including gloves, N–95 respirator masks, gowns, goggles, face shields, or other equipment required for safety.

(2) PUBLIC HEALTH EMERGENCY.—The term "public health emergency" means an emergency with respect to COVID–19 declared by a Federal, State, or local authority.

(3) STATE HOME.—The term "State home" has the meaning given that term in section 101(19) of title 38, United States Code.

MODIFICATIONS TO VETERAN DIRECTED CARE PROGRAM OF DEPARTMENT OF VETERANS AFFAIRS

SEC. 20006. (a) TELEPHONE OR TELEHEALTH RENEWALS.—For the Veteran Directed Care program of the Department of Veterans Affairs (in this section referred to as the "Program"), during a public health emergency, the Secretary of Veterans Affairs shall—

(1) waive the requirement that an area agency on aging process new enrollments and six-month renewals for the Program via an in-person or home visit; and

(2) allow new enrollments and sixth-month renewals for the Program to be conducted via telephone or telehealth modality.

(b) NO SUSPENSION OR DISENROLLMENT.—During a public health emergency, the Secretary shall not suspend or dis-enroll a veteran or caregiver of a veteran from the Program unless—

(1) requested to do so by the veteran or a representative of the veteran; or

(2) a mutual decision is made between the veteran and a health care provider of the veteran to suspend or dis-enroll the veteran or caregiver from the Program.

(c) WAIVER OF PAPERWORK REQUIREMENT.—During a public health emergency, the Secretary may waive the requirement for signed, mailed paperwork to confirm the enrollment or renewal of a veteran in the Program and may allow verbal consent of the veteran via telephone or telehealth modality to suffice for purposes of such enrollment or renewal.

(d) WAIVER OF OTHER REQUIREMENTS.—During a public health emergency, the Secretary shall waive—

(1) any penalty for late paperwork relating to the Program; and

(2) any requirement to stop payments for veterans or caregivers of veterans under the Program if they are out of State for more than 14 days.

(e) AREA AGENCY ON AGING DEFINED.—In this section, the term "area agency on aging" has the meaning given that term in section 102 of the Older Americans Act of 1965 (42 U.S.C. 3002).

PROVISION BY DEPARTMENT OF VETERANS AFFAIRS OF PROSTHETIC APPLIANCES THROUGH NON-DEPARTMENT PROVIDERS DURING PUBLIC HEALTH EMERGENCY

SEC. 20007. The Secretary of Veterans Affairs shall ensure that, to the extent practicable, veterans who are receiving or are eligible to receive a prosthetic appliance under section 1714 or 1719 of title

38, United States Code, are able to receive such an appliance that the Secretary determines is needed from a non-Department of Veterans Affairs provider under a contract with the Department during a public health emergency.

WAIVER OF PAY CAPS FOR EMPLOYEES OF DEPARTMENT OF VETERANS AFFAIRS DURING PUBLIC HEALTH EMERGENCIES

SEC. 20008. (a) IN GENERAL.—Notwithstanding any other provision of law, the Secretary of Veterans Affairs may waive any limitation on pay for an employee of the Department of Veterans Affairs during a public health emergency for work done in support of response to the emergency.

(b) REPORTING.—

(1) IN GENERAL.—For each month that the Secretary waives a limitation under subsection (a), the Secretary shall submit to the Committee on Veterans' Affairs of the Senate and the Committee on Veterans' Affairs of the House of Representatives a report on the waiver.

(2) CONTENTS.—Each report submitted under paragraph (1) for a waiver or waivers in a month shall include the following:

(A) Where the waiver or waivers were used, including in which component of the Department and, as the case may be, which medical center of the Department.

(B) For how many employees the waiver or waivers were used, disaggregated by component of the Department and, if applicable, medical center of the Department.

(C) The average amount by which each payment exceeded the waived pay limitation that was waived, disaggregated by component of the Department and, if applicable, medical center of the Department.

(c) EMPLOYEE OF THE DEPARTMENT OF VETERANS AFFAIRS DEFINED.—In this section, the term "employee of the Department of Veterans Affairs" includes any employee of the Department of Veterans Affairs, regardless of the authority under which the employee was hired.

PROVISION BY DEPARTMENT OF VETERANS AFFAIRS OF PERSONAL PROTECTIVE EQUIPMENT FOR HOME HEALTH WORKERS

SEC. 20009. (a) PROVISION OF EQUIPMENT.—

(1) IN GENERAL.—During a public health emergency, the Secretary of Veterans Affairs shall provide to employees and contractors of the Department of Veterans Affairs personal protective equipment necessary to provide home care to veterans under the laws administered by the Secretary.

(2) SOURCE OF EQUIPMENT.—Personal protective equipment may be provided under paragraph (1) through the All Hazards Emergency Cache of the Department or any other source available to the Department.

(b) DEFINITIONS.—In this section:

(1) HOME CARE.—The term "home care" has the meaning given that term in section 1803(c) of title 38, United States Code.

(2) PERSONAL PROTECTIVE EQUIPMENT.—The term "personal protective equipment" means any protective equipment required to prevent the wearer from contracting COVID–19, including gloves, N–95 respirator masks, gowns, goggles, face shields, or other equipment required for safety.

CLARIFICATION OF TREATMENT OF PAYMENTS FOR PURPOSES OF ELIGIBILITY FOR VETERANS PENSION AND OTHER VETERANS BENEFITS

SEC. 20010. Amounts paid to a person under the 2020 Recovery Rebate in the Coronavirus Aid, Relief, and Economic Security Act shall not be treated as income or resources for purposes of determining eligibility for pension under chapter 15 of title 38, United States Code, or any other benefit under a law administered by the Secretary of Veterans Affairs.

AVAILABILITY OF TELEHEALTH FOR CASE MANAGERS AND HOMELESS VETERANS

SEC. 20011. The Secretary of Veterans Affairs shall ensure that telehealth capabilities are available during a public health emergency for case managers of, and homeless veterans participating in, the Department of Housing and Urban Development–Department of Veterans Affairs Supportive Housing program (commonly referred to as "HUD–VASH").

FUNDING LIMITS FOR FINANCIAL ASSISTANCE FOR SUPPORTIVE SERVICES FOR VERY LOW-INCOME VETERAN FAMILIES IN PERMANENT HOUSING DURING A PUBLIC HEALTH EMERGENCY

SEC. 20012. In the case of a public health emergency, nothing in subsection (e)(1) of section 2044 of title 38, United States Code, may be construed as limiting amounts that may be made available for carrying out subsections (a), (b), and (c) of such section.

MODIFICATIONS TO COMPREHENSIVE SERVICE PROGRAMS FOR HOMELESS VETERANS DURING A PUBLIC HEALTH EMERGENCY

SEC. 20013. (a) RULE OF CONSTRUCTION.—In the case of a public health emergency, no authorization of appropriations in section 2014 of title 38, United States Code, may be construed as limiting amounts that may be appropriated for carrying out subchapter II of chapter 20 of such title.

(b) GRANTS AND PER DIEM PAYMENTS.—In the case of a public health emergency, the Secretary of Veterans Affairs may waive any limits on—

(1) grant amounts under sections 2011 and 2061 of title 38, United States Code; and

(2) rates for per diem payments under sections 2012 and 2061 of such title.

(c) PARTICIPANT ABSENCE.—Notwithstanding Veterans Health Administration Handbook 1162.01(1), dated July 12, 2013, and amended June 30, 2014, and titled "Grant and Per Diem (GPD) Program", or any other provision of law, for the duration of a public health emergency, the Secretary—

(1) shall waive any requirement to discharge a veteran from the grant and per diem program of the Veterans Health Administration after the veteran is absent for 14 days; and

(2) may continue to pay per diem to grant recipients and eligible entities under the program for any additional days of absence when a veteran has already been absent for more than 72 hours.

SEC. 20014. The amounts provided by sections 20003 through 20013 of this title in this Act are designated by the Congress as being for an emergency requirement pursuant to section 251(b)(2)(A)(i) of the Balanced Budget and Emergency Deficit Control Act of 1985.

TITLE XI DEPARTMENT OF STATE

ADMINISTRATION OF FOREIGN AFFAIRS

DIPLOMATIC PROGRAMS

For an additional amount for "Diplomatic Programs", $324,000,000, to remain available until September 30, 2022, to prevent, prepare for, and respond to coronavirus, including for necessary expenses to maintain consular operations and to provide for evacuation expenses and emergency preparedness: Provided, That such amount is designated by the Congress as being for an emergency requirement pursuant to section 251(b)(2)(A)(i) of the Balanced Budget and Emergency Deficit Control Act of 1985.

UNITED STATES AGENCY FOR INTERNATIONAL DEVELOPMENT

FUNDS APPROPRIATED TO THE PRESIDENT

OPERATING EXPENSES

For an additional amount for "Operating Expenses", $95,000,000, to remain available until September 30, 2022, to prevent, prepare for, and respond to coronavirus: Provided, That such amount is designated by the Congress as being for an emergency requirement pursuant to section 251(b)(2)(A)(i) of the Balanced Budget and Emergency Deficit Control Act of 1985.

BILATERAL ECONOMIC ASSISTANCE

FUNDS APPROPRIATED TO THE PRESIDENT

INTERNATIONAL DISASTER ASSISTANCE

For an additional amount for "International Disaster Assistance", $258,000,000, to remain available until expended, to prevent, prepare for, and respond to coronavirus: Provided, That such amount is designated by the Congress as being for an emergency requirement pursuant to section 251(b)(2)(A)(i) of the Balanced Budget and Emergency Deficit Control Act of 1985.

DEPARTMENT OF STATE

MIGRATION AND REFUGEE ASSISTANCE

For an additional amount for "Migration and Refugee Assistance", $350,000,000, to remain available until expended, to prevent, prepare for, and respond to coronavirus: Provided, That such amount is designated by the Congress as being for an emergency requirement pursuant to section 251(b)(2)(A)(i) of the Balanced Budget and Emergency Deficit Control Act of 1985.

INDEPENDENT AGENCIES

PEACE CORPS

For an additional amount for "Peace Corps", $88,000,000, to remain available until September 30, 2022, to prevent, prepare for, and respond to coronavirus: Provided, That such amount is designated by the Congress as being for an emergency requirement pursuant to section 251(b)(2)(A)(i) of the Balanced Budget and Emergency Deficit Control Act of 1985.

GENERAL PROVISIONS—THIS TITLE

(INCLUDING TRANSFER OF FUNDS)

SEC. 21001. The authorities and limitations of section 402 of the Coronavirus Preparedness and Response Supplemental Appropriations Act (division A of Public Law 116–123) shall apply to funds appropriated by this title as follows:

(1) Subsections (a), (d), (e), and (f) shall apply to funds under the heading "Diplomatic Programs"; and

(2) Subsections (c), (d), (e), and (f) shall apply to funds under the heading "International Disaster Assistance".

SEC. 21002. Funds appropriated by this title under the headings "Diplomatic Programs", "Operating Expenses", and "Peace Corps" may be used to reimburse such accounts administered by the Department of State, the United States Agency for International Development, and the Peace Corps, as appropriate, for obligations incurred to prevent, prepare for, and respond to coronavirus prior to the date of enactment of this Act.

SEC. 21003. The reporting requirement of section 406(b) of the Coronavirus Preparedness and Response Supplemental Appropriations Act, 2020 (division A of Public Law 116–123) shall apply to funds appropriated by this title: Provided, That the requirement to jointly submit such report shall not apply to the Director of the Peace Corps: Provided further, That reports required by such section may be consolidated and shall include information on all funds made available to such Federal agencies to prevent, prepare for, and respond to coronavirus.

SEC. 21004. Section 7064(a) of the Department of State, Foreign Operations, and Related Programs Appropriations Act, 2020 (division G of Public Law 116–94) is amended by striking "$100,000,000" and inserting in lieu thereof "$110,000,000", and by adding the following before the period at the end: ": Provided, That no amounts may be used that were designated by the Congress for Overseas Contingency Operations/Global War on Terrorism pursuant to the Concurrent Resolution on the Budget or the Balanced Budget and Emergency Deficit Control Act of 1985".

SEC. 21005. The Department of State, Foreign Operations, and Related Programs Appropriations Act, 2020 (division G of Public Law 116–94) is amended under the heading "Emergencies in the Diplomatic and Consular Service" in title I by striking "$1,000,000" and inserting in lieu thereof "$5,000,000".

SEC. 21006. The Department of State, Foreign Operations, and Related Programs Appropriations Act, 2020 (division G of Public Law 116–94) is amended under the heading "Millennium Challenge Corporation" in title III by striking "$105,000,000" in the first proviso and inserting in lieu thereof "$107,000,000".

SEC. 21007. Notwithstanding any other provision of law, and in addition to leave authorized under any other provision of law, the Secretary of State and the Administrator of the United States Agency for International Development may, in order to prevent, prepare for, and respond to coronavirus, provide additional paid leave to address employee hardships resulting from coronavirus: Provided, That this authority shall apply to leave taken since January 29, 2020, and may be provided abroad and domestically: Provided further, That the Secretary and the Administrator shall consult with the Committee on Appropriations and the Committee on Foreign Relations of the Senate and the Committee on Appropriations and the Committee on Foreign Affairs of the House of Representatives prior to implementation of such authority: Provided further, That the authority made available pursuant to this section shall expire on September 30, 2022.

SEC. 21008. The Secretary of State, to prevent, prepare for, and respond to coronavirus, may exercise the authorities of section 3(j) of the State Department Basic Authorities Act of 1956 (22 U.S.C. 2670(j)) to provide medical services or related support for private United States citizens, nationals, and permanent resident aliens abroad, or third country nationals connected to such persons or to the diplomatic or development missions of the United States abroad, who are unable to obtain such services or support otherwise: Provided, That such assistance shall be provided on a reimbursable basis to the extent feasible: Provided further, That such reimbursements may be credited to the applicable Department of State appropriation and shall remain available until expended: Provided further, That the Secretary shall prioritize providing medical services or related support to individuals eligible for the health program under section 904 of the Foreign Service Act of 1980 (22 U.S.C. 4084): Provided further, That the authority made available pursuant to this section shall expire on September 30, 2022.

SEC. 21009. Notwithstanding section 6(b) of the Department of State Authorities Act of 2006 (Public Law 109–472; 120 Stat. 3556), during fiscal year 2020, passport and immigrant visa surcharges collected in any fiscal year pursuant to the fourth paragraph under the heading "Diplomatic and Consular Programs" in the Department of State and Related Agency Appropriations Act, 2005 (title IV of division B of Public Law 108–447; 8 U.S.C. 1714) may be obligated and expended for the costs of providing consular services: Provided, That such funds should be prioritized for United States citizen services: Provided further, That not later than 90 days after the expiration of this authority, the Secretary of State shall provide a report to the Committee on Appropriations and the Committee on Foreign Relations of the Senate and the Committee on Appropriations and the Committee on Foreign Affairs of the House of Representatives detailing the specific expenditures made pursuant to this authority: Provided further, That the amount provided by this section is designated by the Congress as being for an emergency requirement pursuant to section 251(b)(2)(A)(i) of the Balanced Budget and Emergency Deficit Control Act of 1985.

SEC. 21010. The Department of State and the United States Agency for International Development are authorized to enter into contracts with individuals for the provision of personal services (as described in section 104 of part 37 of title 48, Code of Federal Regulations and including pursuant to section 904 of the Foreign Service Act of 1980 (22 U.S.C. 4084)) to prevent, prepare for, and respond to coronavirus, within the United States and abroad, subject to prior consultation with, and the notification procedures of, the Committee on Appropriations and the Committee on Foreign Relations of the Senate and the Committee on Appropriations and the Committee on Foreign Affairs of the House of Representatives: Provided, That such individuals may not be deemed employees of the United States for the purpose of any law administered by the Office of Personnel Management: Provided further, That not later than 15 days after utilizing this authority, the Secretary of State shall provide a report to the Committee on Appropriations and the Committee on Foreign Relations of the Senate and the Committee on Appropriations and the Committee on Foreign Affairs of the House of Representatives on the overall staffing needs for the Office of Medical Services: Provided further, That the authority made available pursuant to this section shall expire on September 30, 2022.

SEC. 21011. Notwithstanding any other provision of law, the Secretary of State and the Administrator of the United States Agency for International Development may authorize any oath of office required by law to, in particular circumstances that could otherwise pose health risks, be administered remotely, subject to appropriate verification: Provided, That prior to initially exercising the authority of this section, the Secretary and the Administrator shall each submit a report to the Committee on Appropriations and the Committee on Foreign Relations of the Senate and the Committee on Appropriations and the Committee on Foreign Affairs of the House of Representatives describing the process and procedures for administering such oaths, including appropriate verification: Provided further, That the authority made available pursuant to this section shall expire on September 30, 2021.

SEC. 21012. (a) PURPOSES.—For purposes of strengthening the ability of foreign countries to prevent, prepare for, and respond to coronavirus and to the adverse economic impacts of coronavirus, in a manner that would protect the United States from the spread of coronavirus and mitigate an international economic crisis resulting from coronavirus that may pose a significant risk to the economy of the United States, each paragraph of subsection (b) shall take effect upon enactment of this Act.

(b) CORONAVIRUS RESPONSES.—

(1) INTERNATIONAL DEVELOPMENT ASSOCIATION REPLENISHMENT.—The International Development Association Act (22 U.S.C. 284 et seq.) is amended by adding at the end the following new section:

[¶ 2243] SEC. 31. "NINETEENTH REPLENISHMENT.

(a) "IN GENERAL.—The United States Governor of the International Development Association is authorized to contribute on behalf of the United States $3,004,200,000 to the nineteenth replenishment of the resources of the Association, subject to obtaining the necessary appropriations.

(b) "AUTHORIZATION OF APPROPRIATIONS.—In order to pay for the United States contribution provided for in subsection (a), there are authorized to be appropriated, without fiscal year limitation, $3,004,200,000 for payment by the Secretary of the Treasury.".

(2) INTERNATIONAL FINANCE CORPORATION AUTHORIZATION.—The International Finance Corporation Act (22 U.S.C. 282 et seq.) is amended by adding at the end the following new section:

[¶ 2244] SEC. 18. "CAPITAL INCREASES AND AMENDMENT TO THE ARTICLES OF AGREEMENT.

(a) "VOTES AUTHORIZED.—The United States Governor of the Corporation is authorized to vote in favor of—

(1) "a resolution to increase the authorized capital stock of the Corporation by 16,999,998 shares, to implement the conversion of a portion of the retained earnings of the Corporation into paid-in capital, which will result in the United States being issued an additional 3,771,899 shares of capital stock, without any cash contribution;

(2) "a resolution to increase the authorized capital stock of the Corporation on a general basis by 4,579,995 shares; and

(3) "a resolution to increase the authorized capital stock of the Corporation on a selective basis by 919,998 shares.

(b) "AMENDMENT OF THE ARTICLES OF AGREEMENT.—The United States Governor of the Corporation is authorized to agree to and accept an amendment to article II, section 2(c)(ii) of the Articles of Agreement of the Corporation that would increase the vote by which the Board of Governors of the Corporation may increase the capital stock of the Corporation from a four-fifths majority to an eighty-five percent majority.".

(3) AFRICAN DEVELOPMENT BANK.—The African Development Bank Act (22 U.S.C. 290i et seq.) is amended by adding at the end the following new section:

[¶ 2245] SEC. 1345. "SEVENTH CAPITAL INCREASE.

(a) "SUBSCRIPTION AUTHORIZED.—

(1) "IN GENERAL.—The United States Governor of the Bank may subscribe on behalf of the United States to 532,023 additional shares of the capital stock of the Bank.

(2) "LIMITATION.—Any subscription by the United States to the capital stock of the Bank shall be effective only to such extent and in such amounts as are provided in advance in appropriations Acts.

(b) "AUTHORIZATION OF APPROPRIATIONS.—

(1) "IN GENERAL.—In order to pay for the increase in the United States subscription to the Bank under subsection (a), there are authorized to be appropriated, without fiscal year limitation, $7,286,587,008 for payment by the Secretary of the Treasury.

(2) "SHARE TYPES.—Of the amount authorized to be appropriated under paragraph (1)—

(A) "$437,190,016 shall be for paid in shares of the Bank; and

(B) "$6,849,396,992 shall be for callable shares of the Bank.".

(4) AFRICAN DEVELOPMENT FUND.—The African Development Fund Act (22 U.S.C. 290g et seq.) is amended by adding at the end the following new section:

[¶2246] SEC. 226. "FIFTEENTH REPLENISHMENT.

(a) "IN GENERAL.—The United States Governor of the Fund is authorized to contribute on behalf of the United States $513,900,000 to the fifteenth replenishment of the resources of the Fund, subject to obtaining the necessary appropriations.

(b) "AUTHORIZATION OF APPROPRIATIONS.—In order to pay for the United States contribution provided for in subsection (a), there are authorized to be appropriated, without fiscal year limitation, $513,900,000 for payment by the Secretary of the Treasury.".

(5) INTERNATIONAL MONETARY FUND AUTHORIZATION FOR NEW ARRANGEMENTS TO BORROW.—

(A) IN GENERAL.—Section 17 of the Bretton Woods Agreements Act (22 U.S.C. 286e–2) is amended—

(i) in subsection (a)—

(I) by redesignating paragraphs (3), (4), and (5) as paragraphs (4), (5), and (6), respectively;

(II) by inserting after paragraph (2) the following new paragraph:

(3) "In order to carry out the purposes of a one-time decision of the Executive Directors of the International Monetary Fund (the Fund) to expand the resources of the New Arrangements to Borrow, established pursuant to the decision of January 27, 1997, referred to in paragraph (1), the Secretary of the Treasury is authorized to make loans, in an amount not to exceed the dollar equivalent of 28,202,470,000 of Special Drawing Rights, in addition to any amounts previously authorized under this section, except that prior to activation of the New Arrangements to Borrow, the Secretary of the Treasury shall report to Congress whether supplementary resources are needed to forestall or cope with an impairment of the international monetary system and whether the Fund has fully explored other means of funding to the Fund.";

(III) in paragraph (5), as so redesignated, by striking "paragraph (3)" and inserting "paragraph (4)"; and

(IV) in paragraph (6), as so redesignated, by striking "December 16, 2022" and inserting "December 31, 2025"; and

(ii) in subsection (e)(1) by striking "(a)(2)," each place such term appears and inserting "(a)(2), (a)(3),".

(B) EMERGENCY DESIGNATION.—The amount provided by this paragraph is designated by the Congress as being for an emergency requirement pursuant to section 251(b)(2)(A)(i) of the Balanced Budget and Emergency Deficit Control Act of 1985.

TITLE XII DEPARTMENT OF TRANSPORTATION

OFFICE OF THE SECRETARY

SALARIES AND EXPENSES

For an additional amount for "Salaries and Expenses", $1,753,000, to remain available until expended, to prevent, prepare for, and respond to coronavirus, including necessary expenses for operating costs and capital outlays: Provided, That such amounts are in addition to any other amounts made available for this purpose: Provided further, That obligations of amounts under this heading in this Act shall not be subject to the limitation on obligations under the heading "Office of the Secretary—Working Capital Fund" in division H of the Further Consolidated Appropriations Act, 2020 (Public Law 116–94): Provided further, That such amount is designated by the Congress as being for an emergency requirement pursuant to section 251(b)(2)(A)(i) of the Balanced Budget and Emergency Deficit Control Act of 1985.

ESSENTIAL AIR SERVICE

In addition to funds provided to the "Payments to Air Carriers" program in Public Law 116–94 to carry out the essential air service program under section 41731 through 41742 of title 49, United States Code, $56,000,000, to be derived from the general fund of the Treasury, and to be made available to the Essential Air Service and Rural Improvement Fund, to remain available until expended, to prevent, prepare for, and respond to coronavirus: Provided, That such amount is designated by the Congress as being for an emergency requirement pursuant to section 251(b)(2)(A)(i) of the Balanced Budget and Emergency Deficit Control Act of 1985.

FEDERAL AVIATION ADMINISTRATION

GRANTS-IN-AID FOR AIRPORTS

For an additional amount for "Grants-In-Aid for Airports", $10,000,000,000, to prevent, prepare for, and respond to coronavirus, to remain available until expended: Provided, That amounts made available under this heading in this Act shall be derived from the general fund of the Treasury: Provided further, That funds provided under this heading in this Act shall only be available to sponsors of airports defined in section 47102 of title 49, United States Code: Provided further, That funds provided under this heading in this Act shall not otherwise be subject to the requirements of chapter 471 of such title: Provided further, That notwithstanding the previous proviso, section 47112(b) of such title shall apply to funds provided for any contract awarded (after the date of enactment) for airport development and funded under this heading: Provided further, That funds provided under this heading in this Act may not be used for any purpose not directly related to the airport: Provided further, That of the amounts appropriated under this heading in this Act—

(1) Not less than $500,000,000 shall be available to pay a Federal share of 100 percent of the costs for which a grant is made under Public Law 116–94: Provided, That any remaining funds after the apportionment under this paragraph (1) shall be distributed as described in paragraph (2) under this heading in this Act;

(2) Not less than $7,400,000,000 shall be available for any purpose for which airport revenues may lawfully be used: Provided, That 50 percent of such funds shall be allocated among all commercial service airports based on each sponsor's calendar year 2018 enplanements as a percentage of total 2018 enplanements for all commercial service airports:Provided further, That the remaining 50 percent of such funds shall be allocated among all commercial service airports based on an equal combination of each sponsor's fiscal year 2018 debt service as a percentage of the combined debt service for all commercial service airports and each sponsor's ratio of unrestricted reserves to their respective debt service: Provided further, That the Federal share payable of the costs for which a grant is made under this paragraph shall be 100 percent:

(3) Up to $2,000,000,000 shall be available for any purpose for which airport revenues may lawfully be used, and: (A) be apportioned as set forth in section 47114(c)(1)(C)(i), 47114(c)(1)(C)(ii), or 47114(c)(1)(H) of title 49, United States Code; (B) not be subject to the reduced apportionments of 49 U.S.C. 47114(f); and (C) have no maximum apportionment limit, notwithstanding 47114(c)(1)(C)(iii) of title 49, United States Code: Provided, That any remaining funds after the apportionment under this paragraph (3) shall be distributed as described in paragraph (2) under this heading in this Act: Provided further, That the Federal share payable of the costs for which a grant is made under this paragraph shall be 100 percent; and

(4) Not less than $100,000,000 shall be for general aviation airports for any purpose for which airport revenues may lawfully be used, and, which the Secretary shall apportion directly to each eligible airport, as defined in section 47102(8) of title 49, United States Code, based on the categories published in the most current National Plan of Integrated Airport Systems, reflecting the percentage of the aggregate published eligible development costs for each such category, and then dividing the allocated funds evenly among the eligible airports in each category, rounding up to the nearest thousand dollars: Provided, That the Federal share payable of the costs for which a grant is made under this paragraph shall be 100 percent:

Provided further, That the Administrator of the Federal Aviation Administration may retain up to 0.1 percent of the funds provided under this heading in this Act to fund the award and oversight by the Administrator of grants made under this heading in this Act: Provided further, That obligations of funds under this heading in this Act shall not be subject to any limitations on obligations provided in Public Law 116–94: Provided further, That all airports receiving funds under this heading in this Act shall continue to employ, through December 31, 2020, at least 90 percent of the number of individuals employed (after making adjustments for retirements or voluntary employee separations) by the airport as of the date of enactment of this Act: Provided further, That the Secretary may waive the workforce retention requirement in the previous proviso, if the Secretary determines the airport is experiencing economic hardship as a direct result of the requirement, or the requirement reduces aviation safety or security: Provided further, That the workforce retention requirement shall not apply to nonhub airports or nonprimary airports receiving funds under this heading in this Act: Provided further, That such amount is designated by the Congress as being for an emergency requirement pursuant to section 251(b)(2)(A)(i) of the Balanced Budget and Emergency Deficit Control Act of 1985.

FEDERAL MOTOR CARRIER SAFETY ADMINISTRATION

MOTOR CARRIER SAFETY OPERATIONS AND PROGRAMS

Of prior year unobligated contract authority and liquidating cash provided for Motor Carrier Safety in the Transportation Equity Act for the 21st Century (Public Law 105–178), SAFETEA–LU (Public Law 109–59), or other appropriations or authorization acts, in addition to amounts already appropriated in fiscal year 2020 for "Motor Carrier Safety Operations and Programs", $150,000 in additional obligation limitation is provided and repurposed for obligations incurred to support activities to prevent, prepare for, and respond to coronavirus.

FEDERAL RAILROAD ADMINISTRATION

SAFETY AND OPERATIONS

For an additional amount for "Safety and Operations", $250,000, to remain available until September 30, 2021, to prevent, prepare for, and respond to coronavirus: Provided, That such amount is designated by the Congress as being for an emergency requirement pursuant to section 251(b)(2)(A)(i) of the Balanced Budget and Emergency Deficit Control Act of 1985.

NORTHEAST CORRIDOR GRANTS TO THE NATIONAL RAILROAD PASSENGER CORPORATION

(INCLUDING TRANSFER OF FUNDS)

For an additional amount for "Northeast Corridor Grants to the National Railroad Passenger Corporation", $492,000,000, to remain available until expended, to prevent, prepare for, and respond to coronavirus, including to enable the Secretary of Transportation to make or amend existing grants to the National Railroad Passenger Corporation for activities associated with the Northeast Corridor, as authorized by section 11101(a) of the Fixing America's Surface Transportation Act (division A of Public Law 114–94): Provided, That amounts made available under this heading in this Act may be transferred to and merged with "National Network Grants to the National Railroad Passenger Corporation" to prevent, prepare for, and respond to coronavirus: Provided further, That such amount is designated by the Congress as being for an emergency requirement pursuant to section 251(b)(2)(A)(i) of the Balanced Budget and Emergency Deficit Control Act of 1985.

NATIONAL NETWORK GRANTS TO THE NATIONAL RAILROAD PASSENGER CORPORATION

(INCLUDING TRANSFER OF FUNDS)

For an additional amount for "National Network Grants to the National Railroad Passenger Corporation", $526,000,000, to remain available until expended, to prevent, prepare for, and respond to coronavirus, including to enable the Secretary of Transportation to make or amend existing grants to the National Railroad Passenger Corporation for activities associated with the National Network as authorized by section 11101(b) of the Fixing America's Surface Transportation Act (division A of Public Law 114–94): Provided, That a State shall not be required to pay the National Railroad Passenger Corporation more than 80 percent of the amount paid in fiscal year 2019 under section 209 of the Passenger Rail Investment and Improvement Act of 2008 (Public Law 110–432) and that not less than $239,000,000 of the amounts made available under this heading in this Act shall be made available for use in lieu of any increase in a State's payment: Provided further, That amounts made available under this heading in this Act may be transferred to and merged with "Northeast Corridor Grants to the National Railroad Passenger Corporation" to prevent, prepare for, and respond to coronavirus: Provided further, That such amount is designated by the Congress as being for an emergency requirement pursuant to section 251(b)(2)(A)(i) of the Balanced Budget and Emergency Deficit Control Act of 1985.

FEDERAL TRANSIT ADMINISTRATION

TRANSIT INFRASTRUCTURE GRANTS

For an additional amount for "Transit Infrastructure Grants", $25,000,000,000, to remain available until expended, to prevent, prepare for, and respond to coronavirus: Provided, That the Secretary of Transportation shall provide funds appropriated under this heading in this Act as if such funds were provided under section 5307 of title 49, United States Code, and section 5311 of title 49, United States Code and apportion such funds in accordance with section 5336 of such title (other than subsections (h)(1) and (h)(4)), section 5311 (other than subsection (b)(3) and (c)(1)(A)), section 5337 and section 5340 of title 49, United States Code, and apportion such funds in accordance with such sections except that funds apportioned under section 5337 shall be added to funds apportioned under 5307 for administration under 5307: Provided further, That the Secretary shall allocate the amounts provided in the preceding proviso under sections 5307, 5311, 5337, and 5340 of title 49, United States Code, among such sections in the same ratio as funds were provided in the fiscal year 2020 appropriations: Provided further, That funds apportioned under this heading in this Act shall be apportioned not later than 7 days after the date of enactment of this Act: Provided further, That funds shall be apportioned using the fiscal year 2020 apportionment formulas: Provided further, That not more than three-quarters of 1 percent, but not to exceed $75,000,000, of the funds for transit infrastructure grants provided under this heading in this Act shall be available for administrative expenses and ongoing program management oversight as authorized under sections 5334 and 5338(f)(2) of title 49, United States Code, and shall be in addition to any other appropriations for such purpose: Provided further, That notwithstanding subsection (a)(1) or (b) of section 5307 of title 49, United States Code, funds provided under this heading are available for the operating expenses of transit agencies related to the response to a coronavirus public health emergency as described in section 319 of the Public Health Service Act, including, beginning on January 20, 2020, reimbursement for operating costs to maintain service and lost revenue due to the coronavirus public health emergency, including the purchase of personal protective equipment, and paying the administrative leave of operations personnel due to reductions in service: Provided further, That such operating expenses are not required to be included in a transportation improvement program, long-range transportation, statewide transportation plan, or a statewide transportation improvement program: Provided further, That the Secretary shall not waive the requirements of section 5333 of title 49, United States Code, for funds appropriated under this heading in this Act or for funds previously made available under section 5307 of title 49, United States Code, or sections 5311, 5337, or 5340 of such title as a result of the coronavirus: Provided further, That unless otherwise specified, applicable requirements under chapter 53 of title 49, United States Code, shall apply to funding made available under this heading in this Act, except that the Federal share of the costs for which any grant is made under this heading in this Act shall be, at the option of the recipient, up to 100 percent: Provided further, That the amount made available under this heading in this Act shall be derived from the general fund and shall not be subject to any limitation on obligations for transit programs set forth in any Act: Provided further, That such amount is designated by the Congress as being for an emergency requirement pursuant to section 251(b)(2)(A)(i) of the Balanced Budget and Emergency Deficit Control Act of 1985.

Maritime Administration

OPERATIONS AND TRAINING

For an additional amount for "Operations and Training", $3,134,000, to remain available until September 30, 2021, to prevent, prepare for, and respond to coronavirus: Provided, That of the amounts made available under this heading in this Act, $1,000,000 shall be for the operations of the United States Merchant Marine Academy: Provided further, That such amount is designated by the Congress as being for an emergency requirement pursuant to section 251(b)(2)(A)(i) of the Balanced Budget and Emergency Deficit Control Act of 1985.

STATE MARITIME ACADEMY OPERATIONS

For an additional amount for "State Maritime Academy Operations", $1,000,000, to remain available until September 30, 2021, to prevent, prepare for, and respond to coronavirus: Provided, That amounts made available under this heading in this Act shall be for direct payments for State Maritime Academies: Provided further, That such amount is designated by the Congress as being for an emergency requirement pursuant to section 251(b)(2)(A)(i) of the Balanced Budget and Emergency Deficit Control Act of 1985.

Office of Inspector General

SALARIES AND EXPENSES

For an additional amount for "Office of Inspector General", $5,000,000, to remain available until expended, to prevent, prepare for, and respond to coronavirus: Provided, That the funding made available under this heading in this Act shall be used for conducting audits and investigations of projects and activities carried out with funds made available in this Act to the Department of Transportation to prevent, prepare for, and respond to coronavirus: Provided further, That such amount is designated by the Congress as being for an emergency requirement pursuant to section 251(b)(2)(A)(i) of the Balanced Budget and Emergency Deficit Control Act of 1985.

DEPARTMENT OF HOUSING AND URBAN DEVELOPMENT

Management and Administration

ADMINISTRATIVE SUPPORT OFFICES

For an additional amount for "Administrative Support Offices", $35,000,000, to remain available until September 30, 2021, to prevent, prepare for, and respond to coronavirus, for the Office of the Chief Financial Officer, including for Department-wide salaries and expenses, Information Technology purposes, and to support the Department's workforce in a telework environment: Provided, That the amounts provided under this heading in this Act shall be in addition to amounts otherwise available for such purposes, including amounts made available under the heading "Program Offices" in this Act: Provided further, That such amount is designated by the Congress as being for an emergency requirement pursuant to section 251(b)(2)(A)(i) of the Balanced Budget and Emergency Deficit Control Act of 1985.

PROGRAM OFFICES

For an additional amount for "Program Offices", $15,000,000, to remain available until September 30, 2021, to prevent, prepare for, and respond to coronavirus: Provided, That of the sums appropriated under this heading in this Act—

(1) $5,000,000 shall be available for the Office of Public and Indian Housing; and

(2) $10,000,000 shall be available for the Office of Community Planning and Development:

Provided further, That such amount is designated by the Congress as being for an emergency requirement pursuant to section 251(b)(2)(A)(i) of the Balanced Budget and Emergency Deficit Control Act of 1985.

PUBLIC AND INDIAN HOUSING

TENANT-BASED RENTAL ASSISTANCE

For an additional amount for "Tenant-Based Rental Assistance", $1,250,000,000, to remain available until expended, to prevent, prepare for, and respond to coronavirus, including to provide additional funds for public housing agencies to maintain normal operations and take other necessary actions during the period that the program is impacted by coronavirus: Provided, That of the amounts made available under this heading in this Act, $850,000,000 shall be available for both administrative expenses and other expenses of public housing agencies for their section 8 programs, including Mainstream vouchers: Provided further, That such other expenses shall be new eligible activities to be defined by the Secretary and shall include activities to support or maintain the health and safety of assisted individuals and families, and costs related to retention and support of participating owners: Provided further, That amounts made available under paragraph (3) under this heading in Public Law 116–94 may be used for such other expenses, as described in the previous proviso, in addition to their other available uses: Provided further, That of the amounts made available under this heading in this Act, $400,000,000 shall be available for adjustments in the calendar year 2020 section 8 renewal funding allocations, in addition to any other appropriations available for such purpose, including Mainstream vouchers, for public housing agencies that experience a significant increase in voucher per-unit costs due to extraordinary circumstances or that, despite taking reasonable cost savings measures, as determined by the Secretary, would otherwise be required to terminate rental assistance for families as a result of insufficient funding: Provided further, That the Secretary shall allocate amounts provided in the previous proviso based on need, as determined by the Secretary: Provided further, That the Secretary may waive, or specify alternative requirements for, any provision of any statute or regulation that the Secretary administers in connection with the use of the amounts made available under this heading and the same heading of Public Law 116–94 (except for requirements related to fair housing, nondiscrimination, labor standards, and the environment), upon a finding by the Secretary that any such waivers or alternative requirements are necessary for the safe and effective administration of these funds, consistent with the purposes described under this heading in this Act, to prevent, prepare for, and respond to coronavirus: Provided further, That the Secretary shall notify the public through the Federal Register or other appropriate means of any such waiver or alternative requirement to ensure the most expeditious allocation of this funding, and in order for such waiver or alternative requirement to take effect, and that such public notice may be provided, at a minimum, on the Internet at the appropriate Government web site or through other electronic media, as determined by the Secretary: Provided further, That any such waivers or alternative requirements shall remain in effect for the time and duration specified by the Secretary in such public notice and may be extended if necessary upon additional notice by the Secretary: Provided further, That to prevent, prepare for, and respond to coronavirus, the notification required by section 223 of Public Law 116–6 and section 221 of Public Law 116–94 shall not apply to the award of amounts provided under paragraph (2) of this heading in Public Law 116–6 or under paragraph (7)(B) of this heading in Public Law 116–94 in support of the family unification program under section 8(x) of such Act: Provided further, That the Secretary may award any remaining unobligated balances appropriated under this heading in prior Acts for incremental tenant-based assistance contracts under section 811 of the Cranston-Gonzalez National Affordable Housing Act (42 U.S.C. 8013), to prevent, prepare for, and respond to coronavirus, without competition, including for extraordinary administrative fees: Provided further, That no less than 25 percent of such amounts shall be allocated proportionally to public housing agencies who received awards in the 2017 and 2019 competitions for such purposes within 60 days of enactment of this Act: Provided further, That the waiver and alternative requirements authority provided under this heading in this Act shall also apply to such incremental tenant-based assistance contract amounts: Provided further, That such amount is designated by the Congress as being for an emergency requirement pursuant to section 251(b)(2)(A)(i) of the Balanced Budget and Emergency Deficit Control Act of 1985.

PUBLIC HOUSING OPERATING FUND

For an additional amount for "Public Housing Operating Fund", as authorized by section 9(e) of the United States Housing Act of 1937 (42 U.S.C. 1437g(e)), $685,000,000, to remain available until September 30, 2021, to prevent, prepare for, and respond to coronavirus, including to provide additional funds for public housing agencies to maintain normal operations and take other necessary actions during the period that the program is impacted by coronavirus: Provided, That the amount provided under this heading in this Act shall be combined with the amount appropriated for the same purpose under the same heading of Public Law 116–94, and distributed to all public housing agencies pursuant to the Operating Fund formula at part 990 of title 24, Code of Federal Regulations: Provided further, That for the period from the enactment of this Act through December 31, 2020, such combined total amount may be used for eligible activities under subsections (d)(1) and (e)(1) of such section 9 and for other expenses related to preventing, preparing for, and responding to coronavirus, including activities to support or maintain the health and safety of assisted individuals and families, and activities to support education and child care for impacted families: Provided further, That amounts made available under the headings "Public Housing Operating Fund" and "Public Housing Capital Fund" in prior Acts, except for any set-asides listed under such headings, may be used for all of the purposes described in the previous proviso: Provided further, That the expanded uses and funding flexibilities described in the previous two provisos shall be available to all public housing agencies through December 31, 2020, except that the Secretary may extend the period under which such flexibilities shall be available in additional 12 month increments upon a finding that individuals and families assisted by the public housing program continue to require expanded services due to coronavirus: Provided further, That the Secretary may waive, or specify alternative requirements for, any provision of any statute or regulation that the Secretary administers in connection with the use of such combined total amount or funds made available under the headings "Public Housing Operating Fund" and "Public Housing Capital Fund" in prior Acts (except for requirements related to fair housing, nondiscrimination, labor standards, and the environment), upon a finding by the Secretary that any such waivers or alternative requirements are necessary for the safe and effective administration of these funds to prevent, prepare for, and respond to coronavirus: Provided further, That the Secretary shall notify the public through the Federal Register or other appropriate means of any such waiver or alternative requirement, to ensure the most expeditious allocation of this funding, in order for such waiver or alternative requirement to take effect, and that such public notice may be provided, at a minimum, on the Internet at the appropriate Government web site or through other electronic media, as determined by the Secretary: Provided further, That any such waivers or alternative requirements shall remain in effect for the time and duration specified by the Secretary in such public notice and may be extended if necessary upon additional notice by the Secretary: Provided further, That such amount is designated by the Congress as being for an emergency requirement pursuant to section 251(b)(2)(A)(i) of the Balanced Budget and Emergency Deficit Control Act of 1985.

NATIVE AMERICAN PROGRAMS

For an additional amount for "Native American Programs", $300,000,000, to remain available until September 30, 2024, to prevent, prepare for, and respond to coronavirus, for activities and assistance authorized under title I of the Native American Housing Assistance and Self-Determination Act of 1996 (NAHASDA) (25 U.S.C. 4111 et seq.), and under title I of the Housing and Community Development Act of 1974 with respect to Indian tribes (42 U.S.C. 5306(a)(1)): Provided, That the amounts made available under this heading in this Act are as follows:

(1) No less than $200,000,000 shall be available for the Native American Housing Block Grants program, as authorized under title I of NAHASDA: Provided, That amounts made available under this paragraph shall be distributed according to the same funding formula used in fiscal year 2020: Provided further, That such amounts shall be used by recipients to prevent, prepare for, and respond to coronavirus, including to maintain normal operations and fund eligible affordable housing activities under NAHASDA during the period that the program is impacted by coronavirus: Provided further, That amounts provided under this heading in this Act may be used to cover or reimburse allowable costs to prevent, prepare for, and respond to coronavirus that are incurred by a recipient, including for costs incurred prior to the date of enactment of this Act: Provided further, That the Secretary may waive, or specify alternative requirements for, any provision of any statute or regulation that the Secretary administers in connection with the use of amounts made available under this paragraph or under the same paragraph in Public Law 116–94 (except for requirements related to fair housing, nondiscrimination, labor standards, and the environment), upon a finding by the Secretary that any such waivers or alternative requirements are necessary to expedite or facilitate the use of such amounts to prevent, prepare for, and respond to coronavirus: Provided further, That any such waivers shall be deemed to be effective as of the date an Indian tribe or tribally designated housing entity began preparing for coronavirus and shall apply to the amounts made available under this paragraph and to the previously appropriated amounts described in the previous proviso; and

(2) Up to $100,000,000 shall be available for grants to Indian tribes under the Indian Community Development Block Grant program under title I of the Housing and Community Development Act of 1974, notwithstanding section 106(a)(1) of such Act, to prevent, prepare for, and respond to coronavirus, for emergencies that constitute imminent threats to health and safety: Provided, That the Secretary shall prioritize, without competition, allocations of these amounts for activities and projects designed to prevent, prepare for, and respond to coronavirus: Provided further, That not to exceed 20 percent of any grant made with funds appropriated under this paragraph shall be expended for planning and management development and administration: Provided further, That amounts provided under this heading in this Act may be used to cover or reimburse allowable costs to prevent, prepare for, and respond to coronavirus incurred by a recipient, including for costs incurred prior to the date of enactment of this Act: Provided further, That, notwithstanding section 105(a)(8) of such Act (42 U.S.C. 5305(a)(8)), there shall be no per centum limitation for the use of funds for public services activities to prevent, prepare for, and respond to coronavirus: Provided further, That the previous proviso shall apply to all such activities for grants of funds made available under this paragraph or under paragraph (4) of this heading in Public Law 116–94: Provided further, That the Secretary may waive, or specify alternative requirements for, any provision of any statute or regulation that the Secretary administers in connection with the use of amounts made available under this paragraph or under paragraph (4) in Public Law 116–94 (except for requirements related to fair housing, nondiscrimination, labor standards, and the environment), upon a finding by the Secretary that any such waivers or alternative requirements are necessary to expedite or facilitate the use of such amounts to prevent, prepare for, and respond to coronavirus: Provided further, That any such waivers shall be deemed to be effective as of the date an Indian tribe began preparing for coronavirus and shall apply to the amounts made available under this paragraph and to the previously appropriated amounts described in the previous proviso:

Provided further, That such amount is designated by the Congress as being for an emergency requirement pursuant to section 251(b)(2)(A)(i) of the Balanced Budget and Emergency Deficit Control Act of 1985.

COMMUNITY PLANNING AND DEVELOPMENT

HOUSING OPPORTUNITIES FOR PERSONS WITH AIDS

For an additional amount for carrying out the "Housing Opportunities for Persons with AIDS" program, as authorized by the AIDS Housing Opportunity Act (42 U.S.C. 12901 et seq.), $65,000,000, to remain available until September 30, 2021, except that amounts allocated pursuant to section 854(c)(5) of such Act shall remain available until September 30, 2022, to provide additional funds to maintain operations and for rental assistance, supportive services, and other necessary actions, in order to prevent, prepare for, and respond to coronavirus: Provided, That not less than $50,000,000 of the amount provided under this heading in this Act shall be allocated pursuant to the formula in section 854 of such Act using the same data elements as utilized pursuant to that same formula in fiscal year 2020: Provided further, That up to $10,000,000 of the amount provided under this heading in this Act shall be to provide an additional one-time, non-renewable award to grantees currently administering existing contracts for permanent supportive housing that initially were funded under section 854(c)(5) of such Act from funds made available under this heading in fiscal year 2010 and prior years: Provided further, That such awards shall be made proportionally to their existing grants: Provided further, That such awards are not required to be spent on permanent supportive housing: Provided further, That, notwithstanding section 859(b)(3)(B) of such Act, housing payment assistance for rent, mortgage, or utilities payments may be provided for a period of up to 24 months: Provided further, That, to protect persons who are living with HIV/AIDS, such amounts provided under this heading in this Act may be used to self-isolate, quarantine, or to provide other coronavirus infection control services as recommended by the Centers for Disease Control and Prevention for household members not living with HIV/AIDS: Provided further, That such amounts may be used to provide relocation services, including to provide lodging at hotels, motels, or other locations, for persons living with HIV/AIDS and household members not living with HIV/AIDS: Provided further, That, notwithstanding section 856(g) of such Act (42 U.S.C. 12905(g)), a grantee may use up to 6 percent of its award under this Act for administrative purposes, and a project sponsor may use up to 10 percent of its sub-award under this Act for administrative purposes: Provided further, That such amounts provided under this heading in this Act may be used to cover or reimburse allowable costs consistent with the purposes of this heading incurred by a grantee or project sponsor regardless of the date on which such costs were incurred: Provided further, That any regulatory waivers the Secretary may issue may be deemed to be effective as of the date a grantee began preparing for coronavirus: Provided further, That any additional activities or authorities authorized pursuant to this Act may also apply at the discretion and upon notice of the Secretary to all amounts made available under this same heading in Public Law 116–94 if such amounts are used by grantees for the purposes described under this heading: Provided further, That up to 2 percent of amounts made available under this heading in this Act may be used, without competition, to increase prior awards made to existing technical assistance providers to provide an immediate increase in capacity building and technical assistance available to grantees under this heading and under the same heading in prior Acts: Provided further, That such amount is designated by the Congress as being for an emergency requirement pursuant to section 251(b)(2)(A)(i) of the Balanced Budget and Emergency Deficit Control Act of 1985.

COMMUNITY DEVELOPMENT FUND

For an additional amount for "Community Development Fund", $5,000,000,000, to remain available until September 30, 2022, to prevent, prepare for, and respond to coronavirus: Provided, That up to $2,000,000,000 of the amount made available under this heading in this Act shall be distributed pursuant to section 106 of the Housing and Community Development Act of 1974 (42 U.S.C. 5306) to grantees that received allocations pursuant to that same formula in fiscal year 2020, and that such allocations shall be made within 30 days of enactment of this Act: Provided further, That, in addition to amounts allocated pursuant to the preceding proviso, an additional $1,000,000,000 shall be allocated directly to States and insular areas, as defined by 42 U.S.C. 5302(a), to prevent, prepare for, and respond to coronavirus within the State or insular area, including activities within entitlement and nonentitlement communities, based on public health needs, risk of transmission of coronavirus, number of coronavirus cases compared to the national average, and economic and housing market disruptions, and other factors, as determined by the Secretary, using best available data and that such allocations shall be made within 45 days of enactment of this Act: Provided further, That remaining amounts shall be distributed directly to the State or unit of general local government, at the discretion of the Secretary, according to a formula based on factors to be determined by the Secretary, prioritizing risk of transmission of coronavirus, number of coronavirus cases compared to the national average, and economic and housing market disruptions resulting from coronavirus: Provided further, That such allocations may be made on a rolling basis based on the best available data at the time of allocation: Provided further, That amounts made available in the preceding provisos may be used to cover or reimburse allowable costs consistent with the purposes of this heading in this Act incurred by a State or locality regardless of the date on which such costs were incurred: Provided further, That section 116(b) of such Act (42 U.S.C. 5316(b)) and any implementing regulations, which requires grantees to submit their final statements of activities no later than August 16 of a given fiscal year, shall not apply to final statements submitted in accordance with sections 104(a)(2) and (a)(3) of such Act (42 U.S.C. 5304(a)(2) and (a)(3)) and comprehensive housing affordability strategies submitted in accordance with section 105 of the Cranston-Gonzalez National Affordable Housing Act (42 U.S.C. 12705) for fiscal years 2019 and 2020: Provided further, That such final statements and comprehensive housing affordability strategies shall instead be submitted no later than August 16, 2021: Provided further, That the Secretary may waive, or specify alternative requirements for, any provision of any statute or regulation that the Secretary administers in connection with the use of amounts made available under this heading in this Act and under the same heading in Public Law 116–94 and Public Law 116–6 (except for requirements related to fair housing, nondiscrimination, labor standards, and the environment), upon a finding by the Secretary that any such waivers or alternative requirements are necessary to expedite or facilitate the use of such amounts to prevent, prepare for, and respond to coronavirus: Provided further, That up to $10,000,000 of amounts made available under this heading in this Act may be used to make new awards or increase prior awards to existing technical assistance providers, without competition, to provide an immediate increase in capacity building and technical assistance to support the use of amounts made available under this heading in this Act and under the same heading in prior Acts to prevent, prepare for, and respond to coronavirus: Provided further, That, notwithstanding sections 104(a)(2), (a)(3), and (c) of the Housing and Community Development Act of 1974 (42 U.S.C. 5304(a)(2), (a)(3), and (c)) and section 105 of the Cranston-Gonzalez National Affordable Housing Act (42 U.S.C. 12705), a grantee may adopt and utilize expedited procedures to prepare, propose, modify, or amend its statement of activities for grants from amounts made available under this heading in this Act and under the same heading in Public Law 116–94 and Public Law 116–6: Provided further, That under such expedited procedures, the grantee need not hold in-person public hearings, but shall provide citizens with notice and a reasonable opportunity to comment of no less than 5 days: Provided further, That, for as long as national or local health authorities recommend social distancing and limiting public gatherings for public health reasons, a grantee may create virtual public hearings to fulfill applicable public hearing requirements for all grants from funds made available under this heading in this Act and under the same heading in Public Law 116–94 and Public Law 116–6: Provided further, That any such virtual hearings shall provide reasonable notification and access for citizens in accordance with the grantee's certifications, timely responses from local officials to all citizen questions and issues, and public access to all questions and responses: Provided further, That, notwithstanding section 105(a)(8) of the Housing and Community Development Act of 1974 (42 U.S.C. 5305(a)(8)), there shall be no per centum limitation for the use of funds for public services activities to prevent, prepare for, and respond to coronavirus: Provided further, That the previous proviso shall apply to all such activities for grants of funds made available under this heading in this Act and under the same heading in Public Law 116–94 and Public Law 116–6: Provided further, That the Secretary shall ensure there are adequate procedures in place to prevent any duplication of benefits as required by section 312 of the Robert T. Stafford Disaster Relief and Emergency Assistance Act (42 U.S.C. 5155) and in accordance with section 1210 of the Disaster Recovery Reform Act of 2018 (division D of Public Law 115–254; 132 Stat. 3442), which amended section 312 of the Robert T. Stafford Disaster Relief and Emergency Assistance Act (42 U.S.C. 5155): Provided further, That such amount is designated by the Congress as being for an emergency requirement pursuant to section 251(b)(2)(A)(i) of the Balanced Budget and Emergency Deficit Control Act of 1985.

HOMELESS ASSISTANCE GRANTS

For an additional amount for "Homeless Assistance Grants", $4,000,000,000, to remain available until September 30, 2022, to prevent, prepare for, and respond to coronavirus, among individuals and families who are homeless or receiving homeless assistance and to support additional homeless assistance and homelessness prevention activities to mitigate the impacts created by coronavirus under the Emergency Solutions Grants program as authorized under subtitle B of title IV of the McKinney-Vento Homeless Assistance Act (42 U.S.C. 11371 et seq.), as amended: Provided, That up to $2,000,000,000 of the amount appropriated under this heading in this Act shall be distributed pursuant to 24 CFR 576.3 to grantees that received allocations pursuant to that same formula in fiscal year 2020, and that such allocations shall be made within 30 days of enactment of this Act: Provided further, That, remaining amounts shall be allocated directly to a State or unit of general local government by a formula to be developed by the Secretary and that such allocations shall be made within 90 days of enactment of this Act: Provided further, That such formula shall allocate such amounts for the benefit of unsheltered homeless, sheltered homeless, and those at risk of homelessness, to geographical areas with the greatest need based on factors to be determined by the Secretary, such as risk of transmission of coronavirus, high numbers or rates of sheltered and unsheltered homeless, and economic and housing market conditions as determined by the Secretary: Provided further, That individuals and families whose income does not exceed the Very Low-Income Limit of the area, as determined by the Secretary, shall be considered "at risk of homelessness" and shall be eligible for homelessness prevention if they meet the criteria in section 401(1)(B) and (C) of such Act (42 U.S.C. 11360(1)(B) and (C)): Provided further, That amounts provided under this heading in this Act may be used to cover or reimburse allowable costs to prevent, prepare for, and respond to coronavirus that are incurred by a State or locality, including for costs incurred prior to the date of enactment of this Act: Provided further, That recipients may deviate from applicable procurement standards when procuring goods and services to prevent, prepare for, and respond to coronavirus: Provided further, That a recipient may use up to 10 percent of its allocation for administrative purposes: Provided further, That the use of amounts provided under this heading in this Act shall not be subject to the consultation, citizen participation, or match requirements that otherwise apply to the Emergency Solutions Grants program, except that a recipient must publish how it has and will utilize its allocation, at a minimum, on the Internet at the appropriate Government web site or through other electronic media: Provided further, That the spending cap established pursuant to section 415(b) of such Act (42 U.S.C. 11374) shall not apply to amounts provided under this heading in this Act: Provided further, That amounts provided under this heading in this Act may be used to provide temporary emergency shelters (through leasing of existing property, temporary structures, or other means) to prevent, prepare for, and respond to coronavirus, and that such temporary emergency shelters shall not be subject to the minimum periods of use required by section 416(c)(1) of such Act (42 U.S.C. 11375(c)(1)): Provided further, That Federal habitability and environmental review standards and requirements shall not apply to the use of such amounts for those temporary emergency shelters that have been determined by State or local health officials to be necessary to prevent, prepare for, and respond to coronavirus: Provided further, That amounts provided under this heading in this Act may be used for training on infectious disease prevention and mitigation and to provide hazard pay, including for time worked prior to the date of enactment of this Act, for staff working directly to prevent, prepare for, and respond to coronavirus among persons who are homeless or at risk of homelessness, and that such activities shall not be considered administrative costs for purposes of the 10 percent cap: Provided further, That in administering the amounts made available under this heading in this Act, the Secretary may waive, or specify alternative requirements for, any provision of any statute or regulation that the Secretary administers in connection with the obligation by the Secretary or the use by the recipient of these amounts (except for requirements related to fair housing, nondiscrimination, labor standards, and the environment unless otherwise provided under this paragraph), if the Secretary finds that good cause exists for the waiver or alternative requirement and such waiver or alternative requirement is necessary to prevent, prepare for, and respond to coronavirus: Provided further, That any such waivers shall be deemed to be effective as of the date a State or unit of local government began preparing for coronavirus and shall apply to the use of amounts provided under this heading in this Act and amounts provided under the same heading for the Emergency Solutions Grant program in prior Acts used by recipients to prevent, prepare for, and respond to coronavirus: Provided further, That the Secretary shall notify the public through the Federal Register or other appropriate means of any such waiver or alternative requirement, and that such public notice may be provided, at a minimum, on the Internet at the appropriate Government web site or through other electronic media, as determined by the Secretary: Provided further, That any additional activities or authorities authorized pursuant to this Act, including any waivers and alternative requirements established by the Secretary pursuant to this Act, may also apply at the discretion and upon notice of the Secretary with respect to all amounts made available for the Emergency Solutions Grants program under the heading "Homeless Assistance Grants" in any prior Act and used by recipients to prevent, prepare for, and respond to coronavirus: Provided further, That up to 1 percent of amounts made available under this heading in this Act may be used to make new awards or increase prior awards made to existing technical assistance providers with experience in providing health care services to homeless populations, without competition, to provide an immediate increase in capacity building and technical assistance available to recipients of amounts for the Emergency Solutions Grants program under this heading in this Act and under the same heading in prior Acts: Provided further, That none of the funds provided under this heading in this Act may be used to require people experiencing homelessness to receive treatment or perform any other prerequisite activities as a condition for receiving shelter, housing, or other services: Provided further, That such amount is designated by the Congress as being for an emergency requirement pursuant to section 251(b)(2)(A)(i) of the Balanced Budget and Emergency Deficit Control Act of 1985.

Housing Programs

PROJECT-BASED RENTAL ASSISTANCE

For an additional amount for "Project-Based Rental Assistance", $1,000,000,000, to remain available until expended, to prevent, prepare for, and respond to coronavirus, including to provide additional funds to maintain normal operations and take other necessary actions during the period that the program is impacted by coronavirus, for assistance to owners or sponsors of properties receiving project-based assistance pursuant to section 8 of the United States Housing Act of 1937 (42 U.S.C. 1437f et seq.): Provided, That the Secretary may waive, or specify alternative requirements for, any provision of any statute or regulation that the Secretary administers in connection with the use of amounts made available under this heading in this Act (except for requirements related to fair housing, nondiscrimination, labor standards, and the environment), upon a finding by the Secretary that any such waivers or alternative requirements are necessary to expedite or facilitate the use of such amounts to prevent, prepare for, and respond to coronavirus, and such waiver or alternative requirement is consistent with the purposes described under this heading in this Act: Provided further, That the Secretary shall notify the public through the Federal Register or other appropriate means of any such waiver or alternative requirement in order for such waiver or alternative requirement to take effect, and that such public notice may be provided, at a minimum, on the Internet at the appropriate Government web site or through other electronic media, as determined by the Secretary: Provided further, That such amount is designated by the Congress as being for an emergency requirement pursuant to section 251(b)(2)(A)(i) of the Balanced Budget and Emergency Deficit Control Act of 1985.

HOUSING FOR THE ELDERLY

For an additional amount for "Housing for the Elderly", $50,000,000, to remain available until September 30, 2023, to prevent, prepare for, and respond to coronavirus, including to provide additional funds to maintain normal operations and take other necessary actions during the period that the program is impacted by coronavirus, for assistance to owners or sponsors of properties receiving project-based assistance pursuant to section 202 of the Housing Act of 1959 (12 U.S.C. 1701q), as amended: Provided, That of the amount provided under this heading in this Act, up to $10,000,000 shall be for service coordinators and the continuation of existing congregate service grants for residents of assisted housing projects: Provided further, That the Secretary may waive, or specify alternative requirements for, any provision of any statute or regulation that the Secretary administers in connection with the use of amounts made available under this heading in this Act (except for requirements related to fair housing, nondiscrimination, labor standards, and the environment), upon a finding by the Secretary that any such waivers or alternative requirements are necessary to expedite or facilitate the use of such amounts to prevent, prepare for, and respond to coronavirus, and such waiver or alternative requirement is consistent with the purposes described under this heading in this Act: Provided further, That the Secretary shall notify the public through the Federal Register or other appropriate means of any such waiver or alternative requirement in order for such waiver or alternative requirement to take effect, and that such public notice may be provided, at a minimum, on the Internet at the appropriate Government web site or through other electronic media, as determined by the Secretary: Provided further, That such amount is designated by the Congress as being for an emergency requirement pursuant to section 251(b)(2)(A)(i) of the Balanced Budget and Emergency Deficit Control Act of 1985.

HOUSING FOR PERSONS WITH DISABILITIES

For an additional amount for "Housing for Persons with Disabilities", $15,000,000, to remain available until September 30, 2023, to prevent, prepare for, and respond to coronavirus, including to provide additional funds to maintain normal operations and take other necessary actions during the period that the program is impacted by coronavirus, for assistance to owners or sponsors of properties receiving project-based assistance pursuant to section 811 of the Cranston-Gonzalez National Affordable Housing Act (42 U.S.C. 8013), as amended: Provided, That the Secretary may waive, or specify alternative requirements for, any provision of any statute or regulation that the Secretary administers in connection with the use of amounts made available under this heading in this Act (except for requirements related to fair housing, nondiscrimination, labor standards, and the environment), upon a finding by the Secretary that any such waivers or alternative requirements are necessary to expedite or facilitate the use of such amounts to prevent, prepare for, and respond to coronavirus, and such waiver or alternative requirement is consistent with the purposes described under this heading in this Act: Provided further, That the Secretary shall notify the public through the Federal Register or other appropriate means of any such waiver or alternative requirement in order for such waiver or alternative requirement to take effect, and that such public notice may be provided, at a minimum, on the Internet at the appropriate Government web site or through other electronic media, as determined by the Secretary: Provided further, That such amount is designated by the Congress as being for an emergency requirement pursuant to section 251(b)(2)(A)(i) of the Balanced Budget and Emergency Deficit Control Act of 1985.

FAIR HOUSING AND EQUAL OPPORTUNITY

FAIR HOUSING ACTIVITIES

For an additional amount for "Fair Housing Activities", $2,500,000, to remain available until September 30, 2021, for contracts, grants, and other assistance, as authorized by title VIII of the Civil Rights Act of 1968, as amended by the Fair Housing Amendments Act of 1988, and section 561 of the Housing and Community Development Act of 1987, to prevent, prepare for, and respond to coronavirus, of which $1,500,000 shall be for the Fair Housing Assistance Program Partnership for Special Enforcement grants to address fair housing issues relating to coronavirus, and $1,000,000 shall be for the Fair Housing Initiatives Program for education and outreach activities under such section 561 to educate the public about fair housing issues related to coronavirus: Provided, That such amount is designated by the Congress as being for an emergency requirement pursuant to section 251(b)(2)(A)(i) of the Balanced Budget and Emergency Deficit Control Act of 1985.

OFFICE OF INSPECTOR GENERAL

For an additional amount for "Office of Inspector General", $5,000,000, to remain available until expended, to prevent, prepare for, and respond to coronavirus: Provided, That the funding made available under this heading in this Act shall be used for conducting audits and investigations of projects and activities carried out with funds made available in this Act to the Department of Housing and Urban Development to prevent, prepare for, and respond to coronavirus: Provided further, That such amount is designated by the Congress as being for an emergency requirement pursuant to section 251(b)(2)(A)(i) of the Balanced Budget and Emergency Deficit Control Act of 1985.

GENERAL PROVISIONS—THIS TITLE

SEC. 22001. Of the amounts made available from the Airport and Airway Trust Fund for "Federal Aviation Administration—Operations" in title XI of division B of the Bipartisan Budget Act of 2018 (Public Law 115–123), up to $25,000,000 may be used to prevent, prepare for, and respond to coronavirus: Provided, That amounts repurposed in this section that were previously designated by the Congress as an emergency requirement pursuant to the Balanced Budget and Emergency Deficit Control Act of 1985 are designated by the Congress as an emergency requirement pursuant to section 251(b)(2)(A)(i) of the Balanced Budget and Emergency Deficit Control Act of 1985.

SEC. 22002. For amounts made available by this Act under the headings "Northeast Corridor Grants to the National Railroad Passenger Corporation" and "National Network Grants to the National Railroad Passenger Corporation", the Secretary of Transportation may not waive the requirements under section 24312 of title 49, United States Code, and section 24305(f) of title 49, United States Code: Provided, That for amounts made available by this Act under such headings the Secretary shall require the National Railroad Passenger Corporation to comply with the Railway Retirement Act of 1974 (45 U.S.C. 231 et seq.), the Railway Labor Act (45 U.S.C. 151 et seq.), and the Railroad Unemployment Insurance Act (45 U.S.C. 351 et seq.): Provided further, That not later than 7 days after the date of enactment of this Act and each subsequent 7 days thereafter, the Secretary shall notify the House and Senate Committees on Appropriations, the Committee on Transportation and Infrastructure of the House of Representatives, and the Committee on Commerce, Science, and Transportation of the Senate of any National Railroad Passenger Corporation employee furloughs as a result of efforts to prevent, prepare for, and respond to coronavirus: Provided further, That in the event of any National Railroad Passenger Corporation employee furloughs as a result of efforts to prevent, prepare for, and respond to coronavirus, the Secretary shall require the National Railroad Passenger Corporation to provide such employees the opportunity to be recalled to their previously held positions as intercity passenger rail service is restored to March 1, 2020 levels and not later than the date on which intercity passenger rail service has been fully restored to March 1, 2020 levels.

SEC. 22003. For the duration of fiscal year 2020, section 127(i)(1)(A) of title 23, United States Code, shall read as if and apply to situations in which: the President has declared an emergency or a major disaster under the Robert T. Stafford Disaster Relief and Emergency Assistance Act (42 U.S.C. 5121 et seq.).

SEC. 22004. No later than September 30, 2020, the remaining unobligated balances of funds made available for the youth homelessness demonstration under the heading "Department of Housing and Urban Development—Community Planning and Development—Homeless Assistance Grants" in the Consolidated Appropriations Act, 2018 (Public Law 115–141) are hereby permanently rescinded, and an amount of additional new budget authority equivalent to the amount rescinded is hereby appropriated, to remain available until September 30, 2021, in addition to other funds as may be available for such purposes, and shall be available, without additional competition, for completing the funding of awards made pursuant to the fiscal year 2018 youth homelessness demonstration.

HIGHWAY SAFETY GRANTS EMERGENCY AUTHORITY

SEC. 22005. (a) IN GENERAL.—The Secretary of Transportation (referred to in this section as the "Secretary") may waive or postpone any requirement under section 402, 404, 405, or 412 of title 23, United States Code, section 4001 of the FAST Act (Public Law 114–94; 129 Stat. 1497), or part 1300 of title 23, Code of Federal Regulations (or successor regulations), if the Secretary determines that—

(1) the Coronavirus Disease 2019 (COVID–19) is having a substantial impact on—

(A) the ability of States to implement or carry out any grant, campaign, or program under those provisions; or

(B) the ability of the Secretary to carry out any responsibility of the Secretary with respect to a grant, campaign, or program under those provisions; or

(2) the requirements of those provisions are having a substantial impact on the ability of States or the Secretary to address the Coronavirus Disease 2019 (COVID–19).

(b) REPORT.—The Secretary shall periodically submit to the relevant committees of Congress a report describing—

(1) each determination made by the Secretary under subsection (a); and

(2) each waiver or postponement of a requirement under that subsection.

(c) EMERGENCY REQUIREMENT.—The amount provided by this section is designated by the Congress as being for an emergency requirement pursuant to section 251(b)(2)(A)(i) of the Balanced Budget and Emergency Deficit Control Act of 1985.

TITLE XIII GENERAL PROVISIONS—THIS ACT

SEC. 23001. Each amount appropriated or made available by this Act is in addition to amounts otherwise appropriated for the fiscal year involved.

SEC. 23002. No part of any appropriation contained in this Act shall remain available for obligation beyond the current fiscal year unless expressly so provided herein.

SEC. 23003. Unless otherwise provided for by this Act, the additional amounts appropriated by this Act to appropriations accounts shall be available under the authorities and conditions applicable to such appropriations accounts for fiscal year 2020.

SEC. 23004. (a) Subject to subsection (b), and notwithstanding any other provision of law, funds made available in this Act, or transferred pursuant to authorization granted in this Act, may only be used to prevent, prepare for, and respond to coronavirus.

(b) Subsection (a) shall not apply to sections 11002, 13002, and 18114 of this Act, reimbursements made pursuant to authority in this Act, or to funds made available in this Act for the Emergency Reserve Fund, established pursuant to section 7058(c)(1) of division J of Public Law 115–31, or to funds made available in this Act for the Infectious Diseases Rapid Response Reserve Fund, established pursuant to section 231 of division B of Public Law 115–245.

(c) This section shall not apply to title VI of this Act.

SEC. 23005. In this Act, the term "coronavirus" means SARS–CoV–2 or another coronavirus with pandemic potential.

SEC. 23006. Each amount designated in this Act by the Congress as being for an emergency requirement pursuant to section 251(b)(2)(A)(i) of the Balanced Budget and Emergency Deficit Control Act of 1985 shall be available (or rescinded or transferred, if applicable) only if the President subsequently so designates all such amounts and transmits such designations to the Congress.

SEC. 23007. Any amount appropriated by this Act, designated by the Congress as an emergency requirement pursuant to section 251(b)(2)(A)(i) of the Balanced Budget and Emergency Deficit Control Act of 1985 and subsequently so designated by the President, and transferred pursuant to transfer authorities provided by this Act shall retain such designation.

BUDGETARY EFFECTS

SEC. 23008. (a) STATUTORY PAYGO SCORECARDS.—The budgetary effects of this division shall not be entered on either PAYGO scorecard maintained pursuant to section 4(d) of the Statutory Pay As-You-Go Act of 2010.

(b) SENATE PAYGO SCORECARDS.—The budgetary effects of this division shall not be entered on any PAYGO scorecard maintained for purposes of section 4106 of H. Con. Res. 71 (115th Congress).

(c) CLASSIFICATION OF BUDGETARY EFFECTS.—Notwithstanding Rule 3 of the Budget Scorekeeping Guidelines set forth in the joint explanatory statement of the committee of conference accompanying Conference Report 105–217 and section 250(c)(7) and (c)(8) of the Balanced Budget and Emergency Deficit Control Act of 1985, the budgetary effects of this division shall be estimated for purposes of section 251 of such Act.

(d) ENSURING NO WITHIN-SESSION SEQUESTRATION.—Solely for the purpose of calculating a breach within a category for fiscal year 2020 pursuant to section 251(a)(6) or section 254(g) of the Balanced Budget and Emergency Deficit Control Act of 1985, and notwithstanding any other provision of this division, the budgetary effects from this division shall be counted as amounts designated as being for an emergency requirement pursuant to section 251(b)(2)(A) of such Act.

This division may be cited as the "Emergency Appropriations for Coronavirus Health Response and Agency Operations".

Attest:

116TH CONGRESS

2D SESSION

H.R. 748

AMENDMENT

Family and Medical Leave Act of 1993, as Amended

[¶3000]

Introduction

The Family and Medical Leave Act (FMLA) in its entirety is reproduced below. The FMLA was amended by the Families First Coronavirus Response Act, (P.L. 116-127) and Coronavirus Aid, Relief and Economic Security Act (CARES Act) (P.L. 116-136). Deleted FMLA material or the text of the FMLA Section prior to amendment appears in the amendment notes following each amended FMLA provision. *Any changed or added material is set out in italics.*

[¶3001] Sec 1. [29 U.S.C. 2601 note]. Short Title

(a) SHORT TITLE.—This Act may be cited as the "Family and Medical Leave Act of 1993".

* * *

[¶3002] Sec. 2. [29 U.S.C. 2601]. Findings and Purposes

(a) FINDINGS.—Congress finds that—

(1) the number of single-parent households and two-parent households in which the single parent or both parents work is increasing significantly;

(2) it is important for the development of children and the family unit that fathers and mothers be able to participate in early childrearing and the care of family members who have serious health conditions;

(3) the lack of employment policies to accommodate working parents can force individuals to choose between job security and parenting;

(4) there is inadequate job security for employees who have serious health conditions that prevent them from working for temporary periods;

(5) due to the nature of the roles of men and women in our society, the primary responsibility for family caretaking often falls on women, and such responsibility affects the working lives of women more than it affects the working lives of men; and

(6) employment standards that apply to one gender only have serious potential for encouraging employers to discriminate against employees and applicants for employment who are of that gender.

(b) PURPOSES.—It is the purpose of this Act—

(1) to balance the demands of the workplace with the needs of families, to promote the stability and economic security of families, and to promote national interests in preserving family integrity;

(2) to entitle employees to take reasonable leave for medical reasons, for the birth or adoption of a child, and for the care of a child, spouse, or parent who has a serious health condition;

(3) to accomplish the purposes described in paragraphs (1) and (2) in a manner that accommodates the legitimate interests of employers;

(4) to accomplish the purposes described in paragraphs (1) and (2) in a manner that, consistent with the Equal Protection Clause of the Fourteenth Amendment, minimizes the potential for employment discrimination on the basis of sex by ensuring generally that leave is available for eligible medical reasons (including maternity-related disability) and for compelling family reasons, on a gender-neutral basis; and

(5) to promote the goal of equal employment opportunity for women and men, pursuant to such clause.

TITLE I—GENERAL REQUIREMENTS FOR LEAVE

[¶3004] Sec. 101. [29 U.S.C. 2611]. Definitions

As used in this title:

(1) COMMERCE.—The terms "commerce" and "industry or activity affecting commerce" mean any activity, business, or industry in commerce or in which a labor dispute would hinder or obstruct commerce or the free flow of commerce, and include "commerce" and any "industry affecting commerce", as defined in paragraphs (1) and (3) of section 501 of the Labor Management Relations Act, 1947 (29 U.S.C. 142 (1) and (3)).

(2) ELIGIBLE EMPLOYEE.—

(A) IN GENERAL.—The term "eligible employee" means an employee who has been employed—

(i) for at least 12 months by the employer with respect to whom leave is requested under section 102; and

(ii) for at least 1,250 hours of service with such employer during the previous 12-month period.

(B) EXCLUSIONS.—The term "eligible employee" does not include—

(i) any Federal officer or employee covered under subchapter V of chapter 63 of title 5, United States Code (as added by title II of this Act); or

(ii) any employee of an employer who is employed at a worksite at which such employer employs less than 50 employees if the total number of employees employed by that employer within 75 miles of that worksite is less than 50.

(C) DETERMINATION.—For purposes of determining whether an employee meets the hours of service requirement specified in subparagraph (A)(ii), the legal standards established under section 7 of the Fair Labor Standards Act of 1938 (29 U.S.C. 207) shall apply.

(D) AIRLINE FLIGHT CREWS.—

(i) DETERMINATION.—For purposes of determining whether an employee who is a flight attendant or flight crewmember (as such terms are defined in regulations of the Federal Aviation Administration) meets the hours of service requirement specified in subparagraph (A)(ii), the employee will be considered to meet the requirement if—

(I) the employee has worked or been paid for not less than 60 percent of the applicable total monthly guarantee, or the equivalent, for the previous 12-month period, for or by the employer with respect to whom leave is requested under section 102; and

(II) the employee has worked or been paid for not less than 504 hours (not counting personal commute time or time spent on vacation leave or medical or sick leave) during the previous 12-month period, for or by that employer.

(ii) FILE.—Each employer of an employee described in clause (i) shall maintain on file with the Secretary (in accordance with such regulations as the Secretary may prescribe) containing information specifying the applicable monthly guarantee with respect to each category of employee to which such guarantee applies.

(iii) DEFINITION.—In this subparagraph, the term "applicable monthly guarantee" means—

(I) for an employee described in clause (i) other than an employee on reserve status, the minimum number of hours for which an employer has agreed to schedule such employee for any given month; and

(II) for an employee described in clause (i) who is on reserve status, the number of hours for which an employer has agreed to pay such employee on reserve status for any given month, as established in the applicable collective bargaining agreement or, if none exists, in the employer's policies.

(3) EMPLOY; EMPLOYEE; STATE.—The terms "employ", "employee", and "State" have the same meanings given such terms in subsections (c), (e), and (g) of section 3 of the Fair Labor Standards Act of 1938 (29 U.S.C. 203 (c), (e), and (g)).

(4) EMPLOYER.—

(A) IN GENERAL.—The term "employer"—

(i) means any person engaged in commerce or in any industry or activity affecting commerce who employs 50 or more employees for each working day during each of 20 or more calendar workweeks in the current or preceding calendar year;

(ii) includes—

(I) any person who acts, directly or indirectly, in the interest of an employer to any of the employees of such employer; and

(II) any successor in interest of an employer;

(iii) includes any "public agency", as defined in section 3(x) of the Fair Labor Standards Act of 1938 (29 U.S.C. 203(x)); and

(iv) includes the General Accounting Office and the Library of Congress.

(B) PUBLIC AGENCY.—For purposes of subparagraph (A)(iii), a public agency shall be considered to be a person engaged in commerce or in an industry or activity affecting commerce.

(5) EMPLOYMENT BENEFITS.—The term "employment benefits" means all benefits provided or made available to employees by an employer, including group life insurance, health insurance, disability insurance, sick leave, annual leave, educational benefits, and pensions, regardless of whether such benefits are provided by a practice or written policy of an employer or through an "employee benefit plan", as defined in section 3(3) of the Employee Retirement Income Security Act of 1974 (29 U.S.C. 1002(3)).

(6) HEALTH CARE PROVIDER.—The term "health care provider" means—

(A) a doctor of medicine or osteopathy who is authorized to practice medicine or surgery (as appropriate) by the State in which the doctor practices; or

(B) any other person determined by the Secretary to be capable of providing health care services.

(7) PARENT.—The term "parent" means the biological parent of an employee or an individual who stood in loco parentis to an employee when the employee was a son or daughter.

(8) PERSON.—The term "person" has the same meaning given such term in section 3(a) of the Fair Labor Standards Act of 1938 (29 U.S.C. 203(a)).

(9) REDUCED LEAVE SCHEDULE.—The term "reduced leave schedule" means a leave schedule that reduces the usual number of hours per workweek, or hours per workday, of an employee.

(10) SECRETARY.—The term "Secretary" means the Secretary of Labor.

(11) SERIOUS HEALTH CONDITION.—The term "serious health condition" means an illness, injury, impairment, or physical or mental condition that involves—

(A) inpatient care in a hospital, hospice, or residential medical care facility; or

(B) continuing treatment by a health care provider.

(12) SON OR DAUGHTER.—The term "son or daughter" means a biological, adopted, or foster child, a stepchild, a legal ward, or a child of a person standing in loco parentis, who is—

(A) under 18 years of age; or

(B) 18 years of age or older and incapable of self-care because of a mental or physical disability.

(13) SPOUSE.—The term "spouse" means a husband or wife, as the case may be.

(14) COVERED ACTIVE DUTY.—The term "covered active duty" means—

(A) in the case of a member of a regular component of the Armed Forces, duty during the deployment of the member with the Armed Forces to a foreign country; and

(B) in the case of a member of a reserve component of the Armed Forces, duty during the deployment of the member with the Armed Forces to a foreign country under a call or order to active duty under a provision of law referred to in section 101(a)(13)(B) of title 10, United States Code.

(15) COVERED SERVICEMEMBER.—The term "covered servicemember" means—

(A) a member of the Armed Forces (including a member of the National Guard or Reserves) who is undergoing medical treatment, recuperation, or therapy, is otherwise in outpatient status, or is otherwise on the temporary disability retired list, for a serious injury or illness; or

(B) a veteran who is undergoing medical treatment, recuperation, or therapy, for a serious injury or illness and who was a member of the Armed Forces (including a member of the National Guard or Reserves) at any time during the period of 5 years preceding the date on which the veteran undergoes that medical treatment, recuperation, or therapy.

(16) OUTPATIENT STATUS.—The term "outpatient status", with respect to a covered servicemember, means the status of a member of the Armed Forces assigned to—

(A) a military medical treatment facility as an outpatient; or

(B) a unit established for the purpose of providing command and control of members of the Armed Forces receiving medical care as outpatients.

(17) NEXT OF KIN.—The term "next of kin", used with respect to an individual, means the nearest blood relative of that individual.

(18) SERIOUS INJURY OR ILLNESS.—The term "serious injury or illness"

(A) in the case of a member of the Armed Forces (including a member of the National Guard or Reserves), means an injury or illness that was incurred by the member in line of duty on active duty in the Armed Forces (or existed before the beginning of the member's active duty and was aggravated by service in line of duty on active duty in the Armed Forces) and that may render the member medically unfit to perform the duties of the member's office, grade, rank, or rating; and

(B) in the case of a veteran who was a member of the Armed Forces (including a member of the National Guard or Reserves) at any time during a period described in paragraph (15)(B), means a qualifying (as defined by the Secretary of Labor) injury or illness that was incurred by the member in line of duty on active duty in the Armed Forces (or existed before the beginning of the member's active duty and was aggravated by service in line of duty on active duty in the Armed Forces) and that manifested itself before or after the member became a veteran.

(19) VETERAN.—The term "veteran" has the meaning given the term in section 101 of title 38, United States Code.

[¶3005] Sec. 102. [29 U.S.C. 2612]. Leave Requirement

(a) IN GENERAL.—

(1) ENTITLEMENT TO LEAVE.——Subject to section 103, an eligible employee shall be entitled to a total of 12 workweeks of leave during any 12-month period for one or more of the following:

(A) Because of the birth of a son or daughter of the employee and in order to care for such son or daughter.

(B) Because of the placement of a son or daughter with the employee for adoption or foster care.

(C) In order to care for the spouse, or a son, daughter, or parent, of the employee, if such spouse, son, daughter, or parent has a serious health condition.

(D) Because of a serious health condition that makes the employee unable to perform the functions of the position of such employee.

(E) Because of any qualifying exigency (as the Secretary shall, by regulation, determine) arising out of the fact that the spouse, or a son, daughter, or parent of the employee is on covered active duty (or has been notified of an impending call or order to covered active duty) in the Armed Forces.

(F) During the period beginning on the date the Emergency Family and Medical Leave Expansion Act takes effect, and ending on December 31, 2020, because of a qualifying need related to a public health emergency in accordance with section 110.

(2) EXPIRATION OF ENTITLEMENT.——The entitlement to leave under subparagraphs (A) and (B) of paragraph (1) for a birth or placement of a son or daughter shall expire at the end of the 12-month period beginning on the date of such birth or placement.

(3) SERVICEMEMBER FAMILY LEAVE.——Subject to section 103, an eligible employee who is the spouse, son, daughter, parent, or next of kin of a covered servicemember shall be entitled to a total of 26 workweeks of leave during a 12-month period to care for the servicemember. The leave described in this paragraph shall only be available during a single 12-month period.

(4) COMBINED LEAVE TOTAL.——During the single 12-month period described in paragraph (3), an eligible employee shall be entitled to a combined total of 26 workweeks of leave under paragraphs (1) and (3). Nothing in this paragraph shall be construed to limit the availability of leave under paragraph (1) during any other 12-month period.

(5) CALCULATION OF LEAVE FOR AIRLINE FLIGHT CREWS.——The Secretary may provide, by regulation, a method for calculating the leave described in paragraph (1) with respect to employees described in section 101(2)(D).

[Leave Taken Intermittently or on a Reduced Leave Schedule]

(b) LEAVE TAKEN INTERMITTENTLY OR ON A REDUCED LEAVE SCHEDULE.—

(1) IN GENERAL.——Leave under subparagraph (A) or (B) of subsection (a)(1) shall not be taken by an employee intermittently or on a reduced leave schedule unless the employee and the employer of the employee agree otherwise. Subject to paragraph (2), subsection (e)(2), and subsection (b)(5) or (f) (as appropriate) of section 103, leave under subparagraph (C) or (D) of subsection (a)(1) or under subsection (a)(3) may be taken intermittently or on a reduced leave schedule when medically necessary. Subject to subsection (e)(3) and section 103(f), leave under subsection (a)(1)(E) may be taken intermittently or on a reduced leave schedule. The taking of leave intermittently or on a reduced leave schedule pursuant to this paragraph shall not result in a reduction in the total amount of leave to which the employee is entitled under subsection (a) beyond the amount of leave actually taken.

(2) ALTERNATIVE POSITION.——If an employee requests intermittent leave, or leave on a reduced leave schedule, under subparagraph (C) or (D) of subsection (a)(1) or under subsection (a)(3), that is foreseeable based on planned medical treatment, the employer may require such employee to transfer temporarily to an available alternative position offered by the employer for which the employee is qualified and that—

(A) has equivalent pay and benefits; and

(B) better accommodates recurring periods of leave than the regular employment position of the employee.

[Unpaid Leave and Its Relationship to Paid Leave]

(c) UNPAID LEAVE PERMITTED.——Except as provided in subsection (d), leave granted *under subsection (a) (other than certain periods of leave under subsection (a)(1)(F))* may consist of unpaid leave. Where an employee is otherwise exempt under regulations issued by the Secretary pursuant to section 13(a)(1) of the Fair Labor Standards Act of 1938 (29 U.S.C. 213(a)(1)), the compliance of an employer with this title by providing unpaid leave shall not affect the exempt status of the employee under such section.

(d) RELATIONSHIP TO PAID LEAVE.—

(1) UNPAID LEAVE.——If an employer provides paid leave for fewer than 12 workweeks (or 26 workweeks in the case of leave provided under subsection (a)(3)), the additional weeks of leave necessary to attain the 12 workweeks (or 26 workweeks, as appropriate) of leave required under this title may be provided without compensation.

(2) SUBSTITUTION OF PAID LEAVE.—

(A) IN GENERAL.——An eligible employee may elect, or an employer may require the employee, to substitute any of the accrued paid vacation leave, personal leave, or family leave of the employee for leave provided under subparagraph (A), (B), or (C) of subsection (a)(1) for any part of the 12-week period of such leave under such subsection.

(B) SERIOUS HEALTH CONDITION.——An eligible employee may elect, or an employer may require the employee, to substitute any of the accrued paid vacation leave, personal leave, or medical or sick leave of the employee for leave provided under subparagraph (C) or (D) of subsection (a)(1) for any part of the 12-week period of such leave under such subsection, except that nothing in this title shall require an employer to provide paid sick leave or paid medical leave in any situation in which such employer would not normally provide any such paid leave. An eligible employee may elect, or an employer may require the employee, to substitute any of the accrued paid vacation leave, personal leave, family leave, or medical or sick leave of the employee for leave provided under subsection (a)(3) for any part of the 26-week period of such leave under such subsection, except that nothing in this title requires an employer to provide paid sick leave or paid medical leave in any situation in which the employer would not normally provide any such paid leave.

[Foreseeable Leave]

(e) FORESEEABLE LEAVE.—

(1) REQUIREMENT OF NOTICE.——In any case in which the necessity for leave under subparagraph (A) or (B) of subsection (a)(1) is foreseeable based on an expected birth or placement, the employee shall provide the employer with not less than 30 days' notice, before the date the leave is to begin, of the employee's intention to take leave under such subparagraph, except that if the date of the birth or placement requires leave to begin in less than 30 days, the employee shall provide such notice as is practicable.

(2) DUTIES OF EMPLOYEE.——In any case in which the necessity for leave under subparagraph (C) or (D) of subsection (a)(1) or under subsection (a)(3) is foreseeable based on planned medical treatment, the employee—

(A) shall make a reasonable effort to schedule the treatment so as not to disrupt unduly the operations of the employer, subject to the approval of the health care provider of the employee or the health care provider of the son, daughter, spouse, parent, or covered servicemember of the employee, as appropriate; and

(B) shall provide the employer with not less than 30 days' notice, before the date the leave is to begin, of the employee's intention to take leave under such subparagraph, except that if the date of the treatment requires leave to begin in less than 30 days, the employee shall provide such notice as is practicable.

(3) NOTICE FOR LEAVE DUE TO COVERED ACTIVE DUTY OF FAMILY MEMBER.——In any case in which the necessity for leave under subsection (a)(1)(E) is foreseeable, whether because the spouse, or a son, daughter, or parent, of the employee is on covered active duty, or because of notification of an impending call or order to covered active duty, the employee shall provide such notice to the employer as is reasonable and practicable.

[Spouses Employed by the Same Employer]

(f)(1) SPOUSES EMPLOYED BY THE SAME EMPLOYER.—

IN GENERAL.—In any case in which a husband and wife entitled to leave under subsection (a) are employed by the same employer, the aggregate number of workweeks of leave to which both may be entitled may be limited to 12 workweeks during any 12-month period, if such leave is taken—

(A) under subparagraph (A) or (B) of subsection (a)(1); or

(B) to care for a sick parent under subparagraph (C) of such subsection.

(2) SERVICEMEMBER FAMILY LEAVE.—

(A) IN GENERAL.—The aggregate number of workweeks of leave to which both that husband and wife may be entitled under subsection (a) may be limited to 26 workweeks during the single 12-month period described in subsection (a)(3) if the leave is—

(i) leave under subsection (a)(3); or

(ii) a combination of leave under subsection (a)(3) and leave described in paragraph (1).

(B) BOTH LIMITATIONS APPLICABLE.——If the leave taken by the husband and wife includes leave described in paragraph (1), the limitation in paragraph (1) shall apply to the leave described in paragraph (1).

[Explanations at ¶100, ¶120, and ¶140.]

2020 Amendment.—Division C, Section 3102(a)(1) of P.L. 116-127, effective April 1, 2020, amended section 102(a)(1) by adding subsection (F) and Section 3102(a)(2) amended section 102(c) by striking "under subsection (a)" and inserting "under subsection (a) (other than certain periods of leave under subsection (a)(1)(F))". Prior to amendment, section 102(c) read as follows:

(c) Unpaid Leave Permitted.—Except as provided in subsection (d), leave granted under subsection (a) may consist of unpaid leave. Where an employee is otherwise exempt under regulations issued by the Secretary pursuant to section 13(a)(1) of the Fair Labor Standards Act of 1938 (29 U.S.C. 213(a)(1)), the compliance of an employer with this title by providing unpaid leave shall not affect the exempt status of the employee under such section.

[¶3006] Sec. 103. [29 U.S.C. 2613]. Certification

(a) IN GENERAL.——An employer may require that a request for leave under subparagraph (C) or (D) of paragraph (1) or paragraph (3) of section 102(a) be supported by a certification issued by the health care provider of the eligible employee or of the son, daughter, spouse, or parent of the employee, or of the next of kin of an individual in the case of leave taken under such paragraph (3), as appropriate. The employee shall provide, in a timely manner, a copy of such certification to the employer.

(b) SUFFICIENT CERTIFICATION.——Certification provided under subsection (a) shall be sufficient if it states—

(1) the date on which the serious health condition commenced;

(2) the probable duration of the condition;

(3) the appropriate medical facts within the knowledge of the health care provider regarding the condition;

(4)(A) for purposes of leave under section 102(a)(1)(C), a statement that the eligible employee is needed to care for the son, daughter, spouse, or parent and an estimate of the amount of time that such employee is needed to care for the son, daughter, spouse, or parent; and

(B) for purposes of leave under section 102(a)(1)(D), a statement that the employee is unable to perform the functions of the position of the employee; and

(5) in the case of certification for intermittent leave, or leave on a reduced leave schedule, for planned medical treatment, the dates on which such treatment is expected to be given and the duration of such treatment;

(6) in the case of certification for intermittent leave, or leave on a reduced leave schedule, under section 102(a)(1)(D), a statement of the medical necessity for the intermittent leave or leave on a reduced leave schedule, and the expected duration of the intermittent leave or reduced leave schedule; and

(7) in the case of certification for intermittent leave, or leave on a reduced leave schedule, under section 102(a)(1)(C), a statement that the employee's intermittent leave or leave on a reduced leave schedule is necessary for the care of the son, daughter, parent, or spouse who has a serious health condition, or will assist in their recovery, and the expected duration and schedule of the intermittent leave or reduced leave schedule.

[Second and Third Opinions]

(c) SECOND OPINION.—

(1) IN GENERAL.——In any case in which the employer has reason to doubt the validity of the certification provided under subsection (a) for leave under subparagraph (C) or (D) of section 102(a)(1), the employer may require, at the expense of the employer, that the eligible employee obtain the opinion of a second health care provider designated or approved by the employer concerning any information certified under subsection (b) for such leave.

(2) LIMITATION.——A health care provider designated or approved under paragraph (1) shall not be employed on a regular basis by the employer.

(d) RESOLUTION OF CONFLICTING OPINIONS.—

(1) IN GENERAL.——In any case in which the second opinion described in subsection (c) differs from the opinion in the original certification provided under subsection (a), the employer may require, at the expense of the employer, that the employee obtain the opinion of a third health care provider

designated or approved jointly by the employer and the employee concerning the information certified under subsection (b).

(2) FINALITY.——The opinion of the third health care provider concerning the information certified under subsection (b) shall be considered to be final and shall be binding on the employer and the employee.

(e) SUBSEQUENT RECERTIFICATION.——The employer may require that the eligible employee obtain subsequent recertifications on a reasonable basis.

(f) CERTIFICATION RELATED TO COVERED ACTIVE DUTY OR CALL TO COVERED ACTIVE DUTY.——An employer may require that a request for leave under section 102(a)(1)(E) be supported by a certification issued at such time and in such manner as the Secretary may by regulation prescribe. If the Secretary issues a regulation requiring such certification, the employee shall provide, in a timely manner, a copy of such certification to the employer.

[¶3007] Sec. 104. [29 U.S.C. 2614]. Employment and Benefits Protection

(a) RESTORATION TO POSITION.—

(1) IN GENERAL.—Except as provided in subsection (b), any eligible employee who takes leave under section 102 for the intended purpose of the leave shall be entitled, on return from such leave—

(A) to be restored by the employer to the position of employment held by the employee when the leave commenced; or

(B) to be restored to an equivalent position with equivalent employment benefits, pay, and other terms and conditions of employment.

(2) LOSS OF BENEFITS.—The taking of leave under section 102 shall not result in the loss of any employment benefit accrued prior to the date on which the leave commenced.

(3) LIMITATIONS.—Nothing in this section shall be construed to entitle any restored employee to—

(A) the accrual of any seniority or employment benefits during any period of leave; or

(B) any right, benefit, or position of employment other than any right, benefit, or position to which the employee would have been entitled had the employee not taken the leave.

(4) CERTIFICATION.—As a condition of restoration under paragraph (1) for an employee who has taken leave under section 102(a)(1)(D), the employer may have a uniformly applied practice or policy that requires each such employee to receive certification from the health care provider of the employee that the employee is able to resume work, except that nothing in this paragraph shall supersede a valid State or local law or a collective bargaining agreement that governs the return to work of such employees.

(5) CONSTRUCTION.—Nothing in this subsection shall be construed to prohibit an employer from requiring an employee on leave under section 102 to report periodically to the employer on the status and intention of the employee to return to work.

[Exemption for Highly Compensated Employees]

(b) EXEMPTION CONCERNING CERTAIN HIGHLY COMPENSATED EMPLOYEES.—

(1) DENIAL OF RESTORATION.——An employer may deny restoration under subsection (a) to any eligible employee described in paragraph (2) if—

(A) such denial is necessary to prevent substantial and grievous economic injury to the operations of the employer;

(B) the employer notifies the employee of the intent of the employer to deny restoration on such basis at the time the employer determines that such injury would occur; and

(C) in any case in which the leave has commenced, the employee elects not to return to employment after receiving such notice.

(2) AFFECTED EMPLOYEES.——An eligible employee described in paragraph (1) is a salaried eligible employee who is among the highest paid 10 percent of the employees employed by the employer within 75 miles of the facility at which the employee is employed.

[Maintenance of Health Benefits]

(c) MAINTENANCE OF HEALTH BENEFITS.—

(1) COVERAGE.——Except as provided in paragraph (2), during any period that an eligible employee takes leave under section 102, the employer shall maintain coverage under any "group health plan" (as defined in section 5000(b)(1) of the Internal Revenue Code of 1986) for the duration of such leave at the level and under the conditions coverage would have been provided if the employee had continued in employment continuously for the duration of such leave.

(2) FAILURE TO RETURN FROM LEAVE.——The employer may recover the premium that the employer paid for maintaining coverage for the employee under such group health plan during any period of unpaid leave under section 102 if—

(A) the employee fails to return from leave under section 102 after the period of leave to which the employee is entitled has expired; and

(B) the employee fails to return to work for a reason other than—

(i) the continuation, recurrence, or onset of a serious health condition that entitles the employee to leave under subparagraph (C) or (D) of section 102(a)(1) or under section 102(a)(3); or

(ii) other circumstances beyond the control of the employee.

(3) CERTIFICATION.—

(A) ISSUANCE.——An employer may require that a claim that an employee is unable to return to work because of the continuation, recurrence, or onset of the serious health condition described in paragraph (2)(B)(i) be supported by—

(i) a certification issued by the health care provider of the son, daughter, spouse, or parent of the employee, as appropriate, in the case of an employee unable to return to work because of a condition specified in section 102(a)(1)(C); or

(ii) a certification issued by the health care provider of the eligible employee, in the case of an employee unable to return to work because of a condition specified in section 102(a)(1)(D); or

(iii) a certification issued by the health care provider of the servicemember being cared for by the employee, in the case of an employee unable to return to work because of a condition specified in section 102(a)(3).

(B) COPY.——The employee shall provide, in a timely manner, a copy of such certification to the employer.

(C) SUFFICIENCY OF CERTIFICATION.—

(i) LEAVE DUE TO SERIOUS HEALTH CONDITION OF EMPLOYEE.——The certification described in subparagraph (A)(ii) shall be sufficient if the certification states that a serious health condition prevented the employee from being able to perform the functions of the position of the employee on the date that the leave of the employee expired.

(ii) LEAVE DUE TO SERIOUS HEALTH CONDITION OF FAMILY MEMBER.——The certification described in subparagraph (A)(i) shall be sufficient if the certification states that the employee is needed to care for the son, daughter, spouse, or parent who has a serious health condition on the date that the leave of the employee expired.

[¶3008] Sec. 105. [29 U.S.C. 2615]. Prohibited Acts

(a) INTERFERENCE WITH RIGHTS.—

(1) EXERCISE OF RIGHTS.——It shall be unlawful for any employer to interfere with, restrain, or deny the exercise of or the attempt to exercise, any right provided under this title.

(2) DISCRIMINATION.——It shall be unlawful for any employer to discharge or in any other manner discriminate against any individual for opposing any practice made unlawful by this title.

(b) INTERFERENCE WITH PROCEEDINGS OR INQUIRIES.——It shall be unlawful for any person to discharge or in any other manner discriminate against any individual because such individual—

(1) has filed any charge, or has instituted or caused to be instituted any proceeding, under or related to this title;

(2) has given, or is about to give, any information in connection with any inquiry or proceeding relating to any right provided under this title; or

(3) has testified, or is about to testify, in any inquiry or proceeding relating to any right provided under this title.

[¶3009] Sec. 106. [29 U.S.C. 2616]. Investigative Authority

(a) IN GENERAL.——To ensure compliance with the provisions of this title, or any regulation or order issued under this title, the Secretary shall have, subject to subsection (c), the investigative authority provided under section 11(a) of the Fair Labor Standards Act of 1938 (29 U.S.C. 211(a)).

(b) OBLIGATION TO KEEP AND PRESERVE RECORDS.——Any employer shall make, keep, and preserve records pertaining to compliance with this title in accordance with section 11(c) of the Fair Labor Standards Act of 1938 (29 U.S.C. 211(c)) and in accordance with regulations issued by the Secretary.

(c) REQUIRED SUBMISSIONS GENERALLY LIMITED TO AN ANNUAL BASIS.——The Secretary shall not under the authority of this section require any employer or any plan, fund, or program to submit to the Secretary any books or records more than once during any 12-month period, unless the Secretary has reasonable cause to believe there may exist a violation of this title or any regulation or order issued pursuant to this title, or is investigating a charge pursuant to section 107(b).

(d) SUBPOENA POWERS.——For the purposes of any investigation provided for in this section, the Secretary shall have the subpoena authority provided for under section 9 of the Fair Labor Standards Act of 1938 (29 U.S.C. 209).

[¶3010] Sec. 107. [29 U.S.C. 2617]. Enforcement

(a) CIVIL ACTION BY EMPLOYEES.—

(1) LIABILITY.——Any employer who violates section 105 shall be liable to any eligible employee affected—

(A) for damages equal to—

(i) the amount of—

(I) any wages, salary, employment benefits, or other compensation denied or lost to such employee by reason of the violation; or

(II) in a case in which wages, salary, employment benefits, or other compensation have not been denied or lost to the employee, any actual monetary losses sustained by the employee as a direct result of the violation, such as the cost of providing care, up to a sum equal to 12 weeks (or 26 weeks, in a case involving leave under section 102(a)(3)) of wages or salary for the employee;

(ii) the interest on the amount described in clause (i) calculated at the prevailing rate; and

(iii) an additional amount as liquidated damages equal to the sum of the amount described in clause (i) and the interest described in clause (ii), except that if an employer who has violated section 105 proves to the satisfaction of the court that the act or omission which violated section 105 was in good faith and that the employer had reasonable grounds for believing that the act or omission was not a violation of section 105, such court may, in the discretion of the court, reduce the amount of the liability to the amount and interest determined under clauses (i) and (ii), respectively; and

(B) for such equitable relief as may be appropriate, including employment, reinstatement, and promotion.

(2) Right of Action.——An action to recover the damages or equitable relief prescribed in paragraph (1) may be maintained against any employer (including a public agency) in any Federal or State court of competent jurisdiction by any one or more employees for and in behalf of—

(A) the employees; or

(B) the employees and other employees similarly situated.

(3) Fees and Costs.——The court in such an action shall, in addition to any judgment awarded to the plaintiff, allow a reasonable attorney's fee, reasonable expert witness fees, and other costs of the action to be paid by the defendant.

(4) Limitations.——The right provided by paragraph (2) to bring an action by or on behalf of any employee shall terminate—

(A) on the filing of a complaint by the Secretary in an action under subsection (d) in which restraint is sought of any further delay in the payment of the amount described in paragraph (1)(A) to such employee by an employer responsible under paragraph (1) for the payment; or

(B) on the filing of a complaint by the Secretary in an action under subsection (b) in which a recovery is sought of the damages described in paragraph (1)(A) owing to an eligible employee by an employer liable under paragraph (1),

unless the action described in subparagraph (A) or (B) is dismissed without prejudice on motion of the Secretary.

(b) Action by the Secretary.—

(1) Administrative Action.——The Secretary shall receive, investigate, and attempt to resolve complaints of violations of section 105 in the same manner that the Secretary receives, investigates, and attempts to resolve complaints of violations of sections 6 and 7 of the Fair Labor Standards Act of 1938 (29 U.S.C. 206 and 207).

(2) Civil Action.——The Secretary may bring an action in any court of competent jurisdiction to recover the damages described in subsection (a)(1)(A).

(3) Sums Recovered.——Any sums recovered by the Secretary pursuant to paragraph (2) shall be held in a special deposit account and shall be paid, on order of the Secretary, directly to each employee affected. Any such sums not paid to an employee because of inability to do so within a period of 3 years shall be deposited into the Treasury of the United States as miscellaneous receipts.

[Time Limitations]

(c) Limitation.—

(1) In General.——Except as provided in paragraph (2), an action may be brought under this section not later than 2 years after the date of the last event constituting the alleged violation for which the action is brought.

(2) Willful Violation.——In the case of such action brought for a willful violation of section 105, such action may be brought within 3 years of the date of the last event constituting the alleged violation for which such action is brought.

(3) Commencement.——In determining when an action is commenced by the Secretary under this section for the purposes of this subsection, it shall be considered to be commenced on the date when the complaint is filed.

(d) Action for Injunction by Secretary.——The district courts of the United States shall have jurisdiction, for cause shown, in an action brought by the Secretary—

(1) to restrain violations of section 105, including the restraint of any withholding of payment of wages, salary, employment benefits, or other compensation, plus interest, found by the court to be due to eligible employees; or

(2) to award such other equitable relief as may be appropriate, including employment, reinstatement, and promotion.

(e) SOLICITOR OF LABOR.——The Solicitor of Labor may appear for and represent the Secretary on any litigation brought under this section.

(f) GENERAL ACCOUNTING OFFICE AND LIBRARY OF CONGRESS.——In the case of the General Accounting Office and the Library of Congress, the authority of the Secretary of Labor under this title shall be exercised respectively by the Comptroller General of the United States and the Librarian of Congress.

[¶3011] Sec. 108. [29 U.S.C. 2618]. Special Rules Concerning Employees of Local Educational Agencies

(a) APPLICATION.—

(1) IN GENERAL.——Except as otherwise provided in this section, the rights (including the rights under section 104, which shall extend throughout the period of leave of any employee under this section), remedies, and procedures under this title shall apply to—

(A) any "local educational agency" (as defined in section 1471(12) of the Elementary and Secondary Education Act of 1965 (20 U.S.C. 2891(12)) and an eligible employee of the agency; and

(B) any private elementary or secondary school and an eligible employee of the school.

(2) DEFINITIONS.——For purposes of the application described in paragraph (1):

(A) ELIGIBLE EMPLOYEE.——The term "eligible employee" means an eligible employee of an agency or school described in paragraph (1).

(B) EMPLOYER.——The term "employer" means an agency or school described in paragraph (1).

(b) LEAVE DOES NOT VIOLATE CERTAIN OTHER FEDERAL LAWS.——A local educational agency and a private elementary or secondary school shall not be in violation of the Individuals with Disabilities Education Act (20 U.S.C. 1400 et seq.), section 504 of the Rehabilitation Act of 1973 (29 U.S.C. 794), or title VI of the Civil Rights Act of 1964 (42 U.S.C. 2000d et seq.), solely as a result of an eligible employee of such agency or school exercising the rights of such employee under this title.

(c) INTERMITTENT LEAVE OR LEAVE ON A REDUCED SCHEDULE FOR INSTRUCTIONAL EMPLOYEES.—

(1) IN GENERAL.——Subject to paragraph (2), in any case in which an eligible employee employed principally in an instructional capacity by any such educational agency or school requests leave under subparagraph (C) or (D) of section 102(a)(1) or under section 102(a)(3) that is foreseeable based on planned medical treatment and the employee would be on leave for greater than 20 percent of the total number of working days in the period during which the leave would extend, the agency or school may require that such employee elect either—

(A) to take leave for periods of a particular duration, not to exceed the duration of the planned medical treatment; or

(B) to transfer temporarily to an available alternative position offered by the employer for which the employee is qualified, and that—

(i) has equivalent pay and benefits; and

(ii) better accommodates recurring periods of leave than the regular employment position of the employee.

(2) APPLICATION.——The elections described in subparagraphs (A) and (B) of paragraph (1) shall apply only with respect to an eligible employee who complies with section 102(e)(2).

(d) RULES APPLICABLE TO PERSONS NEAR THE CONCLUSION OF AN ACADEMIC TERM.——The following rules shall apply with respect to periods of leave near the conclusion of an academic term in the case of any eligible employee employed principally in an instructional capacity by any such educational agency or school:

(1) LEAVE MORE THAN 5 WEEKS PRIOR TO END OF TERM.—If the eligible employee begins leave under section 102 more than 5 weeks prior to the end of the academic term, the agency or school may require the employee to continue taking leave until the end of such term, if—

(A) the leave is of at least 3 weeks duration; and

(B) the return to employment would occur during the 3-week period before the end of such term.

(2) LEAVE LESS THAN 5 WEEKS PRIOR TO END OF TERM.——If the eligible employee begins leave under subparagraph (A), (B), or (C) of section 102(a)(1) or under section 102(a)(3) during the period that commences 5 weeks prior to the end of the academic term, the agency or school may require the employee to continue taking leave until the end of such term, if—

(A) the leave is of greater than 2 weeks duration; and

(B) the return to employment would occur during the 2-week period before the end of such term.

(3) LEAVE LESS THAN 3 WEEKS PRIOR TO END OF TERM.——If the eligible employee begins leave under subparagraph (A), (B), or (C) of section 102(a)(1) or under section 102(a)(3) during the period that commences 3 weeks prior to the end of the academic term and the duration of the leave is greater than 5 working days, the agency or school may require the employee to continue to take leave until the end of such term.

(e) RESTORATION TO EQUIVALENT EMPLOYMENT POSITION.——For purposes of determinations under section 104(a)(1)(B) (relating to the restoration of an eligible employee to an equivalent position), in the case of a local educational agency or a private elementary or secondary school, such determination shall be made on the basis of established school board policies and practices, private school policies and practices, and collective bargaining agreements.

(f) REDUCTION OF THE AMOUNT OF LIABILITY.——If a local educational agency or a private elementary or secondary school that has violated this title proves to the satisfaction of the court that the agency, school, or department had reasonable grounds for believing that the underling act or omission was not a violation of this title, such court may, in the discretion of the court, reduce the amount of the liability provided for under section 107(a)(1)(A) to the amount and interest determined under clauses (i) and (ii), respectively, of such section.

[¶3012] Sec. 109. [29 U.S.C. 2619]. Notice

(a) IN GENERAL.——Each employer shall post and keep posted, in conspicuous places on the premises of the employer where notices to employees and applicants for employment are customarily posted, a notice, to be prepared or approved by the Secretary, setting forth excerpts from, or summaries of, the pertinent provisions of this title and information pertaining to the filing of a charge.

(b) PENALTY.——Any employer that willfully violates this section may be assessed a civil money penalty not to exceed $100 for each separate offense.

[¶3013] Sec. 110. [29 U.S.C. 2620]. *Public Health Emergency Leave*

(a) DEFINITIONS.—The following shall apply with respect to leave under section 102(a)(1)(F):

(1) APPLICATION OF CERTAIN TERMS.—The definitions in section 101 shall apply, except as follows:

(A) ELIGIBLE EMPLOYEE.—(i) IN GENERAL.—In lieu of the definition in sections 101(2)(A) and 101(2)(B)(ii), the term "eligible employee" means an employee who has been employed for at least 30 calendar days by the employer with respect to whom leave is requested under section 102(a)(1)(F).

(ii) RULE REGARDING REHIRED EMPLOYEES.—For purposes of clause (i), the term "employed for at least 30 calendar days", used with respect to an employee and an employer described in clause (i), includes an employee who was laid off by that employer not earlier than March 1, 2020, had worked for the employer for not less than 30 of the last 60 calendar days prior to the employee's layoff, and was rehired by the employer.

(B) EMPLOYER THRESHOLD.—Section 101(4)(A)(i) shall be applied by substituting "fewer than 500 employees" for "50 or more employees for each working day during each of 20 or more calendar workweeks in the current or preceding calendar year".

(2) ADDITIONAL DEFINITIONS.—In addition to the definitions described in paragraph (1), the following definitions shall apply with respect to leave under section 102(a)(1)(F):

(A) QUALIFYING NEED RELATED TO A PUBLIC HEALTH EMERGENCY.—The term "qualifying need related to a public health emergency", with respect to leave, means the employee is unable to work (or telework) due to a need for leave to care for the son or daughter under 18 years of age of such employee if the school or place of care has been closed, or the child care provider of such son or daughter is unavailable, due to a public health emergency.

(B) PUBLIC HEALTH EMERGENCY.—The term "public health emergency" means an emergency with respect to COVID–19 declared by a Federal, State, or local authority.

(C) CHILD CARE PROVIDER.—The term "child care provider" means a provider who receives compensation for providing child care services on a regular basis, including an "eligible child care provider" (as defined in section 658P of the Child Care and Development Block Grant Act of 1990 (42 U.S.C. 9858n)).

(D) SCHOOL.—The term "school" means an "elementary school" or "secondary school" as such terms are defined in section 8101 of the Elementary and Secondary Education Act of 1965 (20 U.S.C. 7801).

(3) REGULATORY AUTHORITIES.—The Secretary of Labor shall have the authority to issue regulations for good cause under sections 553(b)(B) and 553(d)(3) of title 5, United States Code—

(A) to exclude certain health care providers and emergency responders from the definition of eligible employee under section 110(a)(1)(A);

(B) to exempt small businesses with fewer than 50 employees from the requirements of section 102(a)(1)(F) when the imposition of such requirements would jeopardize the viability of the business as a going concern; and

(C) as necessary to carry out the purposes of this Act, including to ensure consistency between this Act and Division E and Division G of the Families First Coronavirus Response Act.

(4) The Director of the Office of Management and Budget shall have the authority to exclude for good cause from the requirements under subsection (b) certain employers of the United States Government with respect to certain categories of Executive Branch employees.

***(b)** RELATIONSHIP TO PAID LEAVE.—*

(1) UNPAID LEAVE FOR INITIAL 10 DAYS.—(A) IN GENERAL.—The first 10 days for which an employee takes leave under section 102(a)(1)(F) may consist of unpaid leave.

(B) EMPLOYEE ELECTION.—An employee may elect to substitute any accrued vacation leave, personal leave, or medical or sick leave for unpaid leave under section 102(a)(1)(F) in accordance with section 102(d)(2)(B).

(2) PAID LEAVE FOR SUBSEQUENT DAYS.—

(A) IN GENERAL.—An employer shall provide paid leave for each day of leave under section 102(a)(1)(F) that an employee takes after taking leave under such section for 10 days.

(B) CALCULATION.—

(i) IN GENERAL.—Subject to clause (ii), paid leave under subparagraph (A) for an employee shall be calculated based on—

(I) an amount that is not less than two-thirds of an employee's regular rate of pay (as determined under section 7(e) of the Fair Labor Standards Act of 1938 (29 U.S.C. 207(e)); and

(II) the number of hours the employee would otherwise be normally scheduled to work (or the number of hours calculated under subparagraph (C)).

(ii) LIMITATION.—An employer shall not be required to pay more than $200 per day and $10,000 in the aggregate for each employee for paid leave under this section.

(C) VARYING SCHEDULE HOURS CALCULATION.—In the case of an employee whose schedule varies from week to week to such an extent that an employer is unable to determine with certainty the number of hours the employee would have worked if such employee had not taken leave under section 102(a)(1)(F), the employer shall use the following in place of such number:

(i) Subject to clause (ii), a number equal to the average number of hours that the employee was scheduled per day over the 6-month period ending on the date on which the employee takes such leave, including hours for which the employee took leave of any type.

(ii) If the employee did not work over such period, the reasonable expectation of the employee at the time of hiring of the average number of hours per day that the employee would normally be scheduled to work.

(c) *NOTICE.—In any case where the necessity for leave under section 102(a)(1)(F) for the purpose described in subsection (a)(2)(A) is foreseeable, an employee shall provide the employer with such notice of leave as is practicable.*

(d) *RESTORATION TO POSITION.—*

(1) IN GENERAL.—Section 104(a)(1) shall not apply with respect to an employee of an employer who employs fewer than 25 employees if the conditions described in paragraph (2) are met.

(2) CONDITIONS.—The conditions described in this paragraph are the following:

(A) The employee takes leave under section 102(a)(1)(F).

(B) The position held by the employee when the leave commenced does not exist due to economic conditions or other changes in operating conditions of the employer—

(i) that affect employment; and

(ii) are caused by a public health emergency during the period of leave.

(C) The employer makes reasonable efforts to restore the employee to a position equivalent to the position the employee held when the leave commenced, with equivalent employment benefits, pay, and other terms and conditions of employment.

(D) If the reasonable efforts of the employer under subparagraph (C) fail, the employer makes reasonable efforts during the period described in paragraph (3) to contact the employee if an equivalent position described in subparagraph (C) becomes available.

(3) CONTACT PERIOD.—The period described under this paragraph is the 1-year period beginning on the earlier of—

(A) the date on which the qualifying need related to a public health emergency concludes; or

(B) the date that is 12 weeks after the date on which the employee's leave under section 102(a)(1)(F) commences.

[Explanations at ¶100, ¶110, ¶120, ¶130, and ¶140.]

2020 Amendment.—Division A, Title III, Part IV, Subtitle C, Section 3604(a) of P.L. 116-136, effective April 1, 2020, amended section 110(a) by adding subsection (4).

Division A, Title III, Part IV, Subtitle C, Section 3605 of P.L. 116-136 amended section 110(a)(1)(A) by adding subsections (i) and (ii). **Note:** Division B, Title IX, Section 19008(2) of P.L. 116-136 also amended section 110(a)(1)(A) by adding a subsection (ii). For the convenience of the reader, this amendment reads as follows:

"(ii) SPECIAL RULE.—For purposes of applying section 102(a)(1)(F) and this section under the Congressional Accountability Act of 1995, in lieu of the definition in section 202(a)(2)(B) of that Act (2 U.S.C. 1312(a)(2)(B)), the term 'eligible employee' means a covered employee (as defined in section 101 of that Act (2 U.S.C. 1301)) who has been employed for at least 30 calendar days by the employing office (as so defined) with respect to whom leave is requested under section 102(a)(1)(F)."

Division A, Title III, Part IV, Subtitle C, Section 3611(1) of P.L. 116-136 amended Section 110(a)(3) by striking "553(d)(A)" and inserting "553(d)(3)", and Section 3611(7) added subsection (C).

Division A, Title III, Part IV, Subtitle C, Section 3601 of P.L. 116-136 amended Section 110(b)(2)(B) by striking clause (ii) and inserting "(ii) LIMITATION.—An employer shall not be required to pay more than $200 per day and $10,000 in the aggregate for each employee for paid leave under this section.". Prior to amendment, Section 110(b)(2)(B)(ii) read as follows:

"(ii) Clarification.—In no event shall such paid leave exceed $200 per day and $10,000 in the aggregate."

Division A, Title III, Part IV, Subtitle C, Section 3611(3) of P.L. 116-136 amended Section 110(c) by striking "subsection (a)(2)(A)(iii)" and inserting "subsection (a)(2)(A)".

2020 Amendment.—Division C, Section 3102(b) of P.L. 116-127, effective April 1, 2020, added section 110.

[¶3014] Sec. 3103 *EMPLOYMENT UNDER MULTI-EMPLOYER BARGAINING AGREEMENTS*

(a) EMPLOYERS.—An employer signatory to a multiemployer collective bargaining agreement may, consistent with its bargaining obligations and its collective bargaining agreement, fulfill its obligations under section 110(b)(2) of title I of the Family and Medical Leave Act of 1993, as added by the Families First Coronavirus Response Act, by making contributions to a multiemployer fund, plan, or program based on the paid leave each

of its employees is entitled to under such section while working under the multiemployer collective bargaining agreement, provided that the fund, plan, or program enables employees to secure pay from such fund, plan, or program based on hours they have worked under the multiemployer collective bargaining agreement for paid leave taken under section 102(a)(1)(F) of title I of the Family and Medical Leave Act of 1993, as added by the Families First Coronavirus Response Act.

(b) EMPLOYEES.—*Employees who work under a multiemployer collective bargaining agreement into which their employers make contributions as provided in subsection (a) may secure pay from such fund, plan, or program based on hours they have worked under the multiemployer collective bargaining agreement for paid leave taken under section 102(a)(1)(F) of title I of the Family and Medical Leave Act of 1993, as added by the Families First Coronavirus Response Act.*

2020 Amendment.—Section 3103 included in Division C of P.L. 116-127, effective April 1, 2020.

[¶3015] Sec. 3104 *SPECIAL RULE FOR CERTAIN EMPLOYERS*

An employer under section 110(a)(1)(B) of the Family and Medical Leave Act of 1993 shall not be subject to section 107(a) of such Act for a violation of section 102(a)(1)(F) of such Act if the employer does not meet the definition of employer set forth in section 101(4)(A)(i) of such Act.

2020 Amendment.—Division A, Title III, Part IV, Subtitle C, Section 3611(4) of P.L. 116-136, effective April 1, 2020, amended section 3104. Prior to amendment, section 3104 read as follows:

"Special Rule for Certain Employers—An employer under 110(a)(B) shall not be subject to section 107(a) for a violation of section 102(a)(1)(F) if the employer does not meet the definition of employer set forth in Section 101(4)(A)(i)."

2020 Amendment.—Section 3104 included in Division C of P.L. 116-127, effective April 1, 2020.

[¶3016] Sec. 3105 *SPECIAL RULE FOR HEALTH CARE PROVIDERS AND EMERGENCY RESPONDERS*

An employer of an employee who is a health care provider or an emergency responder may elect to exclude such employee from the application of the provisions in the amendments made under of section 3102 of this Act.

2020 Amendment.—Section 3105 included in Division C of P.L. 116-127, effective April 1, 2020.

TITLE II—LEAVE FOR CIVIL SERVICE EMPLOYEES

[¶3018] Sec. 201. [5 U.S.C. 6381]. Leave Requirement

(a) CIVIL SERVICE EMPLOYEES.—

(1) IN GENERAL.——Chapter 63 of title 5, United States Code, is amended by adding at the end the following new subchapter:

SUBCHAPTER V—FAMILY AND MEDICAL LEAVE

[¶3020] [5 U.S.C. 6381] Definitions

For the purpose of this subchapter—

(1) the term 'employee' means any individual who—

(A) is an 'employee', as defined by section 6301(2), including any individual employed in a position referred to in clause (v) or (ix) of section 6301(2), but excluding any individual employed by the government of the District of Columbia any individual employed on a temporary or intermittent basis, and any employee of the Government Accountability Office or the Library of Congress; and;

(B) has completed at least 12 months of service as an employee (within the meaning of subparagraph (A));

(2) the term 'health care provider' means—

(A) a doctor of medicine or osteopathy who is authorized to practice medicine or surgery (as appropriate) by the State in which the doctor practices; and

(B) any other person determined by the Director of the Office of Personnel Management to be capable of providing health care services;

(3) the term 'parent' means the biological parent of an employee or an individual who stood in loco parentis to an employee when the employee was a son or daughter;

(4) the term 'reduced leave schedule' means a leave schedule that reduces the usual number of hours per workweek, or hours per workday, of an employee;

(5) the term 'serious health condition' means an illness, injury, impairment, or physical or mental condition that involves—

(A) inpatient care in a hospital, hospice, or residential medical care facility; or

(B) continuing treatment by a health care provider;

(6) the term 'son or daughter' means a biological, adopted, or foster child, a stepchild, a legal ward, or a child of a person standing in loco parentis, who is—

(A) under 18 years of age; or

(B) 18 years of age or older and incapable of self-care because of a mental or physical disability;

(7) the term 'covered active duty' means—

(A) in the case of a member of a regular component of the Armed Forces, duty during the deployment of the member with the Armed Forces to a foreign country; and

(B) in the case of a member of a reserve component of the Armed Forces, duty during the deployment of the member with the Armed Forces to a foreign country under a call or order to active duty under a provision of law referred to in section 101(a)(13)(B) of title 10, United States Code.

(8) the term 'covered servicemember' means—

(A) a member of the Armed Forces (including a member of the National Guard or Reserves) who is undergoing medical treatment, recuperation, or therapy, is otherwise in outpatient status, or is otherwise on the temporary disability retired list, for a serious injury or illness; or

(B) a veteran who is undergoing medical treatment, recuperation, or therapy, for a serious injury or illness and who was a member of the Armed Forces (including a member of the National Guard or Reserves) at any time during the period of 5 years preceding the date on which the veteran undergoes that medical treatment, recuperation, or therapy;

(9) the term 'outpatient status', with respect to a covered servicemember, means the status of a member of the Armed Forces assigned to—

(A) a military medical treatment facility as an outpatient; or

(B) a unit established for the purpose of providing command and control of members of the Armed Forces receiving medical care as outpatients;

(10) the term 'next of kin', used with respect to an individual, means the nearest blood relative of that individual;

(11) the term 'serious injury or illness'—

(A) in the case of a member of the Armed Forces (including a member of the National Guard or Reserves), means an injury or illness that was incurred by the member in line of duty on active duty in the Armed Forces (or existed before the beginning of the member's active duty and was aggravated by service in line of duty on active duty in the Armed Forces) and that may render the member medically unfit to perform the duties of the member's office, grade, rank, or rating; and

(B) in the case of a veteran who was a member of the Armed Forces (including a member of the National Guard or Reserves) at any time during a period described in paragraph (8)(B), means an injury or illness that was incurred by the member in line of duty on active duty in the Armed Forces (or existed before the beginning of the member's active duty and was aggravated by service in line of duty on active duty in the Armed Forces) and that manifested itself before or after the member became a veteran; and

(12) the term 'veteran' has the meaning given the term in section 101 of title 38, United States Code.

[¶3021] Sec. 6382. [5 U.S.C. 6382] Leave requirement

(a)(1) Subject to section 6383, an employee shall be entitled to a total of 12 administrative workweeks of leave during any 12-month period for one or more of the following:

(A) Because of the birth of a son or daughter of the employee and in order to care for such son or daughter.

(B) Because of the placement of a son or daughter with the employee for adoption or foster care.

(C) In order to care for the spouse, or a son, daughter, or parent, of the employee, if such spouse, son, daughter, or parent has a serious health condition.

(D) Because of a serious health condition that makes the employee unable to perform the functions of the employee's position.

(E) Because of any qualifying exigency arising out of the fact that the spouse, or a son, daughter, or parent of the employee is on covered active duty (or has been notified of an impending call or order to covered active duty) in the Armed Forces.

(2) The entitlement to leave under subparagraph (A) or (B) of paragraph (1) based on the birth or placement of a son or daughter shall expire at the end of the 12-month period beginning on the date of such birth or placement.

(3) Subject to section 6383, an employee who is the spouse, son, daughter, parent, or next of kin of a covered servicemember shall be entitled to a total of 26 administrative workweeks of leave during a 12- month period to care for the servicemember. The leave described in this paragraph shall only be available during a single 12-month period.

(4) During the single 12-month period described in paragraph (3), an employee shall be entitled to a combined total of 26 administrative workweeks of leave under paragraphs (1) and (3). Nothing in this paragraph shall be construed to limit the availability of leave under paragraph (1) during any other 12-month period.

(b)(1) Leave under subparagraph (A) or (B) of subsection (a)(1) shall not be taken by an employee intermittently or on a reduced leave schedule unless the employee and the employing agency of the employee agree otherwise. Subject to paragraph (2), subsection (e)(2), and subsection (b)(5) or (f) (as appropriate) of section 6383, leave under subparagraph (C) or (D) of subsection (a)(1) or under subsection (a)(3) may be taken intermittently or on a reduced leave schedule when medically necessary. Subject to subsection (e)(3) and section 6383(f), leave under subsection (a)(1)(E) may be taken intermittently or on a reduced leave schedule. In the case of an employee who takes leave intermittently or on a reduced leave schedule pursuant to this paragraph, any hours of leave so taken by such employee shall be subtracted from the total amount of leave remaining available to such employee under subsection (a), for purposes of the 12-month period involved, on an hour-for-hour basis.

(2) If an employee requests intermittent leave, or leave on a reduced leave schedule, under subparagraph (C) or (D) of subsection (a)(1) or under subsection (a)(3), that is foreseeable based on planned medical treatment, the employing agency may require such employee to transfer temporarily to an available alternative position offered by the employing agency for which the employee is qualified and that—

(A) has equivalent pay and benefits; and

(B) better accommodates recurring periods of leave than the regular employment position of the employee.

(c) Except as provided in subsection (d), leave granted under subsection (a) shall be leave without pay.

(d) An employee may elect to substitute for leave under subparagraph (A), (B), (C), or (D), or (E) of subsection (a)(1) any of the employee's accrued or accumulated annual or sick leave under subchapter I for any part of the 12-week period of leave under such subsection, except that nothing in this subchapter shall require an employing agency to provide paid sick leave in any situation in which such employing agency would not normally provide any such paid leave. An employee may elect to substitute for leave under subsection (a)(3) any of the employee's accrued or accumulated annual or sick leave under subchapter I for any part of the 26-week period of leave under such subsection.

(e)(1) In any case in which the necessity for leave under subparagraph (A) or (B) of subsection (a)(1) or under subsection (a)(3) is foreseeable based on an expected birth or placement, the employee shall provide the employing agency with not less than 30 days' notice, before the date the leave is to begin, of the employee's intention to take leave under such subparagraph, except that if the date of the birth or placement requires leave to begin in less than 30 days, the employee shall provide such notice as is practicable.

(2) In any case in which the necessity for leave under subparagraph (C) or (D) of subsection (a)(1) is foreseeable based on planned medical treatment, the employee—

(A) shall make a reasonable effort to schedule the treatment so as not to disrupt unduly the operations of the employing agency, subject to the approval of the health care provider of the employee or the health care provider of the son, daughter, spouse, parent, or covered servicemember of the employee, as appropriate; and

(B) shall provide the employing agency with not less than 30 days' notice, before the date the leave is to begin, of the employee's intention to take leave under such subparagraph, except that if the date of the treatment requires leave to begin in less than 30 days, the employee shall provide such notice as is practicable.

(3) In any case in which the necessity for leave under subsection (a)(1)(E) is foreseeable, whether because the spouse, or a son, daughter, or parent, of the employee is on covered active duty, or because of notification of an impending call or order to covered active duty, the employee shall provide such notice to the employer as is reasonable and practicable.

[¶3022] Sec. 6383. [5 U.S.C. 6383] Certification

(a) An employing agency may require that a request for leave under subparagraph (C) or (D) of section 6382(a)(1) be supported by certification issued by the health care provider of the employee or of the son, daughter, spouse, or parent of the employee, as appropriate. The employee shall provide, in a timely manner, a copy of such certification to the employing agency.

(b) A certification provided under subsection (a) shall be sufficient if it states—

(1) the date on which the serious health condition commenced;

(2) the probable duration of the condition;

(3) the appropriate medical facts within the knowledge of the health care provider regarding the condition;

(4)(A) for purposes of leave under section 6382(a)(1)(C), a statement that the employee is needed to care for the son, daughter, spouse, or parent, and an estimate of the amount of time that such employee is needed to care for such son, daughter, spouse, or parent; and

(B) for purposes of leave under section 6382(a)(1)(D), a statement that the employee is unable to perform the functions of the position of the employee; and

(5) in the case of certification for intermittent leave, or leave on a reduced leave schedule, for planned medical treatment, the dates on which such treatment is expected to be given and the duration of such treatment.

(c)(1) In any case in which the employing agency has reason to doubt the validity of the certification provided under subsection (a) for leave under subparagraph (C) or (D) of section 6382(a)(1), the employing agency may require, at the expense of the agency, that the employee obtain the opinion of a second health care provider designated or approved by the employing agency concerning any information certified under subsection (b) for such leave.

(2) Any health care provider designated or approved under paragraph (1) shall not be employed on a regular basis by the employing agency.

(d)(1) In any case in which the second opinion described in subsection (c) differs from the original certification provided under subsection (a), the employing agency may require, at the expense of the agency, that the employee obtain the opinion of a third health care provider designated or approved jointly by the employing agency and the employee concerning the information certified under subsection (b).

(2) The opinion of the third health care provider concerning the information certified under subsection (b) shall be considered to be final and shall be binding on the employing agency and the employee.

(e) The employing agency may require, at the expense of the agency, that the employee obtain subsequent recertifications on a reasonable basis.

(f) An employing agency may require that a request for leave under section paragraph (1)(E) or (3) of section 6382(a) be supported by a certification issued at such time and in such manner as the Office of Personnel Management may by regulation prescribe.

[¶3023] Sec. 6384. [5 U.S.C. 6384] Employment and benefits protection

(a) Any employee who takes leave under section 6382 for the intended purpose of the leave shall be entitled, upon return from such leave—

(1) to be restored by the employing agency to the position held by the employee when the leave commenced; or

(2) to be restored to an equivalent position with equivalent benefits, pay, status, and other terms and conditions of employment.

(b) The taking of leave under section 6382 shall not result in the loss of any employment benefit accrued prior to the date on which the leave commenced.

(c) Except as otherwise provided by or under law, nothing in this section shall be construed to entitle any restored employee to—

(1) the accrual of any employment benefits during any period of leave; or

(2) any right, benefit, or position of employment other than any right, benefit, or position to which the employee would have been entitled had the employee not taken the leave.

(d) As a condition to restoration under subsection (a) for an employee who takes leave under section 6382(a)(1)(D), the employing agency may have a uniformly applied practice or policy that requires each such employee to receive certification from the health care provider of the employee that the employee is able to resume work.

(e) Nothing in this section shall be construed to prohibit an employing agency from requiring an employee on leave under section 6382 to report periodically to the employing agency on the status and intention of the employee to return to work.

[¶3024] Sec. 6385. [5 U.S.C. 6385] Prohibition of coercion

(a) An employee shall not directly or indirectly intimidate, threaten, or coerce, or attempt to intimidate, threaten, or coerce, any other employee for the purpose of interfering with the exercise of any rights which such other employee may have under this subchapter.

(b) For the purpose of this section—

(1) the term 'intimidate, threaten, or coerce' includes promising to confer or conferring any benefit (such as appointment, promotion, or compensation), or taking or threatening to take any reprisal (such as deprivation of appointment, promotion, or compensation); and

(2) the term 'employee' means any 'employee', as defined by section 2105.

[¶3025] Sec. 6386. [5 U.S.C. 6386] Health insurance

An employee enrolled in a health benefits plan under chapter 89 who is placed in a leave status under section 6382 may elect to continue the health benefits enrollment of the employee while in such leave status and arrange to pay currently into the Employees Health Benefits Fund (described in section 8909), the appropriate employee contributions.

[¶3026] Sec. 6387. [5 U.S.C. 6387] Regulations

The Office of Personnel Management shall prescribe regulations necessary for the administration of this subchapter. The regulations prescribed under this subchapter shall, to the extent appropriate, be consistent with the regulations prescribed by the Secretary of Labor under title I of the Family and Medical Leave Act of 1993.

(2) TABLE OF CONTENTS.—The table of contents for chapter 63 of title 5, United States Code, is amended by adding at the end the following:

SUBCHAPTER V—FAMILY AND MEDICAL LEAVE

* * *

[Employees Paid from Nonappropriated Funds]

(b) EMPLOYEES PAID FROM NONAPPROPRIATED FUNDS.—Section 2105(c)(1) of title 5, United States Code, is amended—

(1) by striking "or" at the end of subparagraph (C); and

(2) by adding at the end the following new subparagraph:

"(E) subchapter V of chapter 63, which shall be applied so as to construe references to benefit programs to refer to applicable programs for employees paid from nonappropriated funds; or".

TITLE III—COMMISSION ON LEAVE

[¶3028] Sec. 301. [29 U.S.C. 2631]. ESTABLISHMENT.

There is established a commission to be known as the Commission on Leave (referred to in this title as the "Commission").

[¶3029] Sec. 302. [29 U.S.C. 2632]. DUTIES.

The Commission shall—

(1) conduct a comprehensive study of—

(A) existing and proposed mandatory and voluntary policies relating to family and temporary medical leave, including policies provided by employers not covered under this Act;

(B) the potential costs, benefits, and impact on productivity, job creation and business growth of such policies on employers and employees;

(C) possible differences in costs, benefits, and impact on productivity, job creation and business growth of such policies on employers based on business type and size;

(D) the impact of family and medical leave policies on the availability of employee benefits provided by employers, including employers not covered under this Act;

(E) alternative and equivalent State enforcement of title I with respect to employees described in section 108(a);

(F) methods used by employers to reduce administrative costs of implementing family and medical leave policies;

(G) the ability of the employers to recover, under section 104(c)(2), the premiums described in such section; and

(H) the impact on employers and employees of policies that provide temporary wage replacement during periods of family and medical leave.

(2) not later than 2 years after the date on which the Commission first meets, prepare and submit, to the appropriate Committees of Congress, a report concerning the subjects listed in paragraph (1).

[¶3030] Sec. 303. [29 U.S.C. 2633]. MEMBERSHIP

(a) COMPOSITION.—

(1) APPOINTMENTS.—The Commission shall be composed of 12 voting members and 4 ex officio members to be appointed not later than 60 days after the date of the enactment of this Act as follows:

(A) SENATORS.—One Senator shall be appointed by the Majority Leader of the Senate, and one Senator shall be appointed by the Minority Leader of the Senate.

(B) MEMBERS OF HOUSE OF REPRESENTATIVES.—One Member of the House of Representatives shall be appointed by the Speaker of the House of Representatives, and one Member of the House of Representatives shall be appointed by the Minority Leader of the House of Representatives.

(C) ADDITIONAL MEMBERS.—

(i) APPOINTMENT.—Two Members each shall be appointed by—

(I) the Speaker of the House of Representatives;

(II) the Majority Leader of the Senate;

(III) the Minority Leader of the House of Representatives; and

(IV) the Minority Leader of the Senate.

(ii) EXPERTISE.—Such members shall be appointed by virtue of demonstrated expertise in relevant family, temporary disability, and labor management issues. Such members shall include representatives of employers, including employers from large businesses and from small businesses.

(2) EX OFFICIO MEMBERS.—The Secretary of Health and Human Services, the Secretary of Labor, the Secretary of Commerce, and the Administrator of the Small Business Administration shall serve on the Commission as nonvoting ex officio members.

(b) VACANCIES.—Any vacancy on the Commission shall be filled in the manner in which the original appointment was made. The vacancy shall not affect the power of the remaining members to execute the duties of the Commission.

(c) CHAIRPERSON AND VICE CHAIRPERSON.—The Commission shall elect a chairperson and a vice chairperson from among the members of the Commission.

(d) QUORUM.—Eight members of the Commission shall constitute a quorum for all purposes, except that a lesser number may constitute a quorum for the purpose of holding hearings.

[¶3031] Sec. 304. [29 U.S.C. 2634]. COMPENSATION

(a) PAY.—Members of the Commission shall serve without compensation.

(b) TRAVEL EXPENSES.—Members of the Commission shall be allowed reasonable travel expenses, including a per diem allowance, in accordance with section 5703 of title 5, United States Code, when performing duties of the Commission.

[¶3032] Sec. 305. [29 U.S.C. 2635]. POWERS

(a) MEETINGS.—The Commission shall first meet not later than 30 days after the date on which all members are appointed, and the Commission shall meet thereafter on the call of the chairperson or a majority of the members.

(b) HEARINGS AND SESSIONS.—The Commission may hold such hearings, sit and act at such times and places, take such testimony, and receive such evidence as the Commission considers appropriate. The Commission may administer oaths or affirmations to witnesses appearing before it.

(c) ACCESS TO INFORMATION.—The Commission may secure directly from any Federal agency information necessary to enable it to carry out this title, if the information may be disclosed under section 552 of title 5, United States Code. Subject to the previous sentence, on the request of the chairperson or vice chairperson of the Commission, the head of such agency shall furnish such information to the Commission.

(d) USE OF FACILITIES AND SERVICES.—Upon the request of the Commission, the head of any Federal agency may make available to the Commission any of the facilities and services of such agency.

(e) PERSONNEL FROM OTHER AGENCIES.—On the request of the Commission, the head of any Federal agency may detail any of the personnel of such agency to serve as the Executive Director of the Commission or assist the Commission in carrying out the duties of the Commission. Any detail shall not interrupt or otherwise affect the civil service status or privileges of the Federal employee.

(f) VOLUNTARY SERVICE.—Notwithstanding section 1342 of title 31, United States Code, the chairperson of the Commission may accept for the Commission voluntary services provided by a member of the Commission.

[¶3033] Sec. 306. [29 U.S.C. 2636]. TERMINATION

The Commission shall terminate 30 days after the date of the submission of the report of the Commission to Congress.

TITLE IV—MISCELLANEOUS PROVISIONS

[¶3035] Sec. 401. [29 U.S.C. 2651]. Effect on Other Laws

(a) FEDERAL AND STATE ANTIDISCRIMINATION LAWS.—Nothing in this Act or any amendment made by this Act shall be construed to modify or affect any Federal or State law prohibiting discrimination on the basis of race, religion, color, national origin, sex, age, or disability.

(b) STATE AND LOCAL LAWS.—Nothing in this Act or any amendment made by this Act shall be construed to supersede any provision of any State or local law that provides greater family or medical leave rights than the rights established under this Act or any amendment made by this Act.

[¶3036] Sec. 402. [29 U.S.C. 2652]. Effect on Existing Employment Benefits.

(a) MORE PROTECTIVE.—Nothing in this Act or any amendment made by this Act shall be construed to diminish the obligation of an employer to comply with any collective bargaining agreement or any employment benefit program or plan that provides greater family or medical leave rights to employees than the rights established under this Act or any amendment made by this Act.

(b) LESS PROTECTIVE.—The rights established for employees under this Act or any amendment made by this Act shall not be diminished by any collective bargaining agreement or any employment benefit program or plan.

[¶3036] Sec. 403. [29 U.S.C. 2653]. Encouragement of More Generous Leave Policies

Nothing in this Act or any amendment made by this Act shall be construed to discourage employers from adopting or retaining leave policies more generous than any policies that comply with the requirements under this Act or any amendment made by this Act.

[¶3037] Sec. 404. [29 U.S.C. 2654]. Regulations

The Secretary of Labor shall prescribe such regulations as are necessary to carry out title I and this title not later than 120 days after the date of the enactment of this Act.

[¶3038] Sec. 405. [29 U.S.C. 2601 note]. Effective Dates.

(a) TITLE III.—Title III shall take effect on the date of the enactment of this Act.

(b) OTHER TITLES.—

(1) IN GENERAL.—Except as provided in paragraph (2), titles I, II, and V and this title shall take effect 6 months after the date of the enactment of this Act.

(2) COLLECTIVE BARGAINING AGREEMENTS.—In the case of a collective bargaining agreement in effect on the effective date prescribed by paragraph (1), title I shall apply on the earlier of—

(A) the date of the termination of such agreement; or

(B) the date that occurs 12 months after the date of the enactment of this Act.

TITLE V—COVERAGE OF CONGRESSIONAL EMPLOYEES

»»→ Caution: Title V (2 U.S.C. 60m and 60n) was repealed by the Congressional Accountability Act of 1995, P.L. 104-1, 109 Stat. 1, effective Jan. 23, 1995. However, congressional employees may bring claims under Title V after that date, depending upon when their cause of action arose.

[¶3040] Sec. 501. [2 U.S.C. 60m]. Leave for Certain Senate Employees

(a) COVERAGE.—The rights and protections established under sections 101 through 105 shall apply with respect to a Senate employee and an employing office. For purposes of such application, the term "eligible employee" means a Senate employee and the term "employer" means an employing office.

(b) CONSIDERATION OF ALLEGATIONS.—

(1) APPLICABLE PROVISIONS.—The provisions of sections 304 through 313 of the Government Employee Rights Act of 1991 (2 U.S.C. 1204-1213) shall, except as provided in subsections (d) and (e)—

(A) apply with respect to an allegation of a violation of a provision of sections 101 through 105, with respect to Senate employment of a Senate employee; and

(B) apply to such an allegation in the same manner and to the same extent as such sections of the Government Employee Rights Act of 1991 apply with respect to an allegation of a violation under such Act.

(2) ENTITY.—Such an allegation shall be addressed by the Office of Senate Fair Employment Practices or such other entity as the Senate may designate.

(c) RIGHTS OF EMPLOYEES.—The Office of Senate Fair Employment Practices shall ensure that Senate employees are informed of their rights under sections 101 through 105.

(d) LIMITATIONS.—A request for counseling under section 305 of such Act by a Senate employee alleging a violation of a provision of sections 101 through 105 shall be made not later than 2 years after the date of the last event constituting the alleged violation for which the counseling is requested, or not later than 3 years after such date in the case of a willful violation of section 105.

(e) APPLICABLE REMEDIES.—The remedies applicable to individuals who demonstrate a violation of a provision of sections 101 through 105 shall be such remedies as would be appropriate if awarded under paragraph (1) or (3) of section 107(a).

(f) EXERCISE OF RULEMAKING POWER.—The provisions of subsections (b), (c), (d), and (e), except as such subsections apply with respect to section 309 of the Government Employee Rights Act of 1991 (2 U.S.C. 1209), are enacted by the Senate as an exercise of the rulemaking power of the Senate, with full recognition of the right of the Senate to change its rules, in the same manner, and to the same extent, as in the case of any other rule of the Senate. No Senate employee may commence a judicial proceeding with respect to an allegation described in subsection (b)(1), except as provided in this section.

(g) SEVERABILITY.—Notwithstanding any other provision of law, if any provision of section 309 of the Government Employee Rights Act of 1991 (2 U.S.C. 1209), or of subsection (b)(1) insofar as it applies such section 309 to an allegation described in subsection (b)(1)(A), is invalidated, both such section 309, and subsection (b)(1) insofar as it applies such section 309 to such an allegation, shall have no force and effect, and shall be considered to be invalidated for purposes 322 of such Act (2 U.S.C. 1221).

(h) DEFINITIONS.—As used in this section:

(1) EMPLOYING OFFICE.—The term "employing office" means the office with the final authority described in section 301(2) of such Act (2 U.S.C. 1201(2)).

(2) SENATE EMPLOYEE.—The term "Senate employee" means an employee described in subparagraph (A) or (B) of section 301(c)(1) of such Act (2 U.S.C. 1201(c)(1)) who has been employed for at least 12 months on other than a temporary or intermittent basis by any employing office.

»»→ Caution: Title V (2 U.S.C. 60m and 60n) was repealed by the Congressional Accountability Act of 1995, P.L. 104-1, 109 Stat. 1, effective Jan. 23, 1995. However, congressional employees may bring claims under Title V after that date, depending upon when their cause of action arose.

[¶3041] Sec. 502. [2 U.S.C. 60n]. Leave for Certain Congressional Employees

(a) IN GENERAL.—The rights and protections under sections 102 through 105 (other than section 104(b)) shall apply to any employee in an employment position and any employing authority of the House of Representatives.

(b) ADMINISTRATION.—In the administration of this section, the remedies and procedures under the Fair Employment Practices Resolution shall be applied.

(c) DEFINITION.—As used in this section, the term "Fair Employment Practices Resolution" means rule LI of the Rules of the House of Representatives.

TITLE VI—SENSE OF CONGRESS

[¶3043] Sec. 601. [Reports]. Sense of Congress

It is the sense of the Congress that:

(a) The Secretary of Defense shall conduct a comprehensive review of current departmental policy with respect to the service of homosexuals in the Armed Forces;

Such review shall include the basis for the current policy of mandatory separation; the rights of all service men and women, and the effects of any change in such policy on morale, discipline, and military effectiveness;

(c) The Secretary shall report the results of such review and consultations and his recommendations to the President and to the Congress no later than July 15, 1993;

(d) The Senate Committee on Armed Services shall conduct (i) comprehensive hearings on the current military policy with respect to the service of homosexuals in the military services; and (ii) shall conduct oversight hearings on the Secretary's recommendations as such are reported.

Internal Revenue Code Sections Added, Amended or Repealed

[¶ 5000]

Introduction

Select Internal Revenue Code provisions amended by the Coronavirus Aid, Relief and Economic Security Act (CARES Act) (P.L. 116-136) are shown in the following paragraphs. Deleted Internal Revenue Code material or the text of the Internal Revenue Code Section prior to amendment appears in the amendment notes following each amended Internal Revenue Code provision. *Any changed or added material is set out in italics.*

[¶ 5001] CODE SEC. 106. CONTRIBUTIONS BY EMPLOYER TO ACCIDENT AND HEALTH PLANS.

* * *

(f) Reimbursements for Menstrual Care Products.—For purposes of this section and section 105, expenses incurred for menstrual care products (as defined in section 223(d)(2)(D)) shall be treated as incurred for medical care.

* * *

[Explanation at ¶ 440.]

Amendments

• 2020, Coronavirus Aid, Relief, and Economic Security (CARES) Act (P.L. 116-136)

P.L. 116-136, §3702(c):

Amended Code Sec. 106 by striking subsection (f) and inserting a new subsection (f). **Effective** for expenses incurred after 12-31-2019. Prior to being stricken, Code Sec. 106(f) read as follows:

(f) Reimbursements for Medicine Restricted to Prescribed Drugs and Insulin.—For purposes of this section and section 105, reimbursement for expenses incurred for a medicine or a drug shall be treated as a reimbursement for medical expenses only if such medicine or drug is a prescribed drug (determined without regard to whether such drug is available without a prescription) or is insulin.

[¶ 5002] CODE SEC. 127. EDUCATIONAL ASSISTANCE PROGRAMS.

* * *

(c) Definitions; Special Rules.—For purposes of this section—

(1) Educational assistance.—The term "educational assistance" means—

(A) the payment, by an employer, of expenses incurred by or on behalf of an employee for education of the employee (including, but not limited to, tuition, fees, and similar payments, books, supplies, and equipment),

(B) in the case of payments made before January 1, 2021, the payment by an employer, whether paid to the employee or to a lender, of principal or interest on any qualified education loan (as defined in section 221(d)(1)) incurred by the employee for education of the employee, and

(C) the provision, by an employer, of courses of instruction for such employee (including books, supplies, and equipment),

but does not include payment for, or the provision of, tools or supplies which may be retained by the employee after completion of a course of instruction, or meals, lodging, or transportation. The term "educational assistance" also does not include any payment for, or the provision of any benefits with respect to, any course or other education involving sports, games, or hobbies.

* * *

[Explanation at ¶ 580.]

Amendments

• 2020, Coronavirus Aid, Relief, and Economic Security (CARES) Act (P.L. 116-136)

P.L. 116-136, §2206(a):

Amended Code Sec. 127(c)(1) by striking "and" at the end of subparagraph (A), by redesignating subparagraph (B) as subparagraph (C), and by inserting after subparagraph (A) a new subparagraph (B). **Effective** for payments made after 3-27-2020.

[¶ 5003] CODE SEC. 220. ARCHER MSAs.

* * *

(d) ARCHER MSA.—For purposes of this section—

* * *

(2) QUALIFIED MEDICAL EXPENSES.—

(A) IN GENERAL.—The term "qualified medical expenses" means, with respect to an account holder, amounts paid by such holder for medical care (as defined in section 213(d)) for such individual, the spouse of such individual, and any dependent (as defined in section 152, determined without regard to subsections (b)(1), (b)(2), and (d)(1)(B) thereof) of such individual, but only to the extent such amounts are not compensated for by insurance or otherwise. *For purposes of this subparagraph, amounts paid for menstrual care products (as defined in section 223(d)(2)(D)) shall be treated as paid for medical care.*

* * *

[Explanation at ¶ 440.]

Amendments

• 2020, Coronavirus Aid, Relief, and Economic Security (CARES) Act (P.L. 116-136)

P.L. 116-136, §3702(b):

Amended Code Sec. 220(d)(2)(A) by striking the last sentence and inserting: "For purposes of this subparagraph, amounts paid for menstrual care products (as defined in section 223(d)(2)(D)) shall be treated as paid for medical care.". **Effective** for amounts paid after 12-31-2019. Prior to being stricken, the last sentence of Code Sec. 220(d)(2)(A) read as follows:

Such term shall include an amount paid for medicine or a drug only if such medicine or drug is a prescribed drug (determined without regard to whether such drug is available without a prescription) or is insulin.

[¶ 5004] CODE SEC. 221. INTEREST ON EDUCATION LOANS.

* * *

(e) SPECIAL RULES.—

(1) DENIAL OF DOUBLE BENEFIT.—No deduction shall be allowed under this section for any amount for which a deduction is allowable under any other provision of this chapter, *or for which an exclusion is allowable under section 127 to the taxpayer by reason of the payment by the taxpayer's employer of any indebtedness on a qualified education loan of the taxpayer*. The deduction otherwise allowable under subsection (a) (prior to the application of subsection (b)) to the taxpayer for any taxable year shall be reduced (but not below zero) by so much of the distributions treated as a qualified higher education expense under section 529(c)(9) with respect to loans of the taxpayer as would be includible in gross income under section 529(c)(3)(A) for such taxable year but for such treatment.

* * *

[Explanation at ¶ 580.]

Amendments

• 2020, Coronavirus Aid, Relief, and Economic Security (CARES) Act (P.L. 116-136)

P.L. 116-136, §2206(b):

Amended the first sentence of Code Sec. 221(e)(1) by inserting before the period ", or for which an exclusion is allowable under section 127 to the taxpayer by reason of the payment by the taxpayer's employer of any indebtedness on a qualified education loan of the taxpayer". **Effective** for payments made after 3-27-2020.

[¶ 5005] CODE SEC. 223. HEALTH SAVINGS ACCOUNTS.

* * *

(c) DEFINITIONS AND SPECIAL RULES.—For purposes of this section—

(1) ELIGIBLE INDIVIDUAL.—

* * *

(B) CERTAIN COVERAGE DISREGARDED.—Subparagraph (A)(ii) shall be applied without regard to—

* * *

(ii) coverage (whether through insurance or otherwise) for accidents, disability, dental care, vision care, *long-term care, or (in the case of plan years beginning on or before December 31, 2021) telehealth and other remote care*, and

* * *

(2) HIGH DEDUCTIBLE HEALTH PLAN.—

* * *

(E) SAFE HARBOR FOR ABSENCE OF DEDUCTIBLE FOR TELEHEALTH.—In the case of plan years beginning on or before December 31, 2021, a plan shall not fail to be treated as a high deductible health plan by reason of failing to have a deductible for telehealth and other remote care services.

* * *

[Explanation at ¶ 430.]

Amendments

• 2020, Coronavirus Aid, Relief, and Economic Security (CARES) Act (P.L. 116-136)

P.L. 116-136, §3701(a):

Amended Code Sec. 223(c)(2) by adding at the end a new subparagraph (E). **Effective** 3-27-2020.

P.L. 116-136, §3701(b):

Amended Code Sec. 223(c)(1)(B)(ii) by striking "or long-term care" and inserting "long-term care, or (in the case of plan years beginning on or before December 31, 2021) telehealth and other remote care". **Effective** 3-27-2020.

(d) HEALTH SAVINGS ACCOUNT.—For purposes of this section—

* * *

(2) QUALIFIED MEDICAL EXPENSES.—

(A) IN GENERAL.—The term "qualified medical expenses" means, with respect to an account beneficiary, amounts paid by such beneficiary for medical care (as defined in section 213(d)) for such individual, the spouse of such individual, and any dependent (as defined in section 152, determined without regard to subsections (b)(1), (b)(2), and (d)(1)(B) thereof) of such individual, but only to the extent such amounts are not compensated for by insurance or otherwise. *For purposes of this subparagraph, amounts paid for menstrual care products shall be treated as paid for medical care.*

* * *

(D) MENSTRUAL CARE PRODUCT.—For purposes of this paragraph, the term "menstrual care product" means a tampon, pad, liner, cup, sponge, or similar product used by individuals with respect to menstruation or other genital-tract secretions.

* * *

[Explanation at ¶ 440.]

Amendments

• 2020, Coronavirus Aid, Relief, and Economic Security (CARES) Act (P.L. 116-136)

P.L. 116-136, §3702(a)(1)-(2):

Amended Code Sec. 223(d)(2) by striking the last sentence of subparagraph (A) and inserting "For purposes of this subparagraph, amounts paid for menstrual care products shall be treated as paid for medical care."; and by adding at the end a new subparagraph (D). **Effective** for amounts paid after 12-31-2019. Prior to being stricken, the last sentence of Code Sec. 223(d)(2)(A) read as follows:

Such term shall include an amount paid for medicine or a drug only if such medicine or drug is a prescribed drug (determined without regard to whether such drug is available without a prescription) or is insulin.

[¶5006] CODE SEC. 401. QUALIFIED PENSION, PROFIT-SHARING, AND STOCK BONUS PLANS.

(a) REQUIREMENTS FOR QUALIFICATION.—A trust created or organized in the United States and forming part of a stock bonus, pension, or profit-sharing plan of an employer for the exclusive benefit of his employees or their beneficiaries shall constitute a qualified trust under this section—

* * *

(9) REQUIRED DISTRIBUTIONS.—

* * *

(I) TEMPORARY WAIVER OF MINIMUM REQUIRED DISTRIBUTION.—

(i) IN GENERAL.—The requirements of this paragraph shall not apply for calendar year 2020 to—

(I) a defined contribution plan which is described in this subsection or in section 403(a) or 403(b),

(II) a defined contribution plan which is an eligible deferred compensation plan described in section 457(b) but only if such plan is maintained by an employer described in section 457(e)(1)(A), or

(III) an individual retirement plan.

(ii) SPECIAL RULE FOR REQUIRED BEGINNING DATES IN 2020.—Clause (i) shall apply to any distribution which is required to be made in calendar year 2020 by reason of—

(I) a required beginning date occurring in such calendar year, and

(II) such distribution not having been made before January 1, 2020.

(iii) SPECIAL RULES REGARDING WAIVER PERIOD.—For purposes of this paragraph—

(I) the required beginning date with respect to any individual shall be determined without regard to this subparagraph for purposes of applying this paragraph for calendar years after 2020, and

(II) if clause (ii) of subparagraph (B) applies, the 5-year period described in such clause shall be determined without regard to calendar year 2020.

* * *

[Explanation at ¶ 610.]

Amendments

• 2020, Coronavirus Aid, Relief, and Economic Security (CARES) Act (P.L. 116-136)

P.L. 116-136, §2203(a):

Amended Code Sec. 401(a)(9) by adding at the end a new subparagraph (I). **Effective** generally for calendar years beginning after 12-31-2019. For a special rule, see Act Sec. 2203(c)(2), below.

P.L. 116-136, §2203(c)(2), provides:

(2) PROVISIONS RELATING TO PLAN OR CONTRACT AMENDMENTS.—

(A) IN GENERAL.—If this paragraph applies to any plan or contract amendment—

(i) such plan or contract shall not fail to be treated as being operated in accordance with the terms of the plan during the period described in subparagraph (B)(ii) solely because the plan operates in accordance with this section, and

(ii) except as provided by the Secretary of the Treasury (or the Secretary's delegate), such plan or contract shall not fail to meet the requirements of section 411(d)(6) of the Internal Revenue Code of 1986 and section 204(g) of the Employee Retirement Income Security Act of 1974 by reason of such amendment.

(B) AMENDMENTS TO WHICH PARAGRAPH APPLIES.—

(i) IN GENERAL.—This paragraph shall apply to any amendment to any plan or annuity contract which—

(I) is made pursuant to the amendments made by this section, and

(II) is made on or before the last day of the first plan year beginning on or after January 1, 2022.

In the case of a governmental plan, subclause (II) shall be applied by substituting "2024" for "2022".

(ii) CONDITIONS.—This paragraph shall not apply to any amendment unless during the period beginning on the effective date of the amendment and ending on December 31, 2020, the plan or contract is operated as if such plan or contract amendment were in effect.

[¶5007] CODE SEC. 402. TAXABILITY OF BENEFICIARY OF EMPLOYEES' TRUST.

* * *

(c) RULES APPLICABLE TO ROLLOVERS FROM EXEMPT TRUSTS.—

* * *

(4) ELIGIBLE ROLLOVER DISTRIBUTION.—For purposes of this subsection, the term "eligible rollover distribution" means any distribution to an employee of all or any portion of the balance to the credit of the employee in a qualified trust; except that such term shall not include—

(A) any distribution which is one of a series of substantially equal periodic payments (not less frequently than annually) made—

(i) for the life (or life expectancy) of the employee or the joint lives (or joint life expectancies) of the employee and the employee's designated beneficiary, or

(ii) for a specified period of 10 years or more,

(B) any distribution to the extent such distribution is required under section 401(a)(9), and

(C) any distribution which is made upon hardship of the employee.

If all or any portion of a distribution during *2020* is treated as an eligible rollover distribution but would not be so treated if the minimum distribution requirements under section 401(a)(9) had applied during *2020*, such distribution shall not be treated as an eligible rollover distribution for purposes of section 401(a)(31) or 3405(c) or subsection (f) of this section.

* * *

[Explanation at ¶ 610.]

Amendments

• 2020, Coronavirus Aid, Relief, and Economic Security (CARES) Act (P.L. 116-136)

P.L. 116-136, §2203(b):

Amended Code Sec. 402(c)(4) by striking "2009" each place it appears in the last sentence and inserting "2020". **Effective** generally for calendar years beginning after 12-31-2019. For a special rule, see Act Sec. 2203(c)(2), below.

P.L. 116-136, §2203(c)(2), provides:

(2) PROVISIONS RELATING TO PLAN OR CONTRACT AMENDMENTS.—

(A) IN GENERAL.—If this paragraph applies to any plan or contract amendment—

(i) such plan or contract shall not fail to be treated as being operated in accordance with the terms of the plan during the period described in subparagraph (B)(ii) solely because the plan operates in accordance with this section, and

(ii) except as provided by the Secretary of the Treasury (or the Secretary's delegate), such plan or contract shall not fail to meet the requirements of section 411(d)(6) of the Internal Revenue Code of 1986 and section 204(g) of the Employee Retirement Income Security Act of 1974 by reason of such amendment.

(B) AMENDMENTS TO WHICH PARAGRAPH APPLIES.—

(i) IN GENERAL.—This paragraph shall apply to any amendment to any plan or annuity contract which—

(I) is made pursuant to the amendments made by this section, and

(II) is made on or before the last day of the first plan year beginning on or after January 1, 2022.

In the case of a governmental plan, subclause (II) shall be applied by substituting "2024" for "2022".

(ii) CONDITIONS.—This paragraph shall not apply to any amendment unless during the period beginning on the effective date of the amendment and ending on December 31, 2020, the plan or contract is operated as if such plan or contract amendment were in effect.

[¶5008] CODE SEC. 414. DEFINITIONS AND SPECIAL RULES.

* * *

(y) COOPERATIVE AND SMALL EMPLOYER CHARITY PENSION PLANS.—

(1) IN GENERAL.—For purposes of this title, except as provided in this subsection, a CSEC plan is a defined benefit plan (other than a multiemployer plan)—

* * *

(B) that, as of June 25, 2010, was maintained by more than one employer and all of the employers were organizations described in section 501(c)(3);

(C) that, as of June 25, 2010, was maintained by an employer—

(i) described in section 501(c)(3),

(ii) chartered under part B of subtitle II of title 36, United States Code,

(iii) with employees in at least 40 States, and

(iv) whose primary exempt purpose is to provide services with respect to children; *or*

(D) that, as of January 1, 2000, was maintained by an employer—

(i) described in section 501(c)(3),

(ii) who has been in existence since at least 1938,

(iii) who conducts medical research directly or indirectly through grant making, and

(iv) whose primary exempt purpose is to provide services with respect to mothers and children.

* * *

[Explanation at ¶ 630.]

Amendments

• 2020, Coronavirus Aid, Relief, and Economic Security (CARES) Act (P.L. 116-136)

P.L. 116-136, §3609(b)(1)-(3):

Amended Code Sec. 414(y)(1) by striking "or" at the end of subparagraph (B); by striking the period at the end of subparagraph (C)(iv) and inserting "; or"; and by inserting after subparagraph (C) a new subparagraph (D). **Effective** for plan years beginning after 12-31-2018.

[¶ 5009] CODE SEC. 3306. DEFINITIONS.

* * *

(v) SHORT-TIME COMPENSATION PROGRAM.—For purposes of this section, the term "short-time compensation program" means a program under which—

* * *

(6) eligible employees may participate, as appropriate, in training (including employer-sponsored training or worker training funded under the *Workforce Innovation and Opportunity Act*) to enhance job skills if such program has been approved by the State agency;

* * *

[Explanation at ¶ 260.]

Amendments

• 2020, Coronavirus Aid, Relief, and Economic Security (CARES) Act (P.L. 116-136)

P.L. 116-136, §2108(f):

Amended Code Sec. 3306(v)(6) by striking "Workforce Investment Act of 1998" and inserting "Workforce Innovation and Opportunity Act". **Effective** 3-27-2020.

ERISA Sections Added, Amended or Repealed

[¶ 6000]

Introduction

All Employee Retirement Income Security Act (ERISA) provisions amended by the Coronavirus Aid, Relief and Economic Security Act (CARES Act) (P.L. 116-136) are shown in the following paragraphs. Deleted ERISA material or the text of the ERISA section prior to amendment appears in the amendment notes following each amended ERISA provision. *Any changed or added material is set out in italics.*

[¶ 6001] Act Sec. 210. PLANS MAINTAINED BY MORE THAN ONE EMPLOYER, PREDECESSOR PLANS, AND EMPLOYER GROUPS

* * *

(f) COOPERATIVE AND SMALL EMPLOYER CHARITY PENSION PLANS.—

(1) IN GENERAL.—For purposes of this title, except as provided in this subsection, a CSEC plan is an employee pension benefit plan (other than a multiemployer plan) that is a defined benefit plan—

* * *

(B) that, as of June 25, 2010, was maintained by more than one employer and all of the employers were organizations described in section 501(c)(3) of the Internal Revenue Code of 1986;

(C) that, as of June 25, 2010, was maintained by an employer—

* * *

(iv) whose primary exempt purpose is to provide services with respect to children; *or*

(D) that, as of January 1, 2000, was maintained by an employer—

(i) described in section 501(c)(3) of the Internal Revenue Code of 1986,

(ii) who has been in existence since at least 1938,

(iii) who conducts medical research directly or indirectly through grant making, and

(iv) whose primary exempt purpose is to provide services with respect to mothers and children.

* * *

[Explanation at ¶ 630.]

Amendments

P.L. 116-136, §3609(a):

Amended ERISA Sec. 210(f)(1) by striking "or" at the end of subparagraph (B); by striking the period at the end of subparagraph (C)(iv) and inserting "; or"; and by inserting after subparagraph (C) a new subparagraph (D) to read as above.

The above amendment applies to plan years beginning after 12-31-2018.

[¶ 6002] AUTHORITY TO POSTPONE CERTAIN DEADLINES BY REASON OF A PRESIDENTIALLY DECLARED DISASTER OR TERRORISTIC OR MILITARY ACTIONS

Act Sec. 518. In the case of a pension or other employee benefit plan, or any sponsor, administrator, participant, beneficiary, or other person with respect to such plan, affected by a Presidentially declared disaster (as defined in section 1033 (h) (3) of the Internal Revenue Code of 1986) *a terroristic or military action (as defined in section 692(c)(2) of such Code), or a public health emergency declared by the*

Secretary of Health and Human Services pursuant to section 319 of the Public Health Service Act, the Secretary may, notwithstanding any other provision of law prescribe, by notice or otherwise, a period of up to 1 year which may be disregarded in determining the date by which any action is required or permitted to be completed underthis Act. No plan shall be treated as failing to be operated in accordance with the terms of the plan solely as the result of disregarding any period by reason of the preceding sentence.

[Explanation at ¶ 640.]

Amendment

P.L. 116-136, §3607:

Amended ERISA Sec. 518 by striking "or a terroristic or military action (as defined in section 692(c)(2) of such Code), the Secretary may" and inserting "a terroristic or military action (as defined in section 692(c)(2) of such Code, or a public health emergency declared by the Secretary of Health and Human Services pursuant to section 319 of the Public Health Service Act, the Secretary may".

The above amendment is effective on the date of enactment (March 27, 2020).

Social Security Act Sections Added, Amended or Repealed

[¶ 7000]

Introduction

Select Social Security Act provisions amended by the Families First Coronavirus Response Act, (P.L. 116-127) and the Coronavirus Aid, Relief and Economic Security Act (CARES Act) (P.L. 116-136) are shown in the following paragraphs. Deleted Social Security Act material or the text of the Social Security Act Section prior to amendment appears in the amendment notes following each amended Social Security Act provision. *Any changed or added material is set out in italics.*

[¶ 7001] *Sec. 903. EMERGENCY TRANSFERS IN FISCAL YEAR 2020 FOR ADMINISTRATION*

* * *

(h)(1)(A) *In addition to any other amounts, the Secretary of Labor shall provide for the making of emergency administration grants in fiscal year 2020 to the accounts of the States in the Unemployment Trust Fund, in accordance with succeeding provisions of this subsection.*

(B) *The amount of an emergency administration grant with respect to a State shall, as determined by the Secretary of Labor, be equal to the amount obtained by multiplying $1,000,000,000 by the same ratio as would apply under subsection (a)(2)(B) for purposes of determining such State's share of any excess amount (as described in subsection (a)(1)) that would have been subject to transfer to State accounts, as of October 1, 2019, under the provisions of subsection (a).*

(C) *Of the emergency administration grant determined under subparagraph (B) with respect to a State—*

(i) not later than 60 days after the date of enactment of this subsection, 50 percent shall be transferred to the account of such State upon a certification by the Secretary of Labor to the Secretary of the Treasury that the State meets the requirements of paragraph (2); and

(ii) only with respect to a State in which the number of unemployment compensation claims has increased by at least 10 percent over the same quarter in the previous calendar year, the remainder shall be transferred to the account of such State upon a certification by the Secretary of Labor to the Secretary of the Treasury that the State meets the requirements of paragraph (3).

(2) *The requirements of this paragraph with respect to a State are the following:*

(A) The State requires employers to provide notification of the availability of unemployment compensation to employees at the time of separation from employment. Such notification may be based on model notification language issued by the Secretary of Labor.

(B) The State ensures that applications for unemployment compensation, and assistance with the application process, are accessible in at least two of the following: in-person, by phone, or online.

(C) The State notifies applicants when an application is received and is being processed, and in any case in which an application is unable to be processed, provides information about steps the applicant can take to ensure the successful processing of the application.

(3) *The requirements of this paragraph with respect to a State are the following:*

(A) The State has expressed its commitment to maintain and strengthen access to the unemployment compensation system, including through initial and continued claims.

(B) The State has demonstrated steps it has taken or will take to ease eligibility requirements and access to unemployment compensation for claimants, including waiving work search requirements and the waiting week, and noncharging employers directly impacted by COVID–19 due to an illness in the workplace or direction from a public health official to isolate or quarantine workers.

(4) Any amount transferred to the account of a State under this subsection may be used by such State only for the administration of its unemployment compensation law, including by taking such steps as may be necessary to ensure adequate resources in periods of high demand.

(5) Not later than 1 year after the date of enactment of the Emergency Unemployment Insurance Stabilization and Access Act of 2020, each State receiving emergency administration grant funding under paragraph (1)(C)(i) shall submit to the Secretary of Labor, the Committee on Ways and Means of the House of Representatives, and the Committee on Finance of the Senate, a report that includes—

(A) an analysis of the recipiency rate for unemployment compensation in the State as such rate has changed over time;

(B) a description of steps the State intends to take to increase such recipiency rate.

(6)(A) Notwithstanding any other provision of law, the Secretary of the Treasury shall transfer from the general fund of the Treasury (from funds not otherwise appropriated) to the employment security administration account (as established by section 901 of the Social Security Act) such sums as the Secretary of Labor estimates to be necessary for purposes of making the transfers described in paragraph (1)(C).

(B) There are appropriated from the general fund of the Treasury, without fiscal year limitation, the sums referred to in the preceding sentence and such sums shall not be required to be repaid.

[Explanation at ¶200.]

2020 Amendments:

Section 4102(a) of the Emergency Unemployment Insurance Stabilization and Access Act of 2020 (P.L. 116-127), effective March 18, 2020, added subsection (h).

Section 3603 of the Coronavirus Aid, Relief, and Economic Security Act (P.L. 116-136), effective March 27, 2020, amended Social Security Act Section 903(h)(2)(B) as added by section 4102 of the Emergency Unemployment Insurance Stabilization and Access Act of 2020 P.L. 116-127), to read as follows: "(B) The State ensures that applications for unemployment compensation, and assistance with the application process, are accessible, to the extent practicable in at least two of the following: in person, by phone, or online.".

[¶7002] *Sec. 903. TRANSFERS FOR FEDERAL REIMBURSEMENT OF STATE UNEMPLOYMENT FUNDS*

* * *

(i)(1)(A) In addition to any other amounts, the Secretary of Labor shall provide for the transfer of funds during the applicable period to the accounts of the States in the Unemployment Trust Fund, by transfer from amounts reserved for that purpose in the Federal unemployment account, in accordance with the succeeding provisions of this subsection.

(B) The amount of funds transferred to the account of a State under subparagraph (A) during the applicable period shall, as determined by the Secretary of Labor, be equal to one-half of the amounts of compensation (as defined in section 3306(h) of the Internal Revenue Code of 1986) attributable under the State law to service to which section 3309(a)(1) of such Code applies that were paid by the State for weeks of unemployment beginning and ending during such period. Such transfers shall be made at such times as the Secretary of Labor considers appropriate.

(C) Notwithstanding any other law, funds transferred to the account of a State under subparagraph (A) shall be used exclusively to reimburse governmental entities and other organizations described in section 3309(a)(2) of such Code for amounts paid (in lieu of contributions) into the State unemployment fund pursuant to such section.

(D) For purposes of this paragraph, the term 'applicable period' means the period beginning on March 13, 2020, and ending on December 31, 2020.

(2)(A) Notwithstanding any other provision of law, the Secretary of the Treasury shall transfer from the general fund of the Treasury (from funds not otherwise appropriated) to the Federal unemployment account such sums as the Secretary of Labor estimates to be necessary for purposes of making the transfers described in paragraph (1).

(B) There are appropriated from the general fund of the Treasury, without fiscal year limitation, the sums referred to in subparagraph (A) and such sums shall not be required to be repaid.

[Explanation at ¶240.]

2020 Amendments:

Section 2103(b) of the Coronavirus Aid, Relief, and Economic Security Act (P.L. 116-136), effective March 27, 2020, added subsection (i).

[¶7003] Sec. 1202. REPAYMENT BY STATES OF ADVANCES TO STATE UNEMPLOYMENT FUNDS

* * *

(b)(10)(A) With respect to the period *beginning on the date of enactment of the Emergency Unemployment Insurance Stabilization and Access Act of 2020 and ending on December 31, 2020.*—

(i) any interest payment otherwise due from a State under this subsection during such period shall be deemed to have been made by the State; and

(ii) no interest shall accrue shall accrue during such period on any advance or advances made under section 1201 to a State.

* * *

[Explanation at ¶210.]

2020 Amendments:

Section 4103 of the Emergency Unemployment Insurance Stabilization and Access Act of 2020 (P.L. 116-127), effective March 18, 2020, amended subsection (b)(10)(A) by striking "beginning on the date of enactment of this paragraph and ending on December 31, 2010" at the end of subparagraph (A) and inserting "beginning on the date of enactment of the Emergency Unemployment Insurance Stabilization and Access Act of 2020 and ending on December 31, 2020."

Fair Credit Reporting Act Sections Added, Amended or Repealed

[¶8000]

Introduction

Select Fair Credit Reporting Act (FCRA) provisions amended by the Coronavirus Aid, Relief and Economic Security Act (CARES Act) (P.L. 116-136) are shown in the following paragraphs. Deleted FCRA material or the text of the FCRA Section prior to amendment appears in the amendment notes following each amended FCRA provision. *Any changed or added material is set out in italics.*

[¶8001] Sec. 1681s-2. Responsibilities of furnishers of information to consumer reporting agencies

(a) **Duty of furnishers of information to provide accurate information**

[Fair Credit Reporting Act, Sec. 623]

(1) PROHIBITION.—

* * *

*(F) **Reporting information during COVID–19 pandemic***

(i) DEFINITIONS.—In this subsection:

(I) ACCOMMODATION.—The term 'accommodation' includes an agreement to defer 1 or more payments, make a partial payment, forbear any delinquent amounts, modify a loan or contract, or any other assistance or relief granted to a consumer who is affected by the coronavirus disease 2019 (COVID–19) pandemic during the covered period.

(II) COVERED PERIOD.—The term 'covered period' means the period beginning on January 31, 2020 and ending on the later of—

(aa) 120 days after the date of enactment of this subparagraph; or

(bb) 120 days after the date on which the national emergency concerning the novel coronavirus disease (COVID–19) outbreak declared by the President on March 13, 2020 under the National Emergencies Act (50 U.S.C. 1601 et seq.) terminates.

(ii) REPORTING.—Except as provided in clause (iii), if a furnisher makes an accommodation with respect to 1 or more payments on a credit obligation or account of a consumer, and the consumer makes the payments or is not required to make 1 or more payments pursuant to the accommodation, the furnisher shall—

(I) report the credit obligation or account as current; or

(II) if the credit obligation or account was delinquent before the accommodation—

(aa) maintain the delinquent status during the period in which the accommodation is in effect; and

(bb) if the consumer brings the credit obligation or account current during the period described in item (aa), report the credit obligation or account as current.

(iii) EXCEPTION.—Clause (ii) shall not apply with respect to a credit obligation or account of a consumer that has been charged-off.

* * *

[Explanation at ¶ 740.]

History: Act of March 27, 2020 (Coronavirus Aid, Relief, and Economic Security Act or the CARES Act, Title IV—Economic Stabilization and Assistance to Severely Distressed Sectors of the United States Economy, Subtitle A—Coronavirus Economic Stabilization Act of 2020) Sec. 4021, Public Law 116-136, 134 Stat. 489; 15 U.S. Code 1681s-2 [Fair Credit Reporting Act, Sec. 623].

.001 Amendments

2020—Subsec. (a)(1)(F). Pub. L. 116-136, § 4021 added subsec. (F).

U.S. Department of Labor, Wage and Hour Division
29 CFR Part 826—Paid Leave under the Families First Coronavirus Response Act

[¶ 9000]

Introduction

The preamble to the Temporary Rule and regulatory text of 29 CFR Part 826, Paid Leave under the Families First Coronavirus Response Act, are reproduced below. The Temporary Rule was issued by the Department of Labor's Wage and Hour Division on April 1, 2020, pursuant to the Families First Coronavirus Response Act (P.L. 116-127). The Wage and Hour Division issued the rule to implement the newly available public health emergency leave under Title I of the Family and Medical Leave Act, and the similarly new emergency paid sick leave available to assist workers facing public health emergencies arising out of the COVID-19 pandemic. The Temporary Rule was published in the *Federal Register* on April 6, 2020 (85 FR 19326), and reads as corrected April 10, 2020 (85 FR 20156). It is effective from April 2, 2020, through December 31, 2020.

AUTHORITY: P.L. 116-127 sections 3102(b) and 5111(3); P.L. 116-136 section 3611(7).

Table of Contents

Preamble

I. Executive Summary

On March 18, 2020, President Trump signed into law the FFCRA, which creates two new emergency paid leave requirements in response to the COVID-19 global pandemic. Division E of the FFCRA, "The Emergency Paid Sick Leave Act" (EPSLA), entitles certain employees to take up to two weeks of paid sick leave. Division C of the FFCRA, "The Emergency Family and Medical Leave Expansion Act" (EFMLEA), which amends Title I of the Family and Medical Leave Act, 29 U.S.C. 2601 *et seq.* (FMLA), permits certain employees to take up to twelve weeks of expanded family and medical leave, ten of which are paid, for specified reasons related to COVID-19. On March 27, 2020, President Trump signed into law the Coronavirus Aid, Relief, and Economic Security Act, Public Law 116-136 (CARES Act), which amends certain provisions of the EPSLA and the provisions of the FMLA added by the EFMLEA.

In general, the FFCRA requires covered employers to provide eligible employees up to two weeks of paid sick leave at full pay, up to a specified cap, when the employee is unable to work because the employee is subject to a Federal, State, or local quarantine or isolation order related to COVID-19, has been advised by a health care provider to self-quarantine due to concerns related to COVID-19, or is experiencing COVID-19 symptoms and seeking a medical diagnosis. The FFCRA also provides up to two weeks of paid sick leave at partial pay, up to a specified cap, when an employee is unable to work because of a need to care for an individual subject to a Federal, State, or local quarantine or isolation order related to COVID-19 or who has been advised by a health care provider to self-quarantine due to concerns related to COVID-19; because of a need to care for the employee's son or daughter whose school or place of care is closed, or whose child care provider is unavailable, due to COVID-19 related reasons; or because the employee is experiencing a substantially similar condition, as specified by the Secretary of Health and Human Services. The FFCRA also requires covered employers to provide up to twelve weeks of expanded family and medical leave, up to ten weeks of which must be paid at partial pay, up to a specified cap, when an eligible employee is unable to work because of a need to care for the employee's son or daughter whose school or place of care is closed, or whose child care provider is unavailable, due to COVID-19 related reasons.

The FFCRA covers private employers with fewer than 500 employees and certain public employers. Small employers with fewer than 50 employees may qualify for an exemption from the requirement to provide paid leave due to school, place of care, or child care provider closings or unavailability, if the leave payments would jeopardize the viability of their business as a going concern.

Under the FFCRA, covered private employers qualify for reimbursement through refundable tax credits as administered by the Department of the Treasury, for all qualifying paid sick leave wages and qualifying family and medical leave wages paid to an employee who takes leave under the FFCRA, up to per diem and aggregate caps, and for allocable costs related to the maintenance of health care coverage under any group health plan while the employee is on the leave provided under the FFCRA. For information on the tax credits, *see https://www.irs.gov/forms-pubs/about-form-7200* see also *https://www.irs.gov/pub/irs-drop/n-20-21.pdf*. For more information on the COVID-19 related small business loans, *see https://www.sba.gov/page/coronavirus-covid-19-small-business-guidance-loan-resources*.

The CARES Act amended the FFCRA by providing certain technical corrections, as well as clarifying the caps for payment of leave; expanded family and medical leave to certain employees who were laid off or terminated after March 1, 2020, but are reemployed by the same employer prior to December 31, 2020; and provided authority to the Director of the Office of Management and Budget (OMB) to exclude certain Federal employees from paid sick leave and expanded family and medical leave.

The FFCRA grants authority to the Secretary to issue regulations for certain purposes. In particular, sections 3102(b), as amended by section 3611(7) of the CARES Act, and 5111(3) of the FFCRA grant the Secretary authority to issue regulations "as necessary, to carry out the purposes of this Act, including to ensure consistency" between the EPSLA and the EFMLEA. The Department is issuing this temporary rule to carry out the purposes of the FFCRA. These new paid sick leave and expanded family and medical leave requirements become effective on April 1, 2020, and expire on December 31, 2020.

Pursuant to the Congressional Review Act (5 U.S.C. 801 *et seq.*), the Office of Information and Regulatory Affairs (OIRA) designated this rule as a "major rule", as defined by 5 U.S.C. 804(2).

II. Background

A. Emergency Paid Sick Leave Act (EPSLA)

The EPSLA requires employers to provide paid sick leave to employees who are unable to work for six reasons having to do with COVID-19 where the employee (1) is subject to a Federal, State, or local quarantine or isolation order related to COVID-19; (2) has been advised by a health care provider to self-quarantine due to concerns related to COVID-19; (3) is experiencing symptoms of COVID-19 and is seeking a medical diagnosis; (4) is caring for an individual who is subject to an order as described in (1), or who has been advised as described in (2); (5) is caring for his or her son or daughter whose school or place of care has been closed or whose child care provider is unavailable due to COVID-19 related reasons; or (6) is experiencing any other substantially similar condition specified by the Secretary of Health and Human Services in consultation with the Secretary of the Treasury and the Secretary of Labor.

Private employers with fewer than 500 employees, as well as public agencies with one or more employees, must comply with the EPSLA, although the Secretary has authority to exempt by rulemaking certain employers with fewer than 50 employees from providing paid sick leave to an employee who is unable to work because the employee is caring for his or her son or daughter whose school or place of care has been closed or whose child care provider is unavailable due to COVID-19 related reasons when compliance with this requirement would "jeopardize the viability of the business as a going concern." FFCRA sections 5100(2)(B)(i)–(ii), 5111(2). The EPSLA applies to employees of covered employers regardless of how long an employee has worked for an employer, except that employers may exclude employees who are health care providers or emergency responders from taking paid sick leave; similarly, the Secretary has the authority to exclude by rulemaking "certain health care providers and emergency responders" from the requirements of the EPSLA. FFCRA sections 5102(a), 5102(e)(1), 5111(1). The CARES Act also added certain exemptions that may apply to Federal employers and employees, which are discussed below.

The EPSLA entitles full-time covered employees to up to 80 hours of paid sick leave, and generally entitles part-time employees to up to the number of hours that they work on average over a two-week period, although special rules may apply to part-time employees with varying schedules. For an employee who takes paid sick leave because he or she is subject to a quarantine or isolation order, has been advised to self-quarantine by a health care provider, or is experiencing symptoms of COVID-19 and is seeking a medical diagnosis, the EPSLA provides for paid sick leave at the greater of the employee's regular rate of pay under section 7(e) of the Fair Labor Standards Act of 1938, as amended, 29 U.S.C. 201 *et seq.* (FLSA) (29 U.S.C. 207(e)), or the applicable minimum wage (federal, state, or local), up to $511 per day and $5,110 in the aggregate. An employee who takes paid sick leave for any other qualifying reason under the EPSLA is entitled to be paid two-thirds of that amount, up to $200 per day and $2,000 in the aggregate. An employer may not require an employee to use other paid leave provided by the employer before the employee uses the paid sick leave, nor may an employer require the employee involved to search for or find a replacement employee to cover the hours during which the employee is using paid sick leave.

The EPSLA also provides that employers who fail to provide paid sick leave as required are considered to have failed to pay minimum wages in violation of section 6 of the FLSA, and that such employers are subject to enforcement proceedings described in sections 16 and 17 of the FLSA. 29 U.S.C. 206, 216, 217. In addition, the EPSLA prohibits employers from discharging, disciplining, or in any other manner discriminating against an employee who takes paid sick leave under the EPSLA, files any complaint under or relating to the EPSLA, institutes any proceeding under or relating to the EPSLA, or testifies in any such proceeding. *See* FFCRA section 5104, as amended by CARES Act section 3611(8). Employers who violate this prohibition are considered to have violated section 15(a)(3) of the FLSA, and are subject to the penalties described in sections 216 and 217 of the FLSA. 29 U.S.C. 215(a)(3), 216, 217. The EPSLA also authorizes the Secretary to investigate and gather data to ensure compliance with the EPSLA in the same manner as authorized by sections 9 and 11 of the FLSA, and the CARES Act section 3611(9) (adding FFCRA section 5105(c)); 29 U.S.C. 209, 211.

The EPSLA requires employers to post a notice of employees' rights under the EPSLA. It permits, but does not require, employers who are signatories to multiemployer collective bargaining agreements to fulfill their obligations under the EPSLA by making contributions to a multiemployer fund, plan, or program, subject to certain requirements. Nothing in the EPSLA diminishes the rights or benefits that an employee is entitled to under any other Federal, State, or local law; collective bargaining agreement; or existing employer policy. Moreover, the EPSLA does not require financial or other reimbursement by an employer to an employee for unused paid sick leave upon the employee's separation from employment.

B. Emergency Family and Medical Leave Expansion Act (EFMLEA)

The EFMLEA requires employers to provide expanded paid family and medical leave to eligible employees who are unable to work because the employee is caring for his or her son or daughter whose school or place of care is closed or whose child care provider is unavailable due to a public health emergency, defined as an emergency with respect to COVID-19, declared by a Federal, State, or local authority.

The EFMLEA applies to different sets of employers and employees from the other provisions of the FMLA. Private employers with fewer than 500 employees must comply with the EFMLEA, although the Secretary has the authority to exempt by rulemaking employers with fewer than 50 employees from EFMLEA's requirements when compliance with the EFMLEA would "jeopardize the viability of the business as a going concern." FFCRA section 3102(b) (adding FMLA section 110(a)(1)(B), (3)(B)). Generally, public agencies as defined at § 826.10(a) must comply with the EFMLEA. As it relates to the Federal government, however, only those *Federal employees covered by Title I of the FMLA* are potentially eligible under the EFMLEA. 29 U.S.C. 2611(2)(B)(i). The EFMLEA applies to employees of covered employers if such employees have been employed by the employer for at least 30 calendar days. This includes employees who were laid off or otherwise terminated on or after March 1, 2020, had worked for the employer for at least thirty of the prior 60 calendar days, and were subsequently rehired or otherwise reemployed by the same employer. CARES Act section 3605 (amending FMLA section 110(a)(1)(A)). As with the EPSLA, employers may, however, exclude employees who are health care providers or emergency responders from taking expanded family and medical leave, and similarly, the Secretary has the authority to exclude by rulemaking "certain health care providers and emergency responders" from the requirements of the EFMLEA.

An employee is entitled to take up to twelve weeks of leave for the purpose described in the EFMLEA. 29 U.S.C. 2611(a)(1). The first two weeks (usually ten workdays) of this leave are unpaid, though an employee may substitute paid sick leave under the EPSLA or paid leave under the employer's preexisting policies for these two weeks of unpaid leave. Unlike FMLA leave taken for other reasons, the following period of up to ten weeks of expanded family and medical leave must be paid. Specifically, after the first two weeks of leave, expanded family and medical leave under the FFCRA must be paid at two-thirds the employee's regular rate of pay. For each day of leave, the employee receives compensation based on the number of hours he or she would otherwise be normally scheduled to work, although special rules may apply to employees with varying schedules. An eligible employee may elect to use, or an employer may require that an employee use, such expanded family and medical leave concurrently with any leave offered under the employer's policies that would be available for the employee to take to care for his or her child, such as vacation or personal leave or paid time off. The total EFMLEA payment per employee for this ten-week period is capped at $200 per day and $10,000 in the aggregate, for a total of no more than $12,000 when combined with two weeks of paid leave taken under the EPSLA.

The EFMLEA provides that if the need for expanded family and medical leave is foreseeable, employees shall provide employers with notice of the leave as soon as practicable. The EFMLEA defines conditions under which employees who take leave are entitled to be restored to their positions, while exempting employers with fewer than twenty-five employees from this requirement under certain circumstances. The FMLA's general prohibitions on interference with rights and discrimination, 29 U.S.C. 2615, as well as the FMLA's enforcement provisions, 29 U.S.C. 2617, apply for purposes of the EFMLEA, except that an employee's right to file a lawsuit directly against an employer does not extend to employers who were not previously covered by the FMLA.

The EFMLEA permits, but does not require, employers who are signatories to multiemployer collective bargaining agreements to fulfill their obligations under the EFMLEA by making contributions to a multiemployer fund, plan, or program, subject to certain requirements.

III. Discussion

The paid leave requirements of the EPSLA and the EFMLEA are described and interpreted by the Secretary in regulations to appear in new Part 826 of Title 29 of the Code of Federal Regulations, and addressed below.

A. General

Section 826.10 contains definitions of terms used in the EPSLA and the EFMLEA as well as in this rule. As a general matter, the FMLA definitions apply to the EFMLEA unless specific definitions were included in the EFMLEA. The majority of the terms found in the EPSLA and the EFMLEA are based on terms that are defined in other statutes and/or their implementing regulations, such as the FLSA. For example, the EPSLA expressly adopts the definition of "person" from the FLSA and the definition of "son or daughter" from the FMLA.

The EFMLEA defines "qualifying need related to a public health emergency" as a need for leave "to care for the son or daughter under 18 years of age of such employee if the school or place of care has been closed, or the child care provider of such son or daughter is unavailable, due to a public health emergency." FFCRA section 3102(b) (adding FMLA section 110(a)(1)(A)). This definition could be read to narrow the FMLA definition of "son or daughter" for purposes of expanded family and medical leave, as the FMLA expressly includes children 18 years of age or older and incapable of self-care because of a mental or physical disability. 29 U.S.C. 2611(12). The EFMLEA does not contain a definition of "son or daughter," however, and therefore the FMLA definition of that term applies to expanded family and medical leave. The EPSLA also adopts the FMLA definition of "son or daughter." As addressed more fully below in the discussion of § 826.20, the Department believes it would create needless confusion and complication to have different rules under the EFMLEA and the EPSLA for when an employee may take leave to care for his or her son or daughter whose school or place of care is closed or child care provider is unavailable due to COVID-19 related reasons. The Department is therefore treating the definitions as the same (*i.e.*, to include children under 18 years of age and children age 18 or older who are incapable of self-care because of a mental or physical disability), pursuant to its statutory authority to issue regulations to ensure consistency between the EPSLA and the EFMLEA.

Only one other definition in the FFCRA—"telework"—bears further discussion here. Section 826.10 defines the word broadly to effectuate the statute's underlying purposes and also outlines when an employee is able to telework. The definition also clarifies that telework is no less work than if it were performed at an employer's worksite. As a result, employees who are teleworking for COVID-19 related reasons must always record—and be compensated for—all hours actually worked, including overtime, in accordance with the requirements of the FLSA. *See* 29 CFR 785.11-13; 785.48; *see also* 29 U.S.C. 206, 207; 29 CFR Part 778. However, an employer is not required to compensate employees for unreported hours worked while teleworking for COVID-19 related reasons, unless the employer knew or should have known about such telework. *See, e.g., Allen v. City of Chicago*, 865 F.3d 936 (7th Cir. 2017), *cert. denied*, 138 S. Ct. 1302, 200 L. Ed. 2d 474 (2018). While the Department's regulations and interpretations of the FLSA generally apply to employees who are teleworking for COVID-19 related reasons, the Department has concluded that § 790.6 and its continuous workday guidance are inconsistent with the objectives of the FFCRA and CARES Act only with respect to such employees.

The FFCRA and these regulations encourage employers and employees to implement highly flexible telework arrangements that allow employees to perform work, potentially at unconventional times, while tending to family and other responsibilities, such as teaching children whose schools are closed for COVID-19 related reasons. But section 790.6 and the Department's continuous workday guidance generally provide that all time between performance of the first and last principal activities is compensable work time. *See* 29 CFR 790.6(a). Applying this guidance to employers with employees who are teleworking for COVID-19 related reasons would disincentivize and undermine the very flexibility in teleworking arrangements that are critical to the FFCRA framework Congress created within the broader national response to COVID-19. As a result, the Department has determined that an employer allowing such flexibility during the COVID-19 pandemic shall not be required to count as hours worked all time between the first and last principal activity performed by an employee teleworking for COVID-19 related reasons as hours worked. For example, an employee may agree with an employer to perform telework for COVID-19 related reasons on the following schedule: 7-9 a.m., 12:30-3 p.m., and 7-9 p.m. on weekdays. This allows an employee, for example, to help teach children whose school is closed or assist the employee's parents who are temporarily living with the family, reserving work times when there are fewer distractions. Of course, the employer must compensate the employee for all hours actually worked—6.5 hours—that day, but not all 14 hours between the employee's first principal activity at 7 a.m. and last at 9 p.m. Section 790.6 and the Department's guidance regarding the continuous workday continue to apply to all employees who are not teleworking for COVID-19 related reasons.

B. Paid Leave Entitlements

Section 826.20 of Title 29 of the Code of Federal Regulations describes the circumstances under which a covered employer must provide paid sick leave and/or expanded family and medical leave to an eligible employee.

Section 826.20(a) explains that an employee may take paid sick leave if the employee is unable to work because of any one of six qualifying reasons related to COVID-19. The first reason for paid sick leave applies where an employee is unable to work because he or she is subject to a Federal, State, or local COVID-19 quarantine or isolation order. Quarantine or isolation orders include a broad range of governmental orders, including orders that advise some or all citizens to shelter in place, stay at home, quarantine, or otherwise restrict their own mobility. Section 826.20(a)(2) explains that an employee may take paid sick leave only if being subject to one of these orders prevents him or her from working or teleworking as described therein. The question is whether the employee would be able to work or telework "but for" being required to comply with a quarantine or isolation order.

An employee subject to one of these orders may not take paid sick leave where the employer does not have work for the employee. This is because the employee would be unable to work even if he or she were not required to comply with the quarantine or isolation order. For example, if a coffee shop closes temporarily or indefinitely due to a downturn in business related to COVID-19, it would no longer have any work for its employees. A cashier previously employed at the coffee shop who is subject to a stay-at-home order would not be able to work even if he were not required to stay at home. As such, he may not take paid sick leave because his inability to work is not due to his need to comply with the stay-at-home order, but rather due to the closure of his place of employment.[1] That said, he may be eligible for state unemployment insurance and should contact his State workforce agency or State unemployment insurance office for specific questions about his eligibility.

Additionally, § 826.20(a)(2) explains that an employee subject to a quarantine or isolation order is able to telework, and therefore may not take paid sick leave, if (a) his or her employer has work for the employee to perform; (b) the employer permits the employee to perform that work from the location where the employee is being quarantined or isolated; and (c) there are no extenuating circumstances that prevent the employee from performing that work. For example, if a law firm permits its lawyers to work from home, a lawyer would not be prevented from working by a stay-at-home order, and thus may not take paid sick leave as a result of being subject to that order. In this circumstance, the lawyer is able to telework even if she is required to use her own computer instead of her employer's computer. But, she would not be able to telework in the event of a power outage or similar extenuating circumstance and would therefore be eligible for paid sick leave during the period of the power outage or extenuating circumstance due to the quarantine or isolation order.

The second reason for paid sick leave applies where an employee is unable to work because he or she has been advised by a health care provider, as defined in 29 CFR 825.102, to self-quarantine for a COVID-19 reason. Section 826.20(a)(3) explains that the advice to self-quarantine must be based on the health care provider's belief that the employee has COVID-19, may have COVID-19, or is particularly vulnerable to COVID-19. And, self-quarantining must prevent the employee from working. An employee who is self-quarantining is able to telework, and therefore may not take paid sick leave for this reason, if (a) his or her employer has work for the employee to perform; (b) the employer permits the employee to perform that work from the location where the employee is self-quarantining; and (c) there are no extenuating circumstances, such as serious COVID-19 symptoms, that prevent the employee from per-

[1] This analysis holds even if the closure of the coffee shop was substantially caused by a stay-at-home order. If the coffee shop closed due to its customers being required to stay at home, the reason for the cashier being unable to work would be because those customers were subject to the stay-at-home order, not because the cashier himself was subject to the order. Similarly, if the order forced the coffee shop to close, the reason for the cashier being unable to work would be because the coffee shop was subject to the order, not because the cashier himself was subject to the order.

forming that work. For instance, if the lawyer in the above example would be able to work while self-quarantining at home, she may not take paid sick leave due to a need to self-quarantine.

The third reason for paid sick leave applies where an employee is experiencing symptoms of COVID-19 and seeking a medical diagnosis. Section 826.20(a)(4) explains that symptoms that could trigger this are: fever, dry cough, shortness of breath, or other *COVID-19 symptoms* identified by the U.S. Centers for Disease Control and Prevention (CDC). Additionally, paid sick leave taken for this reason must be limited to the time the employee is unable to work because he or she is taking affirmative steps to obtain a medical diagnosis. Thus, an employee experiencing COVID-19 symptoms may take paid sick leave, for instance, for time spent making, waiting for, or attending an appointment for a test for COVID-19. But, the employee may not take paid sick leave to self-quarantine without seeking a medical diagnosis. An employee who is waiting for the results of a test is able to telework, and therefore may not take paid sick leave, if: (a) his or her employer has work for the employee to perform; (b) the employer permits the employee to perform that work from the location where the employee is waiting; and (c) there are no extenuating circumstances, such as serious COVID-19 symptoms, that may prevent the employee from performing that work. An employee may continue to take leave while experiencing any of the symptoms specified at § 826.20(a)(4), however; or may continue to take leave after testing positive for COVID-19, regardless of symptoms experienced, provided that the health care provider advises the employee to self-quarantine. In addition, an employee who is unable to telework may continue to take paid sick leave under this reason while awaiting a test result, regardless of the severity of the COVID-19 symptoms that he or she might be experiencing. In the case of an employee who exhibits COVID-19 symptoms and seeks medical advice but is told that he or she does not meet the criteria for testing and is advised to self-quarantine, he or she is eligible for leave under the second reason, provided he or she meets all the requirements spelled out above.

The fourth reason for paid sick leave applies where an employee is unable to work because he or she needs to care for an individual who is either: (a) subject to a Federal, State, or local quarantine or isolation order; or (b) has been advised by a health care provider to self-quarantine due to concerns related to COVID-19. This qualifying reason applies only if but for a need to care for an individual, the employee would be able to perform work for his or her employer. Accordingly, an employee caring for an individual may not take paid sick leave if the employer does not have work for him or her. Furthermore, if the employee must have a genuine need to care for the individual. Accordingly, § 826.20(a)(5) explains that paid sick leave may not be taken to care for someone with whom the employee has no personal relationship. Rather, the individual being cared for must be an immediate family member, roommate, or a similar person with whom the employee has a relationship that creates an expectation that the employee would care for the person if he or she self-quarantined or was quarantined. Additionally, the individual being cared for must: (a) be subject to a Federal, State, or local quarantine or isolation order as described above; or (b) have been advised by a health care provider to self-quarantine based on a belief that he or she has COVID-19, may have COVID-19, or is particularly vulnerable to COVID-19.

The fifth reason for paid sick leave applies when the employee is unable to work because the employee needs to care for his or her son or daughter if: (a) the child's school or place of care has closed; or (b) the child care provider is unavailable, due to COVID-19 related reasons. Again, the employee must be able to perform work for his or her employer but for the need to care for his or her son or daughter, which means an employee may not take paid sick leave if the employer does not have work for him or her. Moreover, an employee may take paid sick leave to care for his or her child only when the employee needs to, and actually is, caring for his or her child. Generally, an employee does not need to take such leave if another suitable individual—such as a co-parent, co-guardian, or the usual child care provider—is available to provide the care the employee's child needs.

The sixth reason for paid sick leave applies if the employee is unable to work because the employee is experiencing any other substantially similar condition specified by the Secretary of Health and Human Services in consultation with the Secretary of the Treasury and the Secretary of Labor.

Section 826.20(b) explains that an employee may take expanded family and medical leave if the employee is unable to work due to a need for leave to care for his or her son or daughter if the child's school or place of care is closed, or the child care provider of such son or daughter is unavailable, for reasons related to COVID-19. The EFMLEA provides that this reason for leave is for closures or unavailability "due to a public health emergency," which the statute defines as "an emergency with respect to COVID-19 declared by a Federal, State, or local authority." FFCRA section 3102(b) (adding FMLA section 110(a)(2)(A), (B)). In keeping with the Department's statutory authority to issue regulations to ensure consistency between the EPSLA and the EFMLEA, the regulatory text uses "for reasons related to COVID-19" to match the regulatory text related to the same reason for taking paid sick leave. In other words, the leave authorized by the EFMLEA is the same as the fifth reason discussed above authorized by the EPSLA, i.e., leave required when an employee is unable to work because of a need to care for his or her son or daughter if the school or place of care of the son or daughter is closed, or the child care provider of the son or daughter is unavailable, due to COVID-19 related reasons.

The Department recognizes that section 3102 of the EFMLEA defines "qualifying need related to a public health emergency" as a need for leave "to care for the son or daughter under 18 years of age of such employee if the school or place of care has been closed, or the child care provider of such son or daughter is unavailable, due to a public health emergency." FFCRA section 3102(b) (adding FMLA section 110(a)(2)(A), (B)). This definition can be read to narrow the FMLA definition of son or daughter, which includes children under 18 years of age or 18 years of age or older and incapable of self-care because of a mental or physical disability. 29 U.S.C. 2611(12). Section 5110(4) of the EPSLA states that the FMLA definition of son or daughter applies when, among other things, the employee is unable to work because the employee is caring for a son or daughter of the employee if: (a) the school or place of care of the son or daughter has been closed; or (b) the child care provider of such son or daughter is unavailable, due to COVID-19 related reasons.

The Department considered interpreting the leave provision of the EFMLEA to apply only when an employee is unable to work because of a need to care for a child under age 18 years of age, and not to apply when a child is 18 years of age or older and incapable of self-care because of a mental or physical disability. The Department also recognizes there could be other interpretations of the "under 18 years of age" phrase within the EFMLEA. However, the Department has decided not to employ these alternative interpretations because it sees significant disadvantages to having different rules under the EFMLEA and the EPSLA for when an employee may take leave to care for his or her son or daughter. Having different rules would introduce unnecessary complexity and incongruity into the leave provisions and could improperly deny leave to employees with a need to care for a child age 18 or older who is incapable of caring for himself or herself because of a mental or physical disability. The Department is therefore treating the definitions as the same pursuant to its authority under section 5111 of the EPSLA and section 110(a) of the FMLA, as amended by the EFMLEA, and the CARES Act, and will issue regulations to ensure consistency between the EPSLA and the EFMLEA.

The Department intends that providing maximum flexibility to employers and employees during the public health emergency should not impact the underlying relationships between an employer and an employee. More specifically, nothing in this Act should be construed as impacting an employee's exempt status under the FLSA. For example, an employee's use of intermittent leave combined with either paid sick leave or expanded family and medical leave should not be construed as undermining the employee's salary basis for purposes of 29 U.S.C. 213 and 29 CFR Part 541.

Section 826.21 explains how much paid sick leave an employee is entitled to under the EPSLA. Under section 5102(b)(2) of the EPSLA, a full-time employee is entitled to 80 hours of paid sick leave, and a part-time employee is entitled to the "number of hours that such employee works, on average, over a 2-week period." Section 5110(5)(C)(i) further provides that if the part-time employee's "schedule varies from week to week . . . the average number of hours that the employee was scheduled per day over the 6-month period ending on the date on which the employee takes the paid sick time" shall be used in place of the "number of hours that such employee works, on average, over a 2-week period" under section 5102(b)(2)(B) to determine the number of paid sick leave hours.

The Department does not believe the EPSLA intended to replace the average number of hours worked "over a 2-week period" with the average number of hours scheduled "per day" as the number of paid sick leave hours because such replacement would create a contradiction within the statute and lead to an absurd outcome. Setting hours of paid sick leave "equal to the average number of hours that the employee was scheduled per day," as section 5110(5)(C)(i) requires, would violate the requirement under section 5102(b)(2)(B) that "hours of paid sick time to which an employee is entitled shall be . . . equal to the number of hours that such employee works, on average, over a 2-week period" for the obvious reason that a day is different from a two-week period. And the number of hours an employee typically works in a day is an order of magnitude lower than the number of hours that an employee typically works in a two-week period. Thus, an employee who works a varied schedule would be entitled to an order of magnitude fewer hours of paid sick leave than if the employee had worked a regular schedule. In light of the FFCRA, the Department can think of no reason why Congress would penalize part-time employees who work varied as opposed to regular schedules.

Rather, the Department believes Congress intended to use the daily average to compute the two-week average. Because there are fourteen calendar days over a two-week period, the Department believes Congress intended for the EPSLA to provide part-time employees whose weekly schedule varies with paid sick leave equal to fourteen times the "number of hours that the employee was scheduled per [calendar] day," averaged over the above-mentioned six-month period. An employer may also use twice the number of hours that an employee was scheduled to work per workweek, averaged over the six-month period.

The EPSLA does not define what it means to be a "full-time" or "part-time" employee. Because paid sick leave is designed to provide leave "over a 2-week period," and the EPSLA provides up to 80 hours of such leave to full-time employees, the Department believes a full-time employee is an employee who works at least 80 hours over two workweeks, or at least 40 hours each workweek. As a result, the Department defines a full-time employee as an employee who is normally scheduled to work at least 40 hours each workweek in § 826.21(a)(2). Further, § 826.21(a)(3) provides that an employee who does not have a normal weekly schedule may also be a full-time employee if he or she is scheduled to work, on average, at least 40 hours each workweek. For consistency purposes, this weekly average should be computed over the same six-month period as the "Varying Schedule Hours Calculation" for certain part-time employees under section 5110(5)(C)(i) of the FFCRA. Thus, § 826.21(a)(3) provides that the average hours per workweek for an employee who does not have a normal weekly schedule should be calculated over the six-months prior to the date on which leave is requested to determine if he or she is a full-time employee. If the employee has been employed for less than six months, the average hours per workweek is computed over the entire period of employment.

Under § 826.21(b), a part-time employee is an employee who is normally scheduled to work fewer than 40 hours each workweek or—if the employee lacks a normal weekly schedule—who is scheduled to work, on average, fewer than 40 hours each workweek. Under § 826.21(b)(1), a part-time employee who works a normal schedule is entitled to paid sick leave equal to the number of hours he or she is normally scheduled to work over a two-workweek period. As discussed above, the Department believes that a part-time employee whose weekly work schedule varies should be entitled to paid sick leave equal to fourteen times the average number of hours that the employee was scheduled to work per calendar day over the six-month period ending on the date on which the employee takes paid sick leave, including hours for which the employee took leave of any type. This computation is possible only if the employee has been employed for at least six months. Thus, § 826.21(b)(2) provides variable-schedule part-time employees with such an amount of paid sick leave.

Section 5110(5)(C)(ii) of the EPSLA further provides that, if a part-time employee with a varying weekly schedule has been employed for fewer than six months, "the reasonable expectation of the employee at the time of hiring of the average number of hours per day that the employee would normally be scheduled to work" should be used "in place of" the average number of hours worked "over a 2-week period" under section 5102(b)(2)(B) to determine the amount of paid sick leave to which an employee is entitled. Again, the Department does not believe that in the EPSLA Congress intended for "the reasonable expectation . . . of the average number of hours per day" to be used "in place of" the average number of hours worked "over a 2-week period." Rather, Congress intended to use the expected daily average number of hours to estimate the two-week average. The Department further believes such "reasonable expectation" is best evidenced by an agreement between the employer and employee at the time of hiring.

Thus, § 826.21(b)(3) states that a part-time employee with a varying schedule who has been employed for fewer than six months is entitled to fourteen times the expected number of hours the employee and employer agreed at the time of hiring that the employee would work, on average, each calendar day. This is equal to twice the average number of hours that the employee would be expected to work each workweek. The agreement could have used any time period—e.g., each workweek, month, or year—to express the average number of hours the employee was expected to work, so long as that daily average could be extrapolated. In the absence of such an agreement, the Department believes that the actual average number of hours the employee was scheduled to work each workday demonstrates "the reasonable expectation . . . of the average number of hours per day that the employee would normally be scheduled to work." FFCRA section 5110(5)(C)(ii). Accordingly, § 826.21(b)(3) further states that, in the absence of an agreement regarding the expected number of hours worked each day, a part-time employee with a varying schedule who has been employed for fewer than six months "is entitled to up to the number of hours of paid sick leave equal to fourteen times the average number of hours per calendar day that the employee was scheduled to work over the entire period of employment, including hours for which the employee took leave of any type." An employer may also use twice the number of hours that an employee was scheduled to work per workweek, on average, over the six-month period.

Section 826.22 explains the amount of pay due to employees who take paid sick leave. If the employee takes paid sick leave because he or she is subject to a Federal, State, or local COVID-19 quarantine or isolation order; has been advised by a health care provider to self-quarantine for COVID-related reasons; or is experiencing COVID-19 symptoms and seeking a medical diagnosis, the employer must pay the employee his or her regular rate of pay (subject to the qualifications described below) for each hour of paid sick leave taken. If an employee takes paid sick leave because of any other COVID-19 qualifying reason, the employer must pay the employee two-thirds of the employee's regular rate of pay (subject to the qualifications described below).

If the employee's regular rate of pay is lower than the Federal, State, or local minimum wage (if applicable to the employee), the employee should instead be paid the highest of such amounts. That means an employee taking paid sick leave because he or she is subject to a Federal, State, or local COVID-19 quarantine or isolation order; has been advised by a health care provider to self-quarantine for COVID-related reasons; or is experiencing COVID-19 symptoms and seeking a medical diagnosis must be paid the highest applicable minimum wage (federal, state, or local). And, an employee taking paid sick leave for any other COVID-19 qualifying reason must be paid at least two-thirds of the highest applicable minimum wage.

The amount an employer is required to pay is capped at $511 per day of paid sick leave taken and $5,110 in total per covered employee for all paid sick leave pay. Furthermore, where an employee is taking paid sick leave at two-thirds pay, the amount of pay is subject to a lower cap of $200 per day of leave and $2,000 in total per covered employee for all paid sick leave that is paid at two-thirds pay.

Section 826.23 explains that expanded family and medical leave is a type of FMLA leave that is available for certain eligible employees between April 1, 2020, and December 31, 2020. As such, § 826.23(a) explains that an eligible employee is entitled to up to twelve workweeks of expanded family and medical leave, as provided under section 102 of the FMLA, during that period. *See* 29 U.S.C. 2612; *see also* 29 CFR 825.200. Section 826.23(b) further clarifies that any time taken by an eligible employee as expanded family and medical leave counts towards the twelve workweeks of FMLA leave to which the employee is entitled under section 102 of the FMLA and 29 CFR 825.200. Because the FFCRA amends the FMLA, and in particular references Section 102(d)(2)(B) of the FMLA, § 826.23 explains that an employee may elect to use, or an employer may require an employee to use, accrued leave that under the employer's policies would be available to the employee to care for a child, such as vacation or personal leave or paid time off concurrently with the expanded family and medical leave under the EFMLEA. Although Section 102(d)(2)(B) is read broader in the traditional FMLA context to include sick and medical leave, the Department notes that the FMLA is in part a medical leave, whereas the leave provided under FFCRA is solely for care for a family (*i.e.*, a child whose school or place of care is closed or whose child care provider is unavailable). The Department believes that this flexibility carries out the purposes of FFCRA by allowing employees to receive full pay during the period for which they have preexisting accrued vacation or personal leave or paid time off, and allowing employers to require employees to take such leave and minimize employee absences.

Section 826.24 explains the amount an employer must pay an employee for each day of expanded family and medical leave under the EFMLEA taken to care for his or her child whose school or place of care is closed, or whose child care provider is unavailable, for a COVID-19 related reason. The payment requirement under the EFMLEA is triggered after two weeks that an employee uses leave for this reason. For each day of expanded family and medical leave after the initial two-week period, the employer must pay an employee taking such leave two-thirds of the employee's regular rate times the number of hours the employee would normally be scheduled to work that day, up to a maximum of $200 per day or $10,000 in total for the additional ten workweeks.

Some employees do not have a regular work schedule. If the employee's "schedule varies week to week to such an extent that an employer is unable to determine with certainty [that] number of hours," section 110(b)(2)(C)(i) of the FMLA, as amended by the EFMLEA, requires the employer to compute pay per day of expanded family and medical leave based on "the average number of hours the employee was scheduled per day over the six-month period ending on the date on which the employee takes such leave, including hours for which the employee took leave of any type." This six-month average of daily hours is possible only if the employee has been employed for at least six months. The Department does not believe Congress intended for the EFMLEA to use this six-month average only where an employee's "schedule varies week to week," but also where the schedule varies day to day. This is because, even if an employee is scheduled for the same number of hours each workweek, day-to-day variations within each workweek could prevent an employer from determining the number of hours an employee would have been scheduled to work on a particular workday.[2] Thus, § 826.24(b) provides that the six-month average set forth in section 110(b)(2)(C) of the FMLA, as amended by the EFMLEA, is to be used to compute pay for each day of expanded family and medical leave taken where an employee's work schedule varies, without a week-to-week requirement, and has been employed for at least six months.

For an employee with a varying schedule of hours who has been employed for fewer than six months, section 110(b)(2)(C)(i) of the FMLA, as amended by the EFMLEA, provides that "the reasonable expectation of the employee at the time of hiring of the average number of hours per day that the employee would normally be

[2] For instance, an employee may always work 40 hours each workweek, but on some weeks the employee works five eight-hour shifts and on other weeks he or she works four ten-hour shifts.

scheduled to work" should be used to compute the amount of pay for each day of expanded family and medical leave he or she takes after the initial unpaid period. The Department believes such "reasonable expectation" is best evidenced by an agreement between the employer and employee at the time of hiring. Thus, § 826.21(b)(2)(ii) explains the number of hours per day used to compute pay for an employee with a varying schedule who has been employed for less than six months is equal to the number of hours that the employee and the employer agreed at the time of hiring that the employee would be expected to work, on average, each workday. The agreement could have expressed the average number of hours over any time period—e.g., each week, month, or year—so long as that daily average could be extrapolated. In the absence of such an agreement, the Department believes that the actual average number of hours the employee was scheduled to work each workday evinces "the reasonable expectation . . . of the average number of hours per day that the employee would normally be scheduled to work." Accordingly, § 826.21(b)(2)(ii) further states that, in the absence of an agreement regarding the expected number of hours worked each day, the employer should use "the average number of hours per workday that the employee was scheduled to work over the entire period of employment, including hours for which the employee took leave of any type" to compute the amount of pay for an employee with a varying schedule who has been employed for fewer than six months.

The Department recognizes that the two-week initial unpaid period of expanded family and medical leave under § 826.60 is different from the ten-day unpaid period set forth in section 110(b)(1)(A) of the FMLA, as amended by the EFMLEA. This deviation is necessary to ensure that expanded family and medical leave provided under the EFMLEA and paid sick leave provided under the EPSLA work together—as Congress intended—to permit an employee to have a continuous income stream while taking FFCRA paid leave to care for his or her child whose school or place of care is closed, or whose child care provider is unavailable, for a COVID-19 related reason.

The EFMLEA provides that, during the unpaid period of expanded family and medical leave, an employee may receive pay by using other paid leave to which he or she may be entitled, including paid sick leave provided by the EPSLA. Paid sick leave may be used for the same reason as expanded family and medical leave, i.e., to care for a child whose school or place of care is closed, or whose child care provider is unavailable, for a COVID-19 related reason. And the amount of pay per hour of paid sick leave is guaranteed to be at least as much as the amount of pay per hour for paid expanded family and medical leave, i.e., two-thirds of the employee's regular rate, up to $200 per day. Furthermore, the entitlement to paid sick leave of an employee with a regular work schedule, i.e., eight hours each day for five days for a total of 40 hours each workweek—is the same as the ten-day period of unpaid expanded family and medical leave. Such an employee is entitled to 80 hours of paid sick leave, which provides pay at two-thirds of the employee's regular rate, as defined in § 826.25, for ten workdays. If the employee were concurrently taking expanded family and medical leave, he or she would be able to take paid expanded family and medical leave at two-thirds the regular rate as soon as the 80 hours of paid sick leave runs out. Thus, paid sick leave and expanded family and medical leave are designed to work in tandem to provide continuous income for an employee to care for his or her child whose school or place of care is closed, or whose child care provider is unavailable, for a COVID-19 related reason. Put another way, the reason for an unpaid initial period of expanded family and medical leave is because an eligible employee already may concurrently use paid sick leave for the same reason and get paid at the same rate. The unpaid period is therefore intended to ensure that the employee has sufficient leave for a constant stream of income at two-thirds the regular rate, up to $200 per day, while taking care of his or her child, but not more paid leave than necessary for that purpose.

As explained above, a ten-day period of unpaid expanded family and medical leave satisfies these purposes for an employee who works a regular 40-hour week. But the twin purposes of providing sufficient, yet not excessive, paid leave are not satisfied with respect to employees who work unconventional hours. For instance, consider an employee who works twelve hours each day for three days each workweek, or a total of 36 hours each workweek. This employee would be entitled to 72 hours of paid sick leave under the EPSLA to care for his or her child, which lasts for two workweeks. The employee, however, would not be able to take paid expanded family and medical leave at the end of two workweeks time because he would have taken only six workdays of such leave, and the ten-day period of unpaid leave would still be in effect. In order to have a continuous income stream until the ten-day unpaid period of expanded family and medical leave expired, the employee would need an additional 48 hours of paid sick leave.

As another example, consider a second employee who works six hours each day for six days each workweek, also for a total of 36 hours each workweek. The second employee would likewise be entitled to 72 hours of paid sick leave under the EPSLA to care for his or her child, which lasts for two workweeks or twelve workdays. The period of unpaid expanded family and medical leave would expire after ten workdays—two workdays before the second employee runs out of paid sick leave. The second employee may transition from paid sick leave to expanded family and medical leave after ten workdays, leaving two days of paid sick leave unused. In other words, the second employee would have two more days of paid leave than necessary to have a continuous income stream at two-thirds the regular rate while caring for his or her child.

In short, there is inconsistency between the provisions for expanded family and medical leave under the EFMLEA and paid sick leave under the EPSLA with respect to the first employee because he or she would be 48 hours short of being able to have continuous income. And there is inconsistency between the two Acts with respect to the second employee because he or she would have more hours of leave than needed for that purpose. Accordingly, pursuant to the Secretary's authority to issue regulations "to ensure consistency" between the two types of paid leave under the FFCRA, § 826.24 states that the unpaid period for expanded family and medical leave lasts for two weeks rather than ten days.[3]

In subsection (d), we made clear that despite the cap on pay, an employee may elect to use, or an employer may require that an employee take leave under the employer's policies that would be available to the employee to care for a child, such as vacation or personal leave or paid time off, concurrently with expanded family and medical leave, and the employer must pay the employee a full day's pay for that day.

Section 826.25 explains how to calculate the regular rate that is used to determine the amount an employer must pay an eligible employee who takes paid sick leave or expanded family and medical leave (after the initial two-week unpaid period). An employee's regular rate is computed for each workweek as defined under section 7(e) of the FLSA, as "all [non-overtime] remuneration for employment" paid to the employee except for eight statutory exclusions, divided by the number of hours worked in that workweek. *See* 29 U.S.C. 207(e); *see also Bay Ridge Operating Co. v. Aaron*, 334 U.S. 446, 458 (1948) (stating that the "regular rate must be computed by dividing the total number of hours worked into the total [non-overtime] compensation received").

The Department's regulations at 29 CFR Parts 531 and 778 explain how to calculate the regular rate in different circumstances. For example, the Department uses the computation of an employee's regular rate with respect to tips in § 531.60. Moreover, the Department clarifies how to compute an employee's regular rate under different compensation arrangements, including commissions and piece rates, at § § 778.110–.122, and explains what types of compensation are excludable from the regular rate, at § § 778.200–.225. The regular rate used to determine the amount of pay due an employee who takes paid sick leave or expanded family and medical leave must be computed using the same methods as those described in 29 CFR Parts 531 and 778.

The regular rate must also be computed on a workweek to workweek basis. *See, e.g.*, § 778.104 ("Each workweek stands alone"). Neither the EPSLA nor the EFMLEA, however, explains which workweek should be used to compute the regular rate that is the basis for determining the amount of pay for leave taken. The Department does not believe it would be appropriate to use the workweek in which an employee takes leave because an employee's hours worked, and therefore regular rate, in such a workweek is unlikely to be representative. Indeed, if the employee takes leave for the entire workweek, the regular rate would equal zero.

Instead, the Department believes the regular rate used to determine the amount of pay under the EPSLA and the EFMLEA should be representative of the employee's regular rate from week to week. Section 826.25 therefore requires an employer to use an average of the employee's regular rate over multiple workweeks.[4] Such an average should be weighted by the number of hours worked each workweek. For example, consider an employee who receives $400 of non-excludable compensation in one week for working 40 hours and $200 of non-excludable compensation in the next week for working ten hours. The regular rate in the first week is $10 per hour ($400 ÷ 40 hours), and the regular rate for the second week is $20 per hour ($200 ÷ 10 hours). The weighted average, however, is not computed by averaging $10 per hour and $20 per hour (which would be $15 per hour). Rather, it is computed by adding up all compensation over the relevant period (here, two workweeks), which is $600, and then dividing that sum by all hours worked over the same period, which is 50 hours. Thus, the weighted average regular rate over this two-week period is $12 per hour ($600 ÷ 50 hours).

To be representative, the period over which the regular rate is averaged should be substantially greater than the two workweeks used in the above example. The Department believes it would be appropriate to compute the average regular rate over the same period used by the EPSLA and the EFMLEA to compute the employee's average number of hours worked per day, *i.e.*, a six-month period ending on the date on which the employee first takes paid sick leave or expanded family and medical leave. The Department has selected this six-month period be-

[3] As a practical matter, the unpaid period for employees who work regular Monday-through-Friday schedules would still be ten days because that is the number of days they would work in two weeks.

[4] The Department notes that § 778.104 states that the FLSA "does not permit averaging of hours over 2 or more weeks" for the purpose of computing the regular rate. But this prohibition against averaging applies when the regular rate is used for its purpose under the FLSA to compute overtime pay due. It does not apply when, as here, the regular rate is used as a metric for an employee's average hourly non-overtime wages.

cause it is sufficiently representative under both the EPSLA and the EFMLEA. And it minimizes regulatory burden by allowing employers to use the same payroll and schedule records to compute both an employee's average number of hours worked per day and average regular rate. Of course, computing an average regular rate used to determine the amount of pay should be computed over a six-month period is not possible if the employee at issue has not been employed for at least six months. In such a case, the average regular rate should be computed over the entire term of the employment.

C. Employee Eligibility for Leave under the EPSLA and the EFMLEA

Section 826.30 sets out the criteria for an employee's eligibility to receive paid sick leave under the EPSLA and/or expanded family and medical leave under the EFMLEA, which have similar, but not identical, eligibility requirements for leave. This section also addresses when employers may elect to exclude certain otherwise-eligible employees from coverage under these Acts.

Sections 826.30(a) and (b) provide that all employees employed by a covered employer are eligible to take paid sick leave under the EPSLA regardless of their duration of employment, and all employees who have been employed by a covered employer for at least thirty calendar days are eligible to take expanded family and medical leave under the EFMLEA, subject to the exceptions described in §§826.30(c)–(d) and .40(b).

Section 826.30(b)(1)(i) further explains that an employee is considered to have been employed for at least thirty calendar days for purposes of EFMLEA eligibility if the employer had the employee on its payroll for the thirty calendar days immediately prior to the day that the employee's leave would begin. For example, for an employee to be eligible to take leave under the EFMLEA on April 1, 2020, the employee must have been on the employer's payroll as of March 2, 2020. Section 826.30(b)(1)(ii) provides that an employee who is laid off or otherwise terminated by an employer on or after March 1, 2020, is nevertheless also considered to have been employed for at least thirty calendar days, provided the employer rehires or otherwise reemploys the employee on or before December 31, 2020, and the employee had been on the employer's payroll for thirty or more of the sixty calendar days prior to the date the employee was laid off or otherwise terminated. "For example, an employee who was originally hired by an employer on January 15, 2020, but laid off on March 14, 2020, would be eligible for leave under the EFMLEA and the EPSLA, if the same employer rehired the employee on October 1, 2020."

The EFMLEA and the EPSLA both provide that an employer may exclude employees who are health care providers or emergency responders from leave requirements under the Acts. Section 826.30(c) reiterates this option and defines which employees are "health care providers" or "emergency responders" whom employers may exclude from eligibility for the EPSLA and the EFMLEA's leave requirements. An employer's exercise of this option does not impact an employee's earned or accrued sick, personal, vacation, or other employer-provided leave under the employer's established policies. Further, an employer's exercise of this option does not authorize an employer to prevent an employee who is a health care provider or emergency responder from taking earned or accrued leave in accordance with established employer policies. Because an employer is not required to exercise this option, if an employer does not elect to exclude an otherwise-eligible health care provider or emergency responder from taking paid leave under the EPSLA or the EFMLEA, such leave is subject to all other requirements of those laws and this Part, and should be treated in the same manner for purposes of the tax credit created by the FFCRA. To minimize the spread of COVID-19, the Department encourages employers to be judicious when using this definition to exempt health care providers and emergency responders from the provisions of the FFCRA.

The Department recognizes that health care providers whom an employer may exempt pursuant to sections 3105 and 5102(a) of the FFCRA is broader than the definition of health care provider under 29 CFR §825.102. Section 5110(4) of the FFCRA adopts the FMLA definition of "health care providers," which includes licensed doctors of medicine or osteopathy and "any other person determined by the Secretary to be capable of providing health care services." 29 U.S.C. 2611(6). The Department defined "health care provider" narrowly in §825.102 to mean medical professionals who are capable of diagnosing serious health conditions in light of the FMLA's requirement for such health care providers to issue certifications regarding the nature and probable duration of serious health conditions. *See* 29 U.S.C. 2613; *see also* 58 FR 31800 ("Because health care providers will need to indicate their diagnosis in health care certificates, such a broad definition was considered inappropriate.").

The term "health care provider" as used in sections 3105 and 5102(a) of the FFCRA, however, is not limited to diagnosing medical professionals. Rather, such health care providers include any individual who is capable of providing health care services necessary to combat the COVID-19 public health emergency. Such individuals include not only medical professionals, but also other workers who are needed to keep hospitals and similar health care facilities well supplied and operational. They further include, for example, workers who are involved in research, development, and production of equipment, drugs, vaccines, and other items needed to combat the COVID-19 public health emergency. Accordingly, the Department is adopting a definition of "health care provider" that is broader than the diagnosing medical professionals under § 825.102 for the limited purpose of identifying employees whom an employer may exclude under sections 3105 and 5102(a) of the FFCRA. The definition of health care provider under § 825.102 continues to apply for other purposes of the FFCRA, such as, for instance, identifying health care providers who may advise an employee to self-quarantine for COVID-19 related reasons under section 5102(a)(2).

The authority for employers to exempt emergency responders is reflective of a balance struck by the FFCRA. On the one hand, the FFCRA provides for paid sick leave and expanded family and medical leave so employees will not be forced to choose between their paychecks and the individual and public health measures necessary to combat COVID-19. On the other hand, providing paid sick leave or expanded family and medical leave does not come at the expense of fully staffing the necessary functions of society, including the functions of emergency responders. The FFRCA should be read to complement—and not detract from—the work being done on the front lines to treat COVID-19 patients, prevent the spread of COVID-19, and simultaneously keep Americans safe and with access to essential services. Therefore, the Department interprets "emergency responder" broadly.

The specific parameters of the Department's definition of "emergency responder" derive from consultation of various statutory and regulatory definitions and from the consideration of input provided to the Department by various stakeholders and public officials. The Department endeavored to include those categories of employees who (1) interact with and aid individuals with physical or mental health issues, including those who are or may be suffering from COVID-19; (2) ensure the welfare and safety of our communities and of our Nation; (3) have specialized training relevant to emergency response; and (4) provide essential services relevant to the American people's health and wellbeing. While the Department endeavored to identify these categories of workers, it was cognizant that no list could be fully inclusive or account for the differing needs of specific communities. Therefore, the definition allows for the highest official of a state or territory to identify other categories of emergency responders, as necessary.

Section 826.30(d) explains that the CARES Act grants authority to the Director of OMB to exclude, for good cause, certain federal government employers from eligibility to take paid sick leave or expanded family and medical leave. As to the EFMLEA, the Director of OMB may exclude certain categories of United States Executive Branch employees from expanded family and medical leave. As to the EPSLA, the Director of OMB may exclude certain categories of federal government employees if they are covered by Title II of the FMLA, occupy a position in the civil service (as defined in 5 U.S.C. 2101(1)), and/or are employees of a United States Executive Agency (as defined in 5 U.S.C. 105), which includes employees of the U.S. Postal Service and the U.S. Postal and Regulatory Commission.

D. Employer Coverage under the EPSLA and the EFMLEA

Section 826.40 addresses which employers are covered by the EPSLA and the EFMLEA, that is, which employers must provide paid leave to employees as described in those Acts.

Section 826.40(a) explains which private employers must provide paid sick leave and expanded family and medical leave to their employees. Specifically, it explains that, subject to the exemption described in § 826.40(b), all private employers that employ fewer than 500 employees at the time an employee would take leave must comply with the EPSLA and the EFMLEA.

This determination is dependent on the number of employees at the time an employee would take leave. For example, if an employer has 450 employees on April 20, 2020, and an employee is unable to work starting on that date because a health care provider has advised that employee to self-quarantine because of concerns related to COVID-19, the employer must provide paid sick leave to that employee. If, however, the employer hires 75 new employees between April 21, 2020, and August 3, 2020, such that the employer employs 525 employees as of August 3, 2020, the employer would not be required to provide paid sick leave to a different employee who is unable to work for the same reason beginning on August 3, 2020.

Section 826.40(a) also addresses how to determine who counts as an employee for this purpose, including discussing categories of workers who do (and do not) count toward the 500-employee threshold. In making this determination, the employer should include full-time and part-time employees, employees on leave, temporary employees who are jointly employed by the employer and another employer, and day laborers supplied by a temporary placement agency. Independent contractors that provide services for an employer do not count towards the 500-employee threshold. Nor do employees count who have been laid off or furloughed and have not subsequently been reemployed. Furthermore, employees must be employed within the United States. For example, if an employer employs 1,000 employees in North America, but only 250 are employed in a U.S. State, the District of Columbia, or a territory or possession of the United States, that employer will be considered to have 250 employees and is thus subject to the FFCRA.

Section 826.40(a) further explains that joint or integrated employers must combine employees in determining the number of employees they employ for this purpose. The FLSA's test for joint employer status applies in determining who is a joint employer for purposes of coverage, and the FMLA's test for integrated employer status applies in determining who is an integrated employer, under both the EPSLA and the EFMLEA.

Section 826.40(a) does not distinguish between for-profit and non-profit entities; employers of both types must comply with the FFCRA if they otherwise meet the requirements for coverage.

Section 826.40(b) describes the small employer exemption pursuant to the Secretary's regulatory authority to exempt small private employers with fewer than 50 employees from having to provide an employee with paid sick leave and expanded family and medical leave to care for his or her child whose school or place of care is closed, or child care provider is unavailable, when such leave would jeopardize the viability of the business as a going concern. The American Institute of Certified Public Accountants (AICPA) allows companies to use the "ongoing concern assumption" to defer some of its prepaid expenses until future accounting periods because the entity can continue in business for the foreseeable future without the intention nor the necessity to liquidate, cease trading, or seek protection from creditors pursuant to laws or regulations. In other words, the business is considered to remain a viable business for the foreseeable future. There is no formula provided by the AICPA to determine the viability of a business as a going concern, but rather the standard considers conditions or events in the aggregate.

The Department believes it is necessary to set forth objective criteria for when a small business with fewer than 50 employees can deny an employee paid sick leave or expanded family and medical leave to care for the employee's son or daughter whose school or place of care is closed, or child care provider is unavailable, for COVID-19 related reasons. To that end, section 826.40(b)(1) explains that a small employer is exempt from the requirement to provide such leave when: (1) such leave would cause the small employer's expenses and financial obligations to exceed available business revenue and cause the small employer to cease operating at a minimal capacity; (2) the absence of the employee or employees requesting such leave would pose a substantial risk to the financial health or operational capacity of the small employer because of their specialized skills, knowledge of the business, or responsibilities; or (3) the small employer cannot find enough other workers who are able, willing, and qualified, and who will be available at the time and place needed, to perform the labor or services the employee or employees requesting leave provide, and these labor or services are needed for the small employer to operate at a minimal capacity. For reasons (1), (2), and (3), the employer may deny paid sick leave or expanded family and medical leave only to those otherwise eligible employees whose absence would cause the small employer's expenses and financial obligations to exceed available business revenue, pose a substantial risk, or prevent the small employer from operating at minimum capacity, respectively.

Section 826.40(b)(2) explains that if a small employer decides to deny paid sick leave or expanded family and medical leave to an employee or employees whose child's school or place of care is closed, or whose child care provider is unavailable, the small employer must document the facts and circumstances that meet the criteria set forth in § 826.40(b)(1) to justify such denial. The employer should not send such material or documentation to the Department, but rather should retain such records for its own files.

In exercising its authority to exempt certain employers with fewer than 50 employees, the Department balanced two potentially competing objectives of the FFCRA. On the one hand, the leave afforded by the FFCRA was designed to be widely available to employees to assist them navigating the social and economic impacts of COVID-19 as well as public and private efforts to contain and slow the spread of the virus. On the other hand, the Department recognizes that FFCRA leave entitlements have little value if they cause an employer to go out of business and, in so doing, deny employees not only leave but also jobs. In § 826.40(b), the Department attempted to extend the leave benefits as broadly as practicable, but not in circumstances that would significantly increase the likelihood that small businesses would be forced to close. The Department rejected alternative arrangements that excessively favored either the extension of leave or exclusion of small businesses or which imposed compliance requirements that were overly burdensome, particularly in economic conditions resulting from COVID-19.

Section 826.40(c) explains which public employers must comply with the EPSLA and the EFMLEA. It uses the term "Public Agency," which as explained in the definitions section, has the same meaning as in section 203(x) of the FLSA. Specifically, public agency means the Government of the United States; the government of a State or political subdivision of a State; or an agency of the United States (including the United States Postal Service and Postal Regulatory Commission), a State, or a political subdivision of a State; or any interstate governmental agency. All covered public agencies must comply with both the EPSLA and the EFMLEA regardless of the number of employees they employ, although such employers may exclude employees who are health care providers or emergency responders as described in § 826.30(c).

Section 826.40(c) provides further information about which parts of the Federal government must comply with these Acts. Because the EFMLEA only amends Title I of the FMLA, only employers of employees covered by Title I of the FMLA are subject to the requirements of the EFMLEA. Employers of federal employees covered by Title II of the FMLA are not subject to requirements of the EFMLEA.

Section 826.40(c) provides certain clarifications as to the EPSLA's and the EFMLEA's applicability to public employers. It explains that all public agencies must provide their eligible employees with paid sick leave, subject to the exceptions set forth in § 826.30(c)–(d). In general, public agencies must also provide their eligible employees with expanded family and medical leave, subject to the exceptions and limitations set forth in § 826.30(b)–(d). However, as § 826.40(c) clarifies, only certain employees of the United States or agencies of the United States ("federal employees") are potentially eligible to take expanded family and medical leave. Those who are potentially eligible are the federal employees covered by Title I of the FMLA. Those who are not potentially eligible for expanded family and medical leave are the federal employees whose FMLA coverage is found elsewhere, including in Title II of the FMLA (codified in Title 5 of the U.S. Code). Section 826.40(c)(i)–(viii) sets forth specific examples of federal employees covered by Title I of the FMLA and therefore potentially eligible for expanded family and medical leave.

E. Intermittent Leave

Section 826.50 outlines the circumstances and conditions under which paid sick leave or expanded family and medical leave may be taken intermittently under the FFCRA. In this section, the Department has imported and applied to the FFCRA certain concepts of intermittent leave from its FMLA regulations. However, it has also modified these concepts and added additional limitations on the use of intermittent leave in circumstances where the Department believes it is incompatible with Congress' objectives to slow the spread of COVID-19.

One basic condition applies to all employees who seek to take their paid sick leave or expanded family and medical leave intermittently—they and their employer must agree. Absent agreement, no leave under the FFCRA may be taken intermittently. Subsection (a) does not require an employer and employee to reduce to writing or similarly memorialize their agreement. But, in the absence of a written agreement, there must be a clear and mutual understanding between the parties that the employee may take intermittent paid sick leave or intermittent expanded family and medical leave, or both. Additionally, where an employer and employee agree that the latter may take paid sick leave or expanded family and medical leave intermittently, they also must agree on the increments of time in which leave may be taken, as explained in subsections (b)(1) and (c).

Section 826.50(c) provides that if an employer directs or allows an employee to telework, subject to an agreement between the employer and employee, the employee may take paid sick leave or expanded family and medical leave intermittently, in any agreed increment of time, while the employee is teleworking. This section intentionally affords teleworking employees and employers broad flexibility under the FFCRA to agree on arrangements that balance the needs of each teleworking employee with the needs of the employer's business. Moreover, as teleworking employees present no risk of spreading COVID-19 to work colleagues, intermittent leave for any qualifying reason furthers the statute's objective to contain the virus.

In contrast, employees who continue to report to an employer's worksite may only take paid sick leave or expanded family and medical leave intermittently and in any increment—subject to the employer and employee's agreement—in circumstances where there is a minimal risk that the employee will spread COVID-19 to other employees at an employer's worksite. Therefore, subsection (b)(1) allows an employer and employee who reports to an employer's worksite to agree that the employee may take paid sick leave or expanded family and medical leave intermittently solely to care for the employee's son or daughter whose school or place of care is closed, or whose child care provider is unavailable, because of reasons related to COVID-19. In this context, the absence of confirmed or suspected COVID-19 in the employee's household reduces the risk that the employee will spread COVID-19 by reporting to the employer's worksite while taking intermittent paid leave. This is not true, however, when the employee takes paid sick leave for other qualifying reasons.

Subsection (b)(2) prohibits employees who report to an employer's worksite from taking paid sick leave intermittently, notwithstanding any agreement between the employer and employee to the contrary, if the leave is taken because the employee: (1) is subject to a Federal, State, or local quarantine or isolation order related to COVID-19; (2) has been advised by a health care provider to self-quarantine due to concerns related to COVID-19; (3) is experiencing symptoms of COVID-19 and is taking leave to obtain a medical diagnosis; (4) is caring for an individual who either is subject to a quarantine or isolation order related to COVID-19 or has been advised by a health care provider to self-quarantine due to concerns related to COVID-19; or (5) is experiencing any other substantially similar condition specified by the Secretary of Health and Human Services. As the Department explains in subsection (b)(2), where paid leave is taken for these reasons, "the employee is, may be, or is reasonably likely to become, sick with COVID-19, or is exposed to someone who is, may be, or is reasonably likely to become, sick with COVID-19." In these situations, the employee may not take intermittent leave due to the unacceptably high risk that the employee might spread COVID-19 to other employees when reporting to the employer's worksite. Once such an employee begins taking paid sick leave for one or more of these qualifying reasons, the employee must continue to take paid sick leave each day until the employee either uses the full amount of paid sick leave or no longer has a qualifying reason for taking paid sick leave. The Department believes that such a requirement furthers Congress' objective to slow the spread of COVID-19.

Finally, subsection (d) clarifies that where an employer and employee have agreed that FFCRA leave may be taken intermittently, only the amount of leave actually taken may be counted toward the employee's leave entitlements. This is consistent with the requirements for intermittent leave use under the FMLA and ensures that employees are able to use the full leave entitlement.

F. Leave to Care for a Child Due to School or Place of Care Closure or Child Care Unavailability—Intersection between the EPSLA and the EFMLEA

Both the EPSLA and the EFMLEA permit an employee to take paid leave when needed to care for his or her son or daughter whose school or place of care is closed, or child care provider is unavailable, due to COVID-19 related reasons. Section 826.60 sets forth how the requirements of the EFMLEA and the EPSLA interact when an employee qualifies for both types of leave.

Generally, when an employee qualifies for leave under both Acts, an employee may first use the two weeks of paid leave provided by the EPSLA. This use runs concurrent with the first two weeks of unpaid leave under the EFMLEA. Any remaining leave taken for this purpose is paid under the EFMLEA.

Section 826.60 further explains that where an employee has already taken some FMLA leave in the current twelve-month leave year as defined by 29 C.F.R. § 825.200(b), the maximum twelve weeks of EFMLEA leave is reduced by the amount of the FMLA leave entitlement taken in that year. If an employee has exhausted his or her twelve workweeks of FMLA or EFMLEA leave, he or she may still take EPSLA leave for a COVID-19 qualifying reason.

Section 826.60(b) addresses an employee's prior use of emergency paid sick leave, which does not prevent the employee from taking expanded family and medical leave. For example, if the employee takes two weeks of paid sick leave for a qualifying reason under EPSLA section 5102(a)(1)–(4) and (6), the employee has exhausted the paid sick leave available to the employee under the EPSLA and may not take additional paid sick leave for any qualifying reason. If the employee then needs to take leave under the EFMLEA, the employee may do so, but the first ten days of expanded family and medical leave may be unpaid. The employee may, however, choose to substitute earned or accrued paid leave, as provided by the employer's established policies.

G. Leave to Care for a Child Due to School or Place of Care Closure or Child Care Unavailability – Intersection between the EFMLEA and the FMLA

Section 826.70 addresses the interaction between the new entitlement to take FMLA leave to care for an employee's child due to school or place of care closure or child care unavailability under the EFMLEA and an employee's entitlement to take FMLA leave for other reasons, such as bonding with a newborn or newly placed child, for the employee's own serious health condition, or to care for a covered family member with a serious health condition. The EFMLEA amended the FMLA to add a sixth reason to take the twelve-week FMLA entitlement: to care for an employee's son or daughter whose school or place of care is closed or child care provider is unavailable due to COVID-19 related reasons.

Eligibility requirements for employees to take expanded family and medical leave under the EFMLEA differ from standard FMLA leave. Not all employees who are eligible to take expanded family and medical leave will be eligible to take FMLA leave for other reasons. Employees only need to have been employed for 30 calendar days in order to be eligible for expanded family and medical leave to care for their child due to school or place of care closure or child care unavailability under the EFMLEA. In contrast, to be eligible to take FMLA leave for other reasons, employees generally need to have worked for the employer for at least twelve months, have 1,250 hours of service in the twelve-month period prior to the leave, and work at a location where the employer has at least 50 employees within 75 miles.

Employer coverage also differs under the EFMLEA and the FMLA. Most significantly, the EFMLEA applies to all employers with fewer than 500 employees, while the FMLA generally does not apply to employers with fewer than 50 employees. Further, employers of health care providers and emergency responders may exclude such employees from the EFMLEA's leave requirements, but not the FMLA's.

An employee's ability to take EFMLEA leave depends on his or her use of FMLA leave during the 12-month FMLA leave year pursuant to 29 C.F.R. § 825.200(b) for a reason unrelated to COVID-19. If an employee has already taken such leave, the employee may not be able to take the full twelve weeks of expanded family and medical leave under the EFMLEA. For example, if the employer uses the calendar year as the twelve-month FMLA leave year and an employee took three weeks of leave in January 2020 for the employee's own serious health condition, the employee would only have nine weeks of expanded family and medical leave available. Additionally, employees are limited to a total of twelve weeks of expanded family and medical leave under the EFMLEA, even if the applicable time period (April 1 to December 31, 2020) spans two twelve-month leave periods under the FMLA. Finally, for employees who are eligible to take leave under the FMLA and the EFMLEA, and who take leave to care for a service member with a serious injury or illness, the total amount of leave available to the employee will be calculated as set forth in 29 CFR 825.127(e).

H. Employer Notice

Section 826.80 addresses the FFCRA requirement that employers post and keep posted a notice of the law's requirements. As required by the FFCRA, the Department made a model notice available on March 25, 2020, and employers may, free of charge, download the poster (WHD1422 REV 03/20) from the WHD website at *https://www.dol.gov/whd*. In addition to posting the notice in a conspicuous place where employees or job applicants at a worksite may view it, an employer may distribute the notice to employees by e-mail, or post the required notice electronically on an employee information website to satisfy the FFCRA requirement. An employer may also directly mail the required notice to any employees who are not able to access information at the worksite, through e-mail, or online. An employer may post or distribute the required information provided in the model notice in a different format, as long as the content is accurate and readable. Although the FFCRA does not require employers to provide a translated notice to employees, the Department has issued a Spanish language version of the poster. For employers who are covered by the EFMLEA but are not covered by the other provisions of the FMLA, posting of this FFCRA notice satisfies their FMLA general notice obligation. *See* 29 U.S.C. 2619; 29 CFR 825.300.

The Department is aware that employers newly affected by the EFMLEA requirements of the FFCRA will not have established policies and practices for administering FMLA leave. In consideration of these employers, the number of employees who will be eligible to use the FMLA for the first time for a limited period of time, and interruptions to normal business operations from emergency conditions, the Department did not adopt in the FFCRA employer notice regulations or employer "specific notice" obligations that are required in the FMLA regulations. The FFCRA regulations do not require employers to respond to employees who request or use EFMLEA leave with notices of eligibility, rights and responsibilities, or written designations that leave use counts against employees' FMLA leave allowances. However, an employer that has established practices for providing individual employees with specific notices compliant with the FMLA regulatory guidance at 29 CFR 825.300 may prefer to apply their existing practices to EFMLEA leave users.

I. Employee Notice of Need for Leave

Section 826.90 addresses an employee's notice to his or her employer regarding the need to take leave. Section 826.90(a) explains that for paid sick leave or expanded family and medical leave to care for the employee's son or daughter whose school or place of care is closed, or whose child care provider is unavailable, due to COVID-19 related reasons, an employer may require employees to follow reasonable notice procedures as soon as practicable after the first workday or portion of a workday for which an employee receives paid sick leave in order to continue to receive such leave. Sections 826.90(b) and (c) explain that it will be reasonable for an employer to require notice as soon as practicable after the first workday is missed, and to require that employees provide oral notice and sufficient information for an employer to determine whether the requested leave is covered by the FFCRA. The employer may not require the notice to include documentation beyond what is allowed by § 826.100.

Section 826.90(d) states that it is reasonable for the employer to require the employee to comply with the employer's usual notice procedures and requirements, absent unusual circumstances. If an employee fails to give proper notice, the employer should give him or her notice of the failure and an opportunity to provide the required documentation prior to denying the request for leave.

J. Documentation of Need for Leave

An employee must provide his or her employer documentation in support of paid sick leave or expanded family and medical leave. As provided in § 826.100, such documentation must include a signed statement containing the following information: (1) the employee's name; (2) the date(s) for which leave is requested; (3) the COVID-19 qualifying reason for leave; and (4) a statement representing that the employee is unable to work or telework because of the COVID-19 qualifying reason.

An employee must provide additional documentation depending on the COVID-19 qualifying reason for leave. An employee requesting paid sick leave under § 826.20(a)(1)(i) must provide the name of the government entity that issued the quarantine or isolation order to which the employee is subject. An employee requesting paid sick leave under § 826.20(a)(1)(ii) must provide the name of the health care provider who advised him or her to self-quarantine for COVID-19 related reasons. An employee requesting paid sick leave under § 826.20(a)(1)(iv) to care for an individual must provide either (1) the government entity that issued the quarantine or isolation order to which the individual is subject or (2) the name of the health care provider who advised the individual to self-quarantine, depending on the precise reason for the request. An employee requesting to take paid sick leave under § 826.20(a)(1)(v) or expanded family and medical leave to care for his or her child must provide the following information: (1) the name of the child being care for; (2) the name of the school, place of care, or child care provider that closed or became unavailable due to COVID-19 reasons; and (3) a statement representing that no other suitable person is available to care for the child during the period of requested leave.

For leave taken under the FMLA for an employee's own serious health condition related to COVID-19, or to care for the employee's spouse, son, daughter, or parent with a serious health condition related to COVID-19, the normal

FMLA certification requirements still apply. *See* 29 CFR 825.306.

K. Health care coverage

Section 826.110 explains that an employee who takes expanded family and medical leave or paid sick leave is entitled to continued coverage under the employer's group health plan on the same terms as if the employee did not take leave. *See* 29 U.S.C. 2614(c); *see also* 29 U.S.C. 1182 and 26 CFR 54.9802-1(e)(2)(i); 29 CFR 2590.702(e)(2)(i) and 45 CFR 146.121(e)(2)(i) (providing that an employer cannot establish a rule for group health plan eligibility or set any individual's premium or contribution rate based on whether an individual is actively at work, unless the employer treats employees who are absent from work on sick leave as being actively at work). This rule defines "group health plan" using the definition under the FMLA. *See* 29 CFR 825.102. Maintenance of individual health insurance policies purchased by an employee from an insurance provider, as described in 29 CFR 825.209(a), is the responsibility of the employee.

Section 826.110(b)–(g) explains what an employer must do to continue group health plan coverage on the same terms as if the employee did not take paid sick leave or expanded family and medical leave. These requirements are similar to the regulatory requirements for employers when employees take FMLA leave for other reasons. In particular, while an employee is taking paid sick leave or expanded family and medical leave, the employer must maintain the same group health plan benefits provided to an employee and his or her family members covered under the plan prior to taking leave—including medical care, surgical care, hospital care, dental care, eye care, mental health counseling, substance abuse treatment, and other benefit coverage. This requirement also applies to benefits provided through a supplement to a group health plan, whether or not the supplement is provided through a flexible spending account or other component of a cafeteria plan.

Likewise, if an employer provides a new health plan (including a new benefit package option) or benefits or changes health benefits or plans while an employee is taking paid sick leave or expanded family and medical leave, the employee is entitled to the new or changed plan/benefits to the same extent as if the employee was not on leave. The employer must give the employee notice of any opportunity to change plans or benefits, and if the employee requests the changed coverage it must be provided by the employer.

Employees in a group health plan who take paid sick leave or expanded family and medical leave remain responsible for paying the same portion of the plan premium that the employee paid prior to taking leave. If premiums are adjusted, the employee is required to pay the new employee premium contribution on the same terms as other employees. The employee's share of premiums must be paid by the method normally used during any paid leave; in many cases, this will be through a payroll deduction. For unpaid leave, or where the pay provided by the EFMLEA or the EPSLA is insufficient to cover the employee's premiums, the rule directs employers to 29 CFR 825.210(c), which specifies how employers can obtain payment. If an employee chooses not to retain group health plan coverage while taking paid sick leave or expanded family and medical leave, the employee is entitled upon returning from leave to be reinstated on the same terms as prior to taking the leave, including family member coverage.

L. Multiemployer plans

An employer that is a signatory to a multiemployer collective bargaining agreement may satisfy its obligations under the EFMLEA and the EPSLA by making contributions to a multiemployer fund, plan, or other program consistent with its bargaining obligations and its collective bargaining agreement. The contributions must be based on the amount of paid sick leave and expanded family and medical leave to which the employee is entitled under the applicable provisions of the FFCRA based on each employee's work under the multiemployer collective bargaining agreement. The fund, plan, or other program must allow employees to obtain their pay for the leave to which they are entitled under the FFRCA.

Alternatively, an employer that is part of a multiemployer collective bargaining agreement may choose to satisfy its obligations under the FFCRA by means other than through contribution to a plan, fund, or program, provided they are consistent with its bargaining obligations and collective bargaining agreement.

M. Return to work

Section 826.130 describes an employee's right to return to work after taking paid leave under the EPSLA or the EFMLEA. In most instances, an employee is entitled to be restored to the same or an equivalent position upon return from paid sick leave or expanded family and medical leave in the same manner that an employee would be returned to work after FMLA leave. *See* the FMLA job restoration provisions at 29 CFR 825.214 and the FMLA equivalent position provisions at 29 CFR 825.215.

However, the new statute does not protect an employee from employment actions, such as layoffs, that would have affected the employee regardless of whether the leave was taken. The employer must be able to demonstrate that the employee would have been laid off even if he or she had not taken leave. This provision tracks the existing provision under the FMLA in 29 CFR 825.216. The employer has the same burden of proof to show that an employee would not otherwise have been employed at the time reinstatement is requested in order to deny restoration to employment.

The EFMLEA amendments to the FMLA specify that the FMLA's restoration provision in 29

U.S.C. 2614(a)(1) does not apply to an employer who has fewer than twenty-five employees if all four of the following conditions are met:

(a) The employee took leave to care for his or her son or daughter whose school or place of care was closed or whose child care provider was unavailable;

(b) The employee's position no longer exists due to economic or operating conditions that (i) affect employment and (ii) are caused by a public health emergency (*i.e.*, due to COVID-19 related reasons) during the period of the employee's leave;

(c) The employer made reasonable efforts to restore the employee to the same or an equivalent position; and

(d) If the employer's reasonable efforts to restore the employee fail, the employer makes reasonable efforts for a period of time to contact the employee if an equivalent position becomes available. The period of time is specified to be one year beginning either on the date the leave related to COVID-19 reasons concludes or the date twelve weeks after the employee's leave began, whichever is earlier.

In addition, as these provisions amend the FMLA, the existing limitation to job restoration for "key" employees is applicable to leave taken under the EFMLEA. The FMLA's key employee regulations are in 29 CFR 825.217.

N. Recordkeeping

Section 826.140 explains that an employer is required to retain all documentation provided pursuant to § 826.100 for four years, regardless of whether leave was granted or denied. If an Employee provided oral statements to support his or her request for paid sick leave or expanded family and medical leave, the employer is required to document and retain such information for four years. If an employer denies an employee's request for leave pursuant to the small business exemption under § 826.40(b), the employer must document its authorized officer's determination that the prerequisite criteria for that exemption are satisfied and retain such documentation for four years. Section 826.140 also explains what documents the employer should create and retain to support its claim for tax credits from the Internal Revenue Service (IRS). A more detailed explanation of how Employers may claim tax credits can be found at *https://www.irs.gov/forms-pubs/about-form-7200* and *https://www.irs.gov/pub/irs-drop/n-20-21.pdf.*

O. Prohibited Acts and Enforcement

Sections 826.150 and 826.151 describe certain acts that are prohibited under the EPSLA and the EFMLEA, as well as enforcement mechanisms.

Section 826.150(a) explains that, under the EPSLA, employers are prohibited from discharging, disciplining, or discriminating against any employee because the employee took paid sick leave, initiated a proceeding under or related to paid sick leave, or testified or is about to testify in such a proceeding.

Section 826.150(b) explains that an employer who violates the paid sick leave requirements is considered to have failed to pay the minimum wage required by section 6 of the FLSA, and an employer who violates the prohibition on discharge, discipline, or discrimination described in section 826.150(a) is considered to have violated section 15(a)(3) of the FLSA. *See* 29 U.S.C. 206, 215(a)(3). With respect to such violations, the relevant enforcement provisions of sections 16 and 17 of the FLSA apply. *See* 29 U.S.C. 216, 217.

For instance, an employee may maintain, on behalf of the employee and any other similarly-situated employees, an action in any federal or state court of competent jurisdiction to recover an amount equal to the federal minimum wage for each hour of paid sick leave denied, an additional equal amount as liquidated damages, and an amount for costs and reasonable attorney's fees. Moreover, the Secretary may bring an action against an employer to recover an amount equal to the Federal minimum wage for each hour of paid sick leave denied, and an additional equal amount as liquidated damages, or to obtain an injunction against the employer. Finally, in the case of a repeated or willful violation, the employer shall also be subject to a civil penalty for each violation, and liable in an additional amount, as liquidated damages, equal to the minimum wage for each hour of paid sick leave denied.

Section 826.151(a) explains that, for purposes of the EFMLEA, employers are subject to the prohibitions that apply with respect to all FMLA leave, which are set forth at 29 U.S.C. 2615. Specifically, employers are prohibited from interfering with, restraining, or denying an employee's exercise of or attempt to exercise any right under the FMLA, including the EFMLEA; discriminating against an employee for opposing any practice made unlawful by the FMLA, including the EFMLEA; or interfering with proceedings initiated under the FMLA, including the EFMLEA.

Section 826.151(b) explains that, for purposes of the EFMLEA, employers are subject to the enforcement provisions set forth in section 107 of the FMLA, with one exception: an employee may not bring a private action against an employer under the EFMLEA if the employer, although subject to the EFMLEA, is not otherwise subject to the FMLA. *See* 29 U.S.C. 2617; 29 CFR 825.400. In other words, an employee can only bring an action against an employer under the EFMLEA if the employer has had 50 or more employees for each working day during each of twenty or more calendar workweeks in the current or preceding calendar year, as required by section 101(4)(A)(i) of the FMLA.

Section 826.152 provides that employees may file complaints alleging violations of the EPSLA and/or the EFMLEA with WHD.

Section 826.153 sets out the Secretary's investigative authority under the EPSLA and the EFMLEA. Under the EPSLA, the Secretary may investigate and gather data in the same manner as authorized by sections 9 and 11 of the FLSA. *See* 29 U.S.C. 209, 211. Under the EFMLEA, the Secretary may investigate and gather data in the same manner as authorized by sections 106(a) and (d) of the FMLA. *See* 29 U.S.C. 2616(a), (d). The provisions authorize, among other things, the Secretary to enter a workplace and have access to, inspect, and copy documents, and/or require witness attendance and testimony, relating to any matter under investigation, from any person or entity being investigated or proceeded against, at any stage of any proceeding or investigation, at any place in the United States. They also permit the Secretary to compel the production of relevant documents or testimony by subpoena as permitted by these provisions of law, including that in the event of any failure or refusal to comply with such a subpoena, the Secretary may obtain from any district court in the United States an order to compel production and/or testimony. Failure to obey such an order may be enforced through contempt proceedings.

P. Effect of Other Laws, Employer Practices, and Collective Bargaining Agreements

Section 826.160 discusses the effect of taking paid sick leave and expanded family and medical leave on other rights, benefits, employer practices, and collective bargaining agreements. The statutory provisions underlying this section appear in the EPSLA.

Section 826.160(a)(1) explains that an employee's entitlement to, or actual use of, paid sick leave is not grounds for diminishment, reduction, or elimination of any other right or benefit to which the employee is entitled under any other federal, state, or local law, under any collective bargaining agreement, or under any employer policy that existed prior to April 1, 2020. *See* 29 U.S.C. 2651(b), 2652. Paid sick leave is in addition to, and not a substitute for, other sources of leave which the employee had already accrued, was already entitled to, or had already used, before the EPSLA became effective on April 1, 2020. Therefore, neither eligibility for, nor use of, paid sick leave may count against an employee's balance or accrual of any other source or type of leave.

Section 826.160(a)(2) explains that an employer may not deny an employee paid sick leave or expanded family and medical leave on the grounds that the employee has already taken another type of leave or taken leave from another source, including leave taken for reasons related to COVID-19. Regardless of how much other leave an employee has taken up to the date he or she requests paid sick leave or expanded family and medical leave, the employer must permit the employee to immediately take any and all paid sick leave or expanded family and medical leave to which he or she is entitled and eligible under the EPSLA and the EFMLEA. However, the preceding analysis does not apply to or affect the FMLA's twelve workweeks within a twelve-month period cap.

The Department interprets "existing employer policy" in section 5107(1)(C) of the FFCRA to include a COVID-19 related offering of paid leave that the employer voluntarily issued prior to April 1, 2020, and under which employees were offered more paid leave than under the employer's standard or current policy. The Department acknowledges that some employers voluntarily offered and provided such leave to help their employees in this time of emergency. Nonetheless, the FFCRA still requires those employers to provide the entirety of the paid sick leave and expanded family and medical leave to which its employees are eligible, regardless of whether an employee took the additional paid leave the employer voluntarily offered. Doing so is necessary to ensure all eligible employees receive the full extent of paid sick leave and expanded family and medical leave to which they are entitled under the EPSLA and the EFMLEA. However, an employer may prospectively terminate such a voluntary additional paid leave offering as of April 1, 2020, or thereafter, provided that the employer had not already amended its leave policy to reflect the voluntary offering. This means the employer must pay employees for leave already taken under such an offering before it is terminated, but the employer need not continue the offering in light of the FFCRA taking effect.

Finally, the Department clarifies that employees do not have any right or entitlement to use paid sick leave or expanded family and medical leave retroactively, meaning they have no right or entitlement to be paid through paid sick leave or expanded family and medical leave for any unpaid or partially paid leave taken before April 1, 2020.

Section 826.160(b) explains the sequencing of paid sick leave with other types of leave. Pursuant to section 5102 of the FFRCA, an employee may choose to use paid sick leave prior to using any other type of paid leave to which he or she is entitled under any other Federal, State, or local law; collective bargaining agreement; or employer policy that existed prior to April 1, 2020. As this decision is at the employee's discretion, § 826.160(b)(2) clarifies that no employer shall require, coerce, or unduly influence an employee to use another source of paid leave before taking paid sick leave. Of course, an employer may not require or influence an employee to use unpaid leave prior to taking paid sick leave; doing so would be akin to denying or attempting to deny the employee the paid sick leave to which he or she is entitled.

Section 826.160(c) explains the sequencing of expanded family and medical leave with other types of leave. No employer shall require, coerce, or unduly influence an employee to use another source of paid leave before taking expanded family and medical leave. However, an eligible employee may elect to use, or an employer may require that an employee use, leave the employee has available under the employer's policies to care for a child, such as vacation or personal leave or paid time off, concurrently. If expanded family and medical leave is used concurrently with another source of paid leave, then the employer has to pay the employee the full amount to which the employee is entitled under the employer's preexisting paid leave policy for the period of leave taken, even if that amount is greater than $200 per day or $10,000 in the aggregate. But the employer's eligibility for tax credits is still limited to the cap of $200 per day or $10,000 in the aggregate.

Section 826.160(d)–(e) explains that an employer has no obligation to provide, and an employee has no right or entitlement to receive, financial compensation or other reimbursement for unused paid sick leave or unused expanded family and medical leave in the event the employee's employment ends after April 1, 2020, but before the FFCRA's expiration on December 31, 2020. Moreover, the Department interprets sections 5107(2) and 5109 of the FFCRA to mean that no employer has an obligation to provide, and no employee or former employee has a right or entitlement to receive, financial compensation or other reimbursement for unused paid sick leave or unused expanded family and medical leave upon or after the FFCRA's expiration on December 31, 2020.

Section 826.160(f) explains that any one individual employee is limited to a maximum of two weeks (80 hours) paid sick leave as described in § 826.160. Thus, the absolute upper limit of 80 hours of paid sick leave to which one could potentially be eligible is per person and not per job. Should an employee change positions during the period of time in which the paid sick leave is in effect, he or she is not entitled to a new round of paid sick leave. Once an employee takes the maximum 80 hours of paid sick leave, he or she is not entitled to any paid sick leave from a subsequent employer. If an employee changes positions before taking 80 hours of paid sick leave, then his or her new employer (if covered by FFCRA) must provide paid sick leave until the employee has taken 80 hours of paid sick leave total regardless of the employer providing it.

IV. Statutory and Regulatory Requirements

A. Administrative Procedure Act

This rule is issued without prior notice and opportunity to comment and with an immediate effective date pursuant to the Administrative Procedure Act (APA). 5 U.S.C. 553(b) and (d).

1. Good cause to forgo notice and comment rulemaking

The APA, 5 U.S.C. 553(b)(B), authorizes an agency to issue a rule without prior notice and opportunity to comment when the agency, for good cause, finds that those procedures are "impracticable, unnecessary, or contrary to the public interest." The FFCRA authorizes the Department to issue regulations under the EPSLA and the EFMLEA pursuant to the good cause exception of the APA. FFCRA sections 3102(b) (adding FMLA section 110(a)(3)), 5111.

The Department is bypassing advance notice and comment because of the exigency created by sections 3106 and 5108 of the FFCRA, which go into effect on April 1, 2020, and expire on December 31, 2020. The COVID-19 pandemic has escalated at a rapid pace and scale, leaving American families with difficult choices in balancing work, child care, and the need to seek medical attention for illness caused by the virus. To avoid economic harm to American families facing these conditions, a decision to undertake notice and comment rulemaking would likely delay final action on this matter by weeks or months, and would, therefore, complicate and likely preclude the Department from successfully exercising the authority created by sections 3106 and 5108. Moreover, such delay would be counter to one of the FFCRA's main purposes in establishing paid leave: enabling employees to leave the workplace now to help prevent the spread of COVID-19.

2. Good cause to proceed with an immediate effective date

The APA also authorizes agencies to make a rule effective immediately, upon a showing of good cause, instead of imposing a 30-day delay. 5 U.S.C. 553(d)(3). The FFCRA authorizes the Department to issue regulations that are effective immediately under the EPSLA and the EFMLEA pursuant to the good cause exception of the APA. FFCRA sections 3102(b) (adding FMLA section 110(a)(3)), 5111; CARES Act section 3611(1)–(2). For the reasons stated above, the Department has concluded it has good cause to make this temporary rule effective immediately and until the underlying statute sunsets on December 31, 2020.

B. Executive Order 12866, Regulatory Planning and Review; and Executive Order 13563, Improved Regulation and Regulatory Review

1. Introduction

Under E.O. 12866, OIRA determines whether a regulatory action is significant and therefore, subject to the requirements of the E.O. and OMB review. Section 3(f) of E.O. 12866 defines a "significant regulatory action" as an action that is likely to result in a rule that (1) has an annual effect on the economy of $100 million or more, or adversely affects in a material way a sector of the economy, productivity, competition, jobs, the environment, public health or safety, or state, local, or tribal governments or communities (also referred to as economically significant); (2) creates serious inconsistency or otherwise interferes with an action taken or planned by another agency; (3) materially alters the budgetary impacts of entitlement grants, user fees, or loan programs, or the rights and obligations of recipients thereof; or (4) raises novel legal or policy issues arising out of legal mandates, the President's priorities, or the principles set forth in the E.O. As described below, this temporary rule is economically significant. The Department has prepared a Regulatory Impact Analysis (RIA) in connection with this rule, as required under section 6(a)(3) of Executive Order 12866, and OMB has reviewed the rule. OIRA has designated this rule as a "major rule", as defined by 5 U.S.C. 804(2).

Executive Order 13563 directs agencies to propose or adopt a regulation only upon a reasoned determination that its benefits justify its costs; the regulation is tailored to impose the least burden on society, consistent with achieving the regulatory objectives; and in choosing among alternative regulatory approaches, the agency has selected those approaches that maximize net benefits. Executive Order 13563 recognizes that some benefits are difficult to quantify and provides that, where appropriate and permitted by law, agencies may consider and discuss qualitatively values that are difficult or impossible to quantify, including equity, human dignity, fairness, and distributive impacts.

2. Overview of the Rule

The rule implements the EPSLA and the EFMLEA, as modified by the CARES Act. The EPSLA requires that certain employers provide two workweeks (up to 80 hours) of paid sick leave to eligible employees who need to take leave from work for specified reasons. The EFMLEA requires that certain employers provide up to twelve weeks of expanded family and medical leave to eligible employees who need to take leave from work because the employee is caring for his or her son or daughter whose school or place of care is closed or child care provider is unavailable due to COVID-19 related reasons. Payments from employers to employees for such paid leave, as well as allocable costs related to the maintenance of health benefits during the period of the required leave, is to be reimbursed by the Department of the Treasury via tax credits, up to statutory limits, as provided under the FFCRA.

3. Economic Impacts

The Department estimated the number of affected employers and quantified the costs associated with this temporary rule. The paid sick leave and the expanded family and medical leave provisions of the FFCRA both apply to employers with fewer than 500 employees. The 2017 Statistics of U.S. Businesses (SUSB) reports that there are 5,976,761 private firms in the U.S. with fewer than 500 employees.[5] This temporary rule says that small employers with fewer than 50 employees may qualify for an exemption from the requirement to provide leave due to school or place of care closings or child care unavailability if the leave payments would jeopardize the viability of their business as a going concern. The 2017 SUSB reports that there are 5,755,307 private firms with fewer than 50 employees, representing 96 percent of all impacted firms (firms with fewer than 500 employees). The employers who are not able to qualify for the exemption discussed above are those with fewer than 500 employees but greater than or equal to 50 employees. Using the SUSB data mentioned above, the Department estimates that there are 221,454 firms that meet this criteria.

Although the rule exempts certain health care providers and emergency responders from the definition of eligible employee for purposes of the FFCRA, their employers may have some employees who do not meet this definition, so these employers may still be impacted by the provisions of the FFCRA.

The Department estimates that employees who work for employers with fewer than 500 employees could potentially benefit from this rule. According to the 2017 SUSB data, the 5,976,761 firms that meet this criteria employ 60,556,081 workers. Not all eligible employees will require use of the paid sick leave or expanded family and medical leave provisions of the FFCRA. The Department lacks data to determine how many employees will use this leave, which type of leave they will use and for what reason, and the wages of those who will use the leave.

Certain health care providers and emergency responders may be excluded from this group of impacted employees. The rule defines health care provider to include anyone employed at any doctor's office, hospital, health care center, clinic, post-secondary educational institution offering health care instruction, medical school, local health department or agency, nursing facility, retirement facility, nursing home, home health care provider, any facility that performs laboratory or medical testing, pharmacy, or any similar institution. According to the SUSB data mentioned above, employers with fewer than 500 employees in the health care and social assistance industry employ 9.0 million workers.[6] This estimate is likely to be the upper bound of potentially exempt health care industry workers, because it could include workers that may not be employed at an institution covered by the exemption. This estimate may not, however, include employees who provide services to the health care industry. The SUSB data does not include further industry breakouts, and so the Department is unable to determine the exact number of workers employed at these organizations with fewer than 500 employees.

The rule defines emergency responders as anyone necessary for the provision of transport, care, healthcare, comfort and nutrition of such patients, or others needed for the response to COVID-19. The rule provides a list of occupations that includes but is not limited to military or National Guard, law enforcement officers, cor-

[5] Statistics of U.S. Businesses 2017, *https://www.census.gov/data/tables/2017/econ/susb/2017-susb-annual.html*, 2017 SUSB Annual Data Tables by Establishment Industry.

[6] Statistics of U.S. Businesses 2017, *https://www.census.gov/data/tables/2017/econ/susb/2017-susb-annual.html*, 2017 SUSB Annual Data Tables by Establishment Industry.

rectional institution personnel, fire fighters, emergency medical services personnel, physicians, nurses, public health personnel, emergency medical technicians, paramedics, emergency management personnel, 911 operators, child welfare workers and service providers, and public works personnel. Because this list consists of occupations spread across various industries, the Department is unable to use the SUSB data to determine the magnitude of potential affected emergency responders. According to the May 2018 BLS Occupational Employment and Wages estimates, these occupations have a combined employment of 4.4 million.[7] This may be an over count or an under count of the potentially exempt emergency responders. The estimate may be an over count because it includes employees who work for employers of all sizes, not just those with fewer than 500 employees. The estimate may be an under count because it does not include military or national guard, as they are not counted in the OES estimates.

i. Costs

This temporary rule implementing the paid sick leave and expanded family and medical leave provisions of the FFCRA will result in four different categories of costs to employers: rule familiarization costs, documentation costs, costs of posting a notice, and other managerial and operating costs. The temporary rule will also result in increased costs to the Department to administer the rule and handle complaints and claims related to the provisions of the Acts.

a. Rule Familiarization Costs

The Department estimates that all employers with fewer than 500 employees will need to review the rule to determine their responsibilities. For those 5,755,307 employers with fewer than 50 employees, they will need to review the rule to determine what the rules are for all businesses, what the small employer exemptions are, and how to either comply or show that the requirements of the rule would jeopardize the viability of their business. The Department estimates that these small employers will likely spend one hour to understand their responsibilities under the rule. For the 221,454 employers with fewer than 500 employees, but greater than or equal to 50 employees, they will likely need to spend one hour to read the rule and determine their responsibilities to provide paid sick leave and expanded family and medical leave. The Department estimates that this will be a one-time rule familiarization cost, as the provisions of the Act sunset on December 31, 2020.

The Department's analysis assumes that the rule would be reviewed by Compensation, Benefits, and Job Analysis Specialists (SOC 13-1141) or employees of similar status and comparable pay. The median hourly wage for these workers is $30.29 per hour.[8] In addition, the Department also assumes that benefits are paid at a rate of 46 percent[9] and overhead costs are paid at a rate of 17 percent of the base wage, resulting in a fully-loaded hourly wage of $49.37.[10] The Department estimates that the total rule familiarization cost to employers with fewer than 50 employees, who spend one hour reviewing the rule, will be $284,139,507 (5,755,307 firms × 1 hour × $49.37). The Department estimates that the total rule familiarization cost to employers with greater than or equal to 50 but fewer than 500 employees will be $10,933,184 (221,454 firms × 1 hour × $49.37). Total rule familiarization costs for all impacted firms will therefore be $295,072,691.

b. Costs of Documentation

Employers with fewer than 50 employees are able to be exempt from providing paid sick leave for child care purposes and expanded family and medical leave under the FFCRA if they are able to show that complying with the requirements would jeopardize the viability of their business as a going concern. These employers will need to demonstrate this burden, and to show that they are exempt. These small employers must document the facts and circumstances to demonstrate this burden if they have employees who are requesting paid sick leave or expanded family and medical leave. Although the employers are not required to send such material or documentation to the Department, they are required to retain such records for their own files. Some employers will not qualify for the exemption. The Department lacks specific data to estimate the number of small employers who will use the exemption, but the Department assumes that until the end of the year, potentially up to 10 percent of these 5,755,307 employers (575,531) will likely document that the requirements of the Act will jeopardize the viability of their businesses. The Department estimates that each of these employers will spend one hour for creating and documenting these records. Costs of documentation for these small employers will therefore be $28,413,965 (575,531 firms × 1 hour × $49.37).

Employers are required to retain all records or documentation provided by the employee prior to taking paid sick leave or expanded family and medical leave. When employees take expanded family and medical leave, employees must pro-

[7] Occupational Employment and Wages, May 2018, *https://www.bls.gov/oes/2018/may/oes131141.htm*. The Department used SOC codes 29-1060 (Physicians and Surgeons), 29-1141 (Registered Nurses), 29-1171 (Nurse Practitioners), 29-2041 (Emergency Medical Technicians and Paramedics), 33-2000 (Fire Fighting and Prevention Workers), and 33-3000 (Law Enforcement Workers), to represent the occupations listed in the rule.

[8] Occupational Employment and Wages, May 2018, *https://www.bls.gov/oes/2018/may/oes131141.htm*.

[9] The benefits-earnings ratio is derived from the Bureau of Labor Statistics' Employer Costs for Employee Compensation data using variables CMU1020000000000D and CMU1030000000000D.

[10] $30.29 + $30.29(0.46) + $30.29(0.17) = $49.37

vide their employers with appropriate documentation in support of such leave. Employers must retain this documentation, as it may be required for tax credits and other purposes under the FFCRA. For the 221,454 employers with between 50 and 500 employees, the Department estimates that they will spend an additional one hour, on average, on documentation associated with this rule. For the 5,755,307 employers with fewer than 50 employees, the Department assumes that they will spend 30 minutes, on average, on documentation associated with this rule. The time spent by small employers will be lower because they have fewer employees, and some of them will be able to use the small business exemption from the requirement to provide leave due to school or childcare closings. The Department believes an average of one hour or 30 minutes is appropriate for the year, because some employers will not have any employees that will request leave, so will therefore not need any documentation, while other employers will have multiple employees requesting this leave. Documentation costs for these employers will therefore be \$153,002,937 (5,755,307 × 0.5 hours × \$49.37) + (221,454 × 1 hour × \$49.37).

Total documentation costs for employers of all sizes are therefore estimated to be \$181,416,902 (\$28,413,965 + \$153,002,937).

c. Costs of Posting a Notice

Section 5103(a) of the FFCRA requires employers to post a notice to inform their employees of the requirements of the EPSLA. The notice must be posted in a conspicuous place on the premises of the employer where notices to employees are customarily posted, or emailed or direct mailed to employees, or posted electronically on an employee information internal or external website. All employers covered by the paid sick leave and expanded family and medical leave provisions of the FFCRA are required to post this notice. The Department estimates that all 5,976,761 employers with fewer than 500 employees will post this notice, and that 99 percent of employers (5,916,993) will post the information electronically while 1 percent (59,768) will physically post the notice on employee bulletin boards. The Department estimates that it will take 15 minutes (or 0.25 hours) for employers posting the provision electronically to prepare and post the provision, and it will take 75 minutes (or 1.25 hours) for employers posting the notice manually to prepare the notice and post it in a conspicuous place where notices to employees are customarily posted. Employers who post electronically will incur a one-time cost of \$73,030,486 (5,916,993 × 0.25 × \$49.37) and those who physically post the notice will incur a one-time cost of \$3,688,433 (59,768 × 1.25 × \$49.37). Therefore, the total cost of posting this notice will be \$76,718,919. Employers may also incur a small cost of manually producing the notices, including paper, printer ink, etc., but the Department believes that this cost will be minimal compared to the cost of the time spent preparing and posting the notice.

d. Other Managerial and Operating Costs

In order to comply with the paid sick leave and expanded family and medical leave provisions of the FFCRA, employers may incur additional managerial and operating costs that the Department is unable to quantify. For example, when employees require the use of this paid leave, employers will need to determine if their employees are eligible for the leave, and will need to calculate the amount that an employee should receive, and will need to make the adjustments to an employee's paycheck, and will also need to adjust bookkeeping practices to track the amount of leave used by an employee. Because the Department lacks data on how many employees will require either paid sick leave or expanded family and medical leave through the end of the year, the total managerial and operation costs incurred by employers cannot be quantified. However, for illustrative purposes, for each employee that requires the use of this leave, the Department estimates it will take an employer two hours to complete these additional tasks. If these tasks are performed by a Compensation, Benefits, and Job Analysis Specialist with a fully-loaded hourly wage of \$49.37, then the cost to each employer per employee requiring leave is \$98.74. The Department estimates that all 5,976,761 firms with fewer than 500 employees could potentially incur this cost, but is unable to determine the extent to which leave will be used by employees given the various eligibility requirements, and therefore cannot estimate the total managerial and operation costs incurred.

There are likely other costs to employers for which the Department is unable to quantify in part because the number of employees who will qualify for leave under the FFCRA and take such leave at each employer is unknown and because the productivity losses caused by employees taking leave likely vary by employer and for each individual employee, but which are discussed qualitatively here. The new paid leave provisions of the Act may result in an increase in the number of employees who take advantage of sick leave and family and medical leave, compared to the number of employees who would use leave absent the new provisions. When an employee takes leave, the overall productivity of the business likely will suffer (although there could be some offsetting productivity improvements if coworkers are less likely to become infected) and, in some instances, the business may face unique operational challenges which could hinder its ability to continue operations for the same duration or at the same capacity as before the employee(s) took leave. These costs are difficult to quantify, but likely will be significant, especially if a large number of employees are eligible for, and take, leave. These costs are not created specifically because of any unique features of this temporary rule, but are directly linked to the statute's leave provisions.

e. Costs to the Department

WHD will also incur costs associated with the paid sick leave and expanded family and medical leave provisions of the FFCRA. Prior to this Act, WHD had not enforced a comprehensive paid sick leave program applicable to a large segment of the U.S. workforce (minus the exemptions). WHD will incur the additional costs of setting up a new enforcement program, administering the program, and processing complaints associated with this new provision. The Department does not have data to assess this cost to the Department.

ii. Cost Summary

As discussed above, the quantified costs associated with the paid sick leave and expanded family and medical leave provisions of the FFCRA and with this temporary rule are rule familiarization costs, costs of documentation, and the cost of posting a notice. Table 1 summarizes all of these costs in 2018 dollars. The Department estimates that total costs in 2020 are $553 million.

Table 1. Costs

Rule Familiarization Costs	$295,072,691
Documentation Costs	$181,416,902
Cost of Posting a Notice	$76,718,919
Total Costs	**$553,208,512**

iii. Transfers

The transfers associated with this rule are the paid sick leave and expanded family and medical leave that employees will receive as a result of the FFCRA. The paid leave will initially be provided by employers, who will then be reimbursed by the Department of the Treasury through a tax credit, up to statutory limits, which is then ultimately paid for by taxpayers (although there may be some offsetting taxpayer effects due to statutory limits, which is then ultimately paid for by taxpayers' reduced reliance on social assistance programs). Such transfers may be reduced if employees opt to use or employers require that employees use certain pre-existing leave (*i.e.*, personal or vacation leave or paid time off) concurrently with any EFMLEA leave. As discussed above, the total number of employees who are potentially eligible for this leave is as high as 61 million, but the number of employees who will actually use the leave will be a smaller share of this total. The Department does not know to what extent employees will be exposed to COVID-19 themselves, will be subject to a Federal, State, or local quarantine, will be caring for an individual exposed to COVID-19, or will need to stay home to take care of a child out of school or child care (and unable to telework), and therefore does not know how many employees will require use of the paid leave provided in the Act. In order to quantify the potential transfer, the Department would need to determine the number of days of leave that would be taken, and the monetary value of those days of leave. The FFCRA requires employers to pay leave based on an employee's regular rate, so the Department would need to determine the regular rate of each employee who requests leave. This estimate could vary greatly depending on the occupations and industries of employees requesting leave. The share of the regular rate used to calculate the transfer would also depend on the reason for which an employee requires the use of paid leave. The Department would also need to determine the number of days each employee would take leave, the type of leave employees would take, and whether EFMLEA leave would run concurrently with certain previously-provided leave, all of which would vary depending on whether they are taking paid sick leave or expanded family and medical leave. If an employee requires the use of paid sick leave to self-quarantine, they will likely take the entire 80 hours allotted, because the CDC's guidelines recommend a quarantine period of two weeks. Additionally, an employee may take up to ten weeks of paid expanded family and medical leave to care for his or her child whose school or place of care is closed or child care provider is unavailable. For school districts that have closed through the end of the 2020 school year, it is likely that these parents would take the entire twelve week allotment. The Department lacks data to determine which employees will need leave, how many days of leave will ultimately be used, and how much pay employers will be required to provide for such leave. Although the Department is unable to quantify the transfer of paid leave, we expect that it is likely to exceed $100 million in 2020.

iv. Benefits

The benefits of the paid sick leave and expanded family and medical leave provisions of the FFCRA are vast, and although unable to be quantified, are expected to greatly outweigh any costs of these provisions. With the availability of paid leave, sick or potentially exposed workers will be encouraged to stay home, thereby helping to curb the spread of the virus and lessen the strain on hospitals and health care providers. If employees still receive pay while on leave, they will benefit from being able to cover necessary expenses, and to continue to spend money to help support the economy. This will have spillover effects not only on the individuals who receive pay while on leave, but also on their communities and the national economy as a whole, which is facing unique challenges due to the COVID-19 global pandemic.

The expanded family and medical leave provisions of the FFCRA will allow parents to care for their children who are out of school, or whose childcare provider is unavailable due to COVID-19 related reasons. This will allow parents to avoid extra childcare costs that they otherwise may have to incur.

Without this paid sick leave and expanded family and medical leave (that is, without the policy of tying some federal COVID-19 assistance to employment arrangements), there could be long-term costs in addition to the short term impacts listed above. For example, there could be substantial rehiring costs for employers when the public health concern has abated and, simultaneously, transition costs to workers as they restart their careers. A spillover effect of these frictions might be increased reliance on social assistance programs.

v. Regulatory Alternatives

The Department notes that the FFCRA delegates to the Secretary the authority to issue regulations to "exclude certain health care providers and emergency responders from the definition of eligible employee" under section 110(a)(1)(A) of the EFMLEA and 5110(1) of the EPSLA; "to exempt small businesses with fewer than 50 employees from the requirements" of section 102(a)(1)(F) of EFMLEA and 5102(a)(5) of the EPSLA "when the imposition of such requirements would jeopardize the viability of the business as a going concern"; and "as necessary to carry out the purposes of the EPSLA to ensure consistency between it and Division C and Division G of the FFCRA."

Because the FFCRA itself establishes the basic expanded family and medical leave and paid sick leave requirements that the Department is responsible for implementing, many potential regulatory alternatives would be beyond the scope of the Department's authority in issuing this temporary rule. The Department considered two regulatory alternatives to determine the correct balance between providing benefits to employees and imposing compliance costs on covered employers. This section presents the two alternatives to the provisions set forth in this temporary rule.

The Department considered one regulatory alternative that would be less restrictive than what is currently being issued and two that would be more restrictive. For the less-restrictive option, the Department considered excluding all small businesses with fewer than 50 employees from the requirements of the FFCRA, assuming that any requirement to provide expanded family and medical leave or paid sick leave for child care to their employees would jeopardize the viability of those small businesses. The Department concluded, however, that requiring small businesses to demonstrate that the viability of their business will be jeopardized if they have to provide paid leave would ensure uniformity among these employers, help the Department administer sections 102(a)(1)(F) of FMLA and 5102(a)(5) of the EPSLA, and would best conform to the FFCRA.

For the first more restrictive alternative, the Department considered requiring small businesses with fewer than 50 employees to maintain formal records in order to demonstrate a need for exemption from the rule's requirements. The Department concluded, however, that this requirement would be unnecessarily onerous for these employers, particularly given that they are not otherwise subject to the FMLA. The Department believes that the requirements issued in this temporary rule will ensure that small employers have the flexibility they need to balance their staffing and business needs during the COVID-19 public health emergency.

For the second more restrictive alternative, the Department considered using a more narrow definition of health care provider and emergency responder for purposes of excluding such employees from the EPSLA's paid sick leave requirements and/or the EFMLEA's expanded family and medical leave requirements. The Department considered only allowing employers to exclude those workers who directly work with COVID-19 patients, but felt that such a limitation would not provide sufficient flexibility to the health care community to make necessary staffing decisions to address the COVID-19 public health emergency. Further, a more narrow definition could leave health care facilities without staff to perform critical services needed to battle COVID-19.

C. Regulatory Flexibility Analysis

The Regulatory Flexibility Act of 1980 (RFA), 5 U.S.C. 601 *et seq.*, as amended by the Small Business Regulatory Enforcement Fairness Act of 1996, Public Law 104-121 (March 29, 1996), requires federal agencies engaged in rulemaking to consider the impact of their proposals on small entities, consider alternatives to minimize that impact, and solicit public comment on their analyses. The RFA requires the assessment of the impact of a regulation on a wide range of small entities, including small businesses, not-for-profit organizations, and small governmental jurisdictions. Agencies must perform a review to determine whether a proposed or final rule would have a significant economic impact on a substantial number of small entities. 5 U.S.C. 603 and 604.

As discussed above, the Department calculated rule familiarization costs, documentation costs, and the cost of posting a notice for all employers with fewer than 500 employees. For employers with fewer than 50 employees, their one-time rule familiarization cost would be $49.37. Their cost for documentation would be $24.69, and the cost of posting a notice would be $12.84. Total cost to these employers would be $111.58. An additional ten percent of employers with fewer than 50 employees will have an additional documentation cost of $49.37 for qualifying for the small employer exemption, bringing their total cost to $160.95. For employers with at least 50 employees but fewer than 500 employees, their one-time rule familiarization cost would be $49.37. Their cost for documentation would be $49.37, and the cost of posting a notice would be $12.84. The average managerial and operational cost to an employer would be $98.74. Total cost to these employers would be $210.32. These estimated costs will be minimal for small business entities, and will be well below one percent of their gross annual revenues, which is typically at least $100,000 per year for the smallest businesses. Based on this determination, the Department certifies that the rule will not have a significant economic impact on a substantial number of small entities.

D. Unfunded Mandates Reform Act of 1995

The Unfunded Mandates Reform Act of 1995 (UMRA) requires agencies to prepare a written statement for rules that include any federal mandate that may result in increased expenditures by state, local, and tribal governments, in the aggregate, or by the private sector, of $165 million ($100 million in 1995 dollars adjusted for inflation using the CPI-U) or more in at least one year. This statement must: (1) identify the authorizing legislation; (2) present the estimated costs and benefits of the rule and, to the extent that such estimates are feasible and relevant, its estimated effects on the national economy; (3) summarize and evaluate state, local, and tribal government input; and (4) identify reasonable alternatives and select, or explain the non-selection, of the least costly, most cost-effective, or least burdensome alternative.

1) Authorizing legislation

This rule is issued pursuant to the FFCRA.

2) Assessment of Quantified Costs and Benefits

For purposes of the UMRA, this rule includes a federal mandate that is expected to result in increased expenditures of more than $165 million in the first year. Based on the cost analysis in this temporary rule, the Department determined that the rule will result in Year 1 total costs for rule familiarization, documentation, and posting of notices totaling $553 million (*see* Table 1). There will be no additional costs incurred in subsequent years.

UMRA requires agencies to estimate the effect of a regulation on the national economy if, at its discretion, such estimates are reasonably feasible and the effect is relevant and material.[11] However, OMB guidance on this requirement notes that such macroeconomic effects tend to be measurable in nationwide econometric models only if the economic effect of the regulation reaches 0.25 percent to 0.5 percent of GDP, or in the range of $51.5 billion to $102.9 billion (using 2018 GDP). A regulation with smaller aggregate effect is not likely to have a measurable effect in macroeconomic terms unless it is highly focused on a particular geographic region or economic sector, which is not the case with this rule. Given OMB's guidance, the Department has determined that a full macroeconomic analysis is not likely to show that these costs would have any measurable effect on the economy.

3) Least Burdensome Option Explained

The Department believes that it has chosen the least burdensome option given the FFCRA's provisions. Although the Department is requiring small employers with fewer than 50 employees to maintain formal records in order to demonstrate a need for exemption from the rule's requirements they are not required to provide any documents to the Department. The Department believes that the requirements issued in this temporary rule will ensure that small employers have the flexibility they need to balance their staffing and business needs during the COVID-19 pandemic.

E. Executive Order 13132 (Federalism)

This rule does not have substantial direct effects on the States, on the relationship between the National Government and the States, or on the distribution of power and responsibilities among the various levels of government. Therefore, in accordance with section 6 of Executive Order No. 13132, 64 FR 43255 (Aug. 4, 1999), this rule does not have sufficient federalism implications to warrant the preparation of a federalism summary impact statement.

F. Executive Order 13175, Indian Tribal Governments

This rule would not have substantial direct effects on one or more Indian tribes, on the relationship between the Federal Government and Indian tribes, or on the distribution of power and responsibilities between the Federal Government and Indian tribes.

G. Paperwork Reduction Act

The Paperwork Reduction Act of 1995 (PRA), 44 U.S.C. 3501 *et seq.*, and its attendant regulations, 5 CFR Part 1320, require the Department to consider the agency's need for its information collections, their practical utility, as well as the impact of paperwork and other information collection burdens imposed on the public, and how to minimize those burdens. The Department is seeking emergency approval related to the collection of information described herein. Persons are not required to respond to the information collection requirements until OMB approves them under the PRA. This temporary rule creates a new information collection specific to paid leave under the FFCRA. The Department has created a new information collection request and submitted the request to OMB for approval under OMB control number 1235-0NEW (Paid Leave under the Families First Coronavirus Response Act) for this action.

Summary: Section 826.140(a) requires covered employer to document and retain information submitted by an employees to support requests for paid sick leave and expanded family and medical leave. Section 826.140(a) further requires any employer that denies a request for leave pursuant to the small business exemption under § 826.40(b) must document and retain the determination by its authorizing officer that it meets

[11] *See* 2 U.S.C. 1532(a)(4).

the criteria for that exemption. Finally, §826.140(c) advises, but does not require, employers to create and maintain certain records for the purpose of obtaining a tax credit from the Internal Revenue Service.

Purpose and Use: WHD and employees use employer records to determine whether covered employers have complied with various requirements under the FFCRA. Employers use the records to document compliance with the FFCRA.

Technology: The regulations prescribe no particular order or form of records, and employers may preserve records in forms of their choosing, provided that facilities are available for inspection and transcription of the records.

Minimizing Small Entity Burden: Although the FLSA recordkeeping requirements do involve small businesses, including small state and local government agencies, the Department minimizes respondent burden by requiring no specific order or form of records in responding to this information collection.

Total annual burden estimates, which reflect the new responses for the recordkeeping information collection, are summarized as follows:

Type of Review: Approval of a new collection.

Agency: Wage and Hour Division, Department of Labor.

Title: Paid Leave under the Families First Coronavirus Response Act.

OMB Control Number: 1235-0NEW.

Affected Public: Private Sector: businesses or other for-profits, farms, and not-for-profit institutions: State, Local and Tribal governments; and individuals or households.

Estimated Number of Respondents: 9,895,325

Estimated Number of Responses: 9,895,325

Estimated Burden Hours: 2,794,216 hours

Estimated Time per Response: Various

Frequency: Various

Other Burden Cost: $4,255,500 (operations/maintenance)

List of Subjects in 29 CFR Part 826

Wages.

Signed at Washington, D.C. this 1st day of April, 2020.

Cheryl M. Stanton,

Administrator, Wage and Hour Division.

[¶9001]

§826.10 General.

(a) *Definitions*. For the purposes of this rule:

Child Care Provider. The term "Child Care Provider" means a provider who receives compensation for providing child care services on a regular basis. The term includes a center-based child care provider, a group home child care provider, a family child care provider, or other provider of child care services for compensation that is licensed, regulated, or registered under State law as described in section 9858c(c)(2)(E) of Title 42; and satisfies the State and local requirements, including those referred to in section 9858c(c)(2)(F) of Title 42. Under the Families First Coronavirus Response Act (FFCRA), the eligible child care provider need not be compensated or licensed if he or she is a family member or friend, such as a neighbor, who regularly cares for the Employee's child.

Commerce. The terms "Commerce" and "industry or activity affecting commerce" mean any activity, business, or industry in commerce or in which a labor dispute would hinder or obstruct commerce or the free flow of commerce, and include "commerce", and any "industry affecting commerce", as defined in paragraphs (1) and (3) of section 501 of the Labor Management Relations Act of 1947 (29 U.S.C. 142 (1) and (3)).

COVID-19. The term "COVID-19" has the meaning given the term in section 506 of the Coronavirus Preparedness Response Supplemental Appropriations Act, 2020.

EFMLEA. The term "EFMLEA" means the Emergency Family and Medical Leave Expansion Act, Division C of the FFCRA.

Employee. The term "Employee" has the same meaning given that term in section 3(e) of the Fair Labor Standards Act of 1938 (FLSA) (29 U.S.C. 203(e)).

Eligible Employee. For the purposes of the EFMLEA, the term "Eligible Employee" means an Employee who has been employed for at least 30 calendar days by the Employer.

Employer:

(i) Subject to paragraph (ii) of this definition, "Employer":

(A) Means any person engaged in Commerce or in any industry or activity affecting commerce that:

(1) In the case of a private entity or individual, employs fewer than 500 Employees; and

(2) In the case of a Public Agency or any other entity that is not a private entity or individual, employs one or more Employees;

(B) Includes:

(1) Any person acting directly or indirectly in the interest of an employer in relation to an Employee (within the meaning of such phrase in section 3(d) of the FLSA (29 U.S.C. 203(d));

(2) Any successor in interest of an employer;

(3) Joint employers as defined under the FLSA, 29 CFR Part 791 of this chapter, with respect to certain Employees; and

(4) Integrated employers as defined under the Family and Medical Leave Act (FMLA), § 825.104(c)(2) of this chapter.

(C) Includes any Public Agency; and

(D) Includes the Government Accountability Office and the Library of Congress.

(ii) For purposes of the EPSLA, "Employer" also specifically identifies the following as an employer:

(A) An entity employing a State Employee described in section 304(a) of the Government Employee Rights Act of 1991;

(B) An employing office, as defined in section 101 of the Congressional Accountability Act of 1995;

(C) An employing office, as defined in 3 U.S.C. 411(c); and

(D) An Executive Agency as defined in section 5 U.S.C. 105, and including the U.S. Postal Service and the Postal Regulatory Commission.

EPSLA. The term "EPSLA" means the Emergency Paid Sick Leave Act, Division E of the FFCRA.

Expanded Family and Medical Leave. The term "Expanded Family and Medical Leave" means paid leave under the EFMLEA.

FFCRA. The term "FFCRA" means the Families First Coronavirus Response Act, Public Law 116-127.

FLSA Terms. The terms "employ", "person", and "State" have the meanings given such terms in section 3 of the FLSA (29 U.S.C. 203).

Paid Sick Leave. The term "Paid Sick Leave" means paid leave under the EPSLA.

Place of Care. The term "Place of Care" means a physical location in which care is provided for the Employee's child while the Employee works for the Employer. The physical location does not have to be solely dedicated to such care. Examples include day care facilities, preschools, before and after school care programs, schools, homes, summer camps, summer enrichment programs, and respite care programs.

Public Agency. The term "Public Agency" means the Government of the United States; the government of a State or political subdivision thereof; any agency of the United States (including the United States Postal Service and Postal Regulatory Commission), a State, or a political subdivision of a State; or any interstate governmental agency. *See* 29 U.S.C. 203(x); 29 U.S.C. 5110(2)(B)(i)(III). A Public Agency shall be considered to be a person engaged in Commerce or in an industry or activity affecting Commerce. *See* 29 U.S.C. 2611(4)(B); 29 U.S.C. 5110(2)(B)(ii). Whether an entity is a Public Agency, as distinguished from a private Employer, is determined by whether the agency has taxing authority, or whether the chief administrative officer or board, etc., is elected by the voters-at-large or their appointment is subject to approval by an elected official. *See* § 825.108 of this chapter.

Public Health Emergency. The term "Public Health Emergency" means an emergency with respect to COVID-19 declared by a Federal, State, or local authority.

School. The term "School" means an "elementary school" or "secondary school" as such terms are defined below, in accordance with section 8101 of the Elementary and Secondary Education Act of 1965 (20 U.S.C. 7801). "Elementary school" means a nonprofit institutional day or residential school, including a public elementary charter school that provides elementary education, as determined under State law. "Secondary school" means a nonprofit institutional day or residential school, including a public secondary charter school that provides secondary education, as determined under State law, except that the term does not include any education beyond grade 12.

Secretary. The term "Secretary" means the Secretary of Labor or his or her designee.

Son or Daughter. The term "Son or Daughter" has the meaning given such term in section 101 of the FMLA (29 U.S.C. 2611). Accordingly, the term means a biological, adopted, or foster child, a stepchild, a legal ward, or a child of a person standing *in loco parentis*, who is under 18 years of age; or 18 years of age or older who is incapable of self-care because of a mental or physical disability.

Subject to a Quarantine or Isolation Order. For the purposes of the EPSLA, a quarantine or isolation order includes quarantine, isolation, containment, shelter-in-place, or stay-at-home orders issued by any Federal, State, or local government authority that cause the Employee to be unable to work even though his or her Employer has work that the Employee could perform but for the order. This also includes when a Federal, State, or local government authority has advised categories of citizens (*e.g.*, of certain age ranges or of certain medical conditions) to shelter in place, stay at home, isolate, or quarantine, causing those categories of Employees to be unable to work even though their Employers have work for them.

Telework. The term "Telework" means work the Employer permits or allows an Employee to perform while the Employee is at home or at a location other than the Employee's normal workplace. An Employee is able to Telework if: (a) his or her Employer has work for the Employee; (b) the Employer permits the Employee to work from the Employee's location; and (c) there are no extenuating circumstances (such as serious COVID-19 symptoms) that prevent the Employee from performing that work. Telework may be performed during normal hours or at other times agreed by the Employer and Employee. Telework is work for which wages must be paid as required by applicable law and is not compensated as paid leave under the EPSLA or the EFMLEA. Employees who are teleworking for COVID-19 related reasons must be compensated for all hours actually worked and which the Employer knew or should have known were worked by the Employee. However, the provisions of § 790.6 of this chapter shall not apply to Employees while they are teleworking for COVID-19 related reasons.

(b) *Effective period.* (1) This part becomes effective on April 1, 2020.

(2) This part expires on December 31, 2020.

[85 FR 20156, Apr. 10, 2020]

[¶9002]

§826.20 Paid Leave Entitlements.

(a) *Qualifying reasons for Paid Sick Leave.* (1) An Employer shall provide to each of its Employees Paid Sick Leave to the extent that Employee is unable to work due to any of the following reasons:

(i) The Employee is subject to a Federal, State, or local quarantine or isolation order related to COVID-19;

(ii) The Employee has been advised by a health care provider to selfquarantine due to concerns related to COVID-19;

(iii) The Employee is experiencing symptoms of COVID-19 and seeking medical diagnosis from a health care provider;

(iv) The Employee is caring for an individual who is subject to an order as described in this paragraph (a)(1)(i) or directed as described in this paragraph (a)(1)(ii);

(v) The Employee is caring for his or her Son or Daughter whose School or Place of Care has been closed for a period of time, whether by order of a State or local official or authority or at the decision of the individual School or Place of Care, or the Child Care Provider of such Son or Daughter is unavailable, for reasons related to COVID-19; or

(vi) The Employee has a substantially similar condition as specified by the Secretary of Health and Human Services, in consultation with the Secretary of the Treasury and the Secretary of Labor. The substantially similar condition may be defined at any point during the Effective Period, April 1, 2020, to December 31, 2020.

(2) *Subject to a Quarantine or Isolation Order.* Any Employee Subject to a Quarantine or Isolation Order may take Paid Sick Leave for the reason described in paragraph (a)(1)(i) of this section only if, but for being subject to the order, he or she would be able to perform work that is otherwise allowed or permitted by his or her Employer, either at the Employee's normal workplace or by Telework. An Employee Subject to a Quarantine or Isolation Order may not take Paid Sick Leave where the Employer does not have work for the Employee as a result of the order or other circumstances.

(3) *Advised by a health care provider to self-quarantine.* For the purposes of this section, the term health care provider has the same meaning as that term is defined in § 825.102 of this chapter. An Employee may take Paid Sick Leave for the reason described in paragraph (1)(ii) of this section only if:

(i) A health care provider advises the Employee to self-quarantine based on a belief that—

(A) The Employee has COVID-19;

(B) The Employee may have COVID-19; or

(C) The Employee is particularly vulnerable to COVID-19; and

(ii) Following the advice of a health care provider to self-quarantine prevents the Employee from being able to work, either at the Employee's normal workplace or by Telework.

(4) *Seeking medical diagnosis for COVID-19.* An Employee may take Paid Sick Leave for the reason described in paragraph (1)(iii) of this section if the Employee is experiencing any of the following symptoms:

(i) Fever;

(ii) Dry cough;

(iii) Shortness of breath; or

(iv) Any other COVID-19 symptoms identified by the U.S. Centers for Disease Control and Prevention.

(v) Any Paid Sick Leave taken for the reason described in paragraph (1)(iii) of this subsection is limited to time the Employee is unable to work because the Employee is taking affirmative steps to obtain a medical diagnosis, such as making, waiting for, or attending an appointment for a test for COVID-19.

(5) *Caring for an individual.* For the purpose of paragraph (1)(iv) of this section, "individual" means an Employee's immediate family member, a person who regularly resides in the Employee's home, or a similar person with whom the Employee has a relationship that creates an expectation that the Employee would care for the person if he or she were quarantined or self-quarantined. For this purpose, "individual" does not include persons with whom the Employee has no personal relationship.

(6) An Employee may not take Paid Sick Leave for the reason described in paragraph (1)(iv) of this section unless, but for a need to care for an individual, the Employee would be able to perform work for his or her Employer, either at the Employee's normal workplace or by Telework. An Employee caring for an individual may not take Paid Sick Leave where the Employer does not have work for the Employee.

(7) *Caring for an individual.* An Employee may take Paid Sick Leave for the reason described in paragraph (a)(1)(iv) of this section if the Employee is unable to perform work for his or her Employer and if the individual depends on the Employee to care for him or her and is either:

(i) Subject to a Quarantine or Isolation Order as described in paragraph (a)(1)(i) of this section; or

(ii) Has been advised to self-quarantine by a health care provider because of a belief that—

(A) The individual has COVID-19;

(B) The individual may have COVID-19 due to known exposure or symptoms; or

(C) The individual is particularly vulnerable to COVID-19.

(8) *Caring for a Son or Daughter.* An Employee has a need to take Paid Sick Leave if he or she is unable to work due to a need to care for his or her Son or Daughter whose School or Place of Care has been closed, or whose Child Care Provider is unavailable, for reasons related to COVID-19 only if no other suitable person is

available to care for the Son or Daughter during the period of such leave.

(9) An Employee may not take Paid Sick Leave to care for his or her Son or Daughter unless, but for a need to care for an individual, the Employee would be able to perform work for his or her Employer, either at the Employee's normal workplace or by Telework. An Employee caring for his or her Son or Daughter may not take Paid Sick Leave where the Employer does not have work for the Employee.

(b) *Qualifying reason for Expanded Family and Medical Leave.* An Eligible Employee may take Expanded Family and Medical Leave because he or she is unable to work due to a need to care for his or her Son or Daughter whose School or Place of Care has been closed, or whose Child Care Provider is unavailable, for reasons related to COVID-19. An Eligible Employee has need to take Expanded Family and Medical Leave for the purposes of this paragraph (b) only if no suitable person is available to care for his or her Son or Daughter during the period of such leave.

(1) An Eligible Employee may not take Expanded Family and Medical Leave to care for his or her Son or Daughter unless, but for a need to care for an individual, the Eligible Employee would be able to perform work for his or her Employer, either at the Eligible Employee's normal workplace or by Telework. An Eligible Employee caring for his or her Son or Daughter may not take Expanded Family and Medical Leave where the Employer does not have work for the Eligible Employee.

(2) [Reserved]

(c) *Impact on FLSA exemptions.* The taking of Paid Sick Leave or Expanded Family and Medical Leave shall not impact an Employee's status or eligibility for any exemption from the requirements of section 6 or 7, or both, of the FLSA.

[85 FR 20156, Apr. 10, 2020]

[¶ 9003]

§ 826.21 Amount of Paid Sick Leave.

(a) *Full-time Employees.* (1) A full-time Employee is entitled to up to 80 hours of Paid Sick Leave.

(2) An Employee is considered to be a full-time Employee under this section if he or she is normally scheduled to work at least 40 hours each workweek.

(3) An Employee who does not have a normal weekly schedule under § 826.21(a)(2) is considered to be a full-time Employee under this section if the average number of hours per workweek that the Employee was scheduled to work, including hours for which the Employee took leave of any type, is at least 40 hours per workweek over a period of time that is the lesser of:

(i) The six-month period ending on the date on which the Employee takes Paid Sick Leave; or

(ii) The entire period of the Employee's employment.

(b) *Part-time Employees.* An Employee who does not satisfy the requirements of § 826.21(a) is considered to be a part-time Employee.

(1) If the part-time Employee has a normal weekly schedule, the Employee is entitled to up to the number of hours of Paid Sick Leave equal to the number of hours that the Employee is normally scheduled to work over two workweeks.

(2) If the part-time Employee lacks a normal weekly schedule under § 826.21(b)(1), the number of hours of Paid Sick Leave to which the Employee is entitled is calculated as follows:

(i) If the part-time Employee has been employed for at least six months, the Employee is entitled to up to the number of hours of Paid Sick Leave equal to fourteen times the average number of hours that the Employee was scheduled to work each calendar day over the six-month period ending on the date on which the Employee takes Paid Sick Leave, including any hours for which the Employee took leave of any type.

(ii) If the part-time Employee has been employed for fewer than six months, the Employee is entitled to up to the number of hours of Paid Sick Leave equal to fourteen times the number of hours the Employee and the Employer agreed to at the time of hiring that the Employee would work, on average, each calendar day. If there is no such agreement, the Employee is entitled to up to the number of hours of Paid Sick Leave equal to fourteen times the average number of hours per calendar day that the Employee was scheduled to work over the entire period of employment, including hours for which the Employee took leave of any type.

[¶ 9004]

§ 826.22 Amount of Pay for Paid Sick Leave.

(a) Subject to paragraph (c) of this section, for each hour of Paid Sick Leave taken by an Employee for qualifying reasons set forth in § 826.20(a)(1)(i) through (iii), the Employer shall pay the higher of:

(1) The Employee's average regular rate as computed under § 826.25;

(2) The Federal minimum wage to which the Employee is entitled; or

(3) Any State or local minimum wage to which the Employee is entitled.

(b) Subject to paragraph (c) of this section, for each hour of Paid Sick Leave taken by an Employee for qualifying reasons set forth in § 826.20(a)(1)(iv) through (vi), the Employer shall pay the Employee two-thirds of the amount described in § 826.24(a).

(c) The limitations on payments are as follows:

(1) In no event shall an Employer be required to pay more than $511 per day and $5,110 in the aggregate per Employee when an Employee takes Paid Sick Leave for qualifying reasons set forth in § 826.20(a)(1)(i) through (iii).

(2) In no event shall an Employer be required to pay more than $200 per day and $2,000 in the aggregate per Employee when an Employee takes Paid Sick Leave for qualifying reasons set forth in § 826.20(a)(1)(iv) through (vi).

[85 FR 20156, Apr. 10, 2020]

[¶9005]

§826.23 Amount of Expanded Family and Medical Leave.

(a) An Eligible Employee is entitled to take up to twelve workweeks of Expanded Family and Medical Leave during the period April 1, 2020 through December 31, 2020.

(b) Any time period of Expanded Family and Medical Leave that an Eligible Employee takes counts towards the twelve workweeks of FMLA leave to which the Eligible Employee is entitled for any qualifying reason in a twelve-month period under § 825.200 of this chapter, *see* § 826.70.

(c) Section 2612(d)(2)(A) of the FMLA shall be applied, provided however, that the Eligible Employee may elect, and the Employer may require the Eligible Employee, to use only leave that would be available to the Eligible Employee for the purpose set forth in § 826.20(b) under the Employer's existing policies, such as personal leave or paid time off. Any leave that an Eligible Employee elects to use or that an Employer requires the Eligible Employee to use would run concurrently with Expanded Family and Medical Leave taken under this section.

[¶9006]

§826.24 Amount of Pay for Expanded Family and Medical Leave.

Subject to § 826.60, after the initial two weeks of Expanded Family and Medical Leave, the Employer shall pay the Eligible Employee two-thirds of the Eligible Employee's average regular rate, as computed under § 826.25, times the Eligible Employee's scheduled number of hours for each day of such leave taken.

(a) In no event shall an Employer be required to pay more than $200 per day and $10,000 in the aggregate per Eligible Employee when an Eligible Employee takes Expanded Family and Medical Leave for up to ten weeks after the initial two-week period of unpaid Expanded Family and Medical Leave.

(b) For the purpose of § 826.24, the "scheduled number of hours" is determined as follows:

(1) If the Eligible Employee has a normal work schedule, the number of hours the Eligible Employee is normally scheduled to work on that workday;

(2) If the Eligible Employee has a work schedule that varies to such an extent that an Employer is unable to determine the number of hours the Eligible Employee would have worked on the day for which leave is taken and has been employed for at least six months, the average number of hours the Eligible Employee was scheduled to work each workday, over the six-month period ending on the date on which the Eligible Employee first takes Expanded Family and Medical Leave, including hours for which the Eligible Employee took leave of any type; or

(3) If the Eligible Employee has a work schedule that varies to such an extent that an Employer is unable to determine the number of hours the Eligible Employee would have worked on the day for which leave is taken and the Eligible Employee has been employed for fewer than six months, the average number of hours the Eligible Employee and the Employer agreed at the time of hiring that the Eligible Employee would work each workday. If there is no such agreement, the scheduled number of hours is equal to the average number of hours per workday that the Eligible Employee was scheduled to work over the entire period of employment, including hours for which the Eligible Employee took leave of any type.

(c) As an alternative, the amount of pay for Expanded Family and Medical Leave may be computed in hourly increments instead a full day. For each hour of Expanded Family and Medical Leave taken after the first two weeks, the Employer shall pay the Eligible Employee two-thirds of the Eligible Employee's average regular rate, as computed under § 826.25.

(d) Notwithstanding paragraph (a) of this section, if an Eligible Employee elects or is required to use leave available to the Eligible Employee for the purpose set forth in § 826.20(b) under the Employer's policies, such as vacation or personal leave or paid time off, concurrently with Expanded Family and Medical Leave, the Employer must pay the Eligible Employee a full day's pay for that day. However, the Employer is capped at taking $200 a day or $10,000 in the aggregate in tax credits for Expanded Family and Medical Leave paid under the EFMLEA.

[¶9007]

§826.25 Calculating the Regular Rate under the Family First Coronavirus Response Act.

(a) *Average regular rate.* The "average regular rate" used to compute pay for Paid Sick Leave and Expanded Family and Medical Leave is calculated as follows:

(1) Use the methods contained in 29 CFR Parts 531 and 778 of this chapter to compute the regular rate for each full workweek in which the Employee has been employed over the lesser of:

(i) The six-month period ending on the date on which the Employee takes Paid Sick Leave or Expanded Family and Medical Leave; or

(ii) The entire period of employment.

(2) Compute the average of the weekly regular rates under paragraph (1), weighted by the number of hours worked for each workweek.

(b) *Calculating the regular rate for commissions, tips, and piece rates.* An Employee's commissions, tips, and piece rates are incorporated into the regular rate for purposes of the FFCRA to the same extent that they are included in the calculation of the regular rate under the FLSA and 29 CFR Parts 531.60 and 778 of this chapter.

[¶ 9008]

§ 826.30 Employee Eligibility for Leave.

(a) *Eligibility under the EPSLA.* All Employees of an Employer are eligible for Paid Sick Leave under the EPSLA, except as provided in paragraphs (c) and (d) of this section and in § 826.40(b).

(b) *Eligibility under the EFMLEA.* All Employees employed by an Employer for at least thirty calendar days are eligible for Expanded Family and Medical Leave under the EFMLEA, except as provided in paragraphs (c) and (d) in this section and in § 826.40(b).

(1) An Employee is considered to have been employed by an Employer for at least thirty calendar days if:

(i) The Employer had the Employee on its payroll for the thirty calendar days immediately prior to the day that the Employee's leave would begin; or

(ii) The Employee was laid off or otherwise terminated by the Employer on or after March 1, 2020, and rehired or otherwise reemployed by the Employer on or before December 31, 2020, provided that the Employee had been on the Employer's payroll for thirty or more of the sixty calendar days prior to the date the Employee was laid off or otherwise terminated.

(2) If an Employee employed by a temporary placement agency is subsequently hired by the Employer, the Employer will count the days worked as a temporary Employee at the Employer toward the thirty-day eligibility period.

(3) An Employee who has been employed by a covered Employer for at least thirty calendar days is eligible for Expanded Family and Medical Leave under the EFMLEA regardless of whether the Employee would otherwise be eligible for leave under the FMLA. Thus, for example, an Employee need not have been employed for 1,250 hours of service and twelve months of employment as otherwise required under the FMLA, *see* § 825.110(a)(1) and (2) of this chapter, to be eligible for leave under the EFMLEA.

(c) *Exclusion of Employees who are health care providers and emergency responders.* An Employer whose Employee is a health care provider or an emergency responder may exclude such Employee from the EPSLA's Paid Sick Leave requirements and/or the EFMLEA's Expanded Family and Medical Leave requirements.

(1) Health care provider—

(i) For the purposes of this definition Employees who may be exempted from Paid Sick Leave or Expanded Family and Medical Leave by their Employer under the FFCRA, a health care provider is anyone employed at any doctor's office, hospital, health care center, clinic, post-secondary educational institution offering health care instruction, medical school, local health department or agency, nursing facility, retirement facility, nursing home, home health care provider, any facility that performs laboratory or medical testing, pharmacy, or any similar institution, Employer, or entity. This includes any permanent or temporary institution, facility, location, or site where medical services are provided that are similar to such institutions.

(ii) This definition includes any individual employed by an entity that contracts with any of these institutions described above to provide services or to maintain the operation of the facility where that individual's services support the operation of the facility. This also includes anyone employed by any entity that provides medical services, produces medical products, or is otherwise involved in the making of COVID–19 related medical equipment, tests, drugs, vaccines, diagnostic vehicles, or treatments. This also includes any individual that the highest official of a State or territory, including the District of Columbia, determines is a health care provider necessary for that State's or territory's or the District of Columbia's response to COVID–19.

(iii) The definition of "health care provider" contained in this section applies only for the purpose of determining whether an Employer may elect to exclude an Employee from taking leave under the EPSLA and/or the EFMLEA, and does not otherwise apply for purposes of the FMLA or section 5102(a)(2) of the EPSLA.

(2) Emergency responders—

(i) For the purposes of Employees who may be excluded from Paid Sick Leave or Expanded Family and Medical Leave by their Employer under the FFCRA, an emergency responder is anyone necessary for the provision of transport, care, healthcare, comfort and nutrition of such patients, or others needed for the response to COVID-19. This includes but is not limited to military or national guard, law enforcement officers, correctional institution personnel, fire fighters, emergency medical services personnel, physicians, nurses, public health personnel, emergency medical technicians, paramedics, emergency management personnel, 911 operators, child welfare workers and service providers, public works personnel, and persons with skills or training in operating specialized equipment or other skills needed to provide aid in a declared emergency, as well as individuals who work for such facilities employing these individuals and whose work is necessary to maintain the operation of the facility. This also includes any individual whom the highest official of a State or territory, including the District of Columbia, determines is an emergency responder necessary for that State's or territory's or the District of Columbia's response to COVID-19.

(ii) [Reserved]

(d) *Exclusion by OMB from EFMLEA.* The Director of the Office of Management and Budget (OMB) has authority to exclude, for good cause, certain U.S. Government Employers with respect to certain categories of Executive Branch Eligible

Employees from the requirement to provide paid leave under the EFMLEA. *See* CARES Act section 4605.

(e) *Exclusion by OMB from EPSLA.* The Director of the OMB has authority to exclude certain Employees, for good cause, from the definition of "Employee" for purposes of the EPSLA. *See* CARES Act section 4605. The categories of Employees the Director of the OMB has authority to so exclude from EPSLA are:

(1) Federal officers or Employees covered under Title II of the FMLA (which is codified in subchapter V of chapter 63 of title 5 of the United States Code);

(2) Other individuals occupying a position in the civil service (as that term is defined in 5 U.S.C. 2101(1)); and

(3) Employees of a United States Executive Agency, as defined in 5 U.S.C. 105, including the U.S. Postal Service and U.S. Postal Regulatory Commission.

[85 FR 20156, Apr. 10, 2020]

[¶ 9009]

§ 826.40 Employer Coverage.

(a) *Private Employers.* Any private entity or individual who employs fewer than 500 Employees must provide Paid Sick Leave and Expanded Family and Medical Leave, except as provided in paragraph (b) or in § 826.30(c).

(1) To determine the number of Employees employed, the Employer must count all full-time and part-time Employees employed within the United States at the time the Employee would take leave. For purposes of this count, every part-time Employee is counted as if he or she were a full-time Employee.

(i) For this purpose, "within the United States" means any State within the United States, the District of Columbia, or any Territory or possession of the United States.

(ii) The number of Employees includes:

(A) all Employees currently employed, regardless of how long those Employees have worked for the Employer;

(B) any Employees on leave of any kind;

(C) Employees of temporary placement agencies who are jointly employed under the FLSA, *see* 29 CFR Part 791 of this chapter, by the Employer and another Employer (regardless of which Employer's payroll the Employee appears on); and

(D) day laborers supplied by a temporary placement agency (regardless of whether the Employer is the temporary placement agency or the client firm).

(iii) The number of Employees does not include workers who are independent contractors, rather than Employees, under the FLSA. Nor does the number of Employees include workers who have been laid off or furloughed and have not subsequently been reemployed.

(2) To determine the number of Employees employed, all common Employees of joint employers or all Employees of integrated employers must be counted together.

(i) Typically, a corporation (including its separate establishments or divisions) is considered a single Employer and all of its Employees must be counted together.

(ii) Where one corporation has an ownership interest in another corporation, the two corporations are separate Employers unless they are joint employers under the FLSA, *see* 29 CFR Part 791 of this chapter, with respect to certain Employees.

(iii) In general, two or more entities are separate Employers unless they meet the integrated employer test under the FMLA. *See* § 825.104(c)(2) of this chapter. If two entities are an integrated employer under this test, then Employees of all entities making up the integrated employer must be counted.

(b) *Exemption from requirement to provide leave under the EPSLA Section 5102(a)(5) and the EFMLEA for Employers with fewer than 50 Employees.*

(1) An Employer, including a religious or nonprofit organization, with fewer than 50 Employees (small business) is exempt from providing Paid Sick Leave under the EPSLA and Expanded Family and Medical Leave under the EFMLEA when the imposition of such requirements would jeopardize the viability of the business as a going concern. A small business under this section is entitled to this exemption if an authorized officer of the business has determined that:

(i) The leave requested under either section 102(a)(1)(F) of the FMLA or section 5102(a)(5) of the EPSLA would result in the small business's expenses and financial obligations exceeding available business revenues and cause the small business to cease operating at a minimal capacity;

(ii) The absence of the Employee or Employees requesting leave under either section 102(a)(1)(F) of the FMLA or section 5102(a)(5) of the EPSLA would entail a substantial risk to the financial health or operational capabilities of the business because of their specialized skills, knowledge of the business, or responsibilities; or

(iii) There are not sufficient workers who are able, willing, and qualified, and who will be available at the time and place needed, to perform the labor or services provided by the Employee or Employees requesting leave under either section 102(a)(1)(F) of the FMLA or section 5102(a)(5) of the EPSLA, and these labor or services are needed for the small business to operate at a minimal capacity.

(2) To elect this small business exemption, the Employer must document that a determination has been made pursuant to the criteria set forth by the Department in § 826.40(b)(1). The Employer should not send such documentation to

the Department, but rather retain the records in its files.

(3) Regardless of whether a small Employer chooses to exempt one or more Employees, the Employer is still required to post a notice pursuant to § 826.80.

(c) *Public Employers*. (1) Any public Employer must provide its Employees Paid Sick Leave except as provided in § 826.30(c) through (d).

(2) Any public Employer must provide its Eligible Employees Expanded Family and Medical Leave, except as provided in paragraph (c)(3) of this section and in § 826.30(c) through (d).

(3) The EFMLEA amended only Title I of the FMLA, resulting in a divide in coverage as to Employees of the United States and of agencies of the United States (Federal Employees). Federal Employees covered by Title I of the FMLA are eligible for Expanded Family and Medical Leave. But most Federal Employees are instead covered under Title II of the FMLA, which was not amended by the EFMLEA. Such Federal Employees are not within the EFMLEA's purview and are therefore not eligible for Expanded Family and Medical Leave. The Federal Employees covered by Title I of the FMLA are therefore eligible for Expanded Family and Medical Leave, subject to the limitations and exceptions set forth in § 826.30(b) through (d), including:

(i) Employees of the U.S. Postal Service;

(ii) Employees of the U.S. Postal Regulatory Commission;

(iii) Part-time Employees who do not have an established regular tour of duty during the administrative workweek;

(iv) Employees serving under an intermittent appointment or temporary appointment with a time limitation of one year or less;

(v) Employees of the Government Accountability Office;

(vi) Employees of the Library of Congress; and

(vii) Other Federal Employees not covered by Title II of the FMLA.

[¶ 9010]

§ 826.50 Intermittent Leave.

(a) *General Rule*. Subject to the conditions and applicable limits, an Employee may take Paid Sick Leave or Expanded Family and Medical Leave intermittently (*i.e.*, in separate periods of time, rather than one continuous period) only if the Employer and Employee agree. The Employer and Employee may memorialize in writing any agreement under this section, but a clear and mutual understanding between the parties is sufficient.

(b) *Reporting to Worksite*. The ability of an Employee to take Paid Sick Leave or Expanded Family and Medical Leave intermittently while reporting to an Employer's worksite depends upon the reason for the leave.

(1) If the Employer and Employee agree, an Employee may take up to the entire portion of Paid Sick Leave or Expanded Family and Medical Leave intermittently to care for the Employee's Son or Daughter whose School or Place of Care is closed, or Child Care Provider is unavailable, because of reasons related to COVID-19. Under such circumstances, intermittent Paid Sick Leave or paid Expanded Family and Medical Leave may be taken in any increment of time agreed to by the Employer and Employee.

(2) An Employee may not take Paid Sick Leave intermittently if the leave is taken for any of the reasons specified in § 826.20(a)(1)(i) through (iv) and (vi). Once the Employee begins taking Paid Sick Leave for one or more of such reasons, the Employee must use the permitted days of leave consecutively until the Employee no longer has a qualifying reason to take Paid Sick Leave.

(c) *Teleworking*. If an Employer directs or allows an Employee to Telework, or the Employee normally works from home, the Employer and Employee may agree that the Employee may take Paid Sick Leave for any qualifying reason or Expanded Family and Medical Leave intermittently, and in any agreed increment of time (but only when the Employee is unavailable to Telework because of a COVID-19 related reason).

(d) *Calculation of leave*. If an Employee takes Paid Sick Leave or Expanded Family and Medical Leave intermittently as the Employee and Employer have agreed, only the amount of leave actually taken may be counted toward the Employee's leave entitlements. For example, an Employee who normally works forty hours in a workweek and only takes three hours of leave each work day (for a weekly total of fifteen hours) has only taken fifteen hours of the Employee's Paid Sick Leave or 37.5% of a workweek of the Employee's Expanded Family and Medical Leave entitlement.

[85 FR 20156, Apr. 10, 2020]

[¶ 9011]

§ 826.60 Leave to Care for a Child Due to School or Place of Care Closure or Child Care Unavailability – Intersection between the EPSLA and the EFMLEA.

(a) An Eligible Employee who needs leave to care for his or her Son or Daughter whose School or Place of Care is closed, or whose Child Care Provider is unavailable, due to COVID-19 related reasons may be eligible to take leave under both the EPSLA and the EFMLEA. If so, the benefits provided by the EPSLA run concurrently with those provided under the EFMLEA.

(1) *Intersection between the EPSLA and the EFMLEA*. An Eligible Employee may take up to twelve weeks of Expanded Family and Medical Leave to care for his or her Son or Daughter whose School or Place of Care has been closed, or whose Child Care Provider is unavailable, due to COVID-19 related reasons.

(2) The first two weeks of leave (up to 80 hours) may be paid under the EPSLA; the subsequent weeks are paid under the EFMLEA.

(3) An Employee's prior use of Paid Sick Leave under EPSLA will impact the amount of Paid Sick Leave that remains available to the Employee.

(4) An Eligible Employee who has exhausted his or her twelve workweek FMLA entitlement, *see* § 826.70, is not precluded from taking Paid Sick Leave.

(b) *Supplementing Expanded Family and Medical Leave with other accrued Employer-provided leave.*

(1) Where an Eligible Employee takes Expanded Family and Medical Leave after taking all or part of his or her Paid Sick Leave for a reason other than that provided in § 826.20(a)(1)(v), all or part of the Eligible Employee's first ten days (or first two weeks) of Expanded Family and Medical Leave may be unpaid because the Eligible Employee will have exhausted his or her Paid Sick Leave entitlement.

(2) Under the circumstances in (b)(1), the Eligible Employee may choose to substitute earned or accrued paid leave provided by the Employer during this period. The term substitute means that the preexisting paid leave provided by the Employer, which has been earned or accrued pursuant to established policies of the Employer, will run concurrently with the unpaid Expanded Family and Medical Leave. Accordingly, the Eligible Employee receives pay pursuant to the Employer's preexisting paid leave policy during the period of otherwise unpaid Expanded Family and Medical Leave.

(3) If the Eligible Employee does not elect to substitute paid leave for unpaid Expanded Family and Medical Leave under the above conditions and circumstances, the Eligible Employee will remain entitled to any paid leave that the Eligible Employee has earned or accrued under the terms of his or her Employer's plan.

[¶ 9012]

§ 826.70 Leave to care for a child due to School or Place of Care closure or child care unavailability—intersection of EFMLEA and the FMLA.

(a) Certain employee are entitled to a total of twelve workweeks of FMLA leave in the twelve-month period defined in § 825.200(b) of this chapter for the following reasons:

(1) The birth of the employee's son or daughter, and to care for the newborn child;

(2) The placement with the employee of a son or daughter for adoption or foster care, and to care for the newly placed child;

(3) To care for the employee's spouse, son, daughter, or parent with a serious health condition;

(4) Because of a serious health condition that makes the employee unable to perform one or more of the essential functions of his or her job;

(5) Because of any qualifying exigency arising out of the fact that the employee's spouse, son, daughter, or parent is a military member on covered active duty status (or has been notified of an impending call or order to covered active duty); and

(6) To care for the Eligible Employee's Son or Daughter whose School or Place of Care is closed, or Child Care Provider is unavailable, due to COVID-19 related reasons.

(b) If an Eligible Employee has already taken some FMLA leave for reasons (a)(1) through (5) during the twelve-month period, the Eligible Employee may take up to the remaining portion of the twelve workweek leave for Expanded Family and Medical Leave. If an Eligible Employee has already taken the full twelve workweeks of FMLA leave during the twelve-month period, the Eligible Employee may not take Expanded Family and Medical Leave. An Eligible Employee's entitlement to take up to two weeks of Paid Sick Leave under the EPSLA is not impacted by the Eligible Employee's use of FMLA leave. For example, if an Eligible Employee used his or her full FMLA leave entitlement for birth and bonding with a newborn, he or she would still be entitled to take Paid Sick Leave (for any covered reason), but could not take Expanded Family and Medical Leave in the same twelve-month period if his or her child's day care closed due to COVID-19 related reasons.

(c) If an Eligible Employee takes fewer than twelve weeks of Expanded Family and Medical Leave, the Employee may take up to the remaining portion of the twelve weeks FMLA leave entitlement for reasons (a)(1) through (5) of this section. For example, if an Eligible Employee takes eight weeks of Expanded Family and Medical Leave to care for his or her Son or Daughter whose School is closed due to COVID-19 related reasons, he or she could take up to four workweeks of unpaid FMLA leave for his or her own serious health condition later in the twelve-month period.

(d) If an employee has taken FMLA leave to care for a covered service member with a serious injury or illness, the remaining FMLA leave entitlement that may be used for Expanded Family and Medical Leave is calculated in accordance with § 825.127(e) of this chapter.

(e) An Eligible Employee can take a maximum of twelve workweeks of Expanded Family and Medical Leave during the period in which the leave may be taken (April 1, 2020 to December 31, 2020) even if that period spans two FMLA leave twelve-month periods. For example, if an Employer's twelve-month period begins on July 1, and an Eligible Employee took seven weeks of Expanded Family and Medical Leave in May and June, 2020, the Eligible Employee could only take up to five additional weeks of Expanded Family and Medical Leave between July 1 and December 31, 2020, even though the first seven weeks of Expanded Family and Medical Leave fell in the prior twelve-month period.

[85 FR 20156, Apr. 10, 2020]

[¶9013]

§826.80 Employer Notice.

(a) Every Employer covered by FFCRA's paid leave provisions is required to post and keep posted on its premises, in conspicuous places a notice explaining the FFCRA's paid leave provisions and providing information concerning the procedures for filing complaints of violations of the FFCRA with the Wage and Hour Division.

(b) An Employer may satisfy this requirement by emailing or direct mailing this notice to Employees, or posting this notice on an Employee information internal or external website.

(c) To meet the requirements of paragraph (a) of this section, Employers may duplicate the text of the Department's model notice (WHD 1422 REV 03/20) or may use another format so long as the information provided includes, at a minimum, all of the information contained in that notice. Prototypes are available at *www.dol.gov/whd*. Employers furnishing notices to sensory-impaired individuals must also comply with all applicable requirements under Federal or State law.

(d) This section does not require translation or provision of the notice in languages other than English.

(e) For Employers who are covered by the EFMLEA but are not covered by the other provisions of the FMLA, posting of this FFCRA notice satisfies their FMLA general notice obligation. *See* 29 U.S.C. 2619; § 825.300 of this chapter.

[¶9014]

§826.90 Employee Notice of Need for Leave.

(a) *Requirement to provide notice.* (1) An Employer may require an Employee to follow reasonable notice procedures after the first workday (or portion thereof) for which an Employee takes Paid Sick Leave for any reason other than that described in § 826.20(a)(1)(v). Whether a procedure is reasonable will be determined under the facts and circumstances of each particular case. Nothing in this section precludes an Employee from offering notice to an Employer sooner; the Department encourages, but does not require, Employees to notify Employers about their request for Paid Sick Leave or Expanded Family and Medical Leave as soon as practicable. If an Employee fails to give proper notice, the Employer should give him or her notice of the failure and an opportunity to provide the required documentation prior to denying the request for leave.

(2) In any case where an Employee requests leave in order to care for the Employee's Son or Daughter whose School or Place of Care is closed, or Child Care Provider is unavailable, due to COVID-19 related reasons, if that leave was foreseeable, an Employee shall provide the Employer with notice of such Paid Sick Leave or Expanded Family and Medical Leave as soon as practicable. If an Employee fails to give proper notice, the Employer should give him or her notice of the failure and an opportunity to provide the required documentation prior to denying the request for leave.

(b) *Timing and delivery of notice.* Notice may not be required in advance, and may only be required after the first workday (or portion thereof) for which an Employee takes Paid Sick Leave or Expanded Family and Medical Leave. After the first workday, it will be reasonable for an Employer to require notice as soon as practicable under the facts and circumstances of the particular case. Generally, it will be reasonable for notice to be given by the Employee's spokesperson (*e.g.*, spouse, adult family member, or other responsible party) if the Employee is unable to do so personally.

(c) *Content of notice.* Generally, it will be reasonable for an Employer to require oral notice and sufficient information for an Employer to determine whether the requested leave is covered by the EPSLA or the EFMLEA. An Employer may not require the notice to include documentation beyond what is allowed by § 826.100.

(d) *Complying with Employer policy.* Generally, it will be reasonable for the Employer to require the Employee to comply with the Employer's usual and customary notice and procedural requirements for requesting leave, absent unusual circumstances.

[¶9015]

§826.100 Documentation of Need for Leave.

(a) An Employee is required to provide the Employer documentation containing the following information prior to taking Paid Sick Leave under the EPSLA or Expanded Family and Medical Leave under the EFMLEA:

(1) Employee's name;

(2) Date(s) for which leave is requested;

(3) Qualifying reason for the leave; and

(4) Oral or written statement that the Employee is unable to work because of the qualified reason for leave.

(b) To take Paid Sick Leave for a qualifying COVID-19 related reason under § 826.20(a)(1)(i), an Employee must additionally provide the Employer with the name of the government entity that issued the Quarantine or Isolation Order.

(c) To take Paid Sick Leave for a qualifying COVID-19 related reason under § 826.20(a)(1)(ii) an Employee must additionally provide the Employer with the name of the health care provider who advised the Employee to self-quarantine due to concerns related to COVID-19.

(d) To take Paid Sick Leave for a qualifying COVID-19 related reason under § 826.20(a)(1)(iv) an Employee must additionally provide the Employer with either:

(1) The name of the government entity that issued the Quarantine or Isolation Order to which the individual being care for is subject; or

(2) The name of the health care provider who advised the individual being cared for to self-quarantine due to concerns related to COVID-19.

(e) To take Paid Sick Leave for a qualifying COVID-19 related reason under § 826.20(a)(1)(v) or Expanded Family and Medical Leave, an Employee must additionally provide:

(1) The name of the Son or Daughter being cared for;

(2) The name of the School, Place of Care, or Child Care Provider that has closed or become unavailable; and

(3) A representation that no other suitable person will be caring for the Son or Daughter during the period for which the Employee takes Paid Sick Leave or Expanded Family and Medical Leave.

(f) The Employer may also request an Employee to provide such additional material as needed for the Employer to support a request for tax credits pursuant to the FFCRA. The Employer is not required to provide leave if materials sufficient to support the applicable tax credit have not been provided. For more information, please consult *https://www.irs.gov/newsroom/covid-19-related-tax-credits-for-required-paid-leave-provided-by-small-and-midsize-businesses-faqs*.

[85 FR 20156, Apr. 10, 2020]

[¶ 9016]

§ 826.110 Health Care Coverage.

(a) While an Employee is taking Paid Sick Leave or Expanded Family and Medical Leave, an Employer must maintain the Employee's coverage under any group health plan (as defined in the Internal Revenue Code of 1986 at 26 U.S.C. 5000(b)(1)) on the same conditions as coverage would have been provided if the Employee had been continuously employed during the entire leave period. All Employers covered by the EPSLA or the EFMLEA are subject to the requirement to maintain health coverage. The term "group health plan" has the same meaning as under the FMLA (see § 825.102 of this chapter). Maintenance of individual health insurance policies purchased by an Employee from an insurance provider, as described in § 825.209(a) of this chapter, is the responsibility of the Employee.

(b) The same group health plan benefits provided to an Employee prior to taking Paid Sick Leave or Expanded Family and Medical Leave must be maintained while an Employee is taking Paid Sick Leave or Expanded Family and Medical Leave. For example, if family member coverage is provided to an Employee, family member coverage must be maintained while an Employee is taking Paid Sick Leave or Expanded Family and Medical Leave. Similarly, benefit coverage for medical care, surgical care, hospital care, dental care, eye care, mental health counseling, substance abuse treatment, etc., must be maintained while an Employee is taking Paid Sick Leave or Expanded Family and Medical Leave if provided in an Employer's group health plan, including a supplement to a group health plan, whether or not provided through a flexible spending account or other component of a cafeteria plan.

(c) If an Employer provides a new health plan or benefits or changes health benefits or plans while an Employee is taking Paid Sick Leave or Expanded Family and Medical Leave, the Employee is entitled to the new or changed plan/benefits to the same extent as if the Employee was not on leave. Any other plan changes (*e.g.*, in coverage, premiums, deductibles, etc.) which apply to all Employees of the workforce would also apply to Employees taking Paid Sick Leave or Expanded Family and Medical Leave.

(d) Notice of any opportunity to change plans or benefits must also be given to an Employee taking Paid Sick Leave or Expanded Family and Medical Leave. If the Employee requests the changed coverage, the Employer must provide it.

(e) An Employee remains responsible for paying his or her portion of group health plan premiums which had been paid by the Employee prior to taking Paid Sick Leave or Expanded Family and Medical Leave. If premiums are raised or lowered, the Employee would be required to pay the new Employee premium contribution on the same terms as other Employees. The Employee's share of premiums must be paid by the method normally used during any paid leave, presumably as a payroll deduction. If leave is unpaid, or the Employee's pay during leave is insufficient to cover the Employee's share of the premiums, the Employer may obtain payment from the Employee in accordance with § 825.210(c) of this chapter.

(f) An Employee may choose not to retain group health plan coverage while an Employee is taking Paid Sick Leave or Expanded Family and Medical Leave. However, when an Employee returns from leave, the Employee is entitled to be reinstated on the same terms as prior to taking the leave, including family or dependent coverages, without any additional qualifying period, physical examination, exclusion of pre-existing conditions, etc.

(g) Except as required by the Consolidated Omnibus Budget Reconciliation Act of 1986 (COBRA), an Employer's obligation to maintain health benefits while an Employee is taking Paid Sick Leave or Expanded Family and Medical Leave ceases under this section if and when the employment relationship would have terminated if the Employee had not taken Paid Sick Leave or Expanded Family and Medical Leave (*e.g.*, if the Employee fails to return from leave, or if the entitlement to leave ceases because an Employer closes its business).

[¶9017]

§826.120 Multiemployer Plans.

(a) *Paid Sick Leave.* In accordance with its existing collective bargaining obligations, an Employer signatory to a multiemployer collective bargaining agreement may satisfy its obligations to provide Paid Sick Leave by making contributions to a multiemployer fund, plan, or other program. Such contributions must be based on the hours of Paid Sick Leave to which each Employee is entitled under the EPSLA according to each Employee's work under the multi-employer collective bargaining agreement.

(b) *Expanded Family and Medical Leave.* In accordance with its existing collective bargaining obligations, an Employer signatory to a multiemployer collective bargaining agreement may satisfy its obligations to provide Expanded Family and Medical Leave by making contributions to a multiemployer fund, plan, or other program. Such contributions must be based on the hours of paid family and medical leave to which each Eligible Employee is entitled under the EFMLEA, according to each Eligible Employee's work under the multiemployer collective bargaining agreement.

(c) *Employee Access.* Any multiemployer fund, plan, or program under section (a) or (b) of this section must enable or otherwise allow Employees to secure payments for Paid Sick Leave or Expanded Family and Medical Leave. If the multiemployer fund, plan, or program does not enable or otherwise allow Employees to secure payments for paid leave to which they are entitled under the FFCRA based on their work under the multiemployer collective bargaining agreement, the multiemployer fund, plan, or program does not satisfy the requirements of the FFCRA.

(d) *Alternative means of compliance.* In accordance with its existing collective bargaining obligations, an Employer signatory to a multiemployer collective bargaining agreement may satisfy its obligations to provide Paid Sick Leave under the EPSLA or Expanded Family and Medical Leave under the EFMLEA by means other than those set forth in paragraph (a) and (b) of this section, provided such means are consistent with its existing bargaining obligations and any applicable collective bargaining agreement.

[¶9018]

§826.130 Return to Work.

(a) *General rule.* On return from Paid Sick Leave or Expanded Family and Medical Leave, an Employee has a right to be restored to the same or an equivalent position in accordance with §§ 825.214 and 215 of this chapter.

(b) *Restoration limitations.* Notwithstanding paragraph (a) of this section:

(1) An Employee is not protected from employment actions, such as layoffs, that would have affected the Employee regardless of whether he or she took leave. In order to deny restoration to employment, an Employer must be able to show that an Employee would not otherwise have been employed at the time reinstatement is requested in order to deny restoration to employment.

(2) For leave taken under the EFMLEA, an Employer may deny job restoration to key Eligible Employees, as defined under the FMLA (§ 825.217 of this chapter), if such denial is necessary to prevent substantial and grievous economic injury to the operations of the Employer.

(3) An Employer who employs fewer than twenty-five Eligible Employees may deny job restoration to an Eligible Employee who has taken Expanded Family and Medical Leave if all four of the following conditions exist:

(i) The Eligible Employee took leave to care for his or her Son or Daughter whose School or Place of Care was closed, or whose Child Care Provider was unavailable, for COVID-19 related reasons;

(ii) The position held by the Eligible Employee when the leave commenced does not exist due to economic conditions or other changes in operating conditions of the Employer that affect employment and are caused by a Public Health Emergency during the period of leave;

(iii) The Employer makes reasonable efforts to restore the Eligible Employee to a position equivalent to the position the Eligible Employee held when the leave commenced, with equivalent employment benefits, pay, and other terms and conditions of employment; and

(iv) Where the reasonable efforts of the Employer to restore the Eligible Employee to an equivalent position fail, the Employer makes reasonable efforts to contact the Eligible Employee during a one-year period, if an equivalent position becomes available. The one-year period begins on the earlier of the date the leave related to a Public Health Emergency concludes or the date twelve weeks after the Eligible Employee's leave began.

[¶9019]

§826.140 Recordkeeping.

(a) An Employer is required to retain all documentation provided pursuant to § 826.100 for four years, regardless whether leave was granted or denied. If an Employee provided oral statements to support his or her request for Paid Sick Leave or Expanded Family and Medical Leave, the Employer is required to document and maintain such information in its records for four years.

(b) An Employer that denies an Employee's request for Paid Sick Leave or Expanded Family and Medical Leave pursuant to § 826.40(b) shall document the determination by its authorized officer that it is eligible for such exemption and retain such documentation for four years.

(c) In order to claim tax credits from the Internal Revenue Service (IRS), an Employer is advised to maintain the following records for four years:

(1) Documentation to show how the Employer determined the amount of paid sick leave and expanded family and medical leave paid to Employees that are eligible for the credit, including records of work, Telework and Paid Sick Leave and Expanded Family and Medical Leave;

(2) Documentation to show how the Employer determined the amount of qualified health plan expenses that the Employer allocated to wages;

(3) Copies of any completed IRS Forms 7200 that the Employer submitted to the IRS;

(4) Copies of the completed IRS Forms 941 that the Employer submitted to the IRS or, for Employers that use third party payers to meet their employment tax obligations, records of information provided to the third party payer regarding the Employer's entitlement to the credit claimed on IRS Form 941, and

(5) Other documents needed to support its request for tax credits pursuant to IRS applicable forms, instructions, and information for the procedures that must be followed to claim a tax credit. For more information, please consult *https://www.irs.gov/newsroom/covid-19-related-tax-credits-for-required-paid-leave-provided-by-small-and-midsize-businesses-faqs*.

[¶9020]

§826.150 Prohibited Acts and Enforcement under the EPSLA.

(a) *Prohibited acts.* An Employer is prohibited from discharging, disciplining, or discriminating against any Employee because such Employee took Paid Sick Leave under the EPSLA. Likewise, an Employer is prohibited from discharging, disciplining, or discriminating against any Employee because such Employee has filed any complaint or instituted or caused to be instituted any proceeding, including an enforcement proceeding, under or related to the EPSLA, or has testified or is about to testify in any such proceeding.

(b) *Enforcement.* (1) *Failure to provide Paid Sick Leave.* An Employer who fails to provide its Employee Paid Sick Leave under the EPSLA is considered to have failed to pay the minimum wage as required by section 6 of the FLSA, 29 U.S.C. 206, and shall be subject to the enforcement provisions set forth in sections 16 and 17 of the FLSA, 29 U.S.C. 216, 217.

(2) *Discharge, discipline, or discrimination.* An Employer who discharges, disciplines, or discriminates against an Employee in the manner described in subsection (a) is considered to have violated section 15(a)(3) of the FLSA, 29 U.S.C. 215(a)(3), and shall be subject to the enforcement provisions relevant to such violations set forth in sections 16 and 17 of the FLSA, 29 U.S.C. 216, 217.

[¶9021]

§826.151 Prohibited Acts and Enforcement under the EFMLEA.

(a) *Prohibited acts.* The prohibitions against interference with the exercise of rights, discrimination, and interference with proceedings or inquiries described in the FMLA, 29 U.S.C. 2615, apply to Employers with respect to Eligible Employees taking, or attempting to take, leave under the EFMLEA.

(b) *Enforcement.* An Employer who commits a prohibited act described in section (a) shall be subject to the enforcement provisions set forth in section 107 of the FMLA, 29 U.S.C. 2617, and § 825.400 of this chapter, except that an Eligible Employee may file a private action to enforce the EFMLEA only if the Employer is otherwise subject to the FMLA in the absence of EFMLEA.

[¶9022]

§826.152 Filing a Complaint with the Federal Government.

A complaint alleging any violation of the EPSLA and/or the EFMLEA may be filed in person, by mail, or by telephone, with the Wage and Hour Division, U.S. Department of Labor, including at any local office of the Wage and Hour Division. No particular form of complaint is required, except that a complaint must be in writing and should include a full statement of the acts and/or omissions, with pertinent dates, that are believed to constitute the violation.

[¶9023]

§826.153 Investigative Authority of the Secretary.

(a) *Investigative authority under the EPSLA.* For purposes of the EPSLA, the Secretary has the investigative authority and subpoena authority set forth in sections 9 and 11 of the FLSA, 29 U.S.C. 209, 211.

(b) *Investigative authority under the EFMLEA.* For purposes of EFMLEA, the Secretary has the investigative authority set forth in section 106(a) of the FMLA, 29 U.S.C. 2616(a), and the subpoena authority set forth in section 106(d) of the FMLA, 29 U.S.C. 2616(d).

[¶9024]

§826.160 Effect on Other Laws, Employer Practices, and Collective Bargaining Agreements.

(a) *No diminishment of other rights or benefits.* (1) An Employee's entitlement to, or actual use of, Paid Sick Leave under the EPSLA is in addition to—and shall not in any way diminish, reduce, or eliminate—any other right or benefit, including regarding Paid Sick Leave, to which the Employee is entitled under any of the following:

(i) Another Federal, State, or local law, except the FMLA as provided in § 826.70;

(ii) A collective bargaining agreement; or

(iii) An Employer policy that existed prior to April 1, 2020.

(2) That an Employee already used any type of leave prior to April 1, 2020, for reasons related to COVID-19 or otherwise, shall not be grounds for his or her Employer to deny him or her Paid Sick Leave and Expanded Family and Medical Leave or for the Employer to delay or postpone the Employee's use of Paid Sick Leave and Expanded Family and Medical Leave. The foregoing is subject to the exception of FMLA leave as provided in § 826.70. An Employer shall permit an Employee to immediately use the Paid Sick Leave and Expanded Family and Medical Leave to which he or she is entitled under the EPSLA and the EFMLEA. However, no Employer is obligated or required to provide, and no Employee has a right or entitlement to receive, any retroactive reimbursement or financial compensation through Paid Sick Leave or Expanded Family and Medical Leave for any unpaid or partially paid leave taken prior to April 1, 2020, even if such leave was taken for COVID-19-reated reasons.

(b) *Sequencing of Paid Sick Leave.* (1) An Employee may first use Paid Sick Leave before using any other leave to which he or she is entitled by any:

(i) other Federal, State, or local law;

(ii) collective bargaining agreement; or

(iii) Employer policy that existed prior to April 1, 2020.

(2) No Employer may require, coerce, or unduly influence any Employee to first use any other paid leave to which the Employee is entitled before the Employee uses Paid Sick Leave. Nor may an Employer require, coerce, or unduly influence an Employee to use any source or type of unpaid leave prior to taking Paid Sick Leave.

(c) *Sequencing of Expanded Family and Medical Leave.* (1) Consistent with section 102(d)(2)(B) of the FMLA, 29 U.S.C. 2612(d)(2)(B), an Eligible Employee may elect to use, or an Employer may require that an Eligible Employee use, provided or accrued leave available to the Eligible Employee for the purpose set forth in § 826.20(b) under the Employer's policies, such as vacation or personal leave or paid time off, concurrently with Expanded Family and Medical Leave.

(2) If an Eligible Employee elects, or an Employer requires, concurrent leave, the Employer must pay the Eligible Employee the full amount to which the Eligible Employee is entitled under the Employer's preexisting paid leave policy for the period of leave taken.

(d) *No creation of requirements upon end of employment.* An Employer has no obligation to provide—and an Employee or former Employee has no right or entitlement to receive—financial compensation or other reimbursement for unused Paid Sick Leave or Expanded Family and Medical Leave upon the Employee's termination, resignation, retirement, or any other separation from employment.

(e) *No creation of requirements upon expiration.* An Employer has no obligation to provide—and an Employee or former Employee has no right or entitlement to receive—financial compensation or other reimbursement for unused Paid Sick Leave or Expanded Family and Medical Leave upon the expiration of the FFCRA on December 31, 2020.

(f) *One time use.* Any person is limited to a total of 80 hours Paid Sick Leave. An Employee who has taken all such leave and then changes Employers is not entitled to additional Paid Sick Leave from his or her new Employer. An Employee who has taken some, but fewer than 80 hours of Paid Sick Leave, and then changes Employers is entitled only to the remaining portion of such leave from his or her new Employer and only if his or her new Employer is covered by the Emergency Paid Sick Leave Act. Such an Employee's Paid Sick Leave would expire upon reaching 80 hours of Paid Sick Leave total, regardless of the Employer providing it, or when the Employee reaches the number of hours of Paid Sick Leave to which he or she is entitled based on a part-time schedule with the new Employer.

¶10,001 Family Medical Leave Act Section to Explanation Table

FMLA Sec.	Explanation
102(a)(1)(F)	¶100; ¶140
102(c)	¶100; ¶120
110	¶110
110(a)(1)(A)	¶110; ¶160
110(a)(1)(A)(ii)	¶110
110(a)(1)(A)(iii)[sic]	¶110
110(a)(1)(B)	¶100; ¶110
110(a)(2)(A)-(D)	¶100
110(a)(3)	¶110
110(a)(3)(A)-(C)	¶110; ¶130
110(a)(4)	¶110
110(b)(1)(B)	¶120
110(b)(2)	¶140
110(b)(2)(B)	¶120
110(b)(2)(C)	¶120
110(c)	¶100
110(d)	¶130

¶10,005 Family Medical Leave Act Sections Added, Amended or Repealed

Families First Coronavirus Response Act, 2020

FMLA Sec.	FFCRA Sec.
102(a)(1)	3102(a)(1)
102(c)	3102(a)(2)
110	3102(b)
110(b)(2)(B)	3102(b)

Coronavirus Aid, Relief and Economic Security Act, 2020

FMLA Sec.	CARES Sec.
110(a)(1)(A)	3605
110(a)(1)(A)(ii)	19008
110(a)(3)	3611(1)
110(a)(3)(A)-(C)	3611(7)(A)-(C)
110(a)(4)	3604(a)
110(b)(2)(B)	3601
110(c)	3611(3)

¶10,010 Act Sections Amending Family Medical Leave Act Sections

Families First Coronavirus Response Act, 2020

FFCRA Sec.	FMLA Sec.
3102(a)(1)	102(a)(1)
3102(a)(2)	102(c)
3102(b)	110; 110(b)(2)(B)

Coronavirus Aid, Relief and Economic Security Act, 2020

CARES Sec.	FMLA Sec.
3601	110(b)(2)(B)
3604(a)	110(a)(4)
3605	110(a)(1)(A)
3611(1)	110(a)(3)
3611(3)	110(c)
3611(7)(A)-(C)	110(a)(3)(A)-(C)
19008	110(a)(1)(A)(ii)

¶10,015 Internal Revenue Code Section to Explanation Table

¶10,020 Internal Revenue Code Sections Added, Amended or Repealed

Coronavirus Aid, Relief and Economic Security Act, 2020

Code Sec.	Act Sec.	Code Sec.	Act Sec.
106(f)	3702(c)	223(d)(2)(D)	3702(a)(2)
127(c)(1)(A)-(C)	2206(a)	401(a)(9)(I)	2203(a)
220(d)(2)(A)	3702(b)	402(c)(4)	2203(b)
221(e)(1)	2206(b)	414(y)(1)(B)-(D)	3609(b)(1)-(3)
223(c)(1)(B)(ii)	3701(b)	3306(v)(6)	2108(f)
223(c)(2)(E)	3701(a)		
223(d)(2)(A)	3702(a)(1)		

¶10,025 Act Sections Amending Internal Revenue Code Sections

Coronavirus Aid, Relief and Economic Security Act, 2020

Act Sec.	Code Sec.
2108(f)	3306(v)(6)
2203(a)	401(a)(9)(I)
2203(b)	402(c)(4)
2206(a)	127(c)(1)(A)-(C)
2206(b)	221(e)(1)
3609(b)(1)-(3)	414(y)(1)(B)-(D)
3701(a)	223(c)(2)(E)
3701(b)	223(c)(1)(B)(ii)
3702(a)(1)	223(d)(2)(A)
3702(a)(2)	223(d)(2)(D)
3702(b)	220(d)(2)(A)
3702(c)	106(f)

¶10,030 ERISA Section to Explanation Table

ERISA Sec.	Explanation
210(f)(1)(D)	¶630
518	¶640

¶10,035 ERISA Sections Added, Amended or Repealed

Coronavirus Aid, Relief and Economic Security Act, 2020

ERISA Sec.	Act Sec.
210(f)(1)	3609
518	3607

¶10,040 Act Sections Amending ERISA Sections

Coronavirus Aid, Relief and Economic Security Act, 2020

Act Sec.	ERISA Sec.
3607	518
3609	210(f)(1)

¶10,045 Social Security Act Section to Explanation Table

SSA Section	Explanation
903(h)(1)(C)(i)	¶200
903(h)(1)(C)(ii)	¶200
903(h)(2)(B)	¶200
903(h)(3)	¶200
903(h)(5)	¶200
903(i)	¶240
1202(b)(10)(A)	¶210

¶10,050 Social Security Act Sections Added, Amended or Repealed

Families First Coronavirus Response Act, 2020

SSA Sec.	FFCRA Sec.
903(h)	4102
1202(b)(10)(A)	4103

Coronavirus Aid, Relief and Economic Security Act, 2020

SSA Sec.	CARES Sec.
903(h)(2)(B)	3603
903(i)	2103(b)

¶10,055 Act Sections Amending Social Security Act Sections

Families First Coronavirus Response Act, 2020

FFCRA Sec.	SSA Sec.
4102	903(h)
4103	1202(b)(10)(A)

Coronavirus Aid, Relief and Economic Security Act, 2020

CARES Sec.	SSA Sec.
2103(b)	903(i)
3603	903(h)(2)(B)

¶10,060 Fair Credit Reporting Act Section to Explanation Table

FCRA Sec.	Explanation
623(a)(1)(F)	¶740

¶10,065 Fair Credit Reporting Act Sections Added, Amended or Repealed

Coronavirus Aid, Relief and Economic Security Act, 2020

FCRA Sec.	Act Sec.
623(a)(1)	4021

¶10,070 Act Sections Amending Fair Credit Reporting Act Sections

Coronavirus Aid, Relief and Economic Security Act, 2020

Act Sec.	FCRA Sec.
4021	623(a)(1)

¶10,075 CARES Act Sections Amending Families First Coronavirus Response Act Sections

This table presents CARES Act, Division A, Title III, Part IV, Subtitle C—Labor Provisions sections that amended FFCRA sections.

CARES Act Sec.	FFCRA Sec.
3601	3102(b)
3602	5102
3603	4102(a)
3604(a)	3102(b)
3604(b)	5112
3605	3102(b)
3606(a)(1)	7001(b)(4)(A)
3606(a)(2)	7001(f)
3606(a)(3)	7001(i)
3606(b)(1)	7003(b)(3)
3606(b)(2)	7003(f)
3606(c)	7003(i)
3611(1)	3102(b)
3611(2)	5111
3611(3)	3102(b)
3611(4)	3104
3611(5)	5110(1)
3611(6)	5110(2)(B)(ii)
3611(7)	3102(b)
3611(8)	5104(1)
3611(9)	5105(c)

Topical Index

M

N

O

P

Q

R

S

T

U

W

Made in United States
North Haven, CT
04 November 2026

21743221R00311